Transitions to Democracy

Transitions to Democracy

A Comparative Perspective

EDITED BY
Kathryn Stoner
and Michael McFaul

The Johns Hopkins University Press
Baltimore

The Johns Hopkins University Press
2715 North Charles Street
Baltimore, Maryland 21218-4363
www.press.jhu.edu

Library of Congress Cataloging-in-Publication Data

Transitions to democracy : a comparative perspective / edited by
Kathryn Stoner and Michael McFaul.
p. cm.
Includes bibliographical references and index.
ISBN 978-1-4214-0813-2 (hdbk. : alk. paper) — ISBN 978-1-4214-
0814-9 (pbk. : alk. paper) — ISBN 978-1-4214-0877-4 (electronic) —
ISBN 1-4214-0813-9 (hdbk. : alk. paper) — ISBN 1-4214-0814-7 (pbk. :
alk. paper) — ISBN 1-4214-0877-5 (electronic)
1. Regime change—History—20th century.   2. Democratization—
History—20th century.   3. Regime change—
Case studies.   4. Democratization—Case studies.
I. Stoner-Weiss, Kathryn, 1965–
II. McFaul, Michael, 1963–
JC489.T72 2013
321.09—dc23   2012023935

A catalog record for this book is available from the British Library.

Special discounts are available for bulk purchases of this book.
For more information, please contact Special Sales at 410-516-6936 or
specialsales@press.jhu.edu.

The Johns Hopkins University Press uses environmentally friendly
book materials, including recycled text paper that is composed of at
least 30 percent post-consumer waste, whenever possible.

Contents

Acknowledgments

This volume started well over five years ago in a conversation regarding the different modes of democratic transition since the end of the Cold War. Observing the transitions in Eastern Europe and the former Soviet Union in particular, we were frustrated with the existing literature on democratization. It was biased toward Western and Southern European and Latin American country cases. The literature also emphasized pacted transitions, even though these were more the exception than the rule in the post–Cold War era. Further, the potential for international influences on democratic transitions was largely ignored. We sought to remedy these and other shortcomings. Finally, we also wanted to provide a volume that would be of use to policy makers and academics, as we explain in the introduction.

To the extent we have succeeded in any of these tasks, it is due to the help of many scholars and policy actors who have aided us along the way. We would like to thank Nadia Schadlow of the Smith Richardson Foundation who saw the value of this project in its earliest days. We are also grateful to the Center on Democracy, Development, and the Rule of Law (CDDRL) at Stanford's Freeman Spogli Institute for International Studies. CDDRL provided us with a venue for three author meetings as well as financial and administrative support. Larry Diamond, the center's current director, was an invaluable source of input and read successive drafts of this volume. We also benefited from the rich community of scholars at the center, many of whom read drafts of chapters or listened to updates on our work in seminars on democratic transitions that we held at the center throughout this project. We thank in particular Francis Fukuyama, Stephen Krasner, Jeremy Weinstein, Stephen Stedman, and Erik Jensen for their constructive criticism and encouragement as we moved this project forward.

Finally, we thank Suzanne Flinchbaugh at the Johns Hopkins University Press for shepherding this project through the publication process. Suzanne was endlessly patient and professional.

Although the list of those to whom we are indebted is long, the errors in conceptualization, fact, or analysis are ours alone.

Introduction

CHAPTER ONE

Transitional Successes and Failures

The International-Domestic Nexus

KATHRYN STONER, LARRY DIAMOND, DESHA GIROD,
AND MICHAEL MCFAUL

This book seeks to discern the interaction between domestic forces and international influences in bringing about democratic transitions. In asking these questions in a variety of country contexts, this study of 15 transitional moments—successes, failures, and those in between—distinguishes itself from the existing, vast literature on "transitology"—the study of how autocratic regimes break down and transit to democracy.

Our understanding of the causal impact of international instruments on domestic outcomes is still evolving.[1] In academia and the think tank world, our appreciation of the international dimensions of democratization has grown, to be sure.[2] But most studies have explained transitions to democracy as a consequence of *domestic* factors alone, rather than also considering the independent or interactive effects of international factors. Such studies tend to fall into two categories, concentrating on either economic or political domestic variables.

In the first category, studies that emphasize socioeconomic conditions, analysts argue that citizens in wealthier countries are more likely to demand democratic governance and that their governments are more likely to respond positively to their demands.[3] A transition to democracy is more likely when either the middle class[4] or both middle and working classes[5] become stronger. Studies emphasizing domestic socioeconomic variables argue that transition to democracy is more likely in countries with citizens who value freedom, tolerance, and democracy as goods in themselves—that is, in countries with a democratic culture.[6] It is reasonable to ask, however, from where such a democratic culture might come. Although it could come from within a particular country, the underemphasis of this group of authors on international influences on democratic transition overlooks the possibility that democratic values and attitudes might come from abroad.

The second category has framed the process of democratic transition as essentially an *elite-led* drama. After the authoritarian regime splits between hard-liners and soft-liners, according to the traditional view, elite actors strategically attempt to maximize their interests while operating under a great deal of uncertainty about the balance of power.[7] Most of the leading accounts of elite-led democratic change, however, were written before the fall of the Berlin Wall and the collapse of communism in Eastern Europe and the Soviet Union. These dramatic events introduced a wave of new country cases (democratic transitional successes and failures) into the potential pool of cases in which to test elite-led theories of successful transition. In light of these new cases, domestic, elite-centered accounts appear incomplete. While some post–Cold War transitions do seem to fit the elite-led model, others have forged a different pattern in which civil societies and mass movements played crucial roles in bringing about change. This pattern is not unique to the post–Cold War era, as careful scrutiny of many transitions during the late 1970s and 1980s in much of Latin America and in countries such as the Philippines and Korea reveals a prominent early role for mass mobilization, which often preceded and even helped to generate splits within the ruling elite.[8]

The predominant explanatory models of democratic transition written from the 1960s to late 1980s, when we lived in a bipolar international system (which was considered a background variable at best), effectively screened out *international* factors. It is this oversight that we seek to remedy in this volume.[9] As late as the early 1990s, the role of international actors was reasonably described as the "forgotten dimension" in the study of democratization.[10] While some prominent political scientists continue this tradition,[11] studies of democratic transition and consolidation have become more internationalized in the past decade.[12]

DEPARTING FROM PAST ANALYSES OF DEMOCRATIC TRANSITION

In this volume, we seek to trace *the interaction between domestic actors and international actors in bringing about transitional opportunities.* Under what circumstances does democracy promotion or technical assistance actually help? When, or do, sanctions against autocracies help bring about transitional opportunities? In sum, what tools of international influence (if any) work and under what set of domestic circumstances? More generally, what other factors and conditions in the international environment may undermine authoritarian rule and help to tip transition dynamics in the direction of democracy?

Researching external dimensions of democratization must involve the insights of both academics and practitioners. Yet the separation between the two worlds remains profound. In attempting to explain exogenous influences on domestic political developments, academics have tended to gravitate toward history (often going back several centuries) rather than grappling with the messy "history of the present."[13] For their part, practitioners borrow few insights from academics, and the two groups are generally "engaged in dissimilar enterprises."[14] In this volume, we have endeavored to bring practitioners and academics together. In many of the country cases that follow, we have paired authors actively engaged in the process of democracy promotion with academics whose work focuses on the theory of democratic transition. We hope that what follows is of use to both communities.

We have also tried to remedy the tendency in the existing analyses to focus on the democracy promotion efforts of individual countries, notably the United States.[15] Along with the unique *American* contribution, the roles of other plausible external actors should be considered. There was a time when the US government was the only major actor in the world promoting democracy, but that time has passed. Today, the European Union (EU), individual European governments and their democracy-promoting foundations and nongovernmental organizations (NGOs), the United Nations, the North Atlantic Treaty Organization (NATO), and hundreds if not thousands of transnational networks and private foundations also engage in efforts to foster or support democratic change. Where possible, we have paired authors from different countries to write the analysis of their particular country case.

In addition to country cases where successful transitional attempts ended in the fall of an autocracy and the establishment of an electoral democracy (even if only temporarily), we must also consider cases of transitional failure—instances of a possible democratic or liberal opening where the attempt was blocked by the existing or a new autocratic regime—in order to better isolate the causal factors of transitional success. Notably, some of our transitional "success" cases are failures when it comes to the consolidation of democracy—for example, the Soviet Union / Russia. Others persist and consolidate as so-called fragile democracies. In this volume, however, we do not concern ourselves with consolidation that may follow the transitional moment. The domestic and international causes of successful consolidation we believe are often different from those at the initial time of transition, and so we leave the issue of consolidation to a later study. Instead, we focus on the causal dynamics of *transition* and move between domestic and international levels of analysis.

DEFINING TRANSITION AND SELECTING COUNTRY CASES

In the tradition of the landmark study of democratic transition of Guillermo O'Donnell and Philippe Schmitter, *Transitions from Authoritarian Regimes* (1986), we define a political transition as "the interval between one political regime and another." We define transitional "success" as a set of events that lead to the downfall of an autocracy and the establishment of at least minimal electoral democracy. We understand transitional "failure" to mean that the existing autocracy was challenged but remained in power or that, while the old autocrat or ruling party may have been ousted, a new autocracy rather than a democracy was installed.

The number of interesting and relevant cases is much greater than our capacities to analyze them. We sought variation in the types and modes of transition. For instance, the cases of South Africa and Poland were pacted transitions, the case of Russia did not involve pacting, and the cases of Serbia and Ukraine saw rapid breakthroughs from semi-autocracy to democracy (via "color revolutions"). Geographically, our cases range from postcommunist Eastern Europe, to Africa, Asia, Latin America, and the Middle East. Finally, we aimed for temporal diversity, including cases from the 1970s, 1980s, 1990s, and 2000s.

To avoid selection bias, we include in our study several cases of failed transitions. Whenever possible, we compare two cases with many shared features (such as geographic location, gross domestic product [GDP] per capita, degree of ethnic homogeneity, moment in history when the "outcome" occurred) but with different outcomes to try to isolate a pivotal factor (international or domestic) that accounts for the divergent outcomes.

We commissioned detailed case studies of the successes and failures and asked our authors to analyze their country case within a carefully defined theoretical and methodological framework. We did this to avoid the tendency to employ a "supply-side" or "outside-in" perspective that would focus first on the external dimension (and usually just the US or the EU dimension) without developing a nuanced explanation of internal democratization in the country being studied. We wanted to capture any interactive effect between domestic and political variables or an independent effect of domestic or international factors contributing to regime change.

We required that authors follow a two-step process in their analysis. First, we asked that they provide a general description of transitional events (or liberal opening) looking only at domestic factors that might explain either the success or the failure of domestic political change in their respective country cases. These factors may include the rise of a reformist group within an otherwise nondemocratic government, the formation of a democratic leadership pact or mass movement outside government, economic or societal changes, changes in institutional makeup and capacity, and the role of "change agents" or "veto players." Importantly, at this stage of the analysis we identify domestic factors and define the interrelations between them, without reference to the possible role of international actors.

The next step in our analysis is to assess whether a given international actor, or set of actors, can be said to have played a tangible role in the factors identified as having caused the domestic change, and if so, how. This approach helps overcome the selection bias inherent in "outside-in" studies, and helps focus the research on understanding the role of international actors (both "positive" and "negative"). We also do not limit our analysis to the role of the United States, the European Union, or the United Nations but look at a panoply of potential international sources of internal change, including global economic influences, nongovernmental actors, and the more elusive and possibly indirect role of norms and ideas in the international system.

Because the list of potential external sources is extensive, we group possible variables into three categories. In the first category we examine the role of regional and international institutions, including the United Nations, the World Bank, International Monetary Fund (IMF), European Union, NATO, Organisation for Security and Co-operation in Europe (OSCE), Council of Europe, the G8, the Organization of American States (OAS), Organization of African Union (OAU), and the Organization of Economic Co-operation and Development (OECD). These organizations rely in the first instance on "transformative engagement" and integration as the mechanism to induce democratic change.[16] The European Union is seen as especially effective in pulling democratizing countries into its orbit and then compelling them to consolidate many democratic practices, procedures, and institutions before being offered EU membership. Does it work? Does the absence of these multilateral institutions make it more difficult to build democracy?

Under this rubric of explanatory factors, we also explored the relationship between security and democratic development and the proposition that a country with secure borders has a better chance at developing a democracy. Because these multilateral institutions often help to reduce regional security risks between states, we should be able to identify a pattern of democracy development between states embedded in international security arrangements and states that are not.

Many of these international institutions also have democracy assistance programs, which we included as potential sources of external influence in our analysis. For instance, the European Union has the European Initiative on Democracy and Human Rights (EIDHR), the Stabilization and Association Process for the Balkan countries, the Euro-Mediterranean Partnership (with substantial funding, through the MEDA program for socioeconomic development and governance reform in North Africa and the Eastern Mediterranean), the European Neighborhood

Policy (which offers a stake in the Single Market and the prospect of enhanced contractual links with the European Union in return for progress on a range of domestic governance reforms), and political conditionality embedded in the Cotonou framework governing EU relations with the African and Pacific group of countries.

In our second general category, we include the impact of the foreign policies of individual states. As the instrument of the world's most powerful country, US foreign policy occupies the center of attention under this rubric, but foreign policies of other states promoting democracy, as well those trying to stifle it, must be included in the analysis. Russia, for example, is a regional hegemon with a lingering influence in nondemocracies such as Belarus and fragile transitional cases such as Georgia and Ukraine.

Finally, in the third category of international factors, we include ideas, scripts, and norms in the international system that can influence internal change. Democracy, both as a normative idea and as an effective method of rule, has appealing qualities. Since the collapse of communism, democracy has faced few if any ideological challengers.[17] Autocratic rulers persist throughout the world, yet few dictators in power try to justify their positions using antidemocratic creeds or doctrines. Pockets of illiberal creeds, racist norms, patrimonial rituals, and antidemocratic ideologies exist throughout the world, but—with the possible newly emergent exception of the so-called China model—only the radical Islamist vision of Osama bin Laden and other forms of jihadist Islam constitute a serious *transnational* alternative to liberal democracy today. Yet, bin Laden's vision for governance is hardly a worldwide challenger to democracy as the most valued political system in the world.

To implement the research design, we devised criteria for conceptualizing the range and estimated impact of external sources of influence across our set of case studies by creating a comprehensive questionnaire or template for every author to follow. While the list of potential external sources of democracy is enormous, a clear advantage of our method lies in its sequencing—identifying internal causes of change first and only then considering any relevant external influence. As such, our study does not prejudge potential sources and paths of external influence.

Each chapter in parts I and II is organized similarly. In the first section of each chapter, the contributors define and describe the *transitional moment* (or potential opening) in the country about which they write—that is, when the old regime becomes vulnerable and, in successful cases, is replaced by a new regime. In the cases of transitional opportunities that fail, the moment of possibility is described.

In the second section, the chapter authors evaluate the *domestic causes* of transitions. At successive author meetings, we devised a range of possible causes using the older literature on democratic transitions according to which military coups, elite splits, and foundational pacts among elites led to democratic outcomes. In these accounts, though, civil society (i.e., the masses) was often overlooked (or was seemingly unimportant) as a significant factor in bringing about transitional moments. Our authors explored beyond the level of elites to assess the possibilities for independent civil society action rather than as just a by-product of elite manipulation. Our research attempted to be exhaustive in seeking evidence of societal involvement.

In the third section of each chapter, the authors evaluate the influence, if any, of external actors in promoting or impeding democratic transition in their respective country case.

In the fourth section of each chapter, the authors discuss the interactions (if any) between domestic and political variables and draw some generalizations regarding the outcome of their country cases and the relative weight of international versus domestic factors in bringing about either democratic transitional success or failure.

The consistent format of the chapters allows us to offer generalizations regarding what makes or breaks transitional opportunities.

BOOK OVERVIEW

We divided the volume into three parts. Part I presents cases with clear and unidirectional transitions to democracy. Part II presents four cases of incremental transition from failure to success. Part III considers four cases where there was a transitional possibility but failed democratic transitional outcomes.

In the first case study in part I (chapter 2), Kathryn Stoner and Michael McFaul give an account of a rapid revolution in the Soviet Union that leads to democracy in 1993. They find that international democracy promotion efforts were in a sense a necessary but insufficient factor in Russia's initial transition to electoral democracy in the early 1990s. The US government, including the nongovernmental organizations it financed and other Western organizations, influenced the outcome of the transition mainly by spreading Western ideas that democracy was the only viable alternative to communist rule. The United States also contributed to the transition by meeting with elites, pressuring them to avoid authoritarian moves, and financing NGO projects that offered technical assistance, such as on how to legalize and administer elections and on federalism, all of which influenced the content of Russia's new political institutions.

In contrast, in chapter 3, Gregory F. Domber describes the pacting that transitioned Poland to a democracy in 1991. Domber reveals that Western assistance helped when Soviet influence waned in the late 1980s. Because Poland faced economic stagnation, the West had leverage over the government and pressured it to negotiate with the resistance movement, Solidarity. Solidarity, however, owed its creation to domestic factors, including an economic crisis that reduced regime legitimacy as well as a "culture of opposition."

Chapters 4 and 5 consider the "mass" revolutions in Serbia and Ukraine, respectively, each of which occurred more than a decade after the breakdown of the Soviet Union. In chapter 4, Ray Salvatore Jennings analyzes the revolution in Serbia, where students led mass mobilization after President Slobodan Milošević declared victory in fraudulent elections. Years of steady Western support for civil society infrastructure, political party development, and independent media preceded the mass mobilization. By the time the election occurred, civic groups already knew how to monitor the election with exit polls and parallel vote tabulation and how to organize protests if the regime cheated.

Next, in chapter 5, Michael McFaul and Richard Youngs analyze the successful transition to democracy in Ukraine in 2004, the Orange Revolution, named for the color associated with the opposition to the regime. Here again, the masses, led by students, organized against the regime after it committed electoral fraud. While the mass mobilization required indigenous networks and legitimacy, McFaul and Youngs demonstrate that the West played an important role by spending years training civil society organizations in exit polling, parallel vote tabulation, and demonstrating; by training independent media; and by offering an "aspirational reference point."

In chapter 6, Edward Aspinall and Marcus Mietzner turn to Indonesia's successful transition to democracy in 1998. They find that the international environment affected democratization in unintended ways: Indonesia suffered an economic decline as a result of integration into the world economy and the "bungled" bailout by the International Monetary Fund. The crisis reduced the legitimacy of the regime, and this propelled mass protests, forcing Indonesia's longtime president Soeharto to resign and his successor to embrace democratic reform. Similar to the situation in the Soviet Union, Poland, Ukraine, and Serbia, indigenous civil society in Indonesia received long-standing technical support from Western donors for a long period preceding the transition moment. Aspinall and Mietzner found that this movement, even if only marginally influencing the emergence of the transition, generated a significant expectation within Indonesia regarding what the country should "transition to" after Soeharto's resignation.

Timothy D. Sisk analyzes, in chapter 7, the transition in South Africa, where apartheid ended with a power-sharing agreement between the white minority and the majority. Domestic pressures to end apartheid and to transition South Africa to democracy included the protest and civic mobilization initiated by the African

National Congress, strong leadership of the movement, and a robust civil society that involved the masses in elite decisions. International pressure strengthened the indigenous movement through declarations that apartheid was immoral and sanctions against the regime. External actors also helped by mediating between the two parties. After the transition in 1994, the international community continued to support the new government by strengthening the capacity of the state, bolstering political parties, and training civil society to oversee elections.

In chapter 8, David Altman concludes part I with a study of successful transition in Chile in the late 1980s. Opposition to Augusto Pinochet united in 1988 to defeat a plebiscite in which Pinochet asked to stay in office for eight more years. This victory led to democratic elections. Altman's study reveals how international organizations offered financial and technical aid to bolster indigenous institutions meant to parallel those shut down by Pinochet.

Part II includes four cases of incremental transition. The first of these is Ghana's transition in chapter 9, by Antoinette Handley. Handley separates Ghana's transition into two phases: from 1988 to 1992 and then from 1992 to 2000. Both democratization phases were driven by decisions made by President Jerry Rawlings in response to donor demands. During the second phase, however, indigenous mobilization by opposition parties—with civil society support from international donors—grew, and the ruling party became less popular. In 2000 Rawlings lost the election and peacefully stepped aside to allow the opposition to take control.

In chapter 10, Alberto Diaz-Cayeros and Beatriz Magaloni present the incremental transition in Mexico. They found that the transition occurred mainly as a result of changes in domestic politics. International actors increased the preeminence of democratic ideals, offered international electoral observers, and provided start-up money for indigenous civil society groups. But Diaz-Cayeros and Magaloni found that, while this help was probably necessary, it was insufficient to promote democracy. The fraudulent elections of 1988 occurred while these international factors were not present. However, they were present during the clean but unfair elections of 1994, when the regime had imbalanced access to campaign funds and the media. These problems were solved with indigenous institutions, such as the Instituto Federal Electoral, by the 1997 congressional elections. When the ruling party stepped down after losing the 2000 presidential election, Mexico was perceived widely to be democratic.

A. David Adesnik and Sunhyuk Kim, in chapter 11, analyze the incremental democratic transition in South Korea. A first attempt occurred in October 1979— at a time when labor unions and students, churches, and the opposition within parliament united to protest dictator Park Chung Hee—but this initial transition attempt failed. At that time, the United States under President Jimmy Carter asked for improvements in human rights but did not call for a regime change. In June 1987 dictator Chun Doo Hwan also faced similar protests. With a growing economy, the government should have been better able to resist the opposition, but Adesnik and Kim suggest that international factors played an important role in halting any suppression. Because the South Korean government valued US opinion so much, and because the government did not want to imperil its prestige at the upcoming 1988 Summer Olympics, it complied with US president Ronald Reagan's demands not to violently repress the protests. The government instead responded by offering free and fair elections and protecting basic rights.

In the final chapter on incremental transitions, chapter 12, Senem Aydın-Düzgit and Yaprak Gürsoy, describe how the Turkish military, which overthrew a democratic government that suffered from instability and economic collapse in the late 1970s, returned the government to civilian rule. Although the United States offered aid for strategic purposes, the Turkish military seemed to understand that the United States wanted to see democracy take hold in Turkey. In the 1983 elections, although the victorious candidate was not preferred by the military, the military returned to the barracks.

In part III of the volume, we present four cases of near transition—that is, four openings of authoritarian regimes with similar socioeconomic conditions as other cases—but with failed democratic outcomes. First, in chapter 13, Kristina Kausch and Richard Youngs detail the transition that failed in Algeria in the early 1990s. Preceding the transition, Algeria's long-standing one-party state was losing legitimacy fast because an economic crisis had befallen the country since the mid-1980s. The crisis led to riots and repression, but when repression failed to stop protests, it prompted the regime to democratize. When the Islamist party outperformed the government's National Liberation Front (Front de Libération Nationale) in local elections, the military feared losing power and overthrew the government. It also canceled upcoming national elections. External actors offered no support for Algeria's attempted democratic transition because they were interested in maintaining current oil contracts with the regime. They seemed to prefer the stability offered by the existing military government to a potentially adversarial Islamist government, even if the Islamists were elected democratically.

In chapter 14, Abbas Milani analyzes the downfall of the shah's regime in Iran and the failure of that transition dynamic in 1978–79 to result in a democratic regime. As Milani explains, the transition attempt failed not for lack of significant societal pressure for democracy. Neither was there an absence of US pressure for democratic reform over time. In fact, Milani reveals, through significant new historical research, the lengthy but fitful and episodic nature of American efforts to press the shah to engage in democratic reform. However, because of the inconsistent nature of American foreign policy toward Iran, and because inflows of oil kept relieving the shah of an immediate need to democratize, when the transition moment came it was too late. By 1978, domestic (liberal) democratic forces were too weak and naïve relative to their exceptionally well-organized and effectively conspiratorial Islamist allies in the movement to bring down the shah. And the United States was too reviled for its past support of the shah to be able to help tip the dynamics of transition toward Iranian democrats. Rather, liberal and secular forces in Iran were outmaneuvered, marginalized, and ultimately destroyed by Ayatollah Khomeini and his Islamist followers, much as Lenin and his fellow Bolsheviks outmaneuvered and consumed the liberals during the Russian Revolution. The outcome of the Iranian transition—a theocratic dictatorship rather than a democracy—underscores not only the limits of international influence but also the importance of timing and classic factors in political history, such as organization and leadership.

Minxin Pei details, in chapter 15, the failed opportunity for transition in China in 1989 after millions protested against the regime throughout most major cities in the country. Pei found that external influences probably facilitated the outbreak of protest: there had been cultural and intellectual exchanges between China and the West, and China belonged to a "democratizing neighborhood"—close to the Philippines, Taiwan, and the Soviet Union, for example. But these factors did not influence the government significantly. Moreover, the West did little to promote democratization after regime hard-liners violently repressed the protesters. The United States sanctioned China, but the sanctions lacked teeth.

Finally, Valerie Bunce and Sharon Wolchik, in chapter 16, offer a similar account of Azerbaijan's failed transitional opportunity during the 2005 parliamentary elections, where opposition parties ran against the incumbent New Azerbaijan Party and its associates. Candidates from the incumbent party decisively defeated the opposition in elections perceived to be fraudulent by domestic and international electoral monitors. Bunce and Wolchik found that external actors interested in oil, including the United States, offered little criticism of these elections and did not give much support to civil society in the country. According to Bunce and Wolchik, civil society could not bring about a successful transition to democracy because the regime dominated the opposition with its patronage and ability to intimidate.

GENERAL FINDINGS

Because we are able to include cases from a broader geographic area than older studies that were focused mainly on Europe and Latin America and new cases arising from the demise of communism in Eastern Europe and the Soviet Union, the conclusions from our 15 country cases are more comprehensive than the older transitology literature. We also are able to make generalizations about why transitions fail and how (or whether) international actors are able to influence these processes. In many cases, democracy promotion by external actors was necessary but insufficient to bring about successful transition. Successful cases usually occurred after indigenous prodemocracy actors rallied the masses against the regime and after indigenous civil society institutions and independent media broadcasted the regime's oppression. These critical changes in domestic politics were often influenced by external actors who trained these prodemocracy actors and supported their infrastructure so they could rally the masses, monitor the regime, and use the independent domestic media. In most failed transitions, these indigenous prodemocracy actors and institutions either failed to emerge or did not receive the same degree of attention from external actors as in successful cases.

Domestic Influences on Successful Transition

Our cases depart from a dominant theme of the transitology literature—that democracy emerges typically when elites negotiate pacts that include democratic institutions. We are skeptical about preconditions and the ability of economic development to deliver democracy. Per capita income, for example, does not predict success across our case studies. Turkey and Azerbaijan had nearly identical per capita incomes in the year of their transitions, but Turkey succeeded at democratizing, whereas Azerbaijan failed. Poland, Chile, Ukraine, and Iran had similar levels of income in the year of transition, but Iran failed at democratizing, whereas the others succeeded. Economic development is not irrelevant in these cases, but we see evidence of a political process with strategic calculations, and these strategies matter more than socioeconomic conditions.

Individual agents mattered in the transitions. For example, what if there was no Gorbachev, no *perestroika*, no attempt to resurrect the Soviet Union? What if the presidents of Mexico and Ghana had not allowed free and fair elections in 2000 or had refused to step down after losing them? What if the shah had recognized more resolutely a decade before his fall the political implications of rapid social change and the need for democratic reform? What if the democrats in Iran had been led by a political figure as savvy and charismatic as Khomeini? In China, the government did not respond to the protests at first because it could not come to agreement between hard-liners and soft-liners. When Deng Xiaoping, leader of the Chinese government, switched sides to support the hard-liners, he tipped the balance of power. What if Deng Xiaoping had sided with the soft-liners?

The pacting model of the early transitology school, though important, is not applicable in several respects. First, pacts were not as pervasive in our case studies as they were to this school—perhaps because this school focused on the particular dynamics of transitions in the two regions that had experienced them at the time: Southern Europe and Latin America. Among our successful cases, pacts figured prominently in only two: Poland's Round Table talks, where elites agreed to a democratic organization of the Polish government, and South Africa's interim constitution of 1993, where the elites agreed to share power with the opposition.

In addition, the military, a key player negotiating pacts in Latin America, was not involved in most of the successful transitions studied here. The only successful transition in which the military played a major role was in Turkey in 1983. Again, the preeminence of the military in the transitology literature may have resulted from selection bias of studying particular regions and time periods.

Nevertheless, the role of the military was not insignificant. One of the more striking features of our success cases was that the military opted not to open fire on protesters, whereas it did in transitions that failed. In Russia, Boris Yeltsin specifically talked to the troops to prevent shooting. In South Korea, diplomatic pressure restrained the government. In Ukraine, neither the state nor the opposition used violence.

We found three domestic factors that were underemphasized by the transitology school. First, whereas O'Donnell and Schmitter noted an elite dominance of the transition process, we see more of a mass element, even if they did acknowledge the resurgence of civil society in driving transitions forward. We find in most cases of success an important role for mass mobilization at varying stages of the process, not simply toward the end. In South Africa, Indonesia, South Korea, Chile, Serbia, Ukraine, and Poland, a well-coordinated opposition exposed failings of the authoritarian regime, encouraged defections from it, and pressured it to change. In other words, mass mobilization, rather than following and interacting with elite divisions, often preceded and provoked them. On the other hand, failed transitions were generally elite led. In Algeria, it was the governing party that decided to open the government to multiparty elections in 1989. The government itself issued a new constitution that eliminated one-party rule, legalized multipartyism, and promised elections. In Azerbaijan, the government decided to allow multiparty parliamentary elections in 2005.

A second factor present in most successful transitions and missing in most failures is the role of indigenous civil society organizations. While not ignored by the original transitions literature, indigenous civil society organizations take on a more substantial and richly textured role in our case studies, not only by mobilizing mass protest but in performing other critical functions that challenged the legitimacy of the regime (such as in exposing corruption) or that unraveled the regime's hegemony. The most vivid example of the latter function is the role that indigenous civil society organizations played in Ukraine and Serbia (and in the Philippines in 1986, if it had been one of our case studies) to monitor elections and publicize fraud. In Mexico, by the 1997 congressional elections, novel indigenous institutions—national electoral observers, the local media, and local NGOs—threatened to expose foul play.

Third, independent media and communications technology were important domestic factors present in many successful transitions and absent in the failed ones. For example, the independent media in Ukraine and Indonesia exposed governmental corruption. In Poland, opposition underground papers facilitated coordination for Solidarity. In Azerbaijan, Algeria, and China, for example, the state controlled the media, and few alternative outlets were available to citizens. In addition, where citizens had mobile phones, text messaging, and the Internet, the masses seemed to mobilize faster, as we saw in Serbia and Ukraine, than in countries with little Internet or mobile phone coverage, including China, where organizers relied on their own underground networks. Better communications technologies might not have democratized China in 1989, but if the demonstrators in Tiananmen Square had been equipped with these technologies, they might have been able to warn each other about the crackdown and avoid the bloody massacre. Yet widespread if still partially suppressed societal access to mobile phones, the Internet, and social media was not sufficient to bring down the Iranian theocratic autocracy in the Green Revolution movement of 2009, whereas the much simpler communication technology of circulating cassette tapes of Khomeini's speeches and messages made a potent contribution to the revolution that brought down the Shah three decades earlier.

These three domestic factors—mass mobilization, indigenous civil society organizations, and independent media and communications technology—emerge as more important in our explanations of transitions than in the earlier literature. While failed transitions lacked these factors, they generally preceded successful transitions. External influences were also important, and our cases reveal how they interacted with these domestic factors.

External Influences on Successful Transition

First, in nearly every successful transition, indigenous groups received some training from external actors for many years before the transition. We see it in Poland, Ukraine, Serbia, Chile, and Ghana but not in China, Algeria, and Iran. External actors did not directly organize and support mass mobilization in these countries;

rather, they provided leaders of the protests with technical support to establish their own opposition organizations and to monitor government and electoral activities.

The training and relationships offered by Western NGOs and the diplomatic relationships offered by Western governments also contributed to the content of post-transition institutions. In Chile, for example, the National Democratic Institute (NDI) had been holding seminars and conferences and funding consultants on free and fair elections since the mid 1980s. In Russia, the United States offered technical assistance to manage elections and also pressured Yeltsin to avoid autocratic moves. In South Africa, while Western governments offered diplomatic support for the negotiations between the white ruling minority and the black majority, international NGOs assisted civil society organizations in the negotiations that undid apartheid, training them in techniques such as civic education and election monitoring. In Poland, the National Endowment for Democracy (NED) supported Solidarity's organizational capacity, while Western governments in general offered aid in exchange for democratic reform.

Second, ideas about democracy advanced by Western countries and their organizations also contributed to the content of the new democratic institutions. What external actors said was sometimes more important than what they paid for democracy promotion. As Stoner claims with regard to Russia, if the United States had been fascist in 1991, it is hard to imagine that Russia would have transitioned to democracy. The same might be said of many of our cases, such as Ghana, where, Handley demonstrates, Rawlings opened up the country in response to Western demands. Ideas also mattered after Soeharto resigned as leader of Indonesia. According to Aspinall and Mietzner, the new president, Jusuf Habibie, was aware of Western expectations and had personal experience living in the West. Aydın-Düzgit and Gürsoy argue that in Turkey the military government understood Western preferences and felt compelled to take them into account. In South Korea, according to Adesnik and Kim, the military dictator Chun Doo Hwan sought international prestige for his country, especially among Western states, and looked forward to hosting the Summer Olympics and to facilitating the first peaceful transition of power. As South Korea was seeking acceptance into the club of advanced industrial countries, it could not afford to be in open defiance of the norms that defined that club.

Third, external actors helped break citizens' dependence on state-controlled media and offered support for independent media. For example, in the Soviet Union, Radio Free Europe, Radio Liberty, and Voice of America, offered critical information to the public about social and economic affairs. According to Stoner, by some estimates half of Soviet citizens listened to Western media at least once a week in 1988. This level of media penetration not only offered information about the country but also helped mobilize citizens against the coup attempt initiated by radical communists against Gorbachev in 1991. The United States also supported Radio Free Europe in Poland, which helped broadcast information about upcoming protests and strikes. In Ukraine, journalists from Internews, who were trained by the US Agency for International Development, financed public-service announcements, local campaign coverage, and talk shows.

Thus, external actors boosted the work of indigenous organizations in cases that succeeded and were little involved in cases that failed. Why did they give less to the transitions that ultimately failed? All of the failures presented here except China were dependent on oil revenues during their transition moments, and the presence of oil may have altered the willingness of external actors to promote democracy. For example, in Algeria and Azerbaijan, external actors did not want to risk the stability of their oil contracts and therefore did little to encourage democratization with diplomacy or to encourage civil society, although the democratic West also greatly feared the consequences of an Islamist electoral victory in Algeria. Oil also constantly lurked in the backdrop of US and other Western calculations in Iran. However, even if external actors had promoted democracy in these cases, it may have had little effect. Because resource-rich governments are usually not financially dependent, external actors have little leverage over these states. As Levitsky and Way have shown elsewhere for competitive authoritarian regimes, Western democratic states are unlikely to exercise effective pressure for democratic change unless they enjoy a reasonably dense set of social and economic linkages with the potential transitional country as well as significant forms of leverage (e.g., in military or economic aid).[18]

POLICY IMPLICATIONS

Our case studies suggest several actionable foreign policies that can trigger democratic change and are not costly. External actors alone cannot undo an authoritarian regime and support the rise of a new democratic one, but working at the margins, they can expose the failings of the current regime and boost the capacity of actors pushing for change, and both of these factors seem necessary to bringing about democracy. At the very least, they seem likely to accelerate it.

First, when a transition is emerging, external actors can help plant the seeds of eventual democratic change by supporting (financially and technically) the organizational capacity of civil society. The prospects for democratization may not always look promising, especially after years of giving support. In Poland, South Africa, Chile, and South Korea, there was a decade-long flow of aid, and at times the effort must have appeared to be failing because it was not producing immediate effects. But we find that continuing to support these civil society actors strengthens their capacity to be serious players who can mobilize when the opportunity presents itself. Predicting very far in advance when political circumstances inside a country will generate propitious circumstances for democratization is difficult, because it takes a long time for civil society to build up the norms, skills, and resources that enable democratic change. If the West had waited until just six months before the elections in South Africa, Poland, Serbia, or Ukraine, those civil societies would not have had enough time to build the societal and civic infrastructure, and the capacity and readiness to support an opposition that can tip political dynamics toward real democratic change. Once the transition moment emerges, it is generally too late to do much to assist parties or social movements. When elections are called, there needs to be an existing capacity that can take advantage of the moment. Parallel vote tabulation, as was used in Ukraine, cannot be taught in one day. In the cases of failed transition, a longer period of commitment to civil society assistance might have helped during the transition moment.

Moreover, by supporting the indigenous civil society early on, external actors can promote an opposition that is more democratic in its orientation. In South Africa, Chile, Poland, and Serbia, frustration that might have been channeled into more violent antiestablishment forms took a more incremental, electoral, civic, peaceful approach. In Iran, the failure of the United States to do much to assist opposition forces left the field open for the Islamists to dominate organizational space.

External actors must be prepared to support democratic actors in civil society for a long period of time, even in the absence of any clear prospect of democratic transition, because donors can never know when the power structure will change. By patiently providing financial and technical assistance as well as moral and normative encouragement, the international community empowers indigenous democratic forces. Such aid may help to tip the balance *within* the political opposition to the authoritarian regime toward a genuine preference for democracy and away from a new authoritarian option. And it may also help to accelerate the resistance to that regime and the erosion of its base of support. Thus, our case studies give support to a policy not only of increasing and intensifying democracy assistance when the transitional moment seems to be emerging but also of initiating and sustaining various forms of democratic assistance even when the prospects for democracy do not appear promising.

Second, when institutions emerge in authoritarian contexts that have the potential to deliver democratic outcomes, donors should support and encourage them. Habibie and Yeltsin merited support and engagement to push forward toward democracy. In Ukraine, the Rada, or parliament, owed some of its strength to Western aid aimed specifically at strengthening the parliament. The Rada was a critical player in revealing electoral fraud. Democratic donors were also right to bet on the emerging transitional dynamics in South Africa after the release of Nelson Mandela, and on the electoral process in Ghana in 2000, even though a long-serving autocrat of uncertain intent, Jerry Rawlings, still stood atop the system.

A third lesson from the case studies is that supporting media and technology development is something external actors can do early on to create an environment that is more conducive to transition. While independent media, including Radio Free Europe and Internews, have encouraged the transitions to democracy in our study, we also believe that new information and communication technologies—such as mobile phones, the Internet, YouTube, blogs, Facebook, and Twitter—can be important networking and organizational tools to facilitate future transitions to democracy (as they evidently did, for example, in Egypt in the spring of 2011). They made a difference in Serbia and Ukraine, and probably the repression of demo-cratic movements would have been much bloodier in Burma in 2007 and in Iran in 2009 had not the visual images of the repression been leaking out rapidly to the international community (and, in Iran, to the domestic population). While it is im-portant to avoid technological determinism—and to be sensitive to the ways that authoritarian regimes like those in China, Iran, and Russia are controlling these technologies and turning them around to sustain their regimes—the media play-ing field can often be leveled and the organizational and coordinating capacity of civil society empowered by the diffusion and enhancement of these technologies.

Finally, we learn several lessons from the failures. First, in the context of a decaying authoritarian regime such as Iran, if democratic countries wait too long to get involved, the outcome can veer toward a new form of authoritarianism. The Iranian case suggests that the West should have engaged on behalf of democratic principles and actors much earlier and especially much more consistently. A simi-lar conclusion might be drawn in the case of China, where there was practically no external involvement; however, in China the West did not have nearly as much leverage as it did with the shah. In China, there was no democratic opposition organization with much coherence or capacity before the student-led movement of 1989.

In addition, however, our collection of country studies indicates that timing does matter. Many of our successful cases of democratic transition—including Chile, Mexico, Ghana, Serbia, and Ukraine—were forged in the crucible of an elec-toral process. That is, competitive elections provided a focal point for opposition mobilization and coalescence. Even in Korea, the anticipation of an election that would be unfair in its structure triggered the mass mobilization that helped—in the context of a critical American diplomatic intervention—to bring down the authoritarian regime. And in Indonesia and South Africa, elections that could have ushered in a new or renewed autocracy instead gave birth to democracy because of domestic mobilization and international engagement. Algeria and Azerbaijan each had the elections as focal points, but other favorable factors were absent or insufficient. Notably, China and Iran lacked any imminent competitive election around which democrats could rally and coalesce to bring down the authoritarian regime.

Without effective domestic or "home grown" organizations and a democratic focus leading to a more favorable balance of power, it is hard to imagine how any amount of external assistance at the transition moment will make much difference. In the transitional situation in Azerbaijan, Western engagement might tip the balance because some indigenous civil society organization already existed. Although Azerbaijan's oil-related corruption insulated it from democratic impulses following the electoral fraud in a way that was different from Serbia's and Ukraine's situation, the West lacked the political will to press Azerbaijan to hold free and fair elections or to help hold the regime accountable when it did not. In Algeria we learn that Western democracies should not push for democracy if they are not prepared to live with the outcome. The mild push for democratization by the West led to an election that brought victory to the well-organized Islamists, who threatened Western interests in the country. International actors thus need a sober and comprehensive assessment of the actors and the balance of power among them before pressing for democratic changes that they are not willing to affirm and sustain down the road.

Finally, our study suggests the need not only for continued engagement and patience but also for humility. If we (in the established democracies) are poor at predicting when a country will be ripe for democratic change, we are also hardly infallible in identifying who "the democrats" are. How many times in history have naïve international actors taken the professions of democratic faith by revolutionaries like Khomeini at face value, or seen the promise of a democratic revolution like Russia's go sour in the post-transition struggle for power and wealth? Yet if Western democrats had cynically concluded that Jerry Rawlings in Ghana or Ernesto Zedillo in Mexico would never allow their dominant party to lose an election, democratic change might not have occurred in either case when it did. If we are unable to identify in advance who the agents of democratization will be and when the times will be ripe for them, then a better approach is to promote democratic principles and process over the long run. Of course, international democrats must be ready to respond with energy, alacrity, and diplomatic pressure and encouragement when electoral moments approach as they did in Chile, Serbia, Ghana, and

Ukraine, or when historical tides suddenly shift as they did in Poland, South Korea, South Africa, and Indonesia. But an important lesson of our studies is the value of patient and persistent international support for domestic civil society. In the end, domestic actors really make (or break) a transition to democracy.

NOTES

Michael McFaul served as senior director and special advisor to the president for Russia and Eurasia in the National Security Council of the United States of America under President Barack Obama in 2009–10. In 2012, he was appointed US ambassador to the Russian Federation. He completed his contribution to this chapter and to this study as a whole before he entered US government service. Views expressed here are his own and do not reflect US policy.

1. To assert that the field is underdeveloped does not mean that important work has not been done already. No one has contributed more to this literature than Thomas Carothers. His books—*In the Name of Democracy: U.S. Policy toward Latin America in the Reagan Years* (Berkeley: University of California Press, 1991); *Assessing Democracy Assistance: The Case of Romania* (Washington, D.C.: Carnegie Endowment for International Peace, 1996); *Aiding Democracy Abroad: The Learning Curve* (Washington, D.C.: Carnegie Endowment for International Peace, 1999); *Critical Mission: Essays on Democracy Promotion* (Washington, D.C.: Carnegie Endowment for International Peace, 2004); and *Promoting the Rule of Law Abroad: In Search of Knowledge* (Washington, D.C.: Carnegie Endowment for International Peace, 2006)—as well as his numerous articles on democracy promotion almost single-handedly have defined this subfield along with several of the major themes and disputes in the literature. Other important studies treating the international dimension of democratization (at least in part) include Samuel P. Huntington, *The Third Wave: Democratization in the Late Twentieth Century* (Norman: University of Oklahoma Press, 1991); Sarah Mendelson and John Glenn, *The Power and Limits of NGOs* (New York: Columbia University Press, 2002); Laurence Whitehead, ed., *The International Dimensions of Democratization* (Oxford: Oxford University Press, 1996); Richard Youngs, *International Democracy and the West: The Role of Governments, Civil Society, and Multinational Business* (Oxford: Oxford University Press, 2004); Michael Cox, John Ikenberry, and Takashi Inoguchi, eds., *American Democracy Promotion: Impulses, Strategies, and Impacts* (Oxford: Oxford University Press, 2000); Francis Fukuyama, *State-Building: Governance and World Order in the Twenty-First Century* (Ithaca, N.Y.: Cornell University Press, 2004); and Larry Diamond, *The Spirit of Democracy: The Struggle to Build Free Societies throughout the World* (New York: Times Books, 2008).

2. See Laurence Whitehead, "Democratization with the Benefit of Hindsight: The Changing International Components," in Edward Newmann and Roland Rich, eds., *The UN Role in Promoting Democracy: Between Ideals and Reality* (New York: United Nations University Press, 2004), 135–66.

3. Seymour Martin Lipset, "Some Social Requisites of Democracy: Economic Development and Political Legitimacy," *American Political Science Review* 53 (March 1959): 69–105; Carles Boix and Susan Stokes, "Endogenous Democratization," *World Politics* 55, no. 4 (2003): 517–49; David Epstein, Robert Bates, Jack Goldstone, Ida Kristensen, and Sharyn O'Halloran, "Democratic Transitions," *American Journal of Political Science* 50 (2006): 551–69. On the other hand, democracy also emerges after economic crises, where dramatic declines in per capita income reduce the legitimacy of the authoritarian regime; see Stephan

Haggard and Robert Kaufman, *The Political Economy of Democratic Transitions* (Princeton, N.J.: Princeton University Press, 1995). See also Diamond, *Spirit of Democracy*, chap. 4.

4. Barrington Moore, *Social Origins of Dictatorship and Democracy: Lord and Peasant in the Making of the Modern World* (Boston: Beacon Press, 1966).

5. Dietrich Rueschemeyer, Evelyne Huber Stephens, and John D. Stephens, *Capitalist Development and Democracy* (Chicago: University of Chicago Press, 1992); Hsin-Huang Michael Hsiao and Hagen Koo, "The Middle Classes and Democratization," in Larry Diamond, Marc F. Plattner, Yun-han Chu, and Hung-mao Tien, eds., *Consolidating the Third Wave Democracies: Themes and Perspectives* (Baltimore: Johns Hopkins University Press, 1997), 312–33.

6. Seymour Martin Lipset, "The Social Requisites of Democracy Revisited," *American Sociological Review* 59 (1994): 1–22; Ronald Inglehart, *Culture Shift in Advanced Industrial Society* (Princeton, N.J.: Princeton University Press, 1990); Robert Putnam with Robert Leonardi and Raffaella Nanetti, *Making Democracy Work: Civic Traditions in Modern Italy* (Princeton, N.J.: Princeton University Press, 1993); Ronald Inglehart and Christian Welzel, *Modernization, Cultural Change and Democracy: The Human Development Sequence* (New York: Cambridge University Press, 2005).

7. Guillermo O'Donnell and Phillipe Schmitter, *Transitions from Authoritarian Rule: Comparative Perspectives* (Baltimore: Johns Hopkins University Press, 1986); Terry Lynn Karl, "Dilemmas of Democratization in Latin America," *Comparative Politics* 23, no. 1 (1990): 1–21; Juan Linz, "The Perils of Presidentialism," *Journal of Democracy* 1, no. 1 (Winter 1990): 51–69; Huntington, *Third Wave*.

8. Larry Diamond, *Developing Democracy: Toward Consolidation* (Baltimore: Johns Hopkins University Press, 1999), 233–39; Ruth Berins Collier and James Mahoney, "Adding Collective Actors to Collective Outcomes: Labor and Recent Democratization in South America and Southern Europe," *Comparative Politics* 29, no. 3 (1997): 285–303.

9. In the seminal study *Transitions from Authoritarian Rule: Southern Europe*, for example, Philippe Schmitter asserted that "one of the firmest conclusions that emerged . . . was that transitions from authoritarian rule and immediate prospects for political democracy were largely to be explained in terms of national forces and calculations. External actors tended to play an indirect and usually marginal role." Schmitter "An Introduction to Southern European Transitions," in Guillermo O'Donnell et al., eds., *Transitions from Authoritarian Rule: Southern Europe* (Baltimore: Johns Hopkins University Press, 1986), 5.

10. In 1991 Geoffrey Pridham pointed out that the role of international structures and actors was "the forgotten dimension in the study of democratic transition." Pridham, "International Influences and Democratic Transition: Problems of Theory and Practice in Linkage Politics," in Pridham, ed., *Encouraging Democracy: The International Context of Regime Transition in Southern Europe* (Leicester: Leicester University Press, 1991), 18.

11. See, for example, Jon Elster et al., *Institutional Design in Post-Communist Societies: Rebuilding the Ship at Seat* (Cambridge: Cambridge University Press, 1998), and Barbara Geddes, "What Do We Know about Democratization after Twenty Years?" *Annual Review of Political Science* 2 (1999): 115–44.

12. See in particular Laurence Whitehead, ed., The International Dimensions *of Democratization* (Oxford: Oxford University Press, 1996); Jon Pevehouse, "Democracy from the Outside-In? International Organizations and Democratization," *International Organization* 56, no. 3 (2002): 515–49; Steven Levitsky and Lucan A. Way, "International Linkage and De-

mocratization," *Journal of Democracy* 16 (July 2005): 20–34; Jeffrey S. Kopsten and David A. Reilly, "Geographic Diffusion and the Transformation of the Postcommunist World," *World Politics* 53, no. 1 (2000): 1–37; Kristian Skrede Gleditsch and Michael D. Ward, "The International Context of Democratization," *International Organization* 60, no. 4 (2006): 911–33; Larry Diamond, "The Democratic Rollback: The Resurgence of the Predatory State," *Foreign Affairs* 87, no. 2 (March–April 2008): 36–48.

13. See in particular Avner Greif, "Coercion and Markets: The Dynamics of Institutions Supporting Exchange," in Claude Menard and Mary Shirley, eds., *Handbook on New Institutional Economics* (Heidelberg: Springer Press, 2005), 85–114; Avner Greif and Eugene Kandel, "Contract Enforcement Institutions: Historical Perspective and Current Status in Russia," in Edward Lazear, ed., *Economic Transitions in Eastern Europe and Russia: Realities of Reform* (Stanford, Calif.: Hoover Institution Press, 1995), 291–321; Moore, *Social Origins of Dictatorship and Democracy*; Charles Tilly, *Coercion, Capital and European States, AD 990–1992* (Malden, Mass.: Wiley Blackwell, 1990).

14. Carothers, *Aiding Democracy Abroad*, 94.

15. See in particular Tony Smith, *America's Mission: The United States and the Worldwide Struggle for Democracy in the Twentieth Century* (Princeton, N.J.: Princeton University Press, 1994); Carothers, *Aiding Democracy Abroad*; Cox, Ikenberry, and Inoguchi, *American Democracy Promotion*; Carothers, *Critical Mission*.

16. On the notion of "transformative engagement," see Richard Youngs, "Engagement: Sharpening European Influence," in Youngs, ed., *New Terms of Engagement*, Global Europe Report (London: Foreign Policy Centre, May 2005), 1–14.

17. Michael McFaul, "Democracy Promotion as a World Value," *Washington Quarterly* 28, no. 1 (Winter 2004–5): 147–63.

18. Levitsky and Way, "International Linkage and Democratization," 20–34.

PART ONE

Successful Transition Cases

CHAPTER TWO

The Soviet Union and Russia

The Collapse of 1991 and the Initial
Transition to Democracy in 1993

KATHRYN STONER, WITH MICHAEL McFAUL

Twenty-five years after Mikhail Gorbachev became general secretary of the Communist Party of the Soviet Union and quickly began the process of political change within the USSR, consolidated democracy in Russia is more elusive than ever. Russia did, however, successfully transit from Soviet-style autocracy, and so we count it among the transitional "success" cases for the purposes of this volume. We argue that the influence of the United States, Europe, or other countries in fostering regime change inside the Soviet Union and then Russia has been relatively limited. The United States played at best only an indirect role in facilitating the collapse of the Soviet system. Indeed, in the final months immediately before the dissolution of the Soviet Union in December 1991, President George H. W. Bush may have actually done more to preserve the old system than to destroy it.

During the second phase of the Soviet-Russian transition between 1991 and 1993, when the basic institutional framework of the new political system was created, Americans did provide information about the various options available to Russian policy makers but offered only limited guidance about what choices to make regarding institutional design. Russians made these decisions on the basis of immediate political interests and not with reference to the long-term viability of Russian democratic consolidation. After the transitional phase of institutional design, American actors helped keep afloat important participants in the democratic process, such as political parties, trade unions, and civic groups, but these efforts at fostering an organized and democratic society within Russia likewise were not sufficient to withstand or impede autocratic rollbacks by both President Yeltsin and later President Putin.

Moreover, at certain moments regarding specific issues, the US government and various American nongovernmental actors were able to affect the course of Soviet and later Russian liberalization in a positive way. Yet, despite some episodic successes, what is more striking are the setbacks or missed opportunities. As we explain in this chapter, the primary sources of transition from communism came from within the Soviet Union, not from without.

DEFINING THE POINT OF TRANSITIONAL "SUCCESS"

Whether December 25, 1991, the date the Soviet Union collapsed, is the date on which to mark the end of Russia's successful transition to a modest form of democracy is contested. Despite the unequivocal demise of the Soviet state in December 1991 and the formal emergence of Russia as a separate state internationally, the transitional struggle did not end quickly or definitively at this point. A debate over the nature of the political system continued between the president of Russia, Boris Yeltsin, elected to this newly created position in June 1991, and the Russian Congress of People's Deputies, which had been elected in 1990. This debate erupted into violence in October 1993 when Yeltsin used force to evict renegade parliamentarians who had refused to follow his decree to disband so that new elections and a referendum for a new constitution to redefine executive-legislative relations could be conducted.

Russia's successful transition thus occurred in two steps. The first step ended on December 25, 1991, with the lowering of the Soviet hammer and sickle flag over the Kremlin and its immediate replacement with the Russian tricolor flag. The second, more definitive step, however, took place after the acceptance of the constitution of 1993 that established completely new democratic political institutions for the country. Although under President Putin the parliament—renamed the Duma—became largely a rubber stamp and he took full advantage of the considerable powers granted to the president in the 1993 constitution, until December 2008 no significant changes were made to Russia's basic formal institutional framework.[1]

That Russia, following its *transition* from communism, has thus far failed to *consolidate* its democracy (and, indeed, under Vladimir Putin's leadership has reverted to a new form of autocracy) is clear, but an issue beyond the scope of this chapter or volume. We focus here only on the internal and external factors by which the initial *transition* occurred in December 1991 and then the second stage in December 1993.

The "gang of eight," or State Committee on the State of Emergency (the Russian acronym was GKChP), attempted to take control of the Soviet Union at four o'clock on the morning of August 19, 1991.[2] A statement was released in the Soviet media that the reformist general secretary of the Communist Party of the Soviet Union Mikhail S. Gorbachev was ill, and that the GKChP would be assuming control of the country. The members of the GKChP included the vice-president of the USSR, the prime minister, the head of the KGB, the minister of defense, the minister of internal affairs, the chairman of the Union of Peasants, the first deputy chairman of the USSR defense council, and the president of the Association of USSR State Industries.

Despite the powerful offices the coup leaders represented, the entire attempted coup of August 19–21, 1991, had a Keystone Kops element to it. The plotters miscalculated the amount of support and mobilization they would actually receive from Soviet citizenry—especially outside Moscow. They also did not anticipate the determination or importance of Boris Yeltsin in the process of change that had already taken place. Inexplicably, they allowed him to slip out of his dacha outside Moscow on August 19. He eventually made his way to the Russian White House, then the seat of the Congress of People's Deputies, of which Yeltsin had served as chairman, before being elected president of Russia in June 1991. He managed to convince the Soviet military to side with him and Russia and not fire on Soviet citizens. The coup attempt unraveled on August 21, 1991. Gorbachev, who had been held (ostensibly) against his will at his southern dacha, returned to Moscow broken politically.[3]

Through the fall of 1991, Yeltsin and his government methodically took over Soviet ministries and other political institutions, moving them under Russian control. Gorbachev, still under the illusion that he could save the Union, continued to try to rally republican leaders around the idea of a loose confederation that he would lead. But the writing on the wall was clear by December 1, as Ukrainians voted in a popular referendum to secede from the Union. The signing of an agreement days later by Russia, Ukraine, and Belarus to create a new Commonwealth of Independent States put the final nail in the coffin of the Soviet Union.

Unlike transitions from authoritarian rule in Latin America, there was no pact between Gorbachev and other members of the old regime that peacefully ended the Soviet Union. There was no deadlock or negotiated outcome that produced democratic breakthrough. The military was not a major player in producing a regime change. There was also remarkably little blood spilled in this first phase of the Russian transition from communism (three people died in central Moscow during the coup attempt). The democratic opposition, led by President Yeltsin, decisively took over the reins of the Russian state through 1991.

The second phase of Russia's democratic breakthrough began in January 1992 and continued to December 1993, when the new (and current) Russian constitution was adopted. This came on the heels of the violent dissolution of the old Russian Congress of People's Deputies by Yeltsin. The coalition of Russian political actors that had come together to declare Russian sovereignty from the Soviet Union in 1990 and the creation of a Russian presidency in 1991 came apart violently in the fall of 1993 after a prolonged and fractious debate over the shape of a new Russian democracy and its institutional underpinnings.

DOMESTIC CAUSES OF TRANSITIONAL BREAKTHROUGH IN 1991
Long-Term Structural Causes

Retrospectively, the internal causes of the collapse of the Soviet Union and the initial breakthrough of democracy were in a sense overdetermined yet paradoxically far from inevitable. The most significant long-term structural factors that created the opportunity for liberalizing reform, although not alone sufficient to cause the collapse of communism in Russia, included the internal incoherence of the institutional structures of the communist system itself; economic decline, partly as a result of the system's institutional failures; societal changes, which led to increased demand for liberalization; negative demographic trends; and ethnic tensions within the 15 republics that composed the Soviet state.

First, although the sophisticated planning mechanism that was able to modernize a predominantly peasant agricultural economy in the 1920s and 1930s was well suited to huge developmental projects, the communist system proved unreliable and unwieldy by the 1980s. The power of ideology also waned in the declining years of the Soviet system. In addition, the Communist Party itself had become a bloated bureaucracy by the mid-1980s following Leonid Brezhnev's death in 1982. The fallacy of the constitutional position of the party as "the leading and guiding force of Soviet life and the nucleus of its political system, of all state organs and public organs," was increasingly in question by the time Gorbachev acceded to power as general secretary in 1985. Indeed, his original plan under *perestroika* was to reconstruct the party and the Soviet political system around it.

Successive leaders tried to make changes to the system before Gorbachev initiated *perestroika*. Nikita Khrushchev, Stalin's immediate successor, was the first in a line of Soviet reformers. His bifurcation of the Communist Party, *sovnarkhoz*, and his limited attempts at political and cultural reform were all undone, however, by Brezhnev when he assumed leadership after Khrushchev's ouster in the early 1960s. Under Brezhnev's long reign, the system stagnated. The large developmental projects that had benefited from the extreme centralization of the party and command economy were largely completed under Stalin. A backward, agrarian country had been rapidly industrialized (even overindustrialized); adult literacy was raised to 98 percent; and the Soviet Union was challenging American hegemony not just on earth but in space by the 1960s.

In contrast, by the 1970s and early 1980s, the system began to decline. *There was a growing crisis of regime legitimacy within Soviet society.* As Moshe Lewin has argued, "The country went through a social revolution as Brezhnev slept."[4] With rapid rises in education levels came increased undermining of the ideology of high mobilization that the system required. The Soviet "social contract"—whereby the state provided cradle to grave services and guaranteed employment—was gradually failing. The adage among Soviet citizens, "we pretend to work, while you pretend to pay us," gained currency through the 1970s. Increasingly, a chasm opened between the promises the regime made in its propagandistic claims regarding the superiority of the socialist way of life and the regime's growing inability to deliver.

Second, as Gorbachev assumed the office of general secretary in March 1985, *the Soviet economic system was badly in need of reform.* Despite Khrushchev's boasts in 1961 that the Soviet economy would surpass the gross national product (GNP) per capita of the United States within 20 years, by 1980 it had attained only about one-third of the US rate.[5] In the 1970s annual growth dipped to less than about 3 percent on average and by 1985 had declined further to 1.6 percent. This steady decline in growth rates was driven by declines in production outputs in previously stellar industries such as coal and steel. Further, oil production was also sliding by the mid-1980s, and agricultural production was "anemic" by 1982, purportedly dipping below plan levels.[6]

Beyond this, an aging capital stock and low investment rates also proved problematic in boosting Soviet production. Soviet firms were not required to live within their means or to adjust production in response to demand for their products. They faced no hard budget constraint.[7] Bureaucrats in Soviet ministries found inputs for production and markets for finished goods. If a manager needed more money to stay apace of the plan, the central government could print it. Money had little meaning or value in the system anyway. By the time of the Soviet collapse, inflation rates approached 100 percent.[8]

The Soviet Union also was not immune to some of the problems that affected the broader world economy—particularly in the 1970s, when world oil prices declined. This economic slowdown, combined with the relentless pressure to fulfill ever-rising production plans, led to further economic inefficiencies. Enterprise managers would pad their reporting of production outputs.[9] This type of behavior, often with the overt (for a fee) or at least tacit acceptance of bureaucrats who were supposed to oversee and stop this activity, helped to fuel the growth of the black market (or shadow) economy and official corruption, further dragging down economic performance.

Third, *social changes as well as negative demographic trends fueled economic problems.* Soviet population growth dropped about 50 percent between 1960 and 1980, causing a decline in the size of the work force and an increase in pensioners in need of state support. Death rates for both men and women were on the increase by the time Gorbachev came to power in 1985. Overall standards of living were rapidly declining from the 1970s onward in comparison to Organisation for Economic Co-operation and Development (OECD) countries, especially in areas like housing (in chronic short supply) and education.[10]

These disturbing statistics may have in some ways contributed to a fourth long-term structural cause of the collapse of the Soviet Union: *there was growing restiveness among the many diverse nationalities throughout the USSR's 15 republics.* The annexation of the Baltics, for example, in the 1939 Soviet-Nazi pact had always been viewed as illegitimate by Lithuanians, Latvians, and Estonians, despite regime attempts to assimilate the native populations into Soviet society and the resettlement of ethnic Russians in these republics. Public demonstrations against Soviet language policy occurred in Lithuania in 1972 and Georgia in 1978. In 1977 an Armenian secessionist group set off a bomb on the Moscow subway. Ethnic friction was also fueled by perceived preferences in appointments to plum jobs, whether for Russians over other ethnicities or for indigenous candidates over Russians. All of this occurred at a time when non-Russian, non-European birthrates within the Soviet Union were increasing four times faster than those of the ethnic Russian majority.[11]

Gorbachev had to deal with these long-term structural problems when he announced his plan of reconstruction or *perestroika* in 1985. They were not, however, alone determinative causes of the ultimate collapse of the Soviet regime in December 1991. The system could have limped forward for an indefinite period had these factors not combined with short-term precipitating factors that contributed to the ultimate downfall of the Soviet regime.

Short-Term Precipitating Factors

Although the Soviet system had been in structural decline for perhaps two decades, its collapse in December 1991 was far from inevitable. Indeed, one leader in the field of Soviet studies wrote confidently in 1986 that, despite all that was wrong in the post-Brezhnev era, "the survival of the Soviet system is not in question, but the utility of many of its policies is."[12] Only five years later, the Soviet Union collapsed spectacularly. While some Soviet specialists, including Timothy Colton and Alexander Dallin, accurately diagnosed what ailed the Soviet system by the mid-1980s, few predicted the timing or the exact mix of problems that would bring about the system's ultimate downfall.[13]

Despite the structural weaknesses that had developed over time as the Soviet system matured, short-term factors—and the role of agency in particular—tipped the system toward collapse between 1985 and the first stage of transition in December 1991.

Role of Agency: Gorbachev

Would the Soviet Union have survived indefinitely, despite all of its problems, if not for the fateful decisions of Mikhail S. Gorbachev? Although Gorbachev cannot bear sole responsibility, his halting economic and social reforms contributed to the timing and peaceful nature of collapse of the system.

Gorbachev was himself a product of the Soviet system. Born in the Stavropol region of Russia in 1931, he advanced through the Komsomol (Communist Youth League) and then the party apparatus to become a provincial party secretary by the late 1970s. In his own autobiography and the various biographies and accounts of his life, we know that he was greatly influenced while a student in Moscow in the 1960s by Khrushchev's troubled but at times innovative rule.[14]

He became a political client of Brezhnev's immediate successor as general secretary, Yuri Andropov, and it was Andropov who first brought Gorbachev from Stavropol to Moscow to work on the enduring problem of Soviet agriculture. Like Andropov, Gorbachev was aware of the failings of the Soviet planning system and the need for rejuvenation. He did not, however, intend to bring the Soviet system down. Indeed, by his own admission, he was a committed communist, proclaiming proudly in 1989, even as he pursued modes of democratization through the partially competitive election of the Soviet Congress of People's Deputies, that "I am a Communist, a convinced Communist! For some that may be a fantasy, but for me, it is my main goal."[15]

Although perhaps best remembered for his attempts to democratize the Soviet system through the introduction of partially free and fair parliamentary elections in 1989 and for his policy of *glasnost* or openness that revolutionized the previously closed Soviet media, Gorbachev actually began *perestroika* by attacking the troubled Soviet economy. But his first foray into economic reform—the antialcohol campaign of 1985–86—proved to have disastrous social effects from which his reputation within the Soviet Union never fully recovered. Gorbachev's other tentative economic reforms included the partial trade liberalization of 1986, the 1988 Law on Enterprises, and the 1988 Law on Cooperatives. Again, as with the antialcohol campaign, these were well-intentioned policies but with evidently unintended and unanticipated negative outcomes.

When he inherited the system in 1985, the Soviet Union was an autarkic state with little external trade beyond other communist countries. By partially liberalizing trade in 1986, Gorbachev enabled a select number of enterprises to engage in private foreign trade. Although this was intended to boost the level of Soviet exports and increase revenue, the result of this incomplete reform was to encourage favoritism and corruption of the process of selecting the enterprises that could participate in the program. Because it was also a relatively limited opportunity to open trade ties, it did little to boost the country's quickly declining GDP. Similarly, the policies on private property embodied in the laws on enterprises and cooperatives had other unintended consequences. While they did little to create private property, they further disrupted the already faltering planning system. The result was that as regulations of enterprise directors were loosened, the availability of certain goods declined rapidly (or at least the legal sale of these goods declined) as some managers resold their products on the black market.[16]

Gorbachev also severely weakened the Communist Party's grip on the economic and political system. His decision to allow limited competition for elected positions to a new super parliament, the Congress of People's Deputies, for example, caused communist candidates to lose seats in open competition with either former party members or new challengers rather than reestablishing the communist power as the intellectual and political guiding force of the system.

In another fateful decision, Gorbachev opted not to stand for popular direct election to the new post of Soviet president that he had created for himself, nor did he participate in open competition for his own seat in the Congress of People's Deputies. Instead, he ran and was "elected" as a representative of the Communist Party in the portion of the CPD seats reserved for members of social organizations. When faced with a strong political challenger in the form of Boris Yeltsin, Gorbachev retreated to the right in the summer and fall of 1990 and then attempted to retreat to the left by the summer of 1991 just as the ill-fated coup attempt by the GKChP took place on August 19 of that year.

Although the decisions that Gorbachev made played a key role in the collapse of the Soviet Union, the actions of Boris Yeltsin, whom Gorbachev brought into the Politburo as first party secretary of the city of Moscow, were also crucial. Yeltsin grew increasingly impatient with the unsteady nature of Gorbachev's *perestroika* program between 1985 and 1987. He formally broke with Gorbachev in his own "secret speech" in October 1987 at a party plenum, where he criticized what he deemed to be the slow pace of *perestroika* and what he saw as a growing cult of personality around Gorbachev himself.[17] Although Gorbachev then tried to end Yeltsin's political career, dismissing him from his posts in Moscow and the Politburo, he clearly underestimated his rival. Yeltsin reemerged in 1989 to win a seat in the

Congress of People's Deputies of the Soviet Union and then in 1990 as leader of a democratic (noncommunist) faction in the newly created and competitively elected Russian Congress of People's Deputies. At about the same time, Gorbachev's foreign minister, Eduard Shevardnaze, and longtime Politburo colleague Aleksandr Yakovlev both formally broke with Gorbachev, warning in December 1990 of the possibility of a coup attempt against him.

Having lost the support of the democratic faction in the Politburo, and surrounded by more conservative forces, Gorbachev proved indecisive. He tacked first toward the conservatives and by January 1991 used mild force in quelling the increasingly restive republics of the Soviet Union. In an incident known as Black Sunday, Gorbachev ordered or at least presided over the attack on unarmed protesters at a television station in Vilnius, Lithuania, during which 14 protesters were killed and another 500 wounded.[18] But by the summer of 1991, Gorbachev appeared more reformist.

Yeltsin capitalized on unrest in the Baltics and led a movement within Russia to declare itself sovereign from the Soviet Union in June 1990. By June 1991 he created distinct Russian political institutions, including a presidency to which he was directly elected in a free and fair competition in June of that year. This was a further challenge to the territorial and political survival of the Soviet Union, for without Russia, how could the Soviet Union survive? Gorbachev again tacked to the left and desperately renegotiated a much looser confederation of republics through the summer of 1991. This, coupled with Yeltsin's immediate ban of the Communist Party on Russian soil, proved to be the main precipitant of the August 19–21 coup attempt against Gorbachev.

The short-term causes of the second phase of breakthrough (December 1991–December 1993) were institutional weakness inherited from the patchwork constitution of 1978, fundamental disagreements over the nature of economic reform, and the choices of individual actors in positions of power.

Institutional Weakness Inherited from an Old Constitution

Boris Yeltsin, although emerging clearly and unequivocally as the leader of the new Russia after the August 1991 coup attempt, was left with a parliament elected in 1990 before the collapse of the Soviet Union. This legislature was large and unwieldy and proved internally factionalized as well as at odds with Yeltsin over economic policy in particular. The creation of the Russian presidency in 1991 strengthened executive power in Russia, but parliamentary power was not correspondingly decreased.

Debate over a new constitutional framework ensued in 1992 and 1993, with disagreement focused on the relative powers of the legislature and executive. Yeltsin, of course, argued in favor of a strong presidency, while the speaker of the Congress of People's Deputies, Ruslan Khasbulatov, favored a strong legislature and parliamentary system. They ultimately produced dueling and irreconcilable constitutional documents by the fall of 1993.

Beyond personalities, however, structurally the Russian Congress of People's Deputies was particularly susceptible to manipulation by a strong and independent speaker. Internally, the parliament was underinstitutionalized and highly fluid. Political party alliances, committee structures, and other institutions that might provide coherence and structure to the formation of parliamentary majorities over particular pieces of legislation proved difficult to form and sustain. This situation enabled Khasbulatov to dominate and lead the parliament without resorting to compromise and negotiation internally.[19]

By the spring of 1993, the governing process in Russia was deadlocked over the distribution of legislative and executive power and could not hold new elections for either president or parliament until the issue was resolved. By March, the parliament moved to lift Yeltsin's decree-making authority and passed other legislation that severely constrained his rule. The conflict seemed intractable. But Yeltsin gambled and won with a popular referendum held on April 25, 1993.

The referendum results, however, were not decisive and reflected the highly polarized nature of Russian politics at the time. In essence, voters were being asked their opinion midstream in the revolution: half supported it, half did not. This electoral result, therefore, did little to defuse the constitutional crisis in Russia. The questions, designed by the Congress, gave the outcome greater legitimacy for Yeltsin since he emerged with a narrow mandate to continue on his current policy path with the confidence of the electorate. He convened a constitutional assembly by July 1993, but the referendum results were largely ignored by parliament as the deputies too continued their efforts to write a constitution more sympathetic to parliamentary rule. Parliament itself, though, was clearly fragmenting, as some deputies resigned in advance of Yeltsin's storming of parliament in October 1993.

Structurally, the 1990 amendments to the constitution that created the Congress and the later change in 1991 that grafted on the presidency had left power relations ambiguous. As Richard Sakwa notes,

> The distinctive feature of the crisis was that while policy initiative lay with the presidential side, control over implementation and administration lay with parliament. This dualism was reflected in the very nature of the struggle, with parliament by necessity reduced to blocking measures: they had the power to impede presidential initiatives but lacked the power to develop policies . . . the Congress had power without responsibility.[20]

Yeltsin was certainly partly to blame for the ongoing disputes with the Congress of People's Deputies. He had shown an inability to build coalitions for his policies with the legislature. Yeltsin also failed to build support among the group of democratic reformers that had helped him win power first as speaker of the Congress of People's Deputies in 1990 and then the presidency in 1991. Indeed, he even had difficulty convincing his own vice-president, Aleksandr Rutskoi, of the value of his economic reforms. Rutskoi tacked to the side of parliament in this debate and soon became a political encumbrance to Yeltsin in his struggle with Khasbulatov and the Congress of People's Deputies.

Fundamental Debates about the Role of the State in the Economy

The sharp political disagreement over the power of the president versus the legislature took place against the backdrop of a crowded economic agenda. In January 1992 Yeltsin's reformist prime minister, Yegor Gaidar, initiated a bold neoliberal economic reform program. On January 2, 1992, prices were liberalized across Russia, causing average price increases of 245 percent throughout the country. Although prices stabilized within a few months, inflation remained high throughout 1992, and there was heavy criticism within the Congress of People's Deputies of this and other aspects of the reform program. These included the initial restriction on credits to failing state enterprises (a policy that was reversed by mid-1992 in response to lobbying by enterprise directors), as well as the speed and nature of the massive privatization program that began in July 1992.

These divisions split relatively neatly such that the Congress under Khasbulatov, himself an economist, and a faction of communists and fascists (the red-brown coalition) opposed the neoliberal agenda, while Yeltsin supported Gaidar and an aggressive neoliberal menu of reforms. The Congress, therefore, was slow in passing laws on privatization, landownership, and bankruptcy, for example. By the winter of 1992, as Yeltsin's temporary decree-making powers were set to expire, he was forced by the Congress to sacrifice Gaidar, his acting prime minister, and to replace him with the more conservative Viktor Chernomyrdin, former Soviet minister of Gas.

Individual Agency in Interaction with Structural Weaknesses:
Yeltsin (the Executive) versus Khasbulatov (the Parliament)

The conflict between president and parliament in this period was not only structurally produced and sharpened by the gravity of the economic choices made during this period but also exacerbated by personalities. Ruslan Khasbulatov used his authority within the Congress as an independent base of power. He replaced Yeltsin as speaker in October 1991, after the attempted coup against Gorbachev (and Yeltsin's earlier election as president of Russia in 1991). He was able to use the power of his role as speaker of the Congress to manipulate the legislative voting process, to control information that reached individual deputies, and to control the access of deputies to trips abroad and even to their parliamentary offices. Some journalists in the Russian media characterized him as dictatorial, and some parliamentarians, complaining that he regularly exceeded the authority of his office, even called for his removal.[21]

The constitution that was ultimately passed by popular referendum in December 1993 established Russia as a presidential republic. The new document was an improvement over what had existed before its adoption—there was a clear outlining of the power of the president versus the new bicameral Federal Assembly (with the 450-seat popularly elected Duma as the lower house and the Federation Council or Senate as the upper house). The constitution, however, threatened the establishment of a "superpresidential" republic in Russia. The president retained the ability to rule by decree in a few areas, although, notably, this power was not applicable to the budget, for example. Although the Duma retained the right to approve the president's choice of prime minister, if it refused to approve a candidate three times consecutively, then the president could disband the Duma and call for new parliamentary elections. Although he came close to testing this rule in 1998, Yeltsin was ultimately kept in check by successive Dumas (elected in 1993 and 1995) that were dominated by the Communist Party of the Russian Federation.

Despite their inauspicious beginning, the December 1993 elections served as the founding elections for Russia's new political system. A majority of Russian voters ratified Yeltsin's draft constitution, giving popular legitimacy to a set of political rules for governing Russia.[22] The new constitution outlined difficult procedures for amendment, meaning that adoption of this constitution was likely to produce a lasting set of political institutions for postcommunist Russia.

The basic rules of the game for elections to the Duma established during this tumultuous period in the fall of 1993 endured for the first four of the (so far) six parliamentary elections. Yeltsin himself was narrowly reelected president in 1996 according to the new constitution and supporting electoral laws. Although relatively short-lived, Russia's democratic breakthrough was complete by December 12, 1993. Unlike phase 1 and the collapse of the Soviet Union in 1991, the second phase of breakthrough in 1993 was violent and tumultuous, but it was ultimately decisive in establishing a (short-lived) democratic regime. The interplay of agency, institutional choices, and fundamental disagreements regarding the nature of the new political and economic system to succeed the Soviet Union worked together to bring the breakthrough to fruition.

EXTERNAL CAUSES OF TRANSITIONAL BREAKTHROUGH

To date, tracing a direct causal link between American foreign policy and Soviet regime change has eluded social scientists, though some indirect influences seem important.[23]

First, compelling evidence exists that the *American defense buildup* and the initiation of the Strategic Defense Initiative in the early 1980s shaped Soviet calculations about reform. Relatedly, the quagmire the Soviet military faced by a *mujahideen* force funded partly by the United States in Afghanistan made a bad economic and social situation worse for Gorbachev. Second, the *collapse of the international oil market* in the 1970s clearly played a crucial role in exposing the weaknesses of the Soviet economic system. Third, *foreign broadcasting* played a surprisingly crucial role in the battle for hearts and minds within Eastern Europe and the former Soviet Union. Fourth, the *diffusion of ideas* from West to East clearly mattered. The democratic principles of the American system also played an inspirational role for Soviet dissidents and influenced the thinking of important reformers in Gorbachev's politburo; Aleksandr Yakovlev, for example, spent time in the 1960s studying as an exchange student at Columbia University. Had Poland not moved steadily toward democracy in the late 1980s or had the United States been a fascist rather than democratic state, it is highly unlikely that democracy would have emerged as the ideology of opposition for Boris Yeltsin and his allies.

Of less importance, and even sometimes to the detriment of transitional success, were trade sanctions against the Soviet Union, halting diplomacy and normative pressure, and financial and technical assistance in the early 1990s.

Moreover, American efforts most certainly did not compel the Soviet leadership to experiment with political reform. Gorbachev made that decision alone. Once the process of political reform gained some momentum as a result of Gorbachev's initiatives, the dynamic of change was driven almost entirely by internal factors. Still, at certain key points external factors (actors, conditions, and policies) provided an incentive for the change that occurred in the Soviet Union between 1985 and 1991 and in Russia between 1991 and 1993.

The Influence of SDI and the Soviet War in Afghanistan on Gorbachev's Decisions

Although much has been made of the influence of President Ronald Reagan's Strategic Defense Initiative (SDI)—a missile defense program that was designed to intercept Soviet missiles in midair before they reached the United States—in bringing down the Soviet Union, analysts disagree on the true effect of the program on Gorbachev's decisions to reform the Soviet Union and also to participate in disarmament talks with the United States in the latter 1980s. Within the spectrum of opinions on the importance of the arms race, however, there is a general consensus that SDI and the US arms buildup in the 1980s did not on their own bring down the Soviet Union.

Peter Schweitzer argues that the military buildup and increasing pressure of the Reagan years were crucial factors precipitating the Soviet collapse: "As the Soviets faced this catastrophic drop in their income, they also faced the prospect of spending more of their dwindling resources on an arms race. U.S. defense procurement budgets rose by 25 per cent in each of the early Reagan years. By the mid 1980's, U.S. military expenditures were exceeding those of the Soviet Union for the first time since the late 1960's."[24]

Similarly, Mira Duric points to the Soviet Union's contradictory statements as evidence that it was concealing its fear of an operational SDI; while Soviet officials publicly declared the SDI to be technologically unfeasible, Soviet leaders also repeatedly criticized the program as a dangerous threat to world peace and stability. They also claimed to have their own missile-defense program, which would be wasteful if the program were actually impossible.[25] Competing views within the Soviet Union partially explain the situation according to Duric, who cites Soviet deputy foreign minister Aleksandr Bessmertnykh's comment that "different people in the government felt differently about the SDI. Those in the foreign ministry including Bessmertnykh, Eduard Shevardnadze and Gorbachev himself, believed that because of the SDI there was 'a good opportunity to work with the military and with the defense sectors of the economy to go further with arms control.' In contrast, the military (defense) part of the government wanted to 'increase the production of their offensive weapons' to counter SDI."[26]

The Soviets could not keep up with US spending. Schweitzer reports that "by 1984 General Secretary Konstantin Chernenko declared that 'the complex international situation has forced us to divert a great deal of resources to strengthening the security of our country.' In 1985 General Secretary Gorbachev pushed for an 8 per cent per year jump in defense spending."[27]

In response, as US defense procurement allocations increased, so too did Soviet defense budgeting. Under Reagan, US defense spending increased from $134 billion in 1980 to $253 billion in 1985, with an emphasis on strategic modernization.[28] Leading Soviet military analysts argued that, even with a projected rise of 45 percent between 1981 and 1985, they could not compete with the US buildup: "It was a shift that further weighed on the already sickly Soviet economy."[29]

Andrew Busch sees SDI as possibly the single biggest factor in the ending of the Cold War:

> Though it did not produce a functioning ballistic defense during the 1980's, SDI funda-mentally altered the strategic context in favor of the United States. . . . SDI quickly be-came an obsession of the Soviet leadership. . . . Having failed to win elimination of the program, the Soviets were prodded by SDI into seeking greater modernization of their own society—which could only be achieved by liberalization. The threat of having to compete with SDI led to greater toleration of reform by the military. Indeed, former Soviet officials have indicated that in many respects, perestroika was a military initia-tive, aimed at redressing the military implications of Soviet technological weakness.[30]

Busch, Duric, and Schweitzer make the strongest arguments for the role played by SDI and the arms race, but others see a more indirect role in Soviet decision making regarding reform.[31] William Wohlforth presents a realist explanation for the fall of the Soviet Union and end of the Cold War. Though he does not spe-cifically mention the arms buildup in the United States under Ronald Reagan, Wohlforth contends that changing perceptions of relative military power had an important role in ending Cold War competition: "Gorbachev may have had numer-ous reasons for seeking to withdraw from the rivalry with the United States, but a necessary precondition was the perception of *reduced capability* to compete."[32]

In separate analyses, Celeste Wallander, Raymond Garthoff, and Sarah Mendel-son see Western pressure on the Soviet collapse only as a contributing factor and not the primary element within the overall context of economic decline. Wallander points to evidence showing that Gorbachev's decision to embark on a path of economic re-form between 1985 and 1987 was little influenced by the American military buildup. Though Gorbachev did look to pursue arms control agreements, which would de-crease the needed defense spending, cuts in defense spending through 1987 were not required for reform at home.[33] Garthoff's study provides further support for this perspective on the role of SDI. He stresses the importance of Gorbachev's agency in wanting to change the relationship between the Soviet Union and the world.[34]

> The West did not, as is widely believed, win the Cold War through geopolitical con-tainment and military deterrence. Still less was the Cold War won by the Reagan military buildup and the Reagan Doctrine, as some have suggested. Instead, "victory" came when a new generation of Soviet leaders recognized how badly their system at home and their polices abroad had failed.[35]

Even more skeptical of the role of SDI, Sarah Mendelson argues that its impact was at best minimal and possibly even strengthened the hands of the hard-liners by reinforcing their self-image as a nation under siege.[36]

Another external conflict that may have hastened domestic reform in the Soviet Union was the 1979 Soviet invasion of Afghanistan. By December of that year, the Soviet army quickly became bogged down in a bloody, disastrous conflict. The United States in 1980 worked with the *mujahideen* resistance fighters to harass Soviet soldiers.[37] Saudi Arabia agreed to contribute matching funds, and China also aided the guerrilla operation.[38] The United States funneled more than $2 billion to the *mujahideen* during the 1980s.[39] By 1985 the United States established National Security Directive 166, shifting the policy goal for Afghanistan from mere harassment to forcing a Soviet withdrawal. From this point, US involvement and funding in Afghanistan escalated.[40] One anonymous Western official described the escalation as "directed at killing Russian military officers," and beginning in 1985, the CIA also started providing the *mujahideen* with satellite reconnaissance data of Soviet targets, intercepts of Soviet communications, and high-technology weaponry.[41] By 1987, Gorbachev announced a decision to withdraw from Afghanistan and the withdrawal was completed by February 1989.

Wallander examines the US role in Afghanistan in light of American aid to guerrillas in other Third World conflicts:

> In Afghanistan . . . the United States provided (along with China, Pakistan, and Saudi Arabia) huge amounts of weaponry assistance to guerillas fighting the Soviet Army. Even so, at the height of the Soviet troop presence in Afghanistan only about 2.1% of Soviet forces were deployed. Soviet casualty rates and losses actually declined after the United States supplied Stinger missiles, which were first deployed in 1986 and became effective in 1987, and Moscow continued to supply the Kabul government $300 million a month even after Soviet troops had withdrawn in 1989. U.S. support for the Afghan rebels certainly made life more difficult for the Soviet Army, and this in turn affected Soviet society's view of the strength of the state and the military forces that sustained it. Afghanistan also helped spur the rise of social movements and organized protest in the Soviet Union, notably the condemnations of the war by mothers of soldiers who were fighting in Afghanistan.[42]

While Wallander does not claim a direct relationship between US pressure on the Soviets in Afghanistan, the Soviet withdrawal, and the subsequent collapse of the Soviet state, she notes that Soviet military commitments abroad, including the war in Afghanistan, "were economically costly, but not on a scale that undermined the Soviet economy or that would have saved the economy had the resources been freed."[43]

Sarah Mendelson agrees that the impact of US intervention in Afghanistan was negligible. Instead, the withdrawal of Soviet troops was caused by the rise of reformist leadership within the Soviet Union; troops would have remained in Afghanistan past 1988 had Gorbachev not come to power.[44]

The International Oil Market

Beyond the pressures of the Cold War and the arms race and the difficulties of the conflict in Afghanistan, the Soviet Union by the mid-1980s was suffering economically. This was in part due to the general inefficiencies of the planning system, and Brezhnev's failures to undertake major reform to address the shortcomings of the overall economy. It was, however, also due to the fall in oil prices that occurred between 1982 and 1986. The Afghan war had been costly in terms not only of the lives of Soviet servicemen but also of Soviet oil revenues, which accounted for a majority share of all domestic revenues.

This fact had not gone unnoticed in the West. According to Yegor Gaidar, Yeltsin's reformist prime minister, Richard Pipes pointed out the vulnerability of the Soviet state in this regard and even recommended using the Soviet dependence on oil prices to destabilize the regime.[45] More explicit are Gaidar's comments regarding the effect of oil on Russian internal politics:

> The timeline of the collapse of the Soviet Union can be traced to September 13, 1985. On this date, Sheikh Ahmed Zaki Yamani, the minister of oil of Saudi Arabia, declared that the monarchy had decided to alter its oil policy radically. The Saudis stopped protecting oil prices, and Saudi Arabia regained its share in the world market. During the next six months, oil production in Saudi Arabia increased fourfold while oil prices collapsed by approximately the same amount in real terms. As a result, the Soviet Union lost approximately $20 billion per year, money without which the country simply could not survive.[46]

World oil prices collapsed from $76 per barrel in 1982 to $20 a barrel in 1986. Desperate for hard currency and pressed to cover its growing trade deficit, the Soviet Union increased its debt burden considerably. The country finally ran out of loan prospects from commercial banks abroad. The head of the State Planning Committee, Yuri Maslyukov, warned that the situation would lead the system to collapse.[47]

Gaidar argues that the financial and hard currency situation in the country by 1989 largely explains Gorbachev's subsequent policy decisions. The desperately needed foreign loans would come only from foreign governments at this point, and "if the Soviet military crushed Solidarity Party demonstrations in Warsaw, the Soviet Union would not have received the desperately needed $100 billion from the West."[48] In sum, Gaidar quite explicitly attributes Gorbachev's decision to let Poland and the East European communist countries peacefully exit the Soviet bloc in the fall of 1989 to falling oil prices and decreased revenue within the Soviet state.

The Influence of Foreign Broadcasting into the Soviet Union

Perhaps the best investment the US government made in its efforts to destabilize the Soviet Union was in Radio Free Europe and Radio Liberty. These radio channels were effective tools in promoting US "psychological warfare" against the USSR. The State Department's Voice of America provided a third branch of attack. Founded in the 1950s and originally funded by the Defense Department, the Voice of America began broadcasting during World War II, with a mission to provide accurate news about America and the war.

After the war, VOA went in decline until its revival during the Cold War. Radio Free Europe and Radio Liberty began operating in 1949 and 1951 respectively. They were privately operated but covertly funded by the CIA. In 1971 the CIA's role was revealed, so Congress began overt funding. Incredibly, Voice of America claimed to reach 127 million listeners in 1988, defined as those who tune in at least once a week, in more than 160 countries. The reach of RFE/RL was less extensive, although it estimated that at about the same time it reached 55 to 56.5 million listeners at least once a week. Within the Soviet Union, "popular surveys showed that nearly 50 percent of the populace in the Soviet Union listened to Western broadcasters at least once a week, 28 percent to VOA and 15 percent each to RL and to the BBC."[49]

Significantly, former KGB agent, Oleg Kalugin testified that "of all the Soviet groups it was the political elite that Radio Liberty most influenced. After years of listening to RL's programming without interference (and in the case of the Party elite, reading the daily transcriptions of broadcasts prepared by the KGB), these Party members understood that the Soviet Union needed fundamental change. This realization laid the groundwork for the reform process that ultimately spelled the end of the USSR."[50]

Voice of America was designed to provide accurate news from the American perspective, while RFE and RL were "supposed to represent the voice of the opposition forces from the countries to which they broadcast."[51] International radio broadcasts quickly became important sources of information in the Soviet bloc. There were several key moments when RFE/RL and VOA proved invaluable in getting around Soviet media controls. One of these was the revelation of Khurschchev's secret speech in February 1956, where he denounced Stalin's crimes. This was followed by his initiation of significant reform. It shocked the Soviet system and perhaps gave disgruntled or disillusioned Soviet citizens hope that things might change.

Foreign media broadcasts also provided Soviet leaders with important information about their own populations and internal challenges to the regime. For example, in the 1950s, "analyses of Soviet youth demonstrated that many were indifferent to the political changes occurring; some students could not even name the First Secretary of the Party, Khrushchev."[52]

The amount of effort and money that the Soviet state spent on jamming the RL and VOA indicated the extent of the Kremlin's concern over the impact of foreign media on the population.[53] In the 1970s, Radio Liberty devoted substantial airtime to reading *samizdat*, eventually establishing a special program specifically for that purpose and allowing the opinions of dissidents to reach millions.[54] Eugene Parta confirms that "the *samizdat* phenomenon and the related human rights movement in the USSR were a major topic of broadcasting. There is a strong correlation between listening to Radio Liberty and approval of this form of dissident activity, decried by a majority of the Soviet population."[55]

The Carter administration expanded radio broadcasting, and total RFE/RL funding rose from $64 million in 1978 to almost $100 million in 1981. The administration also made an effort to reach listeners in the satellite republics by increasing broadcasts in seven languages.[56] "Yet this does not tell the whole story, as the data indicate that information from Western broadcasts was often spread by 'word of mouth,' which served to amplify broadcast impact to a much larger part of Soviet society."[57]

Yeltsin too should have sent foreign broadcasters a note of thanks during the August 1991 coup attempt against Gorbachev. In Moscow, many citizens gained information from fuzzy images of CNN that they were able to pick up through the microwave relay running through Moscow to the Kremlin:

> "The morning of August 19, at about 8 a.m., when they cut off Ekho Moskvy, the situation [of those trying to follow events] seemed almost hopeless," wrote Moscow media critic Lydia Polskaya. "You couldn't listen endlessly to the 'appeal' of Yanayev! But at about 10 a.m., without any hope, I pushed the button for the fourth channel, where I can get CNN, and I was stunned: there were Americans working as if nothing had happened.... That's how I survived for three days, knowing for certain what was happening not far from my home."[58]

In his comprehensive study of Radio Liberty and Western broadcasting into the Soviet Union, Parta reports on a Vox Populi survey indicating that as many as 30 percent of Muscovites may have heard Radio Liberty broadcasts between August 19 and

21 and that this accounted for thousands making their way to the streets to join Boris Yeltsin at the White House.[59] Further testimony to the importance of the outside press during the attempted coup comes from Leonid Ionin in *Nezavisimaya Gazeta*:

> Radio Liberty and the BBC defeated the KGB and the CPSU. . . . If the high-level plot-ters had followed the tested recipe of General Yaruzelski [in declaring martial law in Poland]—seized the newspapers, radio stations, television, cut off telephones and iso-lated the White House from Moscow and Moscow from the rest of the Soviet Union and the world—they most likely would have succeeded. Any other way, they were doomed.[60]

The influence of the media on Soviet citizens had an intangible effect on their attitudes toward the regime and may have contributed to the cognitive divide that developed under Brezhnev in the 1970s. It also exposed Soviet leaders to the truth of the regime's failings. The information it provided helped defeat the coup plot-ters in 1991, which contributed to the Soviet collapse.

Trade Sanctions and Conditionality

After World War II, the United States came to believe that American "security inter-ests would be served best if the Soviet Union, Eastern Europe and People's Repub-lic of China were isolated from, rather than integrated into, the liberal world econ-omy."[61] For a policy of economic denial to be effective, however, the United States needed the cooperation of other Western governments. Western European countries were reluctant to cut important trade ties to the East and impede postwar economic recovery. Even so, by 1948 the West European states, led by Britain and France, had initiated their own selective export bans on strategic goods; in 1949 they coordinated their efforts and compiled the Anglo-French list of prohibited items. Under US pres-sure, Italy and West Germany agreed to abide by the more restrictive American list.

Despite these measures, Western Europe still faced a coordination problem; each country expressed a reluctance to ban export of an item unless all other coun-tries did the same. Moreover, they were wary that the appearance of economic warfare would provoke a military confrontation with the Soviet Union.[62] After a series of negotiations, in November 1949 the United States and West European allies agreed to form the Coordinating Committee for Multilateral Export Bans (CoCom).[63] CoCom was to be an independent association, disassociated from NATO, the Organisation for European Economic Co-operation (OEEC), and other transatlantic institutions.[64] In the following years, the list of prohibited ex-ports continued to expand under US pressure and growing European fear of inva-sion in the aftermath of the Korean War.

By the mid-1950s, however, European support for CoCom was waning; Britain proposed a 50 percent cut in items on the control list and called for greater economic integration with the East. In a new set of negotiations, the list was cut in half, and the allies agreed to focus attention on items of industrial and military significance.[65] Despite the revisions to CoCom policy, the United States continued its stricter unilateral embargo. Although the embargo was largely ineffective as an economic weapon without European cooperation, continued economic warfare "demonstrated, to the Soviets and the rest of the international community, the profound discontent of the United States with Soviet foreign and domestic policies and the willingness of the United States to stand in opposition to them."[66]

But by the mid-1960s, pragmatic considerations led American leaders to reconsider the efficacy of continued unilateral economic warfare. A 1963 Policy Planning Council report showed that the Soviet bloc was generally self-sufficient, and that the US embargo had only a minimal effect on Soviet military capacity. Trade liberalization would have no appreciable effect but could carry significant political benefits as a bargaining chip.[67] Evaluations of CoCom's effectiveness in the 1960s vary, largely due to a lack of clarity about its mission. Though the Soviet Union did increase its military power during the period, the controls do appear to have delayed "Soviet acquisition of military relevant Western technology," helping the West maintain its lead in the arms race.[68]

In 1972 the United States started negotiations in full to normalize trade relations with the East. The Nixon administration used Most Favored Nation (MFN) status and the relaxation of export controls to leverage political concessions from the Soviets. At the 1972 Nixon-Brezhnev summit, the Strategic Arms Limitation Talks (SALT) I treaty was signed and Brezhnev promised to pressure the North Vietnamese to negotiate a political settlement. In return, the Nixon administration agreed to triple bilateral trade and relax the unilateral export controls.

Nixon's MFN initiative though was defeated when seventy-two senators cosponsored the Jackson Amendment to the Trade Reform Act of 1974, which "prohibited the extension of credits or MFN to nonmarket economies that restricted or taxed emigration by their citizens." The Soviets responded by relaxing emigration restrictions (particularly on Russian Jews) but made clear that the amendment's passage would be met with Soviet displeasure.[69] Despite Nixon's pleading, the amended act passed in 1975 and was signed by President Ford. In response, the Soviets abrogated the entire trade agreement of 1972, contending that the emigration amendment went beyond the act's provisions. In the following years, popular and congressional sentiment in the United States grew suspicious of détente and wary of increasing trade links. As a result, in the absence of MFN status or other credits from the United States, the Soviet government had little economic reason to change its foreign policies.

President Carter came to power promising to abandon tactical linkage, but his administration quickly reversed itself, deciding to pursue economic diplomacy. When Congress still would not grant MFN status, the administration believed that it could influence Soviet behavior with other economic instruments. In response to Soviet human rights abuse and intervention in Somalia, the United States placed critical energy extraction technology on the embargo list. The United States also retroactively retracted a license for a US company to export a computer for a Soviet press agency during the 1980 Moscow Olympics.[70] However, Western allies refused to cooperate, and West Europeans stepped in to supply the Soviets both the computer and the needed energy technology. "Because the Soviets experienced little difficulty in acquiring Western computing systems or energy technology, the Carter administration's 1978 foreign policy controls did not provide leverage."[71]

During this period of general trade liberalization, CoCom continued to exist but experienced a decrease in effectiveness. Lax enforcement, confusion in interpretation of the control list, rapidly changing technology, and an increase in requested exceptions undermined its effectiveness and legitimacy. The United States had ceased to serve as an effective leader for the organization as its behavior appeared inconsistent and undisciplined; by the 1970s, it alone requested a majority of all control-list exceptions, sparking copycat behavior from other member states.[72]

After the 1979 Soviet invasion of Afghanistan, the United States showed a renewed interest in sanctions and economic warfare. In January 1980 the Carter administration announced a grain embargo, a potentially devastating move in a poor harvest year that was "intended to punish the Soviets for their foreign policy and, more important, to send a signal of U.S. resolve regarding future Soviet aggression."[73] In cutting agricultural exports, the United States hoped to inflict economic damage on the Soviet Union. However, the move backfired when other countries failed to follow suit. As a result, the United States simply lost a significant share of exports to the USSR as Argentina, Australia, and Canada took America's place. "American trade pressure on the Soviet Union was with regard to agricultural products, unsuccessful."[74]

Also early in 1980 the administration decided additionally to boycott the upcoming Moscow Olympics and to embargo fertilizer shipments. The measures were seen as conditional, with the administration prepared to lift them in exchange for Soviet good behavior. By March, the United States had prepared a new export control list that prohibited all exceptions on exports to the Soviet Union and further restricted technology transfer to lower-grade technologies and "process know-how" of militarily significant sectors.[75]

The Reagan administration placed an even greater emphasis on strengthening the strategic embargo, especially by placing greater limits on the transfer of Western technology and know-how.[76] The Western European allies, always lukewarm at best on economic embargoes involving the Soviet Union, predictably were less enthusiastic. At a January 1982 meeting, CoCom member states reaffirmed the strategic embargo but resisted Reagan's efforts to tighten restrictions.[77] Conflict between the United States and Europe escalated when Poland imposed martial law and cracked down on Solidarity.[78] In 1981 further conflict arose regarding a proposed natural gas pipeline from Siberia to Western Europe, which the Reagan administration opposed. In June 1982, after the Europeans refused to suspend activity on the pipeline, Reagan extended American pipeline sanctions to cover the activities of US firms acting in Europe, effectively halting construction. Western European governments pledged to proceed regardless, forcing companies to defy the United States. In response, the United States imposed retaliatory sanctions.[79]

Though most observers deem the set of sanctions between 1980 and 1982 a clear failure, some argue that the pipeline sanctions had a marginally negative effect on the Soviet economy. For instance, Peter Schweitzer argues that despite the eventual construction of the pipeline, sanctions were somewhat effective within the greater context of Reagan's offensive posture:

> In tandem with the geopolitical counteroffensive in Eastern Europe, the Administration fired the first volleys of what would become a secret economic war against the Kremlin. Using Poland as a justification, the Administration in 1982 imposed sanctions on Moscow, intended to cut off most of the technologies needed for a massive new natural-gas pipeline from Siberia, and for an energy program on the Sakhalin Islands being co-developed with Japan. The sanctions went to the heart of Soviet income: energy exports, which accounted for 80 per cent of Soviet hard-currency earnings. U.S. sanctions, which Western Europe resisted, did not stop construction of the pipeline, but delayed it two years, and cut it back in size. The Kremlin was out $15 to $20 billion.[80]

Trade sanctions did have some effect on Gorbachev's thinking, as he indicates in his memoirs:

> It was—and still is—my conviction that there can be no fruitful cooperation between two nations without economic ties. Apart from our grain imports, there were practically no such ties between the United States and the Soviet Union. We were isolated from each other by political decision and restrictions aimed at preventing the transfer of new technologies. The notorious CoCom lists impeded not only the United States but also many other countries from co-operating with us on a modern technological and economic level. Linking trade to human rights caused many difficulties for those who genuinely wanted to do business with us.[81]

In addition, during President George H. W. Bush's July 1991 visit to Moscow, Gorbachev "reminded Bush of the serious obstacles that the discriminatory laws of the United States and the CoCom lists were creating for our economy."[82]

Trade pressure may have helped the United States to achieve some of its political aims. During the 1980s, "the United States government made clear the areas in which it was looking for changes with regard to Soviet domestic and international behavior."[83] The first issue was the Soviet human rights record, particularly with regard to questions of dissent and restrictions on Jewish emigration. The USSR was a signatory to the Conference on Security and Cooperation in Europe (CSCE) and the Helsinki Final Act, agreements that bound the Soviet Union to some Western conceptions of human rights. "The West saw CSCE as a broad multilateral negotiating process aimed at not only lessening East-West tension but gradually encouraging the possibility for development of freedom and democracy (as they defined them) in Eastern Europe."[84] In the short term, Washington was looking for greater tolerance of dissent and emigration liberalization.[85]

Though it is unclear to what extent reforms were motivated by external pressure, tolerance of dissidence increased greatly under Gorbachev's policy of *glasnost* starting in 1987. Some evidence suggests that the Soviets were influenced by international human rights regimes: "In an article in *Pravda* in September, Gorbachev suggested that the United Nations play a leading role in the promotion and protection of human rights. He also stressed that governments had a duty to make their laws conform with international standards. In 1987 the Soviet Union also ratified the UN convention against torture."[86]

In his 1986 assessment of the internal well-being of the Soviet system, Timothy Colton argued that sanctions may be necessary as an occasionally used instrument to express moral outrage or concern or to raise the cost to Moscow of making undesirable foreign policy decisions. Actively promoting systemic reform, however, would come as a "result of trends and pressures internal to Soviet society."[87] Because of the minuscule proportion of US imports to the Soviet Union (0.1 percent in 1985) most sanctions would have relatively little effect on the state of the overall Soviet economy.[88]

Diplomacy, Normative Pressure, and Persuasion

Clearly, democracy promotion in the Soviet Union and then Russia was always an objective of American foreign policy, but never the primary objective. When the Soviet regime began to shake, George H. W. Bush and most (but not all) of his senior foreign policy advisers placed territorial preservation ahead of democratization as a US national interest. Bush also acquired tangible benefits for American national security from Gorbachev. He believed that helping Gorbachev stay in power, therefore, was more important than fostering regime change.

For most of the Clinton era, though, fostering economic reform trumped supporting democratic change. Clinton was also willing to sacrifice American influence over shaping Russia's internal developments in the pursuit of other foreign policy goals, be it NATO expansion or the war against Serbia. In these various lists of priorities, promoting democratization has not only ranked lower than other issues, but the pursuit of higher-ranking issues actually hindered the parallel pursuit of democracy promotion by US and other actors and later may even have impeded the development of democratization inside Russia after 1999.

But even if American presidents *had* made democratic regime change in the USSR and Russia their priority, they lacked any coherent strategy for achieving this goal. No game plan, no set of priorities, and no guidance existed about the sequence of political reforms or the relationship between reform plans for fostering capitalism and democracy. Would or should the project of democracy building in the largest country in the world cost $50 million, $1 billion, or 100 billion? Would it take 2, 10, or 20 years? No senior US official tried to answer these questions, nor could they. After all, the Russian experts in government at this time were experts in arms control and communism, not democratization.

Though initially skeptical of Gorbachev's true intentions, George H. W. Bush eventually embraced Gorbachev as a Soviet leader ready to deliver on foreign policy outcomes that the United States desired, be it the fall of the Berlin Wall, German unification, or Soviet troop withdrawal from Afghanistan. The Bush administration did not want to weaken or undermine the present leadership in the Kremlin. Besides, Gorbachev's political alternative, Boris Yeltsin, did not look appealing. At a White House visit in 1989, Yeltsin allegedly arrived drunk and acted boorishly, creating the impression that he was untrustworthy and unstable. Yeltsin's call for Russian sovereignty in 1990 made him particularly suspect for many Bush administration officials, since this move breached one of the principal rules of the game of the international system in which states recognize one another's right to exist.

Consequently, even as Yeltsin grew in strength, President Bush maintained a firm policy of noninterference in the internal affairs of the Soviet Union. Regarding the battle between the Soviet Union and Russia and the very personalized contests between Gorbachev and Yeltsin, the White House firmly sided with the internationally recognized leader of the USSR, Gorbachev. For Bush and National Security Advisor Brent Scowcroft, the paramount importance of stability in the US-Soviet relationship and the sense that Gorbachev could deliver for them on matters of importance to the United States led them to stand by their man and not actively promote regime change. Scowcroft recommended that the United States "avoid involvement in Soviet domestic political wars."[89] Others in the Bush team, including Secretary of Defense Dick Cheney, Deputy Undersecretary of Defense Lewis "Scooter" Libby, Assistant Secretary of Defense for International Security Policy Stephen J. Hadley, and some senior CIA analysts, wanted the United States to do more to aid Yeltsin and the democrats, but on this issue Scowcroft evidently prevailed. As Bush wrote in his diary in March 1991, "My view is, you dance with who is on the dance floor—you don't try to influence this succession, and you especially don't do something that would [give the] blatant appearance of [encouraging] destabilization."[90]

In fact, Bush went out of his way to aid the Soviet Union's survival, including most famously in a speech in Kiev in August 1991 when he warned that the dangers of ethnic conflict within the Soviet Union (including conflict with Russia) could fuel state collapse. Bush clearly proclaimed, "We support the struggle in this great country for democracy and economic reform." But he also warned advocates of Ukrainian independence that

> freedom cannot survive if we let despots flourish or permit seemingly minor restrictions to multiply until they form chains, until they form shackles. . . . Yet freedom is not the same as independence. America will not support those who seek independence in order to replace a far off tyranny with a local despotism. They will not aid those who promote a suicidal nationalism based upon ethnic hatred. We will support those who want to build a democracy.[91]

Later the same month, Yeltsin and his democratic allies defeated a coup attempt against right-wing members of Gorbachev's government. Only on the second day of the coup did Bush forcefully denounce the coup plotters,[92] though in truth the coup was an internal matter in which Russian democrats acted without external assistance. Just a few months later, the Soviet Union disappeared, and, despite Bush's warning, Ukraine and the fourteen other republics became independent countries.

Although Bush did not develop a close relationship with Yeltsin, his successor as president of the United States, Bill Clinton did. Wilsonian ideals infused President Clinton's thinking about Russia. In an address devoted to US-Russia relations on the eve of his first trip abroad as president to meet Yeltsin in Vancouver in April 1993, Clinton argued:

> Think of it—land wars in Europe cost hundreds of thousands of American lives in the twentieth century. The rise of a democratic Russia, satisfied within its own boundaries, bordered by other peaceful democracies, could ensure that our nation never needs to pay that kind of price again. I know and you know that, ultimately, the history of Russia will be written by Russians and the future of Russia must be charted by Russians. But I would argue that we must do what we can and we must act now. Not out of

charity but because it is a wise investment. . . . While our efforts will entail new costs, we can reap even larger dividends for our safety and our prosperity if we act now.[93]

During his first meeting with Yeltsin as president at the Vancouver summit, Clinton not only pledged financial support for the Yeltsin government in Russia but openly endorsed the Russian president as America's horse in the showdown between the president and parliament, saying to Yeltsin in front of the press, "Mr. President, our nation will not stand on the sidelines when it comes to democracy in Russia. We know where we stand. . . . We actively support reform and reformers and you in Russia."[94] When the conflict with parliament escalated into violence in October 1993, Clinton yet again defended Yeltsin's use of military force and demonized the parliament as antireformist communists. In his first public reaction to Yeltsin's dissolution of parliament, Clinton affirmed, "I support him fully."[95] Clinton officials said Yeltsin's precarious hold on power was a reason for the US Congress to support with even greater speed the administration's $2.5 billion aid package for the region. US officials subsequently praised the new constitution ratified by popular referendum in December 1993.

Democracy, Financial and Technical Assistance

The rhetorical devotion to democracy's advance especially during the Clinton administration was not matched by actual deeds, however. Facilitating economic reform, not democratic transition, became the real focus of Clinton's aid to Russia after the Soviet collapse. Beginning with a first meeting on February 6, 1993, a senior group in the new administration met for three months to devise an overall strategy toward Russia and the other newly independent states.[96]

At this early stage, officials at the Treasury Department (including Larry Summers and David Lipton) and on the National Security Council (NSC) staff had different priorities, and despite the lead of Clinton's special ambassador at large to the former Soviet states Strobe Talbott in these talks, the State Department was relatively less important in this area, primarily because Talbott by all accounts (including his own) had little expertise in economic matters. During his tenure, he focused primarily on traditionally defined strategic issues in the US-Russian relationship, which had been the subject of many of the books he had written earlier in his career. Many former Clinton officials reported that Talbott was not engaged in the technical issues of privatization, stabilization, or social policy reform.[97]

In retrospect, the former acting prime minister of Russia in 1992, Yegor Gaidar, believed that the absence of a major political figure behind the aid effort had negative consequences. "I don't think that the leaders of the major Western powers were unaware of the magnitude of the choices they faced. The trouble, in my view, was that there was no leader capable of filling the sort of organizing and coordinating role that Harry Truman and George C. Marshall played in the post war restoration of Europe."[98]

In the early years, Summers and Lipton provided the intellectual guiding principles for assistance to Russia in the Clinton administration. They prevailed in large part because they had a plan for reform, a theory behind it, and a clear idea of the tools needed to implement it. These two Treasury officials believed in the imperative of sequencing economic reform ahead of political reform. As Lipton recalls, "Our view was that America should make clear its support for reform in Russia. We thought that U.S. support for reform in Russia with Yeltsin, with the elites, with the public would be helpful to people who wanted to carry out reform."[99] The thinking was that if Russia could not stabilize its economy, then democracy would have no chance.

After the failed putsch in August 1991 and the dissolution of the USSR in December of that year, there was a consensus within the Russian government that Yeltsin had a popular mandate to initiate radical economic reform. It is not surprising that Yeltsin's supporters within the United States endorsed this idea as well. Finally, Russian economic reformers believed that they had a finite reserve of time before trust in Yeltsin and support for reform would wane. Driven by this perceived time constraint, Russia's reformers wanted to transform the economy as fast as possible to make reforms irreversible before they were forced out of office. Their American counterparts, particularly in the Treasury Department, shared their view.

The budgets to support economic versus political reform reflected these priorities. The International Monetary Fund (IMF), which focused almost exclusively on economic reform, played the central role in aiding Russia in the beginning of the 1990s and throughout the decade.[100] US bilateral assistance—the package of aid handled directly by the US government and not by the multilateral financial institutions—also reflected the "economics first" strategy. Of the $5.45 billion in direct US assistance to Russia between 1992 and 1998, only $130 million or 2.3 percent was devoted to programs involved directly in democratic reform.[101] When US government expenditures channeled through the Department of Commerce, the Overseas Private Investment Corporation, the US Export-Import Bank, and the US Trade and Development Agency are added to the equation, the primacy of economic reform becomes even more clear.

There were no officials working on democratization to serve as counterparts to the Clinton officials in the Treasury engaged in assisting with Russian economic reform. Instead, the job of promoting democracy was delegated to lower-level officials working primarily at the US Agency for International Development (USAID).

Clinton never made democracy a top issue in US-Russian relations. The United States and Russia had established joint commissions on defense conversion, the environment, and trade at the 1993 Vancouver summit but did not create a similar working group for political reform.

Given the strong rhetoric from senior US officials about the importance of Russian democracy, the relatively small amount of aid for democracy and rule of law assistance is curious. It may be that democracy promotion was deemed too politically sensitive and might imperil progress in the area of economic reform. Another argument is that democracy assistance did not need as much money because this kind of aid was cheaper to provide than economic assistance. As Brian Atwood explains, "Democracy programs don't cost that much money. Even if it's a case of running a successful election, you may spend 15–20 million dollars on the mechanical equipment and ballots: that's not a lot of money."[102]

USAID did join with the National Endowment for Democracy to fund the operations of the International Republican Institute, the National Democratic Institute, and the Free Trade Union Institute (funded by the AFL-CIO) in Russia. USAID also supported democratic assistance programs run by ABA-CEELI, ARDO-Checchi, the International Foundation for Electoral Systems (IFES), Internews, the Eurasia Foundation, and a host of other nongovernmental organizations (NGOs).[103] These groups focused on fostering the development of political parties, business associations, trade unions, and civic organizations, as well as promoting electoral reform, the rule of law, and an independent press. Their budgets were only shadows of the amounts spent on economic and technical assistance. NGOs, though, did help introduce Russian politicians to the effects of different types of voting systems. For instance, in 1992 NDI convened a series of working-group meetings on the relationship between electoral systems and parties, which included electoral experts on the American single-mandate system as well as the Portuguese, German, and Hungarian electoral regimes.[104] NDI also translated into Russian electoral laws from several countries. All of Russia's key decision makers on the electoral law at the time and senior officials from Yeltsin's presidential administration participated in these meetings. Facilitated by Western actors, the Western idea of proportional representation was brought to Russia and incorporated into law.

THE INTERACTION BETWEEN FACTORS IN BRINGING ABOUT DEMOCRATIC BREAKTHROUGH IN THE SOVIET UNION AND THEN RUSSIA

Although the West provided invaluable assistance at important junctures, this assistance did not cause the collapse of the Soviet Union or the democratic breakthrough of 1993. Ultimately, Russians brought the Soviet Union down and provided a democratic opening, although perhaps a short-lived one. This is despite the fact that US officials truly did seem to want this second Russian revolution to succeed.

More than two decades later, it is striking just how little real power the United States exercised over democratic change in the Soviet Union and then Russia. The United States emerged from the Cold War as the world's only superpower and has often been described as the most powerful country in history. Dramatic change in the Soviet Union and Russia occurred, to be sure. But the US role in facilitating this revolution has been much less than advertised. US policy did help Russia integrate with the West, and some American interventions (in particular the media) did prod domestic transformation in the intended direction, but there was no Marshall Plan; the United States did not provide Russia with a blueprint on how to build democracy from scratch. It can be neither blamed nor credited for the demise of the Soviet Union and Russia's initial transition to a fragile democracy in 1993.

Why and what lessons can we draw from this case about the interaction between democratic and international factors in bringing about regime collapse and democratic transition?

Ultimately, transition came from within, not from external factors. Still, at crucial junctures, external policies and decisions clearly influenced internal decision making. The sustained American efforts to encourage economic distress within the Soviet Union by driving up the cost of the arms race and by pursuing SDI clearly had an indirect effect on Gorbachev's decision making in the mid 1980s. But by this point the Soviet system was already in deep decline largely because communism had exhausted itself as an economic model. The ill-fated attempt to take over Afghanistan hastened the system's demise, and the US support of the *mujahideen* created an additional obstacle for the Soviet military, but the United States had little influence over the dramatic decline in world oil prices and expanding Soviet debt. These factors had a much greater impact on decisions Gorbachev made to reform the system.

There was an important transfer of ideas over constitutions and the distribution of authority between the president and parliament, electoral systems, and economic reform. But the United States was limited in its efforts to promote democracy by the strength of internal political actors with whom it chose to partner. When their influence on the process declined again, so did that of the United States. Further, while American NGOs may have been helpful in designing institutions associated with democratic states, to date they have done little to affect how these institutions actually function.

The Soviet empire is gone and will never be reconstituted. The market in Russia is also now permanent. Doubt, however, still remains about the future of democratic institutions. The US role in the overall drama was relatively limited. At the end of the day, when we finally are able to determine whether Russia's democracy has succeeded or failed, it will be Russians who should be blamed or praised.

NOTES

1. Two minor changes were made to the constitution of 1993 in 2008. These amendments extended the term of the Duma to five years from four, and the term of the president of Russia from four to six years.

2. See John Dunlop, *The Rise of Russia and the Fall of the Soviet Union* (Princeton, N.J.: Princeton University Press, 1993), chap. 5, for the most authoritative account of the coup attempt.

3. Dunlop (ibid., 202–3) provides some evidence that Gorbachev may have been able to act more freely when he was supposedly in custody in Crimea than he did. He allegedly had his communications system intact and could have contacted Yeltsin and Moscow, but may have been adopting a wait-and-see posture before declaring himself a prisoner of the GKChP.

4. Moshe Lewin, *The Gorbachev Phenomenon: A Historical Interpretation* (Berkeley: University of California Press, 1991), xx.

5. Timothy J. Colton, *The Dilemma of Reform in the Soviet Union* (New York: Council on Foreign Relations, 1986), 47.

6. Ibid., 35.

7. For an explanation of hard versus soft budget constraints, see, for example, Anders Aslund, *How Capitalism Was Built: The Transformation of Central and Eastern Europe, Russia, and Central Asia* (New York: Cambridge University Press, 2007), 15.

8. Ibid., 19.

9. Colton, *Dilemma of Reform*, 52.

10. Ibid., 36.

11. Ibid., 45.

12. Ibid., 32.

13. Ibid.; Alexander Dallin, "Causes of the Collapse of the USSR," *Post-Soviet Affairs* 8, no. 4 (1992): 279–302; Janos Kornai, *The Socialist System: The Political Economy of Communism* (Princeton, N.J.: Princeton University Press, 1992).

14. See, for example, John Dunlop, *The Rise of Russia and the Fall of the Soviet Union* (Princeton, N.J.: Princeton University Press, 1995); Archie Brown, *The Gorbachev Factor* (New York: Oxford University Press, 1997); and Mikhail S. Gorbachev, *Memoirs* (New York: Doubleday, 1995).

15. As cited in the *New York Times*, 1989, and at http://quotes.liberty-tree.ca/quote/mikhail_gorbachev_quote_e403.

16. See Anders Aslund, *Russia's Capitalist Revolution: Why Market Reform Succeeded and Democracy Failed* (Washington, D.C.: Peterson Institute for International Economics, 2007).

17. Timothy J. Colton, *Yeltsin: A Life* (New York: Basic Books, 2008).

18. Dunlop, *The Rise of Russia and the Fall of the Soviet Empire*, 11.

19. See Josephine Andrews, *When Majorities Fail: The Russian Parliament of 1990–1993* (New York: Cambridge University Press, 2002).

20. Richard Sakwa, *Russian Politics and Society*, 4th ed. (London: Routledge, 2008), 47.

21. Ibid.

22. While it seems that a majority of voters did support the constitution, it is not clear that 50 percent of eligible voters participated in the referendum, the required minimum to make the election valid. Some electoral observers amassed serious evidence suggesting that the turnout numbers had been falsified (A. E. Sobyanin and V. Sukhovolsky, "Democracy Restricted by Falsifications," unpublished manuscript, Moscow, 1995).

23. We are particularly grateful to Rachel Silverman for her able research assistance in helping us to complete this section of the report.

24. Peter Schweizer, "Who Broke the Evil Empire?" *National Review*, May 30, 1994, 4.

25. Mira Duric, *The Strategic Defence Initiative: US Policy and the Soviet Union* (London: Ashgate, 2003), 42–44.

26. Ibid., 44.

27. Peter Schweizer, *Victory: The Reagan Administration's Secret Strategy That Hastened the Collapse of the Soviet Union* (New York: Atlantic Monthly Press, 1994), 4.

28. Andrew E. Busch, "Ronald Reagan and the Defeat of the Soviet Empire," *Presidential Studies Quarterly* 27, no. 3 (Summer 1997): 452.

29. Schweizer, *Victory*, 195–96.

30. Busch, "Ronald Reagan and the Defeat of the Soviet Empire," 4.

31. Archie Brown presents the strongest argument against the idea that SDI played an important role in ending the Cold War, instead arguing that new leadership and new ideas played the decisive role in the change. He also rejects realist explanations for the end of the Cold War, as articulated by William Wohlforth and others. Given that even a successful SDI would not change the balance of power for at least 20 years, Brown maintains that it did not necessitate immediate changes in Soviet policy. Brown argues, "The Soviet Union's existing force of inter-continental ballistic missiles with multiple warheads was more than ample to make any potential American reliance on SDI catastrophically risky." Archie Brown, *Seven Years That Changed the World: Perestroika in Perspective* (Oxford: Oxford University Press, 2007), 273. In an earlier book, *The Gorbachev Factor*, 226–27, Brown also discussed the interplay of individual agency with SDI, specifically with regard to Gorbachev's role. He argues that while SDI may have slightly influenced Gorbachev's thinking, it would not have had a similar effect on other leaders had Gorbachev specifically not been in power in the late 1980s.

32. William Wohlforth, "Realism and the End of the Cold War," *International Security* 19, no. 3 (1994): 96.

33. Celeste A. Wallander, "Western Policy and the Demise of the Soviet Union," *Journal of Cold War Studies* 5, no. 4 (Fall 2003): 146–47.

34. Raymond Garthoff, *The Great Transition* (Washington, D.C.: Brookings Institution Press, 1994), 769.

35. Ibid., 753.

36. Sarah Mendelson, *Changing Course: Ideas, Politics and the Soviet Withdrawal from Afghanistan* (Princeton, N.J.: Princeton University Press, 1998), 70–71.

37. Ibid., 68–69.

38. Steve Coll, "Anatomy of a Victory: CIA's Covert Afghan War; $2 Billion Program Reversed Tide for Rebels," *Washington Post*, July 19, 1992, 2.

39. Ibid., 3.

40. Mendelson, *Changing Course*, 69, 96.

41. By 1986, the United States sought to undermine Soviet reliance on air power in Afghanistan and shipped Stinger antiaircraft missiles to the *mujahideen*. Blowpipe missiles, the British equivalent, were also provided. Between September 1986 and August 1987, 1,150 missiles were shipped to Pakistan and 863 were received in Afghanistan. However, accounts of their effectiveness are mixed, and Soviet casualty rates did not increase after the missiles' deployment. Coll, "Anatomy of a Victory," 2.

42. Wallander, "Western Policy and the Demise of the Soviet Union," 165.

43. Ibid., 167.

44. Mendelson, *Changing Course*, 11–12.

45. Yegor Gaidar, *Collapse of an Empire: Lessons for Modern Russia* (Washington, D.C.: Brookings Institution Press, 2008), 107.

46. Ibid., 4–5.

47. Ibid., 5–6.

48. Ibid., 6.

49. Joshua Muravchik, *Exporting Democracy: Fulfilling America's Democracy Abroad* (Washington, D.C.: American Enterprise Institute, 1991): 190–91.

50. "Cold War Broadcasting Impact," report on a conference organized by the Hoover Institution and the Cold War International History Project of the Woodrow Wilson International Center for Scholars at Stanford University, October 13–16, 2004, 37.

51. Muravchik, *Exporting Democracy*, 191.

52. "Cold War Broadcasting Impact," 33.

53. David S. Foglesong, *The American Mission and the "Evil Empire": The Crusade for a "Free Russia"* (New York: Cambridge University Press, 2008), 145.

54. Arch Puddington, *Broadcasting Freedom: The Cold War Triumph of Radio Free Europe and Radio Liberty* (Lexington: University of Kentucky Press, 2003), 171–72.

55. Eugene Parta, *Discovering the Hidden Listener: An Empirical Assessment of Radio Liberty and Western Broadcasting to the USSR during the Cold War* (Stanford, Calif.: Hoover Institute Press, 2007), 53.

56. Western broadcasters and listeners within the Soviet bloc were ingenious in discovering methods by which they could avoid jamming. In a 2004 report, it was estimated that between 1978 and 1990, these forms of Western media reached as many as 25 million listeners inside the Soviet Union every day and over twice that many in an average week. VOA purportedly had the largest audience during this time frame, apparently reaching 15 percent of the adult population of the Soviet Union per week. See Foglesong, *The American Mission*, 170, and "Cold War Broadcasting Impact," 15.

57. "Cold War Broadcasting Impact," 15–16.

58. Scott Shane, *Dismantling Utopia: How Information Ended the Soviet Union* (Chicago: Ivan R. Dee, 1994), 264.

59. Parta, *Discovering the Hidden Listener*, xv.

60. Shane, *Dismantling Utopia*, 266.

61. Michael Mastanduno, *Economic Containment: CoCom and the Politics of East-West Trade* (Ithaca, N.Y.: Cornell University Press, 1992), 64.

62. Ibid., 75–77.

63. Ibid., 78–80.

64. Ibid., 81–93.

65. Ibid., 93–94.

66. Ibid., 97.

67. Ibid., 126–28, 132–33.

68. Ibid., 119–20.

69. Ibid., 149.

70. Ibid., 153–55.

71. Ibid., 155–56.

72. Ibid., 170–75.

73. Ibid., 223

74. Mohammed Ishaq, *The Politics of Trade Pressure: American-Soviet Relations, 1980–1988* (London: Ashgate, 1999), 71–72.

75. Mastanduno, *Economic Containment*, 223–26.

76. Ibid., 234–36.

77. Ibid., 243–44.

78. Ibid., 245–47. See also the chapter 3 on Poland by Gregory Domber in this volume.

79. Ibid., 247–60.

80. Peter Schweitzer, "Who Broke the Evil Empire?" *National Review*, May 30, 1994.

81. Gorbachev, *Memoirs*, 448.

82. Ibid., 622.

83. Ishaq, *Politics of Trade Pressure*, 124–26.

84. Ibid., 125.

85. Ibid., 128.

86. Ibid., 135.

87. Colton, *The Dilemma of Reform in the Soviet Union*, 220.

88. Ibid., 222. See also Philip Hanson, *Western Economic Statecraft in East-West Relations* (London: Royal Institute of International Affairs, 1988).

89. George H. W. Bush and Brent Scowcroft, *A World Transformed* (New York: Vintage Books, 1998), 499.

90. Ibid., 500.

91. President George H. W. Bush, "Remarks to the Supreme Soviet of the Republic of Ukraine in Kiev, Soviet Union, August 1, 1991, http://bushlibrary.tamu.edu/papers/1991/91080102.html.

92. On the first day of the coup, Bush stressed, "There's very little we can do right now. . . . We're not going to overexcite the American people or the world. And so, we will conduct our diplomacy in a prudent fashion, not driven by excess, not driven by extreme." August 19, 1991, pp. 5–7, http://bushlibrary.tamu.edu/papers/1991/91080102.html.

93. President Bill Clinton, "A Strategic Alliance with Russian Reform," April 1, 1993, in *US Department of State Dispatch* 4, no. 13 (April 5, 1993): 189–94.

94. Serge Shmemann, "Summit in Vancouver: The Overview," *New York Times*, April 5, 1993, A1.

95. "Clinton Sends Yeltsin His Full Support," Associated Press, September 23, 1993.

96. Participants included President Clinton, National Security Adviser Anthony Lake and his deputy, Samuel Berger; Vice President Gore and his national security adviser, Leon Fuerth; senior NSC staffers for this region Toby Gati and Nicholas Burns; Ambassador-at-Large for the NIS Strobe Talbott; and presidential adviser George Stephanopoulos. See Jeremy D. Rosner, *The New Tug of War* (Washington, D.C.: Brookings Institution Press, 2005), 49–50.

97. Brian Atwood, former Clinton administration official, interview by McFaul, Washington, D.C., January 19, 2001.

98. Yegor Gaidar, *Days of Defeat and Victory* (Seattle: University of Washington Press, 1999), 152.

99. David Lipton, interview by McFaul, Washington, D.C., January 19, 2001.

100. Between 1992 and 1999, the IMF loaned $22 billion to Russia, which was roughly three-quarters of all multilateral lending to Russia in the 1990s. See Augusto Lopez-Claros, "The Role of International Financial Institutions during the Transition in Russia," unpublished manuscript, September 2002.

101. Our calculations are based on analyses of budgets described in the annual reports of the aid compiled by the Office of the Coordinator of US Assistance to the NIS called US Government Assistance to and Cooperative Activities with the Newly Independent States of the Former Soviet Union (US Department of State, 1992–99).

102. Atwood interview.

103. Regrettably, no comprehensive history or assessment of these programs in Russia has been written. On some individual sectors, see James Richter, "Evaluating Western Assistance to Russian Women's Organizations," 54–90, and Leslie Powell, "Western and Russian Environmental NGOs: A Greener Russia?" 126–51, both in Sarah Mendelson and John Glenn, eds., *The Power and Limits of NGOs: A Critical Look at Building Democracy in Eastern Europe and Eurasia* (New York: Columbia University Press, 2003); Lisa McIntosh Sundstrom, "Strength from Without? Transitional Influences on NGO Development in Russia" (Ph.D. diss., Stanford University, 2001); "Democracy Assistance and Political Transition in Russia: Between Success and Failure," *International Security* 25 (Spring 2001): 68–106.

104. In the interest of full disclosure, Michael McFaul headed the NDI office in Moscow at this time.

CHAPTER THREE

Poland

International Pressure for a Negotiated
Transition, 1981–1989

GREGORY F. DOMBER

Early on the morning of December 13, 1981, General Wojciech Jaruzelski, the leader of the communist Polish United Workers' Party (PZPR), declared martial law and jailed thousands of political activists linked to the Independent Self-Governing Trade Union "Solidarność." Over the next eight years, the Communist government and the democratic opposition struggled over power against a backdrop of increasingly dire domestic economic conditions. By the second half of the 1980s, General Secretary of the Communist Party of the Soviet Union Mikhail Gorbachev began pursuing a policy of "new thinking" in relations with Eastern Europe—decreasing economic subsidies, thereby weakening Poland's economic position but increasing independence, which allowed the PZPR to pursue political reforms without fear of interference. While Jaruzelski pursued a policy of slow political normalization, officially suspending martial law in 1983 and declaring a final amnesty for interned Solidarność activists in 1986, the PZPR did not succeed in resolving endemic economic malaise and social instability.

A DEMOCRATIC BREAKTHROUGH

Over these tenuous years, the United States and Western Europe enacted policies meant to pressure the PZPR to hasten and expand political liberalization. In December 1981 President Ronald Reagan imposed economic sanctions, and then, from 1983 onward, Washington utilized a "step-by-step" policy of lifting particular sanctions in return for small steps towards political pluralism. While Western European nations did not initially adopt stringent sanctions, in 1986 the European Economic Community (EEC) threatened to rescind pending economic and political improvements unless all remaining political prisoners were released, creating a unified front. Beyond punitive sanctions, Poland's inability to service its massive international debt decreased possibilities for further Western loans, cutting the domestic economy off from renewed lending.

Simultaneously, American nongovernmental organizations (NGOs) provided needed monetary and material support to Solidarność through a network of Polish émigrés sympathetic to the democratic opposition, supplying it with the money, ink, printing presses, radios, transmitters, and computers needed to reorganize itself as an underground institution. The creation of the National Endowment for Democracy (NED) in November 1983 provided a deep new funding source of Western support to Solidarność, privileging it against other opposition groups and helping to maintain the movement's domestic legitimacy.

In 1988 in a tense atmosphere charged by two consecutive waves of strikes, Jaruzelski's government understood that it could no longer delay substantive economic reforms and keep a lid on social instability. But, in order to gain the public support it needed to implement painful price reforms, the PZPR was forced to seek agreement with Solidarność. Including Solidarność in a new arrangement also greatly increased the chances of renewed Western economic support. Negotiations with Solidarność culminated in the Round Table Agreements signed April 1989, which allowed for semi-free elections. In the wake of the opposition's electoral victory in June 1989, Solidarność leaders took advantage of political infighting within the communist government to forge an opposition-led coalition. At the end of August 1989 Tadeusz Mazowiecki became Poland's first noncommunist prime minister since World War II. While Jaruzelski remained president and the PZPR retained leadership positions in the ministries of internal affairs and defense, Poland passed a monumental threshold, successfully completing a democratic breakthrough.

Overall, Poland's dire domestic economic and political problems—exacerbated by pressure from the West, magnified by its enormous international debt, and intensified by Gorbachev's reform-minded government—lingered unresolved and finally grew to a breaking point at which Jaruzelski was forced to turn to the indigenous opposition for help. In part because of the significant support it had received from the United States and Western Europe, Solidarność was the only group that could provide the legitimacy the government needed. While the sources of the democratic revolution in 1989 were primarily domestic, internal problems magnified by outside interference opened the door for the Round Table process and Poland's democratic breakthrough.

DOMESTIC EVENTS

Shortly after the end of World War II, the PZPR consolidated political power, transforming Poland into a socialist state and a satellite of the Soviet Union for the remainder of the Cold War. Three important domestic trends, however, differentiated Poland from other members of the Eastern bloc. First, the Polish Catholic Church, which had a long tradition of safeguarding Polish national identity, maintained significant independence from the state and often acted as a mediator between society and the government. The church's strength grew exponentially when the bishop of Kraków, Karol Wotyła, became Pope John Paul II and made a triumphant pilgrimage to Poland in 1979. Second, a pattern of economic crisis followed by government concessions emerged first in 1956 when workers took to the streets in response to price increases and successfully pressured the PZPR into removing the general secretary. The pattern was repeated after strikes on the Baltic Coast in December 1970 and outside Warsaw in 1976, showing that workers could effect changes in economic policy and at the highest leadership levels. Third, by the mid-1970s, Poland had a small but mature and dedicated indigenous political opposition movement, including the Workers' Defense Committee, Helsinki monitoring groups, independent *samizdat* publishing houses, and a nascent free trade-union movement.

Each of these three domestic trends culminated in a series of strikes in August 1980 including the Lenin Shipyard in Gdańsk. Unlike earlier strikes, which primarily demanded economic concessions, the 1980 strike leaders, most prominently Lech Wałęsa, called for the creation of independent trade unions, an overtly political demand in a Marxist system where government legitimacy was based on claims of representing workers' concerns. The regional strikes quickly became a nationwide phenomena, and the PZPR opted to negotiate. On August 31, 1980, PZPR and strike representatives signed the Gdańsk Accords, clearing the way for the creation of the Independent Self-Governing Trade Union "Solidarność." Within a year Solidarność had between 8 million and 10 million members from all parts of society (including party members) in a population of about 38 million and a loose institutional structure with local, regional, and national offices. From August 1980 to December 1981, Solidarność activists mobilized nationwide and regional strikes to pressure the government to fulfill the Gdańsk Accords, bringing the Polish economy to a standstill and creating an intense atmosphere of crisis.

Under acute pressure from the Soviet Union to regain control of the country and the implicit threat of a Soviet invasion, Jaruzelski declared martial law on December 12, 1981, and mobilized elite units of the security services to capture Solidarność leaders. The operation was a near complete success. More than 3,000 activists were imprisoned, with only a few nationally known leaders eluding capture. A few small occupation strikes were called, but the security services reacted swiftly and violently to break them. Within a week of the declaration, Solidarność was in shambles, and the PZPR was in control of the country again.

With full military and political control, Jaruzelski turned to Poland's most pressing problem: economics. Oversimplifying, the economy suffered from high inflation, decreasing productivity, lack of consumer goods, market disequilibrium within the system, deficits in foreign trade, substantial debt repayment problems, and inefficiencies in the management system. These problems, though common across Eastern Europe, were more acute in the Polish case because of recurrent political crises. According to figures compiled by the PZPR, national production income, consumption, and imports all decreased from 1980 through 1983. Through the end of 1982, all major economic indicators showed losses between 10 and 33 percent when compared to data from 1978.[1] In more macroeconomic terms, real GDP per capita measured in 2004 złoty dropped precipitously in 1981 and 1982 before growing from 1983 to 1986. Overall it took from 1983 to the middle of 1987 to recover from the losses incurred in 1981 and 1982.[2]

In the face of Western sanctions in response to martial law, the PZPR turned toward the East for economic support. Jaruzelski's requested and received sharp increases in Soviet aid and turned toward his major trading partners and allies in COMECON—the Council for Mutual Economic Assistance, which encompassed most of the Soviet bloc—for improved support and concessions.[3] The PZPR also pursued a series of tepid economic reforms, called the "First Stage," which were meant to improve productivity by allowing for more market mechanisms within particular industries and decreasing bureaucracy, particularly through increased worker self-management and self-financing by individual enterprises. In 1986 the government announced the "Second Stage" economic reforms, taking further steps to decentralize economic decision making and to allow for greater coordination with foreign companies. In both cases, the reform efforts bore little fruit, primarily because attempts to decease bureaucratic oversight and to decentralize led to the creation of new government bodies, which suffered from the inefficiencies and corruption of the system it was replacing.[4]

These economic efforts from December 1981 to mid-1987 were combined with gradual political liberalization. Wałęsa was released from prison in November 1982 after a series of meetings between Archbishop Józef Glemp and Jaruzelski.[5] A contingent of other unthreatening political prisoners was released in a limited amnesty in December 1982 at the same time that the PZPR took the symbolic step of suspending martial law in order to focus on Poland's economic problems.[6] Pope John Paul II was allowed to make a pilgrimage to Poland in June 1983 but only after lengthy negotiations with Vatican representatives confirmed that the pope would moderate his political messages to promote understanding between the government and the people rather than fan social discontent.[7] On July 22, 1983 (the anniversary of the founding of the People's Republic of Poland), martial law was officially lifted, and another limited amnesty of political prisoners was announced but only after legal changes institutionalized many of the government's new powers. Another limited amnesty was implemented in July 1984, with many prominent activists finding themselves returned to prison within a few months. Under intense pressure from the international community in the summer of 1986, the PZPR declared a final amnesty, releasing all political prisoners (without reinterning them) in September 1986.

During this period of political evolution from December 1981 to September 1986, Solidarność rebuilt itself as an underground organization. The handful of national leaders who remained at large resurrected the movement in secret and organized annual strikes on May 1 and August 31, which initially brought significant numbers of workers onto the street but did not succeed in forcing political breakthroughs. The Solidarność underground also rebuilt its "independent" publishing networks saturating the country with *samizdat*. Casual acts of resistance, including antigovernment graffiti, work absenteeism, attending illegal theater performances and artists openings, and reading and distributing *samizdat* became commonplace. After the September 1986 amnesty, Solidarność maintained its underground structures but also created semipublic groups reconstituting old leadership structures.

By the end of 1986, the democratic opposition and the government had come to a modus vivendi of sorts. Solidarność remained illegal, but its former leaders were allowed to live openly. They were harassed and detained by security services but no longer imprisoned for long periods of time. By early 1987, Poland's economic situation was also turning a corner, with GDP finally returning to pre-1980 levels. The overall situation, however, remained tense. As the PZPR reported in August 1987, "General anxiety is rising due to the prolonged economic crisis. An opinion is spreading that the economy instead of improving is getting worse. As a result there arises an ever greater dissonance between the so-called official optimism of the authorities ('after all it's better') and the feeling of society. . . . Social dissatisfaction is growing."[8]

This tense calm was fractured in early 1988 by labor disturbances. In response to price increases, steelworkers at a mill southeast of Warsaw held a protest rally on April 22 calling for pay increases and greater freedom for unions. Soon after, municipal workers in Bydgoszcz held wildcat strikes, which ended only after local party leaders agreed to raise wages. After seeing this success, workers at the Lenin

Steelworks outside of Kraków went on strike, demanding wage increases but also requiring that workers removed for opposition activities be reinstated. Workers outside Warsaw then followed through on threats, striking to raise pay and relegalize Solidarność. A week later the Lenin Shipyard in Gdańsk declared its own strike.[9]

In response, the PZPR utilized tested strikebreaking methods. Riot police stormed the gates of the Lenin Steelworks, beating, arresting, and carrying away workers.[10] Elite units of the militia amassed outside of the Lenin Shipyard, shining bright lights and beating their truncheons against police trucks in a show of force meant to intimidate workers.[11] Authorities harassed Solidarność leaders, detaining about twenty-five activists and briefly jailing some. Under strong government pressure, the strikes concluded on May 10 with workers peacefully exiting the shipyard with their goals unmet, despite the fact that Wałęsa had joined them behind the gates.[12] As one historian has summarized, "It looked as though [the PZPR] were no longer in imminent danger, the strike wave would not be repeated any time soon, and the prestige of Wałęsa and Solidarity had suffered a serious blow."[13]

In mid-August, however, a second wave of strikes swept across Poland, beginning with the July Manifesto Coal mine. Within a week's time, nine other mines had joined. In addition, workers were again occupying the Lenin Shipyard, portions of the Lenin Steelworks, and numerous other small industries. These events were particularly dangerous for the PZPR because coal exports provided a significant source of foreign currency. Second, many of the striking workers were in their teens and twenties with only vague memories of the 1980 strikes, proving that another generation of workers had been radicalized. Finally, most strike committees called for the reemergence of Solidarność, making these strikes more political than the previous round.

In the middle of the second wave of strikes, the PZPR Politburo discussed a possible new direction: initiating talks with Wałęsa. Meeting on August 21, the Politburo clearly feared that strikes would both intensify and spread, leading to "spillover effects" or as Minister of the Interior Czesław Kiszczak defined them, "points of explosion." Politburo members also recognized that "the population . . . locates its sympathies on the side of Solidarność."[14] Disagreements over relegalizing Solidarność continued, but contacts with the opposition intensified. When the Politburo met again on August 28, it decided to negotiate directly with Wałęsa and his inner circle, utilizing the issue of trade union pluralism as a bargaining chip. "In the situation when the summer strikes were obviously stronger than the strikes in the spring, and Jaruzelski—despite being in charge of preparations— had not decided to introduce an exceptional state [*stan wyjątkowy*], initiating a dialogue with moderate opposition appeared to be the optimal solution. 'It is a bold path, but it is the path forward,' [Jaruzelski] declared . . . adding simultaneously that 'tomorrow the situation will be worse.' "[15] On August 31, 1988, the eighth anniversary of the Gdańsk accords, Kiszczak met with Wałęsa, and in the presence of Bishop Jerzy Dąbrowski invited him to further talks, contingent upon all existing strikes ending.

The strikes came to an end on September 4, and formal negotiations between the opposition and the government began in secret on September 16, just outside of Warsaw in the village of Magdalenka. By then each side was talking about the possibility of "round table" negotiations to decide Poland's path forward. In his opening remarks, Kiszczak explained:

> The "round table" could take a stance and eventually correct the economic model, which should ensure that reforms are effectively realized, achieve economic equilibrium, and dissolve the debt issue. The economic reform program's success, through assuring equal chances and workloads to all forms of ownership, depends upon the degree of its comprehension and social acceptance.[16]

For the government, the key issue was the economy and finding a way to get opposition support for the painful measures (particularly price rationalization) needed to get the economy working again. The government knew that changes would succeed only if they had "social acceptance." The talks broke without agreement when Wałęsa demanded that Solidarność be legalized as a part of the Round Table agreements. However, after Wałęsa appeared on national television to debate the head of the state-sponsored workers' union, government public opinion polls showed 73 percent of the population favored legalizing Solidarność, suggesting that Solidarność was a viable partner to provide necessary PZPR reforms a measure of social acceptance.[17]

On December 20–21, 1988, and January 16–17, 1989, the PZPR held its Tenth Party Plenum, and Jaruzelski was able to push through a motion to relegalize Solidarność. However, some party members loudly complained that this decision had been forced upon them. The issue became so contentious that during an emergency Politburo meeting Jaruzelski asked for a vote of confidence. Despite the divisive vote (32 of 178 Central Committee members voted against and 14 abstained), Jaruzelski and his fellow reformers remained in office and won the debate to legalize Solidarność. With Wałęsa's precondition met, Jaruzelski cleared the final hurdle for full-scale negotiations.

The Round Table negotiations began on February 6 and ran through April 4, 1989, with working groups focusing on political, economic, and social reform. On one side sat members of the political opposition—primarily activists linked with Solidarność—and representatives from the church. The government side was made of a coalition dominated by the PZPR but which included two minor parties: the United Peasant Party (ZSL) and the Social Democrats (SD)—remnants of early communist attempts to create a national front government. Key political agreements in the accords included forming a new office of the president, creating a 100-member upper house of parliament (Senat), and setting guidelines for semi-free elections: all seats in the Senat were open to competition, while the opposition could compete for 35 percent of Sejm (the existing lower house of parliament) seats. Only candidates from the government coalition, including high-level PZPR reformers who would run unopposed on a so-called national list, could run for the remaining 65 percent of seats. Elections were called for June 4 and 18.

Solidarność candidates won 99 seats in the Senat and all 161 Sejm seats open to them. Equally surprisingly, few of the government candidates reached a necessary threshold of 50 percent support to keep from appearing on the ballot for June 18, including all but two of the prominent PZPR reformers who ran on the national list. Voters took the time to cross out the names on the list, showing their disgust for these party leaders, reformers or not.

As the January events attest, cohesion in the PZPR-led government coalition was falling apart; however, it was not until after elections in June that cracks in the party caused a full political crisis when the satellite parties (SD and ZSL) began to pursue their own self-interest. As the US embassy reported two days after the first round of elections, the opposition "quietly claims to have at least 10 perspective Peasant's Party (ZSL) deputies in its pockets. The glue that has held the ruling coalition together—the permanence and inevitability of PZPR rule—has been eliminated."[18] Government cohesion continued to fray in July as members of the coalition refused to vote for Jaruzelski as president (an implicit part of the Round Table deal), forcing Solidarność parliamentarians to support his candidacy.

With the opposition's new role of kingmaker, Solidarność began to pursue the possibility of forming its own government. Under Wałęsa's leadership (who had not run for public office but remained the head of the Solidarność union) the opposition blocked Jaruzelski's nominee for prime minister from forming a government and steadfastly fought against PZPR pressure to create a grand coalition government in which opposition members would hold cabinet positions but the PZPR would retain the premiership. Wałęsa also quietly instructed Solidarność activists to begin secret negotiations with the ZSL and SD about possibilities for a Solidarność-led coalition.[19] In August these negotiations succeeded. With a new coalition of Solidarność, ZSL, and SD parliamentarians, well-known Catholic intellectual and longtime Solidarność adviser Tadeusz Mazowiecki was elected prime minister and charged with forming a government. Solidarność had successfully overseen Poland's transformation to the point of democratic breakthrough.

INTERNATIONAL EVENTS
Pressure on the PZPR

Both the Carter and Reagan administrations viewed the formation of Solidarność in August 1980 as an important move toward increased pluralism, directly challenging and weakening the communist system. So in the months between August 1980 and December 1981 the United States supported developments in Poland. For example, less than two weeks after the Gdańsk Accords, President Jimmy Carter announced that Poland would receive $670 million in credits for FY 1980–81, an increase of $120 million over FY 1979–80. Similarly, just a week before the declaration of martial law, the Reagan White House was finalizing an agreement to increase aid to $740 million including $100 million in emergency aid for animal feed, because according to the CIA "our national security interests are well served by gambling $740 million (or other sums) in credits in the hope that it will allow the Polish experiment to continue and in the knowledge that the experiment's very survival will contribute to the long-term unraveling of the Soviet position in Eastern Europe."[20]

When Jaruzelski turned the mechanisms of state power against Solidarność, the US government reversed course and pressured the PZPR to return to its previous policies. On December 17, 1981, Reagan condemned the use of military force, focusing particularly on the abuse of human rights as violations of the Helsinki Final Act. This was contrasted by West European voices, particularly the West Germans, who were openly sympathetic toward martial law. From December 1981 to September 1986, American diplomats regularly invoked the Helsinki Agreements as a pretext for raising concerns about treatment of specific individuals and more generalized calls for political amnesty. In 1982 the United States Information Agency promoted the global distribution and airing of the documentary "Let Poland Be Poland" to keep international attention focused on human rights abuses. Reagan also frequently spoke out in public against Jaruzelski's government, including a memorable speech to the British Parliament in June 1982, which called for the West to improve efforts at promoting democracy. Although public attention waned after the first year of martial law, the United States refused to hold high-level meetings with Polish officials, most notably when the White House snubbed Jaruzelski during his visit to the fortieth opening session of the United Nations in 1985. West European leaders maintained similar restrictions on high-level contacts until 1985.

In addition to these political steps, the Reagan administration invoked a series of economic sanctions. Initially Washington stopped consideration of the $100 million in emergency aid and blocked sending $47 million in dairy products left in the FY 1980–81 account. This provided a real sting to the PZPR, because its poultry industry (an important source of protein) was near collapse and in need of the feed. The Poles, however, stayed the course. When it became clear that the initial sanctions had not effected change, the Reagan administration increased sanctions to include halting the renewal of Export-Import Bank insurance credits, suspending all LOT flights to and from the United States, suspending Poland's rights to fish in American waters, and working with NATO to increase restrictions on technology trade. By the end of 1982 Poland had lost Most Favored Nation (MFN) status, and Washington was blocking its pending request for International Monetary Fund (IMF) membership.

These sanctions were seen as reversible if the PZPR met three clear demands: end martial law, free all political prisoners, and begin a dialogue with representatives of the people. By spring 1983, sanctions had sparked few changes, so the White House decided on a new negotiating stance labeled the "step-by-step" approach. Under this approach individual sanctions could be lifted in return for specific changes in Warsaw that progressed toward, but did not necessarily fulfill, America's three demands.[21] The step-by-step approach remained policy from mid-1983 to February 10, 1987, when Reagan lifted the final sanctions in response to the complete political amnesty announced in September 1986.

Because Polish-American trade was relatively small compared to trade with Western Europe, the Reagan administration knew that its primary point of leverage was not trade but the PZPR's massive international debt. During the 1970s, Poland's government took advantage of improved East-West relations fostered by détente to gain loans and credits from both Western governments, coordinated through an informal group known as the Paris Club, and private Western banks, coordinated through the London Club. While loans had provided easy money to artificially prop up Poland's economy, by 1980 Poland owed around $23 billion, which was beginning to come due. According to calculations by the State Department after the declaration of martial law, even with the economy in shambles Polish exports could pay for all necessary Western imports. However, the Warsaw government did not have enough hard currency to cover its debt payments. To keep their economy afloat the Poles needed public and private debt rescheduling and new export and agricultural credits from the West. In this analysis, Western economic leverage after December 1981 came from "continuing trade relationships; debt service relief, both public and private; and access to new credits, both public and private."[22]

Initially, Washington used the threat of blocking Paris Club talks to pressure the PZPR to lessen internal repression. However, by early 1983 and with little hope that Poland would be able to pay in full, some other creditor nations were expressing "their doubts about the appropriateness of delaying a Polish rescheduling,"[23] pressuring the United States to allow talks. By August 1983 the United States dropped its reservations, because it believed US allies were "prepared to move on their own."[24] Negotiations opened later in the year, and in July 1985 the Paris Club announced that it had agreed to reschedule $12 billion in debts owed from 1982 to 1984, followed by another agreement in November rescheduling $1.37 billion in debt from 1985.[25] Despite these successes at rescheduling, Poland remained highly indebted with the total amount owed growing to more than $40 billion by 1989. At the same time, Poland's ability to repay the debt decreased from a debt service ratio of 1.88 in 1981 to 0.76 in 1988. Overall, the "debt service burden constrained sustained economic growth."[26] Most importantly for international considerations, however, Poland's substantial debt hurt its creditworthiness, limiting the PZPR's ability to gain any new loans. Private banks in particular were loath to open up new funding sources after having lost money on the large loans floated a decade earlier.[27]

Poland's international economic problems did not come only from the West; in the second half of the 1980s, the USSR decreased subsidies for COMECON partners. By the end of 1982, Eastern Europe had become an economic liability for the Soviet Union, primarily because COMECON partners purchased raw materials and energy at subsidized prices "that had not kept pace with world market prices."[28] While previous leaders had shouldered these burdens, Gorbachev set out to reverse course, writing to members of the Soviet Politburo in June 1986 that "a genuine turning point in the entire system of collaboration with our allies is needed."[29] Six months later, Gorbachev was becoming increasingly frustrated with his allies, explaining to the Politburo, "It is pointless to shout that we are wrong to give [gas, oil, and raw materials] to them so cheaply. We need to shift to mutually beneficial trade. And we should hold more firmly to the principle of each communist party being responsible for what happens in its country."[30] While Poland had turned to the Soviets for increased aid in the aftermath of martial law, by the Gorbachev era that source of economic support was drying up.

Gorbachev's new relationship with Poland was not without its benefits. While the punitive side of Soviet "new thinking" meant decreases in subsidies, Gorbachev's new policy also meant that the USSR gave East Europeans more room to exercise their own discretion when dealing with domestic problems. Unlike 1980 to 1981, when the Kremlin powerfully interjected itself to push for a conservative response to the ongoing crisis, Gorbachev made clear that he would not interfere in Poland's domestic affairs. Moreover, he pursued increasingly radical domestic political reforms of his own, leading East European reformers including Jaruzelski by example. Finally, Gorbachev pursued improved economic and political relations with Western Europe hoping to create a "common European home," illustrating that East Europeans could take similar steps to improve economic coordination with the West.[31] Thus, although the Soviet Union was cutting economic subsidies, Gorbachev provided the PZPR with leeway to pursue domestic political reforms and improvements with the West. He even forged a close relationship with Jaruzelski, as the two tried to reform their political and economic systems.[32] In line with his ideals of new thinking that emphasized self-determination, Gorbachev did not dictate changes to be made by the PPZR; instead, he offered council and supportive advice in the second half of the 1980s. The possibility of Soviet intervention, either military or economic, however, continued to hang over Poland's move toward democratic breakthrough.[33] What was notable about Soviet policy in the late 1980s was not that they somehow guided the process, but that Gorbachev broke with tradition to not intervene, to be absent as an actively controlling interest in Poland.[34]

Returning to Western policy, after February 1987, when the United States lifted its final sanctions, Washington's main point of economic pressure returned to the incentive side of the equation. Meeting in Warsaw in October 1988, Deputy Secretary of State John Whitehead outlined possible economic support in light of increasing dialogue between Solidarność and the PZPR. "Step-by-step passed the test," in Whitehead's words, "and it is necessary currently to elevate relations to a new level."[35] This new level included the possibility of appropriations for scientific-technical cooperation, increased Credit Commodity Corporation (CCC) credits, new Overseas Private Investment Corporation (OPIC) and Export-Import Bank credits, tax relief for Polish exports to the United States usually reserved for developing countries, increased development of joint ventures, and support for Poland's programs in the IMF, World Bank, and Paris Club with America's "specific influence."[36]

When George H. W. Bush became president in January 1989, he continued with a reserved incentives program. On his visit to Poland in July 1989 (after the Round Table and elections), Bush signed agreements to improve the Generalized System of Preferences (GSP) tariffs, allow OPIC investment incentive measures, expand agreements for tourism, and fund the building of cultural centers. The president also proposed new measures to support scientific (energy sector) coordination, legal assistance to improve American business's foundation for investment, a housing privatization and development program to promote home ownership and increase the housing stock, and three environmental initiatives worth $15 million. The administration also pledged to back "two economically viable project loans . . . totaling $325 million" through the World Bank. The most significant new unilateral initiative launched by the Americans, however, was a $100 million "Polish-American Enterprise Fund," which would provide funds for private sector development, privatizing state firms, increased technical assistance and training programs, funding export projects, and encouraging joint ventures between private Polish and American investors.[37] Shortly after Mazowiecki took power, US commitments in aid to Poland rose to more than $1.2 billion, and the European Union made funds available through food aid and a stabilization fund.

Support for *Solidarność*

While working to pressure the PZPR to pursue more democratic policies, the United States and the West simultaneously supported Solidarność. From August 1980 to December 1981, both the Carter and Reagan administrations were weary about direct aid to Solidarność for fear of provoking a conservative response. American trade unionists were much less reserved. Less than a week after the Gdańsk agreements were signed, AFL-CIO president Lane Kirkland announced the creation of the Polish Workers Aid Fund (PWAF), which grew to nearly $250,000 by November 1981.[38] To determine how to spend these funds, the AFL-CIO turned to Solidarność for guidance and before December 1981 used them precisely as requested: for fax machines, office equipment, and printing supplies.[39]

When martial law was declared, some Solidarność members were caught outside of Poland and, rather than returning, they decided to work for the opposition in exile. On July 29, 1982, the Solidarność Coordinating Office Abroad opened its doors in Brussels led by Jerzy Milewski.[40] Two Poles who had been active in the underground printing movement and who had been attending a book fair in Western Europe in December 1981, Mirosław Chojecki and Sławomir Czarlewski, took charge of the Coordinating Office's efforts to provide aid to opposition activists. The Coordinating Office initially projected an annual operating budget of $800,000 for support—"material and equipment (photographic, broadcasting, communications, printing, etc.)"—to the underground.[41] Funded primarily by European trade unions, especially a French contribution of 8 million francs ($1 million),[42] Chojecki began meeting with Poles who were allowed to travel to Western Europe and to exchange information about the internal situation for money and small items to be smuggled back in to Poland. For larger items like printing presses Chojecki's preferred method was to dismantle them, disguise them, and send them with the help of sympathetic truck drivers who were delivering a steady stream of humanitarian aid. The parts would be picked up by opposition activists and reassembled. In addition to printing supplies, Chojecki successfully sent in radios and even an early computer during the Coordinating Office's first year.[43]

While the AFL-CIO and its Free Trade Union Institute (FTUI) were supportive of Milewski's Coordinating Office, they did not make a major financial commitment to Brussels at first. Instead, the AFL-CIO teamed up with a newly formed entity, the Committee in Support of Solidarity (CSS), codirected by Irena Lasota (a Pole who was active in the democratic opposition in the late 1960s), to publicize human rights abuses and to funnel support to those members of the opposition who were not interned. Lasota sent parcels to friends in the opposition disguised as care packages. She included censored books and small amounts of cash (in American dollars) hidden in common objects. To aid independent publishers, Lasota purchased containers of Hershey's syrup, emptied the contents, cleaned them, and refilled them with printing ink. Because there were so many care packages being sent, she assumed that the government could not possibly search all incoming mail and that a fair amount of support would reach the intended recipients.[44] Lasota also utilized AFL-CIO funds to send needed technology through trusted intermediaries in Western Europe, including: audio recorders, cassette recorders, accessory tapes, transistors, short wave radios, two-way radios, mobile antennas, base station antennas, and various printing and communications equipment.

At the end of 1983, the opposition gained an important new ally: the National Endowment for Democracy. With this new source of money, American labor significantly increased its direct aid to Solidarność. From 1984 through 1989, the AFL-CIO's FTUI funneled about $300,000 per year in NED funds to Solidarność's Coordinating Office in Brussels, providing roughly two-thirds of the office's annual operating budget.[45] When Congress appropriated $1 million in additional funds to go to Solidarność in FY 1988 and FY 1989, these funds too, went through FTUI. Once in the hands of Solidarność's Brussels office, American money was dispersed mainly to union structures in Poland for their daily work of organizing, for supporting those who could not work, and for publishing independent news. From 1984 through 1989, FTUI also provided about $100,000 per year to former Solidarność member Mirosław Dominczyk to smuggle printing materials, communications equipment, and money to regions and local union organizations that the AFL-CIO felt were being underserved by aid directed through Brussels.[46]

NED also provided funds for sections of the opposition, which were not directly linked to Solidarność. Beginning in FY 1984, the Institute for Democracy in Eastern Europe (IDEE), another organization run by Irena Lasota, received grants to support the Consortium of Independent Publishers, which included all the major underground publishing houses. In total, from 1984 to 1989, IDEE received just over $800,000 in NED funds to support underground publishing in Eastern Europe, with the vast majority of funds going to Poland.[47]

NED funds also supported Polish émigrés working as publishers in Western Europe. This included Eugeniusz Smolar's ANEKS publishing house and the *Uncensored Poland News Bulletin*, both located in London, as well as various publications produced by the Independent Poland Agency in Lund, Sweden. Both of these groups translated and distributed Polish *samizdat* for a Western audience and produced underground literature that was smuggled into Poland. Between FY 1986 and 1989, ANEKS, *Uncensored Poland News Bulletin*, and the Independent Poland Agency received over $350,000 in NED funds administered by Freedom House and the Polish America Congress Charitable Foundation (PACCF). A small literary journal founded in Paris in December 1982, *Zeszyty Literackie*, which benefited from $100,000 in NED grants from FY 1984 to 1989, was published both for the émigré Polish population and to be smuggled back into Poland.[48]

NED also focused funds on a variety of humanitarian and human rights efforts. In addition to two $1 million Congressional allocations that went through NED to the International Rescue Committee to support a Solidarność Social Fund in 1987 and 1989, NED also allocated $90,000 annually to provide material assistance to political prisoners and their families. POLCUL, a foundation created by a wealthy Polish-Australian philanthropist, was also funded to provide annual awards of about $500 to Polish artists, writers, journalists, lawyers, actors, intellectuals, and scientists. In 1985 and 1986 the Aurora Foundation administered NED grants totaling $120,000 for the Polish Legal Defense Fund to provide legal support to democracy activists on trial. Between FY 1986 and 1989, NED also provided $50,000 to the Polish Helsinki Watch Committee, through a grant administered by PACCF.[49]

As a final category of its efforts, NED funded groups working to promote educational, cultural, and scientific activities that were neglected, criminalized, or censored by the Polish state, activities often referred to as "independent culture." From 1986 to 1989, NED provided $100,000 per year (through subgrants to PACCF) to OKN, which was an umbrella group for organizations operating in Poland. Each group published its own weeklies, as well as hard-to-find or illegal academic books and textbooks. More central to its mission, OKN organizations provided "scholarships" to students and academics who were involved in politically sensitive research. Money also funded youth programs and the well-known "Flying Universities": secret lectures and discussions held in private apartments or churches to teach censored subjects. For artists, money produced plays and theater events, supported music performances, paid for literary contests, and sponsored art exhibits (more than 40 in 1987 involving more than 100 artists). The committees also supported libraries and archives that collected and lent censored literature, as well as projects for recording oral histories.[50] As an offshoot of these cultural and artistic activities, NED provided a total of $170,000 from 1986 to 1989 to produce and distribute videos—recordings of independent theater productions, popular lecture series from the Flying University, interviews with underground leaders, coverage of special events like the papal pilgrimage, movies banned in Poland, and documentaries on martial law and the opposition movement—to be shown in private homes at so-called Flying home cinemas.[51] None of these activities were overtly political but helped promote widespread dissidence.

Without complete records from West European nations who were also supporting the opposition through their own governmental organizations, private initiatives, and trade unions, it remains difficult to accurately calculate the total sum of money going to the opposition. However, it is safe to assume that, as with the Coordinating Office's budget, American funds accounted for somewhere between half and two-thirds of all money flowing into Poland. Total amounts of NED money going to Poland began at under $500,000 per year in 1984 and grew to just over $900,000 in 1986. Because of increased congressional interest, Poland received about $1,900,000 in congressional funds in 1987 and 1988 and just over $3,300,000 in 1989. Overall from FY 1984 to 1989, NED administered just under $10 million in congressional funding to promote democracy in Poland.

INTERPLAY BETWEEN DOMESTIC AND INTERNATIONAL FACTORS

Poland's transformation was primarily a function of internal dynamics. The trends that led to the creation of Solidarność in August 1980 were purely domestic. There were no exogenous shocks or changes in Western or Eastern policies that provoked this crisis. Despite the fact that the 1981 American economic sanctions were immediately painful for the Polish government, in the first three years after the declaration of martial law, sanctions had little effect on PZPR actions and decisions. Economically, sanctions caused Poland to turn decisively to the East, weakening Western economic leverage. Western political pressure also backfired. Rather than forcing the Poles into a conciliatory dialogue with the West, the PZPR reacted to American political pressure by doing all it could to stymie and restrict political relations, provoking a series of diplomatic crises by declaring US diplomats persona non grata and rejecting the American choice for ambassador knowing that this would further retard bilateral relations.[52] In the years directly after the declaration of martial law, the PZPR knowingly and willingly did everything in its power to torpedo bilateral ties, steps that contradict a supposition that Warsaw was liberalizing to improve relations with Washington. Against this background, the PZPR's limited steps toward liberalization between 1982 and 1985 come into focus as responses to domestic rather than international pressure.

Outside this general trend, the American government did have limited success with its step-by-step policy. In December 1984 Ambassador John R. Davis and Assistant Secretary of State for European Affairs Lawrence Eagleburger negotiated with Adam Schaff, a communist intellectual with close ties to the PZPR, for the release of high-profile political prisoners in return for removing sanctions.[53] Eleven high-profile prisoners were released after only one day of trial as part of an amnesty announced on July 22, 1984. In return, as agreed, the Americans allowed Poland's national airline, LOT, to resume regularly scheduled flights to the United States and announced that scientific-technical exchanges would resume.[54] Unfortunately, bilateral reconciliation and the period of time the democracy activists remained free were both short-lived, suggesting that sanctions provided only minimal leverage to change the situation on the ground.

Beginning in mid-1985, however, Western political and economic pressure began to show progress. In the face of unsuccessful attempts to improve Poland's economy through internal reforms and increased cooperation with COMECON, the PZPR leadership found its country in an economic catch 22: Poland needed to increase foreign exports to earn Western currency to service its immense foreign debt and rebuild the economy; but to increase foreign exports, the Poles needed new Western credits to buy needed technology and raw materials.[55] To alleviate the situation, the PZPR rewrote regulations regarding joint enterprises with Western investors and worked to reinvigorate political relations with Japan and Western Europe, most notably Italy, West Germany, France, and the United Kingdom (Poland's largest Western trading partners). This initiative included numerous lower-level visits between Polish and West European officials throughout 1985, culminating with Jaruzelski's summit with French president François Mitterrand in December 1985, the general's first visit to a Western capital since the declaration of martial law.[56] The Polish Ministry of Foreign Affairs summed up its sense of success in a year-end review, stating, "We brought about significant progress in the process of normalizing relations with developed capitalist nations. The results gained were quantitatively and qualitatively much greater than those during 1982–1984."[57]

Contrary to the PZPR's hopes, improved relations with Western Europe became entwined with domestic political concerns in the middle of 1986. In early 1986, the PZPR publicly hinted that it was considering another limited amnesty for political prisoners. At that time the EEC was pursuing talks with East European countries about starting EEC-COMECON trade and restarting bilateral ties with individual countries, both of which had been dormant since 1980. The EEC held exploratory negotiations with Poland on July 14–15, 1986.[58] As the PZPR decided on whom to release and whom to hold, the EEC (led by Great Britain) sent a demarche explaining that if the upcoming amnesty was not complete, Western European countries would summarily end all of the political and economic deals under discussion. In effect, Poland would lose all of the gains it had made with Western Europe since the beginning of 1985, returning to square one in its push to gain new Western investment. On August 6, a PZPR report stated that "the exclusion from the amnesty of the most active members of the opposition" would "have an unfavorable impact upon our potential to conduct an active and effective policy towards Western Europe." Regarding economic consequences,

> the meaning of [not releasing the political prisoners] will grow as a condition complicating Poland's payment situation and [will create] increasing difficulties in the evolution of a deadline for financial obligations to Western nations. . . . Poland's international position in the economic and payment matters may succumb to later weaknesses.[59]

In the face of these dire consequences, the PZPR Politburo decided to resolve the issue: "Not embracing the [amnesty law] as part of a frontal action against the opposition and the judicial process will provide an opportunity [for the West] to malign the good name of Poland, to continue restrictions, and to slow the development of economic and political relations. On the other hand, embracing the law will permit us to develop actions in international policies, which should bring improvements on a great many levels and will be fruitful with positive results for the country."[60] Six weeks after the political amnesty was announced, all remaining political prisoners were freed.

In the two years following the final release of political prisoners, international economic concerns continued to weigh on the PZPR. As a group of World Bank economists reported to the PZPR in the summer of 1987, Poland's two main economic problems were indebtedness and its negative balance of payments. To improve its situation, the bank highly recommended that the PZPR make the economy more pro-export and work to normalize prices.[61] However, Poland was still in the same catch-22. Meeting with East German leader Erich Honecker in late 1987, Jaruzelski lamented that, while Western sanctions had been lifted, the change meant only about $20 million more per year. In Jaruzelski's words, "This doesn't deserve comment. That's nothing." Regarding the possibility for new credits, he complained, "in practice the [Western] blockade is continuing."[62] So even though political messages had changed from the West, the Europeans and Americans were not making new credits available. The Poles would have to bail themselves out of their economic crisis, further necessitating the price increases announced on April 1, 1988, which led directly to the strikes that spring and summer.

In 1988 Solidarność's positive image in the West clearly played a key role in the PZPR's decision to negotiate with Wałęsa and move toward the Round Table. Although Wałęsa and Solidarność were chosen primarily because of their domestic legitimacy, the PZPR also hoped that negotiations would improve Poland's image internationally and open up more economic opportunities. In explaining their decision to the party aktiv to talk with Solidarność in September 1988, the PZPR leadership stressed the international economic situation:

> Talks and preparatory activities for the "round table" allow us to gain the political initiative and deprive our political adversary and the West of the argument that we don't want to talk, that the dialogue is being simulated and understanding is a façade . . . ; [and] Wałęsa is being played out in the political game of the West toward Poland. . . . Thus, undertaking talks with him is depriving the West of an essential argument in its propaganda war with us.[63]

Although it is unclear if there was a quid pro quo between the government and the opposition about seeking Western economic support in return for opening negotiations, representatives from both sides increased their meeting schedules with Western governments once the Round Table negotiations were announced. From a brief comparison of PZPR and Solidarność requests made in Washington in May 1989, it is clear that both sides of the political divide in Poland were asking for improved economic packages from the West.[64] The decision to seek negotiations with Solidarność in August 1988 and to pursue the Round Table negotiations was at the least partially a response to long-term international economic pressure.

Direct Western support to Solidarność also influenced domestic developments. When Wałęsa spoke to an AFL-CIO convention in November 1989, "He thanked the United States, its people, its labor movement and its government for being 'our most steadfast allies.' "[65] Beyond the realm of political theater (Wałęsa visited Washington to ask for financial aid and had reason to be flattering), Polish democracy activists openly admitted the centrality of international support. As Konstanty Gebert, an underground editor and independent publisher throughout the 1980s, summarized when asked about the role of the West to his work: "Money. We could not have done it on our own."[66]

Extrapolating from these types of comments it is reasonable to assume that American financial and political support for Solidarność did almost certainly influence internal dynamics *within* the opposition. Throughout the 1980s, the democratic opposition was by no means monolithic. Some groups that gained substantial followings, including Fighting Solidarity (Solidarność Walcząca) and the Confederation for an Independent Poland (Konfederacja Polski Niepodległy), maintained more radically anticommunist positions than Wałęsa and his circle of advisers, such as violently overthrowing the communist system and declaring complete independence from Soviet domination. Groups popular among students, like Freedom and Peace (Wolność i Pokój) and Orange Alternative (Pomarancza Alternatywa), successfully organized youth to protest but articulated no specific political or democratic platform. Nonetheless, they provided alternative visions for the opposition's best path forward.

Western support for the moderate wing of Solidarność closely linked with Wałęsa (and other activists aligned with their centrist point of view) privileged its position within Poland. By sending most of its aid through the Solidarność Coordinating Office in Brussels (more than 60 percent of all NED funds for democracy in Poland were allocated directly through this channel controlled by the moderate wing), the United States gave Wałęsa and his colleagues the power of the purse. As Chojecki understood, he had power within opposition circles because he had access to American money.[67] As the major recipient of foreign money, moderates within Solidarność could decide which opposition groups other than its own received foreign support, limiting radical opposition groups' ability to push their own, separate agendas. Moreover, American and international financial support allowed a portion of Solidarność to be more active than it would have been without outside sources of money, magnifying what they could do. Radios allowed moderate activists to communicate more quickly than they could through slower written channels. Smuggled computers made editing and layout work easier. More ink and more printing presses allowed underground publishers to produce more *samizdat*. More money allowed for scholarships for independent artists to produce more politically sensitive or subversive theatrical productions. Because Solidarność was the main conduit for American support, it could choose the people and efforts within Poland that received money, enhancing its standing against other opposition voices.

However, the ability to magnify, augment, or boost a domestic trend does not mean that American money was essential. For example, in the spring of 1989 while Solidarność adviser Bronisław Geremek visited Washington, the AFL-CIO provided him with $100,000 to fund the ongoing election campaign.[68] It is doubtful, however, that boosting opposition activities was essential to Solidarność's electoral victory. Solidarność candidates won an overwhelming victory, winning all but one seat open to them. Moreover, nearly all Communist candidates did not receive the necessary percentage of votes to secure seats in the first round of voting. Most telling, voters took time to individually cross names off of a so-called National List to ensure that they would be removed from government, despite the fact that Wałęsa and other prominent Solidarność members had asked voters to support these high-level PZPR reformers. Given the opportunity to choose their leaders, Polish citizens overwhelmingly voted against the communist system. As Ambassador Davis surmised at the time, "The party, despite its touted superior organization, is vastly disliked and nearly incapable of persuading an electorate through traditional campaign techniques, with which it has had no experience. . . . It is difficult to see how the party's core will be able to elect many—or any—candidates to the Senate."[69] While many voters were motivated to go to the polls to vote *for* Solidarność, the elections in June 1989 were essentially a referendum *against* 40 years of Communist rule. No amount of money could have changed the outcome.

In a separate crucial stage of Poland's democratic breakthrough, however, American money appears to have played a pivotal role. On May 3, 1988, in between the spring and summer strikes, Solidarność issued a communiqué committing to "discharge financial assistance" for up to six months to workers who had lost their jobs as a result of strikes and to cover financial losses "as a result of repressions" against workers. By early June the Coordinating Office had already forwarded "all money currently at our disposal," so Jerzy Milewski wrote to FTUI to request that it "speed up the transfer of the first quarterly installment of $250,000" and "to arrange for the prompt transfer of the second $250,000 quarterly installment." In addition to paying workers already affected by government repression, the money was meant to support "emergency funds to cover future events which are expected, but not specifically predictable."[70] FTUI thus helped affected workers at a crucial time in Poland's furtive steps toward a negotiated power-sharing agreement.

When Kiszczak met with Wałęsa on August 31, 1988, the PZPR agreed to open negotiations with the opposition on the condition that all the miners, shipyard workers, and other strikers around the country return to work; however, the process of getting strikers to return to work was easier said than done. When Wałęsa traveled to the Lenin Shipyard after meeting with Kiszczak, workers "whistled, booed and raised charges of cowardice." From their perspective, he had received no definite concessions, only a vague agreement to continue negotiations toward trade union pluralism.[71] Demands for neither pay increases nor legalizing Solidarność had been met. As one young worker lamented, "We walked out in May with empty hands. We're going to walk out again with nothing to show for it."[72] Even the Lenin Shipyard's strike committee chairman, a longtime Wałęsa supporter, was quoted as saying, "After 11 days of strikes we have advanced so little. . . . It is a bitter decision." The Gdańsk strikers acquiesced to Wałęsa's request only after "nightlong debates and a narrow vote."[73]

At the July Manifesto Mine in Silesia, workers were so reticent to end their strike that they demanded Wałęsa personally visit. The head of Solidarność was greeted by cheers but soon met "some very sharp moments and a sharp exchange, even swearing at first." Again "charges of betrayal" surfaced. As in Gdańsk, the final decision to end the strike came down to a contentious and close vote. As one Polish commentator opined, "Wałęsa thought he could stride right in and the miners would follow him. . . . But he got a good lesson. It took him eight hours to convince them."[74]

Certainly Wałęsa's clout, charisma, and ability to seize the political moment went a long way to convincing both young and old workers that the government would follow through with its promises to begin negotiations and to legalize Solidarność; however, strikers' demands were economic as well as political. They had demanded recognition of Solidarność *and* pay increases. Moreover, the centrality of economic matters in the earlier strikes in April and May clearly showed how essential these issues were to workers. As one shipyard worker related, "We found it hard to understand [Wałęsa's] reasoning. . . . He was talking about the state of the economy, but our economic situation was also very difficult."[75] In addition, one of the most contentious issues between workers and management involved demands "for assurances of personal safety and job security"; workers were afraid of reprisals and economic repression.[76] Solidarność had recently received $500,000 from the US government (a sum greater than the usual annual NED allocation to Solidarność for the year) to help in precisely this manner. Because of American support, Solidarność could economically support striking workers to guarantee that they received at least some pay.

CONCLUSION

The victory for international pressure in 1986 and the positive role played by American money in 1988 show the very complex ways long-term domestic trends and short-term international actions interacted to cause notable political shifts. In the case of economic pressure, the stagnation that forced the Poles to seek Western economic help was driven by long-term weaknesses in Poland's centrally planned economy. Combined with payments to creditors, the economy was overburdened. When it became clear that Poland's socialist brothers could not and would not bail them out, Jaruzelski had nowhere else to turn than the West; Poland's long-standing economic ties to Western European countries made them the most likely candidates. By early 1986, the PZPR was pleased by the advances it had made in relations with West Europeans. The EEC demarche in July 1986 called all of this progress into question and unified American and European economic pressure tactics for the first time since 1980.

International pressure to declare a complete and final amnesty for political prisoners in 1986 accelerated an existing domestic trend. In line with the modest steps toward liberalization that it had taken since 1981, the Jaruzelski government was already moving toward a modus vivendi with the opposition. Although it feared possible crisis down the road, the PZPR remained in full control; to the party, democracy activists looked increasingly fractured and irrelevant. By 1986 Solidarność no longer enjoyed the massive public appeal it had during 1980–81, or even the popular support it initially commanded as a coordinated underground group able to spark nationwide disturbances in May and August 1982. According to PZPR calculations, releasing a few more democratic activists did not give the opposition the upper hand.[77] By fall 1986, Moscow was sending significant signals to Warsaw that improved relations with Western Europe and internal political liberalization not only would be tolerated but were actually desirable. The PZPR would not have released all political prisoners in September 1986 on its own; Western pressure accelerated preexisting internal trends by a few months or perhaps a year. Similarly, PZPR hopes that talks with Solidarność would improve the possibilities of increased economic support from the West clearly buttressed reformers' calls to move toward the Round Table negotiations.

In the case of striking workers in spring and summer 1988, Wałęsa only narrowly succeeded in getting them to return to work. In a situation in which the vote to cease strikes was so close and so contentious, workers' economic motivations certainly played an important, perhaps pivotal role. Because Congress had already allocated $1,000,000 for FY 1988 to Solidarność (in addition to the usual NED allotment), money was available, and FTUI could respond quickly to Milewski's and Solidarność's requests for support. Foreign monetary support provided Solidarność the means to provide some economic security to workers, easing their economic concerns and the sense of uncertainty of ending a strike before their demands had been fully met. Without international support, Solidarność would not have had this safeguard to ease workers' concerns about ending their occupation strikes, and Wałęsa's pleas to end the strike for the possibility of open negotiations with the PZPR might not have been heeded. If the strikes had not ended, it is doubtful that the Magdalenka meetings would have taken place and the Round Table negotiations would have begun the following April.

Overall, Poland appears to be a clear case of international intervention tipping the scales in favor of democratic breakthrough. Given that the mechanisms for international interference were limited—compared particularly to cases where possible or actual military force was utilized—the effects of these influences appeared only when the balance of domestic forces was relatively equal. Economic pressure culminated in the fall of 1986 to accelerate the creation of a new, stable relationship between the opposition and the government that had been developing over a long period of time. In late 1988, American money gave the Solidarność leadership another tool to shore up loyalty among workers at a moment when strikers were reticent to return to their jobs with only a promise of future political improvements and against fears of economic reprisals. International efforts did not restructure the domestic political landscape, but at specific points in time external pressures did tilt the existing order to accelerate and insure democratic transformation.

NOTES

1. Informacja o skutkach gospodarczych wywołanych restrykcjami wprowadzonymi przez państwo zachodnie przeciwko Polsce, June 9, 1983, Archive of Modern Records, Warsaw (hereafter AAN), KC PZPR, V/203, 13.

2. For statistics, see Global Financial Data's Poland Real Per Capita GDP in 2004 Zlotych, www.globalfinancialdata.com/.

3. For information on Poland's trade within COMECON, see Vienna Institute for Comparative Economic Studies, *COMECON Foreign Trade Data 1980* (Westport, Conn.: Greenwood Press, 1981), esp. 130, 133, 136; for requests to Moscow, see Pilna Notatka z wizyty w Moskwie Delegacji Partyjno-Państwowej z I Sekretarzem KC PZPR, Prezesem Rady Ministrów tow. Wojciechem Jaruzelskim, w dniach 1–2 marca 1982 r., March 5, 1982, AAN, KC PZPR, V/172, 555–61; and for information on requests to COMECON following martial law, see AAN, KC PZPR, XIA/1394, 3–30.

4. For a full discussion of these economic reforms, see Ben Slay, *The Polish Economy: Crisis, Reform, and Transformation* (Princeton, N.J.: Princeton University Press, 1994), 50–85.

5. For correspondence between Glemp and Jaruzelski, see records for the June 29, 1982, Politburo meeting in AAN, Sygn. 1833, Mikr. 3002, 1–16. For information on internal decision making, see Mieczysław Rakowski, *Dzienniki Politycne 1981–1983* (Warsaw: Wydawnictwo ISKRY, 2004), 362. For the final decision, see Protokoł nr. 56 z posiedzenia Biura Politycznego KC PZPR w dniu 18.xi.1982, November 18, 1982, AAN, KC PZPR, V/182, 217–52.

6. Protokoł nr. 56 z posiedzenia Biura Politycznego KC PZPR w dniu 18.xi.1982.

7. Wytyczne Polityki Wyznaniowej, February 4, 1983, AAN, KC PZPR, V/191, 11–16; Węzłowe Zadania Polityki Zagranicznej PRL w 1983 r., ca. January 1983, AAN, KC PZPR, V/190, 8–27, esp. 17; untitled report [re: Ikonowicz's visit to the Vatican], April 1983, AAN, XIA/1417; Korespondencja z człokami BP i Sekretarzami KC PZPR, 1983, 1–15; Report on the internal situation, Wydział Informacyjna KC PZPR, May 23, 1983, AAN, KC PZPR, V/198, 207–21; John Kifner, "Free Prisoners, Pope Asks Poland," *New York Times*, April 30, 1983, A4; and Rakowski, *Dzienniki 1981–1983*, 460, 494.

8. Report, "A Synthesis of the Internal Situation and the West's Activity," August 28, 1987, in Paweł Machcewicz, "Poland 1986–1989: From 'Cooptation' to 'Negotiated Revolution' New Documents," *Cold War International History Project Bulletin* 12–13 (Fall–Winter 2001): 98.

9. Information in this paragraph is based on reporting by John Tagliabue for the *New York Times*. In particular, see "Polish Workers Strike and Win a Raise," April 26, 1988, A3; "Steel Strike Widens Polish Labor Unrest," April 27, 1988, A3; "Steel Strikes Spreading in Poland; Talks with Official Unions Fail," April 30, 1988, A1; and "Thousands at Gdansk Shipyard Join Polish Strike," May 3, 1988, A1.

10. Tagliabue, "Security Forces Crush a Walkout at Mill in Poland," *New York Times*, May 6, 1988, A1.

11. Tagliabue, "Young and Wary Strikers Take Solace from Wałęsa," *New York Times*, May 7, 1988, A1.

12. Tagliabue, "Gdansk Workers Reject Polish Offer to End Strike," *New York Times*, May

10, 1988, A10; and "Gdańsk Workers End 9-day Strike; Key Demand Unmet," *New York Times*, May 11, 1988, A1.

13. Andrzej Paczkowski, *The Spring Will Be Ours* (University Park: Pennsylvania State University Press, 2003), 490.

14. "From the Meeting of the Political Bureau held on 21 August 1988 under the chairmanship of the 1st Secretary of the KC PZPR, comrade Wojciech Jaruzelski," in the documents briefing book prepared for the conference, "Poland, 1986–1989: The End of the System," Miedzeszyn-Warsaw, Poland, October 20–24, 1999; quoted at 13 and 10. Copies are available though the National Security Archive.

15. Antoni Dudek, *Reglamentowana Rewolucja* (Krakow: Arcana Historia, 2004), 166. The term *exceptional state* is a euphemism for martial law.

16. "Spotakanie Robocze w Magdalence, 16 września 1988 r., godz. 15.15–19.00," in Krzysztof Dubiński, *Magdalenka: Transakcja epoki* (Warsaw: Sylwa, 1990), 19.

17. Andrzej Friszke, *Polska: Losy Państwa i Narodu 1939–1989* (Warsaw: Wydawnictwo ISKRY, 2003), 448.

18. Cable from Amembassy Warsaw to SecState, "Election '89—Solidarity's Victory Raises Questions," June 6, 1989, National Security Archive (hereafter NSA), Washington, D.C., End of the Cold War, Poland 1989 Cables.

19. Dudek, *Reglamentowana Rewolucja*, 376–77.

20. Memorandum from Robert M. Gates to the Director of Central Intelligence, "Assistance to Poland: Tuesday's NSC Meeting," December 4, 1981, NSA, Soviet Flashpoints Originals, box 1.

21. The approach was codified Memo "Next Steps on Poland," attached to Memo from William Clark to the President, "Poland: Next Steps," May 5, 1983, Ronald Reagan Presidential Library, Simi Valley, Calif. (hereafter RRPL), Paula Dobriansky Files, box 3, Poland Memoranda 1981–1983 [May 1–12 1983].

22. Action Memorandum from Robert Hormats and Lawrence Eagleburger to the Secretary, "Western Economic Leverage on Poland and Secure Phone Call to Regan," December 17, 1981, NSA, Soviet Flashpoints, box 26, December 1–22, 1981.

23. Memorandum from David Pickford, "Senior Interdepartmental Group on International Economic Policy (SIG-IEP)" with attachments, January 10, 1983, RRPL, Executive Secretary NSC, National Security Decision Directives, box 91286, NSDD 66 [4 of 5].

24. Briefing Memorandum, "Western Policy towards Poland," August 10, 1983, NSA, End of the Cold War, box 1, September 6–9, 1983: Shultz's Trip to Madrid.

25. Christoph Bobinski, "New Chapter Opens in Poland's Debt Saga," *Financial Times*, July 17, 1985, A2; and David Buchan, "West Signs Rescheduling Accord with Poles," *Financial Times*, November 11, 1985, A2.

26. Batara Simatupang, *The Polish Economic Crisis: Background, Causes and Aftermath* (London: Routledge, 1994), 196.

27. Lee Kjelleran, interview, December 2007.

28. Valerie Bunce, "The Empire Strikes Back: The Evolution of the Eastern Bloc from a Soviet Asset to a Soviet Liability," *International Organization* 39, no. 1 (Winter 1985): 1–46, quoted at 15.

29. "Memorandum from Mikhail Gorbachev to the Politburo on Topical Questions Regarding Collaboration with Socialist Countries, June 26, 1986," in Svetlana Savranskaya, Thomas Blanton, and Vladislav Zubok, eds., *Masterpieces of History: The Peaceful End of the Cold War in Europe, 1989* (Budapest: Central European University Press, 2010), 232.

30. "Notes of the CPSU CC Politburo Session, January 27, 1987," in ibid., 242.

31. For a full discussion of the effects of "new thinking" and the "common European home," see Svetlana Savranskaya, "The Logic of 1989: The Soviet Peaceful Withdrawal from Eastern Europe," in Savranskaya, Blanton, and Zubok, *Masterpieces of History*, 6.

32. Anatoly Chernyaev, *My Six Years with Gorbachev*, trans. and ed. Robert English and Elizabeth Tucker (University Park: Pennsylvania State University Press, 2000), 62.

33. For a further discussion of this phenomena, particularly the opposition's relationship with Gorbachev, see Gregory F. Domber, "Ending the Cold War, Unintentionally," in Frédéric Bozo, Marie-Pierre Rey, N. Piers Ludlow, and Leopoldo Nuti, eds., *Overcoming the Iron Curtain: Visions of the End of the Cold War in Europe, 1945–1990* (Oxford: Bergham Books, 2011).

34. For one attempt to understand the important effects of this policy, see Jacques Levesque, *The Enigma of 1989: The USSR and the Liberation of Eastern Europe* (Berkeley: University of California Press, 1997). The noninterference by the Soviet Union opens up interesting possibilities for further study of the dynamics of intra-bloc relations on democratic breakthrough. Given the historical uniqueness of the Soviet presence in Eastern Europe and the fact that this chapter is primarily focused on Western influences on Poland, an analysis of the relative importance of the lack of Soviet influence or interference has been limited.

35. Notatka Informacyjna dot. wizyty w Polsce zastępcy Sekretarza Stanu USA Johna Whiteheada (12–14 października 1988 r.), October 15, 1988, Archive of the Polish Ministry of Foreign Affairs (hereafter MSZ), Warsaw, Poland, 42/92, W-6, Dep III (1988), AP 220-25-88, quoted at 7.

36. Ibid., 9–10.

37. Explanations of all of these initiatives are included in declassified briefing materials for Bush's Trip, ca. July 1989, NSA, End of the Cold War, scanned incoming Freedom of Information Act (FOIA) documents. For a full discussion of American policy toward Poland in 1989 within the broader context of superpower relations, see Gregory F. Domber, "Skepticism and Stability: Reevaluating U.S. Policy toward Poland's Democratic Transformation in 1989," *Journal of Cold War Studies* 13, no. 3 (Summer 2011): 52–82.

38. "Statement on the Polish Workers Aid Fund," September 4, 1980, George Meany Memorial Archives (hereafter GMMA), College Park, Md., Information Department, AFL-CIO Press Releases 1980, box 45, 45/3. Most of the individual donations are less than $20, with larger donations from individual unions up to $10,000. See AFL-CIO International Affairs Department Files, Inactive Records, "After Nov. 24 PWAF [Polish Workers Aid Fund]" and "Letters of Contribution from Individuals to the AFL-CIO Polish Workers Aid Fund, 1981."

39. See "Report to the ICFTU on visits to Warschau and Gdańsk, 15/9–18/9/1980," undated, GMMA, AFL-CIO, International Affairs Department, Inactive Records, "Wałęsa, Lech." According to internal accounting, $152,000 was spent on office supplies and material for Solidarność before December 13; see "Note to Editors," June 14, 1982, GMMA, AFL-CIO, Information Department, AFL-CIO Press Releases 1937–95, box 49, 49/2.

40. Solidarity International Press Release, July 18, 1982, GMMA, AFL-CIO, unprocessed records, "Solidarność 1982 #2."

41. Letter from Jerzy Milewski to Lane Kirkland, dated August 1, 1982, GMMA, AFL-CIO, International Affairs Department Files, Inactive Records, "Milewski, Jerzy."

42. For a full exploration of Western trade union support to Solidarność, see Idesbald Goddeeris, ed., *Solidarity with Solidarity: Western European Trade Unions and the Polish Crisis, 1980–1982* (New York: Lexington Books, 2010).

43. Mirosław Chojecki, interview, December 7, 2007.

44. Irena Lasota, interview, June 19, 2007.

45. This $300,000 figure is substantiated by research done in Poland based on sources from the Polish underground. According to Andrzej Friszke, in his article "Tymczasowo Komisja Koordynacyjna," the Coordinating office received $200,000 yearly from 1983 to 1984, and then $300,000 for 1985 and 1986. Adrian Karatnycky, director of AFL-CIO's Poland programs from 1984 onward confirmed this funding range when he referred to "our traditional $300,000 allotment to Solidarność from FTUI's unrestricted NED funds." See memo from Adrian Karatnycky to Tom Kahn, "Eastern Europe and the USSR," November 29, 1989, GMMA, AFL-CIO, International Affairs Department, unprocessed records, "Adrian Chron 1989."

46. This brief overview comes from the author's interview with Adrian Karatnycky, November 21, 2007. For further information on the project, see Arch Puddington, "Surviving the Underground: How American Unions Helps Solidarity Win," *American Educator* (Summer 2005), www.aft.org/pubs-reports/american_educator/issues/summer2005/puddington.htm.

47. Levels of funding come from NED annual reports, available at its headquarters' library. Other information on IDEE's activities is based on the author's interview with Lasota.

48. Funding levels come from NED annual reports. Specific information on PACCF activities and grants came from NED grant files located at the Polish American Congress's offices in Washington, D.C. I am indebted to Casimir Lenard for making these files available.

49. Ibid.

50. The information about OKN is compiled from three annual reports from 1986, 1987, and 1988. See the files located in the Polish American Congress Files (hereafter PAC), Washington, D.C., Books 4, "Grant #86-181-E-047-25.0 OKNO" and "Grant #87-181-E-047-17.1 OKNO," as well as PAC, NED 89/90, "OKNO 1988."

51. The information in this paragraph is culled from various reports from Agnieszka Holland in PAC, Books 4, "NED Grant #86-181-E-047-50 Polish Video Film."

52. Letter from John Davis to Stefan Olszowski with attached note, December 19, 1984, MSZ, 2/89, W-6, Dep III (1985), AP 10-5-85. For more general information on the ambassador controversy, see informal notes and brief records in MSZ, 2/89, W-6, Dep III (1985), AP 10-5-85.

53. Memorandum from Paula Dobriansky to Robert McFarlane, "Poland: Response to Unofficial Emissary Schaff," February 9, 1984, RRPL, NSC, European and Soviet Affairs Directorate, box 91186, Vatican; and Memorandum from Robert McFarlane to the President, "Poland: Response to Unofficial Emissary Schaff," February 16, 1984, PPRL, NSC, European and Soviet Affairs Directorate, box 91186, Vatican. See also Adam Schaff, *Notatki Kłopotnika* (Warsaw: Polska Oficyna Wydawnicza BGW, 1995). These eleven political prisoners were all prominent members of the opposition: Jacek Kuron, Adam Michnik, Henryk Wujec, Zbigniew Romaszewski, Andrzej Gwiazda, Seweryn Jaworski, Marian Jurczyk, Karol Modzielewski, Grzegorz Palce, Andrzej Rozpłochowski, and Jan Rulewski.

54. "Statement by Principal Deputy Press Secretary Speaks on United States Sanctions against Poland, August 3, 1984," *Public Papers of the President, 1984* (Washington, D.C.: Government Printing Office, 1984), available on the Reagan Library's Web site, www.reagan.utexas.edu.

55. Węźłowe Zadania Polityki Zagranicznej PRL w 1986 r., ca. January 1986, AAN, KC PZPR, V/294, 9–31; Informacja o wspólnych przedsięwzięciach z udziałem kapitału obcego

w krajach socjalistycznych, November 14, 1985, AAN, KC PZPR, V/292, 91–96; and Wydział Ekonomicny Opinia dot.: projektu ustawy o spółkach z udziałem kapitału zagranicznego, December 30, 1985, AAN, KC PZPR, V/292, 109–11.

56. On March 6, 1985, West German foreign minister Hans Dietrich Genscher made an unofficial visit to Warsaw. During Soviet General Secretary Chernenko's funeral, Jaruzelski met briefly with German Chancellor Helmut Kohl, UN Secretary General Perez de Cuellar, President Allessandro Pertini of Italy, and President Mauno Koivisto of Finland. Visits to Warsaw by West German minister of economics Martin Bangemann, British foreign minister Geoffrey Howe, Italian prime minister Bettino Craxi, and Japanese foreign minister Shintao Abe followed in March, April, May, and June.

57. "Bilans Polityki Zagranicznej PRL w 1985 r.," ca. December 31, 1985, AAN, KC PZPR, V/294, 32–53, quoted at 40.

58. John Maslen, "The European Community's Relations with the State-Trading Countries of Eastern Europe 1984–1986," in *Yearbook of European Law* (Oxford: Clarendon Press, 1987), 338–40.

59. "Notatka w sprawie implikacji naszej sytuacji wewnętrznej dla stosunków Polski z państwami Europy Zachodniej," August 6, 1986, AAN, KC PZPR, V/314, 85–92, quoted at 88.

60. "Propozycje w sprawie rozszerzenia zakresu stosowania ustawy z dnia 17 lipca 1986 r. o szczególnym postępowaniu wobec sprawców niektórych przestępstw," September 9, 1986, published in Antoni Dudek and Andrzej Friszke, eds., *Polska 1986–1989: koniec systemu*, vol. 3 (Warsaw: Wydawnictwo Trio, 2002), 13–19, quoted at 14–15.

61. "Wyciąg Tez i Opinii Raportu Banku Swiatowego 'Polska: Reforma, Dostowanie i Wzrost,'" September 9, 1987, AAN, KC PZPR, V/365.

62. "Zapis stenograficzny rozmowy Ericha Honeckera z Wojciechiem Jaruzelskim 16 wrzesnia 1987 r. (fragmenty)," in Dudek and Friszke, *Polska 1986–1989*, 48.

63. "Teleprinter Message from the Political and Organizational Committee of the PZPR Central Committee to Members and Associate Members of the Politburo and Central Committee Secretaries, on 'The Question of Talks with the Opposition,'" September 2, 1988, in the conference briefing book "Poland, 1986–1989: The End of the System."

64. See numerous cables dealing with PZPR and Solidarność activists trips to Washington and Western Europe in Greg Domber, ed., *Ku zwycięstwu "Solidarności": Korespondencja Ambasady USA z Departamentem Stanu, styczeń-wrzesień 1989* (Warsaw: Instytut Studiów Politycznych, 2006).

65. Lawrence Knutsen, "Wałęsa to Address a Joint Session of Congress," Associated Press, November 15, 1989.

66. Konstanty Gebert, interview, August 3, 2006.

67. Chojecki interview.

68. Puddington, "Surviving the Underground." Presumably this money came from NED funds already allocated to Poland.

69. Cable from Amembassy Warsaw to SecState, "Election '89—The Year of Solidarity," April 19, 1989, NSA, End of the Cold War, Poland 1989 Cables.

70. Letter from Jerzy Milewski to Lane Kirkland, June 6, 1988, GMMA, AFL-CIO, International Affairs Department, unprocessed records, "FTUI."

71. John Tagliabue, "Wałęsa takes to Coal Country to Press for an End to Strikes," *New York Times*, September 3, 1988, A1.

72. John Tagliabue, "Appeal by Wałęsa fails to Resolve All Polish Strikes," *New York Times*, September 2, 1988, A1.

73. Jackson Diehl, "Gdańsk Strikes End, but Others Continue; Polish Union Split over Government Talks," *Washington Post*, September 2, 1988, A23. For a transcript of those discussions, see Tomasz Tabako, *Strajk '88* (Warsaw: NOWA, 1992), 295–328.

74. William Echikson, "Who'll Pay the Price if Wałęsa's Risk Doesn't Pay Off?" *Christian Science Monitor*, September 6, 1988, 7.

75. John Tagliabue, "Workers Heed Wałęsa and Agree to End Last of Strikes," *New York Times*, September 4, 1988, A1.

76. Tagliabue, "Wałęsa Takes to Coal Country," A1. These concerns also appear in the transcript of Wałęsa's meeting with the strike committee; see, for example, Tabako, *Strajk '88*, 314–15.

77. Dudek, *Reglomentowana Rewolucja*, 57–73.

CHAPTER FOUR

Serbia

Evaluating the Bulldozer Revolution

RAY SALVATORE JENNINGS

In 1987 Slobodan Milošević showed promise as a modern liberator. The former Yugoslav communist apparatchik rose to power swiftly, enjoying immense initial support, but he ultimately retained the authority he achieved with violence, xenophobic propaganda, clientelism, and misappropriation of the country's wealth as his popularity declined. He ruled as Yugoslavia's constituent republics devolved into separate nations, through four wars and a NATO bombing campaign that pitted his regime against the West. The stirring electoral victory of his opposition and subsequent protests that removed Milošević from the presidency on October 5, 2000, came after 13 years during which the autocrat often seemed invulnerable and incorrigible. His defeat was hailed inside and outside of Serbia as a decisive moment of revolutionary democratic change, even though few of the individuals who played critical roles in the electoral breakthrough of 2000 characterize the subsequent consolidation of democratic gains after Milošević's defeat as equally compelling or successful.

As is the case in most revolutions of this kind, Milošević's fall was dramatic. Elections for the Yugoslav presidency and federal assembly took place on September 24, 2000. Parallel-vote counts revealed that Milošević had tampered with the election and had lost to the rival Democratic Opposition of Serbia (DOS) candidate, Vojislav Koštunica. The regime refused to concede. Milošević instead insisted on a second round of elections and then an annulment of election results. Street demonstrations and strikes ensued, including a pivotal slowdown in work at the Kolubara coal mines in central Serbia, which provided 70 percent of the republic's energy reserves. International condemnation, even from Serbia's traditional ally

Russia, crescendoed as Milošević maneuvered. By midday on October 5, more than 500,000 protestors converged on Belgrade, assisted and directed by opposition party activists, civic groups, and student organizers. Opposition party operatives helped commandeer a bulldozer, now famous as an icon of the revolution, while organizing crowds to surround and occupy key institutions in the capital including the Serbia Radio Television (RTS) building, the Federal Parliament, the Central Bank, Belgrade city hall, and Milošević's party headquarters. Security forces and paramilitary formations declined to act in the regime's defense and by nightfall DOS and its supporters were in de facto control on the ground. The following day Milošević yielded, and by October 7 Kostunica was sworn into office.

Mass movements of the "regime change" variety often originate with political and civic elites mobilizing the public, as witnessed in Russia, Ukraine, and Georgia, for example. In Serbia, the work of free media outlets, civic activists, and the political opposition were as responsible for mobilizing the public as they were, in turn, mobilized by it. Well into 2000, most civic and opposition leaders were nearly as distrusted as the regime. They were unprepared to marshal growing anger over economic conditions, corruption, and the severity of the extralegal crackdown on regime critics during and after the 1998–99 war in Kosovo. Not until the student movement OTPOR (Resistance!) began to push civic and political leaders toward each other, helping define and mature their roles, did the public warm to their alternative leadership. Preparing to visit the Kolubara miners during the postelection crisis that fall, Kostunica remarked that "there are sometimes historic situations in which parties and political leaders do not lead the people, but the people to a large extent lead them. This is one such situation."[1]

Yet it is unlikely that these internal developments would have had the same character or that the nature and timing of breakthrough would have occurred as it did without the influences of external factors. Direct democracy assistance supported OTPOR and the formation of DOS, while lending durability to opposition parties and alternative media. Democracy aid also helped to expose manipulation of election results and to ensure that revelations about vote fraud reached large segments of the public after elections were held. Regional activists helped diffuse their knowledge of lessons learned from breakthroughs in neighboring countries, encouraging civic leaders to form an effective network of activists called Izlaz (Exit!), for example. Military intervention as well as economic, legal, and diplomatic sanctions inconsistently, and sometimes counterproductively and at great cost, contributed to a sense of political decay around the financially exhausted regime. Even the defection of security forces on October 5 may be traced, in part, to the capability of the opposition to organize mass protests and to cultivate important allies in and around the regime—a capability marginally influenced by external factors.

External influences supported a struggle for democracy that was already prevalent inside Serbia, however. They did not independently originate this struggle or create the courageous and creative community of activists that produced it. Nor did external forces create the kind of critical mass of public disaffection over conditions in Serbia in 2000 that the opposition eventually exploited. Breakthrough would likely have been accomplished without significant outside help although the character and timing of such an event is open to question.

After a summary of historical events within Serbia that contextualize the efforts of both domestic and international opponents of the Milošević regime, I consider the role of internal and external factors in regime change. Then I examine the causal relationships among the internal influences and external factors contributing to breakthrough and consider the question of what breakthrough might have looked like in the absence of external influence.

HISTORICAL CONTEXT PRECEDING DEMOCRATIZATION

By 1990, Slobodan Milošević's concentration of power within the Serbian republic of Yugoslavia was well underway. The republic of Slovenia would leave the Yugoslav Communist Party in response, collapsing the already moribund institution. Multiparty elections throughout Yugoslavia's constituent republics followed, and unsurprisingly nationalist candidates won in every major poll, leveraging discontent with declining living standards throughout the 1980s and alarm over Milošević's Serbo-centric policies in Belgrade. The populist and ethno-nationalist tensions that resulted would eventually provoke four wars that would tear the country apart and reduce Yugoslavia to a rump state of two former Yugoslav republics, a dominant Serbia and smaller Montenegro, over the course of Milošević's tenure.

The first significant challenge to the Milošević regime occurred in early 1991. On March 9, police lost control of a protest organized by students and the opposition politician Vuk Draskovic of the Serbian Renewal Movement (SPO). Army intervention was necessary to clear the streets, but after the army withdrew despite orders from Milošević to remain, protestors regrouped and succeeded in retaking the city center of Belgrade for ten days. Milošević was forced to grant tactical concessions, including the release of jailed activists and the reassignment or resignation of five top officials. Milošević would not entrust the army to quell dissent again. Instead, the number of police within the republic would rise to more than 80,000 by 1996, and new secret police units were established that were under Milošević's direct control.

A second period of intensified resistance began in early 1996. Opposition parties formed a political coalition called Zajedno (Together) to contest elections that

November. The results of the polls at the federal level disappointed the opposition, and Zajedno nearly dissolved in a muddle of recriminations over the loss of parliamentary seats. But the first round of local election results offered hope with the surprising news of opposition victories in 14 of the republic's largest towns and cities. The regime's awkward response and denial of these local gains inspired a growing and determined resistance. Street demonstrations throughout the winter forced Milošević to concede and to finally recognize local election results on February 11, 1997, after 78 days of protest. These new "platforms" in towns now controlled by the opposition and the lessons learned by protestors over the period would prove useful in later resistance to Milošević. To Sonja Licht, then director of the Fund for an Open Society in Belgrade, it was the advent of pluralist politics and the beginning of "real democratic change" in Serbia.[2]

But events in Kosovo and in wartime Belgrade would draw the dividing line between this second and a third episode of resistance. By the spring of 1998, ethnic Albanian rebels pressing for the independence of the Kosovo region of southern Serbia had escalated their violent attacks on Serbian security forces in the territory. The regime's response was severe and indiscriminate, targeting both the militants and Albanian Kosovar civilians. For most Serbs, control over Kosovo was important for cultural and historical reasons, and the political opposition, civic groups, and resistance-minded students found it difficult to consolidate dissent even within their own ranks. Moreover, even general criticism of the regime during the Kosovo crisis was quickly labeled traitorous, and as international condemnation of Belgrade's moves in Kosovo grew, state media consistently equated dissent of all kinds with foreign-inspired subversion. An 11-week NATO bombing campaign that targeted sites throughout Serbia between March and June 1999 ended Belgrade's political and military presence throughout most of the province.

What many activists remember of the period is how the politics of hope and victory evident in 1997 and early 1998 rapidly turned into desperate survivalism. Mass arrests, conscription, and harassment of activists and opposition political figures occurred on an unprecedented scale. Nearly all alternative media outlets that were critical of the regime were closed or experienced suspicious technical difficulties with their signals. Assassinations of regime critics also took place, prompting many key opposition figures and civic activists not already pressed into military service or under arrest to leave the country. The formerly legalistic and semi-autocratic regime had become despotic—not without consequences.

The semi-autocratic nature of the regime worked both for and against Milošević. Over the decade, Milošević allowed pockets of easily controlled, nominally open political space to expand and contract to reassure international interlocutors, co-opt his political opposition, and portray himself as an aspiring democrat. But consistent and comprehensive control of social alternatives eluded Serbian authorities, witnessed in the rapid growth of a student movement called OTPOR by 1999 and the stubborn survival of alternative media outlets despite the hard dictatorship of the regime's past 24 months. Moreover, a reliance on legalistic authority inclined the regime to resort to the passage of repressive laws on civic activity, university education, and media expression when threatened, providing signature moments for mobilization of the opposition. As the regime became more tyrannical from 1998 onward, violations of the regime's own political norms only served to reveal its weaknesses, not its strengths.

During this time, it became clear the lengths the regime would go to in order to preserve itself. Democratic Party (DS) leader Zoran Djindjic would be particularly struck by how willing the regime was to use extralegal means to survive. After the Kosovo War, he would openly muse that the opposition may have to resort to bold measures to remove Milošević, as it did during its postelection seizure of power on October 5.[3]

By late 1999, bitterness with Milošević had grown intense. Deprivations brought about by wars in Croatia, Bosnia, and Kosovo, as well as the NATO bombing, the regime's unprecedented crackdown on its critics, unpaid salaries, and a dismal economy led to poll numbers showing that nearly half of those responding were repelled by current political figures—within the government and in the political opposition. Tellingly, the loss of control over Kosovo merited far less concern than issues of personal well-being closer to home.[4]

After a July 2000 announcement that elections for the Yugoslav presidency and the federal assembly would take place on September 24, 18 political parties and civic organizations eventually, and with great effort, formed the Democratic Opposition of Serbia. The creation of the DOS and the selection of the relative unknown Vojislav Kostunica to lead the coalition were no small achievements, given the dispiriting rivalries within the political opposition on display just months earlier. Kostunica was an inspired choice for many reasons, not the least of which were his ethnonationalist credentials.

Ethnic chauvinism and selective historical memory merged to create powerful, revisionist sociopolitical memes throughout the Balkans in the 1990s. In Serbia, populism and appeals to ethnic solidarity were indispensable to Milošević as he consolidated his authority and ridiculed his critics. By 1995, however, increasing numbers of nationalist ideologues sensed betrayal in the regime's poor treatment of Serbian refugees from wars in Croatia and Bosnia and political neglect of Kosovo's Serbian population. Milošević's disinterest in the plight of Serbs remaining in postwar Croatia and Bosnia also troubled the regime's nationalist allies. By the end of the war in Kosovo, the regime was barely able to rally traditional bases of support with jingoistic appeals. The political opposition, however, was able to leverage the soft nationalism of an unassuming Vojislav Kostunica to attract attention away from the regime during the 2000 campaign.

DOS's parallel vote tallies on election night would show that Kostunica won with 51.71 percent of the vote to 38.24 percent for Milošević on September 24. Turnout was just over 70 percent.[5] As Milošević unsuccessfully tried to discredit the results, civic and political resistance grew. On October 5 more than 500,000 people were in the streets of Belgrade, with hundreds of thousands more protesting in Serbia's other major towns and cities. The numbers were "a critical fact on the ground" says former Yugoslav army general Miroslav Hadžić. Many police units were ordered to defend government buildings and assets but ultimately did not. "Those were self-preservation decisions. The number of people was critically important."[6]

Leaders of the political opposition approached Milošević allies after vote fraud was revealed, including the directors of Serbian State Security, the Federal Customs Administration, and the head of the Yugoslav Army. On October 4 Djindjic also met with Milorad Ulemek, a notorious paramilitary member and henchman of the regime who would later be convicted of Djindjic's 2003 assassination and the attempted murder of Vuk Draskovic. Ulemek struck a bargain with Djindjic that he and his secret police unit known as the Red Berets would stand down as long as the police were not attacked.[7] Djindjic returned from that meeting and others with Interior Ministry officials during the night enormously relieved, remembers Djindjic aide Aleksandar Joksimovic. "He said to me, on the morning of October 5, 'Don't worry it's over.'"[8] Ulemek was the wild card, not the police or the military. Djindjic had been signaled that the army would remain in its barracks and that the resolve of loyal police units would weaken if he "had numbers in the street."[9] With Ulemek out of the picture, the challenge was to maintain discipline and ensure turnout, something about which Djindjic had a high level of confidence, according to Joksimovic.[10] Without the support of key personalities within the army, secret police, interior ministry, and paramilitary formations, Milošević's ability to retain authority in the face of overwhelming numbers of organized protestors was lost within hours.

On June 28, 2001, Milošević was subsequently extradited to the International Criminal Tribunal for the former Yugoslavia, headquartered in The Hague on charges of crimes against humanity and other war crimes. He died in his cell on March 12, 2006, several months before his 48-month-long trial was to end.

INTERNAL FACTORS

Internal factors were decisive influences on the success of the breakthrough in Serbia. Without the persistence of many in the political and civic opposition, the commitment of free media professionals, and the courage of citizens, the breakthrough attempt in Serbia would not have succeeded. External democracy assistance broadened and deepened opposition to Milošević but, as Thomas Carothers suggests, "the aid campaign was a facilitator of change, not an engine of it."[11] Several examples of these domestic factors are worth examining.

OTPOR

The student-based resistance movement, OTPOR, appeared in 1998. It was as much a reaction to the failure of students that year to roll back restrictive university legislation as it was to be an inspired new attempt to overcome the shortcomings of past resistance efforts and channel the public's readily visible and growing discontent with the regime into social action. The organization did not begin to actively recruit large numbers of activists until after NATO airstrikes subsided in June 1999. By August 2000, OTPOR counted 80,000 members in 130 branches, and the student initiative had become more of a people's movement composed of pensioners, academics, laborers, housewives, and veterans as well as youth.[12]

Many of OTPOR's most effective mobilization tactics entailed humorous, choreographed, street-theater-style events calculated to avoid creating an "us" verses "them" attitude with other citizens or critical parts of the regime. On holidays, OTPOR had members of the organization bring cakes and sweets to police stations. OTPOR also did the same for conscripts and officers in barracks on Army Day. When the pensioners had strikes, OTPOR joined them. When the Serbian state information minister labeled the organization a "neo-fascist terrorist group" in May 2000, OTPOR activists made light of how diminutive youths in t-shirts fell short of the terrorist stereotype. When a confrontation with police was necessary, women were in the front ranks of such marches instead of toughs. As part of the training for actions, protestors were advised that, if arrested, they should gently engage police during captivity. "This is how we knew, since May [2000], that there was wavering loyalty in the police and army. He was finished by then," maintains Srdja Popovic. "It was all over but the technical part."[13] As one OTPOR activist remarked, "The day I saw my OTPOR t-shirt on the clothesline that my mother had previously refused to wash, I knew he was finished."

OTPOR became a critical "third way" between a political opposition and a civic sector regarded by OTPOR's founders and many citizens as inept and enfeebled. As OTPOR grew in influence inside Serbia, so did the value of the international support it received. The total amount of funding provided to OTPOR in the two-month period of August and September 2000 reached $1.5 million, much of it offered with little to no supervision and for initiatives that originated among a close-knit group of creative activists.[14]

Foreign assistance did alter OTPOR's course. The founders of OTPOR claimed inspiration for their mobilization approach to some degree from the peace researcher Gene Sharp but primarily as an affirmation of something they intuitively grasped from earlier episodes of resistance and were already applying before they became aware of Sharp's work. Their largest funders were the US-based National Endowment for Democracy (NED), the United States Agency for International Development's Office of Transition Initiatives (USAID/OTI), the Fund for an Open Society, and the British Embassy, but support they received from all sources enabled the movement to expand its training and outreach efforts, maintain a growing number of support staff, plan and hold increasing numbers of protest events, and print and distribute larger runs of posters, leaflets, t-shirts, stickers, and branding symbols like the clenched fist logo that became their ubiquitous icon. Illustrative of this support was USAID's provision of 80 tons of adhesive paper to produce the stark "Gotov Je!" (He's Finished!) and clenched-fist logo stickers that appeared in the cities and towns of Serbia before the September 2000 election in one of OTPOR's boldest and best-remembered campaigns. OTPOR had the presence, innovation, and insight to effectively mobilize the public. External aid enabled it to operate in a capacity and on a scale it otherwise would have had difficulty attaining.

The Political Opposition

The Serbian public could hardly be blamed for regarding their political opposition as feckless. Attempts to form coherent coalitions to challenge Milošević, including the Democratic Movement of Serbia (DEPOS) in 1992, Zajedno in 1996, and the Alliance for Change in 1998 and 2000, failed and revealed how parties allied in their opposition to Milošević were poles apart in their positions on leadership, election boycotts, outreach, and policy. Often the failures resulted from petty bickering and unsuccessful efforts to broker a truce between the two main opposition parties, the DS and the SPO.

By late 1999, international observers and civic leaders inside Serbia worried that, despite the public's growing resentment of the regime, Milošević would prevail in any upcoming election if a viable bloc did not emerge to challenge him.

Public opinion polling by the US-based National Democratic Institute (NDI) that year revealed two countervailing trends. The percentage of respondents that held Milošević responsible for the deplorable conditions inside Serbia had risen to 70 percent; yet a majority of respondents also "felt that the parties in the opposition 'were self-interested, uncooperative, likely to fall apart, temporary.'"[15] Neither DS leader Zoran Djindjic nor SPO leader Vuk Draskovic registered as strong alternative candidates in the polls. Convincing them of this was another matter.

In October 1999, NDI public opinion polling consultant Douglas Schoen presented his conclusions to leading members of the Serbian opposition in Budapest. As Schoen writes, the polling "showed that a truly united opposition would best Milošević's ruling Socialist Party (SPS) by a thumping 46 percent to 26 percent." "It was time to unify behind a common candidate or risk four more years of Milošević as president," he added.[16] According to NDI's chief of party at the time, Paul Rowland, the meeting did not go well; especially after Schoen reminded them that the chances of opposition victory would be greatly reduced if any of the established opposition figures were to lead an opposition bid.[17]

Schoen and NDI continued to poll, sometimes on a weekly basis, and to share their findings with the major opposition parties that remained in disarray well into 2000. Data included information on which topics would resonate with voters, the fluctuations of opinion among Serbia's major cities and towns, and which political figures might lead a viable opposition challenge. Only with the galvanizing July 2000 announcement of upcoming elections in September did the opposition rally, however, forming the DOS and selecting the little-known but respected Vojislav Kostunica as its leading candidate. Kostunica was not charismatic, but he enjoyed surprising popularity in NDI's surveys. He brought focus, calm dignity, and incorruptible nationalist credentials to the indocile opposition.[18]

Schoen's last preelection poll showed Kostunica ahead at 56 percent to Milošević's 26 percent, a margin that both comforted the opposition and made it clear that Milošević would not win in a fair election. The NDI and the International Republican Institute (IRI) quickly reoriented the majority of their resources to get-out-the-vote initiatives, advising the Kostunica campaign, developing parallel vote count capacities and election monitoring training in anticipation of a contested election.

It is unlikely that this aid alone, originating primarily with US sources, served as the tipping point for the creation of DOS and the selection of Kostunica. What is clear is that the external resources that were provided to the opposition before and during the campaign enhanced the effectiveness of the opposition after DOS was formed. The accumulation of technical and human capital within party organizations as a consequence of polling data, campaign advising, and material and operational support, as well as preparations to increase turnout, to monitor the election, and to protect the vote, contributed to the success of breakthrough, shaping both the timing and the character of regime change that October.

Media Assistance

By the early 1990s, Milošević had managed to consolidate control over most print and nearly all broadcast outlets with a few notable exceptions. At least five alternative print publications had small circulations but loyal readers. Alternative voices in radio included Radio Bajina Basta, Radio Smederevo, Radio Kragujevac, and Radio Boom 93 (Pozarevac), as well as Radio Television Studio B, Radio Index, and Radio B-92 in Belgrade. Radio B-92 was particularly vital, with its irreverent and defiant prankster ethic that mimicked the young *rokeri* street milieu of its audience in the early 1990s.

It was not until the civic protests of 1997 that audience share for alternative media outlets began to grow, however. Public suspicion of state-controlled media's poor coverage of the elections controversy that year created greater interest in alternative sources of news and information. In addition, 19 municipal-owned radio and television stations emerged from the shadow of regime influence that May after the opposition took control of the towns it had won in local elections. A newly formed Association of Independent Electronic Media (ANEM) would incorporate many of these radio stations into its membership. Operating largely around the hub of Radio B-92 and its director Veran Matic, ANEM affiliates began to use the Internet and a few donated satellite decoders to rebroadcast four hours of B-92-produced news and Serbian-language BBC World Service programming in 1998. B-92 would email an encrypted copy of its program to the BBC, which in turn would uplink the stream to a satellite over Serbia that affiliates could downlink through decoders for local broadcast. For the first time, independent media could rival the reach of the regime. "It was a reawakening—the real beginning," said Sonja Licht, then director of the Fund for an Open Society in Belgrade. "For the first time in a long time it looked like we had a real chance."[19]

Media assistance increased in 1997, prompted by the opposition's political gains and the success of Radio B-92 and its ANEM affiliates. Additionally, Rich and Suzy McClear, respected media professionals who served as advisers to the US-based International Research and Exchanges Board (IREX) helped sell Matic's idea for an expanded ANEM to the US Embassy's Democracy Commission and USAID/OTI, giving technical legitimacy to B-92's ambitious, yet undeveloped goals for a radio network. The United States increased media grant funding to almost $2 million, five times what was provided in 1996. Support from the Fund for an Open Society offices in Belgrade and Budapest along with European Union and bilateral donors easily doubled this amount. The United States provided early grants of assistance to free media that year through the Democracy Commission and USAID/OTI. Additional sources of significant assistance that came later were typically channeled through the NED, NDI, IREX, and Internews.

The priority of most funders was to develop broadcast media in Serbia, especially radio. Print outlets were too incapacitated by the regime's control of newsprint and distribution networks to displace their state-connected counterparts. ANEM became a favorite partner. By June 1998, ANEM's radio broadcasts had reached 33 stations thanks to technical upgrades, operational support, the provision of additional satellite link equipment, and programming assistance that leveraged the capacities and creative abilities of B-92 and the network's affiliates.

By October 1998, however, the heightened tensions and radicalization of Serbian politics during the confrontation with the West over Kosovo shifted the trajectory of free media into reverse. The regime closed 3 ANEM affiliates after charging them with taking part in the "psychological war by Western forces." An additional 20 ANEM stations would struggle with various forms of legal and financial harassment. In March 1999, shortly after NATO bombing began, B-92's offices were seized and would remain in regime hands until after breakthrough. By August, Matic would start B2-92 in its place, with operations based in small offices and private homes in Belgrade.

Donors retrenched, reorienting much of their media assistance to ensure the availability of independent news and information inside Serbia and the survivability of alternative media outlets. The "Ring Around Serbia" (RAS) system of FM transmitters based in the surrounding territories of Kosovo, Bosnia, Croatia, and Romania was established to broadcast content from Radio Free Europe, Voice of America, the BBC, Deutsche Welle, and Radio France International into Serbia. Later, international advisers helped Matic negotiate access to Romanian and Bosnian transmitters to relay Serbian-origin broadcasts terrestrially back into Serbia. IREX, Norwegian Peoples Aid (NPA), and British sources stocked spare terrestrial transmitters as well as satellite link equipment inside Serbia to replace those that the regime confiscated and to use, as needed, to disseminate news of street violence and word of a regime crackdown. The European Union, USAID/ OTI, George Soros's Fund for an Open Society, and the Swedish Helsinki Commission continued to underwrite the operations costs of the Belgrade Media Center and to use it as a resource and venue for donor programs offering legal advice, technical assistance, and technical training for journalists and civic groups during this period.

By late 1999, Matic continued the Internet stream through the BBC to the few stations still operating within the ANEM network, and he received support to develop a second steam of 24-hour satellite programming that would be available to anyone in Serbia with a satellite dish. Internet equipment upgrades, like switching equipment allowing streaming audio and video, were critical. This external assistance and its own perseverance and expertise helped ANEM regain a broadcasting footprint of 32 radio stations by May 2000 using B2-92's Internet and satellite downlink capabilities. "With the Internet we knew we could not be stopped," said Matic reflecting on his station's use of the medium. "We felt safer. It was a great feeling."[20] ANEM affiliates and the independent Radio Index would be instrumental in relaying the results of parallel vote counts and evidence of electoral manipulation. A network of taxi radios and a previously neutral sports radio station were also used to relay logistical information for the Belgrade protests on October 5.

It is unlikely that the courageous and creative professionals who staffed and maintained media outlets in Serbia would have attained the same degree of durability, impact, and reach without external assistance, despite their innovation and resolve. The ability of indigenous outlets to survive and claim sufficient media space in the lead-up to and in the midst of the democratic breakthrough meant free media would contribute to the accumulation of revolutionary potential and become a catalyst of that potential as coverage of electoral results mobilized mass protests that October.

Civic Campaigns

Civil society groups in Serbia were nearly as divided and distrusted as the political opposition. Not until early 2000 did a coordinated front of civic groups begin to join in a campaign to mobilize voters throughout Serbia. Until that time, most donors provided small grants to an atomized civic community that included powerful organizations such as the Humanitarian Law Center, the Center for Anti-War Action, the Belgrade Circle, the Center for Development of the Non-Profit Sector, Helsinki Committee for Human Rights, the Autonomous Women's Center, and others. But it was difficult for any single or small group of organizations to have an impact despite international support for operational costs, training, materials, and other technical assistance.

Yet, in August 2000, at the height of the civic campaign then known as Izlaz 2000, 150 nongovernmental organizations and media outlets were participating in a coordinated get-out-the-vote and voter education effort. It was an unprecedented development in Serbia among many organizations that were typically wary of being "politicized." What accounted for the collaborative endeavor?

First, a longer-term learning process fueled by the diffusion of lessons from other democratic transitions in the region contributed to a growing understanding of a common interest in the democratization of the country. Second, the constellation of forces that involved a united opposition, a profoundly unpopular autocrat, popular unrest, and a real chance of regime change was an irresistible alignment for many groups intent on democratizing political processes in Serbia. Third, the campaign's activities were to officially be political but not partisan, encouraging citizens to participate in upcoming elections and to understand and protect the electoral process. Fourth, the campaign was initiated by a diverse cadre of capable and respected Serbian organizations including the Foundation for Peace and Conflict Management, the Trade Unions "Independence," Civic Initiatives, and the Center for Free Elections and Democracy (CeSID). The gravitas of these founding groups lent credibility to the enterprise. Finally, the campaign's primary international supporters included the Canadian International Development Agency (CIDA), the Fund for an Open Society, the Know How Fund of Great Britain, the Dutch and Swiss embassies in Belgrade, the German interest section in Belgrade, the German Marshall Fund of the United States, NDI, USAID/OTI, IRI and USAID's Europe & Eurasia Bureau. Many of these donors had consistently advocated the joining of civic forces in the past and now worked through the Izlaz campaign's Donors' Forum and Campaign Coordination Board to centrally fund civic action related to the election. Together donors provided an estimated $8 million toward civic campaign activities, including the "Vreme Je!" (It's Time!) initiative.[21]

CeSID was particularly important in the breakthrough effort in 2000. From past experience in the 1992 and 1997 election debacles, both international and domestic observers knew Milošević would steal the vote, particularly if the expected result promised to be uncertain. CeSID, with a budget of $1.8 million from the NED, NDI, USAID/OTI, the Swedish International Development Agency (SIDA), and the Australian and German embassies, directed several get-out-the-vote initiatives and media campaigns as well as recruitment drives for election workers. Along with the Yugoslav Lawyers Committee for Human Rights and the Belgrade Center for Human Rights, CeSID developed handbooks and manuals for election monitors and poll workers. But it was CeSID's preparations for gathering and protecting election results, together with DOS's own parallel vote tallies, that verified the opposition's victory. While the IRI funded the training of nearly 16,000 election monitors and helped DOS develop its own poll watching system, it was primarily NDI that helped CeSID develop a network of seven backup locations and servers to secure election data provided by poll watchers deployed throughout the country.

External actors helped persuade other civic groups to join in the Izlaz 2000 campaign once it was established by local organizations. By channeling support through the initiative and sharing experiences from other breakthrough efforts in the region, they helped the campaign achieve the proportions its founder's envisioned. And without additional external aid facilitating the work of election monitors and CeSID, definitive knowledge of the stolen elections may not have transformed the revolutionary potential of Milošević's critics into a revolutionary situation, a situation where the organizational capacities of the political opposition, media, and civic groups could then effectively contribute to a breakthrough outcome.[22]

THE ROLE OF EXTERNAL VARIABLES

Of the five external factors that had a bearing on regime change, direct democracy assistance provided the most cogent and sustained influence, while diffusion follows in order of importance, trailed by the less consistent influences of diplomatic and legal sanctions, economic and trade sanctions, and military intervention. All five factors are examined in this section, with the greatest amount of attention being given to democracy promotion assistance and diffusion.

Military Intervention

NATO airstrikes on targets throughout Serbia were initially conceived of as an air campaign of a few days duration that would quickly convince Milošević to reduce the size his police and military operations in Kosovo. Instead, beginning in April 1999, Milošević intensified his anti-insurgent activities in the province, eventually displacing 1.3 million Kosovar Albanians from their homes and 800,000 residents out of Kosovo altogether.[23] An 11-week air campaign targeted electrical grids, water networks, telephone exchanges, security facilities, state-media infrastructure, roads, and bridges in every major city throughout Serbia. It was NATO's first combat operation in its 50 years of existence, and it flew nearly 40,000 sorties in a war that proceeded without a UN resolution authorizing the attacks.[24]

The intent was to drive Milošević from Kosovo, not from office. In doing neither initially, Milošević not only escalated his attacks in Kosovo but leveraged his response to airstrikes into wartime measures that effectively reversed nearly all opposition gains over the previous 36 months. "Collateral damage" killed upward of 500 civilians in errant NATO bombardment of prisons, clinics, refugee convoys, residential areas, bus depots, and train trestles. More than 100,000 lost their jobs when factories were destroyed or closed as a result of the NATO air campaign.[25] Critics in the civic and political opposition, including OTPOR, joined in a chorus of dissent over the bombing, less in solidarity with the regime as it was driven by outrage and, in some quarters, expediency. Few risked the condemnation and potential harm that would come in publicly blaming Milošević for the airstrikes or in mentioning the regime's operations in Kosovo that precipitated the crisis. As Milošević closed media outlets, including the popular alternative radio station Radio B-92, director Veran Matic remembers thinking, "It was the end. We were through."[26]

Yet anger at the West and at Milošević after the bombing were not mutually exclusive. The regime's expenditures on the war, capital arrogation of state industries, and the exhaustive effects of war-related diplomatic and economic sanctions accelerated economic and political decline. Service delivery worsened, unemployment increased, and salaries to public workers and reservists, including many with recent fighting experience in Kosovo, went unpaid. Almost as infuriating as airstrikes were the regime's transparently false postwar claims that Serbia had won the confrontation with the West, that war damage was being actively repaired, and that conditions were improving within the country.[27] State-controlled media's attempts to suggest victory and recovery were regarded as outlandish and, combined with Milošević's questionable wartime dictatorial behavior, as eroding credibility among many of his supporters.

At great cost and somewhat counterintuitively, Western military intervention had a multiplier effect with other influences on breakthrough by helping to crystallize widespread anger at a number of worsening social and economic ills that the regime could not remedy and that the opposition eventually capitalized on. Growing dissidence and disaffection helped to reanimate the regime's opposition that, in turn, struggled to turn the public's anger into active resistance.

Economic and Trade Sanctions

An arms embargo was in place around Yugoslavia (then composed of the two remaining republics of Serbia and Montenegro) as early as 1991 with the adoption of UN Resolution 713 condemning Yugoslavia's actions in Croatia. UN Resolution 787 followed in 1992, imposing economic and trade sanctions and freezing the country's foreign assets in response to Milošević's support for Serbian separatist forces in Bosnia. By 1993, most UN member states complied with these prohibitions, precluding access to industrial export markets, spare parts, raw materials, and consumer goods. At the time, it was a rare display of broad international consensus toward an outlaw state. The blockade, however, was imperfect and led to the creation of a sanctions-evading nouveau riche criminal class with strong ties to the regime. After the signing of the Dayton Accords ending the Bosnia war in 1995, most restrictions were lifted with the exception of outer-wall prohibitions against membership in international financial institutions and participation in multilateral organizations. By 1999 and the Kosovo War, however, nearly all previous arms, economic, and trade restrictions were reimposed with the addition of a prohibition on oil sales to Serbia and a ban on commercial air traffic.

In the short run, sanctions and a weakened economy were a net positive for Milošević. Economic decline created dependency on the regime for infrequent wages and benefit payments. The sense of foreign persecution that Milošević sharpened through his control of the media as a basis for regional wars and ethnic solidarity was well served by the ongoing sense of isolation imposed by UN resolutions and bilateral prohibitions. The opportunities the gray and black market afforded helped create a loyal and obedient insulating layer of enterprising retainers around Milošević with an interest in keeping sanctions in place. The government under Milošević could export capital without close scrutiny and move large amounts of funds internally to shore up lagging support in sectors and areas of the country where dissent began to emerge. Internal critics were accused of being vassals to foreign centers of power—the same powers that were blamed for the immiseration of the public.[28]

By 1999, however, three phases of capital arrogation had largely run their course, and the regime's beneficiaries would begin to believe that it was no longer possible to extract much more out of the system. Hard-currency accounts of Serbian citizens had been confiscated and exhausted by 1994. From 1995 onward, an intensification of high-level corporate theft and expropriation of public funds resulted in sharp declines in formal employment and public service delivery. By 1997 and the third round of expropriation, Milošević resorted to selling state assets, including Serbia Telecom, in order to raise the resources necessary to maintain his patronage networks.[29] Additional plans to sell breweries, the state power company, a department store chain, and the national airline to foreign investors were stalled only by new sanctions and the ensuing inflation with the Kosovo War.[30] When a new Serbian civic group of economists called G17 gained access to critical financial documents after Milošević's defeat, they found that only $250 million remained in state reserves.[31]

This exhaustion of liquidity had the effect of creating tension and doubt within Milošević's trusted circle of allies. By November 1999, it appeared fear of unrest and betrayal as a result of this relentless decline in spoils motivated Milošević to dismiss air force chief Ljubisa Velickovic, army chief of staff Momcilo Perisic, Socialist Party chief Milorad Vucelic, head of State Security Jovica Stanisic, and more than a dozen top officers in the security services. Figures like Perisic would later turn on Milošević and assist the opposition in organizing both an electoral challenge and successful demonstrations on October 5.

By late 1999 and 2000, the cumulative effects of inequalities of wealth between a circle of rich elites and average citizens, confiscated foreign currency accounts, unpaid benefits and salaries, inflation, and a lack of access to consumer
goods began to incite health workers, teachers, and bus and train drivers as well
as Kosovo war veterans. G17 economists and financial experts were uncovering
and publishing the tragic dimensions of Serbia's economy and how little actual
reconstruction was actually taking place after NATO airstrikes, despite regime
claims to the contrary. Radio B-92 and its network of associated radio stations
also produced compelling programming revealing the growing gap between the
Serbian government's claims and economic reality, amplifying overall dissent and
contributing to the erosion of the mythos surrounding the regime in the process.
This gap in opposing claims about economic reality may have been a reflection of
Milošević's own delusional understanding about domestic economic conditions.
Richard Miles, then US chief of mission to Yugoslavia, describes how he pressed
Milošević on the high price of basic staples during a meeting in 1998. "We ended
up having a furious argument about the price of eggs," with the Serbian president
maintaining that they were much less expensive than they really were.[32]

By 2000, the ill effects and causes of poor economic performance and capital
flight from Serbia were increasingly undeniable. "As we understood these things,
we prepared for our own Gdansk," says Danko Cosic, a founder of the Belgrade-
based CeSID. "Serbs learned who the enemy was within that year, and it was not
sanctions and bombs but the regime that was responsible for how we lived."[33]
Milošević called for elections that September instead of waiting until they were required the following year for a number of reasons. The political opposition was in
disarray, the regime's ability to leverage its economic control into critical patronage
was weakening, and few resources existed for the repair of critical infrastructure
that was damaged from the Kosovo War or was deteriorating from long-term neglect. Milošević also knew that his government's ability to ensure adequate electrical supplies for the coming winter was uncertain. Ultimately, economic decline
caused by both internal expropriation and external pressure contributed to the
accelerated timing of the election and to the levels of anger and dissatisfaction that
helped the opposition DOS coalition prevail in breakthrough elections.[34]

Diplomatic and Legal Sanctions

Before 1997, much of the West still valued Milošević as a guarantor of stability and
security in the Balkans as a result of his assistance in brokering the 1995 Dayton
Accords. In May 1997, however, US secretary of state Madeleine Albright signaled
that the United States would no longer continue to ignore the behavior of the re-

gime toward its internal critics. Subsequent diplomatic and legal sanctions by the United States and others that followed suit began to diminish the regime's internal cohesion and constrain its political alternatives abroad. These sanctions were not without controversy, however.

Many figures in the Serbian opposition complained that the May 1999 Hague indictment of Milošević and four others for actions in Kosovo foreclosed a chance for Milošević's negotiated and peaceful exit from power. Also a source of contention was the not-so-private discord between US envoys Robert Gelbard and Richard Holbrooke about how and whether to engage Milošević, even after Albright began to put distance between the United States and the regime. Other confusing signals were sent by the US State Department as it attempted to pick a horse in the Serbian opposition to support. Attention would swing between a preference for Draskovic or Djindjic until June 2000. Impatient and unsuccessful efforts by the United States and Britain to "create a decisive moment" in 2000 before elections were announced in July were also confusing and often overrode the sensibilities of the opposition. The delay of any significant engagement with the civic and political opposition until 1997 and the evacuations and bombing that followed just 24 months later made the use of soft power and diplomatic persuasion more difficult in any case.

On the positive side, a Hague indictment gave Milošević an expiration date and made him an international outlaw. After the indictment was issued, the UN was more easily able to penetrate the labyrinth of bank accounts Milošević and his allies used in Cyprus, although this proved less fruitful than anticipated. A travel ban on nearly 800 individuals in Milošević's coterie, threats of financial ruin for Milošević allies, and direct contacts with several Milošević associates and family friends successfully peeled away support as well, as in the case of TV Pink proprietor Zeljko Mitrovic.[35]

Diplomacy also became more byzantine after 1998. It was a poorly kept secret that the British and Americans had developed a larger, extensive "white list" and a "black list" of individuals who might (or might not) expect to face criminal charges, bankruptcy, and a permanent loss of travel privileges if they did not distance themselves from Milošević. This alarmed many of the regime's business and media allies as Milošević's ability to improvise and revive his political standing diminished. Adding to this uncertainty was the effort by the British Foreign Office to bring together nearly all major figures in Milošević's civic and political opposition beginning in 1999. The initiative, called the New Serbia Forum, created a comprehensive plan for a post-Milošević Serbia, including provisions to punish the corrupt and those who committed atrocities under the *ancien régime*.[36]

In addition to sticks, carrots were also used. After the indictments, promises by the United States and European countries of easily obtainable travel visas, the lifting of outer-wall sanctions, easier access to Europe's markets, and improved relations were also made, all in the event of an opposition victory in any upcoming poll. But in the wake of NATO bombing, the intended impact of these gestures was deflected by the insular political culture of the moment within Serbia that regarded such overtures and commitments as unreliable.

While the influence of diplomatic and legal sanctions were variable overall, their most potent contribution was to impart a growing sense of entropy surrounding the regime. As international consensus for regime change hardened and international critics appeared to number Milošević's days, patronage networks and the aura of invincibility surrounding the autocrat weakened, making the September 2000 election as much a referendum on Serbia's future as it was a plebiscite on Milošević's ability to continue in office.

Diffusion

Valerie Bunce and Sharon Wolchik define diffusion as a "process wherein new ideas, institutions, policies, models or repertoires of behavior spread geographically" from one country to another.[37] In Serbia, diffusion was the most consistent external influence on breakthrough over the decade, factoring in as early as 1991. While it was the most sustained influence, it was not the most important. Direct democracy assistance would prove most influential largely due to the intensity and breadth of assistance from 1997 onward. In Serbia's case, being in the neighborhood of several other instances of regime change encouraged diffusion among activists and countries sharing postcommunist structural similarities as well as the same existential questions about their economies, security, and sovereignty.

A first wave of breakthroughs in the region occurred between 1988 and 1992 and included East Germany, Poland, Hungary, the Czech Republic, and Slovenia. A second wave from 1996 to 1998 saw Bulgaria, Romania, and Slovakia shake off their own autocrats in electoral breakthroughs. Serbia was a tougher case, however. For most of the decade Milošević was adept at pirouetting around his international critics and blunting the force of his domestic opponents, giving him a longevity in office that other regional autocrats lacked. After 1998 Serbia became increasingly isolated, especially after the evacuation of most aid groups and embassies the following year at the outset of the Kosovo War. No outside monitors observed elections, and networks of contacts among civic actors with the outside world diminished as the confrontation with NATO radicalized Serbian politics and xenophobia eroded both an ability and a willingness to embrace outside help, especially from Western sources.

Regional activists from breakthroughs in Bulgaria, Slovakia, and Croatia were well placed to pierce the insulation surrounding Serbia. They could more easily enter the country and were more trusted and safer to deal with than Western contacts. These activists and advisers also enjoyed credibility from their own struggle and a history of being influenced, in turn, by Serbia's protests in 1996–97. The IRI helped bring in the Slovak Marek Kapusta of the Pontis Foundation to work with OTPOR. In a rare acknowledgment of outside influence, two founders of OTPOR, Srdja Popovic and Ivan Marovic, maintain it was Kapusta who helped refine and develop the complementary two-pronged "Vreme Je!" (It's Time!) and "Gotov Je!" (He's Finished!) campaigns that OTPOR and Izlaz 2000 so effectively deployed.[38] "We invented the two-track approach on Kapusta's advice about what the donors would like—one easy campaign for the civic groups, not hard edged, and one advocating an extraconstitutional change of government," admitted Marovic. The Slovak Pavol Demes of the German Marshall Fund (GMF) helped Izlaz 2000 organizers understand and emulate the Slovak OK98 civic movement and experience. Demes, Kapusta, and the Slovakian ambassador to Serbia at the time helped mediate with and raise funds from Western donors as well as negotiate the gulf between Serbian civic groups and the Serbian political opposition as well.

After CeSID organizers traveled to Bulgaria and Poland in 1997 and 1999 to witness elections and speak with civic organizers there, Kapusta and Croatian activists worked alongside the NDI to help CeSID develop the vote-tallying mechanisms the organization employed to protect polling data in September. Additionally, the East-West Foundation brought regional civic and political leaders together to compare experiences, including one famous meeting in Bratislava in July 2000, when the announcement of September elections was made. According to Steven Grand, then the GMF's director of programs, key Serbian figures in the room wanted to boycott, but regional activists and political leaders in attendance helped them to reconsider.[39] Ultimately, such influences convinced the political opposition to eventually unite and contest elections.

Pressure to work in a united fashion, amplified by similar efforts by international donors, may have been one of the most important contributions of these regional activists and politicians. They were able to leverage their credibility to advance an inclusive social movement model that overcame the sometimes caustic relationships between civic and political leaders in Serbia. Most importantly, they were on the ground and spent long periods with Serbian opposition actors when most representatives of international organizations could not. They were "affirmers" and "refiners" who could speak of their own successes and failures of unity, such as the Slovak debacle in 1994, when opposition gains collapsed as consensus among the victorious parties unraveled.

In more than 80 interviews with Serbian opposition political leaders, media professionals, and civic activists, the importance of diffusion was consistently cited. Regional breakthroughs and actors reminded them "they too could do it," that there were proven ways to go about regime change, that they were not alone, and that it was okay to tailor the advice and encouragement received from regional allies and international sources to the Serbian context. Kapusta, for one, was impressed by OTPOR's use of humor against the regime; it was something new for the veteran of Slovakia's struggle for democracy.[40]

Direct Democracy Assistance

While small amounts of direct democracy promotion assistance from the NED and the Fund for an Open Society became available in 1988 and 1991 respectively, it was not until 1997 that significant democracy aid flowed to those in the opposition community within Serbia and Montenegro. By 1999, the amount of these resources more than trebled. Democracy promotion assistance from all sources totaled nearly $150 million in the period 1988–2000, including the value of consulting, training, polling, and direct aid composed of goods and support costs. Nearly two-thirds of this amount was expended in 1999 and 2000 alone. Four features of this assistance were most responsible for making this variable the most convincing external factor contributing to breakthrough.

Coordination

Five major international democracy promotion conferences among aid providers active in Serbia took place after 1997. Among funders supporting independent media in Serbia, coordination meetings took place every six months. In 1999 and 2000 the GMF began regular coordination meetings in Washington that were attended by the USAID, State Department personnel, and representatives of several implementing organizations. Coordination among foreign assistance professionals in the field was also unusually effective. Expatriate staff of embassies, donor agencies, and implementing organizations that were evacuated from Serbia to Budapest and Szeged, Hungary, as well as to Skopje, Macedonia, just before NATO airstrikes constituted informal and congenial "offshore" communities where tactical and strategic information was regularly exchanged after March 1999.

The results of consensus among capitals and coordination in the field included a single application form that Serbian media outlets and civic organizations could use to apply for grants from most funders as well as general agreement on reporting formats. Multidonor collaboration on large media support projects, elections training, and civil society support was also made easier with this frequent consultation. (Consensus also made it possible to avoid exhausting the human and diplomatic capital that is often consumed in the struggle to develop strategic coherence in high-profile aid venues.) As a consequence, there was limited turnover in the personnel of embassies, donor agencies, or implementing organizations throughout the period despite the hardships of these posts and their temporary, "offshore" offices. This valuable reservoir of institutional knowledge and the relationships these professionals developed in Serbia before their evacuation provided continuity and the basis for enduring partnerships with Serbian activists during the absence of most aid providers through the breakthrough period.

"Venture Capital" Assistance

International consensus on regime change as of 1999 came as an enormous relief for many Serbian activists. An emphasis on more confrontational antiregime initiatives and on "whatever worked" also encouraged the growth of "venture capital" approaches to aid initiatives. By design, much of the aid provided by the NED, the USAID/OTI, and the Fund for an Open Society was already of this type. But other, more traditional forms of aid also became entrepreneurial. Typical reporting and accounting mechanisms for most types of assistance were relaxed and grant-processing times shortened by early 2000. To Paige Alexander, vice-president of IREX at the time and an implementer of media assistance in Serbia, this flexibility and a willingness to suspend some of USAID's more cumbersome approval processes "made it possible to effectively and reactively target opportunities as they arose even when we were not in Serbia."[41]

Arm's-Length Engagement

The expatriate democracy promotion community was absent from Serbia during the most intense period of breakthrough mobilization. Many embassies and foreign organizations experienced two brief evacuations before a third and final exit took place in March 1999. Most Western embassies and aid offices would not return until 2001. These withdrawals from Serbia under tense circumstances had the effect of prompting international assistance providers to rely more on the judgment of their courageous local staff members who remained in the country and their local partners' descriptions of opportunities and appropriate priorities. Moreover, beneficiaries like OTPOR sometimes reprogrammed the fungible aid they received to new emerging challenges inside Serbia—often with their donors' assent. OTPOR activists and financial managers would often reorient the USAID/OTI funds they obtained to the demands of the moment, for example, whether it was for operations costs or for demonstrations, legal aid, printing, matériel expenses, or travel costs.

Creative Financing

The regime sharpened its scrutiny of Western assistance and traditional funding channels as international antagonism toward Milošević grew more intense. By the time the evacuation of Western embassies and organizations was completed and NATO airstrikes began, many Serbian partners requested greater circumspection in the way they received support to avoid the criminal penalties and social stigma associated with Western aid. As Michael Dobbs of the *Washington Post* would write in 2000, it was an informal but well-understood rule within many organizations never to talk about Western support. "To have done so would have played straight into the hands of the Milošević propaganda machine, which routinely depicted opposition leaders as 'traitors' or 'NATO lackeys.' "[42] Most groups still requested aid but insisted that it be discreet. As a result, the provision of some types of democracy assistance became more clandestine.

Before their final evacuation, the British Embassy used its diplomatic pouch to provide important satellite decoder equipment to Radio B-92 for its network affiliates. Civic groups also describe how they would send trusted individuals to the German and Dutch embassies to pick up grant funds under the guise of seeking a visa. After evacuation, the Norwegian and Hungarian embassies carried local staff salaries, grant funds, and equipment for USAID grantees in their diplomatic vehicles over the border from Budapest to Belgrade. Other Western support to partners inside Serbia was routed to their foreign bank accounts to avoid detection by the regime's financial police. Another method entailed wiring funds to the foreign accounts of Belgrade-based travel agencies that would then launder these donor funds into hard currency made available over the counter to grantees inside Serbia. OTPOR's financial manager Slobodan Homen frequently forwarded the Western funding his organization received in its bank accounts in Vienna to the foreign accounts of supporters living in Belgrade with currency on hand that, in turn, made cash available to OTPOR inside Serbia.

The EU, USAID, NPA, and the Fund for an Open Society procured and then protected communications and data-processing equipment for use during the 2000 election campaign and subsequent protests, including the staging of a back-up, high-powered terrestrial radio transmitter at Radio Pancevo, nine miles distant from Belgrade. There was also extraordinary international cooperation on initiatives to circumvent the regime's blockade of Serbian airwaves, including the development of the controversial RAS and Platforms for External Broadcasting (Pebbles) systems of radio transmitters located in neighboring countries that beamed alternative information programming into Serbia.

Not all Western democracy assistance was conducted by hidden means, but this discretion and the multiple streams of funding that did come into Serbia helped ensure that assistance would continue even in the face of hard dictatorship and in ways that would not compromise local partners. Training of election monitors and municipal officials, public opinion research, political party development, and media production activities often proceeded as before—either conducted from offices such as USAID's temporary location just over the border in Szeged, Hungary, or inside Serbia using local expertise or third-country nationals. More often than not, however, less than overt means were employed to support the requests for assistance that came from inside Serbia in the regime's final 18 months.

Together these sources of aid constituted a multifront, redundant, and ad hoc arrangement of providing support that contributed to the durability of the assistance effort. A high level of coordination among these assistance providers, their arm's-length partnerships with Serbian counterparts, and a general agreement on the singular goal of regime change kept such a diverse array of international organizations from otherwise creating havoc in Serbia.

CAUSAL ANALYSIS: INTERNAL AND EXTERNAL FACTORS

External influences and internal factors combined to contribute to a breakthrough outcome in Serbia that either alone could not have accomplished. Among foreign influences, *direct democracy assistance* and *diffusion* made the most straightforward contributions toward breakthrough. Their impact accumulated over time, with diffusion having incremental influence over the decade and direct democracy assistance beginning to have a substantial influence only after 1997. By 2000, the cumulative effects of both factors were conspicuous and had deepened the well of revolutionary potential in Serbia at the time elections were announced. Both factors were particularly important, for example, to the successful efforts of CeSID, Izlaz 2000, the DOS coalition, and free media outlets in getting out the vote and then protecting and broadcasting election results, contributing to Milošević's removal from power 11 days later. The defections of security forces can also be traced to the organizational capabilities of regime critics and the survival of free media in Serbia that year. Both were augmented by external democracy assistance and the support of experienced, regional activists.

Other external factors such as *economic and trade sanctions, diplomatic and legal sanctions,* and *military intervention* had an inconsistent influence on internal factors and on breakthrough in general. *Economic and trade sanctions and military intervention* contributed to economic failure and the general sense of entropy surrounding the regime in its last 24 months. *Diplomatic and legal sanctions* also added to the sense of political decay around the regime as indictments and covert efforts to peel away support from Milošević enjoyed some success. In addition, diplomatic pressure over the decade helped maintain lacunae of democratic expression in Serbia, influencing the semi-autocratic character of the regime—at least until the war in Kosovo. All three of these external influences may have also contributed to the timing of the announcement of September elections in July 2000. Milošević knew that his political options were shrinking, that his circle of allies was closing, and that his regime would be insolvent well before his term expired.

Among all internal factors, Serbia's particular mix of nationalism and historical memory was the least influenced by any external factor. Milošević's early ability to successfully use ethnic chauvinism to his advantage had diminished by 2000. Ethnic nationalism, still a salient characteristic of Serbia's political culture that year, was far more ably employed by Kostunica to capture the imagination of the voting public, and his campaign made use of this advantage. External influence had little to do with this development.

What then is the balance of external and internal influences on breakthrough in Serbia? Internal structural influences like economic failure, semi-autocracy, and ethnic nationalism would have been insufficient to trigger breakthrough. The internal factors of a democratic civic and political opposition as well as free media were required to instrumentalize those factors. Discontent with economic conditions, disillusionment with hard dictatorship, and the perception that Milošević's nationalist credentials were disingenuous created conditions that were ripe for mobilization. But only after this growing anger was given voice by movements such as OTPOR, Izlaz 2000, the DOS coalition, and free media would catalytic events like the announcement of elections and revelations of vote fraud ignite the revolutionary potential that internal influences helped to create.

Yet, while it is likely that the sum total of influence from all of these internal factors would have amounted to breakthrough eventually, it is unlikely that breakthrough would have had the same character or timing without the contributions of external factors. External factors helped to intensify public dissatisfaction with the regime and, at least for a time, helped preserve semi-autocracy. Most importantly, external influences contributed to the growing sophistication, endurance, and capabilities of the democratic civic and political opposition. External factors also ensured that revelations about vote fraud reached the public and contributed to the mass mobilization that helped convince security forces to defect. It is also likely that Milošević's catalytic call for elections resulted because of the decay of his regime and his perception that the opposition could not mount a coherent challenge to his candidacy or easily frustrate vote fraud. External influence contributed to reversals of fortune on both counts.

CONCLUSION

External factors shaped the character of breakthrough, supplying the kinds of resources that ultimately contributed to a peaceful transition of power. These external influences supported a struggle for democracy that was already prevalent
inside Serbia, however. They did not independently originate this struggle nor
create the courageous community of activists that produced it. Nor did external
forces single-handedly create the degree of public disaffection over conditions in
Serbia that the opposition eventually exploited. Breakthrough would likely have
been accomplished without significant outside help although the character and
timing of such an event is open to question.

But what would such a breakthrough have looked like? An examination of coun-
terfactual scenarios is instructive.

This did not have to be an electoral breakthrough. While elections provided
an opportunity to depose Milošević in September 2000, a showdown was in the
works over that summer. One alternative breakthrough scenario would have mass
protests emerging that fall, less an outgrowth of opposition mobilization than a
spontaneous public expression of desperate dissent. External aid, without the galvanizing event of prospective elections or an organized political opposition would
have been much reduced. A regime crackdown using police and security forces
under Milošević's control to dissipate protests would likely have followed. Police
may have withdrawn if the army hinted it would intervene on behalf of protestors,
avoiding a "rock, paper, scissors" situation resembling events in Romania, where
the army clashed with police after the latter had attacked protestors in 1989.[43]
Milošević could have then been forced out through the combined efforts of citizens in the streets and regime insiders disturbed over the autocrat's inability to
govern. Without the unity-inducing effects of an election campaign, however, the
role of civic leaders and the political opposition would have been uncertain and the
breakthrough might have come at great cost, been violent, and created an ambivalent result that would have complicated subsequent efforts to consolidate gains
after regime change.

Another scenario might have included a pacted breakthrough where a compromise resulted from "stalemate and dissensus" among regime and opposition
elites.[44] As Adam Przeworski describes it, democracy may prevail when it becomes
"the only game in town."[45] Although in the case of Serbia a stalemate may have
simply signaled a return to more robust semi-autocracy. Strategic concessions
would have probably split and turned the civic and political opposition in on itself
once more, undermining its attractiveness to the public. But with the regime suffering a crisis of legitimacy and liquidity, it is likely the opposition would have

slowly gained on Milošević, forcing significant compromise and possibly regime change at the next best opportunity. A coup by the regime's remaining soft-liners could also not be ruled out, bringing about a new leadership that could then more easily negotiate shared powers, a transfer of authority, or the holding of elections.

Yet another scenario would have included a situation where the opposition and civic actors received much of their funding from opposition-inclined diaspora sources, Serbian business interests, and other domestic patrons. Serbian activists did generally see this as "plan B" in the event of international withdrawal or disinterest, but it was regarded as a less than satisfactory alternative. Such sources typically offered funds with serious strings attached and in smaller sums than could be obtained through aid channels. Moreover, this kind of assistance did not include difficult to procure equipment and technical support for media initiatives or for protecting the vote, and it did not include the kind of external pressure on the regime that contributed to Milošević's vulnerability. It would have helped with party outreach and much of the work of OTPOR and initiatives like Izlaz 2000, however. In the event of an election, and even without an election, significant forces could have rallied with such resources to challenge and undermine the authority of the regime. The outcome, however, would have been far more uncertain.

As it was, however, the election was close. With all the external and internal pressures noted contributing to breakthrough and with turnout over 70 percent, Kostunica received only 51.7 percent of the vote, barely over the threshold that would necessitate a run-off with Milošević. The constellation of internal and external influences present was sufficient to win the election that September, to safeguard its results, and to remove Milošević through mass protests in October. But it was only through this partnership of factors that the Bulldozer Revolution occurred in the manner and at the time that it did, belatedly adding Serbia to the wave of democratic breakthroughs in the region.

NOTES

Jennings was country director of the United States Agency for International Development, Office of Transition Initiatives in Serbia and Montenegro from 1997–2000.

1. For context, see Lenard J. Cohen, *Serpent in the Bosom: The Rise and Fall of Slobodan Milosevic*, rev. ed. (Boulder, Colo.: Westview Press, 2002), 422. Original quote by Kostunica in *FoNet News Agency Bulletin*, October 2, 2000.

2. Sonja Licht, now director of the Belgrade Fund for Political Excellence, interviews, June 2006 and April 2007.

3. Aleksandra Joksimovic, former aide to Zoran Djindjic, interview, April 2007.

4. See Cohen, *Serpent in the Bosom*, 357, for greater detail on survey results.

5. For turnout figures and background on the presidential vote tallies see International Foundation for Electoral Systems (IFES) data and sourcing at www.electionguide.org/results.php?ID=949.

6. Miroslav Hadžić, former Yugoslav Army general, interview, Belgrade, April 2007. Hadžić now heads the Serbian Center for Civil Military Relations.

7. Others features of the bargain were rumored to be general amnesty for Ulemek and his organization as well as noninterference in the Red Beret's future activities. It was an agreement that Djindjic may have paid for with his life once he moved against Ulemek several years later.

8. Aleksandra Joksimovic, interview, Belgrade, April 2007.

9. Corroborated by both Joksimovic and Hadžić in interviews, April 2007. Quote by Hadžić.

10. Discipline was imperiled at one point when a highly placed DOS operative, Nebojsa Covic, lead several protestors up the steps of the Parliament building prematurely and off script, injuring several policemen. While this did not rally regime defenses, this move and the subsequent burning of the Parliament building sealed Covic's reputation as being unpredictable.

11. Tom Carothers, *Ousting Foreign Strongmen: Lessons From Serbia* (Washington, D.C.: Carnegie Endowment for International Peace, July 28, 2008), 4.

12. Srdja Popovic, Ivan Marovic, and Slobodan Homen, three of the dozen original founders of OTPOR, general background interviews, Belgrade, April 2007.

13. Popovic interview.

14. Homen interview. He is the former international liaison and financial director of OTPOR.

15. See Douglas E. Schoen, *Power of the Vote* (New York: Regan Books, 2007), 131.

16. Ibid., 136.

17. Paul Rowland, interview, April 2007.

18. Milošević likely did not count on a rapid response and the selection of an opposition candidate for the Yugoslav presidency when he announced elections that July. DS leader Djindjic had to be convinced to take a secondary, operational role in DOS—"and it was not easy." Paul Rowland, National Democratic Institute, phone interview, June 2006.

19. Sonja Licht, interviews, June 2006 and April 2007.

20. Veran Matic, interview, April 17, 2006.

21. Pavol Demes and Joerg Forbrig, "Civic Action and Democratic Power Shifts: On Strategies and Resources," in Joerg Forbrig and Pavol Demes, eds., *Reclaiming Democracy: Civil Society and Electoral Change in Central and Eastern Europe* (Washington, D.C., and Bratislava: German Marshall Fund of the United States, 2007), 175–90. Available at www.gmfus.org//doc/ReclaimingDemocracy_web5.pdf.

22. See Mark Thompson and Philip Kuntz, "Stolen Elections and the October Revolution in Serbia," in Mark K. Thompson, *Democratic Revolutions: Asia and Eastern Europe* (London: Routledge, 2004), 86, for one explanation of this transformation.

23. UN High Commissioner for Refugees, cited in Elizabeth Becker and David Rhode "Refugees Are Skeptical of Pledges," *New York Times*, June 4, 1999, 1, 3, 31.

24. Ivo Daalder and Michael O'Hanlon, *Winning Ugly: NATO's War to Save Kosovo* (Washington, D.C.: Brookings Institution Press, 2000), 4.

25. Steve Erlanger, "Economy: Serbs Face Bleak Future after War," *Guardian*, May 4, 1999, www.guardian.co.uk/world/1999/may/04/2.

26. Veran Matic, interview, April 2007.

27. See Sabrina P. Ramet, *The Three Yugoslavias: State-Building and Legitimation, 1918–*

2005 (Bloomington: Indiana University Press; Washington, D.C.: Woodrow Wilson Center Press, 2005), 520.

28. See Michael Palairet, "The Economic Consequences of Slobodan Milosevic," *Europe-Asia Studies* 53, no. 6 (2001): 903–19.

29. Ibid., 914.

30. Chuck Sudetic, *Serbia: The Milosevic Factor,* 14, International Crisis Group Yugoslavia Project, February 24, 1998, draft report.

31. See Louis Sell, *Slobodan Milosevic and the Destruction of Yugoslavia* (Durham, N.C.: Duke University Press, 2002), 334, on this point. The G17 would eventually form a political party from amongst its members.

32. Richard Miles, former US chief of mission to the Federal Republic of Yugoslavia (1993–98), interview, July 2007.

33. Danko Cosic, interview, April 2007.

34. See Damjan de Krnjevic-Miskovic, "Serbia's Prudent Revolution," *Journal of Democracy* 12, no. 3 (2001): 96–110.

35. James O'Brien, US Balkans envoy, interview, March 2006.

36. See "The New Serbia Forum: A Programme for the Reconstruction of Yugoslavia," British Association for Central and Eastern Europe, October 2000.

37. Valerie Bunce and Sharon Wolchik, "International and Post-Communist Electoral Revolutions," *Communist and Post-Communist Studies* 39, no. 3 (September 2006): 285.

38. Popovic and Marovic interviews.

39. Steven Grand, interview, September 2007.

40. See Fredo Arias-King, "Revolution Is Contagious: Interview with Marek Kapusta," *Demokratizatsiya,* January 2007.

41. Paige Alexander, Vice President of International Research and Exchanges Board (IREX), interview, July 2006.

42. See Michael Dobbs, "US Advice Guided Milosevic Opposition," *Washington Post,* December 11, 2000, A01.

43. See A. L. Binnendijk and Ivan Marovic, "Power and Persuasion: Non-violent Strategies to Influence State Security Forces in Serbia (2000) and Ukraine (2004)," *Communist and Post-Communist Studies* 39 (2006): 426.

44. Guillermo O'Donnell and Phillippe C. Schmitter, *Transitions from Authoritarian Rule: Tentative Conclusions about Uncertain Democracies* (Baltimore: Johns Hopkins University Press, 1986), 72.

45. Adam Przeworski, *Democracy and the Market* (Cambridge: Cambridge University Press, 1991).

CHAPTER FIVE

Ukraine

External Actors and the Orange Revolution

MICHAEL MCFAUL AND RICHARD YOUNGS

The analytical framework for explaining the Orange Revolution in this chapter is derived from a theory of democratization that centers analysis on the conflict and the distribution of power between autocratic elites and democratic challengers. It disaggregates variables to develop a nuanced understanding of the proximate causes of the Orange Revolution. This involves identifying factors that both weakened the *ancien régime* and those that empowered the democratic opposition. We locate as crucial explanants the existence of a competitive authoritarianism, an unpopular leader, division among the armed forces, a successful opposition campaign that exposed fraud and was able to communicate information about the falsified vote, and the capability to mobilize masses to protest the fraudulent election.

Crucially, our assessment of the role played by external factors is then structured around this account of regime change, as we consider international policies toward Ukraine. We examine the interplay between internal and external dimensions. The analysis reveals that external factors played a more than trivial role in shaping the Orange Revolution, both in constraining autocratic power and in strengthening democratic power. But it also suggests that this role was more subtle than might have appeared. Precise causal chains between international initiatives and domestic decisions are hard to pinpoint, even if civic actors themselves referred to the importance of outside assistance at various levels. Structuring analysis around the interplay of domestic and international factors, disaggregated across the different causal factors of democratic breakthrough, helps locate exactly where international factors did but also did *not* have significant impact.

THE ORANGE REVOLUTION AS A TRANSITIONAL TURNING POINT

The fall 2004 presidential election triggered a pivotal moment in Ukrainian history. Initially, the campaign and election results resembled other fraudulent votes in semi-authoritarian regimes.[1] The incumbent president, Leonid Kuchma, and his chosen successor, Prime Minister Victor Yanukovych, deployed state resources, national media, and private funding from both Ukrainians and Russians to defeat the opposition candidate, Victor Yushchenko. When this effort to win the vote failed, Kuchma's government tried to steal the election by adding more than one million extra votes to Yanukovych's tally in the second round of voting held on November 21, 2004.[2]

In response to this fraud, Yushchenko called his supporters to come to Independence Square in Kyiv and protest the stolen election. First thousands, then hundreds of thousands answered his call. They remained on the square, with some living in a tent city on Khreshchatyk, Kyiv's main thoroughfare, until the Supreme Court annulled the official results of the second round on December 3, 2004, and set a date for the rerunning of the second round for December 26, 2004. In this round, Yushchenko won 52 percent of the vote, compared to 44 percent for Yanukovych. The victors in this dramatic struggle memorialized this set of events by calling it the Orange Revolution.[3]

THE DOMESTIC STORY

Ukraine's level of economic development, literacy, and urbanization, as well as its cultural proclivities for democratic rule, geographical proximity to Europe, and dearth of oil may all have been necessary preconditions for the Orange Revolution to occur. But, in the fall of 2004, it was real people, motivated by ideas and empowered by real resources, who struggled with each other to produce the Orange Revolution. A few crucial factors explain the democratic breakthrough.

First, before 2004 the degree of authoritarian control enjoyed by the regime was compromised. President Leonid Kuchma aspired to construct a system of managed democracy"—formal democratic practices but informal control of all political institutions—similar to President Putin's model of government in Russia.[4] But the Ukrainian president never achieved as much success as his Russian counterpart.

Kuchma and his regime did not control or own major segments of the Ukrainian economy. Ukraine's business tycoons or oligarchs were not completely united by the *ancien régime*.[5] And crucially, especially after the electoral success of Our Ukraine in the 2002 parliamentary vote, Ukraine's opposition had a foothold in an important institution of state power. The regime's popularity had begun to ebb. No factor undermined Kuchma's standing more than the murder of journalist Giorgy Gongadze, the founder of the Internet publication, *Ukrainska Pravda.*

In contrast to Russia or Armenia, the line between civilian government and the military remained clear in Ukraine. Consequently, when faced with mass social mobilization against the regime during the Orange Revolution, Kuchma could not invoke tradition or call upon a loyal special forces unit to disperse protesters. Kuchma threatened to use force. A week into the protest, troops from the Ministry of the Interior armed and mobilized, with the intention of clearing the square.[6] But Orange Revolution sympathizers from within the intelligence services warned the opposition of the impeding attack, and commanders within the regular army pledged to protect the unarmed citizens if these interior troops tried to march into the center of town. These defections made clear that the guys with the guns—that is, the military, the intelligence services, and police—could not be trusted to carry out a repressive order. These splits helped to convince Kuchma to call off the planned police activity, even though Yanukovych was urging the Ukrainian president to take action.

Second, a united opposition—or at least the perception of one—was crucial for the 2004 democratic breakthrough in Ukraine. In the previous decade, division, disorganization, and the absence of a single charismatic leader had crippled Ukraine's democratic forces. Ironically, Kuchma helped opposition unity when he dismissed Viktor Yushchenko as prime minister in 2001. At the time, Yushchenko cut an image of a technocratic economist, not a revolutionary. Those who knew him best worried that he did not have the drive or temperament to become a national political leader.[9] But he was a popular prime minister with a record of achievement, an image of not being corrupt, an appealing biography, and a handsome appearance. Crucially, in 2004 Yulia Tymoshenko—an opposition leader with more charisma than Yushchenko but also more baggage—agreed not to run independently for president but instead backed Yushchenko.[10]

Third, voter mobilization was crucial and extensive. The Yushchenko campaign believed that a higher voter turnout helped its cause and therefore devoted huge resources to get-out-the-vote efforts. In addition to party efforts, the nongovernmental organization Znayu carried out massive voter education and get-out-the-vote efforts, recognized by friends and foes as a positive contributor to Yushchenko's electoral success. The youth groups Black Pora, Yellow Pora, and its closely affiliated Freedom of Choice Coalition, as well as the Committee of Ukrainian Voters (CVU) also organized extensive get-out-the-vote campaigns, while groups such as Internews-Ukraine placed public service announcements on television educating Ukrainian voters about their electoral rights, which was also an indirect method for increasing voter turnout. In the second round, voter turnout reached an amazing 80.4 percent; in the rerun of the second round (the third time Ukrainians were asked to go to the polls that fall), turnout was still very high, 77.2 percent.

A fourth component of the opposition's success was the ability to provide quickly an accurate and independent account of the actual vote after polls closed. The CVU played the central role in monitoring all rounds of the 2004 presidential vote. CVU also conducted a parallel vote tabulation during all three rounds. In addition, the Ukrainian nongovernmental organization (NGO) Democratic Initiatives coordinated the National Exit Poll.

The Supreme Court used evidence of fraud collected by the CVU and other NGOs to annul the official results and call for a replay of the second round of the presidential election later that month. It is unlikely that either the defecting Central Election Commission (CEC) members or the justices who made up the Supreme Court majority would have acted the way they did if hundreds of thousands of protestors were not on the streets by the time of their deliberations. At the same time, we do know that a necessary condition for the court's decision was hard evidence that the results had been falsified in a systematic manner. This evidence came from Our Ukraine election monitors and commission members, CVU monitors, and several other NGOs. The effort to document violations and then take legal action to prosecute the offenders was much greater in this vote than in previous elections and proved critical to Our Ukraine's case before the Supreme Court.[11]

Fifth, the existence of a modicum of media independence was another important ingredient that created momentum for the Orange Revolution. *Ukrainska Pravda* and Ukraine's other independent media outlets did not fold or begin to practice self-censorship after Gongadze's death, but continued to investigate and expose Kuchma's alleged crimes, often under very threatening circumstances.[12] This critical media, while not national in reach, did help to set a polarized stage for the 2004 electoral showdown.

During the 2004 campaign, Kuchma's regime controlled or enjoyed the loyalty of most national media outlets. By 2004, Ukraine boasted several independent television networks, but all the major channels were owned or controlled by oligarchs loyal to Kuchma and Yanukovych.[13] Through a system of *temniki*, or secret commands, Kuchma and his staff directed the news coverage on all of these channels, resulting in a massive asymmetry of television exposure for Yanukovych compared to that for Yushchenko.[14] Russian television stations ORT, RTR, and NTV, which enjoy considerable audiences in Ukraine, also gave favorable coverage to Yanukovych.

But important independent outlets did remain and developed in the run up to the 2004 presidential campaign. In 2003, a wealthy Yushchenko ally, Petro Poroshenko, acquired the rights to a small television station and then transformed it into Channel Five. Poroshenko then hired a team of professional journalists, whose aim was to provide an outlet for media coverage of the entire campaign and not just Yanukovych. Channel Five did provide positive coverage of the Yushchenko campaign, but Channel Five's audience was much smaller than the major channels', roughly 8 million viewers, and its signal reached only approximately 30 percent of the country.[15] Radio Era provided news that was not shaped by the government. External stations such as Radio Liberty, the BBC, and the Voice of America were also important channels of independent news for those with the ability to receive short-wave broadcasts—a small fraction of the Ukrainian population.

Compared to the previous electoral breakthrough in Georgia 2003, Ukraine's opposition had one major advantage—the Internet. In fact, the Orange Revolution may have been the first in history organized in large measure on the Web. During the critical days after the second round vote, *Ukrainska Pravda* displayed the results of the exit poll most sympathetic to Yushchenko as well as detailed news about other allegations of fraud. The Web site also provided practical information to protestors. During the second round, *Ukrainska Pravda* grew to 350,000 readers and one million hits a day.[16] Other portals also provided critical information that helped to make the Orange Revolution. The Maidan.org site was a clearinghouse of information and coordination for protestors.

Sixth, and most striking, was the extensive popular mobilization to "protect the vote." Months in advance of the presidential election, Our Ukraine campaign leaders made plans to organize street demonstrations in what they believed was the likely event that the election results would be falsified.[17] The appearance of truckloads of tents, mats, and food supplies, which had been secured weeks before clearly demonstrated the opposition's preplanning. Yushchenko appeared on television to call upon his supporters to come to Kyiv and occupy the square immediately after the falsified second round results had been released.

Yushchenko and his team benefited tremendously from the support of the Kyiv city government and the city's mayor, Oleksandr Omelchenko. While at first reluctant to take sides, the Kyiv government eventually allowed the protest and provided logistical support for the provision of food, water, and sanitation. They also opened more than a dozen government buildings for out-of-town protesters to use as warm shelter. Had political leaders loyal to the *ancien régime* been in charge of the capital, they could have severely constrained the opposition's capacity to sustain the Orange Revolution.

Civil society and the "middle class" more broadly helped increase the numbers on Maidan from the several thousand who planned to show up to the million or so who spontaneously joined the protest. Our Ukraine and its partners made preparations for tens of thousands to protest a rigged election, but they did not anticipate that their act of civil disobedience would eventually swell to more than a million people. A central feature of the mobilization's success was a commitment to nonviolence.

THE INFLUENCE OF EXTERNAL FACTORS

A combination of many factors produced a democratic breakthrough. In accordance with this account of Ukraine's 2004 democratic breakthrough, the role of external factors can be disaggregated in finer detail and process-traced in relation to the key causal variables of regime change.

Preventing Full Autocracy

Western linkages, coupled with aid to institutions that checked presidential power, helped keep Ukraine between dictatorship and democracy, a regime type that proved conducive for the Orange Revolution. The causal chains of influence were often indirect, but domestic actors themselves pointed to the impetus given by external assistance at both the macrolevel of their representing normative models and the microlevel of tactical training.

The West—the United States, Canada (a bigger player in Ukraine than in other European countries because of the sizable Ukrainian émigré community there), and Europe—remained a constant pull on Ukrainian government officials. Kuchma was a ruthless leader who erected a corrupt and criminal regime, but he refrained from attempting to construct a truly repressive tyranny because he wanted a cooperative relationship with the United States and Europe. Strikingly, even in the face of harsh criticism, Kuchma sent Ukrainian troops to Iraq, maintained ties to NATO and the European Union, and (unlike Milosevic in Serbia) avoided becoming a pariah in the West. Maintaining links to the West was a policy priority for Kuchma, which in the margins constrained his antidemocratic behavior at home.

Kuchma's desire to be part of the West created opportunities of leverage for American and European diplomats. The lure of partnership with the European Union was a major factor in discouraging any move toward full autocracy. Just how powerful an influence the EU played in this crucial regard is open to question, however. Even if the EU exerted a generally positive magnetic pull, significant limitations persisted in the scale of inducement and partnership offered to Ukraine.

A stress on regular and institutionalized engagement was the guiding philosophy of EU strategy. The EU signed a Partnership and Cooperation Agreement with

Ukraine in 1994, which included a commitment to support the development of democratic norms. This commitment was reiterated and made more explicit in the EU's Common Strategy on Ukraine, adopted in 1999.[18] Europe sought to influence through positive inducements rather than coercive pressure against Kuchma. Serious sanctions were discussed but never applied.[19]

Such caution was encouraged by the fact that Kuchma continued to be seen by several European governments as providing a useful bridge to Moscow.[20] Indeed, Russia-related concerns ensured that this European approach of engagement and inducement was itself limited. A membership prospect was not offered to Ukraine at the crucial meeting of the European Council in Helsinki in December 1999, when other Central and East European states were formally recognized as candidates. EU documents and statements from the early 1990s routinely suggested that Ukraine was making progress toward democratic consolidation, when events on the ground suggested that Kuchma's commitment to reform was increasingly doubtful.

Some EU member states held back any significant deepening of relations with Ukraine, worried that these could be interpreted as intrusion by Moscow. Before 2004, Kuchma himself was scathing of the limited EU incentives on offer to Ukraine, the president having pushed for a free trade agreement and a "Europe Agreement" (the more generous, preaccession type agreements the EU operated with other Central and Eastern European states).[21] Ukraine even lagged behind Russia in the depth of its relations with the EU right up to the early 2000s. Across a swathe of policy areas—loans from the European Investment Bank, the granting of market economy status (which conditioned the degree of trade preferences for exports to the EU market), cooperation with Europol, education links, and visa facilitation—Ukraine was accorded less than the EU offered Moscow.[22]

Conversely, some member states argued that the EU should offer Ukraine a deeper and democracy-conditioned partnership, as a means of bolstering reformists. In 2002 the United Kingdom and Sweden first proposed offering Ukraine a further reaching set of relations, through what became the European Neighborhood Policy. Indeed, the ENP was seen by these states as a way of dealing specifically with "the Ukraine problem."[23] The ENP offered Ukraine incorporation into a wide range of EU policies and programs, within the framework of a partnership formally committed to the fostering of democratic norms. At the bilateral level, in 2002 Lithuania signed a new Strategic Partnership with Ukraine, also with a focus on political reform. Poland pressed for the EU to change its "Russia first" policy to a "Ukraine first" policy.

The Polish government argued strongly that the EU had been guilty of neglecting Ukraine for fear of incurring Russia's wrath and that European policy risked failing to halt Ukraine's slide into Belarus-like isolation. Polish diplomats admit that they failed in their attempt to boost EU offers to Ukraine both before Poland's formal accession in May 2004 and after this—and were angrily disappointed with other member states' resistance. This discrepancy was nested within a broader clash between assertive new EU-entrant Poland and some of the existing member states. For these states, the ENP was seen as a means of tying down Kuchma to the reform commitments he had repeatedly made but failed to implement. The EU concluded negotiations for a Neighborhood Action Plan with the Kuchma government a few months before its fall.

The EU appeared to have done enough over the decade of Kuchma's rule to serve as a reference point for the leader's Western-oriented aspirations and hence encourage at least a formal commitment to basic human rights and democratic procedure—even if the EU was less generous than it might have been in the depth of partnership and cooperation it offered Ukraine. There is only modest evidence that a variation in EU policy offers was linked in any very specific sense to Ukraine's degree of political openness; European influence was imported by the Kuchma regime in the form of a more subjective judgment on the latter's part that longer-term partnership with the EU would be more likely if some semicompetitive political processes were retained.

Similarly, the US pursued a policy of constructive if sometimes critical engagement.[24] After Gongadze's murder, the Bush administration did deny Kuchma a presidential visit to Washington, which the Ukrainian president had desperately desired. At the Prague NATO summit attended by Bush and Kuchma, the official language was changed from English to French so that the two presidents, whose countries' names begin with the same letter in English but different letters in French, would not have to sit next to each other. Kuchma understood the snub. And more generally, American ambassadors in Ukraine were extremely active in engaging the Ukrainian democratic forces, especially after the murder of Gongadze, in a manner that Ukrainian government officials called meddlesome. Yet, direct contact with Kuchma never ended, and active courtship of some of Kuchma's closest confidants, including Kuchma's billionaire son-in-law, Viktor Pinchuk, continued during the Orange Revolution. The American strategy was to keep the regime leaders interested in the West, so as to raise the costs of seriously bad behavior during the 2004 presidential vote. US State Department officials stated clearly in 2003 that "the conduct of the presidential campaign and election" was "the primary focus on U.S.-Ukraine relations."[25]

Western assistance and moral support also helped sustain pockets of pluralism within the regime and independent, opposition actors outside of the state. Within the state, the independence of the Rada was especially critical in checking executive power. Technical assistance provided by a United States Agency for International Development (USAID) grantee, the Indiana University Parliamentary Development Project, helped make this institution more effective. Party development efforts by the International Republican Institute (IRI) and the National Democratic Institute (NDI) also helped insure that Kuchma's party did not win an overwhelming majority of seats in the parliament as occurred in the Russian Duma during the Putin era. NDI and IRI worked with several parties that won representation in the Rada and, in doing so, helped maintain this institution's independence from the president. State Department officials also went out of their way to court the Rada speaker during the crisis. As Ambassador John Tefft testified, "We welcomed Rada Speaker Lytvyn to Washington five days before the run-off to underscore our support for a legislative body committed to ensuring an outcome that reflected the will of the people."[26]

European funding was of greater magnitude than US assistance but was focused more on government and state institutions. The EU's Technical Assistance to the Commonwealth of Independent States (TACIS) aid program prioritized support for "legislative approximation"—a distinctive European approach aimed at harmonizing a swathe of Ukrainian legislation to EU norms and standards. It was here that the EU had its most tangible impact, when in 2002 Ukraine adopted a formal "national program of approximation" with EU legislation. This package included numerous governance-related reforms that further loaded the dice against Ukraine's competitive authoritarianism morphing into full-blown autocracy.

European policy could be seen in this sense to have played a vital role during the Kuchma years in locking Ukraine into a dynamic of "governance convergence" with the EU. This did not seek directly to undermine Kuchma but was a key factor in ensuring that some degree of formal political space and constitutional guarantees remained in Ukraine. Critics accused the EU of sanctioning semi-authoritarianism; more positively it could be seen as contributing eventually to democratic transition, nearly 14 years after Ukrainian independence.

Russian leaders and organizations played the exact opposite role to their US and EU counterparts, encouraging autocratic methods as an effective strategy for holding on to power. Years before the 2004 Ukrainian presidential election, Putin embraced Kuchma without criticizing his antidemocratic ways. Through the provision of subsidized gas, Russia provided direct financial support to Ukraine's government. Putin's own system of growing autocratic rule provided a model for Kuchma to emulate. Obviously, Russian ideological and financial assistance was not sufficient to build a stable authoritarian regime in Ukraine, yet it did delay change. Ukraine's geographic proximity and significant Russian-speaking population facilitated the flow of ideas and resources about Russia's regime as an alternative to the Western model of democracy. After the second round, Putin tried to strengthen Ukraine's "managed democracy" by quickly acknowledging Yanukovych as the winner in the presidential vote, even before the official results were released. Throughout the Orange Revolution, Putin stood firmly on the side of Yanukovych and against reconciliation, flatly denouncing the idea of rerunning the elections.[27]

Fostering the Regime's Unpopularity

Kuchma's own actions, monitored by independent media, drove his government's decline in popularity. Indirectly and marginally, Western reactions to Kuchma's behavior helped magnify Kuchma's image as an illegitimate and criminal leader. Most importantly, American and European leaders strongly denounced the manner in which Kuchma handled the investigation into Gongadze's murder.[28] The Bush administration further downgraded contacts with the Kuchma regime after it become known that the Ukrainian government had tried to sell its Kolchuga air defense radar system to Iraq.[29] European impatience with Kuchma's stalling of long-promised reforms also increased, and the Gongadze murder did elicit a slightly harsher tone of criticism from European governments. High-level visits were reduced: only German chancellor Gerhard Schröder met with Kuchma in 2003, and by early 2004 contacts at the most senior level had dried up.

The most prominent role was adopted by Poland and Lithuania. These two states pressed for a more positive signal to be given toward Ukraine's potential membership to the EU and for a tougher line toward Russian influence in Ukraine. In the autumn of 2004, Lithuania took the lead in initiating EU Council discussions on offering stronger relations with Ukraine. It was backed by six other new Central and Eastern European member states, the Nordic countries and Austria.[30] This group of member states met frequently on an ad hoc basis immediately before the elections. Already in early November, the Polish foreign minister switched a planned visit to Kuchma and prime minister Yanukovych to meet Yushchenko instead.[31]

The extent to which concrete EU positions contributed directly to the unpopularity of the Kuchma government was, however, again tempered by the caution of several governments. Indeed, at this stage most European states actually encouraged Ukrainian reformers still to focus on trying to join the government and gain moderate change from within the parameters of the regime—this even as Kuchma had begun tightening controls on the media and the judiciary and making it clearer than ever that he would seek to block such "reform from within." Kuchma was manipulating political conditions early on in the run-up to the elections of autumn 2004—rigging mayoral elections, threatening students that they would lose their accommodation if they voted for Yushchenko[32]—but the EU stuck to its line of preferring to encourage reform from within the regime.

Some liberal reformers complained bitterly at Europe's reluctance to intervene as tensions deepened early in the autumn of 2004.[33] Many complained that the ENP Action Plan offered backing and protection to Kuchma, just when the latter's position was under challenge. While Central and Eastern European member states, along with the Nordic states and the United Kingdom, argued for a more assertive and critical EU involvement at this stage, they were reined back by Germany, France, and Spain.[34]

The perception was that the Kuchma regime had contributed to Ukraine's isolation from the European sphere—even through several EU member states had carefully *avoided* making any firm promises that if Ukraine did democratize it would be allowed into the EU. In terms of external influences, another lesson is to be found here in the difference between perception and the actual substance of Western policies.

The Kremlin did not invest major resources in trying to improve Kuchma's international image, but Russian officials coordinated and sponsored various activities aimed at helping Yanukovych win the election. At the urging of the Kremlin, Russian businesspeople contributed to Yanukovych's campaign.[35] Some reports claimed that Russian sources provided $300 million to the Yanukovych campaign with the lion's share coming from Gazprom.[36] Several Russian public relations consultants, including several closely tied to the Kremlin, worked directly for the Yanukovych campaign, while others participated in projects in Ukraine designed to bolster indirectly the Yanukovych efforts. For instance, in 2004, Russian public relations professionals created the "the Russian House" in Kyiv, which organized public events to emphasize Russia's positive and pivotal role for Ukrainian economy and security. To help Yanukovych, Putin personally traveled twice to Ukraine in the fall of 2004. A Russian-sponsored election-monitoring group observed the Ukrainian vote and declared the first and second rounds free and fair.

THE INTERPLAY BETWEEN INTERNATIONAL AND DOMESTIC FACTORS

Although international carrots and sticks alone did not bring about the Orange Revolution, there were several areas where the actions of international actors in combination with domestic factors appear crucial in bringing about Ukraine's successful transitional moment in 2004.

External Contributions to a United and Effective Opposition

Assessing the role of external actors on the formation of a united and effective opposition in Ukraine (or anywhere else) is a difficult task because of the nature and sensitivity of the work. The nature of the work is difficult to evaluate because the process of making an impact occurs indirectly over extended periods of time and in parallel to local inputs. The transfer that took place between groups like the International Republican Institute and the National Democratic Institute on the one hand and Our Ukraine on the other was essentially one of ideas and know-how, the most difficult variables to trace systematically.[37] Assessing this work is sensitive, because Ukrainian actors do not want to taint their reputations or legitimacy by reporting that Western actors contributed to their domestic success, while Western actors seek to protect their partners and also maintain a claim of acting as nonpartisans. Recognizing these huge constraints, observations about the role of external actors on the development of Ukraine's opposition coalition can still be made.

There is no evidence that the United States or any European government contributed financial resources directly to the campaign of Viktor Yushchenko and Our Ukraine.[38] Our Ukraine did receive financial contributions from citizens living in the United States and Canada. The greatest source of foreign funding for the Yushchenko campaign came from Russia.[39] The Yushchenko campaign also hired American and Russian campaign consultants. But foreign governments or foreign NGOs receiving financial support from Western governments did not pay for these professional services. Ukrainians did.

The EU had conspicuously declined to support the popular demonstrations that erupted in 2000. Nor did it offer material support for the democratic opposition that took shape in organized and systematic fashion after 2001. At the 2002 elections, no EU support was forthcoming for reformers, and the latter were outmaneuvered by Kuchma for positions and representation after the poll. By 2004 a small amount of party training was being offered on a bipartisan basis, and some indirect logistical support provided in-kind aid for prodemocracy protestors. Germany, Spain, and France eschewed direct political aid projects in the run-up to or in the wake of the first round of the 2004 elections. The role of quasi-independent party foundations such as the Westminster Foundation for Democracy, the German Stiftungen, or the Dutch Alfred Mözer Foundation represented the more notable aspect of European political assistance. In interviews, actors in the Orange Revolution reported favorably on the demonstration effects that Serbia 2000 and Georgia 2003 had on their own mobilization efforts. Contacts between youth activists from Serbia, Slovakia, and Georgia provided inspiration to their counterparts in Ukraine, even if the transfer of technical knowledge about civic resistance is more difficult to measure. The most tangible backing for democracy activists came not from Western official initiatives but through links between Pora and its Serbian counterpart, OTPOR (Pora was too high profile to receive either European or US funding).[40]

While his role was praised *ex poste*, EU foreign policy representative Javier Solana was initially reluctant to get involved in supporting the Orange Revolution. The more activist states complained at Solana's passivity; Solana's team was concerned that it lacked a clear mandate supported by all EU governments. One civil society representative lamented that Solana focused on events in Ukraine only after being pushed hard by Poland and when he belatedly saw "history being written." The triumvirate that was eventually assembled of Solana, Aleksander Kwasniewski, and Valdas Adamkus, the Polish and Lithuanian presidents, respectively, focused on mediating more than bolstering support for the opposition. There was general agreement that it was Kwasniewski who served as the crucial interlocutor, based on a long-standing mutual confidence with Kuchma. Solana was generally recognized as having played a valuable mediating role, while maintaining a line of "we do not meddle, or take sides." This tempered the degree to which EU intervention served as a rallying point for the uniting of an erstwhile fractious opposition.

The Our Ukraine campaign had greater organizational reach than any other party in Ukraine. Our Ukraine leaders accomplished this feat primarily on their own through years of hard work. At the same time, Our Ukraine political leaders reported that the development of their organizational capacity benefited from years of close relationships with the National Democratic Institute and the International Republican Institute.[41] Well before the formation of the Our Ukraine bloc in 2002, IRI and NDI also worked closely with many of the individuals who later assumed senior positions in the Our Ukraine organization and campaign. After the creation of the party, NDI and IRI provided additional training assistance, though using different strategies. IRI conducted multiparty training programs focused almost exclusively on regional party leaders outside of Kyiv, while NDI provided trainers to programs organized by Our Ukraine, a service they provided to other parties as well.[42] NDI staff members also focused more of their efforts on working with Our Ukraine's senior leadership in Kyiv. Measuring systematically the results of these interactions, be it NDI's engagement with senior party officials or IRI regional training efforts, is beyond the scope of this study. That there were purposive efforts by both IRI and NDI to strengthen Our Ukraine's campaign abilities is without question.

Indirectly, both NDI and IRI also helped to increase the respectability of Yushchenko in Washington. IRI organized a trip to Washington for Yushchenko and his senior staff in February 2003, at which time the Ukrainian presidential candidate met with key Bush administration officials and members of Congress. Significantly, he met Senator Richard Lugar, who would eventually play a key role in helping to impede American endorsement of the second round result of the 2004 vote.[43] Former secretary of state Madeleine Albright, chair of NDI's board, traveled to Ukraine in February 2004 to meet with Yushchenko and other Our Ukraine officials. Upon her return to Washington, she also spoke favorably about Yushchenko's candidacy. These kinds of contacts helped assure the Bush administration that the Ukrainian opposition was viable and worth supporting. Our Ukraine ties with other European parties also bolstered Yushchenko's image in the West. More generally, elite networks between Our Ukraine leaders and Western leaders nurtured Our Ukraine allies in the West when debates erupted in Washington and European capitals about how to respond to the Orange protestors.[44]

Turnout in regions supportive of Yushchenko were much higher in the 2004 election than in previous elections. Several American and European organizations, including IRI, NDI, the International Renaissance Foundation (the Ukrainian affiliate of the Soros Foundation), Freedom House, Internews, and the Eurasia Foundation contributed direct financial assistance to the get-out-the-vote projects organized by their Ukrainian partners.[45]

External Contributions to Exposing Fraud

Many of the Ukrainian activities that contributed to the exposure of fraud had significant assistance from external actors. In fact, the West's central contribution to the Orange Revolution was in the form of long-term support of voters' rights groups, think tanks, youth groups, and other civil activist organizations and media organizations that would be instrumental in monitoring, polling, conducting parallel vote tabulations and exit polls, disseminating information about voters' rights and violations of those rights.

NDI provided the original idea for a Ukrainian election monitoring organization and also substantial technical and financial assistance to CVU throughout its support for the 2004 election.[46] In 2004 other Western donors, including most importantly the International Renaissance Foundation, also contributed major financial resources to CVU.[47] The PVT technology used by CVU was also imported from the United States.[48]

CVU was the largest and most visible NGO effort supported by Western funds dedicated to exposing fraud, but not the only effort. At the end of its voter education and voter mobilization campaigns, the Znayu campaign, supported financially by the US-Ukraine Foundation and Freedom House, also turned to exposing fraud, including one leafleting campaign that threatened CEC officials about the legal consequences of committing electoral fraud.[49] Yellow Pora, Black Pora, Chysta Ukraina, and hundreds of smaller NGOs also used various tactics to expose fraud. Freedom House funded many of the NGO activities at the regional level through its Citizen Participation in Elections in Ukraine program.[50] Our Ukraine also worked hard to expose fraud, first by training its party representatives serving on CEC commissions on the rules for vote counting and mechanisms for recording irregularities, and second by organizing a parallel network of election monitors. NDI played a major role in training Our Ukraine monitors.[51]

Democratic Initiatives Foundation's exit poll, which also played a critical role in undermining the legitimacy of the second round official results, was also an imported technology. Its use in Ukraine was funded almost entirely by Western donors, including the International Renaissance Foundation, Eurasia Foundation, Counterpart, and several Western embassies.[52] IRF even financed the participation of Russian and Polish polling experts in the exit poll project.[53]

In addition to Ukrainian poll watchers, the Organization for Security and Co-operation in Europe (OSCE), IRI, NDI, and the US-Ukraine Foundation deployed international election monitoring teams to observe the Ukrainian election. Most innovatively, NDI and Freedom House cooperated to bring to Ukraine the European Network of Election Monitoring Organizations (ENEMO), which comprised 1,000 observers from 17 electoral monitoring organizations in formerly communist countries. ENEMO brought trained electoral monitors, experienced in exposing postcommunist vote rigging (many observers also spoke Russian) and at a fraction of the cost that it would have taken to bring in Americans or Western Europeans. All of these international teams released critical reports about the election process, which were instrumental in generating a unified American and European condemnation of the voting procedures.

The contribution made by European governments to exposing fraud was slightly more circumspect. Interviews uncovered that the French government was particularly ambivalent and tardy in backing protestors' claims that the second round results were fraudulent.[54] Conversely, the British, Dutch, and Swedish governments did join the United States in funding exit polls. It was only after the electoral fraud had been exposed by local groups that the EU, according to one account, "changed to a stick approach" and threatened "serious consequences."[55] France and Germany did send observers to the OSCE mission that monitored the rerun of the election. Yushchenko found strong fraud-reversing assistance from European governments only once momentum toward democratic breakthrough had already taken hold. Here, international influences were imported as a useful secondary back-up, not a factor that was primary in igniting the initial steps toward regime change.

External Contributions to Independent Media

At various stages in their careers, many of the key independent journalists had contact with Western donor programs, most notably USAID-funded media projects.[56] When asked ex post what type of democracy assistance had proved most useful and pertinent, both EU officials and members of the Orange coalition referred to European media training and support. They suggested that, while such support was low key during the Kuchma years, it had helped change journalists' perspectives and provided professional know-how, factors that acted as background "enablers" of the pro-reform role adopted by some Ukrainian media in late 2004.

External Inputs into Internal Mass Mobilization

Several weeks in advance, Our Ukraine planned the first actions of civic resistance after the second round of voting. There is no evidence that it received any Western intellectual or financial assistance in making these preparations. Nor did US or European government sources support its two-week operation on the Maidan. The assertion that demonstrators were paid a daily wage for their efforts is a myth. In line with their preference for "reform from within," European politicians did not encourage mass mobilization. Solana actually called for demonstrators not to impede the working of government ministries. External actors reacted late rather than interacting proactively with domestic dynamics.

External inputs into facilitating mass mobilization were more indirect. Most importantly, a model for "electoral revolution" existed and had succeeded in two postcommunist countries in the previous three years—Serbia in 2000 and Georgia in 2003. Serbian and Georgian activists from OTPOR and Kmara helped reinforce these demonstration effects through direct interaction with their Ukrainian counterparts.[57] Civic mobilization training programs received at least partial funding from Western sources, including the International Renaissance Foundation, Freedom House, the US-Ukraine Foundation, the German Marshall Fund, NDI, the Westminster Foundation, the Swedish International Development Agency (SIDA), and grants from Western embassies in Kyiv.[58] Black Pora and Yellow Pora received direct financial assistance from several Western sources, including the Westminster Foundation, the German Marshall Fund, and several Western embassies. USAID and its implementers, however, never provided direct assistance to these youth groups, as they were considered too radical and partisan.[59]

External Contributions to Crisis Mediation

In parallel to these activities was a mediation effort between Kuchma, Yanukovych, and Yushchenko that was facilitated by Presidents Aleksander Kwasniewski of Poland, Valdas Adamkus of Lithuania, and Javier Solana of the European Union. Kwasniewski was especially influential in pressing for a negotiated but "right" solution to the crisis; Solana followed his lead. The Bush administration deliberately did not seek a public role in the negotiations but stayed closely involved behind the scenes through contacts with Kwasniewski, Solana, and Adamkus. This international effort helped diffuse tensions between polarized enemies. Somewhat contrary to subsequent impressions, European efforts were more significant at this level of elite mediation rather than at the level of proactive support for the Orange coalition.

Western mediators also helped persuade Yushchenko to accept constitutional changes that would weaken the power of the president and strengthen the power of the parliament, a compromise that certainly made it easier for Kuchma and Yanukovych to agree to a third round of elections. That is, the EU pushed for a "pacted" solution, based on Yushchenko agreeing to cede some presidential powers to the parliament in order to placate Kuchma's allies, who would thus retain influence. Views on the deal struck with Kuchma and Yanukovych differed. Some saw it as both necessary and a means of guaranteeing against an overbearing presidency in the future. But many civil society activists in Ukraine lamented that the EU "gave too much away" in December 2004 to the Yanukovych camp, with reformists judging that it did so specifically in order to reach a negotiated position between France and Germany, on the one hand, and the new member states, the Nordics, and the UK, on the other hand. European diplomats protested that in practice negotiations were not so clear-cut, with the speed of events representing the overwhelming factor in November and December 2004 and with even the more enthusiastic European backers of the Orange Revolution accepting that some form of deal had to be struck.

Hence, whether the roundtable negotiations were *necessary* for the breakthrough, however, is disputable. Critics of the negotiations, including Yulia Timoshenko, have argued that the Western-anchored mediation efforts were not central to the outcome and actually tied the opposition's hands after breakthrough.[60] Ironically, after the 2006 parliamentary elections, Yanukovych became prime minister again, this time with more enhanced powers as a result of the Orange Revolution.

External Facilitators of Divisions within the Security Services

Identifying a direct Western impact on division within the security forces is difficult. Some have claimed that those soldiers who participated in NATO's Partnership-for-Peace programs were more likely to support the demonstrators than those who did not.[61] To date, however, the evidence marshaled to support this claim is far from convincing. There is certainly no evidence that Western governments undertook purposive action to provoke the kind of divisions within the security services that are identified above as a key variable in the account of Ukraine's democratic transition. EU states actually expressed concern over defections from security service insiders; these were viewed more as a potential source of instability than a positive precursor to democratic transition.

Western actors did contribute indirectly to keeping the peace during the stand-off between armed forces and the Orange demonstrators. Nevertheless, the number of protesters on the streets was the decisive deterrent to violence, not a phone call from Washington. Anecdotal evidence suggests that the Kremlin supported Yanukovych's desire to use force to clear the streets. Some press accounts even claim that Russia sent its own special forces to Kyiv to assist in the protection of the presidential administration building, which at one point was under threat of forceful takeover by Orange leaders.[62] Press reports also claim that Putin sent his special forces unit, Vympel, to Kyiv in order to evacuate safely Kuchma and his family along with secret documents, if the moment to flee arose.[63] Definitive evidence of Russian military involvement never materialized, and statements made subsequently by Orange Revolution leaders implied that the Russian military threat was greatly exaggerated.[64] Moscow's ability to influence the internal cohesion and actions of Ukrainian armed forces was just as limited as the West's.

CONCLUSION

The set of conditions needed to produce Ukraine's democratic breakthrough was large and complex. Of this long list of factors, external actors played a role in influencing only a few. Given the extremely precarious distribution of power, however, these *imported* inputs from the West were consequential in tipping the balance in favor of the democratic challengers.

With regard to policies, actions, and programs aimed at weakening the semi-autocratic regime, the Ukrainian experience suggests that it is hard for outsiders to foster splits within the *ancien régime* and also difficult for them to influence directly the popularity of the regime. The West played no measurable role in fostering splits within the security forces. Anecdotal evidence suggests that Western criticism of Kuchma contributed to his declining popularity at home, but no hard data exist to isolate the independent causal role of foreign rebuke.

More generally, however, the West did seem to play a role in impeding the full-scale consolidation of autocracy. Western resources helped strengthen institutions such as the Rada, which checked presidential power. Western long-term aid to civil society also helped keep semi-autocracy in Ukraine from becoming a full autocracy. Russia provided technical assistance and resources for constructing a stronger autocracy, but these resources were insufficient. It also remains unclear if Kuchma actually wanted to construct a full-blown autocracy. In the margins, Western engagement of Kuchma, his aides, and his family members raised the costs of completely turning away from democracy.

The EU represented an aspirational reference point for at least some members of the regime, and retaining engagement with the EU constituted one vital pole of Kuchma's multivector foreign policy. The depth of partnership promised to Ukraine by the EU was admonished as insufficient by reformists both within and outside the regime. And the EU did not categorically condition its cooperation on prior democratic transition because it was keen to counterweight Moscow's strategic influence. But the general perception existed within the regime that partnership with the EU—and keeping open the prospect of eventual EU accession—required at least some of the formal aspects of competitive politics to be retained. At the margins, this was one factor that discouraged any slide into full autocracy. The EU's focus on economic governance and technical harmonization was not about preparing overtly and directly for democratic transition—indeed, as argued, in some ways it was designed to head off abrupt and destabilizing regime change. But arguably it did lock Ukraine into an area of Euro-governance that provided some of the legal and procedural mechanisms that enabled the Orange coalition to establish its first foothold.

Regarding policies, actions, and programs aimed at strengthening the opposition, the Ukrainian experience suggests that it is difficult to influence the effectiveness of opposition candidates in elections. In the margins, external actors can encourage unity among the democratic opposition, but the real drivers of unity will always be local actors. Western imports were crucial in exposing electoral fraud. The ideas and technology for exposing fraud—exit polls, a parallel vote tabulation, and poll monitors—were imported from the United States. Funding for these activities came largely from Western sources, and the presence of international monitors provided moral support for local monitors. External actors also contributed to the development of independent media in Ukraine. One of the most effective media outlets, *Ukrainska Pravda*, relied almost exclusively on external financial support. EU officials would later opine that their most positive influence before 2004 was in supporting the modicum of media independence that oiled the wheels of the Orange Revolution at crucial junctures in late 2004. Finally, imported ideas and resources strengthened electoral mobilization, both before and after the vote. If financial assistance for these mobilization activities came from American and West European sources, intellectual and inspirational input came from Serbs, Georgians, and Slovaks. Tracing the intellectual origins of civic resistance ideas back even further, Indian and American ideational inputs—that is, the ideas and practices of Mahatma Gandhi and Martin Luther King Jr.—are also present in the making of the Orange Revolution.

In short, it was a general feeling of being "left behind"—as the EU expanded to Ukraine's immediate neighbors—that was one, albeit secondary factor that motivated protestors. Kuchma himself probably did conclude that an attempt to force through a rigging of the elections in 2004 would have consequences for relations with Europe, even though he himself had enjoyed much support from EU governments up until that point. European influence had impact more at this level than in terms of concrete responses to democratic backsliding after 2000. Members of the Orange coalition would commonly refer to the presence of European Union flags on the Maidan during the 2004 protests as evidence of EU influence. Again, this symbolized the influence of aspiration and hope—that, as became painfully evident after 2004, were not founded on any concrete policy promises or inducements that the EU had provided for democratic transition.

Far from orchestrating democratic protest behind the scenes, most international actors were in reactive mode once mass mobilization began to impact events in the autumn of 2004. European democracy assistance proper did not play a prominent role in Ukraine. This was forthcoming at a low level and did not support the political activism that directly undermined Kuchma. US funding was slightly more "forward leaning" but also of facilitative rather than determinant value. The EU arguably set a broad set of incentives that loosely filtered into Ukrainian identity and aspirations and then intervened in a way that had more identifiable impact only when the regime was already on its way out, because of the strength of domestic-led pressure for change. European governments did not purposively encourage democratic protest, certainly until this was already potent.

European influence discouraged any temptation the Kuchma regime might have had to completely close the modicum of political space that existed in Ukraine before 2004. But it did not guarantee against some meaningful reversals in political and civil rights during that period. Nor did it actively seek to hasten the arrival of democracy, at least until the confluence of domestic events presented the denouement of late 2004. The EU's focus on legislative harmonization before the Orange Revolution might have helped eventually to load the dice in democracy's favor, but many civil society actors criticized it for shoring up Kuchma for longer than was necessary and diverting attention from the more serious political abuses that occurred after 2001.

NOTES

1. On this kind of regimes, see Steven Levitsky and Lucan Way, "Elections without Democracy: The Rise of Competitive Authoritarianism," *Journal of Democracy* 13 (April 2002): 51–65.

2. For details, see Andrew Wilson, *Ukraine's Orange Revolution* (New Haven: Yale University Press, 2005), chap. 6.

3. The symbolic codification of the Orange Revolution as a pivotal moment in Ukrainian history is well underway. See Laura Arzhakovska, *Revolyutsiya Duxa* (Lviv: Ukrainian Catholic University, 2005); and the movie, *Ukraiha: proriv do demokratii* (Kiev: O. Dovzhnko, Fond Rozvitku Ukrains'kogo Kino/Pro TV, 2005).

4. On the Russian model in comparative perspective, see Lucan Way, "Authoritarian State Building and the Sources of Regime Competitiveness in the Fourth Wave: The Cases of Belarus, Moldova, Russia, and Ukraine," *World Politics* 57 (January 2005): 231–61.

5. Anders Aslund, "The Ancien Regime: Kuchma and the Oligarchs," in Anders Aslund and Michael McFaul, eds., *Revolution in Orange: The Origins of Ukraine's Democratic Breakthrough* (Washington, D.C.: Carnegie Endowment for International Peace, 2006), 9–28.

6. Taras Kuzio, "The Opposition's Road to Success," *Journal of Democracy* 16, no. 2 (April 2005): 125; and interview with Security Service of Ukraine chief Ihor Smeshko, in *The Orange Revolution*, documentary film written, directed and produced by Steve York (Washington, D.C.: York Zimmerman Inc., 2007).

7. Yurii Lutsenko, MP and one of key organizers of the Maidan protests, interview, Kyiv, November 2005.

8. C. J. Chivers, "How Top Spies in Ukraine Changed the Nation's Path," *New York Times*, January 17, 2005, 1.

9. Interviews with Roman Bezsmertny, MP, Our Ukraine; and Alexander Moroz, MP, Chairman of the Socialist Party, Kyiv, July 2002.

10. Yulia Timoshenko, interview, Kyiv, February 2006.

11. Interviews with Mikhola Katarynchuk and Yuri Kliuchkovsky, Our Ukraine MPs, Kyiv, November 2005. They argued the Our Ukraine case before the Supreme Court.

12. Olena Prytula, *Ukrainska Pravda* editor, interview, Kyiv, June 2002.

13. Marta Dyczok, "Was Kuchma's Censorship Effective? Mass Media in Ukraine before 2004," *Europe-Asia Studies* 58, no. 2 (March 2006): 215–38.

14. For the specific percentages, see International Renaissance Foundation, *Promotion of the Fair and Open Election of 2004* (Kyiv: IRF, January 2005), 14–19.

15. Adrian Karatnycky, "Ukraine's Orange Revolution," *Foreign Affairs* 84, no. 2 (March–April 2005).

16. Olena Prytula, "The Ukrainian Media Rebellion," in Aslund and McFaul, *Revolution in Orange*, 110.

17. Interviews with Taras Stetskiv and Vladimir Grynev, Kiev, January 2006. See also interviews with Maidan organizers in York, *Orange Revolution*.

18. European Council Common Strategy of December 11, 1999, on Ukraine, 1999/877/CFSP, *Official Journal of the European Communities* L331, no. 1 (December 23, 1999).

19. Richard Youngs, "Ukraine," in Ted Piccone and Richard Youngs, eds., *Strategies for*

Democratic Change: Assessing the Global Response (Washington, D.C.: Democracy Coalition Project, 2006), 104.

20. P. Kubicek, "The European Union and Ukraine: Real Partners or Relationship of Convenience," in P. Kubicek, ed., *The European Union and Democratization* (London: Routledge, 2003), 155.

21. Iryna Solonenko, "European Neighbourhood Policy—The Perception of Ukraine," *Foreign Policy Dialogue* 7, no. 19 (July 2006): 45, www.deutsche-aussenpolitik.de.

22. Marius Vahl, "A Privileged Partnership? EU-Russian Relations in a Comparative Perspective, Danish Institute for International Studies," Working Paper no. 2006/3.

23. K. Smith, "The Outsiders: The European Neighbourhood Policy," *International Affairs* 81, no. 4 (2005): 768.

24. Carlos Pascual, US Ambassador to Ukraine, 2000–3, interview, Kyiv, June 2002.

25. Ambassador John Tefft, Deputy Assistant Secretary for European and Eurasian Affairs, "Ukraine's Election: Next Steps," testimony before the House International Relations Committee, December 7, 2004, 6, www.state.gov/p/eur/rls/rm/39542.htm.

26. Ibid.

27. Daniel Williams, "Putin Opposes Rerun in Ukraine," *Washington Post*, December 3, 2004, A16.

28. Pascual interview. See also Ambassador Stephen Pifer, Deputy Assistant Secretary for European and Eurasian Affairs, testimony before the House International Relations Committee, May 12, 2004, 3 (copy provided to McFaul).

29. Michael Wines, "Report of Arms Sale by Ukraine to Iraq Causes Consternation," *New York Times*, November 7, 2002.

30. M. Emerson et al., "The Reluctant Debutante," in M. Emerson, ed., *Democratisation in the European Neighbourhood* (Brussels: Centre for European Policy Studies, 2005), 17.

31. O. Sushko and O. Prystayko, "Western Influence," in Aslund and McFaul, *Revolution in Orange*, 131.

32. For an overview, see Karatnycky, "Ukraine's Orange Revolution."

33. K. Barysch and C. Grant, "Ukraine Should Not Be Part of a 'Great Game,'" *Open Democracy*, December 7, 2004.

34. Emerson et al., "The Reluctant Debutante," 18; G. Gromadzki, R. Lopata, and K. Raik, "Friends of Family? Finnish, Lithuanian and Polish Perspectives on the EU's Policy towards Ukraine, Belarus and Moldova," *FIIA Report* 12 (2005): 31–32.

35. Sergei Markov, interview, Moscow, September 2005.

36. These numbers are reported in Jackson Diehl, "Putin's Unchallenged Imperialism," *Washington Post*, October 25, 2004, A19.

37. Because tracing causality in this sector is so difficult, few have tried. Serious attempts include Carothers, *Confronting the Weakest Link: Aiding Political Parties in New Democracies* (Washington, D.C.: Carnegie Endowment for International Peace, 2006); and Sarah Mendelson, "Democracy Assistance and Political Transition in Russia," *International Security* 25, no. 4 (Spring 2001): 68–106.

38. Interviews with Kathryn Stevens, Director, Office of Democracy & Governance USAID Ukraine; Chris Holzen, Resident Director, Ukraine, International Republican Institute; David Dettman, Resident Director, Ukraine, National Democratic Institute; Taras Stetskiv, MP and Our Ukraine campaign manager, Kyiv, November 2005.

39. Interview with a board member of a major Russian corporation, which gave funds to the Yushchenko campaign, Moscow, June 2005. The businessman asked not to be identified.

40. T. Kuzio, "The Opposition's Road to Success," *Journal of Democracy* 16, no. 2 (2005): 127.

41. Interviews with Stetskiv and Katarynchuk.

42. Interviews with Dettman and Holzen, and Tetiana Sobeleva, NDI trainer, Kyiv, November 2005.

43. Interviews with Lorne Craner, President, International Republican Institute, and Steve Nix, Director of Former Soviet Union Programs, International Republican Institute, Washington, D.C., October 2005.

44. Zbigniew Brzezinski, Lech Walesa, Ambassador William Miller (former US ambassador to Ukraine), and Adrian Karatnycky are examples of private citizens with close ties to Our Ukraine who played active roles in shaping Western debates about the Orange Revolution.

45. Interviews with Eric Boyle, Regional Director, Kiev Regional Office, The Eurasia Foundation; Yevhen Bystrytsky, Executive Director, International Renaissance Foundation; Juhani Grossman, Senior Program Officer, Civic Participation in Elections in Ukraine, Freedom House; Petro Koshukov, Codirector of Znayu project; Inna Pidluska, President, Europa XXI Foundation, Kyiv, November 2005.

46. On this technology, see Eric Bjornlund, *Beyond Free and Fair: Monitoring Elections and Building Democracy* (Baltimore: Johns Hopkins University Press, 2004).

47. The figures are listed in International Renaissance Foundation, *Promotion of the Fair and Open Election of 2004.*

48. Interview with CVU leaders Oleksandr Popov and Yevgen Poberezhny, Kiev, November 2005. On this method for exposing fraud, see Larry Garber and Glenn Cowan, "The Virtues of Parallel Vote Tabulations," *Journal of Democracy* 4, no. 2 (April 1993): 95–107.

49. Interviews with Koshukov and Dimitri Potekhin, Kieve, 2005.

50. Interview with Grossman and several Ukrainian recipients who received these funds.

51. Vadim Galaychuk, General Director, Moor & Krosondovich, and Coordinator for Our Ukraine Election Monitoring Program, interview, Kyiv, November 2005.

52. See www.ukma.kiev.ua/pub/DI/partners.html.

53. International Renaissance Foundation, *Promotion of the Fair and Open Election of 2004,* 74.

54. A. Guillemoles, *Même la neige etait orange: La révolution ukrainienne* (Paris: les Petits Matins, 2005), 75–77.

55. Sushko and Prystayko, "Western Influence," 132.

56. Interview with Andrei Shevchenko, Channel Five, and Kateryna Myasnykova, Executive Director, Independent Association of Broadcasters, Kyiv, November 2005; and Natalya Ligachova, Project Director and Chairman of the Board, Telekritika, Kyiv, February 2006.

57. Andriy Kohut, Member of Board, (Black) Pora!, interview, Kyiv, March 2005.

58. Altogether, in the year before the 2004 vote, the International Renaissance Foundation, the local Ukrainian arm of the Soros foundation, contributed $1,653,222 to NGOs implementing election related projects. See International Renaissance Foundation, *Promotion of the Fair and Open Election of 2004,* 1. Yellow Pora was a recipient of several IRF grants.

59. Interviews with several USAID officials and Pora members, March and November 2005.

60. Timoshenko interview. See also Youngs, "Ukraine," 100.

61. See, for instance, comments of Major General Nicholas Krawciw, US Army, retired, made at an American Enterprise Institute event in Washington, D.C., "Ukraine's Choice:

Europe of Russia?" December 10, 2004, during panel discussion entitled, "Ukraine's Armed Forces: On the Way to Join NATO?"

62. United Press International, "Russian Troops in Ukraine Capital," November 24, 2004.

63. Nikolai Petrov and Andrei Ryabov, "Russia's Role in the Orange Revolution," in Aslund and McFaul, *Revolution in Orange*, 151.

64. Ibid.

CHAPTER SIX

Indonesia

Economic Crisis, Foreign Pressure, and Regime Change

EDWARD ASPINALL AND MARCUS MIETZNER

Among the major countries that shook off authoritarianism during the third wave of democratization, Indonesia presents a rather unique case as far as external influences on processes of regime change are concerned. Although international influences played a significant role in Indonesia's democratic transition, President Soeharto's demise in 1998 was not the consequence of diplomatic pressure or other deliberately targeted, external democracy promotion. For much of his rule, Soeharto had enjoyed considerable support from Western governments, which appreciated him as a reliable anticommunist ally, a force for stability in Southeast Asia, and a pragmatic economic manager supportive of foreign investment. Even the end of the Cold War, which had led to increased criticisms of Soeharto's human rights record and growing external support for Indonesia's civil society, had not seriously threatened his New Order regime. Condemnation of Soeharto's repressive methods by Western powers was muted, and foreign donors concentrated mostly on politically harmless development projects.

With political pressure ineffective, the real threat to Soeharto's autocracy grew in the form of Indonesia's gradual integration into the world economy. Against the background of the regime's increasing dependence on investment flows and stable stock markets, the Asian economic crisis was the trigger for the events that caused Soeharto's fall. Rather accidentally, the regime's decline was accelerated by the intervention of the International Monetary Fund. As we show, the IMF's economic rescue program was designed to save rather than harm the Soeharto government, but it unintentionally helped to undermine the government's credibility, worsen the economic crisis, and link economic recovery to political reform. Accordingly, Indonesia's democratic transition was *not* a case of regime change successfully induced by external threats, sanctions, or incentives. Rather, it was triggered by a regional economic disaster and further stimulated by the bungled IMF aid package. Beyond that, domestic players dominated the scene.

Interpreting these events, we therefore distinguish analytically between *unintended* and *intended* external influences. The external factors that played a direct and triggering role in Indonesia's democratic transition were not intended to bring about democratic change, but they had this unintended effect. On the other hand, international efforts that were intended to promote democratic reform played little role in triggering the collapse of the Soeharto regime. This is not to say, however, that these efforts were irrelevant to the transition. On the contrary, international support for Indonesian civil society and a changing international environment that favored democratic reform were important background factors that interacted with and reinforced even stronger domestic developments pushing in the same direction. As a result of these factors, Indonesia's polity in the mid-1990s had an ideological context that ensured that, once the political transition began, it led to democratization rather than toward reconstituted authoritarianism. In other words, international support for democratic forces helped to "till the soil" in preparation for democratic transition but did not play an important direct role in the transition events.

In developing these arguments, our chapter is divided into four parts. First, after briefly describing Indonesia's transitional moment, we provide an overview of the political, economic, and social foundations of the New Order regime, explaining the domestic and international factors that allowed Soeharto to rule Indonesia for such a long period of time without notable opposition. In the second section, we give an account of the key domestic events that led to the fall of the regime, allowing readers to better contextualize the analysis presented later in the chapter. Third, we discuss international factors in the disintegration of the Soeharto regime. While pointing to some important external impacts on Indonesia's transition, we emphasize the need not to overstate the significance of pro-democracy development assistance. In the fourth section, we analyze the interplay between international and domestic factors, highlighting in particular the linkages between the Asian economic crisis, the IMF intervention, and the domestic pressures on Soeharto to reform. The conclusion, finally, reviews the main arguments of this chapter and connects them to the larger comparative discussion of this volume. While we believe that the Indonesian case does not deliver evidence for the effectiveness of targeted international efforts in unseating an authoritarian

External influences are most important AFTER the transition [handwritten annotation]

regime, it does indicate that external advocacy and support for reformist domestic forces can improve the chances for a successful democratic transition outcome *after* the autocracy has been removed.

INDONESIA'S TRANSITIONAL MOMENT IN HISTORICAL PERSPECTIVE

In a hastily arranged ceremony on the morning of May 21, 1998, President Soeharto resigned after ruling Indonesia for 32 years as the head of his authoritarian "New Order" regime. A few months earlier, most commentators had been describing his position as unassailable.[1] Earlier in the decade, he had brushed aside mounting domestic dissent, overcome internal divisions in his regime, and ignored growing international criticisms of its human rights record. His regime was solid, it retained formidable repressive capacity, and it was delivering strong economic growth. Most importantly, opposition was weak and disorganized.

Within the space of six months, all this crumbled. The Asian financial crisis of 1997–98 hit Indonesia hard, causing the collapse of its economy and an IMF-led bailout of US$43 billion in pledged funds.[2] The economic meltdown also escalated calls for political reform, prompting a wave of mass protests and, ultimately, splintering the regime. Unable to put down unrest without resorting to extreme military violence, Soeharto stepped down. His deputy, B. J. Habibie, took over as president and immediately began dismantling authoritarian political structures and replacing them with democratic ones. While there has been considerable scholarly debate about the extent and timing of Indonesia's democratic transition,[3] for us the collapse of the Soeharto government was the critical moment in the transition: it did not itself constitute democratization, but after it, there were no serious attempts to construct a nondemocratic alternative. Consequently, the collapse of the regime and its dynamics that prefigured Indonesia's democratic transition outcome are the focus of our analysis. First, however, we consider the foundations of Soeharto's reign of 32 years at the apex of his "New Order" regime, which makes him one of the longest-lasting noncommunist authoritarian rulers in the post–World War II era.

Established in the wake of a left-wing coup attempt and a subsequent purge of the Left in which the army and its allies killed approximately 500,000 people,[4] the New Order regime drew on significant repressive capacity to secure its authority over subsequent decades. The military was the main component of the regime in the late 1960s and early 1970s, presiding over a praetorian state. Even as Soeharto began to build an independent autocracy in the 1970s, he continued to use the military to maintain power. Present at all levels of the civilian administration, military officers exercised intense surveillance and control of society.[5] They repressed regime opponents, controlled the media, and helped Soeharto to build a political structure that shepherded most potential critics into bodies controlled by the regime. Repression and co-optation thus went hand in hand, with a range of political, religious, and other civil society organizations surviving, but with their leaders aware of their inability to overtly challenge the regime.[6] At the same time, the regime and its structures were kept together by the distribution of patronage rewards, with the whole system resembling a pyramidal structure for the distribution of rents, controlled from the top by Soeharto himself.[7] Punishments for those who opposed the system were heavy, but the rewards for those who participated could be significant.

The regime also enjoyed performance legitimacy, achieving strong rates of economic growth. Real income per capita grew from US$70 in 1969 to US$1,100 in 1997.[8] Between 1973 and 1983, much of the growth was driven by the international oil boom, which provided Soeharto with ample funds to overcome domestic economic downturns and political crises. From the mid-1980s, however, Indonesia partly deregulated its economy and built up a manufacturing sector oriented to export to the world market. It attracted much foreign investment in sectors like textiles, clothing, and footwear, which became major employers, and the country became less dependent on oil exports.[9]

Soeharto and his New Order regime also had strong international support, in accordance with the regime's Cold War origins. The government received military aid from the United States and its allies,[10] countries that also furnished it with political endorsement, including for some of its most controversial actions such as the 1975 invasion of the former Portuguese colony of East Timor. The immediate geographic environment was also supportive: for most of the Soeharto period, Indonesia's closest Southeast Asian neighbors were ruled by sympathetic authoritarian and semi-authoritarian leaders, such as Singapore's Lee Kuan Yew, Malaysia's Mahathir Mohammad, and the Philippines' Ferdinand Marcos. Furthermore, Indonesia took a leading role in the formation of the Association of Southeast Asian Nations (ASEAN), a body that strongly emphasized political stability and economic development, and viewed noninterference in members' internal affairs as a key principle.

Equally important was international economic support for the regime. Soon after Soeharto came to power in 1965, a multicountry donor group, the International Governmental Group on Indonesia (IGGI), was formed to support Indonesia's economic stabilization and, later, its development. IGGI included Western European countries, Japan, the United States, the World Bank, and other donors. It ensured a massive flow of development assistance to Indonesia: at the second meeting of the organization in 1968, for example, the United States and Japan pledged US$163.9 million and US$110 million respectively.[11] However, even more important than direct grants were loans. In the 1990s, Indonesia received every year around US$5–7 billion in credits and loans from the IGGI and, later on, from its successor organization, the Consultative Group on Indonesia (CGI). Moreover, foreign investment grew substantially over the regime's 32 years. Between 1990 and 1994 alone, foreign capital inflow rose from US$5.997 billion to US$9.062 billion.[12] At first, such investment was overwhelmingly concentrated in the hydrocarbons, mining, and timber industries, but by the 1990s it had grown massively in manufacturing and was increasing rapidly in the financial and services sector as well. By 1995, 67 percent of all transactions at the Jakarta Stock Exchange were made by foreign investors.[13] But the sharp increase in foreign investment as such had no liberalizing effect on the regime. Transnational corporations investing in Indonesia were not interested in promoting democracy; in fact, they profited from tight labor regulations and high levels of social control.

DOMESTIC INFLUENCES ON THE REGIME CHANGE

Early signs that the New Order regime was experiencing legitimacy problems became visible in the late 1980s and early 1990s. These signs, at first only faint, were related to the aging of the regime and its leader and to some of its prior successes. On the one hand, Soeharto was 71 when he was reelected for his sixth presidential term in 1993, and reports about his health assumed increasing prominence in media and elite discussions. Speculation about, and jockeying in anticipation of, his succession intensified. At the same time, the New Order was taking on increasingly sultanistic features, with Soeharto's personal dominance becoming ever more pronounced, and his children, other family members, and an inner circle of cronies and loyalists turning more venal in their building of business empires, and more dominant in official politics and the military. These factors produced a bout of tension in the military from the late 1980s, when a group of officers became increasingly disgruntled with Soeharto and his inner circle and took independent action to secure key positions in anticipation of succession.[14]

At the same time, there were initial indications that, after decades of stability and economic growth, ordinary Indonesians had grown weary of their long-time ruler. Although many Indonesians remained grateful for continued economic progress, the fading memories of the chaotic and violent 1960s had made them much less susceptible to the government's anticommunist rhetoric and its claim that only it could safeguard stability. Economic growth had fueled an increasingly robust urban middle class and a stronger industrial working class, both of which began to show signs of restiveness. Adding to the difficulties of the regime, Soeharto also began to face growing international criticism of his government's poor human rights record.

This combination of circumstances prompted Soeharto and other regime actors to initiate partial liberalization in the early 1990s. Known by its Indonesian term, *keterbukaan* or "openness," in this Indonesian version of *glasnost*, regime leaders promised to be more tolerant of societal criticism. In a pattern typical of liberalization in authoritarian regimes, however, the loosening of political controls triggered escalating opposition, with increased mobilization by students, labor, nongovernmental organizations (NGOs) and other groups, and a more critical media. Eventually, once the oppositional mood had spread to one of the regime's tolerated political parties, the PDI (Partai Demokrasi Indonesia, Indonesian Democracy Party), which elected Megawati Soekarnoputri, the popular daughter of Soeharto's predecessor, to its leadership, the aging autocrat responded by reversing the *keterbukaan* policy and clamping down once more on critics. In 1994 he banned three prominent news magazines, followed in 1996 by the removal of Megawati from the leadership of her party and a crackdown on the subsequent protests.

By 1997, then, there was a widespread sense of political stagnation, even paralysis.[15] Soeharto was still firmly in control, with the regime dominated by his loyalists in the military, government, and business. The opposition was repressed, marginalized, or co-opted. Given the regime's sultanization, however, it was also experiencing growing legitimacy problems. There was perceptible public dissatisfaction with Soeharto's government, which was nevertheless mixed with continuing gratitude for his delivery of economic growth and a large dose of resignation and apathy. Most Indonesians, despite their resentment of aspects of the New Order, found it hard to imagine any way to challenge the regime, let alone replace it. This political lethargy was compounded by the minimal international pressure on the regime.

The Asian economic crisis of 1997 and 1998 eventually broke this status quo, sparking an eruption of societal protest that forced Soeharto to resign. Now 76 years old and in power for more than three decades, he gave every impression of being overextended by the crisis. At first, he seemed strangely indifferent to the social hardship caused by it, often looking out of touch, tired, and simply incapable. Later, in early 1998, he took actions that aggravated the crisis, such as resisting IMF prescriptions for policy change. With the president rapidly losing his aura of unassailable strength and competence, public confidence in the regime collapsed, making way for growing belief that its overthrow was now feasible.

The regional economic crisis had such consequences in large part because of its severity. Beginning with the collapse of the Thai baht in May 1997, the crisis rapidly spread to neighboring countries, hitting Indonesia the hardest. The collapse of 1997–98 caused a contraction in Indonesia's economy of around 18 percent, making it one of the most severe anywhere in modern history.[16] Significantly, the fall occurred after almost 30 years of annual growth rates that were in the range of 5 to 10 percent and an average of 7 percent in the 1990s.[17] For much of his rule, Soeharto's claim to power had depended on his ability to provide economic growth, low prices for basic commodities, and satisfactory public services. But with prices now skyrocketing, unemployment rising, foreign capital fleeing, and public services declining, Soeharto's authority all but evaporated. As middle-class Indonesians stormed supermarkets to stock up on goods, and the poor were hit by mass layoffs and inflation, their "contract" with Soeharto—which had allowed him to rule with an iron first if he delivered economic benefits in return—dissolved.

The economic disaster was aggravated by Soeharto's declining health and his inability to offer coherent concepts to overcome it. In December 1997 several national dailies falsely hinted that the president had died, triggering a steep drop in the rupiah. As it turned out, Soeharto had suffered a mild stroke and had to rest for several days, during which the political elite intensively discussed succession. Soeharto, however, tried to tough it out. Although he invited the IMF into Indonesia in October 1997 in order to save his regime, Soeharto resisted that body's demands for economic reform. This added to the impression that his stubbornness was dooming Indonesia to economic catastrophe. Amid growing public protest, Soeharto had himself reelected to his seventh presidential term in March 1998 and ensured the appointment of his trusted aide B. J. Habibie as his vice-president. He also installed a highly nepotistic cabinet, defying both international creditors and growing domestic criticism. With Soeharto unwilling to reform and no economic solution in sight, investors continued to move funds offshore. The economic crisis had finally become inseparable from a political one.[18]

It was at this point that the initiative passed to the streets. Most importantly, students organized a wave of large demonstrations around the country, openly calling for regime change and garnering much support from other actors. Violent riots by the urban poor, many of them targeting the country's entrepreneurial Chinese minority, were another crucial precipitating factor in the regime transition. Initially, these riots occurred in small towns in Java, and spread to the North Sumatran capital of Medan in early May. But after troops shot dead four students in Jakarta's Trisakti University on May 12, the mob violence reached the capital. The Trisakti incident caused widespread rioting in Jakarta and the Central Java town of Solo, with countless properties destroyed, some women raped, and more than 1,000 people dead, and presented an image of a country descending into lawlessness. Subsequently, students occupied the parliament building in Jakarta, and the public sensed that Soeharto's end was near.

Under massive pressure, the ruling elite fractured. The first serious cracks in the regime occurred in early May after the Medan riots, when key New Order bureaucrats, politicians, and entrepreneurs began to prepare their transition into the post-Soeharto era. After the Jakarta unrest, the floodgates of the regime broke, culminating with the resignation of 14 cabinet members. Finally, the commander of the armed forces, General Wiranto, told Soeharto that while the military remained loyal, it was not prepared to violently quell the protests.[19] In short, the final splitting of the regime was a response to the crisis, not a cause of it. It was only when the student movement and urban riots had made Indonesia virtually ungovernable that the exodus of Soeharto loyalists began, destroying the president's efforts to cling to power.

Our analysis of important events leading to the Indonesian transition reveals a pattern marked by both international and domestic dynamics: an externally induced economic crisis triggered a society-led process of mobilization that in turn splintered the regime, forcing its long-serving leader to resign. But the collapse of the Soeharto regime was, of course, only the key moment in Indonesia's democratic transition, not its culmination. After he came to power, Soeharto's successor, B. J. Habibie, realized that he had to introduce fundamental democratic reforms if he wanted to remain in power.[20] In short order, he liberalized the press, civil society, and the party system and prepared democratic elections for June 1999, capping Indonesia's transition.[21] In the intervening months, mass mobilizations and the leaders of rapidly forming political parties continued to place pressure on Habibie, and there was remarkably little serious consideration of a nondemocratic alternative by members of Indonesia's ruling elite. The democratic direction of Indonesia's transition, therefore, was largely set by the dynamics that produced Soeharto's fall; the subsequent construction of democratic institutions (which was largely completed with the fourth round of constitutional amendments in 2002) merely finalized a process already prefigured in those critical days of May 1998.

INTERNATIONAL INFLUENCES ON THE REGIME CHANGE: THE ASIAN ECONOMIC CRISIS, IMF INTERVENTIONS, AND THE END OF THE COLD WAR

For much of his rule, Soeharto had enjoyed the support of Western capitals, which issued only token "recommendations" for greater political openness and less repression. Even once the 1997–98 economic crisis began, there was strikingly little diplomatic pressure designed to bring about reform. Most foreign powers had benefited from Soeharto's largely stable and predictable government, and they knew that he had survived previous crises. Accordingly, throughout the crisis, no major foreign government openly suggested that Soeharto should step down until his departure appeared inevitable. For example, the first official US statement (by Secretary of State Madeleine Albright) calling for Soeharto to stand aside did not come until May 20, reflecting Soeharto's hopeless domestic situation rather than representing part of a decisive international push for his resignation.[22] Although Soeharto's resignation was thus not the result of intervention or pressure by foreign governments, international factors nevertheless played a tremendously important role in both triggering and worsening the crisis that led to his downfall. However, these factors were more structural and "accidental" in nature than part of a purposely designed democratization strategy. Beyond that, geopolitical shifts and democracy promotion did play a background role, helping only indirectly to provide a context in which Indonesia's intertwined economic and political crisis would be resolved by way of a democratic transition.

First and foremost, there is no doubt that the Asian economic crisis triggered the domestic political upsurge that left Soeharto with no choice but to leave office. The fact that the regional financial meltdown had such extraordinary consequences for Indonesia was, in turn, the result of the country's increasing exposure to the global financial system. Beginning with the deregulating policies of the mid-1980s, Indonesia had transformed itself from a predominantly oil-dependent economy into an increasingly successful exporter of manufactured goods connected to global trade markets and capital flows. For example, in an IMF index that measured the share of foreign assets and liabilities as a percentage of GDP, Indonesia in 1990 scored 59.3 and 72.9 respectively, indicating a medium-range level of integration into the world's financial system, much higher than China (19.3/38.9), India (27.7/29.9), Brazil (34.1/45.1), or Turkey (39.5/48.9).[23] Indonesia's broadening financial linkages helped drive its economic growth in the early 1990s, but it also made the country vulnerable to the world's stock markets and their shifting assessments of political and economic risk.

So long as Indonesia was booming, its dependence on international money flows was seen as an advantage. Impressed by continuously high growth rates, investors tended to overlook the many structural and regulatory problems in Indonesia's economy. These included severe deficiencies in the banking sector, which was riddled with bad loans. In the same vein, Indonesia's growing foreign debt (which at the time of the crisis stood at 147 percent of GDP) did not create concerns in times of expanding industrial output and exports.[24] Indonesian companies had borrowed heavily in dollars on world markets, something they could afford to do while the rupiah was stable. Most market players ignored the possibility that un-expected fluctuations in the rupiah could trigger a rush to buy dollars and cause the currency to collapse. However, this is exactly what happened in 1997–98 when investors alarmed by developments in Thailand began to look at Indonesia with newly skeptical eyes.

A second important international factor was the IMF-led effort to rescue Indo-nesia's economy from meltdown. Despite the absence of direct foreign pressure on Soeharto to resign, this particular intervention was important in deciding the outcome of the political crisis. This was ironic, given that the program was *not* intended to remove Soeharto from office; rather, it was crafted to stabilize Indo-nesia's economy and, by implication, its government. But miscalculations in its implementation meant that the IMF worsened the crisis instead of alleviating it. While most economists today agree that this was the result of errors of judgment on the part of the IMF, in Indonesia and elsewhere conspiracy theories about the IMF's role have been rampant.[25] Consequently, the analysis of this failed rescue package is crucially important for evaluating international influences on the 1998 regime change.

When Indonesia first asked the IMF to help with emergency credits in October 1997, a memorandum was signed that required Indonesia to take various reform steps, including closing 16 troubled banks and addressing corruption in the wider banking sector. The rupiah and the economy continued to slide, however, and thus a second deal was negotiated in January 1998. This package went further, abolish-ing a slew of Soeharto family and crony projects, such as the national car project and the cloves monopoly, each run by one of Soeharto's sons. The package thus did not simply focus on the country's macroeconomic settings, as in most countries where the IMF intervened with emergency programs, but also called for the elimi-nation of crony business interests. From this perspective, the IMF did indeed play a highly political role, even if its packages did not call for human rights, individual freedoms, or democratic reforms.

The political consequences of the IMF packages were twofold. First, by high-lighting the issues of corruption and cronyism, the IMF linked the resolution of the economic crisis to the political sphere. This was an association that Soeharto had tried hard to avoid, insisting that the current difficulties were merely a techni-cal matter of fiscal management. In the eyes of the Indonesian public, however, the IMF's stress on fighting corrupt practices substantiated its suspicion that Soe-harto was now a political liability for the country rather than an asset. Soeharto's domestic opponents, for their part, quickly took up and amplified the IMF's (per-haps unintended) message that the economy was being destroyed by Soeharto's crony capitalism. This notion itself seemed to be confirmed when Soeharto and his supporters resisted several of the IMF-dictated attempts to dismantle their business interests. For instance, when his son's bank was closed after the October package, it was almost immediately reopened under a new name. Hence, a perception grew in international markets that Soeharto opposed the IMF's prescription, hardening his image as a stubborn and inflexible autocrat unwilling to reform.

Second, and even more importantly, the IMF packages failed to address the substance of the economic crisis and in fact accelerated Indonesia's descent into instability. For instance, the IMF demanded the closure of the 16 ill-fated banks without guaranteeing deposits held in other banks. Fearing that other banks would soon be shut as well, millions of Indonesians rushed to withdraw their savings, providing the deathblow to the already ailing banking system, which now required tens of billions of dollars to be revived. Similarly, the symbolic anti-crony measures in January 1998 "contained no hint of any plan for tackling a primary source of worry about the rupiah—the increasingly crippling foreign debt of Indonesian companies."[26] As a result, the rupiah crashed even more. In a further blunder, the IMF requested that fuel prices be increased in May, rejecting government requests that this be done at a later stage. This price hike triggered the riots in Medan in early May 1998, the beginning of a wave of urban unrest that continued until Soeharto resigned three weeks later.

Given this long list of missteps, it comes as no surprise that critics have accused the IMF of deliberately intending to unseat Soeharto. Fueling the suspicions, Michel Camdessus, the managing director of the IMF during the crisis, has admitted, "We created the conditions that obliged President Soeharto to leave his job." However, in a caveat often left unmentioned by those who quote Camdessus's admission, the latter added: "That was not our intention."[27] But if it was not the IMF's goal to remove Soeharto, why did it pursue policies that focused on rooting out KKN (the Indonesian acronym for collusion, corruption, and nepotism popularized by the protestors)?

To be sure, the anticrony measures in the IMF packages were inserted only after considerable debate within the fund, the World Bank, and the governments of the advanced economies. In his account of these debates, Paul Blustein notes that such measures were eventually included primarily because of "pressure from members of the IMF board representing Western industrial countries."[28] In particular, US administration officials "wanted reforms to extend well beyond the typical Fund program."[29] IMF staff adopted this expansive approach partly because it believed symbolic action was needed against the cronyism that they saw as central to Indonesia's economic woes, but also because they were influenced by economic reformers *inside* the Soeharto government. In Blustein's account, Indonesian economists and even some technocrat ministers who were frustrated with their inability to tackle vested interests encouraged the fund to incorporate "an attack on the monopolies and subsidies that had flourished thanks to KKN."[30] A senior and well-informed US diplomat confirmed that some of Soeharto's advisers viewed institutions like the cloves monopoly "highly offensive" to their sense of rational economic order, and they privately urged the IMF to take strong measures against them and were delighted when it did so.[31] These technocrats were influential because some of them had long-standing links in US economic policy-making circles, links that were a legacy of one of the oldest and most influential aspects of US development assistance in Indonesia: the training of a corpus of Indonesian economists from the 1950s onward.[32]

The position of the IMF and the US administration hardened after Soeharto defied the fund on various reform issues and the crisis spiraled out of control. Even so, in January 1998, as the rupiah collapsed and President Clinton and other world leaders telephoned Soeharto, "the dominant message was that Suharto could lead his country out of the mess, but doing so would require demonstrating a renewed commitment to IMF discipline and structural reforms of the KKN-riddled economy."[33] After the failure of the January reform package, Robert Rubin and Larry Summers in the US Treasury took a firmer stance and personally concluded that Indonesia needed political reform and that Soeharto probably had to go. There is little evidence, however, that this view dictated the subsequent policy agenda, with important voices in the State Department and Pentagon warning that Soeharto remained a powerful player and that the IMF should limit itself to a macroeconomic agenda.[34] In practical terms, the growing frustration with Soeharto translated into a "short leash" in the economic domain: when a renewed pact with the IMF was negotiated in April, it "included a long list of commitments and target dates for action," as well as "step-by-step monitoring."[35] Soon the debates were rendered moot: within two months, Indonesia had gone from economic downturn to full political crisis, and events were moving too quickly for the IMF or other international actors to keep pace. When US secretary of state Madeleine Albright finally called on Soeharto to step down on May 20, his domestic political support base had already collapsed.

Several other international factors also influenced the course of events in 1997–98, all of them linked to growing international criticism of the Soeharto regime over the preceding decade, coinciding with the end of the Cold War. Although these factors were not decisive in the democratic breakthrough, they contributed to it by nurturing reformist ideas in Indonesian society that pushed the transition in a democratic direction and helped to constrain the country's authoritarian rulers.

To appreciate these factors, it is first necessary to briefly review the increased international pressures directed at the Soeharto regime from the early 1990s. The end of the Cold War meant that the United States and other Western powers suddenly found authoritarian military-based regimes like Soeharto's less important as allies against communism, and there was growing emphasis on human rights and democracy in international political affairs. This had its effect in Indonesia with, for example, a chorus of international criticism greeting the infamous Santa Cruz massacre in East Timor in 1991. Various governments criticized the Soeharto regime over the massacre; the Dutch tried to make further development assistance conditional on improved human rights protection, while the United States suspended its International Military Education and Training (IMET) programs for Indonesian military officers (while continuing arms sales). Soeharto responded to this and similar pressure with both symbolic concessions and resistance. For example, he established the surprisingly critical National Human Rights Commission but at the same time punished the Netherlands for its pro-democracy interventions by refusing to accept further Dutch assistance and disbanding the IGGI, the multicountry donor coordination group. Soeharto and his officials knew that Indonesia remained very important for the world's major powers, as a guarantor of regional security, as a site for investment, and supplier of raw materials. Moreover, Western capitals continued to praise Soeharto's government for the stability and economic progress it had brought, and foreign development assistance and investment continued to pour in. Even so, the regime's leaders now also knew that they were facing an international environment that was less sympathetic to its authoritarian features than in the past. Senior military officers and other officials increasingly warned of the dangers of *globalisasi* and of the need to increase Indonesia's "national resilience" in the face of negative international influences.

As well as direct criticism, a second and arguably more important source of pressure on the regime was growing transnational civil society links and foreign donor support for Indonesian NGOs. From the 1970s, an increasingly large NGO sector emerged in Indonesia, with the government estimating by 1996 that there were 8,000 such groups.[36] Almost all NGOs were supported, directly or indirectly, by foreign funds. Initially, most foreign donors had supported Indonesian NGOs involved in microcredit, health, and development work.[37] However, by the early 1990s, more NGOs were being encouraged to campaign on human rights, environmental, labor, and other controversial political issues.[38] While private overseas donors (especially European NGOs) took the lead in funding the most critical NGO activism,[39] major US-based foundations with branch offices in Jakarta also began to venture into more politically sensitive work. For instance, the Asia Foundation pursued what its Indonesia director later referred to as a "let a thousand flowers bloom" approach which aimed to fund alternative voices on controversial topics of public debate.[40] By the mid-1990s, even the usually more conservative office of the US Agency for International Development in Indonesia developed a small "democracy and governance" program, supporting various Indonesian groups that promoted rule of law and the empowerment of civil society.[41] It is important to note, however, that with the exception of some of the smaller (especially European) NGOs, most foreign donors did not believe they were helping to build an anti-Soeharto movement. Indeed, as one of the consultants involved in designing the USAID democracy-building project formulated it, the project "didn't shape the basic [US] policy which was to support Soeharto who had done so many good things for the U.S."[42] According to the Asia Foundation's Indonesia director, support for civil society groups was not aimed at dramatic political transformation but at assisting the gradual opening up of civil society, which foundation staff believed was already underway: "We assumed that Indonesia was on the right track for a long-term, evolutionary process."[43]

Consequently, foreign-funded NGOs did not play a leading role in the antiregime mobilizations of 1998. Led by a small intellectual elite that lacked organized links to the bulk of the population, NGOs were ill-equipped to pose a direct political threat to the regime. In part, their isolation directly resulted from the conditions that foreign donors placed upon their grants. Most NGOs were required to be program oriented and apolitical, and even those funded to publicly raise sensitive issues were not expected to lead an opposition movement against the government (and almost all foreign donors—especially those with wide-ranging programs in Indonesia—would have defunded any organization that tried to do so). As a result, the 1998 mobilizations that forced Soeharto to resign were not driven by NGOs but by the student movement—which did not control formal institutions or receive foreign funds and therefore had much less to lose.[44]

Nevertheless, the foreign funding of critical NGOs since the 1980s had not been without effects on Indonesian society. These groups had helped to delegitimize the New Order and disseminate important ideas about human rights, political reform, and individual liberties in Indonesia, contributing to a climate in which the student movement could successfully mobilize against the government. For instance, the idea of human rights was a prominent theme in the student protests. When military officers under the command of the president's son-in-law Prabowo Subianto in early 1998 abducted several activists—some of whom were never again seen alive—this event catalyzed the students' human rights campaign, echoing and compounding the outrage expressed in the media and general public. In retrospect, it is apparent that the notion of human rights had gained such popular resonance in Indonesia partly because of local bodies that possessed strong international linkages. Indonesia's premier human rights organization, LBH (Lembaga Bantuan Hukum, Legal Aid Institute) had been funded for 20 years by Dutch NGOs and other pro-reform agencies.[45] Another institution that had helped to promote ideas of human rights in the regime's last years was the previously mentioned National Human Rights Commission, which also operated with foreign funding.[46] If the students were the shock troops of Indonesia's political transition, their ideological bullets had been prepared—at least in part—by years and even decades of less dramatic political activism by numerous intellectuals, lawyers, and activists, many of whom had—directly or indirectly—received financial and other support from overseas.

Another factor in the transition was the increased presence of the international media in Indonesia, which helped to constrain the regime's leaders and contributed to their decision "not to shoot." The potential power of filmed evidence of human rights violations had already been demonstrated in 1991, when foreign journalists had smuggled out tapes showing the Santa Cruz massacre in East Timor, forcing Soeharto to set up a military tribunal to punish the perpetrators. This time around, teams from CNN, BBC, and other global networks moved freely on the streets of Jakarta, interviewing demonstrators and observing military movements. Juwono Sudarsono, defense minister in several post-Soeharto cabinets, confirmed that "heightened satellite TV news attention during the May upheavals did result in the army restraining itself from excessive use of force against demonstrators."[47] Expelling or limiting the media would have destroyed remaining international confidence in the government, accelerating capital flight. It was ironically the international media, operating without major restrictions amid the growing chaos, that restricted Soeharto's room to maneuver.

Against the backdrop of the foreign media presence in Indonesia during the crisis, it is also probable that considerations about the international response influenced the decisions of key actors in the transition. The political protagonists were aware that the tides of international opinion, especially in the West, were flowing against Cold War regimes, especially military-based ones such as the New Order. Most importantly, Soeharto's relatively swift surrender must have at least partly been due to concerns that his international reputation could suffer if he exited amid a bloodbath. In his more than three decades as president, he had increasingly enjoyed the international stage and took pride in his relationships with other heads of state and multilateral organizations. Thus, although Soeharto's personal views about his resignation have never been made public, it is very likely that fear for his international image likely played at least a part in his decision not to order a final crackdown on his opponents. In addition, the possible impact of such a move on the stock markets, the IMF, and the willingness of foreign governments to extend further aid to Indonesia was arguably also on Soeharto's mind.[48]

In addition, anxieties over international repercussions probably contributed to the decision by the armed forces chief, General Wiranto, not to take power when

Soeharto resigned. Several days before his resignation, Soeharto had issued Wiranto with letters that authorized him to exercise emergency powers if he chose to do so, an opening that would have allowed him to establish and expand his personal authority. Wiranto's inner circle did discuss the possibility of a military-dominated government as an alternative to Habibie's installation as president, but the armed forces commander eventually ruled this scenario out.[49] While domestic opinion was overwhelmingly hostile to such an option, and Wiranto therefore would have found it very difficult to assume government, it is likely that international factors were also a consideration. In his autobiographical account of the events, Wiranto proudly published a letter by the commander of the US Pacific Command, Joseph W. Prueher, who praised him for "bringing about the orderly transfer of leadership in Indonesia, and in a way consistent with the Constitution."[50] Apparently, the opinions of his international counterparts mattered greatly to Wiranto.

Finally, Habibie's decision to immediately liberalize the political system after Soeharto resigned was to an extent a reflection of international expectations and his own experiences outside Indonesia. To be sure, domestic dynamics left him no other choice if he wanted to stay in power, but Dewi Fortuna Anwar, one of his closest advisers, has insisted that "liberalizing Indonesia's political system was also seen by President Habibie as a means to attract international support for Indonesia's recovery effort and transform Indonesia's international image after three decades of authoritarian rule."[51] Moreover, Habibie had lived in Germany from 1955 to 1974, witnessing firsthand the development of the postwar democracy there, and it seems clear that this experience was in the back of his mind when crafting Indonesia's postauthoritarian polity.[52]

THE INTERPLAY OF INTERNAL AND EXTERNAL
FACTORS IN THE TRANSITION

Obviously, all these international factors could affect Indonesia's transition only because they interacted with domestic events. The most consequential interaction was not the confluence of domestic and international factors favoring reform but rather an underlying structural tension or contradiction: that between Indonesia's ossified political structure and Indonesia's integration into the world market and its consequent vulnerability to external shocks. As we have demonstrated, the fact that a monetary crisis could have such a destructive effect on Indonesia's domestic politics was due to Soeharto's own reforms of the economy since the 1980s. Indonesia's increased integration into the world economy had made Indonesia attractive to foreign investors and the stock markets but had also made it vulnerable to their capricious preferences. During the crisis, financial brokers decided that

Soeharto was no longer capable of safeguarding his own economy or their investments, and they pulled out billions of dollars in a matter of days, precipitating the political crisis that brought Soeharto down.

It would be wrong, however, to conclude that the global markets punished Indonesia for its undemocratic polity and thus successfully exerted the kind of external pressure that foreign governments had been unable to impose during over a decade of (admittedly muted) international criticism of the regime and growing support for Indonesian civil society. Significantly, the other two economies most seriously hit by the rejection of the markets were consolidating democracies: Thailand and Korea. Obviously, in making their financial decisions, investors did not discriminate between aging autocracies and democratic systems. In fact, their actions hurt the latter seriously. Thailand's democracy fell into a deep crisis as a result of the economic downturn, helping to set the scene for Thaksin Shinawatra's "electoral authoritarianism" from 2001 onward.[53] Korea's polity, by contrast, survived the monetary disaster but took many years to recover.

Given that investors did not desert Indonesia simply because of its autocratic regime, other considerations must have been dominant. At first, these were mostly related to calculations of economic risk in light of the wider Asian meltdown—the accumulation of bad debt and manipulation in Indonesia's banking sector were from the start of critical importance. To the extent that these problems were themselves a product of the corruption that had grown unconstrained under Soeharto's rule, they did have a political dimension. However, it is important to be cautious in directly linking corruption to the economic crisis. Hal Hill, an expert on Indonesia's economy, has pointed out that

> corruption was a serious problem, but it is difficult to advance the argument that it was a key precipitating variable. More plausible is the thesis that the particular forms corruption, and the political system in general, had assumed by the 1990s rendered the Suharto government unwilling—indeed unable—to move decisively and swiftly once the crisis had hit.[54]

Authoritarian regimes frequently collapse during economic crises, in part because they lack the flexibility to adjust nimbly to them.[55] It was precisely this inflexibility that made Soeharto's regime unable to survive. In particular, once the effects of the international crisis had already begun to be felt in Indonesia, Soeharto's failure to provide a clear blueprint for his succession preoccupied and unsettled international stock markets and ordinary Indonesians alike. For more than 30 years, the markets had entrusted their funds to a strong, healthy, and middle-aged Soeharto, whose authority seemed unchallenged. But now the autocrat was 76 years old and in questionable health, and there was no reassuring scenario for the time after his death. Arguably, had Soeharto groomed a successor early and arranged for an orderly transition in time, the investors would have reacted differently.

In this regard, there was one element of the regime's corruption that did come into play once the crisis had started to unfold: the nepotism in the Soeharto clan. For many years, multinational companies had not objected to establishing joint ventures with Soeharto's children: the obligatory bribes were predictable and often even tax-deductible in their home states—Germany, for example, abolished this latter practice only in 1999.[56] With Soeharto's own future in doubt by early 1998, however, his entire patronage system looked like a shaky foundation on which to build long-term business plans. Many foreign-owned power plants, mining operations, or infrastructure projects required investments of 20 years or more, and nobody knew if a post-Soeharto government would honor the contracts signed with his children. In short, it was the increasing unpredictability of Indonesia's domestic politics that made international investors nervous, much more so than the underlying deficiencies and corrupt mechanisms in its economic structures.

If the direct impact of the financial crisis on Indonesia's political transition can be traced to the country's economic transformation and its increased integration into the world economy, the impact of the IMF-led emergency intervention in 1997 and 1998 was much more "accidental" in nature. Aiming to restabilize the Indonesian economy, the IMF program went so badly wrong that it assisted in a regime change not intended by its inventors. Such a direct external intervention with unintentional consequences poses difficult challenges to scholarship on international influences on democratization processes, which tends to focus on deliberate foreign pressure or "leverage."[57] As we have argued, the IMF's approach was partly driven by a transnational linkage of a particular type: one between economists and economic policy makers in Indonesia and the West, specifically the United States. In the Indonesian case, technocratic reformers inside Soeharto's government and senior US policy makers had forged close relations during decades of economic cooperation, technical assistance, and policy discussions, and influential individuals in both groups viewed the financial crisis as an opportunity to rationalize the Indonesian economy and purge it of some of the most egregious crony influences. However, the political impact of their plans went far beyond what they had intended. Overall, it is hard to avoid the conclusion that mutual misapprehension and misunderstanding were the key elements in the domestic-international interaction that marked the IMF intervention in Indonesia's democratic transition. In Blustein's words, Soeharto's "downfall was not the result of a Machiavellian scheme to topple an autocrat; it was the upshot of an international rescue attempt gone badly, embarrassingly and radically awry."[58]

The impact of other interactions between foreign and domestic factors on the

Indonesian transition was much more indirect and difficult to measure. During the 1990s, a democratic mood had gradually grown in Indonesian society, undermining the legitimacy of the New Order regime and ensuring that, once its final crisis came, the successor regime was likely to be democratic. During that decade, there was a subtle change of political discourse in Indonesia. For instance, by the mid-1990s notions of democratic change were no longer the political taboos they had been in the 1980s. In the major newspapers, in the Jakarta seminar circuit, and in the newsletters and bulletins published by NGOs and (often foreign-funded) think tanks, various ideas about political reform circulated widely. Many factors played a part in this mood shift. Most important, however, were domestic changes, including Indonesia's economic and social transformation, and the fading salience of the regime's founding rationale. Playing a secondary role in this mix were international factors, such as the donor support provided to Indonesian NGOs and other civil society groups, as well as the changing international atmosphere that followed the end of the Cold War. These international factors thus helped to set the scene for Indonesia's democratic transition, but they did so by making an indirect and minor contribution to an ideational shift that—in turn—also had only an indirect effect on the domestic political context of the regime change. In this regard we see in Indonesia another case of "international systemic changes and diffuse social processes that have very likely influenced the trajectory and scope of democratization but whose effects cannot be measured by empirical evidence."[59]

Certainly, it is hard to make a case for a *direct* connection between democracy promotion activities by foreign actors and the fall of Soeharto. In the popular movement that forced Soeharto to resign, none of the groups that had been funded by foreign donors throughout the years played a significant role. The marginality of these NGOs was illustrated nicely by the Suara Ibu Peduli (SIP, Voices of Concerned Mothers) initiative. Staging small demonstrations against the regime in February 1998, this group of prominent Jakarta women's activists complained about high milk prices and distributed flowers to passers-by and security forces. Many of the SIP leaders had been recipients of Ford Foundation grants in the past, a fact that was reportedly a source of some pride in the foundation.[60] SIP members' activism was also inspired by international ideas of women's rights and civil liberties. But while their protest gained much publicity and evoked public sympathy, adding to the general mood of collapsing confidence in Soeharto, it was also emblematic of the inability of (foreign-funded) NGOs to organize real political pressure: the SIP group was tiny, and it was made up of highly educated, elite Jakartan women who had little contact with ordinary Indonesians. Moreover, they were no match for the repressive apparatus of the New Order. Bundled quickly into police cars, the SIP women did not pose a credible threat to the regime.[61] This example shows that foreign support for middle-class NGO activism was important at the symbolic level, and in the arena of political discourse. This was not a small matter, and it did influence the transition. Yet the fact remains that the forces that successfully drove the regime change were *not* part of the community of foreign-funded groups. At most, such groups played a support role—such as SIP itself, when it helped to organize food deliveries to the students who occupied Indonesia's parliament building in the days leading to Soeharto's resignation.[62]

CONCLUSION

Our analysis of international and domestic factors in Soeharto's fall—as well as the interplay between them—has contributed a cautionary note to the debate on the role of foreign pressure or incentives in democratization processes. A first major conclusion is that the 1998 regime change in Indonesia provides little evidence that diplomatic interventions, democracy promotion, or externally induced social change can directly cause the disintegration of authoritarian governments. Especially if such regimes are deeply entrenched in society, bolstered by strong economic performance, and able to offer patronage to key political constituencies, international reform initiatives alone are unlikely to threaten incumbent rulers. As the Indonesian case shows, change is much more likely to occur through internal regime dynamics (e.g., the inability of the autocrat to arrange for his succession and thus secure the long-term survival of the polity), or through an unintended external shock (e.g., the Asian economic crisis). While international motives tend to mix with domestic ones in movements for regime change, they mostly play a supportive rather than a leading role.

But a second major lesson that arises from the material presented in this chapter is that foreign donor support for pro-democracy NGOs, geopolitical shifts, and ideational influences from abroad have the potential to predispose states toward successful democratization *after* the authoritarian regime has been removed. Unable to contribute directly to Soeharto's fall, critical civil society groups nurtured by Western sponsors and discourses helped to ensure that the Indonesian regime change translated into a democratic breakthrough rather than the reconstitution of another autocracy. Students inspired by global ideas of human rights, activists promoting concepts of social justice and democratic participation, and ordinary citizens curious about the political rights other nations had enjoyed for decades formed a formidable hurdle for anyone considering a revival of repressive rule. Habibie's rapid political reforms were mostly the result of his awareness that anything other than radical institutional change would not have satisfied the demands of Indonesia's vibrant civil society and newly emerging political forces. Encouraged by overwhelming international support for democracy in Indonesia after Soeharto's departure, these groups were determined to hold on to their democratic gains and sideline New Order elements from the postauthoritarian polity.

In this context, it is essential to note that our discussion has made no judgments about the importance of post-Soeharto foreign aid programs in stabilizing Indonesia's transition and path to democratic consolidation. With Soeharto's political exit, international donors poured billions of dollars into Indonesia, supporting political, economic, and social reforms.[63] Obviously, the nature of such programs has been fundamentally different from those implemented under the New Order, as development agencies now operate almost without restrictions throughout Indonesia, including in politically sensitive conflict areas. Evaluating the effectiveness of these projects, and their overall impact on Indonesia's democratization, is beyond the scope of our chapter, which aimed to assess the role of foreign interventions in *triggering*, not *sustaining* democratic change. While analyzing the latter would require a separate study, there is a general consensus that post-1998 international aid programs have made a significant contribution to the stabilization of Indonesia's young democracy.[64] Donors have provided crucial electoral assistance, supported the creation of vital new institutions such as the Constitutional Court and the Corruption Eradication Commission, and funded widely praised conflict prevention and postconflict recovery programs. As our case study has shown, however, foreign aid operations and diplomatic interventions in existing (and long-lasting) authoritarian regimes are a much more complex issue, and their impact is not nearly as clear-cut and significant as their supporters commonly believe.

NOTES

1. Geoff Forrester, for example, predicted in late 1997 that "the presidency is Soeharto's for as long as he lives—or for as long as he wishes." See Geoff Forrester, "Towards March 1998, with Determination," in Hal Hill and Thee Kian Wee, eds., *Indonesia's Technological Challenge* (Singapore: Institute of Southeast Asian Studies, 1998), 55–74, quote at 71.

2. Of these US$43 billion, "only" around US$18 billion was eventually disbursed. See Stephen Grenville, "The IMF and the Indonesian Crisis," *Bulletin of Indonesian Economic Studies* 40, no. 1 (2004): 79–80.

3. See, for instance, Richard Robison and Vedi R. Hadiz, *Reorganising Power in Indonesia: The Politics of Oligarchy in an Age of Markets* (London: RoutledgeCurzon, 2004); Vedi R. Hadiz, "Reorganising Political Power in Indonesia: A Reconsideration of So-Called 'Democratic Transitions,'" *Pacific Review* 16, no. 4 (2003): 591–611.

4. John Roosa, *Pretext for Mass Murder: The September 30th Movement and Suharto's Coup d'Etat in Indonesia* (Madison: University of Wisconsin Press, 2006).

5. Harold Crouch, *The Army and Politics in Indonesia*, rev. ed. (Ithaca, N.Y.: Cornell University Press, 1988); Marcus Mietzner, *Military Politics, Islam, and the State in Indonesia: From Turbulent Transition to Democratic Consolidation* (Singapore: Institute of Southeast Asian Studies, 2009).

6. Edward Aspinall, *Opposing Suharto: Compromise, Resistance and Regime Change in Indonesia* (Stanford, Calif.: Stanford University Press, 2005), esp. 4–10, 145–77.

7. Harold Crouch, "Patrimonialism and Military Rule in Indonesia," *World Politics* 31, no. 4 (July 1979): 571–87; Richard Robison, *Indonesia: The Rise of Capital* (Sydney: Allen & Unwin, 1986).

8. Tulus Tambunan, *The Development of Industry and Industrialization Policy since the New Governance Era to the Post-Crisis Era* (Jakarta: Kadin, 2006), 2.

9. Anne Booth, "Development: Achievement and Weakness," in Donald K. Emmerson, ed., *Indonesia beyond Soeharto: Polity, Economy, Society, Transition* (Armonk, N.Y.: M. E. Sharpe, 1999): 112–13.

10. Between 1975 and the early 1990s, Indonesia procured weaponry worth US $1.25 billion from American contractors. See www.fas.org/asmp/profiles/indonesia.htm#Arms%20Sales%20Tables.

11. Annette Clear, "Democracy and Donors in Indonesia" (Ph.D. diss., Columbia University, 2002), 81.

12. Alexander Irwan, "Financial Flows and the Environmental Strategy in Indonesia in the 1990s" (Washington, D.C.: World Resources Institute, 1998), 5.

13. Ibid., 6.

14. Jun Honna, "Military Ideology in Response to Democratic Pressure during the Late Suharto Era: Political and Institutional Contexts," in Benedict R. O'G. Anderson, ed., *Violence and the State in Suharto's Indonesia* (Ithaca, N.Y.: Cornell University, 2001), 54–89.

15. Greg Fealy, "Indonesian Politics, 1995–1996: The Making of a Crisis," in Gavin W. Jones and Terrence H. Hull, eds., *Indonesia Assessment: Population and Human Resources* (Singapore: Institute of Southeast Asian Studies, 1997), 19–38.

16. Anne Booth has shown that Indonesia's 1998 economic collapse occurred much faster than its comparable breakdown in the 1920s and 1930s, when the decline dragged out during a period of five years. See Anne Booth, "Growth Collapses in Indonesia: A Comparison of the 1930s and the 1990s," *Itinerario (European Journal of Overseas History)* 3, no. 4 (2002): 73–99.

17. Hal Hill, *The Indonesian Economy since 1966: Southeast Asia's Emerging Giant* (Cambridge: Cambridge University Press, 1996).

18. Andrew MacIntyre, "Political Institutions and Economic Crisis in Thailand and Indonesia," in T. J. Pempel, ed., *Politics of the Asian Economic Crisis* (Ithaca, N.Y.: Cornell University Press, 1999), 143–62.

19. Takashi Shiraishi, "The Indonesian Military in Politics," in Adam Schwarz and Jonathan Paris, eds., *The Politics of Post-Suharto Indonesia* (New York: Council on Foreign Relations Press, 1999), 73–86.

20. R. William Liddle, "Indonesia's Democratic Opening," *Government and Opposition* 34, no. 1 (1999): 94–116, 111.

21. Marcus Mietzner, "The Ambivalence of Weak Legitimacy: Habibie's Interregnum Revisited," *Review of Indonesian and Malaysian Affairs* 42, no. 2 (2008): 1–34.

22. Secretary of State Madeleine K. Albright, commencement address to the United States Coast Guard Academy, New London, Connecticut, May 20, 1998. As released by the Office of the Spokesman, US Department of State.

23. International Monetary Fund, *Indonesia: Selected Issues*, IMF Country Report No. 07/273 (Washington, D.C.: IMF, 2007), 13.

24. Binny Buchori and Sugeng Bahagijo, "The Case for Debt Relief," *Inside Indonesia* 61

(January 2000), www.insideindonesia.org/edition-61-jan-mar-2000/the-case-for-debt-relief
-3007580.

25. See, for example, Fadli Zon, *The IMF Game: The Role of the IMF in Bringing Down the Suharto Regime in May 1998* (Jakarta: Institute for Policy Studies, 2004); Steve H. Hanke, "On the Fall of the Rupiah and Suharto," *Globe Asia*, January 27, 2007.

26. Paul Blustein, *The Chastening: Inside The Crisis That Rocked the Global Financial System And Humbled the IMF* (New York: Public Affairs, 2001), 216.

27. David E. Sanger, "Longtime I.M.F. Director Resigns in Midterm," *New York Times*, November 10, 1999. Our thanks to Ross McLeod for drawing our attention to the original source of this quotation.

28. Blustein, *The Chastening*, 101.

29. Ibid., 101–2.

30. Ibid., 101.

31. Confidential interview, March 28, 2008. According to the same diplomat, Larry Summers, the US deputy secretary of the Department of Treasury, had known Soeharto's top economics adviser Widjojo Nitisastro for several decades.

32. Bradley R. Simpson, *Economists with Guns: Authoritarian Development and U.S.-Indonesian Relations, 1960–1968* (Stanford, Calif.: Stanford University Press, 2008).

33. Blustein, *The Chastening*, 209.

34. Ibid., 227–31. This assessment was confirmed by a senior US diplomat interviewed in Washington, D.C., March 28, 2008.

35. John Bresnan, "The United States, the IMF, and the Indonesian Financial Crisis," in Adam Schwarz and Jonathan Paris, eds., *The Politics of Post-Suharto Indonesia* (New York: Council on Foreign Relations Press, 1999), 87–112, 96.

36. *Republika*, November 4, 1996.

37. In American development circles, these aid projects were jokingly referred to as "silkworm" programs, alluding to a particular grant that had focused on income generation for Indonesian silkworm farmers. R. William Liddle, interview, Jakarta, January 29, 2008.

38. For discussions of the increased NGO activism of this period, see Philip Eldridge, *Non-government Organisations and Democratic Participation in Indonesia* (Kuala Lumpur: Oxford University Press, 1995); Bob S. Hadiwinata, *The Politics of NGOs in Indonesia: Developing Democracy and Managing a Movement* (London: RoutledgeCurzon, 2002); Aspinall, *Opposing Suharto*, 86–115.

39. Asmara Nababan, former executive secretary of the International NGO Forum on Indonesian Development (INFID), interview, Jakarta, February 8, 2008.

40. Douglas Ramage, interview, Jakarta, February 8, 2008.

41. The money USAID offered for pro-democracy programs was only a small proportion of the total US aid budget in Indonesia. In 1997, the year before the transition, USAID Indonesia allocated US\$5.9 million for its goal of "Increased Effectiveness of Selected Institutions which Support Democracy," out of a total budget of US\$56.7 million. USAID, Fiscal Year 1997 Congressional Presentation, www.usaid.gov/pubs/cp97/countries/id.htm.

42. Liddle interview.

43. Ramage interview.

44. Edward Aspinall, "The Indonesian Student Uprising of 1998," in Arief Budiman, Barbara Hatley, and Damien Kingsbury, eds., *Reformasi: Crisis and Change in Indonesia* (Clayton: Monash Asia Institute, 1999), 212–38; Dave McRae, *The 1998 Indonesian Student Movement*, Working Papers on Southeast Asia No. 110 (Melbourne: Monash University, 2001).

45. Indonesian Legal Aid Foundation, *Taking Part in Democratization: YLBHI's Four Years Plan, 1994–1998* (Jakarta: Indonesian Legal Aid Foundation, 1994).

46. Among others, the commission received funding from the Asia Foundation to cover its basic operating costs (even its electricity bills) from 1996. Ramage interview.

47. Email communication with Juwono Sudarsono, April 22, 2008.

48. Soeharto's longtime security czar, Admiral Sudomo, told the veteran journalist Allan Nairn "that Suharto fell because they failed to open fire early and thoroughly on the Jakarta student demonstrators, because they feared further US aid cutoffs." These comments can be found on Allan Nairn's blog site. See www.allannairn.com/2007_12_01_archive.html.

49. Mietzner, *Military Politics*, 133.

50. Wiranto, *Witness in the Storm: A Memoir of an Army General (Ret.)* (Jakarta: Delta Pustaka Press, 2003), 197.

51. Email communication with Dewi Fortuna Anwar, April 21, 2008.

52. According to Anwar, "Habibie often used Germany as a referent point every time he had to make key decisions on political issues, such as political liberalisation and decentralisation." Email communication with Anwar.

53. Duncan McCargo and Ukrist Pathmanand, *The Thaksinization of Thailand* (Copenhagen: NIAS Press, 2005).

54. Hal Hill, *The Indonesian Economy in Crisis: Causes, Consequences and Lessons* (Singapore: Institute of Southeast Asian Studies), 69.

55. Stephan Haggard and Robert R. Kaufman, *The Political Economy of Democratic Transitions* (Princeton, N.J.: Princeton University Press, 1995); Stephan Haggard, *The Political Economy of the Asian Financial Crisis* (Washington D.C.: Peterson Institute for International Economists, 2000), 125.

56. Klaus Dieter Oehler, "Die Branche Korruption Wächst," *Kölner Stadt-Anzeiger*, August 13, 2005.

57. See, for instance, Steven Levitsky and Lucan A. Way, "International Linkage and Democratization," *Journal of Democracy* 16, no. 3 (2005): 20–34.

58. Blustein, *The Chastening*, 233.

59. Diane Ethier, "Is Democracy Promotion Effective? Comparing Conditionality and Incentives," *Democratization* 10, no. 1 (2003): 99–120, quote at 99.

60. Interviews with Sidney Jones, Jakarta, January 30, 2008, and Hans Antlov, Jakarta, February 8, 2008.

61. Naturally, its foreign donors had a different perspective on SIP's relevance. According to Mercy Corps, SIP "initiated protests that helped to change the history of the world's fifth most populous nation." See Mahfirlana Mashadi, "When Mothers Speak, Milk Prices Come Down—And So Does a Government," November 7, 2002, www.mercycorps.org/countries/indonesia/173.

62. Myra Diarsi, "Sekian Dapur Umum," *Jurnal Perempuan* 4 (June 1998): 1–2.

63. For much of the post-Soeharto period, Indonesia has been the largest recipient of US development aid in Asia. In 2007, however, it was overtaken by Pakistan. Thomas Lum, "U.S. Foreign Aid to East and South Asia: Selected Recipients" (Washington, D.C.: Congressional Research Service, 2008), 18.

64. Annette Clear, "International Donors and Indonesian Democracy," *Brown Journal of World Affairs* 9, no. 1 (2002): 141–55.

CHAPTER SEVEN

South Africa

Enabling Liberation

TIMOTHY D. SISK

From a racially exclusive, white minority autocracy under the invidious system of *apartheid* (or racial segregation), South Africa made the transition to majority-rule democracy. The transition involved domestic drivers of democratization as an endogenous process as well as external influences and culminated with the 1996 constitution. I argue that international normative socialization, tangible economic incentives and sanctions, direct foreign aid, and indirect mediation reinforced and enabled domestic drivers of democratization in the liberation struggle in South Africa. These international influences essentially enabled the success of the domestic antiapartheid liberation struggle, whose aim was the replacement of exclusive *Herrenvolk* democracy with a more inclusive, nonracial democracy.[1]

Interaction among domestic and international variables was seen in the alignment of normative solidarity between the external and internal antiapartheid movement, inducements and sanctions that helped precipitate a "ripe" moment for negotiations on a democratic transition, and a robust international engagement during the period of change that left local actors essentially in control of the transition but that underpinned the efforts of moderate political elites to negotiate a new social contract. In sum, domestic resistance and rebellion in pursuit of liberation drove democratization in process; however, the international antiapartheid movement (and resulting actions by governments and international organizations) was critically reinforcing of internally led change in the South African case.

THE TRANSITIONAL OUTCOME OF 1996

South Africa's celebrated transition from apartheid and autocracy to democracy, which unfolded roughly from late 1989 through to the conclusion of a new constitutional settlement in 1996 has often been described in popular discourse as nothing short of a "miracle."[2] Since the celebrated "liberation" elections of April 26–27, 1994, South Africa features fully functioning democratic institutions with a reasonably inclusive parliament, a coherent executive branch led by an indirectly elected president, and an independent and at times assertive judiciary. Its civil society is vibrant, the press is independent, and democracy has been deepened in practice at the local level through decentralization and local-election processes. The constitutional settlement reached in 1996 remains a widely legitimate charter and enjoys continued broad acceptance; thus, prima facie, South Africa's transition appears to be an unmitigated success. Indeed, the South Africa transition continues to be viewed as a both process and an outcome model for other conflict-torn societies to learn from and to potentially emulate.

While it is too early to demonstrate that democracy is unambiguously consolidated in South Africa—the government is a dominant party regime (or de facto one-party state) with feeble parliamentary opposition[3]—there is little concern among informed insiders that the country will soon follow the precipitous slide into autocracy that has afflicted neighboring Zimbabwe. Remarkably, South Africa—once the recipient of extensive international assistance to democratize—now boasts a significant capacity itself for advancing democratic negotiation and dialogue, election management, and electoral observation in Africa and in offering political and technical assistance to other societies riven by deep ethnic or religious divisions.[4]

Without denigrating the palpable achievements of the transition and the courage of the leadership of the time in avoiding a possibly much worse outcome—a deeper and more devastating civil war—the description of the transition as "miraculous" is a rhetorical obfuscation of a much more complicated process. Interactions among historically contingent domestic drivers of change and considerable international influences account for the relative success of democratization in South Africa. Indeed, the miracle metaphor is also mitigated by the reality that the transitional period was riddled with crises and was accompanied by brutally bloody political violence: more than 16,000 deaths in transition-related violence occurred during the rocky period of negotiated regime transformation from 1990 to 1994. Despite the deeply violent nature of the liberation struggle and the transitional period, South African protagonists negotiated their way through the "turbulent" transition, and in the post-apartheid era political violence has dwindled to relatively low levels for nascent democratic regimes.[5]

A dramatic historical turn from apartheid to democracy unfolded in the early 1990s, after decades of escalating tensions and violence. On February 2, President F. W. de Klerk declared that bans on political opposition would be lifted, Mandela would be freed, and negotiations on democratization would commence; a "New South Africa," a democratic transformation, would be created. The "New South Africa" came into being because of three major factors: a sense of shared and common destiny, a high degree of intergroup economic interdependence, and the abject failure of grand apartheid's attempts to territorialize and reify race and ethnicity.[6] A confluence of events yielded a moment ripe for the turn to negotiation in 1989. Peace talks began formally in February 1990, after an extensive period of prenegotiation (1986 to 1990) in which politicians, businessmen, and civil society leaders began to meet privately and explore solutions to the violence and to South Africa's deep social problems of race and inequality. Among the causes of apartheid's collapse were the inability of the white minority government to sustain the economy in a globalizing world, foreign sanctions and diplomatic incentives for change, and the inability of the state's security apparatus to contain insurrection.

Initially, the talks that began in 1990 were bilateral—between the National Party (NP) and African National Congress (ANC) led by F. W. de Klerk and Nelson Mandela, respectively—but they eventually became more broadly based to include other parties such as the Zulu-based Inkatha Freedom Party, homeland leaders, and other opposition parties. Perhaps the most important interim negotiated agreement was the first, known as the Groote Schuur "Minute" of May 1990. This first accord linked commitment to renunciation of the ANC's armed struggle with normalization of political freedoms, the return of exiles, the release of political prisoners and the eventual move to full enfranchisement and elections. The pact defined "nonracial democracy" in a united South Africa as the ultimate outcome of the talks. Subsequent pacts were reached in 1990, 1991, 1992, and 1993.

The talks broadened in 1992 and 1993 to include white parties to the right of the NP (notably, the white right-wing Freedom Front). African opposition to the left of the ANC such as the Pan Africanist Congress (PAC) at first opposed talks but also was eventually included in multiparty negotiation. All along, the process of negotiation was smoothed by small, moderate, bridge-building parties such as the Democratic Party (DP). Former homeland governments also participated in the multiparty talks, making the peace process eventually (and especially at the time of the April 1994 elections that ended apartheid) widely inclusive of all the major political forces in the country. This broad inclusion is pointed to as a key element in the success of the transitional negotiations.[7]

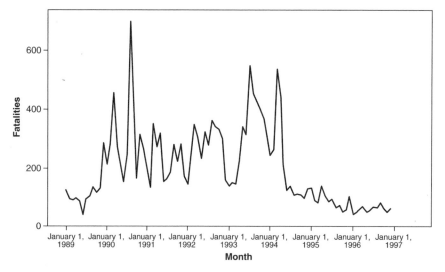

Fig. 7.1. Political Violence in South Africa's Turbulent Transition. *Source*: South African Survey (1997) (Johannesburg: South African Institute of Race Relations), as reported in Adrian Guelke, "Interpretations of Political Violence during South Africa's Transition," *Politikon* (South African Journal of Political Studies) 27, no. 2 (2000): 241.

The transition was deeply and widely violent. Political violence was an endemic feature of the transitional period, to the extent that there was an undeclared internal war (fig. 7.1). There were several crisis-inducing events that threatened the talks beginning in June 1990, just after the Groote Schuur pact. Inkatha Freedom Party (IFP)–ANC faction fighting—mostly the youth wings—was extensive, especially in greater Johannesburg and the KwaZulu Natal region. In the first three months after the onset of formal NP-ANC talks, violence escalated rapidly; some 951 people died in the strife from June to August 1990, for example. The epicenters of the violence were in KwaZulu-Natal, where the IFP and the ANC battled for control of the province, and in the greater Johannesburg area (now called Gauteng) where much of the strife was centered on IFP-loyal migrant workers' hostels whose mostly male residents came into conflict with those in neighboring, informal township settlements that supported the ANC. While there were some ethnic overtones (Zulu-Xhosa), the violence was more party-political than ethnic, as illustrated by the within-group struggles among the Zulu in KwaZulu-Natal. Both parties organized self-defense units or loose militias that often engaged in running battles with each other and with the police. The police were widely accused—and, it was later shown—to be acting as a "third force" stoking the enmity by arming and aiding the IFP.[8]

White right-wing militias and political parties, rogue elements of the South African Police and intelligence services, and members and often the leadership of the IFP all openly rejected the NP-ANC agreements and fomented violence to bring down the peace process. Similarly, for much of the negotiations, outbidders (extremists) on the ANC's left, such as the PAC, rejected the talks, and members of its armed wing continued to wage a feeble armed struggle. Occasionally, PAC cadres carried out attacks as well. The violence often tracked major turning points in the negotiation process. Violence was used in the negotiations strategically to derail the peace process, to prove political power, and to destabilize and marginalize opponents.[9] The April 1993 assassination of ANC and South African Communist Party leader Chris Hani by a white right-wing gunman failed to derail the talks despite widespread public protests. Efforts by white right-wingers to disrupt talks on an interim constitution in June 1993 failed to prevent the Interim Constitution from being sealed that month. Significantly, a white right-wing bombing campaign and an eleventh hour ANC-IFP shootout in downtown Johannesburg (the Shell House massacre) in the early months of 1994 failed to prevent the celebrated elections in April that brought Mandela to power and ended apartheid.

Much credit for the successful conclusion of the bloody transition goes to the ANC. The ANC leadership, particularly, changed its view and recognized that much of the violence was aimed at derailing its pursuit of power. The ANC's changed position was summed up by key negotiator Kader Asmal, who said in November 1993: "We cannot hold the peace process hostage to violence and to the will of violent men."[10] Thus, a settlement was clinched in June 1993—the interim constitution—despite the ongoing strife on the street. This agreement was a quintessential political pact, or mutual security agreement, in which democratization occurs with the explicit protection of the interests of the incumbent regime and its military and security forces.[11] Such pact making and consensus seeking continued after the elections of 1994 and through the period of constitution making by the elected Constitutional Assembly (which also acted as an interim parliament) until the adoption of a permanent constitution and its eventual certification by the Constitutional Court in October 1996.

The linchpin feature of the 1993 interim constitution was the agreement by the ANC on a period of transitional power sharing with the former rulers and a pledge to ensure the jobs and livelihood of the civil service, South African Defense Force (SADF, now SANDF), and the police. The power-sharing pragmatism was backed up by political finesse, manifested by the ANC concessions of early 1994 to the right-wing Freedom Front and the IFP. These concessions to potential spoilers of the pact brought these parties into the Government of National Unity at the

TABLE 7.I.
The 1994 Liberation Election Results

Party	Seats (%)
African National Congress	312 (63.7)
National Party	99 (20.2)
Inkatha Freedom Party	48 (9.8)
Freedom Front	14 (2.8)
Democratic Party	10 (2.0)
Pan-Africanist Congress	5 (1.0)
African Christian Democratic Party	2 (0.04)

eleventh hour and averted a bloody showdown during the celebrated liberation elections of April 1994 (table 7.1).[12]

The transitional Government of National Unity gave way in 1996 when the National Party found it uncomfortable to serve as partner under a guiding ANC, indirectly responsible for government policy, while serving as the official opposition in parliament. This led to the NP's unilateral withdrawal from the power-sharing government after the end of constitutional talks in 1996, but—remarkably—the collapse of power sharing in South Africa did not rattle markets or cause panic because the basic bargaining of political rights for economic stability was not threatened by the end of a grand coalition.[13] This is perhaps true because, as Frueh argues, by that point in the transition the country had already undergone significant social identity change.[14] As Strand concludes with regard to the subsequent constitution-making process that unfolded from 1994 to 1996, which culminated in the transition to a new social contract, the process of democratization and the institutional agreements reached amounted to an internal bargain, one that provided mutual "guarantees of cooperation."[15]

CHALLENGING APARTHEID AND AUTOCRACY: DOMESTIC DRIVERS

The origins of apartheid as autocracy are deeply rooted in South African history, and the process of democratization can be fully understood only in terms of broad social processes that unfolded throughout much of the twentieth century. Among the immediate domestic variables triggering transition were an escalating cycle of revolt and repression from the mid-1970s onward and lasted through the 1980s and eroded the white minority's capacity to rule. In considering domestic drivers of democratization in South Africa, it is important to distinguish between these deep-seated and longer-term structural variables— particularly changes in the socioeconomic class of the Afrikaners (Afrikaans-speaking whites)—and more immediate precipitating events, such as the failure of the 1984 constitutional reforms to quell black resistance and particular crises of the transition that ultimately served to spur the process forward.

Apartheid as Autocracy

Underlying democratization in South Africa were the historical inequities that were grounded in slavery, colonialism, and conquest that characterized the history of the country from the first arrival of Dutch East India Company settlers in 1652 and the social structure of race and class that evolved during the period of colonial conquest.[16] Setting the stage for internal conflict and social structure was a common-seen pattern of racial domination in other European settler societies in Africa (e.g., Kenya), but the differences among the settler populations—between "English-speaking whites" and the Afrikaners (descendants of the mostly Dutch-speaking settlers)—are a unique feature of South Africa. After the Anglo-Boer Wars, in 1910 South Africa emerged as a unified country through the formation of the Union of South Africa. This forged not only a single unified territory, but established the state and determined the structure of executive and legislative authority, and subsequent legislation in the 1920s and 1930s further limited the franchise initially beyond property and residency requirements and eventually on the basis of state-determined racial identity. Union had two other historical antecedents for democratization: one was the overall grouping together of "Brit" (English-speaking whites) and "Boer" (Afrikaners) into a broader category of "white South Africans," who enjoyed a fully functioning democracy among themselves; and, second, it created a political culture of formal-legal institutionalism and especially a generalized respect for the rule of law (which lasted until periods of widespread civil disobedience that began in antiapartheid "defiance campaign" of the early 1950s) and relative judicial independence.

From within the white electorate, Afrikaner nationalists (led by the National Party) rose to power through the whites-only ballot box in 1948 as a result of a wave of ethnic nationalism and by mobilizing constituents on the so-called poor white problem, which emphasized the plight of relatively unskilled, mostly Afrikaner white South Africans who were enduring grinding poverty. Apartheid had both "petty" segregationist aspects (e.g., separate amenities, barring of mixed marriage, and laws against miscegenation) and "grand" elements that sought to redefine the state and territory as a racially exclusive. National Party apartheid social engineers sought to solve the demographic challenge of a black majority through the creation of a set of ten territorially separated "homelands" in which the principal African

ethnic groups would find nominal independence and citizenship.[17] The homelands were created along ethnic lines reflecting the ten major linguistic groups of
the black majority. Some of these homelands were presented to the international
community as separate countries from South Africa, but these were never recognized by outsiders and eventually the collapse of apartheid brought the collapse of
the independent homelands as well. The grand apartheid scheme was brought to
its fruition by the charismatic and controversial prime minister Hendrik Verwoerd
(1958–66); in 1961, South Africa left the British Commonwealth and declared an
independent republic in place of the erstwhile Union. Among the most egregious
apartheid acts was the stripping of Colored voters in the Cape Province from voters' rolls in 1950 and passage of the Population Registration Act, which determined the racial classification of every individual.

Apartheid sparked an internal revolt by the disenfranchised black majority,
embodied in the antiapartheid struggle of the African National Congress (ANC,
founded in 1912), which rebelliously opposed the white minority state with
nonracial nationalism and socialism. From near the very beginning of rule by the
NP, South Africa was gripped by a bloody period of revolt, reform, and repression.
The National Party began to expand and more systematically implement policies
of racial segregation. Apartheid was implemented over a period of 40 years (1948–
88) in what was an eventually futile attempt to prevent a rapidly modernizing
South Africa from becoming a multiethnic society in which the majority black
population would necessarily win the right to vote.

The myriad personal and structural injustices inflicted by apartheid precipitated a revolutionary backlash. In response to black exclusion and racial segregation, an African nationalist armed opposition arose to first reform and later to
defeat the white minority regime through a revolution of national liberation. The
ANC, which led the antiapartheid movement, emulated the nationalist ideology
and strategies of other liberationist movements in Africa, and it forged an enduring alliance with the South African Communist Party and other opponents
of the regime.[18] During the Cold War, the ANC received some modest support
from the Soviet Union, although it was always a mostly African nationalist organization that was wary of the full embrace of the internationalized communist ideology. Likewise, virulent black racial nationalism—espoused by the Pan Africanist
Congress—was also disavowed by the ANC; from the 1950s especially, the ANC
devoted itself to a "nonracial" ideology in response to the imposed racial and ethnic
divisions of apartheid. Over time, the ANC has included many white, Asian, and
Coloured moderates, and its ethos was reflected in the landmark Freedom Charter
of 1955, which declared "that South Africa belongs to all who live in it, black and

white, and that no government can justly claim authority unless it is based on the will of all the people . . . and we pledge ourselves to strive together, sparing neither strength nor courage, until the democratic changes here set out have been won."[19]

Apartheid cruelty stimulated a wide antiapartheid revolutionary struggle that was led mostly by the ANC but that also included key figures such as Afrikaner clergyman Beyers Naudé (who was later banned by the apartheid state) and acclaimed human rights advocate Helen Suzman.[20] Key turning points were the 1960 Sharpeville incident, the 1976 Soweto uprising, and the death in prison of activist Steven Biko in 1977.[21] The ANC pursued nonviolent struggle until 1961 when its fight against apartheid turned armed and explicitly revolutionary; the ANC allied itself with the South African Communist Party and eventually with the powerful internal trade unions (COSATU, the Congress of South African Trade Unions).[22] Nelson Mandela, leader of the ANC, was sentenced to prison for sabotage in 1964 and imprisoned for 27 years. At his 1964 "Rivonia" treason trial, he declared in concluding his oratory as the accused:

> During my lifetime I have dedicated myself to this struggle of the African people. I have fought against white domination, and I have fought against black domination. I have cherished the ideal of a democratic and free society in which all persons live together in harmony and with equal opportunities. It is an ideal which I hope to live for and to achieve. But if needs be, it is an ideal for which I am prepared to die.[23]

Antiapartheid resistance featured strikes and other nonviolent tactics as well as counterregime violence, and it continued intermittently during this period; the "struggle" revolutionaries were committed but limited by a highly capable internal police state and a superior military force. An increasingly embattled apartheid regime responded to black mobilization with internal repression and a regional policy of destabilizing its neighbors. The apartheid regime in the 1970s and 1980s was a bellicose, autocratic, regional hegemon—a fearful and aggressive state, which also fomented civil war and political strife in Angola, Botswana, Mozambique, Zambia, Zimbabwe, and Mozambique in order to keep its own internal opposition at bay. Particularly, by the mid-1980s, the confrontation in Angola began to be perceived as a Vietnam-type experience in which the costs of conflict began to weigh heavily on Afrikaners and sentiments of invincibility began to wane.

The 1980s: Popular Upsurge and Precursor of Change

Violence in South Africa sharply escalated in the late 1980s. In the critical Kwa-Zulu Natal homeland, putative home of the country's largest ethnic group, the ANC was challenged by the breakaway Inkatha Freedom Party, a Zulu nationalist movement led by traditional leader Chief Mangosutho Buthelezi. Many viewed the IFP as a puppet of the regime, with its attacks on the ANC abetted by the apartheid police. Between 1984 and 1990, an estimated 5,500 died in political violence in South Africa in struggles between the antiapartheid resistance and the police and in ANC-IFP faction fighting in Kwa-Zulu Natal, which seriously escalated in 1988 and spread to the Johannesburg urban megalopolis. By the late 1980s, it appeared to even the most informed observers that South Africa was heading for all-out civil war, coupled with regime-abetted Zulu-Xhosa faction fighting among the black population (the Xhosa are the second largest black ethnic group and are prominent in the ANC).

The escalating violence, coupled with the international responses, precipitated three critical changes among the dominant white community and in the regime's key leadership. First, it prompted an early attempt at reform without surrender, characterized by the 1979 speech to Parliament given by then prime minister (later president under 1984 constitutional changes) Pieter W. Botha, who declared that whites must "adapt or die." Second, in some ways, the system of apartheid had worked in the sense that state-sponsored capitalism successfully served as a vehicle for Afrikaner economic advancement, and the population became more urbanized, professional, and educated. Third, the effects of sanctions—economic and cultural—began to have specific and tangible effects on white perceptions about the sustainability of apartheid.[24]

The political economy experienced massive capital flight that tracked the rising tensions. Between 1960 and 1964, following Sharpeville, capital flight first emerged as a critical challenge, and in the ensuing years the economic consequences of repression—together with the real costs of defense expenditures, which grew from 1 to 5 percent of GDP from 1960 to 1980—began to weigh heavily on overall performance.[25] Particularly, the South African economy was vulnerable to the effects of sanctions as a result of its industrialization policy and the reliance on financing its growth through primary-commodity exports; over time, the country became a net exporter of capital.[26] After the Soweto uprising, capital flight and a sharp curtailment of new investment began to impose real costs on the capacity of the state to oversee sufficient economic growth to meet the needs of population growth. Policies of import substitution and state-financed parastatal corporate spending did little to quell the growing dissatisfaction among the leading industrialists and business leaders.

Feeble and ill-considered half-measure reforms in the early 1980s that made minor changes to apartheid but left the system basically intact generated new frustrations over white minority rule. From 1984 to 1989, resistance against apartheid grew domestically and internationally. The trade unions under the banner of

COSATU grew more assertive in defiance of apartheid and in pressing for wage increases and social services. The South Africa Council of Churches and many other local and national civil society groups defied authorities in massive protests, while young militants made the townships "ungovernable." An internal umbrella coalition called the United Democratic Front allied with the ANC in exile to pose a formidable challenge to the regime.[27] The popular uprising reflected a still-prevalent political culture in South Africa around destabilizing "mass action." Thus, despite having control over the formal reins of power, a repressive police state, the largest army in Africa, and six nuclear weapons (since dismantled), the apartheid government could not control the streets. It lacked autonomy from the military under Botha (the military was described as a state within a state, in both legitimacy and critical capacities). Kane-Berman referred to the conditions on the ground as a "violent equilibrium."[28] In the end, though the apartheid state appeared to be strong, it was in reality quite weak.[29]

The immediate domestic precipitants of democratization in South Africa were the polarization of politics in the late 1980s, coupled with splits in the dominant elite. From the ANC perspective, revolutionary rhetoric reached a crescendo at the 1985 Kabwe conference, to which the regime responded with the declaration of a nationwide state of emergency in 1986. Critically, a split within the Afrikaner ranks led to a more enlightened, reformist wing, driven in part by the Consultative Business Movement, an organization of leading industrialists who saw their survival best secured by the scrapping of apartheid and relief from escalating international sanctions, and a more hard-line, Afrikaner nationalist movement that coalesced under the banner of the Conservative Party. In whites-only elections in 1987, the CP emerged as the official opposition in parliament and leading reformists such as Frederick van zyl Slabbert held secret meetings with the ANC in exile. Thus, splits in the ruling elite were the immediate precursors of regime change.

INTERNATIONAL INFLUENCES ON DEMOCRATIZATION

The principal international influences include the moral outcry over entrenched racial segregation that was the antiapartheid movement, economic and cultural sanctions, informal international facilitation, external technical assistance, a United Nations Observer mission (UNOMSA, the United Nations Observer Mission to South Africa, 1992–94), and light-touch mediation in the final hours of transition. The critical variables in transition were the close linkages of the antiapartheid movement with postindependence African regimes, which helped set international agendas of condemnation, support of sympathetic Western governments and social movements within Western countries, and the endorsement of the ANC as "sole representative" at the UN together with the broader UN anti-apartheid framework.

International influences on South Africa's democratic transition were both direct and indirect and involved specific measures that contributed to the survival of the autocratic apartheid regimes, conditionalities for change as reflected in anti-apartheid divestment and other sanctions policies by Western regimes, diplomatic and multilateral engagement to support the transitional talks, and modest international mediation at several critical points in the process. In this section, I consider the extensive international engagement with South Africa in which external influences changed the environment and decision-making dynamic of apartheid-era elites and their supporters and also review the evolution of antiapartheid sanctions. Then I discuss ways in which the international community engaged in and supported the transitional period.

The Internationalized Antiapartheid Campaign

Normatively, as the world was moving progressively in the direction of individualized human rights in the second half of the twentieth century, South Africa moved in the opposite direction. As a result, the antiapartheid movement grew internationally commensurate with each new round of revolt and repression. International condemnation of South Africa increased with the rise of anticolonial nationalist regimes in Africa,[30] which contributed to the rising salience of the apartheid issue on the international agenda. At the same time, there developed a moral and religious movement that associated apartheid's policies with heretical interpretation of Christian religious doctrine (and which eventually led to the ouster of the Dutch Reformed Church from the World Council of Churches).

The backdrop of international pressure in South Africa was set by the now-celebrated "Winds of Change" speech by British prime minister Harold Macmillan in Cape Town in early 1960; the United Kingdom was South Africa's principal foreign investor at the time, and the message of postcolonial transition was sweeping Africa. Not long after, the Sharpeville massacre reinforced external voices against apartheid, and the incident and violent police response—captured in photos run in newspapers around the world—prompted a global response. In April 1960 the United Nations Security Council passed the landmark resolution 134, which called "upon the Government of the Union of South Africa to initiate measures aimed about racial harmony based on equality . . . and to abandon its policies of apartheid and racial discrimination."[31] In the same year, the Norwegian Nobel Committee awarded the 1960 Nobel Peace Prize to Albert Luthuli, a teacher and politician, for his outspoken and nonviolent opposition to apartheid and his consumer boycott campaign against South Africa exports (supported by newly independent African leaders such as Julius Nyerere of Tanzania).

Also in 1960, the Anti-Apartheid Movement was founded in the United Kingdom to begin global advocacy of boycotting exports and advancing South Africa's exclusion and expulsion from international organizations and trade. In response to these pressures, South Africa withdrew from the Commonwealth. International pressure against South Africa then shifted the bright spotlight of the Olympic Games. Efforts to expel South Africa from the games emerged first in 1962, and the country was excluded from the 1964 Tokyo Games; South Africa's participation in global sport continued as an international issue into the 1968 Games in Mexico City. In addition to the sporting boycott, efforts were launched to extend an academic boycott and the cancellation of cultural exchanges.

A 1961 General Assembly Resolution first referenced apartheid as "repugnant." In 1962 the UN established the Special Committee against Apartheid through a General Assembly Resolution; while the committee had little leverage on South Africa, it sparked a moral crusade that ultimately undermined international support for country, though a few Cold War–oriented allies (such as the United States) saw the government as a bulwark against global communist expansion. Although initial efforts to impose economic sanctions against South Africa found little support in Western governments, by the mid-1970s public mobilization for divestment in South Africa and for the imposition of sanctions grew steadily; after the 1976 Soweto incidents, there was a flurry of efforts internationally to isolate and punish the apartheid regime and specifically to call for expansion of the franchise. During this period, a few Western countries, notably Sweden, began to funnel aid directly to the ANC, trade unions, and South Africa civil society, reportedly investing $400 million in support between the 1960s and 1994.[32]

Sanctions

A significant turning point in the pressures against South Africa unfolded in the wake of Soweto: by November 1977, United Nations Security Council Resolution 134 imposed an arms embargo against the country, which further weakened the regime.[33] Although South Africa later developed an extensive domestic production capacity for weapons, the arms embargo was yet another stage in an escalating set of sanctions, condemnations, and repudiation of the apartheid regime. In response, South Africa began to consider halting President P. W. Botha's reforms, in particular the 1983 Tricameral Constitution, which slightly expanded the franchise to Coloureds and Asians yet continued to exclude the black majority. When uprisings began in late 1984 and were carried in media outlets worldwide, sanctions pressure again increased.[34] In mid-October 1984, the Norwegian Nobel Committee named Archbishop Desmond Tutu the year's Nobel Peace Prize Laureate; in his December acceptance speech, Tutu sharply criticized "constructive engagement" with the white minority regime (then US policy under the Reagan administration), and the pressures on the white minority regime grew commensurately.[35]

Perhaps the most significant turning point of international pressures on South Africa was the passage in 1986 of the Comprehensive Anti-Apartheid Act (P.L. 99-440)—over the veto of President Reagan—which overturned the US policies of constructive engagement, and which combined sanctions and threats of additional sanctions together with specific conditionality provisions for the regime's opening of negotiations to democratize. It required US companies in South Africa to follow "Sullivan Code" nondiscriminatory principles, prohibited new investments, limited export of critical materials, suspended air service between South Africa and the United States, and prohibited oil exports, among other provisions. Specifically, the legislation called for the "the unbanning of groups willing to suspend terrorism and to participate in negotiations and a democratic process." Indeed, the late 1980s saw the antiapartheid movement emerge as a truly internationalized social movement with political, economic, and cultural facets. During this time, one of the most significant interventions was the role of the Commonwealth Eminent Persons Group on Southern Africa, which called the government to task because it had "in truth not yet prepared to negotiate fundamental change, nor to countenance the creation of genuine democratic structures."[36]

Sanctions had a significant effect on the South African economy. A critical turning point came in 1985, when South Africa experienced a severe foreign debt crisis, and international banks, led by Chase Manhattan, withdrew substantial credit line, refused to roll over loans, and called in short-term loans. A dramatic currency crisis ensued, with a rapidly falling currency, and the government was forced to suspend its financial and foreign exchange markets and declare a moratorium on debt repayment.[37] Trade sanctions were increasingly imposed by Western governments as well as by the newly independent and Soviet-allied states. As Price notes, "By mid-1988 it had become apparent that under conditions of international financial isolation and forced debt repayment the import cost of sustaining a growth rate of only 2 percent exceeded foreign exchange capability. . . . Economic expansion in the sanctions environment meant a short period of growth, followed by a balance-of-payments crisis, followed by a decline."[38] There is broad agreement among scholars and analysts that, while the actual sanctions applied to South Africa were not sufficiently injurious to lead to regime change, the threat of additional sanctions (and the psychological effects of the sport and cultural boy-cotts)[39] did make a direct contribution to the dramatic political change that led to the negotiated transition to democracy.[40]

The fall of the Berlin Wall in April 1989 and the end of the Cold War was felt at the tip of southern Africa. As Giliomee writes, the fall of the Berlin Wall

> presented de Klerk with what he saw as a "God-sent opportunity." The NP could not tell its constituency that without Soviet backing the ANC, with its ally, the South African Communist party, no longer constituted a major threat to stability. . . . But the fall of the Wall was a double-edged sword. Anti-communism had long been the main reason why Western governments accepted and even bolstered white rule in South Africa.[41]

The Cold War overlay that had so polarized the antiapartheid debate from the 1950s through the 1980s withered away, changing the calculus of National Party elites and setting the stage for the negotiated transition to democracy. In addition, agreements to resolve the Namibian question (the Quadripartite Agreement) were signed in Geneva in December 1988.

External Assistance to the Transition

International efforts to aid the transition in South Africa actually began well be-fore the direct negotiations to democratize began. In 1984, the US Agency for International Development began a program of assistance, providing some 500 grants totaling $66 million, as did the European Community—which funded the Kagiso Trust, a foundation designed to support the victims of apartheid that ulti-mately ended up directly supporting organizations closely allied with the United Democratic Front and the ANC.[42] There were also externally facilitated "track two" negotiation processes facilitated by outsiders that allowed for the initial, informal, and unofficial dialogue between the ANC in exile and "insider partials" within South Africa beginning in 1985 and lasting until the return of exiles in 1990.[43] As a principal condition, sanctions against South Africa lasted until the dramatic unbanning of the ANC and other antiapartheid parties, the release of Nelson Man-dela, and the onset of direct negotiations over a phased transition to democracy.

The dramatic escalation of violence in mid-1990 and into 1991 and 1992, however, heightened the need for direct involvement in what was otherwise an essentially domestic process of political change. International nongovernmental organizations publicized the political violence in South Africa and sought external intervention to stem human rights abuses by security forces.[44] During this time, influential international scholars and specialists in mediation and dispute resolution systems design from nongovernmental organizations were dispatched to run training programs and consult with community members to help mitigate the violence through direct monitoring, mediation, training, and observation.[45] After the escalation of violence in Boipatong in mid-1992, which caused the ANC to temporarily withdraw from talks, the UN secretary-general Boutros Boutros Ghali dispatched Cyrus Vance as a special representative of the secretary-general on a fact-finding mission that was also aimed at keeping the talks on track. Vance met with the major political protagonists and essentially mediated among the players while talks were officially suspended.[46]

Importantly, the Vance mission led to the deployment in August 1992 of UN-OMSA; approximately 60 UN personnel, augmented by observers from the Organization of African Unity, the European Union, and the Commonwealth (such that the total number of observers reached about 100). UNOMSA used internal "National Peace Accord" structures in a way that continues to be an example of how international monitors can multiply the effect of their presence by employing internal dispute resolution processes.[47] As Peter Gastrow concludes, "Despite the continued existence of no-go areas, and despite ongoing high levels of intolerance, the peace structures, strengthened by the international observers, have helped spread the concepts of political pluralism and tolerance in South Africa."[48]

During the course of transition, there were myriad external pressures to negotiate, and international engagement (but not direct intervention) in the negotiations was otherwise quite high. In donor assistance during the period, significant resources were channeled by all the major OECD countries and the European Union to South African civil society organizations.[49] This support was successful in bolstering civil society organizations such as IDASA (then Institute for Democratic Alternatives in South Africa, now the Institute for Democracy in Southern Africa), the Black Sash, the Legal Resources Center, the Institute for Multiparty Democracy, the Center for Policy Studies, and the Center for Conflict Resolution.[50] Such donor assistance was sometimes controversial—for example, the dispute of US Agency for International Development's policies of specifically targeting support to black-led organizations within South Africa and minority-led organizations within the United States, or "reverse discrimination" as some critics called the approach.[51]

Two other areas of intervention during the talks deserve special mention. One was the widespread sharing of knowledge on alternative constitutional (or institutional) options through exchanges of scholars and by exposing South Africans to the debates on democratic institutions in deeply divided societies (to which many South African scholars contributed).[52] This information sharing—while not always helpful, especially in a few instances of "technical assistance" that may have

in fact inflamed differences between the local actors[53]—was directly and exceptionally influential on debates about the relative merits of transitional and permanent
power sharing.

The second engagement was again provided by the Norwegian Nobel Committee in October 1993 in its joint award of the Nobel Peace Prize to F. W. de Klerk
and Nelson Mandela. Indeed, this intervention at a key moment in the talks (on the
cusp of agreement on a transitional constitution and a specific timetable leading
up to the 1994 elections) is an often overlooked aspect of international engagement during this period. The committee, under the direction of Francis Sejersted,
specifically used the prize to spur the further conclusion and implementation of
agreements (as was also the case in prizes to protagonists in Northern Ireland
and in the Israeli-Palestinian conflict).[54] In accepting the prize jointly in Oslo in
December 2003, the key elites that drove the South African transition—Mandela
and de Klerk and their deputies—were internationally recognized as legitimate
advocates of a peaceful solution.

As the 1994 elections loomed amid continuing political violence, and as the
boycott threats of Inkatha promised a violent election, international engagement
was further heighted in the run-up to this critical turning point in the democratization process. Perhaps most effective was quiet US diplomacy that set the stage
for the eventual inclusion of the IFP into the election process at the eleventh hour.
Close observers to the negotiations sensed that calls for international mediation
were met with widespread skepticism from all but the IFP (a weaker party with
ostensible interest in mediator entry to gain concessions from its stronger foe,
principally the ANC). Both the government and the ANC were skeptical of international mediation, as then US ambassador to South Africa Princeton Lyman
reports in his memoirs.[55] Finally, rather than allowing a Japanese mediator clearly
advocated by the IFP, the ANC called for the involvement of two eminent persons
on the world stage, Lord Carrington and Henry Kissinger.

With the IFP's vowing to spoil the poll and violence escalating in the closing
months of the transition, Lord Carrington and Kissinger were eventually brought
in to mediate between the NP, ANC, and IFP. The mediation attempt was an un-
qualified failure; after several days, the two left without agreement on their terms
of reference; in reality, despite inviting Kissinger into the process, the ANC, represented by Mandela and Ramphosa, made the decision to call off the mediation
(affirming their skepticism that the mediation itself was a last-minute effort for
concessions principally by the IFP). A modest Kenyan professor—Washington
Okumu—who was curiously part of the Carrington-Kissinger mission, stayed behind and brokered a last-minute accord on April 19 in which the IFP agreed to
contest the poll and accept the settlement.[56] But this was less mediation than face-

saving by the IFP (and especially Buthelezi, who reported a religious insight in prayer with Okumu), which had been outmaneuvered in the negotiation and was threatened with political oblivion if it failed to contest the liberation elections of April 26–28. Hastily, poll workers pasted an IFP option at the bottom of the ballots for the landmark liberation poll. From Okumu's mediation, little was new with the exception of a promise for future mediation, a deal that ultimately the ANC failed to abide by.[57]

International monitoring and reporting of South Africa's transitional elections were extensive. Over a period of some 18 months in the run-up to the polls, some 2,500 observers were eventually present to oversee the electoral process. International observers trained and assisted local official and unofficial (i.e., civil society) monitors, directly supported the capacity of the Independent Electoral Commission and Independent Mediation Commission, and made preparations for balloting and for counting and proclamation. While international observers did not echo the statement by the Independent Electoral Commission that the polls were "free and fair"—indeed, many observers believe the final results were essentially negotiated—they did endorse the polls as "reflecting the will of the people of South Africa."[58] The palpable irregularities in the poll and the ambiguous statements of the observer missions on the credibility of the elections reflected a conundrum over whether international observers should undermine local efforts to certify elections in the event that, even if imperfect, they are making a positive contribution to political change.

THE INTERACTION OF DOMESTIC AND EXTERNAL VARIABLES

There is good reason, in hindsight, to reaffirm that the transition to democracy in South Africa was an essentially endogenous process of pact making to exit a costly civil conflict. Apartheid collapsed of its own internal contradictions and as a result of an escalating conflict that ended in stalemate through which democratization negotiations became a strategy for exit. At the same time, clearly international influences did have an effect on this process, and especially the calculus of the apartheid regime, as key elites contemplated a negotiated transition. Apartheid's fundamental repugnancies and the "total response" police-state actions and concomitant human rights abuses from the 1960s to the 1980s brought international influence to bear on the need for fundamental reform. Thus, the international community had a direct impact on the onset of the transition, on helping the country through this difficult period, and deepening democracy in the postapartheid era. Thus, even this most celebrated of "internal settlements" cannot be seen as a solely endogenous process.

In sum, the international community structured sanctions and incentives to leverage the apartheid regime into negotiation, and it helped provide credible commitment during the negotiation period through its direct support to civil society (which helped create social cohesion), through an observer mission, and in occasional direct mediation. International action enabled liberation through its moral and direct support to the ANC-led antiapartheid struggle; in turn, the just nature of the struggle facilitated broad international consensus and collective purpose.

South Africa perhaps represents an ideal case of "international socialization" in understanding international and domestic linkages in a democratization process. International engagement was prompted by a sharp divergence of norms between global processes and local conditions; as the world was becoming more attuned to universal human rights and civil rights, South Africa was seeking to suppress legitimate black majority demands for political voice and voting rights. Conversely, in adopting the Freedom Charter, the ANC and regime challengers closely reflected emerging international norms of multicultural nationalism and principles of nondiscrimination and equal opportunity. Thus, the close resonance between the antiapartheid movement in the international community and the regime's opposition was a central characteristic of international influences on democratization; in sum, both in South Africa and abroad, the transition to democracy was ultimately a shared goal of upending the apartheid state.

CONCLUSION

International engagement in support of democratic transition took both hard (or coercive) and soft (or incentive-oriented) approaches. Through coercive measures, outsiders contributed to the demise of the authoritarian regime and the onset of talks. Thereafter, engagement was primarily seen in terms of reassurance and persuasion, direct financial support to critical social organizations, technical assistance to key institutions, and repeated election monitoring. In terms of learning, South Africa also represents an example in which domestic actors absorbed and adapted a wide range of experiences from abroad: from deliberations on constitutional models, to negotiation and bargaining concepts and approaches, to the institutional borrowing of the truth-and-reconciliation approach to transitional justice. In the final phase, too, international support to civil society took the form of financial support and capacity development in the critical areas of parliamentary processes, election management, rule of law and judicial strengthening, and support to institutions and processes of local democracy.

Evaluating the effects of international influence requires the separation of the democratization process into specific phases. Clearly, the case represents an example in which sanctions were generally proved to be an effective instrument in the demise of an authoritarian regime and the onset of a democratization process. Support to the transition is more mixed: while external engagement was critical in specific turning points or moments, the principal drivers of democratization were domestic. Thus, in this case, international influences are best described as "enabling" of liberation of the black majority from apartheid (and, as some have suggested, liberating whites from fear) and of reinforcing the fundamentally internal dynamics that determined the pathway from apartheid to democracy.

NOTES

The author thanks Joel Barkan, Antoinette Handley, and Christoph Zuercher for comments and suggestions on an earlier draft of this chapter.

1. The term *Herrenvolk* (or "mastering people" [author's translation]) democracy refers to the fact that in segregated South Africa, there was an essentially democratic regime for the minority white South Africans, but the franchise was limited on the basis of color (as prescribed in the notorious Population Registration Act of 1950), with some excluded from the franchise and with others participating only in a limited or separate way (after 1984, Coloureds and Indians/Asians were offered the opportunity to participate under what was known as the Tricameral Constitution). The concept was developed by Pierre L. van den Berghe, *The Ethnic Phenomenon* (New York: Elsevier, 1981), to describe apartheid-era South Africa and racial politics in pre-civil-rights era United States.

2. For analysis of the "miracle" metaphor and efforts to explain or debunk this characterization, see Adrian Guelke, *South Africa in Transition: The Miracle Misunderstood* (London: I. B. Tauris, 1999), and Patti Waldmeir, *Anatomy of a Miracle: The End of Apartheid and the Birth of the New South Africa* (New York: W. W. Norton, 1997).

3. Indeed, the liberationist African National Congress increased its majority in the first two post-transition elections—1999 and 2004—winning with 69.68 percent of the popular vote in the 10-years-after-apartheid April 2004 poll, and in the 2009 elections it prevailed with an only slightly reduced vote share, 65.90 percent.

4. Among the countries where the South African transition model or where South African specialists have had a fairly direct and significant influence on transitional processes are Burundi, Lebanon, Nepal, Northern Ireland, and Iraq.

5. The description of the transition as turbulent was coined by Pauline Baker; see "A Turbulent Transition," *Journal of Democracy* 1, no. 4 (1990): 7–24.

6. Timothy Sisk, *Democratization in South Africa: The Elusive Social Contract* (Princeton, N.J.: Princeton University Press, 1995).

7. See ibid.; for a countervailing interpretation of the transition as "conflict inducing," see Marina Ottaway, *South Africa: The Struggle for a New Order* (Washington, D.C.: Brookings Institution Press, 1993). For a South African perspective, see Steven Friedman, ed., *The Long Journey: South Africa's Quest for a Negotiated Settlement* (Braamfontein: Ravan Press, 1993).

8. See the Final Report of the Truth and Reconciliation Commission at www.info.gov.za/otherdocs/2003/trc/rep/pdf.

9. Timothy Sisk, *International Mediation in Civil Wars: Bargaining with Bullets* (London: Routledge, 2009), 83–112.

10. Quoted in Sisk, *Democratization in South Africa*, 243.

11. Ibid.

12. For an evaluation of the 1994 elections and the implications for democratization, see Andrew Reynolds, ed., *Elections '94 South Africa: The Campaign, Results, and Future Prospects* (London: James Curry, 1994); Roger Southall, "The South African Elections of 1994: The Remaking of a Dominant-Party State," *Journal of Modern African Studies* 32, no. 4 (1994): 629–55; and R. W. Johnson and Lawrence Schlemmer, *Launching Democracy in South Africa: The First Open Election, April 1994* (New Haven: Yale University Press, 1996).

13. Timothy Sisk and Cristophe Stefes, "Power Sharing as an Interim Step in Peace Building; Lessons from South Africa for Other Societies," in Philip Roeder and Donald Rothchild, eds., *Sustainable Peace: Power and Democracy After Civil Wars* (Ithaca, N.Y.: Cornell University Press, 2005).

14. Jamie Frueh, *Political Identity and Social Change: The Remaking of the South African Social Order* (Albany: State University of New York Press, 2003).

15. Per Strand, "Decisions on Democracy: The Politics of Constitution-Making in South Africa, 1990–1996" (Ph.D. diss., Uppsala University, 2000), 294.

16. For an authoritative history, see Leonard Thompson, *A History of South Africa*, 3rd ed. (New Haven: Yale University Press, 2001).

17. See T. Dunbar Moodie, *The Rise of Afrikanerdom: Power, Apartheid, and Afrikaner Civil Religion* (Berkeley and Los Angeles: University of California Press, 1980), for an account and a description of apartheid as a civil religion, and Leonard Thompson, *The Political Mythology of Apartheid* (New Haven: Yale University Press, 1985), on the ideological basis of apartheid.

18. On the relationships between the ANC and the South African Communist Party, see Stephen Ellis, *Comrades against Apartheid: The ANC and the South African Communist Party in Exile, 1960–1990* (Bloomington: University of Indiana Press, 1992).

19. www.anc.org.za/ancdocs/history/charter.html.

20. Suzman personified a liberal voice within the South African political tradition, reflected in the policies of the then Progressive Federal Party and subsequently by the Democratic Party. This tradition had a significant effect of defining alternative white political discourse through the language on international human rights; see Jeffrey Butler, Richard Elphick, and David Welsh, eds., *Democratic Liberalism in South Africa: Its History and Prospects* (Cape Town: David Philip, 1987).

21. As Tom Lodge, *Black Politics in South Africa since 1945* (London: Longman, 1983), 225, describes "Sharpeville was a turning point in the struggle, when protest finally hardened into resistance and when African politicians began thinking in terms of a revolutionary strategy."

22. See Steven Friedman, *Building Tomorrow Today: African Workers in Trade Unions* (Johannesburg: Ravan Press, 1987), for an account of the pivotal role of the trade unions in the antiapartheid struggle.

23. www.anc.org.za/ancdocs/history/rivonia.html.

24. See Heribert Adam and Hermann Giliomee, eds., *Ethnic Power Mobilized: Can South Africa Change?* (New Haven: Yale University Press, 1979).

25. Robert M. Price, "Security versus Growth: The International Factor in South African Policy," *Annals of the American Society of Political and Social Science* 489 (1987): 103–22; Stephen R. Lewis Jr., *The Economics of Apartheid* (New York: Council on Foreign Relations, 1990).

26. Jeffrey Herbst, "South Africa: Economic Crises and the Distributional Imperative,"

in Stephen J. Stedman, ed., *South Africa: The Political Economy of Transformation* (Boulder, Colo.: Lynne Rienner, 1994), 30.

27. Tom Lodge, "State of Exile: The African National Congress of South Africa, 1976–1986," in Philip Frankel, Noam Pines, and Mark Swilling, eds., *State, Resistance, and Change in South Africa* (London: Croom Helm, 1988); Tom Lodge et al., *All, Here, and How: Black Politics in South Africa in the 1980s* (New York: Ford Foundation and Foreign Policy Association, 1991).

28. John Kane-Berman, preface to Charles Simkins, ed., *The Prisoners of Tradition and the Politics of Nation-Building* (Johannesburg: South African Institute of Race Relations, 1988), i.

29. Pierre du Toit, *South Africa's Brittle Peace: The Problem of Post-Settlement Violence* (New York: Palgrave, 2001).

30. See Thomas Ohlson and Stephen John Stedman with Robert Davies, *The New Is Not Yet Born: Conflict Resolution in Southern Africa* (Washington, D.C.: Brookings Institution Press, 1994), 39–52, on the relationship between decolonization and apartheid in South Africa.

31. The text of the United Nations Security Council Resolution 134 is found at www .un.org/documents/sc/res/1960/scres60.htm.

32. Christopher Landsberg, "Voicing the Voiceless: Foreign Political Aid to Civil Society in South Africa," in Marina Ottaway and Thomas Carothers, eds., *Funding Virtue: Civil Society Aid and Democracy Promotion* (Washington, D.C.: Carnegie Endowment for International Peace, 2000), 115.

33. For a concise summary on South Africa at the UN, see Milton J. Esman, "A Survey of Interventions," in Milton J. Esman, and Shibley Telhami, eds., *International Organizations and Ethnic Conflict* (Ithaca, N.Y.: Cornell University Press, 1995), 35–38.

34. For a detailed account on sanctions and their effects on the white attitudes toward transition, see Robert M. Price, *The Apartheid State in Crisis: Political Transformation of South Africa, 1975–1990* (New York: Oxford University Press, 1991), 220–46.

35. For an insider's account of the US constructive engagement policy, see Princeton Lyman, *Partner to History: The U.S. Role in South Africa's Transition to Democracy* (Washington, D.C.: United States Institute of Peace Press, 2002), 30–36.

36. Commonwealth Secretariat, *Mission to South Africa: The Commonwealth Report; The Findings of the Commonwealth Eminent Persons Group on Southern Africa* (London: Penguin Books for the Commonwealth Secretariat, 1986), 132. See, too, *South Africa: Time Running Out; The Report of the Study Commission on U.S. Policy toward Southern Africa* (1981).

37. Xavier Carim, Audie Klotz, and Olivier LeBleu, "The Political Economy of Financial Sanctions," in Neta Crawford and Audie Klotz, eds., *How Sanctions Work: Lessons From South Africa* (London: Macmillan, 1999), 3–37.

38. Price, *The Apartheid State in Crisis*, 275.

39. On the effects of the sport boycott, see John Nauright, *Long Run to Freedom: Sport, Cultures and Identities in South Africa* (London: Leicester University Press, 1997).

40. Neta Crawford and Audey Klotz, eds., *How Sanctions Work: Lessons from South Africa* (London: Macmillan, 1999). Waldmeir, *Anatomy of a Miracle*, 134, notes that the effect of the sanctions on de Klerk's decision to inaugurate democratization talks with the ANC was both direct, in the increasing pressure of isolation and threat of escalating sanctions, and indirect, particularly in the influence of the business community, which needed access to international markets, technology, and capital. On the cultural sanctions, Waldmeir observes

"The white elite, which had ruled unchallenged as polecat of the world for decades already, was tiring of that dubious distinction."

41. Hermann Giliomee, *The Afrikaners: Biography of a People* (Cape Town: Tafelberg, 2003), 629.

42. Price, *The Apartheid State in Crisis*, 233–35.

43. See Daniel Lieberfeld, "Evaluating the Contributions of Track-Two Diplomacy to Conflict Termination in South Africa, 1984–90," *Journal of Peace Research* 39, no. 3 (2002): 355–72, for analysis of these externally facilitated efforts.

44. Human Rights Watch, *The Killings in South Africa: The Role of the Security Forces and the Responses of the State* (New York: Human Rights Watch, 1991); Amnesty International, *South Africa: State of Fear* (New York: Amnesty International, 1992).

45. Peter Gastrow *Bargaining for Peace: South Africa and the National Peace Accord* (Washington, D.C.: United States Institute of Peace Press, 1996); Susan Collin Marks, *Watching the Wind: Conflict Resolution in South Africa's Transition* (Washington, D.C.: United States Institute of Peace Press, 2000).

46. Donald Rothchild, *Managing Ethnic Conflict in Africa: Pressures and Incentives for Cooperation* (Washington, D.C.: Brookings Institution Press, 1997), 203.

47. See Gastrow, *Bargaining for Peace*, and Collin Marks, *Watching the Wind*.

48. Gastrow, *Bargaining for Peace*, 74.

49. For a detailed account of the donor support to South Africa during this period, see Christopher Landsberg, *The Quiet Diplomacy of Liberation: International Politics and South Africa's Transition* (Johannesburg: Jacana Media, 2004). Landsberg describes various national donor support to civil society and argues that donors tended to focus on "elite" civil society; he notes that donors include Sweden, Norway, Denmark, Switzerland, and the German party foundations (Ebert Stiftung, Adenauer Stiftung, and the Hans Seidel Foundation). After 1994, the United Nations Development Program also began to directly fund South African civil society organizations. See his "Voicing the Voiceless: Foreign Political Aid to Civil Society in South Africa," in Marina Ottaway and Thomas Carothers, eds., *Funding Virtue: Civil Society Aid and Democracy Promotion* (Washington, D.C.: Carnegie Endowment for International Peace), 115–20.

50. See the report of the Carnegie Commission on Deadly Conflict, *A House No Longer Divided: Progress and Prospects for Democratic Peace in South Africa* (1997); the Commission's work is archived at www.wilsoncenter.org/subsites/ccpdc/pubs/house/hsfr.htm. Julie Hearn, "Aiding Democracy? Donors and Civil Society in South Africa," *Third World Quarterly* 21, no. 5 (2000): 815–30, has argued that support to civil society was a critical element in the success of the 1994 elections in South Africa.

51. See Lyman, *Partner to History* 282, for an account from the US policy maker's point of view. See Creative Associates International, Inc., *Program Evaluation: USAID/South Africa* (Washington, D.C.: United States Agency for International Development, April 21, 1995), for a full review of the USAID program during the transitional period.

52. Particularly the work of Arend Lijphart, *Power-Sharing in South Africa*, Policy Papers in International Affairs, no. 24 (Berkeley: University of California, Berkeley, Institute of International Studies, 1985), and Donald Horowitz, *A Democratic South Africa? Constitutional Engineering in a Divided Society* (Berkeley and Los Angeles: University of California Press, 1991), who proposed differing yet equally influential sets of detailed, contextualized proposals for a constitutional settlement in South Africa.

53. Specifically, there were widespread concerns about the role of Mario Oriani-Ambro-

sini, an international constitutional "expert" who was seen as a hard-line adviser to IFP chief Buthelezi; see Lyman, *Partner to History*, 139, for a discussion of the advisor's threat regarding a potential IFP boycott of the electoral process.

54. Francis Sejersted, "The Nobel Peace Prize in a Changing World: New Definitions, New Dilemmas," Occasional Paper, David M. Kennedy Center for International Studies, Brigham Young University, 1993.

55. Lyman, *Partner to History*, 202–9.

56. Ohlson and Stedman with Davies, *The New Is Not Yet Born*, 63; Waldmeir, *Anatomy of a Miracle*, 249–50.

57. In bringing Buthelezi on board at the last minute, the coordinated work of the United States, Britain, and Germany working together was essential. As former US ambassador during the period, Princeton Lyman, relates: "The United States emerged as a principal actor in this period . . . With Britain and Germany, sharing assessments and ideas was critical. Both Britain and Germany had histories of support to Buthelezi and strong domestic constituencies on his side. It was important that we stay together" (Lyman, *Partner to History*, 276).

58. As quoted in J. Abink and Gerti Hesseling, *Election Observation and Democratization in Africa* (London: Macmillan 2000), 53.

CHAPTER EIGHT

Chile

Coordinating a Successful Democratic Transition

DAVID ALTMAN, WITH RAFAEL PIÑEIRO
AND SERGIO TORO

In the academic literature concerning the Chilean transition, we find that some questions have not been answered satisfactorily: What was the international impact on the Chilean transition to democracy? How much influence was there from international aid both from countries themselves and from organizations outside Chile? Where was this aid coming from, how was it manifesting itself, what was its goal, and to whom did it go? How significant was the organizational power of the opposition groups in enabling the cooperation to become efficient and important? The bias toward internal phenomena due to the influential lead roles played by local actors has caused interest to wane in regards to the international impact.

This chapter seeks to fill this gap by focusing on how the interaction between international factors and the political strategies of local actors influenced the success of the Chilean transition. In terms of the international context, we argue that the transition process was mainly conditioned by changes in the international politics of the US government and its relations with the military regime and by the strong international economic crisis that hit Chile and most of the region in the early eighties. Both events contributed to a political opening and the articulation of a democratic opposition—a process that during the early years of Pinochet's regime was fraught with difficulty, mainly because of the drastic restrictions on political and civil liberties.

Strengthened by international assistance in terms of both financial and technical resources, the idea of resistance to the regime through the creation of parallel entities that would counterbalance the regime's institutions flourished. Faced with the impossibility of securing national funds, these parallel entities arose under the auspices of different international organizations. Institutions from European countries, the United States, and Canada concentrated their efforts in conjoining the opposition to combat a regime that no longer had international legitimacy. Therefore, if we were to venture an explanation on this phenomenon, we could see that there was a correlation between the internal and external events that assisted in inducing three elements that today are recognized as having been influential on the Chilean transition: the coordination between two sectors, which before the coup, were strongly antagonistic (the Socialist Party and Christian Democrats); the creation of a strong and functional organization of private research centers, which acted in parallel to the institutions that the regime interfered with (e.g., universities); and the coordination between those who were exiled and those who were in the country, with the aim of preparing the transition to democracy. This point is endorsed by Ricardo Núñez when he indicates: "The assistance helped in regrouping the previously dispersed intellectual and political strength, to establish a programmatic accumulation that would allow us to better understand what the transition would entail."[1]

This chapter is based primarily on interviews with key actors in the Chilean transition and a systematic analysis of the existing political and historical research on the subject.

THE TRANSITIONAL MOMENT: THE FALL OF PINOCHET

The seventeen-year-old military regime of Augusto Pinochet came officially to an end in 1990. Pinochet had seized power from Salvador Allende as part of a military junta in 1973. Pinochet's regime was highly repressive of the Chilean population, although economically reformist. Indeed, neoliberal economic reform carried out under Pinochet has made Chile an economic standout in Latin America. The regime was highly repressive, nonetheless, but began to liberalize in the 1980s following the passage of constitutional reform. By many accounts, 1983 could be considered the beginning of the transition to democracy, insofar as it is then that the regime starts to decline. Although the political events of the subsequent two years showed that this politics of liberalization was merely a "strategic withdrawal" for Pinochet, the new freedoms that had been granted to social action, to the means of communication, and to political opposition would not disappear.[2]

The 1980 Constitution carried a provision for a plebiscite to vote on whether President Pinochet should have another eight-year term. As a result, a plebiscite took place on October 5, 1988, which Pinochet assumed he would win. Although the government delayed in releasing the results, Pinochet finally accepted defeat.

Todd ya ₽

The "no" option won with 55.99 percent of the vote versus the 44.01 percent obtained by the "yes" option for Pinochet. New presidential elections and congressional elections took place in December 1989. Pinochet peacefully left the presidency in March 1990, transferring presidential power to the newly elected president of Chile, Patricio Aylwin. Thus, despite the violent nature of the military regime under Pinochet, the moment of transition itself was relatively orderly and peaceful.

DOMESTIC CAUSES OF TRANSITION

It is difficult to understand the process of Chilean transition and the international impact that contributed to its demise if we do not first observe the political process of the dictatorial regime. Unlike what happened in the Argentine transition, where the regime collapsed following political, economic, and military (the Falkland/Malvinas War) failures, or in Uruguay, where the conversion to democracy was the product of a long and arduous negotiation between the military and political parties, in Chile, transition developed within the institutional standards that the regime itself had established—almost unilaterally—in the 1980 constitution. Specifically, the rules of the transition—consciously or unconsciously—were foreshadowed by the military government itself and its process of institutionalizing power and the rules of succession for the head of the regime.

Socialist Salvador Allende was elected president by Congress in November 1970,[3] and in fact, it was not the first time a committed socialist became the president of a nation through democratic means. It was, however, one of the most symbolic leftist victories in the Western world of the day. His policies constituted a drastic move toward the economic regulation of the country. The whole program of reforms was called La vía chilena al socialismo (The Chilean Path to Socialism). The economy was rapidly disjointed because of price controls, increased salaries, and nationalization of industries (some of which excel, such as foreign copper firms) and of 60 percent of the private banks.[4]

The Cold War was at its peak during the late 1960s and early 1970s. It is not surprising then that events in a relatively faraway country like Chile were also impacted by this international atmosphere. While there were signs of an active role of the United States in Chilean affairs, the new, partially declassified documents of the American records show this intriguing and obscure dimension of American foreign policy in its reality.[5] The election of Allende was a particularly hard hit for the American side of the equation, which was openly hostile to the possibility of a second Marxist regime (in the wake of Cuba) in the Western Hemisphere, and efforts to undermine Allende's government were taken, even before he assumed office.[6]

But as the popular saying goes: "It takes two to tango." Virtually all relevant political sectors in Chile seem to have received foreign economic collaboration, at least for some years from 1963 to 1973. Thus, the United States was not the only relevant international player in Chile at the time. The Soviet Union also had a relevant role in subsidizing communist parties beyond its borders, and the Chilean Communist Party received important resources as well.[7] However, neither the United States nor the USSR seems to have been willing to have another Cuba in the region, though for different reasons.

Whereas in other countries in the region the armed forces seized power in stages during the early 1970s, in Chile the coup was the exact opposite: the coup on September 11, 1973, took just a few hours and even included a massive rocket attack (from aircraft jets) on the presidential palace in the heart of Santiago, the capital city of the country.

The Chilean military's main ideology was the *doctrine of national security*.[8] On October 8, 1973, Decree Law 77 announced that the main goals of the new military government were "to extirpate Marxism from Chile, to restore the country morally and materially toward economic development and social justice, and to vitalize new institutional forms that bring about a modern democracy that is free from the vices that favored the actions of its enemies."[9] In short, the military defined its goals in opposition to those that Allende's socialist government had embraced.

Unlike other military regimes in the region, the Chilean dictatorship attempted a clear refounding of the country and its institutions. These refounding attempts had a distinct effect in the transition to civilian rule in 1990, and in order to fully grasp the nature of the transition to democracy in Chile, we have first to understand the previous military regime, and its stance toward the democratic regime it overthrew in 1973. Yet, it is hard to create anew the entire institutional framework of a country based solely on a negative doctrine (National Security), so something else was needed. A significant ideological substantiation of the regime was provided by the Chicago Boys,[10] and the Gremialistas.[11]

The Military Regime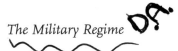

The first years of the dictatorship were characterized by fierce political persecution and repression. Shielded in the guise of a "war against Marxism," the regime sought to silence any opposition using all means at its disposition. With the deep conviction that his actions were justified because of the country's collapse during the government of Salvador Allende, Pinochet noted "we have practically freed the nation from Marxists."[12] This idea of seeking what Huneeus calls "historical legitimacy" justified the long years of human rights abuses.[13] Thus, international complaints of large-scale human rights violations were decisive in the regime's quick loss of political legitimacy abroad.

By March 1974 "the UN Commission of Human Rights took the highly unusual step of authorizing its Chairman to address a cable to the Chilean military authorities expressing the members' concern for the protection of the lives of political prisoners and calling for strict observance of the principles of the United Nations Charter and the International Covenants on Human Rights. The Economic and Social Council of the United Nations (ECOSOC), by consensus, quickly seconded that demand."[14] The obscene degree of human rights violations circa 1975 prompted the UN Human Rights Commission to send a team of observers to Chile, an initiative promoted by Great Britain, West Germany, France, the Netherlands, and Austria.

In July, the day before the group was to arrive in Chile, Pinochet reneged on his pledge to allow the visit, thus precipitating a deterioration in foreign relations, particularly with the United States. This adverse international situation meant further difficulties in obtaining credits from multilateral organizations, in renegotiating the foreign debt, and in accessing foreign bilateral credits and assistance, and it further kindled efforts to organize an economic boycott of Chile.[15]

Such was the distressing atmosphere that "as the 30th UN General Assembly approached, for the first time, the Junta seriously considered the worst-case scenario that Chile might be expelled from the United Nations." In July 1975 Pinochet explicitly requested the United States to veto such a vote, should it be necessary. He also requested the American executive to direct aid to Chile through indirect channels (such as other countries: Brazil, Korea, Taiwan, or Spain), acknowledging US Congress opposition to such aid.

In 1975 the UN General Assembly expressed its "profound distress" at the authorities' practice of institutionalized torture,[16] and in 1976 the UN Ad-Hoc Working Group on Chile concluded that cases of torture, as crimes against humanity, committed by the military government should be prosecuted by the international community.[17] Also, during 1976 some US senators called in several members of the Chilean exile, academicians, to the congressional hearings related to human rights violations in the Southern Cone. These congressional hearings triggered the US Congress decision (later on ratified by President Gerald Ford) to cut all military aid to the Southern Cone military regimes because of their systematic violations of human rights. By the late 1970s, state terrorism shifted from massive to selective tactics.

By 1977, four years after the September 11, 1973, military coup, the regime was gradually becoming less legitimate in the eyes of the international community. The systematic condemnations from the United Nations in regard to the human rights situation in Chile contributed to the change in tone of the relationship with the United States. This was due in part to Carter's assuming the presidency but also to the murder of Chilean ambassador Orlando Letelier[18] in September 1976 in Washington, D.C., mandated by the Chilean National Intelligence Directorate (DINA)."[19] Presumably this assassination constituted the most famous act of international terrorism committed in the United States prior to (the North American) 9/11 and may have been the biggest mistake of the Chilean military regime in terms of international relations.

The election of Jimmy Carter to the White House and the UN condemnation of Chile because of its systematic human rights violations pushed Pinochet to seek an aura of legitimacy through popular mobilization via a plebiscite. That plebiscite was held on January 1978 as a response to the increasingly frosty international environment facing Pinochet. The text of the 1978 plebiscite was possibly the most loaded text ever used in this type of plebiscite: "In the face of international aggression unleashed against the government of our country, I support President Pinochet in his defense of the dignity of Chile, and I reaffirm the legitimate right of the Republic to conduct the process of institutionalization in a manner befitting its sovereignty." Such a plebiscite was a gross imitation of something related to a vote, given that there were no minimal conditions set for a transparent vote whatsoever. Of course, as was expected, Pinochet "won" with a support of almost 80 percent of the population (official numbers).[20]

Furthermore, Huneeus affirms that the international isolation perceived by the regime also had repercussions on national security, given Chile's conflicts with Peru and Argentina.[21] For example, the Kennedy amendment, approved by the US Congress in 1974, forbade any security assistance or arms sales to Chile. In 1976 this amendment was expanded to include other countries through the International Security Assistance and Arms Export Control Act, which prohibited transfers to any country that systematically violated human rights, except in extraordinary circumstances. Senator Ricardo Núñez, leader of the Socialist Party during the transition notes:

> The "Kennedy" amendment was not an issue that made it impossible for them (for the Armed Forces) to gain access to the arms market, the "Kennedy" amendment turned them into the parasitic Armed Forces of an atrocious dictatorship that didn't report to them . . . they realized that the subject of democracy was not unimportant if they wanted to re-legitimize themselves in the political and social life of the country.[22]

By the mid 1970s American relations with Chile were clearly multidimensional. While the executive, the State Department, and the Central Intelligence Agency fully engaged in subversive and antidemocratic actions in Chile, as later demonstrated by declassified documents, the American Congress took action to stop Pinochet's brutality. Stemming from the political actions taken primarily by the US Congress, an abrupt decline in military and economic aid to Chile began in 1977 (table 8.1).

The 1980 Plebiscite and the Debt Crisis: The Time Bomb

The "victory" achieved by the 1978 plebiscite—summoned by the dictatorship in response to the UN condemnations of the human rights violations—produced an aura of glory and legitimacy for the regime and General Pinochet (rather artificially) that helped to catalyze the idea of the need to move forward with the institutionalization of the military regime. This plebiscite and the idea to approve a new constitution advancing the institutionalization of the regime—in order to secure a "protected democracy"—captured in the Chacarillas Plan disclosed on September 9, 1977, was, in a way, a response to international pressure and the controversy regarding the legitimacy of the regime. Thus, in the midst of an economic boom, on September 11, 1980, a new Chilean constitution was put up for a vote.

As indicated, Pinochet's program was far more sophisticated than a mere survival plan to counteract international or domestic pressures, and, in a legalistic country such as Chile, this refounding purpose had to be amalgamated into a new constitution; indeed, the regime had already declared in 1973 that it embodied the executive, legislative, and *constituent* powers of the nation. The plebiscite of 1980, again on a September 11, was held without any sort of international monitoring and with no freedom whatsoever. As expected, the regime again "won." The new constitution stated, in transitory clause 14, that Pinochet would be president for eight years and that after those eight years (in 1988) Chileans would have to face another plebiscite (transitory clause 27) to decide whether Pinochet remained (for another eight years, up to 1994) or a transition was required. The plebiscite of 1988 was thus set in motion. These transitional clauses were an auto-imposed limitation in the exercise of power by the military regime. Thus, Chile is the case of an autocratic regime binding itself by a constitution of its own making.[23] As in 1978, the constitutional plebiscite counted on a high level of participation (6,271,868 citizens) and succeeded in obtaining an overwhelming 68 percent majority support for the new constitution (table 8.2).[24]

In this setting of economic growth and apparent success of the "neoliberal" model driven by the Chicago Boys, the dictatorial government thought itself capable of managing the process initiated in the 1980 constitution to establish a new regime with a limited plurality and with strong control over the groups akin to the dictatorship. However, these plans were seriously altered by a second international

TABLE 8.1.

Assistance per Capita (Military and Economic) from the United States
to the Countries of South America, 1974–1988 (in millions of 2006 US dollars)

Country	1974	1975	1976	1977	1978	1979	1980	1981	1982	1983	1984	1985	1986	1987	1988
Argentina	0	0.01	0	0.01	0	0.01	0	0	0	0	0.01	0	0	0.12	0.02
Bolivia	35.35	17.12	19.57	24.99	26.69	23.18	12.27	4.63	6.56	19.66	22.99	14.13	19.93	19.86	22.1
Brazil	0.57	0.43	0.16	0.1	0.05	0.04	0.04	0.02	0.01	0	0	0.01	0.01	0.06	0.03
Chile	3.33	29	23.2	8.5	1.66	2.9	1.99	2.11	1.09	0.43	0.24	0.17	0.15	0.14	0.17
Colombia	7.52	3.55	4.69	0.93	0.69	0.75	1.78	0.39	0.19	0.23	0.45	0.59	0.58	0.58	0.47
Ecuador	3.95	3.66	2.02	1.43	1.9	1.92	3.24	4.49	5.06	5.5	5.59	9.49	10.51	7.55	3.29
Paraguay	7.82	9.5	7.27	3.11	3.06	8.08	2.58	3.79	2.15	1.68	1.32	1.6	1.43	1.3	1.72
Peru	4.09	3.35	4.47	3.9	8.55	9.95	6.72	8.98	5.58	8.94	14.85	6.75	4.76	4.95	5.22
Uruguay	1.12	14.4	0.72	0.57	0.21	0.16	0.01	0.05	0.53	0.59	0.33	0	7.72	6.38	0.03
Venezuela	0.74	0.4	0.15	0.02	0	0	0	0.01	0.02	0.01	0.04	0.07	0.01	0	0.02

Source: USAID Economic Analysis and Data Services, http://qesdb.usaid.gov/gbk/us_assistance_per_capita_07.xls.

TABLE 8.2.
Plebiscites under the Pinochet Regime, 1973–1990

Date	Turnout (%)	Result (% in favor)	Issue
January 4, 1978	91.43	78.69	Support of President Pinochet's policies
September 11, 1980	92.96	68.52	Constitution
October 5, 1988	97.53	44.01	General Pinochet for president for 8-year term
June 30, 1989	91.30	91.26	Constitutional reforms

event, which would mark the future of the dictatorship and its anticipated process of institutionalization.

The so-called debt crisis that affected the Latin American countries was also felt in Chile. Unemployment rose from 11.3 percent in 1981 to 19.6 percent in 1982, and the GDP registered a decline of close to 14 percent.[25] This crisis also entailed serious financial problems for Chilean companies, whose viability was called into question. The radical change in the country's economic situation brought to light the weaknesses of the economic model imposed by the dictatorship and at the same time impelled an important social movement, which broke through the constraints the regime was trying to impose.

Because of Chile's outward-oriented development (based on exports and unilateral liberalization of foreign trade and supported by strong external borrowing, especially from the private sector), the crisis had a strong impact on employment, particularly on the popular sector. Unemployment generated significant political unrest, mainly because it broke one of the strongholds of the regime's legitimacy, its economic accomplishments. Certainly repression was part of the response to the political unrest. However, the cost of sustaining the repression of a mobilized society made some opening necessary to maintain the regime's stability.

Consequently, faced with the impossibility of increasing repression and with the lack of effectiveness of intensifying the economic model, the dictatorship opted to distance itself from the liberal orthodoxy of the Chicago Boys and to initiate the process of a budding political liberalization. This process was manifested with the appointment of Sergio Onofre Jarpa as minister of the interior and the establishment of what Huneeus calls the regime's "politics of liberalization."[26]

Among the measures that characterize the "politics of liberalization" carried out by Jarpa, the following stand out: a relaxation of the exile (which allowed the return of important political leaders who opposed the regime) and press censorship, and an attempt to engage in dialogue with the opposition. It was thus that, at the insistence of Archbishop Santiago Juan Francisco Fresno, a dialogue was set in motion between Jarpa, social and special interest group leaders, and leaders of the opposition group Democratic Alliance (a union of right-wing, left-wing, and center politicians who opposed the dictatorship).

Thus, a significant impact on Pinochet's regime—the debt crisis in Latin America—resulted in the creation of a niche for the regime's political opposition, which significantly altered its plans of a "protected" democracy and, in effect, initiated the process of transition toward democracy. Although the plans for presidential succession within the regime, as established by the 1980 constitution, remained intact, the political setting in which they took place was very different from that which was expected by the supporters of the dictatorship. After 1983 the opposition had the means of strengthening itself and gathering politically, so that in 1988—for the ensuing plebiscite—it had become a political force capable of defeating Pinochet at the ballot.

The Plebiscite of 1988: The Beginning of the End

In the context of totalitarian or authoritarian regimes, the evidence of a plebiscitary failure is provided only when the government acknowledges its defeat. But if the (nondemocratic) government succeeds in its plebiscitary efforts, we may lack the tools for knowing, and empirically showing, that the plebiscite was held fairly.[27] Yet, there is less than a handful of examples where authoritarian regimes acknowledge their defeat at the ballot box. Indeed, to our knowledge, during the twentieth century there were only two such instances worldwide: Uruguay in 1980 and Chile in 1988. The simplest and most obvious question is, Having roughly all the tools to rig a plebiscite, why do authoritarian regimes accept their loss when they hold one? Was it a political maneuver to pursue other results? Which factors determined the acceptance of the results of those plebiscites? Was it merely the surprise factor, international leverage, or simply a political miscalculation?[28]

With the help of international cooperation, the opposition camp succeeded in building a parallel tallying system for the plebiscite.[29] Also, an important fact to bear in mind is that by 1988 Chile was one of the last countries in the American continent still under control of a military regime, and thus world attention was focused on it. Unlike the Uruguayan experience of 1980, the 1988 plebiscite in Chile had a significantly long and, most importantly, fair campaign for both camps.[30] On the day of the plebiscite, the National Democratic Institute (NDI) sent a large delegation of observers headed by Adolfo Suárez, Misael Pastrana, Bruce Babbitt, and Peter Dailei to monitor the sanctity of the vote, the freedom to vote, and control the process.

The fear of fraud was present in the minds of the opposition and the international community. It was thus that a specialist sent by the NDI, Glen Cowan, suggested it would be necessary to protect not the total tally but rather the individual tables in order to later force the government to release individual table votes to compare with their own. In this way the opposition placed its representatives at all the tables and created centers for gathering information that was later fed to a central command office. Yet, the day of the plebiscite did not pass free of tensions. Just the day before the election, a blackout in Santiago predisposed the opposition camp to sharpen its senses; extreme caution was required at each of the more than 22,000 polling stations throughout the country.

Notwithstanding the assistance of international cooperation for the 1988 plebiscite, Chileans themselves were also learning from other international experiences, especially those within the region. During a personal interview of former Uruguayan president Julio María Sanguinetti, he stated that, immediately after the military defeat in the Uruguayan plebiscite of 1980, Genaro Arriagada was sent to Montevideo on behalf of former Chilean president Eduardo Frei to learn about the Uruguayan experience and how the Uruguayans defeated the military at the ballot boxes.[31]

THE IMPORTANCE OF INTERNATIONAL AID

Both the economic crisis and international condemnation undermined the legitimacy of the regime. These factors were those that conditioned the relationship between international and local actors who later made possible the return to democracy. However, a complete understanding of the international factors requires an analysis of the effects of direct international aid on the actors involved in the transition, especially the opposition. For the most part, foreign cooperation took place among think tanks, civil organizations, and unions.[32] Much cooperation was by means of projects whose outcomes had to be reported on, and yet other ways were through unrestricted donations, free to be used as needed. This aid came primarily from Western European countries, Canada, and the United States. There was also cooperation from the USSR toward the Communist Party and other left-wing groups, but the objectives of the Comintern were nowhere close to the idea of a peaceful transition. Ricardo Núñez points out:

> The Communist Party in the Soviet Union and Cuba helped the Communist Party and the MIR in a different way, and they had a different strategy, the socialist faction of Eastern Europe held a different strategy for our country's release from dictatorship. Chile was merely a platform—indeed insignificant to the Cold War—and the Communist Party had no other alternative, even when many of its leaders admit-

ted in whispers that Chile did not have the conditions to turn into a Vietnam or a Nicaragua.[33]

Meanwhile, the recipient institutions answered to the nongovernmental organizations and the centers created by the Chilean intellectuals. The mechanism for collaboration was primarily through the presentation of research projects and the development of activities. One such example was the famous *economic dialogues* held by the Center of Study for Development (CED), which was able to bring together for the first time liberal economists, government supporters, and organizations of the opposition to discuss subjects that were controversial for the time, such as the right to private property and the redistribution of wealth. Financed by American sources, the main aim of the institution was to reduce the existing differences between the groups, and hence bring their postures closer together primarily on subjects related to the economy of the country. Boeninger points out: "At the CED we organized seminars, meetings between liberals and government supporters, DC, PS, Unionists, etc., and those were projects that were enabled by the financial aid of American foundations."[34]

Table 8.3, shows the group of foreign institutions that supported the Chilean transition. Each institution had its own method of assisting, although most were intermediaries for funding from their own governments. American cooperation during the transition took place in many fronts. On the one hand there was direct pressure from the US government with the aim of forcing the Pinochet regime to liberalize. The need of the authoritarian regime for an infusion of funds surpassing $2 billion, with the aim of furthering the biannual development plan,[35] gave the US Treasury the opportunity to demand this liberalization, setting as a condition to the aid a definitive end of the martial law imposed by the regime. Sigmund points out: "The June 1985 loans from the World Bank provided an opportunity to compel the Chileans to liberalize to some degree, since the lifting of the state of siege was a condition of U.S. support."[36]

Another source of support was from the organizations that were receiving funds from the National Endowment for Democracy (NED). One of the most active of these was the National Democratic Institute (NDI), which established itself in Chile in May 1985 and sponsored conferences, seminars, and visits by external consultants to promote free elections.[37] The NDI also had an active role in the 1988 plebiscite, sending to Chile a group of observers, among whom were Kenneth Wollack, Lewis Manilow, and Larry Garber. The NED funds also helped finance projects in institutions such as the Latin American Corporation for Economic Studies (CIEPLAN, which also received funds from the Canadian International Development Research Centre (IDRC); Latin American School of Social Sciences

TABLE 8.3.
Type, Name, and Provenance of the Main Collaborating Institutes during the Transition

	United States	Germany	Canada	Sweden	France	The Netherlands	USSR
			Public Funds				
Through supporting organizations	NED: National Democratic Institute NED: National Republican Institute	Friedrich Ebert Konrad Adenauer Hans Seidel Friedrich Neuman					Comintern
Through independent governmental organizations	Inter-American Foundation		International Development Research Centre (IDRC) Canadian International Development Agency	Swedish International Development Agency (SIDA) Swedish Agency for Research Cooperation with Developing Countries (SAREC)			

Category		Private Funds	
Through private organizations	NED: Center for International Private Enterprise NED: Free Trade Union Institute		OXFAM Netherlands Organization for International Assistance Humanist Institute for Development Cooperation
Directly from the government	Agency for International Development	Mitterrand government	
Organizations	Ford Foundation Rockefeller Foundation		
Unions	American Institute for Free Labor Department		Landsorganisationen i Sverige Tjänstemännens Centralorganisation

(FLACSO); and even the Center of Study for Development (CED). Private foundations such as the Ford Foundation also contributed to the transition. CIEPLAN and the Interdisciplinary Program for Research in Education (PIIE) were among its beneficiaries. The Rockefeller Foundation did the same for the CED.

German aid was far superior at all levels, almost five times as much as the support sent by the United States. According to Pinto-Duschiszky,[38] between 1984 and 1988, German foundations contributed 26.05 million dollars, a figure much higher than the 6.77 million from the United States. The largest contribution was from the Christian Democrat foundation, Konrad Adenauer, with almost $24 million. These funds helped solidify projects from opposition institutions such as the Corporation for University Advancement (CPU), the Chilean Institute for Humanistic Studies (ICHECH), and the Eduardo Frei Foundation. The other German political foundation—related to the social democrats—that made a significant investment in Chile was the Friedrich Ebert Foundation. Although the amount of money destined to cooperation in this country was inferior to that doled out by the Konrad Adenauer Foundation, both set the standard for common cooperation with the opposition.

Other substantial aid came from Sweden, Canada, and the Netherlands. The Swedish International Development Cooperation Agency (SIDA) and the Swedish Agency for Research Cooperation with Developing Countries (SAREC) were prominent in their support of opposition activities both in and out of the country. The most distinctive feature of Sweden's cooperation is that it also harbored 13,900 Chilean political refugees,[39] a fact that contributed to the strong ties of solidarity with that country. Likewise, the Swedish Labor Unions such as LO and TCO also supported their Chilean counterparts, particularly through cooperation in dialogues and union leadership. The Canadian IDRC was also prominent through its funding of research activities on subjects related to the economy and public policy, particularly those developed by CIEPLAN. Joaquín Vial, a researcher at this institute mentions the international aid provided by the IDRC: "Its contribution (IDRC), moreover, enabled us to track the economic situation, a vital task which allowed a group of researchers to observe events and develop tools for monitoring economic developments in great detail. In addition to forming opinion, it thus facilitated the transfer of power to informed people who were prepared to assume the responsibility of governing the country."[40]

The Netherlands was also another prominent case in regard to international cooperation, specifically dealing with the protection of human rights. One of the salient features of Dutch cooperation was the exceptional strategy of triangulation for Chile. Indeed, from the start cooperation in the realm of human rights was addressed from one government to the next, a strategy that was not well received considering the repression of the state itself toward opposition groups. In this way they decided to supersede aid—especially for Chile and Uganda—reconveying it through nongovernmental channels.[41] The idea was, precisely, to reach the victims of the human rights violations directly, bypassing the victimizing government. Thus, the gamble was to develop contracts with private Dutch institutions, such as the Netherlands Organization for International Assistance (NOVIB), and the Humanist Institute for Development Cooperation (HIVOS), so that they in turn would support the Chilean ones.

Other governments also contributed, although their support was not quite as significant in monetary terms. For example, Mitterrand's France supported some activities in the Center for the Studies of Contemporary Reality (CERC) and the Academy for Christian Humanism.[42] Boeninger indicates: "Those who least collaborated with opposition institutions were the French and the British."[43]

International Cooperation in the Organization and Reconvening of the Opposition

We would see that there was a correlation between the internal and the external events that assisted in inducing three elements that today are recognized as having been influential to the Chilean transition: the coordination between two sectors, which before the coup were strongly antagonistic (the Socialist Party and the Christian Democrats); the creation of a strong and functional organization of private research centers, which acted in parallel to the institutions that the regime interfered with (e.g., universities); and the coordination between those who were exiled and those who were in the country, with the aim of preparing the transition to democracy.

The Union of Two Camps

If we could find a defining moment in international aid it would be the rapprochement of two camps that were highly antagonistic before 1973. During Salvador Allende's government, the supporters of the Popular Unity and those of the Christian Democrats opposed each other vehemently, being unable to reach even minimal consensus in order to save the democratic regime. Although this confrontation left many open wounds and resentment, the hard lesson of the military coup made both postures come to the conclusion that the only escape from totalitarianism was to put aside their differences and maximize their similarities.[44]

This objective was successfully captured by the supporting organizations. Núñez says in regard to the German Social Democrat Foundation, Friedrich Ebert:

"The Foundation understood that here was a specific solution, particular and unique, which was that the Socialists in Chile had the possibility of engaging with the Christian Democrats in order to overthrow a dictatorship."[45]

Thus, the international community never stopped thinking about how crucial this unification was to further a return to democracy. Lectures and seminars were organized that aimed to bring the two postures together. Already in 1976, in Venezuela, the Democratic Action and COPEI parties were successful in facilitating a reunion between Socialists, Communists, and Mapu with the Christian Democrats. The Swedish and German foundations were doing the same by organizing or supporting activities both in Chile and abroad.

The Konrad Adenauer Foundation (KAF) indicates in its institutional presentation: "After the military coup in 1973 and until the return to democracy in 1989, KAF lent its support through multiple activities destined to maintaining and developing the democratic structures. At the same time it dedicated itself to promote a rapprochement between the opposition forces and collaborated in paving the way toward the difficult transition to democracy."[46] This perhaps is one of the clearest objectives of the international cooperation.

Another salient factor of this reunion was the Christian Democrat's following of certain paradigms that had originated abroad, especially in Spain and Italy. Núñez indicates: "The way in which the Christian Democrats behaved is related to the way in which the Christian Democrats behaved in Italy and in the Spanish transition in particular. . . . Adolfo Suárez arrives in Chile and becomes a determining factor in strengthening the idea of unity among the Christian Democrats and the Socialists."[47] Indeed, the influence of Adolfo Suárez was paramount to the union of the Chilean opposition, insofar as he had been able to manage a transition in Spain, where he knew how to bring together such dissimilar tendencies as Social Democrats, Christian Democrats, and Liberals.

Other means of reunion were through activities in the opposition think tanks. The multiple activities developed during this time period, contributed significantly to restore mutual trust and understanding. Once again the CED was a pioneer in creating the program of "Political Compromise, National Project, and Democracy," which became a meeting place for political leaders.[48]

Strong Organizations as Facilitators of International Aid

The dictatorship brought forth one of the most interesting phenomena in regard to organizations. The closure of public places—especially universities—where Chilean intellectuals and academics could develop their work, meant finding new ways of continuing their work. In the beginning, most intellectuals sought refuge in international organizations such as the Latin American School of Social Sciences (FLACSO) or the Center for Economic Research and Education (CIDE).[49] Later, other organizations arose created by the opposition themselves, such as the Chilean Institute of Humanistic Studies (ICHEH) and the Center for Socio-Economic Research (ISEC). By the end of the seventies, there was an array of highly functional organizations engaged in the academic debate of politics and public policy. The Latin American Corporation for Economic Studies (CIEPLAN), the socialist Center for Social and Economic Studies (VECTOR), the Center for Social and Educational Studies (SUR), the Latin American Center for the Research of Political Economy (CLEPI), the Center of Study for Development (CED), and other institutions grouped under the aegis of the Academia de Humanismo Cristiano, including Centro de Estudios de la Realidad Contemporánea (CERC), Programa Interdisciplinario de Investigación en Educación (PIIE), and the Program for Work Economy (PET), all represented places offering a critical and functional mass that could propose political alternatives to the dictatorship.

The interesting thing is that each of these institutions was composed of people with some sort of political affinity. As noted by Puryear, "Each tended to have a single, relative cohesive political viewpoint, reflecting the traditional tendency of Chilean institutions to organize around political subcultures."[50] Likewise, this organization transcended its walls; direct contact with the different social sectors and, in particular, with the party leaders, established a well-prepared and confident organizational power.

It was this organization that allowed for the facilitation of international cooperation. International organizations tended to find their Chilean counterparts through these think tanks. Thus the NDI established itself with the CED and CIEPLAN (institutions tied to the Christian Democrats), the Konrad Adenauer Foundation with the ICHEH and with the two former ones, the Friedrich Ebert Foundation with VECTOR.

Ganuza notes: "It was paramount to international collaboration that Chile has a strong organization, because the donor institutions could find their counterparts in the country . . . but Chilean society was also a society where there were strong churches, which were very important for the international movement."[51]

Indeed, the Catholic Church was very important both internationally and inside the country, by becoming a strong element pressing for change in the regime. Cardenal Raúl Silva Henríquez was the founder of the Solidarity Vicarage, a church institution that succeeded in harboring within the country many who were persecuted by the government. Rev. Robert S. Pelton, C.S.C., from the University of Notre Dame was one of those in charge of smuggling documents (inside his cassock) from the vicarage to the safe haven of the Library of the University of Notre Dame.[52]

Likewise, the successor to Silva Henríquez, Francisco Fresno, collaborated for the creation of the National Agreement for the Transition to True Democracy amid the conflicts and protests of 1983. This agreement, composed of the whole political spectrum, received full support from the United States' Department of State for achieving a basis of agreement and consensus between all those who were aiming for a peaceful solution to the conflict. Representatives of six of the signing parties met with leaders of the United States for a conference in the Woodrow Wilson Center. The International Relations Committees of both the House and the Senate approved a resolution supporting the National Agreement and a peaceful Chilean transition.[53]

Exile and International Cooperation

One form of international aid was the harboring of Chilean refugees in European and South American countries.[54] Be it through exile or refugee programs, the Chilean diaspora became one of the most numerous in many of the host countries. The influence of this exile was felt in three ways. The first was the mere presence of Chilean refugees who contributed in a big way to the international community's becoming aware of what was happening inside the country. To this end, solidarity committees and organizations that broadcast the Chilean cause against the regime were created.[55] A grave mistake was made by the regime when it expelled noted intellectuals from the country, thus launching some of the key figures of the transition. Regarding this point, Genaro Arriagada says: "The dictatorship made serious mistakes. When it expelled (José) Zalaquett,[56] it created the future president of Amnesty International, or when it expelled Eugenio Velasco[57] and Jaime Castillo (Velasco)[58] it created two human rights leaders in the international community."[59] Many of them, like Letelier, became strong advocates and lobbyists for democratization in Chile and the concomitant condemnation of the dictatorship in the international arena.

The countries that received the most of the exiles and refugees were Venezuela, Spain, France, Italy, Sweden, and Canada, and, to a lesser degree, Australia, the United States, and countries in the Soviet bloc. Some of these countries supported their activities in exile. Recalling the 40 years of Chilean activity, the German foundation Friedrich Ebert states: "The FES program to support activities of the leaders in exile was based on three precepts: to provide grants to the leadership groups of the democratic parties in exile with the aim of allowing them to develop their political work, to avoid a fragmentation of the parties in exile and the structures that still existed in Chile, and to facilitate understanding between the groups."[60]

Another key element was the role that Roberts ascribes to the impact of the exile on socialist leaders.[61] In particular, he notes that their exposure to debates that were sponsored by Eurocommunists and Social Democrats during the eighties enabled the moderation of the Chilean Socialist Party. Senator Ricardo Núñez also notes:

> The exile (Chilean) was fortunate in never distancing itself from the dynamics being lived inside the country . . . it was very political . . . certain elements that flourish in international politics such as the substantial modifications experienced by the European Left—after Eurocommunism—allowed us all to prepare for the fall of the Berlin Wall and, from the point of view of the Left, enabled us to be prepared for a process of generation of different political forces . . . it allowed us to understand even better the phenomena that were occurring in the Latin American and, primarily, European Left. I feel that was the great contribution that the Chilean exile made toward transition.[62]

Thus, one of the cornerstones of the Chilean transition was the moderation of the Socialist Party. The fact that the opposition to the dictatorship could act in a unified manner is due in part to the impact the Western European Left had on the moderation of Socialist leaders. The agreements reached between Christian Democrats and Socialists, and their capacity to reach strategic consensus against the regime would have been unthinkable without this process of moderation of the Chilean Socialists.

A last point is the interrelation between the exiles and the internal resistance. The activities that encompassed both groups were primarily supported by international cooperation enabling the reunion of those inside and outside the country so they could plan their resistance to the regime. "Carlos Altamirano, Ricardo Núñez, and Jorge Arrate would meet with Ricardo Lagos and other people who attended the meetings which we sponsored."[63] As a matter of fact, many Chilean intellectuals and politicians were outside the country, but their ability to relate with those inside the country contributed to the strengthening of the movement.[64]

INTERPLAY BETWEEN INTERNAL AND EXTERNAL FACTORS: INTERNATIONAL AID FOR A RETURN TO DEMOCRACY

Pinochet's dictatorship was conditioned by various international political and economic factors. Both the economic crisis in 1982 and international condemnation during all his government's rule undermined the legitimacy of the regime. These factors were those that conditioned the relationship between international and local actors who later made possible the return to democracy. Indeed, the accession of Patricio Aylwin to the presidency in 1990, signaled an end to one of the most relevant and unifying phases of international cooperation in Chile. Unlike in any other time period, a single common objective succeeded in uniting a variety of public and private organizations that, through their programs of technical, financial, and political assistance, argued for the removal of the ruling military regime and a return to democracy.

However, a complete understanding of the international factors requires an analysis of the effects of direct international aid on the actors involved in the transition, especially the opposition.

Starting in 1983, the most significant international impacts to the transition arose from the international political, technical, and financial support granted to the democratic opposition. This helped to consolidate the union of two groups that had been radically opposed in 1973 (the Christian Democrat Party and the parties of the Popular Union), which allowed for a strong democratic opposition united in its objective of redemocratization. It also enabled the democratic forces to show themselves as agents capable of governing and maintaining political and economic stability in a democratic Chile.

Many countries were engaged in this cause. Organizations in Germany, the Netherlands, Sweden, Canada, and the United States among others worked—even in coordination with each other—to support the groups opposing the regime. An example of this is described in *Thinking Politics* by Jeffrey Puryear, who during the period of the military regime led the regional Ford Foundation office for the Andes and Southern Cone.[65] According to the author, one of the goals of this international cooperation was the creation of a critical mass of think tanks, so they could act as a significant force in the reconfiguration of democracy. Hence, Puryear attempts to demonstrate that the collaboration was able to achieve a great political impact at a critical moment in Chilean history by establishing and maintaining a framework of highly specialized professionals who were able to play an important role upon the return of democratic rules.[66] Thus, aid came to the opposition from multiple sources with multiple aims, although the greater part of this was related to research centers whose main or perhaps only means of funding came from donor institutions in Europe and the United States.[67]

Paul Sigmund, who is also concerned with the role of North American funding of the opposition groups, argues that this support allowed a counterbalance to the regime's control of funding resources and means.[68] For example, the US Congress's approval of a budget directly aimed at the promotion of democracy in Chile through the National Endowment for Democracy indicated the United States' interest in pressuring the regime toward liberalization and respect for human rights.

Nonetheless, the true effect of international cooperation on the Chilean political process is not that evident. For many key figures of the transition, international cooperation—although important—never became its main trigger. Boeninger indicates that "just as the military coup was not a product of CIA malice, but rather internal confrontation, the return to democracy was not a result of international cooperation."[69]

Likewise, there are those who point out that the international aid to the Chilean transition played a subordinate role to domestic political forces. As Genaro Arriagada indicates, "If the dictatorship doesn't have internal opposition, international aid is not triggered. The fundamental actor is internal opposition. International aid is subordinate and of relatively less importance. You can't overthrow a dictatorship from the outside."[70]

Therefore, what role did international aid have in the success of the transition? How significant was its impact on the return to democracy? Enrique Ganuza proposes an opposing view to that stated by the two key actors of Chilean transition previously mentioned.[71] "How could it be of little importance? International aid was crucial! Many countries received refugees and cooperated so that internal opposition could articulate itself. Almost all the resources of the opposition were purely from international aid."

Although these statements may be seen as opposing and even somewhat contradictory, the correlation between the two postures may be a good mechanism to understand the impact of international influence on the recovery of democracy. Certainly, a cooperation without formal, well-organized negotiators could have become the inefficient product of the groups' inability to absorb those resources and apply them adequately. The opposite is also true, for a permanent internal articulation and even survival of opposition groups could not have happened without the international aid that came from different countries. Further, the fact that international funds did not proceed from a single country allowed the groups opposing the government to articulate themselves with a certain level of autonomy. Each organization undertook its own agendas for research and political activism without the aid being subjected to conditions. Thus, international cooperation adapted itself to the plans of the recipients and not the other way around.

CONCLUSION

Although much has been written on the Chilean transition to democracy, not much analysis has been made of the international impact to this process. A discerning view of these factors allows one to appreciate that the international political impact had great significance and can help us to better understand the Chilean transition.

International demands and pressure to protect human rights led the regime to feel its legitimacy being undermined both internationally and nationally. This probably impelled it to begin a path of institutionalization. This path, born of the logic to establish a regime that restricted pluralism, a "protected democracy," was seriously altered by the impact of a regional economic crisis that forced the regime to allow for platforms of free expression. Hence, within the rules established by the regime itself, the Chilean transition began as the result of an international trigger, the debt crisis.

These two international impacts set the stage where the democratic opposition and the supporters of the dictatorship competed to impose their vision of the type of government that should rule Chile. In this competition, the international factor is once again transformed into political cooperation that had a role in supporting the democratic opposition. Thus, we can extrapolate some conclusions about the characteristics and functioning of the political cooperation on the Chilean transition.

As Whitehead confirms, the characteristics of European cooperation led the political organizations to look to Europe for aid, while the primarily military profile of North American aid prompted the military to look toward Washington.[72] In the case of Chile, this seems to have been the trend. Although the support of the NED was very important, one could argue that unlike the European cooperation—which primarily supported the democratic opposition—the aid provided, and especially the potential loss of said aid, by the United States to the government had a tremendous impact on the preferences of the regime's supporters toward democratization.

It is evident that collaboration with the political forces of the opposition came primarily from parties or other organizations that saw themselves as their counterparts abroad. The support that the Socialists, the Christian Democrats, and the Communists gave to the Social Democratic Party, the Christian Democratic Party (PDC), and the Communist Party in Chile is perceived as a natural course of events. In this way, as Whitehead suggests, the similarity of the European party systems to those of Latin America, especially that of Chile, favored cooperation. However, the same is not the case for the American political cooperation with Chile. Aid from NED was possible only through the NDI and its ties to leaders of the Christian Democrats. Although the Democratic Party in the United States is not the counterpart to the PDC in Chile, American aid became effective thanks to the exhaustive contacts between the leaders of both parties.

More importantly, however, the main lesson that we can extract from the Chilean case is that the central attribute that made international cooperation a functional element of the strategy of the democratic opposition was—as Whitehead suggests—that local agents had the liberty to act on behalf of their own interests and objectives. This enabled the aid to strengthen their ability to oppose the regime without losing their legitimacy within Chilean society. In other words, it allowed them to establish themselves as "authentic" organizations rather than puppets of foreign interests. Had there not been strong preexisting organizations with strate-gic autonomy from outside influences, international cooperation would not have had as favorable an impact on the Chilean transition.

NOTES

This research is framed within FONDECYT's Project No. 1110368 and the Millennium Nucleus for the Study of Stateness and Democracy in Latin America, Project No. NS100014. All caveats apply.

1. Ricardo Núñez, interview, March 2008. Núñez, a key actor of Chilean Transition, is currently senator for the Socialist Party.

2. Ibid.

3. According to the Chilean Constitution of the time, if no presidential candidate ob-tained a majority of the popular vote, Congress would choose one of the two candidates with the highest number of votes as the winner. Tradition was for Congress to vote for the candidate with the highest popular vote, regardless of margin.

4. Thomas E. Skidmore and Peter H. Smith, *Modern Latin America*, 6th ed. (New York: Oxford University Press, 2001), 127. See also Pilar Vergara, "Changes in the Economic Func-tions of the Chilean State under the Military Regime," in Arturo Valenzuela and Samuel Va-lenzuela, eds., *Military Rule in Chile: Dictatorship and Oppositions* (Baltimore: John Hopkins University Press, 1986), 90.

5. www.gwu.edu/~nsarchiv/news/20001113/#docs.

6. On October 16, 1970, an official command was issued to the CIA base in Chile, pro-nouncing: "It is firm and continuing policy that Allende be overthrown by a coup. It would be much preferable to have this transpire prior to 24 October but efforts in this regard will continue vigorously beyond this date. We are to continue to generate maximum pressure to-ward this end, utilizing every appropriate resource. It is imperative that these actions be im-plemented clandestinely and securely so that the USG and American hand be well hidden" (www.gwu.edu/~nsarchiv/NSAEBB/NSAEBB8/ch05-01.htm). But, US covert operations in Chile did not end there. Allende was subjected to destabilization efforts while in govern-ment, the coup was catalyzed by the United States, and after the military regime overthrew the democratically elected government, US efforts were aimed to bolster the military regime of Augusto Pinochet. On September 16, 1973, Kissinger talking to President Nixon told him: "We didn't do it [referring to the coup]. I mean we helped them . . . created the conditions as great as possible" (www.gwu.edu/~nsarchiv/NSAEBB/NSAEBB123/Box%2022,%20File% 203,%20Telcon,%209-16-73%2011,50%20Mr.%20Kissinger-The%20Pres%202.pdf).

7. See Centro de Estudios Públicos, ed., "Chile en los Archivos de la URSS (1959–1973): Documentos del Comité Central del PCUS y del Ministerio de Relaciones Exteriores de la URSS," *Estudios Públicos* 72 (Spring 1998): 391–476; Olga Ulianova and Eugenia Fediakova, "Algunos aspectos de la ayuda financiera del PC de la URSS al comunismo chileno durante la Guerra Fría," *Estudios Públicos* 72 (Spring 1998): 113–48; Joaquín Fermandois, *Chile y el mundo, 1970–1973* (Santiago: Ediciones Universidad Católica de Chile, 1985); Staff Report of the Select Committee to Study Governmental Operations, *Covert Action in Chile, 1963–1973: Staff Report* (Washington, D.C.: US Government Printing Office, 1975).

8. Barbara Stallings and Phillip Brock, "The Political Economy of Adjustment: Chile, 1973–1990," in Robert Bates and Anne Krueger, eds., *Political and Economic Interactions in Economic Policy Reform: Evidence of Eight Countries* (Cambridge, Mass.: Blackwell, 1993).

9. Pilar Vergara, *Auge y Caída del Neoliberalismo en Chile* (Santiago: FLACSO-Salesianos, 1985), 20.

10. The Chicago Boys were a group of young economists whose programs were the precursors of Chile's radical market-oriented reforms and who participated in the economic policy-making process from the beginning. In 1956, the Department of Economics at the University of Chicago and its counterpart from the Universidad Católica de Chile established an agreement that allowed promising young economists from Chile to pursue graduate studies in Chicago. Although they gained preeminence during the mid-1970s, they started to work together during the late 1960s from their own research center, the Centro de Estudios Socio-Económicos, where they prepared an economic program for the right-wing candidate Jorge Allesandri in the 1970 elections. This experience and subsequent collaborations culminated in the draft of an economic development program that came to be known as "The Brick" (El Ladrillo). On September 12 (only one day after the coup), "The Brick" was distributed among prominent members of the armed forces. Rossana Castiglioni, *The Politics of Social Policy Change in Chile and Uruguay: Retrenchment versus Maintenance, 1973–1998* (New York: Routledge, 2005), 28–29.

11. The Gremialistas, on the other hand, was a political movement founded in the late 1960s by Jaime Guzmán within Universidad Católica de Chile, in opposition to the reform of higher education taking place at the time. Although he failed, as a result of these actions the Labor Movement came into being. Guzmán was influenced by different schools of thought, including Osvaldo Lira, from Franco's Spain, with corporatist ideas.

12. Revista Hoy, February 23, 1988, cited by La Nación, at www.lanacion.cl/noticias/site/artic/20041207/pags/20041207144254.html.

13. For Huneeus, the regime sought three forms of legitimacy over its government: the historical legitimacy that sought to make an example of the failure of the Unidad Popular as well as liberal democracy's inability to contain Marxism, the economic legitimacy that tried to maintain good economic performance, and the legal legitimacy through the ratification of government through popular consultations and the approval of the constitution by a plebiscite. Carlos Huneeus, *El Régimen de Pinochet* (Santiago: Editorial Sudamericana, 2000).

14. Thomas M. Franck, "Of Gnats and Camels: Is there a Double Standard at the United Nations?" *American Journal of International Law* 78, no. 4 (1984): 826.

15. Robert Barros, *Constitutionalism and Dictatorship: Pinochet, the Junta, and the 1980 Constitution* (Cambridge: Cambridge University Press, 2002), 163.

16. Resolution No. 3448 of the General Assembly of the United Nations of December 9, 1975.

17. Frances Webber, "The Pinochet Case: The Struggle for the Realization of Human Rights," *Journal of Law and Society* 26, no. 4 (1999): 528.

18. At the time of the coup, Orlando Letelier was secretary of defense in Salvador Allende's government. After being arrested and tortured, he was released thanks to international pressure. He went to exile first in Venezuela and then, from 1975, in the United States (where he developed an intense activism against the regime of Pinochet). On September 21, 1976, in Washington he was killed by agents of the DINA (the Chilean secret service).

19. Upon the occasion of the visit to Chile of the assistant secretary of state for Inter-American affairs, Terence Todman, the regime announced the dissolution of the DINA and the creation of the National Information Center (CNI).

20. David Altman, *Direct Democracy Worldwide* (New York: Cambridge University Press, 2011), 102–4.

21. Huneeus, *El Régimen de Pinochet*.

22. Núñez interview.

23. Barros, *Constitutionalism and Dictatorship*; Claudia Heiss and Patricio Navia, "You Win Some, You Lose Some: Constitutional Reforms in Chile's Transition to Democracy," *Latin American Politics and Society* 49, no. 3 (2007): 163–90.

24. Data extracted from Huneeus, *El Régimen de Pinochet*.

25. Sources: Instituto Nacional de Estadísticas; Banco Central de Chile; and Castiglioni, *The Politics of Social Policy Change in Chile and Uruguay*.

26. Huneeus, *El Régimen de Pinochet*.

27. Altman, *Direct Democracy Worldwide*, 88–89.

28. See ibid.

29. Most notable among these were the National Endowment for Democracy and the German *Stiftungs*.

30. On February 2, 1988, 13 political parties and movements signed an agreement calling for the "no" vote. This coalition was named Concertación de Partidos por el NO, which was the springboard for the Concertación de Partidos por la Democracia that governed Chile from 1990 to 2011.

31. Julio María Sanguinetti, interview, Montevideo, February 22, 2008.

32. What is surprising is the lack of universities among those receiving international aid for the transition to democracy.

33. Núñez interview.

34. Edgardo Boeninger, interview, January 2008. Boeninger was a key actor of Chilean transition, former ministerial secretary general to the presidency during the first post-authoritarian regime.

35. Paul Sigmund, *The United States and Democracy in Chile* (Baltimore: John Hopkins University Press, 1993), 153.

36. Ibid.

37. National Democratic Institute, *La transición chilena hacia la democracia: El plebiscito presidencial de 1988* (Washington, D.C.: NDI, 1989).

38. Michael Pinto-Duschinsky, "Foreign Political Aid: The German Political Foundations and Their US Counterparts," *International Affairs* 67, no. 1 (1991): 33–63.

39. Luis Roniger and Mario Sznajder, "Exile Communities and Their Differential Institutional Dynamics: A Comparative Analysis of the Chilean and Uruguayan Political Diasporas," *Revista de Ciencia Política* 27, no. 1 (2007): 43–66.

40. International Development Research Centre, *The Path to Power* (Ottawa: IDRC Reports, 1992), 2.

41. Peter Baehr, "Concern for Development Aid and Fundamental Human Rights: The Dilemma as Faced by the Netherlands," *Human Rights Quarterly* 4, no. 1 (1982): 39–52.

42. Jeffrey Puryear, *Thinking Politics: Intellectuals and Democracy in Chile, 1973–1988* (Baltimore: Johns Hopkins University Press, 1994), 52.

43. Boeninger interview.

44. Robert Funk, "La lógica del aprendizaje político durante la consolidación democrática," in Manuel Alcántara and Leticia Ruiz, eds., *Chile: Política y modernización democrática* (Barcelona: Ediciones Bellaterra, 2006), 111–28.

45. Andreas Wille, *Hacia la democracia social . . . Cuatro Décadas de la Fundación Friedrich Ebert en Chile* (Santiago: FES, 2007), 25.

46. KAF, "Objetivos de la Fundación en Chile" (n.d.), www.kas.de/chile/es/pages/8005/.

47. Núñez interview.

48. Puryear, *Thinking Politics*.

49. The exile nourished other Latin American academies that took advantage of the opportunity to incorporate those affected by the repression—for example, FLACSO (Facultad Latinoamericana de Ciencias Sociales—the Latin American School of Social Sciences) in Argentina and the CIDE (Centro de Investigación y Docencia Económicas—Center for Economic Research and Education) in Mexico. In this respect, we might include the Kellogg Institute at the University of Notre Dame as one of the most prominent centers for Latin American intellectuals at the time. David Altman, "From Fukuoka to Santiago: Institutionalization of Political Science in Latin America," *PS-Political Science and Politics* 39, no. 1 (2006): 197.

50. Puryear, *Thinking Politics*, 48.

51. Enrique Ganuza, interview, March 2008. Ganuza was director of the Latin American and the Caribbean Division for the Swedish International Cooperation Agency during the eighties and is the current resident representative of the United Nations Development Programme in Chile.

52. Personal communication.

53. Sigmund, *The United States and Democracy in Chile*.

54. The political importance of Chilean exile reveals the significance that United Nations High Commissioner for Refugees (UNHCR) gave the protection of victims of political persecution in Chile. On September 20, 1973, just nine days after the coup, the UNHCR opened an office in Santiago and mobilized many efforts to facilitate the withdrawal from Chile of those politically persecuted by the regime and their reception in different countries. More than 20,000 people were assisted by UNHCR in those years (UNHCR, 2000).

55. Roniger and Sznajder, "Exile Communities and Their Differential Institutional Dynamics."

56. Attorney for the defense of human rights, who was exiled in 1976.

57. Politician of the Radical Party, exiled in 1976.

58. Prestigious attorney, who was exiled in 1976.

59. Genaro Arriagada, interview, March 2008.

60. Wille, *Hacia la democracia social*, 21.

61. Kenneth M. Roberts, *Deepening Democracy? The Modern Left and Social Movements in Chile and Peru* (Stanford, Calif.: Stanford University Press, 1998).

62. Núñez interview.

63. Ganuza interview.

64. Edgardo Boeninger, *Democracia en Chile: Lecciones para la Gobernabilidad*, 2nd ed. (Santiago: Editorial Andrés Bello, 1998).

65. Puryear, *Thinking Politics*.

66. Ibid., 9.

67. Ibid., 51.

68. Sigmund, *The United States and Democracy in Chile*, 167.

69. Boeninger interview.

70. Arriagada interview.

71. Ganuza interview.

72. Laurence Whitehead, "International Aspects of Democratization," in Guillermo O'Donnell, Philippe C. Schmitter, and Laurence Whitehead, eds., *Transition from Authoritarian Rule: Comparative Perspectives* (Baltimore: Johns Hopkins University Press, 1986), 3–46.

PART TWO

Incremental Transition Cases

CHAPTER NINE

Ghana

*Democratic Transition, Presidential Power,
and the World Bank*

ANTOINETTE HANDLEY

Ghana is widely regarded as a signal success in the African "wave" of democratizations of the 1990s. Since the country's return to constitutional rule in 1992, it has continued to maintain high levels of political competition and contestation within a stable and relatively free political environment.[1] Particularly impressive were the closely contested 2008–9 elections where, despite a very narrow margin of defeat and considerable political tension, the ruling New Patriotic Party (NPP) ceded power to the National Democratic Congress (NDC).[2] These elections also represented a second electoral turnover of power, Huntington's crucial measure of democratic consolidation.[3] Ghana thus represents an important case of a successful transition.

Over the entire period of the transition, domestic and international factors interacted in important ways but ultimately it may be that it was domestic perceptions of international factors that were decisive. Part of what makes this outcome so remarkable is that the Ghanaian transition was not initiated by a particularly insecure regime. On the contrary, while the ruling Provisional National Defense Council (PNDC) was vulnerable financially, in most other respects it was remarkably strong. After decades of severe economic and political crisis, Rawlings and his government had successfully reestablished a baseline level of stability for the country and overseen the recovery of the economy. As a result, Rawlings's government was popular with a broad stratum of the society and likely, in any case, to win a national ballot. This context was crucial to the initial decision to liberalize. It is less important in accounting for what was probably the more important decision—that is, not to reverse that liberalization when it resulted in the ruling party's electoral defeat.

This chapter draws on primary and secondary documents concerning the transition as well as detailed interviews and correspondence with more than 20 actors, many directly involved in the transition, including international diplomats, pro-democracy activists, and high-ranking members of the regime, including Rawlings himself. After reviewing the moment of transition, I consider the domestic modalities of the transition, the role of international pressures, and then the interaction between the various factors. I conclude by considering the wider implications of the argument.

A TRANSITION IN TWO PHASES

Ghana's transition unfolded gradually and in two distinct phases (table 9.1). In the first (1988–92), while there was some pressure from below, political change was primarily directed from the top down. In particular, it was the executive decision to move toward multiparty elections in 1992 that must be explained. Liberalization in Ghana represented a pragmatic response to an area of key (financial) vulnerability by an otherwise remarkably successful regime. This is not to say that the move was undertaken willingly; rather, then president Jerry Rawlings's perhaps misplaced perception that ongoing support from the international financial institutions (IFIs) depended vitally on political reform motivated him to return the country to constitutionalism. This consideration was reinforced by evidence that, if Rawlings did hold elections, he would likely win them. For students of Africa, aware that the World Bank routinely privileged progress on economic reform over the niceties of political reform, and conscious too of how unusual it is for the World Bank to punish a lack of political reform with a cessation of funding, this conclusion may come as a surprise. Nevertheless, I argue that Rawlings took the donors at their word and grudgingly embarked on escalating political reforms.

In the second phase (1992–2000), growing political freedoms and rising levels of competition facilitated a more evenhanded contest of power. Here the dynamics of liberalization took on a momentum of their own; opposition political parties grew more organized and astute, while the popularity of the ruling Provisional National Defense Council waned. Again, in this second phase, international support for democracy was important, this time helping to strengthen the domestic electoral process, but again, less important overall than the man at the center of power, Rawlings, and his decision making. Here the key moment was not the holding of any particular election but rather Rawlings's willingness to step down in 2000 when he reached his term limit and the third successive national election

TABLE 9.1.
Landmarks in Ghana's Transition

Phase 1		
1988–89	District Assembly elections; contested on a no-party basis	Political liberalization
1991–92	Consultative Assembly meets to draft new constitution	
April 18, 1992	Referendum to ratify draft constitution	
November 3, December 29, 1992	First multiparty national elections for parliament and the presidency; some dispute on how free and fair they are. NDC, led by Rawlings, wins.	First election (disputed)
Phase 2		
1996	Second multiparty presidential and parliamentary elections; widely regarded as free and fair. NDC, led by Rawlings, wins again.	Second election (free and fair)
2000	Third set of elections results in an alternation in power: Opposition NPP, led by Kufuor, wins the election and takes office.	First election-based alternation in power
2008	Fifth set of elections results in the narrow defeat of the ruling NPP. The NDC, under the leadership of Atta Mills, returns to power.	Second election-based alternation in power

handed power to his political opponents. In this phase, it is this decision to step down that must be explained, a difficult task. Here I argue that Rawlings was essentially trapped by the logic of earlier decisions, by the ongoing mobilization of bias in favor of the democratic process,[4] and by the unacceptable consequences he would have faced if he had chosen to overrule the electorate.

DOMESTIC DYNAMICS

The PNDC, under the leadership of Flight Lieutenant Rawlings, came to power by means of a military coup in 1981 in the midst of a severe economic crisis.[5] After initial, failed heterodox reforms, the PNDC turned to the World Bank and adopted a structural adjustment program (SAP) in 1983. These reforms and the renewed access to international finance that they permitted enabled the country's economic recovery over the course of that decade.[6] They subsequently led to its political liberalization too.

Any account of Ghanaian politics in this period must start with Rawlings himself as he was central to decision making in the PNDC. Rawlings was and is a controversial figure in Ghanaian politics, an undeniably charismatic leader who set himself up as a champion of the poor and hitherto marginalized. He was scathing about the corruption and elitism that he associated with the conduct of multiparty politics in Ghana and vowed to revolutionize the country's politics by demolishing the structural barriers that had long prevented meaningful participation by ordinary Ghanaians in political decision making. The democracy that he espoused however was a grass-roots, populist form of democracy. He is not and has never been a friend of Western liberal democracy, and this too shaped the nature of his regime, especially its first decade. Opposition figures (even those within the PNDC) and pro-democracy activists were detained and tortured.[7] In describing the atmosphere of the late 1980s and early 1990s, Gyimah-Boadi described how civil society "ha[d] been largely subdued through systematic political repression."[8]

Boafo-Arthur describes "feeble but persistent calls [in the late 1980s] . . . to return the country to constitutional rule" by various civil society organizations (CSOs) that were "not backed by any sustained public agitations . . . strong enough to compel the PNDC to concede."[9] Ghana's "culture of silence" was exacerbated by severe restrictions on the freedom of information and citizens' ability to contest the political process. State newspapers hewed closely to the official line and it was difficult for the unofficial press to survive.[10] As the transition unfolded, Ghanaian civil society and pro-democracy activists were emboldened by widening political freedoms and did receive some modest support from donors and the international community. However, for the most part, this support—and indeed popular political mobilization for democracy—followed rather than preceded the liberalization of politics in the first phase.

Instead, much of the impetus for change came from within the state. Political liberalization began in 1987 with the launch of the government's "Blue Book,"[11] paving the way for the holding of no-party District Assembly elections in the late 1980s.[12] These elections began to generate a sense of potential political reawakening, particularly as they were followed, in 1990, by a series of seminars held in each of the regions to debate the future of the Ghanaian polity. Because they were organized by the government, the seminars were regarded with suspicion by opposition-minded Ghanaians. There were significant constraints on what views could be expressed in these fora. Nonetheless, opponents of the regime did manage to use them to make their opposition to the "no-party" system clear, and something that one might call "civil society" began to revive.[13]

In the mid-1990s, a group of leftist activists began to try to organize a wide democratic front to unite Ghanaians to press for a return to constitutional rule and multiparty elections.[14] They successfully persuaded key liberal figures from the ranks of their former political rivals to join them. These efforts culminated in the launch in August 1990 of the Movement for Freedom and Justice (MFJ).[15] Over the next 20-odd months, the MFJ publicly and persistently articulated the case for multiparty democracy, in an environment where Rawlings's government continued to be hostile to that project. Moreover, MFJ reiterated a wide range of demands for greater political freedom.[16] These initiatives were all very impressive given the circumstances.[17] The MFJ's formation was part of a growing agitation for multiparty rule from a range of civil society actors including students, the Trades Union Council (TUC), professional associations such as the Ghana Bar Association, and the churches.[18]

Despite all of this, at no point did the MFJ and the other forces of civil society ever pose a real threat to the continued viability of the PNDC regime. If one considers the relatively modest scope of these organizations and that relatively few people were ever drawn into their core operations (especially by comparison with democratization movements elsewhere around the world), this was not an especially formidable opposition movement. Thus, while Rawlings was under some domestic pressure to democratize, he could probably have ignored these voices for some time.

However, if he was going to democratize at all, there were at least two good reasons to do so in the early 1990s. First, the economic recovery of the 1980s, along with Rawlings's own considerable personal popularity, made it likely that the PNDC would win even a genuinely free election. Sandbrook and Oelbaum cite two important surveys undertaken by the government in mid-1990 and late 1991. The very fact that these were commissioned is a significant indication that government was considering democratizing. Crucially, these surveys found that the PNDC would probably win an election, were one to be held.[19] Politically, the position of Rawlings and his team seemed relatively secure in terms of the popular vote. Second, taking no chances, Rawlings "fashioned security guarantees for himself and his fellow coup plotters by legislating immunity for the PNDC from prosecutions."[20] These two factors lowered the risks to the regime of liberalizing.

Accordingly, in May 1991 Rawlings confirmed that he would permit a return to multiparty elections;[21] in June he granted amnesty to all political exiles; and in late August the Consultative Assembly was inaugurated to draft a new constitution. While civil society was an important watchdog during this process,[22] local pro-democracy activists were largely unable to play a more dynamic role.

In preparation for the election, the ruling PNDC effectively transformed itself into a political party, renaming itself the NDC. The ruling party's election campaign enjoyed the advantages of an already established "brand" and organizational structure, as well as incumbency. Rawlings's partisans pressed into service many of the tools at the state's disposal, including the budget, as part of their electoral campaign.[23]

The opposition forces faced a tougher challenge: they had to start building the profile and platform of their new political parties from scratch, with little name recognition or access to the media to assist them. Most crucially perhaps, they had very little time to organize and remained divided among themselves all the way up to the elections (party politics was legalized just six months before the election date).[24]

And so, in that first election, Rawlings and his ruling party triumphed, winning close to 60 percent of the votes. Some in the opposition cried foul, but most election observers felt that the election results *did* fairly reflect popular sentiment. This vindicated those within the ruling party who had advocated political reform, and Rawlings became "the first sub-Saharan African military ruler to transform himself into the head of a civilian government through genuinely contested multiparty elections."[25]

The second phase of the transition, 1992–2000, provided an extended opportunity for behind-the-scenes reforms that greatly improved the legitimacy of Ghana's electoral process. This phase was significant chiefly for what did not occur: in 2000, a third set of national elections removed Rawlings's NDC from power, but no political turmoil erupted.

Some of the most important reforms in this second period were undertaken under the judicious guidance of the director of Ghana's Electoral Commission, Dr. Afari-Gyan.[26] With the support of bilateral donors, he oversaw the establishment of an Inter-Party Advisory Committee (IPAC) as "a forum for debating issues pertaining to implementation of the electoral program, electoral reform, [and] regulations designed to ensure an equitable and transparent election."[27] It was a stroke of genius: by involving high-level party officials in key decisions concerning the elections, IPAC secured not only their input on how to improve those processes but also their consent to the outcomes. As Jeffries points out, it is notable that the NDC government was prepared to support these reforms.[28] These incremental improvements paved the way for the second and successful set of elections, held in 1996, that would be widely regarded as free of significant unfairness.

Beyond the electoral process, progress on other markers of democratization was patchy but notable. The political space for opposition continued to open up,[29] albeit slowly and not without some reverses. While the constitution guaranteed the freedom of the press and there was a lively and wide-ranging set of views presented by a range of newspaper titles, private newspapers continued to face structural disadvantages.[30] In 1995 the deregulation of broadcasting permitted a proliferation of private radio stations.[31] The state itself was also being restructured: the Commission for Human Rights and Administrative Justice was established to protect the rights of ordinary Ghanaians and provide institutionalized redress against abuses by the state. By the time of the 1996 elections, the environment for opposition-minded actors was significantly more open than it had been four years earlier. The polls were energetically contested in an atmosphere markedly freer than in the previous election, and there was an almost 80 percent turnout of voters on election day.[32]

Again, the electoral process did receive some external financial support: $23 million was donated by international donors to ensure the smooth running of the elections.[33] Domestic and international poll observers were supported by international donors and by a coalition of Ghanaian actors, including many of those from CSOs that had been active in the struggle for democracy.[34]

Ghana's Electoral Commission continued to draw praise for its oversight of the elections. The actual conduct of the 1996 elections and perceptions of its fairness were improved by innovations that included the development of a new voters' roll; the use of voter identity cards, transparent ballot boxes, and cardboard voting screens; and the counting and public posting of votes at each polling station.[35]

In the contest for votes, the NDC continued to enjoy the advantage of its incumbency status.[36] It was no great surprise when the NDC won the national elections for a second time in 1996. Nonetheless, the structured and legitimate contestation of political power that the elections represented, and the revival of the party system that they facilitated, began to transform the tenor and conduct of politics in Ghana. Jeff Haynes reminds us that, "for the first time in nearly 20 years, the government had to answer publicly for its programs and policies."[37] This engendered a different kind of politics in Ghana, one that shaped the behavior not only of the government but of its opponents too.

In this second phase of Ghana's transition, what was critical was not so much what Rawlings and the PNDC did (i.e., continue to stage polls and respect the outcomes as long as they were winning) but what they did not do (namely, suspend the process when they did not win). The critical "turnover" test came with the third set of national elections in 2000 when voters favored the opposition.[38] When the results handed power to John Kufour and the opposition NPP, Rawlings, in accord with the constitution, stepped down from office.

From a review of domestic-level factors only, it is not entirely clear why. Granted, this was not the first time that he had "done the right thing": over a decade previously, as the leader of the Armed Forces Revolutionary Council, Rawlings had once before handed over power to a democratically elected government. As Jeffries argues, while Rawlings was highly skeptical of the merits of multiparty democracy, he does seem to have been "genuinely committed to maintaining social order and political stability"[39]—and to overturn the electoral results at this late stage would have been seriously destabilizing for the country. His behavior in 2000, therefore, was not totally unprecedented or out of character.

According to the Ghanaian constitution, Rawlings was not eligible to pursue a third term of office. Instead, first in June 1998 and nearly two years later again at Swedru, Rawlings had declared his support for his then deputy Atta Mills to serve as his successor. With these measures, Rawlings essentially blocked the way for his own wife to seek the party's nomination or for himself to stand again.[40] Finally, in December of that year after the results of the first round of presidential voting were largely in, Rawlings admitted in a radio interview that the NPP would probably win the next round, thus signaling, according to Paul Nugent, "an apparent willingness to bow to the verdict of the electorate."[41] Trapped by the logic of the reforms that he had set in motion, by his already announced choice of successor for leadership of the NDP, and by the quiet but steady process of liberalization and resurgence of the opposition that this facilitated, Rawlings graciously accepted the election results. Nonetheless, this decision remains one that is difficult to explain purely with recourse to domestic politics.

INTERNATIONAL FACTORS

The international context within which Ghana began its political liberalization was more favorable to multiparty democracy than it had been for decades. The collapse of the Soviet model from the late 1980s undermined the legitimacy of forms of governance that did not fit the Western, liberal mold—and, in particular, of those systems that did not involve multiparty elections. The triumph of Western liberalism[42] made it increasingly difficult for African governments to defend "no party" or populist forms of government. These trends were epitomized in the Harare Declaration that in 1991 affirmed "the individual's inalienable right to participate by means of free and democratic political processes in framing the society in which he or she lives."[43] This larger normative shift was especially significant for Ghana, which had long been sympathetic to alternative or leftist projects.[44] The inability of the Soviet Union to provide financial support to Ghana in its profoundest moment of economic crisis reinforced Ghana's policy turn to the West in the early 1980s, at least with respect to economics.

Across the rest of Africa, the end of the Cold War (and hence the end of financial and strategic support for African client states), along with worsening economic conditions across the continent contributed to a wave of regime transitions in the 1990s.[45] Bratton and van de Walle describe how, over a five-year period, the number of countries across the continent holding competitive elections quadrupled.[46] In their view, many undemocratic governments collapsed as the direct result of the financial crisis of the state, which grew increasingly incapable of (financially)

TABLE 9.2.
Ghana's Top Ten Trading Partners (ranked by total of both
imports and exports in Ghana cedis, 1986–87, and US dollars,
1996–97)

Rank	1986 and 1987	1996 and 1997
1	United Kingdom	United Kingdom
2	United States	Switzerland
3	China	United States
4	Nigeria	Netherlands
5	Netherlands	Japan
6	Japan	France
7	Togo	Italy
8	Soviet Union*	Belgium
9	Switzerland	Nigeria
10	France	Spain

Source: Quarterly Digest of Statistics, Republic of Ghana.
  *The Soviet Union was an important trading partner for Ghana until the late 1980s but obviously vanished from the list around this time; notably, its "spot" on the list was not replaced by Russia or any of the other former socialist states.

supporting a clientelist system. This logic could well have played out too in Ghana, given the extent of that country's economic crisis in the early 1980s. However, because the PNDC was one of the earliest adopters of a SAP on the subcontinent and rapidly became one of the favored sons of the World Bank, the Ghanaian government secured access to a new revenue stream both in excess of, and in advance of, that available to many other regimes across the continent, significantly bolstering the government's internal position vis-à-vis its citizens.

Ghana's international relationships for the transition period were therefore dominated by the West. During the 1980s and 1990s, the United Kingdom and the United States in particular featured consistently among Ghana's major trading partners; accordingly, along with their historical profile and their activist predispositions, these two states represented the most potent potential source of pressure (as far as individual states go) on the Ghanaian government.[47] While the Netherlands, Japan, and China were also important trading partners, these states employed a much more hands-off approach (table 9.2).

When we turn from trade to aid,[48] the United States again ranks highly. As can be seen in table 9.3, by the mid-1990s there was some overlap between Ghana's major bilateral donors and its major trading partners:[49] Japan, the United States, and the United Kingdom ranked consistently high in both rankings,[50] but again Japan did not energetically seek to shape Ghanaian politics.

Until 1996, democracy-related aid from the United States focused on elections,[51] with support funneled through the International Foundation for Election

TABLE 9.3.
Ghana's Major Bilateral Donors, 1995 (ranked by total annual net in millions of US dollars)

Rank	Country	Annual Net
1	Japan	122
2	United States	54
3	Germany	44
4	Denmark	35
5	Netherlands	30
6	France	23
7	Canada	23
8	United Kingdom	21

Source: Julie Hearn, "Foreign Political Aid, Democratization, and Civil Society in Ghana in the 1990s," *CDD-Ghana Research Paper*, 26 (Accra, Ghana: Center for Democracy and Development, Ghana, 2000), 8.

Systems (IFES) and the National Democratic Institute (NDI). The NDI, for example, supported a network of Ghanaian election observers and also ran programs for parliament and civil society.

For the German foundations, according to Hearn, strengthening democracy was the "primary objective."[52] The Friedrich Ebert Foundation in particular supported civil society organizations in Ghana, including the unions and the Ghana Journalists Association (GJA). They also hosted conferences and seminars in the mid-1990s focused on democratization. Direct support for democracy was less evident from the Konrad Adenauer Foundation and the Friedrich Naumann Foundation, which supported private-sector organizations. This is not unique to the Germans. Most financial aid in this period went not to those CSOs focused on political reform but rather to those associated with economic reform.[53]

The United Kingdom's overall level of aid to Ghana was surprisingly low given the trade figures and the embassy's prominence. In the late 1990s, British aid focused on "government structures and the media,"[54] providing support to state institutions and structures that would support "good governance." The British also funded the training of local journalists. Nonetheless, it was clear that the British, like the Americans, favored a return to constitutional and multiparty rule, and they pressed Rawlings's government to this end. For example, the forthright Baroness Lynda Chalker, director of the Overseas Development Administration (ODA), reportedly visited Ghana a couple of time a year and on these occasions would "lecture Rawlings on democracy."[55] The British also provided support to CSOs, including the GJA, but the United States, Germany (via the foundations), and the World Bank were the biggest donors to civil society.[56] Of all of Ghana's bilateral donors, the United States reportedly provided the most extensive and carefully thought-out support to civil society.[57]

All of this, considered in isolation, sounds reasonable. However, those who study aid comparatively are unequivocal that, in international terms, both the amount of aid specifically directed at fostering democratization and the total aid packages (including everything that could even indirectly be considered to be providing support to democratization) were small. What little "political" aid Ghana received tended to constitute support for "good governance" (often defined as the efficient operation of the state and public sector organs) rather than democracy per se.[58] The overall aid preferences did not look very different for the smaller European donors.

When it came to elections specifically (particularly those in 1992 and 1996), there was more substantial donor support, for the polls themselves, for observers, and for the Electoral Commission. The European Union, the Canadian International Development Agency (CIDA), the British ODA, the Danish International Development Agency (DANIDA), US Agency for International Development (USAID), and the IFES, for example, all supported IPAC and attended IPAC meetings.[59] The Europeans also supported voter education programs, as well as the work of Ghana's National Commission for Civic Education.[60]

This picture of low overall levels of aid, most of it linked to the economic reforms, can be explained by an international backdrop of dramatically declining overall levels of aid to sub-Saharan Africa. In the post–Cold War era, Africa effectively lost out to Eastern Europe as the darling of democratization-minded donors.[61] No longer seen as strategically important,[62] Africa came to be regarded primarily as a developmental challenge, with a concomitant stress on SAPs and economic recovery, and thus African countries received a surprisingly low level of democracy-related assistance.[63]

Despite all of this, Crawford argues that "Ghana provide[d] a particularly favorable context for democracy promotion measures."[64] The reason was Ghana's economic collapse in the 1980s and the country's consequent overwhelming reliance on the aid associated with the adoption of SAPs. For much of the 1980s and 1990s, Ghana was the site of the World Bank's largest lending program in Africa;[65] in turn, bank lending constituted the single largest aid contribution to Ghana. Ghana's relative poverty, its structural dependence on the large flows of finance associated with the country's adherence to structural adjustment, and its long-standing and economically consequential trade and diplomatic ties with Western states rendered it peculiarly vulnerable to even subtle pressures from the relevant states and actors.

And there is little doubt that there was pressure from key bilateral donors for Ghana to democratize. US ambassador Raymond Ewing described his embassy as "very interested in seeing Ghana develop politically towards a more democratic system."[66] Much of this pressure was applied indirectly and by means of strong

hints about the consequences that would follow any abandonment of political reform.[67] A key example was the speech given by President Clinton at a state dinner
for Rawlings where Clinton joked about the political predicament that he shared
with Rawlings: "He [Rawlings] was elected President by his fellow citizens in 1992.
He was re-elected in 1996. He loves his country, and he loves being President of
his country. His Constitution prevents him from running again." The implication
was clear: if Rawlings wanted to preserve his legacy—and if he wanted ongoing US
support—he, like Clinton, had to step down when his term limit ended.[68]

To recap, three features of bilateral aid to Ghana are noteworthy: first, overall levels of aid to Ghana were relatively modest, particularly by comparison with
many other parts of the world. Second, even within these modest aid budgets,
there was less focused and direct support for the broad project of democratization
than one might expect. Third, much of this funding began only *after* the transition
had already commenced. It can hardly be seen to have directly fostered democratization. What is striking is that despite all of this, Ghana's leadership came
to believe that continued support from the West and, in particular the ongoing
flow of IMF and World Bank funds, required progress on the political front. In a
conversation with this author, Rawlings claimed that he was compelled to "force
democracy down the throats" of reluctant and wary Ghanaians because "the State
Department was saying that there'll be no more IMF and World Bank facilities for
us [if we don't]."[69]

Granted, part of the power of aid lay in Ghana's acute financial vulnerability. Economic accounts of the time are clear that the economic reforms had not
succeeded in delivering the hoped-for revival of private-sector investment.[70] Instead, the ongoing recovery of the Ghanaian economy continued to depend on
public-sector spending—which required ongoing IFI support. The other part of
the power of aid lay in the coordination of aid priorities among Ghana's major
donors. One US diplomat described for example an informal monthly luncheon
in Accra where representatives from the major embassies would meet and discuss
their impressions of events in Ghana.[71] More formal and public coordination took
place via the Paris Club of donors. Donors acted together to reward moves to democratize. In the aftermath of the 1992 elections, for example, donors at the Paris
Club in June 1993 pledged $2.1 billion to Ghana. One of Ghana's leading scholars
of the country's foreign relations, Boafo-Arthur, judged this sum "an absolute vote
of confidence" in the country's new path.[72]

Perhaps the clearest evidence of concerted donor pressure and Ghanaian re-
sponsiveness, however, came in late 1991, early 1992 when donors had agreed
among themselves that, at their next Consultative Group meeting in Paris, one
of the items on the agenda would focus pressure on the Ghanaian government to

TABLE 9.4.
*Ghana's Major Multilateral Sources of Funds (net annual development
assistance in millions of US dollars)*

	1992	1993	1994	1995
World Bank	195	168	202	172
European Union	62	63	42	54

Source: Julie Hearn, "Foreign Political Aid, Democratization, and Civil Society in Ghana in the 1990s," *CDD-Ghana Research Paper*, 26 (Accra, Ghana: Center for Democracy and Development, Ghana, 2000), 9.

hold elections. This proposal would not have been kept hidden from the Ghanaians. Even as the donors were preparing to board the plane to Paris, the Ghanaian government announced the formation of the Consultative Assembly and the timetable for elections.[73]

However, it is misleading to consider only bilateral aid flows, which paled by comparison with multilateral giving, especially from the IMF and World Bank (table 9.4).[74] As Hearn points out, in the early 1990s loans from the World Bank alone "averaged 30 percent of Ghana's aid, rising to 37 percent in 1995."[75] Jeff Herbst has argued that the phenomenal influence of the IFIs rested not just in their substantial budgets but also in their gatekeeping roles.[76] A wide range of bilateral donors watched, and followed, the policy lead of the World Bank and its granting decisions. What it decided was immensely consequential for Ghana. However, what was crucial in Rawlings's calculations here were his own perceptions (or misperceptions?) of how World Bank and IMF lending decisions were made. For reasons that are not entirely clear, Rawlings determined that the US State Department's preference for multiparty democracy in Ghana weighed decisively in IFI lending decisions, though he may have been conflating and misreading distinct multilateral policy developments.

In 1989 a new clause was introduced into the Lomé Convention, the agreement that regulated trade relations between European states and developing countries: article 5 of the Convention now prioritized respect for human rights and signaled the emergence of a new set of political concerns even in economic areas traditionally regarded as outside of the realm of politics.[77] Boafo-Arthur reminds us that in the same year the World Bank's 1989 report on adjustment in Africa signaled the onset of political conditionalities, a shift in emphasis for the bank that had hitherto focused exclusively on economic factors. Henceforth the World Bank would consider a wider set of "political barriers to economic development."[78] The new language of "governance" did not provide direct or explicit support for democratization but did emphasize regime characteristics, such as transparency and accountability. This new emphasis was also articulated at a country-program level; Aidoo points, for example, to the World Bank's 1992 country strategy paper for Ghana where the bank "advocated broader participation [for Ghanaians] in political life."[79] Consequential bias was effectively being mobilized on the international front.[80]

Rawlings was not alone in his assumptions about the preferences of the IFIs. It is widely held in Ghana that it was the World Bank that forced the PNDC to liberalize its politics and make the transition to multiparty democracy. This contention is surprising and, on the face of it, unlikely. The World Bank abjures involvement in the partisan politics of the countries to which it lends. Only relatively recently had the bank begun to pay attention to the political conditions that might facilitate economic reform, and even here, in much of its work across Africa the bank has privileged progress on economic reform above a consideration of political concerns.

Rawlings's claim about the World Bank's influence is also hard to verify directly. First, there is no publicly accessible paper trail that might establish the truth or falsity of this assertion. The bank's resident representative for the period under question, Ravi Kanbur, refused this author's request for an interview on the subject, referring her instead to a chapter that he had written critical of aid and economic conditionalities more broadly[81]—a response that is hard to interpret for what it says about the bank's particular stance on political reform in Ghana.

There is, however, a good deal of mostly indirect evidence that key Ghanaian decision makers believed that continued World Bank support depended on political reform. Perhaps the key evidence comes from Jerry Rawlings himself. In his wide-ranging conversation with the author, Rawlings directly attributed (or blamed, in his view) the move to multiparty democracy on the need to secure the next tranche of funding from the bank and to threats from donors (the United States in particular) that this would not be forthcoming if suitable political progress was not made.[82]

On reflection, one can reconstruct how this view might have arisen. I have argued that there was a high level of donor coordination epitomized, for example, by regular meetings between the USAID director and the World Bank mission in Ghana. I have also alluded to subtle shifts in World Bank policy concerning governance that Ghanaian decision makers might have read as explicit support for democracy per se.[83] In an interview with Maame Gyekey-Jandoh, Daniel Boakeye, an economist with the World Bank, described the dynamics as follows:

> The World Bank did not directly insist that Ghana change from military to civilian rule, but it promoted "good governance" for many years. Good governance has many dimensions—political, economic, social accountability—and the Bank tries to promote all these aspects of governance progressively. The Bank has a rating under

Country Policy and Institutional Assessment (CPIA). This assessment is often shared with governments, where based on certain criteria such as the extent of rule of law, human rights protection (basically democratization), particular countries are given more aid if they are perceived to be progressing with regard to the criteria for the assessment. In effect, there is no hard and fast rule about not supporting military regimes, but when the good governance conditions are adhered to, aid is scaled up.[84]

From the Ghanaian government's perspective, the subtle distinction between "good governance" and "democracy" was elided—and thence the connection to aid conditionality. According to Eugene Nyambal, senior strategy officer with the International Finance Corporation, Rawlings "understood that to get continuous flow of money from the IMF, he needed to be less authoritarian and have a more open society. . . . Without money, Rawlings' government would have been weakened, and since the US had to agree to loans, Rawlings' move to democracy pleased the US and opened the doors for further aid."[85]

Again, what is crucial here is the coordination among donors. Haynes claims that "the IMF and World Bank, as well as foreign governments including those of Britain and America, made it plain that aid and loan flows could be reduced, held up or even halted unless moves towards democracy began."[86] These arguments were confirmed by my discussions with Rawlings on these matters.

I should caution that interviews can be confusing here: in conversation, Ghanaian sources often elide the World Bank, IMF, and the United States, not necessarily seeing them as distinct actors. This tendency in itself is telling: pressure would have come principally from the United States (for elections) and the World Bank (for "good governance"), but it could well have been experienced as coming from all of them (and from other aligned donors such as Germany and the United Kingdom, too), almost indistinguishably.[87] These connections are made clear by Eugene Nyambal, in a continuation of the interview cited earlier:

> There were no explicit political conditionalities, but rather policy or institutional-based conditionalities; this is because the Bank and IMF are apolitical organizations. But because they are the foreign policy arm of the United States, if a country does not have good relations with the US, it cannot get loans from the IMF.[88]

According to Paa Kwesi Amissah-Arthur, deputy finance minister in the PNDC, via "snapshots of single interventions . . . it was still clear that democracy issues were important to Western government and multilateral institutions."[89] Beyond such fora as the Paris Club, there is little evidence that the donors' messages concerning democratization were being directly administered via the IFIs. Nonetheless, it is clear that more important donors were pressing the need for political reform with Ghana's decision makers and that those decision makers understood the ongoing flow of IFI funds to be directly connected to and contingent on political liberalization. The multilateral donors—and the World Bank in particular—contributed a great deal to the state's budget in the short term and to the country's economic recovery in the medium term. Even a relatively small signal from this source would have been disproportionately influential.

THE INTERPLAY BETWEEN INTERNAL AND EXTERNAL FACTORS

For the first phase one of the transition, foreign-funded support of democratic activists and democratization (e.g., funding for CSOs or the independent media) was not in and of itself a significant factor. For the most part, such funding was limited and post facto, much of it only really starting in the late 1990s, and most aid was directed instead to supporting economic liberalization.[90] To the extent that some funding went to civil society, it most often went to private-sector institutions rather than actors more explicitly concerned with democratization.[91]

What was crucial in the end was the perceived role of the World Bank—hardly the most obvious ally for democratic activists. Put more precisely, it was the leverage associated with the overall flow of aid, rather than the relatively small amount of bilateral aid directly intended to foster democratization, that was decisive-along with a consistent and coherent message from allied donors and the connection that the Ghanaian executive drew between continued World Bank funding and ongoing democratization. Without these pressures, directed right at Ghana's (financial) Achilles' heel, the bravery and struggles of civil society activists within Ghana would probably have been insufficient, on their own, to accomplish a successful transition.

The dynamics in the second phase were different. As the course of economic reform began to falter over the course of the 1990s, the government's reliance on the IFIs deepened. This effectively weakened the position of the state at a time when the momentum of reform and the strength of opposition and democratically minded actors (both in and out of government) were quietly growing. These dynamics essentially presented Rawlings with an unpalatable set of choices in 2000: he could reject the results of the third election, but if he did so, he would probably risk many of the significant accomplishments that his government had achieved over his years in office and which had contributed to his own reputation. He may well have been able to cling to power, but the money and the international support that had made Ghana's political and economic recovery possible would, he believed, almost certainly drain away, and those advances would be hard to sustain in such an event. It was an unpalatable prospect, and one he ultimately walked away from.

CONCLUSION

How are we to judge Rawlings and his government and the impact of international forces on their decision making? A comparison with the Ugandan case might be instructive. Rawlings's model of no-party democracy was, as Richard Crook points out, inspired by the same "populist theories of participatory, community-led democracy which idealized the consensual character of 'traditional' village life and rejected the relevance of political parties" as those championed by President Yoweri Museveni of Uganda.[92] There are suggestive similarities—and differences—between these two cases. Both Museveni and Rawlings had come to power by military means but had not headed up military governments once in office; both had enjoyed remarkable success in stabilizing their respective societies, politically and economically, pulling them each back from the brink of total collapse and had been feted internationally for their accomplishments. Both countries had embarked on SAPs under the tutelage of the World Bank—and yet in Ghana's case, the country successfully made the transition to multiparty democracy, whereas Uganda did not. How are we to understand this difference?

Because of the opacity of World Bank operations, we do not know how behind-the-scenes World Bank pressures on the two countries may have differed. There are some compelling reasons why Rawlings might both have come under greater donor pressure to reform and have been less able to resist that pressure than Museveni—and these reasons center on security.

As devastating as Ghana's political conflicts of the 1960s and the 1970s were, they had mostly been confined within the country's borders and, while occasionally violent, had not spawned sustained and regionalized military combat. This was not the case with Uganda. Museveni's Uganda had to grapple not only with the devastating legacy of the Amin and Obote years (including the war with Tanzania) and the ongoing conflict in the north of the country but also—and perhaps more crucially—with its ongoing entanglements in a series of other regional conflicts. In the 1990s, a stable Ugandan state was regarded by many donors as vital to the ongoing stabilization of Uganda itself and to the resolution of regional conflicts. Because of his dominant role within that state, and because of the military and tactical skill that he has showed, Museveni himself was regarded by many as indispensable to that stabilization project.

The ongoing predations of the Lord's Resistance Army in northern Uganda received wide and sensationalistic international coverage. The horrors of Rwanda in 1994 provided a dramatic demonstration of just how devastating the consequences of instability and the interlocking conflicts of the Great Lakes region could be. It seems entirely plausible that Museveni, in response to donor pressure to democratize, would have been able to counter that it was regional and domestic stability that ought to be the priority in this context rather than a headlong rush to Western-style democracy.[93]

Rawlings could make no comparable arguments. While there continued to be political tensions in Ghana over the course of the 1990s, there was nothing equivalent to the low-grade civil war being waged in Uganda's North. Again, in contrast with the Great Lakes region, Africa's west coast was relatively calm. Granted, the situation in Cote d'Ivoire unraveled spectacularly in the late 1990s, but there was not a strong sense that that conflict was directly connected to either Ghana or Rawlings himself. Rawlings could not plausibly have put himself forward as central to the resolution of any potentially destabilizing regionalized conflict in order to deflect pressure for political reform.[94]

For donors concerned with political stability, Ghana's long-standing two-party system quickly produced a clear institutionalized competitor and potential successor to Rawlings and his NDC. The same scenario did not appear likely in Uganda—raising the question therefore of who would lead that state should Museveni be forced to step down? Making a final judgment about what ultimately shaped Uganda's and Ghana's divergent outcomes will require detailed archival work; it appears, however, that while both leaders may have come under some pressure to reform, Museveni would have been able to argue that security concerns trumped democratic niceties, thus calling the donors' bluff that they would cut aid if there was no political reform. Rawlings, by contrast, blinked.

The result of these different contexts—and their different outcomes—is that Ghana has successfully completed another set of democratic elections and achieved its second democratically effected regime change. Multiparty politics in that country has weathered some significant tensions including an extremely closely contested election, and both the NPP and the NDC, its two major parties, have survived a leadership succession. Uganda, by contrast, continues to be ruled by the same man, Yoweri Museveni, and Ugandans grumble increasingly about the once-respected leader's inability to delegate and his apparent determination to stay in office. More troubling, when the time comes to find a successor to Museveni, there is little reason to believe that this will be democratically or smoothly accomplished. While democracy has not solved all of the problems that Ghanaians face, the succession problem at least is not one of those. For this, we may well have Rawlings and his misperceptions to thank.

NOTES

1. One should not be too complacent about the outcomes in Ghana. While there has been remarkable progress in that country over the past 20 years, there are still considerable obstacles to the full realization of democracy. Political competition in Ghana is still characterized by patronage and dominated by elites; the full participation of the country's poorest citizens in political decision making remains constrained. Jeff Haynes, "The Possibility of Democratic Consolidation in Ghana," *Democratization* 6, no. 1 (1999): 49.

2. For accounts of these elections and their implications, see E. Gyimah-Boadi, "Another Step Forward for Ghana," *Journal of Democracy* 20, no. 2 (2009): 138–52; Abdul-Gafaru Abdulai and Gordon Crawford, "Consolidating Democracy in Ghana: Progress and Prospects?" *Democratization* 17, no. 1 (2010): 26–67.

3. Samuel P. Huntington, *The Third Wave: Democratization in the Late Twentieth Century* (Norman: University of Oklahoma Press, 1991).

4. Many thanks to Jeff Herbst for this point. As he has noted, one can see in the Ghanaian transition "a set of predominant values, beliefs, rituals, and institutional procedures ('rules of the game') that operate[d] systematically and consistently to the benefits of certain persons and groups at the expense of others." Peter Bachrach and Morton Baratz, *Power and Poverty: Theory and Practice* (New York: Oxford University Press, 1970), 43. In this case, there was an important set of convergences around the value of Western-style democracy and multiparty elections, from both international and certain domestic actors.

5. For an excellent account of this period and its difficulties, see Douglas Rimmer, *Staying Poor: Ghana's Political Economy, 1950–1990* (Oxford: Pergamon Press, 1992).

6. Jeffrey Herbst, *The Politics of Reform in Ghana, 1982–1991* (Berkeley: University of California Press, 1993).

7. Amnesty International, Human Rights Watch, and the British All Party Parliamentary Human Rights Group played an important role in keeping a spotlight on political detainees and hence helping to protect them to some degree at this time. Kwesi Pratt Jr., interview, December 12, 2007; Akoto Ampaw, interview, December 17, 2007.

8. E. Gyimah-Boadi, "Ghana: Adjustment, State Rehabilitation and Democratization," in Thandika Mkandawire and Adebayo Olukoshi, eds., *Between Liberalisation and Oppression: The Politics of Structural Adjustment in Africa* (Dakar, Senegal: CODESRIA, 1995), 226.

9. Kwame Boafo-Arthur, "Prelude to Constitutional Rule: An Assessment of the Process," in Kwame A. Ninsin and Francis K. Drah, eds., *Ghana's Transition to Constitutional Rule* (Accra, Ghana: Ghana Universities Press, 1991), 42–43.

10. Mike Oquaye, "Government and Politics in Contemporary Ghana (1992–1999): A Study" (Accra, Ghana: African Governance Institute, 2000), 40.

11. Formally known as Unattributed, "District Political Authority and Modalities for District Level Elections" (Accra, Ghana: National Commission for Democracy, 1987).

12. The prohibition on parties aside, these bodies were far from democratic as one-third of their membership was appointed by the state. Kwamena Ahwoi, interview, December 11, 2007; Jerry John Rawlings, interview, December 15, 2007.

13. Civil society organizations spoke in favor of multiparty democracy including the Ghana National Association of Teachers, the Ghana Registered Nurses Association, the Ghana Medical Association, and the churches. For a critical review of the idea of civil society and how it is deployed in Ghana, see Lindsay Whitfield, "Civil Society as Idea and Civil Society as Process: The Case of Ghana," *Oxford Development Studies* 31, no. 3 (2003): 379–400.

14. Hon. John Ndebugre was a key proponent of this idea. John Akparibo Ndebugre, interview, December 13, 2007; A. Owusu Gyimah, interview, December 14, 2007.

15. Owusu Gyimah, unpublished mimeo, 2007; Ndebugre interview; Ampaw interview; Akoto Ampaw, speech delivered at symposium organized by Movement for Freedom and Justice at the YMCA, August 27, 1990.

16. For example, the MFJ published a comprehensive list of the names of all those being held as political prisoners and being detained without trial, to serve as added pressure for their release. Owusu Gyimah, unpublished handwritten mimeo, undated.

17. Movement activists received very little outside funding, if any at all, although they did set up committees among their supporters in London and in the United States. Ndebugre interview; Pratt interview.

18. Thomas Maxwell Aidoo, "The Context and Provenance of Democratization in Ghana, 1990–1992," *Historia Actual Online* 9 (2006): 10–11.

19. Richard Sandbrook and Jay Oelbaum, "Reforming the Political Kingdom: Governance and Development in Ghana's Fourth Republic," *Critical Perspectives*, no. 2 (1999): 11.

20. Antoinette Handley and Greg Mills, "From Military Coups to Multiparty Elections: The Ghanaian Military-Civil Transition," in *Working Paper Series* (The Hague: Conflict Research Unit, Netherlands Institute of International Relations, 2001), 22.

21. Aidoo, "The Context and Provenance of Democratization in Ghana, 1990–1992," 14.

22. They pressed for a more thoroughgoing transition to democracy, for the replacement of the National Commission for Democracy with a nonpartisan electoral commission, for the dropping of all conditions for return of exiles, and for an end to government's unilateral control over the composition of the proposed Consultative Assembly.

23. Richard Sandbrook and Jay Oelbaum, "Reforming Dysfunctional Institutions through Democratisation? Reflections on Ghana," *Journal of Modern African Studies* 35, no. 4 (1997): 603–46; Sandbrook and Oelbaum, "Reforming the Political Kingdom." To be fair, it should also be said that one of the NDC's strongest advantages was the government's record of successful economic reform, economic recovery, and broader political stabilization.

24. Haynes, "The Possibility of Democratic Consolidation in Ghana," 112.

25. Robin Luckham, "Crafting Democratic Control over the Military: A Comparative Analysis of South Korea, Chile and Ghana," *Democratization* 3, no. 3 (2007): 237.

26. The commission is highly regarded by a wide range of observers. See, for example, Daniel A Smith, "The Structural Underpinnings of Ghana's December 2000 Elections," in *Critical Perspectives*, no. 6 (Legon, Ghana: Ghana Center for Democratic Development, 2001), 26; Gordon Crawford, "Democratisation in Ghana: Assessing the Impact of Political Aid (1997–2003)," paper presented at the ECPR Marburg conference, September 18–20, 2003, 4.

27. Ernest Dumor, "Keynote Address: The 1996 Elections and Democratic Consolidation," in Joseph R. A. Ayee, ed., *The 1996 General Elections and Democratic Consolidation in Ghana* (Legon, Ghana: Department of Political Science, University of Ghana, undated), 26.

28. Richard Jeffries, "The Ghanaian Elections of 1996: Towards the Consolidation of Democracy?" *African Affairs* 97, no. 387 (1998): 197.

29. Oquaye, "Government and Politics in Contemporary Ghana (1992–1999)," 55.

30. Ibid., 42–44. For a fascinating discussion of both private and government-owned newspapers in Ghana, see Jennifer Hasty, *The Press and Political Culture in Ghana* (Bloomington: Indiana University Press, 2005).

31. Chris Ogbondah, "Democratization and the Media in West Africa: An Analysis of Recent Constitutional and Legislative Reforms for Press Freedom in Ghana and Nigeria," *West Africa Review*, no. 6 (2004): 9–10.

32. Joseph R. A. Ayee, "The 1996 Elections: An Overview," in Ayee, *The 1996 General Elections and Democratic Consolidation in Ghana*, 46.

33. Haynes, "The Possibility of Democratic Consolidation in Ghana," 116.

34. Oquaye, "Government and Politics in Contemporary Ghana (1992–1999)," 8; Haynes, "The Possibility of Democratic Consolidation in Ghana," 116; Joseph R. A. Ayee, "Election Management and Democratic Consolidation: The Electoral Commission of Ghana," in Ayee, *The 1996 General Elections and Democratic Consolidation in Ghana*, 65. Both the Electoral Commission and IPAC were supported by funding from USAID, IFES, and the British government. Smith, "The Structural Underpinnings of Ghana's December 2000 Elections," 5.

35. Ayee, "Election Management and Democratic Consolidation," 62–63.

36. Antoinette Handley, *Business and the State in Africa: Economic Policymaking in the Neo-Liberal Era* (Cambridge: Cambridge University Press, 2008).

37. Haynes, "The Possibility of Democratic Consolidation in Ghana," 105.

38. These elections were supported by international donors to the tune of $8.4 million. Crawford, "Democratisation in Ghana," 32. For a detailed analysis of the 2000 elections, see Joseph R. A. Ayee, ed., *Deepening Democracy in Ghana: Politics of the 2000 Elections* (Accra, Ghana: Freedom Publications, 2001). For a more critical analysis, see Smith, "The Structural Underpinnings of Ghana's December 2000 Elections."

39. Jeffries, "The Ghanaian Elections of 1996," 197.

40. See a discussion of the internal NDC politicking in Paul Nugent, "Winners, Losers and Also Rans: Money, Moral Authority and Voting Patterns in the Ghana 2000 Elections," *African Affairs* 100, no. 400 (2001): 413–15. See also Ivor Agyeman-Duah, *Between Faith and History: A Biography of J. A. Kufuor* (Banbury, Oxfordshire: Ayebia Clarke Publishing, 2003), 73. This decision is difficult to interpret for what it signified about Rawlings's intention to step out of active politics. On the one hand, by blocking his wife's ambitions, Rawlings did appear to be locking his household out of the race for political power. On the other hand, by sponsoring a candidate who was little known to the public and lacked a strong independent base within the party, Rawlings may have been attempting to fashion a new "puppet" through whom he could continue to exercise power. As Agyeman-Duah notes, "Atta Mills . . . promised Ghanaians that if he were elected, he would consult Rawlings 24 hours a day." Agyeman-Duah, *Between Faith and History*, 82.

41. Nugent, "Winners, Losers and Also Rans," 406.

42. Francis Fukuyama, *The End of History and the Last Man* (Toronto: Maxwell Macmillan Canada, 1992).

43. Commonwealth Heads of Government, "Harare Commonwealth Declaration," Commonwealth Secretariat, www.thecommonwealth.org/Internal/20723/34457/harare_commonwealth_declaration/.

44. In its early days, the Rawlings government had associated itself with and even self-consciously modeled itself on leftist regimes, such as the Sandanistas in Nicaragua, Fidel Castro's Cuba, Muammar Qaddafi's Libya and Yoweri Museveni's Uganda.

45. Michael Bratton and Nicolas van de Walle, *Democratic Experiments in Africa: Regime Transitions in Comparative Perspective* (Cambridge: Cambridge University Press, 1997), 3.

46. Ibid., 7.

47. A more thorough analysis of Ghanaian trading patterns and how these might have served as an indirect source of pressure on Ghanaian decision making is hindered by the absence of reliable trade statistics for the crucial period between 1988 and 1995.

48. In the section that follows I draw heavily on the analysis of Gordon Crawford and Julie Hearn respectively.

49. This ranking, drawn from 1995 figures, is fairly representative of the period under question.

50. Much of the Japanese aid is developmental and focused on service provision, and therefore of less direct relevance to the transition politics. Julie Hearn, "Foreign Political Aid, Democratization, and Civil Society in Ghana in the 1990s," in *CDD-Ghana Research Paper* (Accra, Ghana: Center for Democracy and Development, Ghana, 2000), 9.

51. Ibid., 14.

52. Ibid., 22.

53. Ibid., 24.

54. Ibid., 10.

55. Cited in Maame Gyekye-Jandoh, "Explaining Democratization in Africa: The Case of Ghana" (Ph.D. diss., Temple University, 2006), 127.

56. Hearn, "Foreign Political Aid, Democratization, and Civil Society in Ghana in the 1990s," 2.

57. Ibid., 12–14.

58. This framework endorsed the principles of good governance because of their role in ensuring the success of the economic reform program, rather than as constituting a political good in their own right.

59. Ayee, "Election Management and Democratic Consolidation," 64.

60. Ibid., 65.

61. Gordon Crawford, "The European Union and Democracy Promotion in Africa: The Case of Ghana," *European Journal of Development Research* 17, no. 4 (2005): 589.

62. Ewing, for example, described US interests in Ghana in the early 1990s as "limited." Charles Stuart Kennedy, "Interview with Raymond C. Ewing," 35, Foreign Affairs Oral History Collection of the Association for Diplomatic Studies and Training, American Memory, Library of Congress, Washington, D.C., 1993.

63. Crawford, "The European Union and Democracy Promotion in Africa," 572–73, 579.

64. Ibid., 572.

65. Hearn, "Foreign Political Aid, Democratization, and Civil Society in Ghana in the 1990s," 8.

66. Kennedy, "Interview with Raymond C. Ewing," 35.

67. Senior Western diplomat, telephone interview, August 20, 2009.

68. Bill Clinton, "Remarks at a State Dinner Honoring President Rawlings of Ghana," transcript, National Archives and Records Administration, Washington, D.C., Weekly Compilation of Presidential Documents, March 1, 1999.

69. Rawlings interview.

70. See, for example, Institute of Statistical Social and Economic Research, "The State of the Ghanaian Economy in 1991" (Legon, Ghana: Institute of Statistical Social and Economic Research, University of Ghana, 1992).

71. Senior US diplomat, telephone interview, March 13, 2008.

72. Kwame Boafo-Arthur, "Ghana: Structural Adjustment, Democratization, and the Politics of Continuity," *African Studies Review* 42, no. 2 (1999): 64.

73. Senior US diplomat interview.

74. Crawford, "Democratisation in Ghana," 26.

75. Hearn, "Foreign Political Aid, Democratization, and Civil Society in Ghana in the 1990s," 19.

76. Personal correspondence with Jeff Herbst.

77. Crawford, "The European Union and Democracy Promotion in Africa," 575.

78. Boafo-Arthur, "Ghana: Structural Adjustment, Democratization, and the Politics of Continuity."

79. Aidoo, "The Context and Provenance of Democratization in Ghana, 1990–1992," 15.

80. Bachrach and Baratz, *Power and Poverty*.

81. Ravi Kanbur, "Aid, Conditionality and Debt in Africa," in Finn Tarp, ed., *Foreign Aid and Development, Lessons Learnt and Directions for the Future* (London: Routledge, 2000): 409–22.

82. American ambassador Edward Brynn terminated US funding for an organization being run by Mrs. Rawlings on the grounds that, rather than being a genuine attempt to empower women, it was politically partisan. The threat to cut off funding then might have seemed very real to the Rawlings household. Charles Stuart Kennedy, "Interview with Edward Brynn," Foreign Affairs Oral History Collection of the Association for Diplomatic Studies and Training, American Memory, Library of Congress, Washington, D.C., 2000, 43.

83. Gyekye-Jandoh, "Explaining Democratization in Africa," 124.

84. Ibid., 117–18.

85. Interview with Maame Gyekye-Jandoh, cited in ibid., 118.

86. Haynes, "The Possibility of Democratic Consolidation in Ghana," 112.

87. In an interview with Lydia Polgreen, Rawlings argued, "We were forced by the State Department—oh yes, forced—to adopt multiparty democracy." Lydia Polgreen, "Ghana's Unlikely Democrat Finds Vindication in Vote," *New York Times*, January 10, 2009.

88. Cited in Gyekye-Jandoh, "Explaining Democratization in Africa," 126–27.

89. Cited in ibid., 121.

90. Hearn, "Foreign Political Aid, Democratization, and Civil Society in Ghana in the 1990s," 2, 5.

91. Ibid., 2.

92. Richard C. Crook, " 'No-Party' Politics and Local Democracy in Africa: Rawlings' Ghana in the 1990s and the 'Ugandan Model,' " *Democratization* 6, no. 4 (1999): 1114.

93. Exchanges concerning the role of security issues vis-à-vis other priorities including the financial exigencies of structural adjustment can be viewed in the interactions between Museveni, his cabinet, and World Bank teams in the video documentary directed by Peter Chappell, *Our Friends at the Bank* (Brooklyn, N.Y.: First Run Icarus Films, 1998).

94. Herbst, personal correspondence. As Paul Nugent points out, regional conflicts instead may have had a salutary effect on Ghana's political leadership. Referring no doubt to the unraveling situation in Ghana's neighbor Ivory Coast, Nugent remarks that "in 2000 Ghanaian politicians were looking over their western border and reminding themselves of the need for strict limits to political contestation." Nugent, "Winners, Losers and Also Rans," 427.

CHAPTER TEN

Mexico

International Influences but "Made in Mexico"

ALBERTO DIAZ-CAYEROS AND BEATRIZ MAGALONI

Studying international influences in the Mexican transition to democracy must take as its point of departure the uneasy relationship of the country with the United States. Sharing a highly permeable border of 3,141 kilometers, Mexican governments have traditionally reacted viscerally to any international meddling in domestic political affairs, especially when coming from the United States. In the environment of the Cold War, the country prided itself on promoting and following a noninterventionist doctrine in international affairs (the so called Calvo doctrine).[1] A reaction against the Monroe Doctrine, the noninterventionist international policy stance was expressed most clearly in Mexico's retention of diplomatic ties with Cuba, in the face of ostracism by the rest of Latin America. This was primarily an assertion of sovereignty rather than an ideological acceptance of socialism or a blessing of autocratic rule per se. In fact, Mexican foreign policy denounced autocratic rule in Spain under Franco and in the numerous military interventions in South America. But in terms of a self-referential assessment of its democratic standing, politicians and diplomats alike jealously limited the scope of international actors to influence Mexico's electoral and political processes.[2]

Of course, Mexicans discussed the shortcomings of their political regime, and democracy was often debated as an aspiration. But the political sensibilities of the time did not tolerate the idea of foreigners' criticizing the regime. As late as 1990 in the long process of democratization, Peruvian author (and unsuccessful candidate to the presidency of his country) Mario Vargas Llosa created an outrage when he affirmed in a widely attended public forum:

I hope not to be too crass in what I am going to say, but I do not think Mexico can be exonerated from the tradition of Latin American dictatorships. I believe that in the case of Mexico, whose democratization I am the first to praise as all of us who believe in democracy, fits into this tradition, with a caveat which is rather damning. Mexico is the perfect dictatorship. The perfect dictatorship is not communism. It is not the Soviet Union. It is not Fidel Castro. The perfect dictatorship is Mexico. It is a camouflaged dictatorship with all the characteristics of a dictatorship: the permanence, not of a man, but of a party, an unmovable party.[3]

He went on to criticize public intellectuals in Mexico for becoming accomplices of the subtle form of co-optation the regime had in place, through their assignment to cultural offices in the public sector; and he suggested that the Mexican autocracy was so admired by autocrats that all dictators in Latin America had tried to create something similar to the Partido Revolucionario Institucional (PRI).[4] This international meddling was too much, even for Mexican intellectuals, who closed ranks right and left to defend the regime, suggesting that the foreign writer did not quite understand the nature of the Mexican political arrangement.[5]

The United States, for its part, usually disregarded the undemocratic nature of the regime and actively supported the PRI governments because this party guaranteed the political stability of its populous southern neighbor. Within the geopolitics of the second half of the twentieth century the PRI was able to deactivate "communist threats" without having to resort to as much brutal repression as other autocracies in Central America and the Southern Cone. Vargas Llosa was, however, right: the Mexican PRI was the "perfect dictatorship" because for years it was able to rule with consent by actively co-opting voters and potential elite opponents,[6] and because it managed to obtain the United States' endorsement despite its undemocratic character.

Until the year 2000, Mexico was ruled by one of the most long-lasting autocratic regimes of the twentieth century. The system was established in 1929, when the predecessor of the PRI became the sole means for achieving high office in Mexico. The peculiarity of the system, compared to other Latin American nations, was that Mexico never succumbed to military rule and always kept running regular elections (sometimes even competitive ones) throughout the period of autocratic rule. This made the Mexican transition to democracy different from other transitions in Latin America in that it occurred primarily within the electoral arena, where mass actors (political parties and their supporters) played a decisive role.[7] The domestic thrust of the transition allowed only marginal influences to international actors. Thus, the democratization in this chapter was essentially "Made in Mexico." We pay, however, less attention to these domestic factors because we want to center our attention on the international sphere. We refer the reader to Magaloni's *Voting for Autocracy* for a comprehensive account of the Mexican transition.

We begin by discussing the dependent variable of the analysis, namely the emergence of electoral democracy understood as the presence of free and fair elections. Given the protracted transition to democracy, the Mexican case can be divided into the failed transition of 1988 and the successful transition of 1996–97, which became consolidated with the presidential defeat in 2000.

Because long-term structural factors and more immediate triggers may help explain both the failed and the successful transitions to democracy, we next explore the most important domestic factors that explain the transition and how they relate to the strategies followed by opposition parties and the electoral behavior of citizens.[8]

Then we discuss the role of international influences in the transition to democracy and the way in which domestic and international actors have interacted to favor democratization. Despite the limited role of international actors, we identify five channels of influence for the Mexican transition to democracy that may be comparable to other cases around the world: public attention to democracy; international electoral observers; seed money for domestic civil society organizations; internationalization of the economy, migration, and remittances; and the spread of democratic ideas.

THE TIMING OF THE MEXICAN TRANSITION TO DEMOCRACY

The Mexico study can be conceptualized as two different cases in one single country. The first case involves an attempted but failed transition in 1988, when Cuauhtémoc Cárdenas, a candidate splitting from the ruling party and supported by a left-wing coalition, mounted a formidable challenge to the autocrats. In that election, the PRI resorted to massive electoral fraud through an infamous crash of the computer system tallying votes, even though it might be the case that the autocratic party may have actually obtained more votes than the opposition. In 1988 Mexico was clearly an autocracy: in the face of ex-ante uncertainty about losing, the PRI decided to play it safe, resorting to fraud.

The second case constitutes a successful transition to democracy that occurred in 1996–97, when electoral institutions guaranteed a free and fair electoral process and the PRI lost control of the legislature. The political significance of such defeat was clearly expressed by the limitation of presidential authority in the budget approved in December of that year. The president could no longer count on a pliant partisan majority to raise taxes and allocate public spending. Even though the office of the president remained in the hands of the PRI, political authority had shifted to Congress. The definite moment marking a full transition occurred three years later, when President Ernesto Zedillo recognized its party's defeat in the presidential race of 2000, resisting pressures from his rank and file not to concede.

Defining the Mexican experience as two cases raises an important issue for the question of timing, namely a problem with the 1994 election, in which the PRI successfully won a relatively clean presidential election, in between the fraud of 1988 and the actual transition in 1996–97. We conceptualize that election as a turning point in Mexican politics because it is when the independence of the IFE (Federal Electorate Institute) is granted.

Figure 10.1 provides some idea of the trends in political authority in Mexico over more than three decades, as indicated by the two most widely used comparative indexes of democracy, the Freedom House ratings of Political and Civil liberties and the Polity IV score measuring institutional attributes regarding the openness and competitiveness of electoral processes. The Freedom House indexes, each within a 1 to 7 scale, are summed in the left axis in an inverted scale, given that this indicator is coded with higher numbers representing less freedom (hence the combined score goes from 2 to 14). The polity score in the right axis represents the combination of the democracy minus the autocracy scores (in a 10-point scale) as calculated by the Polity project (hence the combined score can range from –10 to 10). A puzzle should be immediately clear from comparing both indexes: although there is not much change in the Mexican political regime before 2000 according to Freedom House, and in fact there is a certain backlash in civil liberties in the most recent years, taking the country back to the same civil liberties score it had in the 1970s, the Polity index (and the political liberties indicator from Freedom House) shows an unambiguous movement toward greater democracy. The difference is most likely attributable to the difficulty in judging how democratic and open the regime was before 1988. During the 1970s and early 1980s, Freedom House ratings tended to consider Mexico much more democratic than the Polity index did, so there was no major backlash in the regime after the 1988 fraud. Moreover, given that the index was already rather high, the transition to democracy in 1997 is suggested by the shift in the Polity indexes by two points sometime around those years. An important aspect that emerges from figure 10.1 is that timing a transition to democracy through moments of discontinuous breaks (such as the rule used by Polity of denoting transition as shifts of 3 or more points) can be fraught with many difficulties, particularly in the case of dominant party systems or electoral autocracies. It is preferable, from our perspective, to use detailed case study knowledge in order to provide a timing of the transition and then to assess whether the indexes reflect such timing.

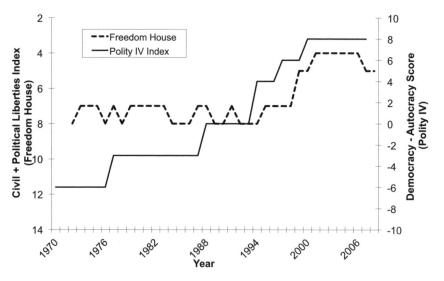

Fig. 10.1. Democratic Regime Evolution in Mexico

Figure 10.2 presents the trends in regime change according to the Polity scores in a format that should be useful in order to highlight the nature of the dependent variable in this study. Because similar figures are used in the rest of the chapter, it is worth explaining the figure. In order to remove proper names and idiosyncratic temporal frames, the graph shows each line as a case, and the time trend is a scale on the horizontal axis divided by zero as the transition moment. It is important to note that this discontinuous break is premised not simply on the possibility of alternation in power or on the likelihood that the hegemonic PRI would lose power, but on a broader sense of whether minimal democratic conditions of free and fair elections were met at a particular point in time. Both the failed and the successful transitions in Mexico occur at time o in the horizontal graph. To the left of o the figure shows the evolution of the indicator before the watershed moment, while to the right it indicates subsequent processes. In subsequent graphs, one may interpret the events on the left as background conditions or even causes of the event to be understood. Trends to the right reflect future events, so they should not be given causal primacy as explanations.

Showing the two independent variables of the study in this form suggests that the cases started from similarly undemocratic conditions. The 1988 attempts at a transition were preceded by a political opening (*apertura*) that did not continue: democratic ratings according to Polity remained at zero for the subsequent five years. Instead, the successful transition in 1997 was preceded by significant openings the previous five years, most crucially the electoral reforms of 1994 and 1996.

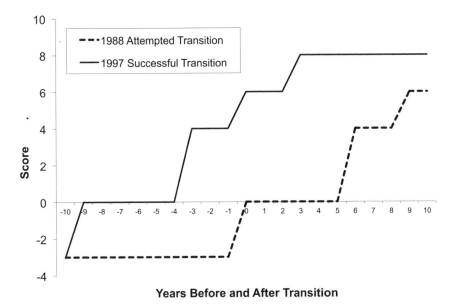

Fig. 10.2. Polity Scores in Mexican Political Transitions

By the year of the transition to democracy, the institutional framework is in place to ensure free and fair elections, so the Mexican Polity score only improves slightly after three years, when the PRI was finally defeated in the 2000 presidential race.

Although it is too early to venture an explanation, the patterns observed in the dependent variable suggest that, at least in the Mexican case, a successful transition occurred only once major institutional reforms had taken place. A moderate *apertura* in 1988 was not enough to bring about a decisive defeat of the incumbent autocrat. Moreover, the gradual *apertura* raised a problem for the opposition, which found it particularly difficult to coordinate effectively, at both the elite and the mass voter levels against the incumbent.

DOMESTIC INFLUENCES IN THE TRANSITION TO DEMOCRACY

Given its slow and protracted nature, the Mexican transition to democracy was not just the product of long-term modernization trends. Table 10.1 shows the evolution of the economy, comparing it to the indicators of regime change from Freedom House and Polity. According to these data, there is no obvious correlation between the processes of economic and political change. Mexico's level of development is relatively high throughout the period. However, the Mexican economy was going through a severe crisis before the 1988 elections, although the transition failed to

TABLE 10.1.
Political Regime and Modernization Indicators: Mexico

Year	Political Liberties	Civil Liberties	Polity Score	GDP	Growth	Agriculture	Inflation
1970	NA	NA	−6	5,127	3.19	12.7	2.6
1971	NA	NA	−6	5,184	1.11	12.6	6.3
1972	5	3	−6	5,444	5.03	11.5	6.5
1973	4	3	−6	5,711	4.90	12.1	13.4
1974	4	3	−6	5,877	2.90	12.0	23.1
1975	4	3	−6	6,053	3.00	11.8	15.6
1976	4	4	−6	6,123	1.15	11.2	19.4
1977	4	3	−3	6,127	0.06	11.2	30.5
1978	4	4	−3	6,455	5.36	10.9	16.0
1979	3	4	−3	6,865	6.36	9.8	19.6
1980	3	4	−3	7,271	5.91	9.0	33.4
1981	3	4	−3	7,719	6.16	9.0	26.0
1982	3	4	−3	7,434	−3.69	8.1	60.9
1983	3	4	−3	6,914	−6.99	8.5	90.5
1984	4	4	−3	7,007	1.35	9.4	59.1
1985	4	4	−3	7,072	0.92	10.1	56.7
1986	4	4	−3	6,653	−5.93	10.3	73.6
1987	3	4	−3	6,595	−0.87	9.7	139.7
1988	4	3	0	6,515	−1.21	7.9	112.7
1989	4	4	0	6,658	2.19	7.8	26.5
1990	4	4	0	6,864	3.10	7.8	28.1
1991	4	3	0	7,026	2.35	7.5	23.3
1992	4	4	0	7,146	1.71	6.7	14.4
1993	4	4	0	7,147	0.03	6.3	9.5
1994	4	4	4	7,328	2.52	6.0	8.5
1995	4	3	4	6,748	−7.91	5.7	37.9
1996	3	4	4	6,948	2.97	6.3	30.7
1997	3	4	6	7,287	4.87	5.7	17.7
1998	3	4	6	7,527	3.31	5.3	15.4
1999	2	3	6	7,701	2.30	4.7	15.1
2000	2	3	8	8,082	4.95	4.2	12.1
2001	2	2	8	7,974	−1.34	4.2	5.9
2002	2	2	8	7,927	−0.59	3.9	7.0
2003	2	2	8	7,938	0.15	3.9	8.6
2004	2	2	8	8,165	2.86	3.9	7.4
2005 *	2	2	8	8,727	2.80	3.8	5.5
2006 *	2	2	8	9,344	4.80	3.9	4.4
2007 *	2	3	8	9,820	3.30	3.6	3.2

Source: Freedom House, Polity VI, and Penn World Tables 6.2.
  * 2005 to 2007 economic data estimated from World Bank World Development Indicators Database; GDP per capita based on purchasing power parity, adjusted by 0.780613 factor to reflect trend and base of the Penn World Tables series.

materialize. In the case of the successful transition in 1996–97, there is a sharp downturn of the economy two years before that, as a consequence of the peso crisis of December 1994. Although poor economic performance alone did not cause the Mexican transition, there is no doubt that the PRI began to weaken at the polls as a result of the economic recession of the 1980s and later the peso crisis of 1995–96. Magaloni has shown that the long-term deterioration of economic performance and the economic volatility of the 1980s and 1990s played a decisive role in the PRI's ultimate demise.[9]

Regarding other short-term precipitating factors, table 10.2 provides a very simplified overview. The table specifies the conditions that were present in the three presidential elections in the 18 years between the attempted but unsuccessful transition and the inauguration of Vicente Fox in 2000 as the first non-PRI Mexican president. The rows of the table present potential variables that may explain the weakening of the authoritarian regime in Mexico, while the entries in each cell provide a brief assessment of how those variables might have played out. The table starts by summarizing the economic conditions, which have already been discussed, highlighting the regime's vulnerability and fragility on economic grounds throughout the period.

Table 10.2 then presents two precipitating factors related to violence. The first indicates whether a political assassination triggered a process of political change, while the second one assesses the risk of war or civil conflict. The 1994 election was a major challenge on both grounds, because the PRI presidential candidate, Luis Donaldo Colosio, was murdered during the campaign (as well as the secretary-general of the party a few months later); while the dawn of January 1, 1994, saw the irruption on the national scene of the Ejército Zapatista de Liberación Nacional (EZLN) movement, a guerrilla organization that at least in its first declaration issued a call to arms and the overthrowing of the illegitimate federal government. The Chiapas uprising was clearly the political challenge with more long-lasting effects, in terms of the way in which it reshaped the beliefs among the public at large of the performance of the Mexican government on grounds of social justice; it signaled the credible possibility of violence taking root as a means to solve deadlocked political conflicts; and it concentrated international attention on the shortcomings of Mexican democracy. The Chiapas conflict had not been solved by the time of the 2000 election, and in fact, additional guerrilla groups, including the Ejército Popular Revolucionario (EPR) in Guerrero, emerged in those years.

With regard to precipitating factors related to elite splits, mass protests, or general unpopularity of the president, the next cells suggest that those conditions were more prevalent in 1988, when the attempted transition failed to materialize than they were in subsequent years. In 1988 many groups, particularly in Mexico City, emerging from the 1985 earthquake and the subsequent revitalization of civil society were organized in the streets carrying out mobilizations and protests. The PRI was not unified, because Cuauhtémoc Cárdenas and the "corriente democratizadora" tried to change the way in which nominations in the party were handled and eventually left the party convinced of the impossibility of reform. President Miguel de la Madrid was relatively unpopular, given that he had presided over the macro-

TABLE 10.2.
Variables Related to Weakening of Authoritarian Regime in Mexico

	1988	1994	2000
Economic crisis	Reduction of inflation since 1987 Pacto de Solidaridad Economica	Tesobono exposure and financial vulnerability	Economic shielding through accumulation of international reserves
Economic growth rate (previous 6 years)	Low	Low	Moderate
Death of political leader	No	PRI[a] candidate assassinated	No
War or civil conflict	No	Chiapas uprising	Unsolved Chiapas conflict, EPR[c] and other guerilla groups
Splits within ruling party	Cuauhtémoc Cárdenas and Democratic Current split	No	No
Mass protests	1985 earthquake in Mexico City	No	No
Presidential approval	Medium	High	High
Media	Monopolistic TV coverage, pervasive corruption	Anticorruption newspapers	Cartelization of media
NGOs	Incipient social movements	Electoral observation	Professionalization in electoral observation
Electoral administration	Crash of computer system, government control of electoral board, self-certification of electoral races	Independent IFE[b] council, but no equity in campaign finance and media access	Highly regulated competition, equal access to media, public campaign finance and fines
Courts	No	No	No

Source: Own coding.
[a]Partido Revolucionario Institucional
[b]Federal Election Institute
[c]Ejército Popular Revolucionario

economic adjustment, cuts in social spending, and in general a lackluster period of economic hardship. Yet none of these factors seems to have been enough to bring the attempted transition to a happy end. In the same vein, the role of independent media, NGOs, or electoral courts does not account clearly for the transition, and in fact there might be serious issues of reverse causation in which media, civil society, and mechanisms of accountability are stronger because democratization is taking place rather than the other way around.

As noted by Magaloni, strategic dilemmas among voters played the key role in sustaining autocratic rule in Mexico, far beyond the time when one could have expected a change in regime on the basis of economic performance.[10] Even as the incumbent failed to deliver economic growth and well-being, voters were caught in strategic dilemmas that prevented them from dislodging the authoritarian regime. First, the ideology of left and right divided the opposition, which was exploited by the incumbent. Second, the division between generational cohorts regarding their memory and learning of the capacity of the PRI made older voters less willing to discard the incumbent despite repeated crises. Third, the overwhelming control of public finance by the president provided the incumbent party with a mechanism for punishing electoral defections, exercised through the vast clientelistic networks. Finally, voters had to cast votes under the shadow of potential violent behavior by the incumbent party. In short, rejecting the PRI was seen by many voters as ideologically undesirable, too rash of a judgment on the historical performance record of the incumbent party, too large a loss of valued resources that the ruling party threatened to withdraw, or too risky from the perspective of the likelihood of violence.

INTERNATIONAL INFLUENCES IN THE TRANSITION TO DEMOCRACY

There is no question that Mexico witnessed a profound transformation in its international position during the two and a half decades that are covered in this study. Mexico passed from being one of the few countries in the world that had not joined the General Agreement on Tariffs and Trade (GATT), the predecessor of the World Trade Organization (WTO), to tying its economic fate to the United States and Canada through the signing of the North American Free Trade Agreement (NAFTA).

Figures 10.3–5 and table 10.3 provide the trends in international trade (measured as imports plus exports as a percentage of GDP), foreign direct investment (FDI), and overseas development assistance (ODA) during the two cases of transitions we are studying. Figure 10.3 suggests a process that was neither conditioned nor disturbed in any way by the regime processes. Figure 10.4 suggests a vast increase in international investment flows that precedes the successful transition

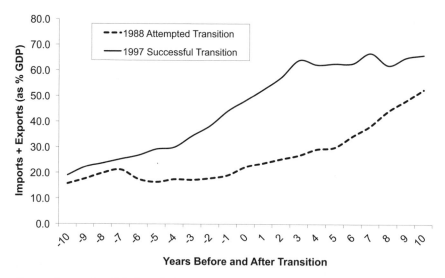

Fig. 10.3. International Trade and Transition to Democracy in Mexico

and continues beyond it, while the ODA trends in figure 10.5 show a marked decline in this type of international flows before the successful transition. Consonant with the findings related to long-term structural factors, these indicators of the exposure and openness of the Mexican economy to international economic forces seem to show no effect on the regime. However, there are other more subtle international influences that are worth exploring further.

International Commodity Prices and Public Finance

A potential explanation of the Mexican transition is related to international forces of world commodity markets. It is worth exploring whether the high dependence of the Mexican government on oil exports for its revenue may have been one of the sources of political change. In particular, Green argues that when the dominant party ceased to have the widely available resources to buy off friends and foes alike, it ended up having to give in to the forces of democratization.[11] In order to gauge this hypothesis, figure 10.6 shows, only for the case of the successful transition of 1997, the trend in oil prices (the simple average of the world price deflated by the US consumer price index) and the fiscal dependence of the federal government on oil (as measured by the share of federal finances coming from oil and gasoline). The graph shows that before the transition the price of oil is relatively stagnant and falls sharply only after the transition, not before it. Moreover, the solid line depicting the share of federal revenues that is being obtained from oil-related revenues exhibits a peak and subsequently a clear decline *after* the tran-

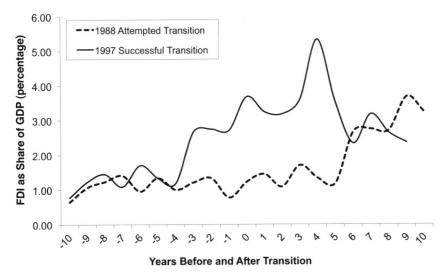

Fig. 10.4. Foreign Direct Investment and Transition to Democracy in Mexico

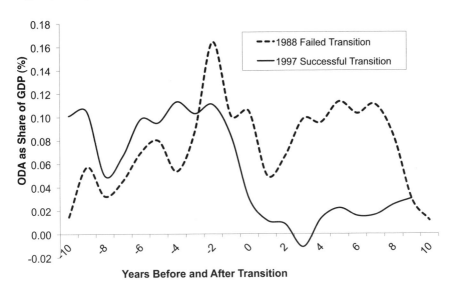

Fig. 10.5. Overseas Development Assistance and Transition to Democracy in Mexico

sition. Hence, the government was highly dependent on oil revenues when the transition occurred, but this would mean that this form of nontax revenue, which yields little accountability,[12] was particularly available precisely at the time of the transition. Thus, although a high price of oil can be a source of easy funding for government largesse, in the Mexican context this was probably not the precipitating factor bringing about political change.

TABLE IO.3.
Political Regime and Internationalization Indicators: Mexico

Year	Polity Score	Trade Openness (% GDP)	FDI (% GDP)	ODA (% GDP)	Media Attention (%)
1970	−6	14.6	0.88	0.23	NA
1971	−6	13.8	0.79	0.11	NA
1972	−6	14.4	0.40	0.13	NA
1973	−6	15.3	0.82	0.11	NA
1974	−6	16.2	0.72	0.08	NA
1975	−6	14.7	0.53	0.06	NA
1976	−6	15.0	0.78	0.07	NA
1977	−3	14.5	0.35	0.05	NA
1978	−3	15.8	0.64	0.01	20.7
1979	−3	17.7	1.06	0.06	31.7
1980	−3	19.9	1.22	0.03	45.3
1981	−3	21.2	1.40	0.05	37.5
1982	−3	17.5	0.95	0.07	64.0
1983	−3	16.4	1.33	0.08	77.2
1984	−3	17.4	1.00	0.05	100.0
1985	−3	17.2	1.21	0.09	67.0
1986	−3	17.9	1.33	0.16	66.4
1987	−3	19.0	0.77	0.10	92.0
1988	0	22.3	1.22	0.10	114.9
1989	0	23.8	1.44	0.05	91.0
1990	0	25.4	1.08	0.07	51.7
1991	0	26.8	1.70	0.10	46.9
1992	0	29.2	1.33	0.10	45.4
1993	0	30.0	1.18	0.11	76.7
1994	4	34.4	2.66	0.10	134.3
1995	4	38.4	2.74	0.11	93.2
1996	4	44.2	2.71	0.08	57.4
1997	6	48.2	3.67	0.03	69.8
1998	6	52.5	3.24	0.01	41.5
1999	6	57.3	3.18	0.01	35.1
2000	8	64.0	3.58	−0.01	79.6
2001	8	62.2	5.33	0.01	44.4
2002	8	62.7	3.52	0.02	35.8
2003	8	62.8	2.33	0.02	30.7
2004	8	66.8	3.18	0.02	39.8
2005	8	62.0	2.64	0.03	35.8
2006	8	65.0	2.36	0.03	50.5
2007	8	66.0	NA	NA	25.0

Source: Trade openness (Imports + Exports), foreign direct investment (FDI), and overseas development assistance (ODA) from the World Bank World Development Indicators Database; LexisNexis search of world and US press of the terms "Democracy W/50 Mexico" divided by "Culture W/50 Mexico" (W/50 searches for the occurrence of the two search terms in the contiguous 50 words, roughly within the same paragraph).

International Public Attention

An additional channel of international influence may have worked through international diplomatic pressure exercised by international organizations and state actors, particularly the US State Department, the European Union, and the Organization of American States (OAS). We find, however, the multilateral channel to be

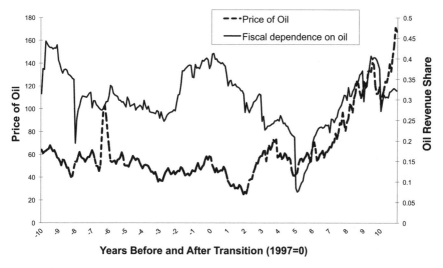

Years Before and After Transition (1997=0)

Fig. 10.6. Oil Dependence and Transition to Democracy in Mexico

weak for the Mexican case. But there is no question that the close attention paid by foreign governments to the evolution of Mexico's democracy after the Zapatista uprising of January 1994 and the initiation of NAFTA that same year played a role in making the Mexican government aware of the close international scrutiny under which the elections were held in July of that year. That channel was reinforced by the role played by international media, which kept Mexico as a prominent news item during that crucial electoral year.

The first appeals to international organizations by Mexican political actors to defend democracy can probably be traced back to the electoral frauds in the state elections of Chihuahua and Durango in 1985 and 1986. The Partido Acción Nacional (PAN) argued that the vote tallies were altered; signatures of electoral authorities were forged; votes stricken from voting lists; and ballots were stuffed, with the connivance of army and police units. The PAN sought a ruling from the Inter-American Human Rights Commission within the OAS. The commission issued a report on Mexican electoral practices in 1990, deciding "neither to accept nor to deny the truth" of the accusations by the PAN.[13] It did note that the failure to have appropriate means of appeal to address such allegations and recommended that legislation should be changed to provide for a free and full exercise of political rights. Despite the unwillingness by the commission and the OAS to play a proactive role in the case, even the mild chiding was taken by the Mexican government as an outrageous meddling. The Mexican delegate to OAS, traditionally an outspoken critic of electoral violations in El Salvador and Chile, angrily rejected the right of any international group to rule on electoral practices in Mexico. The

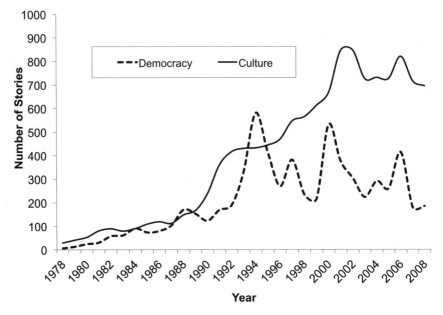

Fig. 10.7. Trends in International News Stories regarding Mexico

Partido de la Revolución Democrática (PRD) also appealed to the United Nations Human Rights Commission in Geneva for alleged electoral frauds in Michoacán and Guerrero in 1989, to little avail.

But attention to issues related to Mexican democratization has not remained constant over the decades; instead there has been a great deal of press coverage related to Mexico's political regime during the past decade. Figure 10.7 shows the trends in international news stories regarding Mexico's democratization, as reported by a search of Lexis-Nexis, a database of international and US media. The search is performed by looking for the simultaneous appearance of the terms "Mexico" and "democracy" within the range of 50 words (roughly one paragraph in a news story). In order to have a meaningful metric of the trends observed, the graph also shows the mentions that are made of "Mexico" and "culture" also within a 50-word range. The attention to Mexico has grown in both lines (also reflecting a wider availability of news stories in the dataset); but it is clear that the interest in democracy is larger at times of democratic challenges, namely elections.

Figure 10.8 provides a measure of international media attention toward Mexico's democratization, both before and after the attempted and the successful transitions. This measure of attention is simply the share of mentions of democracy and Mexico as a percentage of the baseline provided by the mentions of culture and Mexico in Lexis-Nexis. The trends are clear: despite heightened media attention,

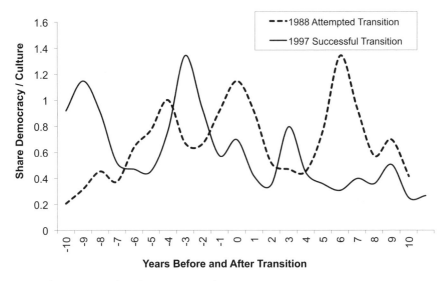

Fig. 10.8. International Media Attention and Transition to Democracy in Mexico

the transition to democracy in 1988 failed. But in 1997 the heightened attention and discussion of democracy seems to precede the moment of political change.

On Electoral Observation

The second channel worked through the role played by international electoral observers during the presidential elections. The independent effect of electoral observation is, however, very hard to gauge, because it is difficult to separate the influence of international observers from the dominant role played by the mobilization of civil society for electoral observation involving domestic rather than international actors. To some extent, the problem in measuring the effect of international electoral observers lies in that their participation is endogenous to the strength of domestic electoral observers that may already have influenced the integrity of the electoral contest: in the case of Mexico, international observers were invited to participate only when the incumbent party was already willing to organize relatively clean elections. However, as Mexican democratic actors negotiated with the hegemonic incumbent party the institutional framework and guarantees of the electoral process, which became embedded in the independent IFE, admitting international observers in a country with such a long history of not permitting international intervention in domestic affairs became a way of providing credibility to some of the agreements already reached among domestic political actors.

International electoral observation can have a positive effect on a transition to democracy when a deadlocked negotiation between the authoritarian incumbent and the opposition is surmounted by appealing to an outside third party to become a guarantor of the integrity of the electoral process. Ex ante the incumbent might claim it will abide by the results of an electoral contest even if it loses, but ex post such promise will not have any credibility. A commitment to respect the rules of democracy could be generated by appealing to domestic actors: empowering civil society to ensure that votes are respected or creating systems of judicial adjudication of conflicts. But it is often the case that an independent judiciary or vigorous civil society are not available arbiters. Hence, allowing a prestigious external actor to give its seal of approval to the electoral process is an available solution to make the opposition believe the incumbent. International observers would not be invited (or accepted to come) had the regime not been willing to bring about some change.

Seed Funding of Domestic Civil Society Organizations

A third channel of international influence was through donors and foundations that provided seed money, ongoing support, and international networks to political parties and emerging civil society organizations. After 1988, Mexican opposition parties on the right and the left started to have access to networks and funding from European political parties (e.g., through the German foundations Friedrich Ebert, Konrad Adenauer, or Friedrich Naumann), as a clearer configuration of a three-party system was established. Social Democratic and Christian Democratic parties in Europe could find in the Partido de la Revolución Democrática and the Partido Accion Nacional clear alternative Mexican counterparts, instead of the amorphous ideological leanings of the PRI.

Arguably an even more important role was played by civil society organizations that became electoral observers through the powerful network of Alianza Cívica. We believe that the support of civil society organizations was perhaps the most important international influence in the Mexican transition to democracy, achieved through the willingness of international donors to take the risk of funding organizations that were initially mostly devoted to human rights issues but gradually shifted their focus to the electoral arena and through the tolerance of the Mexican government for the emergence of independent civil society organizations, under the shadow of international scrutiny.

The Spread of Democratic Ideas

Finally, a channel of international influence can be identified in the realm of ideas. The role played by public intellectuals, the media, and other actors to form overall public opinion on the issue of democratic reform was influenced by the ideas on democratization that were generated by the social sciences not only within the country but also outside Mexico. Although the transmission of democratic ideas is difficult to measure, the support of academic exchanges and scholarship programs such as the British Council or the Fulbright Program enabled young academics, journalists, and leaders of civil society to become exposed to democratic ideas and challenge Mexican "exceptionalism" in the political realm.

To explore diffusion effects in the realm of ideas, we examined texts on democratization published by the main political magazines read by the Mexican intelligentsia and many politicians during the years of the transition (*Nexos, Vuelta, Proceso, Siempre!, Voz y Voto,* and *Este Pais*), and some of the professional academic journals (*Politica y Gobierno, Estudios Sociologicos, Revista Mexicana de Sociologia*) that may have influenced the way in which scholars and intellectuals conceived the Mexican transition to democracy. We found that most of the democratic theory published at the time was homegrown, from Mexican authors, though they were reading predominantly Spanish and French social science, and some translations of US academic debates (often referred to as transitology).

THE INTERACTION OF DOMESTIC AND INTERNATIONAL ACTORS

One advantage of studying the Mexican experiences in the transition to democracy is that it comprises two "cases" within one country: the first, a failed attempted transition in 1988; and the second, a successful transition to democracy after 1996–97. These two cases allow us to focus on the strategic elements of regime transition while holding relatively constant certain structural variables, including political culture, modernization, Catholicism, and even international influences. Those factors did not change so dramatically between 1988 and 1996 to explain democratization.

The successful transition in 1996–97 was not brought about by international forces but as the result of a massive voter defection from the PRI and the enactment of electoral reforms in 1994 and 1996 that made electoral competition more transparent and fairer. The fate of Mexican democracy was in the hands of voters, political parties, and their leaders who built that electoral architecture and mobilized citizens to participate and ultimately forced the incumbent party to accept its defeat at the polls. The loss of control of the lower chamber by the PRI happened three years before the victory of Vicente Fox in 2000 and the most decisive institutional changes occurred before 1997. Hence, the time of the Mexican transition to democracy was 1996–97.[14]

International influences had a marginal role owing to the peculiarities of Mexico's protracted regime change. The international channels were mostly absent in 1988, when a transition to democracy failed to materialize. It is impossible to know for sure whether the challenger in that election, Cuauhtémoc Cárdenas, won the presidential race. But there is no question that the PRI resorted to massive electoral fraud. However, international factors failed to forcibly support the cause of democracy in that decisive year. International actors could have tilted the outcome of postelectoral conflicts if they had been willing to condemn the authoritarian nature of the regime. Not only had the United States always endorsed the PRI, but in 1988 it had a strategic interest in preventing the victory of a candidate that had actively campaigned against IMF-sponsored stabilization measures and market reforms.

The PRI's candidate, Harvard-trained Carlos Salinas de Gortari, was highly sympathetic to the market-oriented policies that had been initiated under his predecessor, Miguel de la Madrid, after Mexico had declared a debt moratorium in 1982. By contrast, Cuauhtémoc Cárdenas had openly rejected the IMF-sponsored stabilization measures and opposed further economic liberalization, including lifting trade barriers and privatizing state-owned companies. Perceived as a dangerous populist reversal, Cárdenas's plea for electoral transparency and for imposing sanctions against the PRI because of the 1988 fraud was not supported by the United States or international financial institutions. Furthermore, it did not help Cárdenas that in the 1988 elections there was almost no international media coverage of the events surrounding the fraudulent elections and that there were no international electoral observers that could buttress the allegations of fraud before the international community.

Although the 1988 electoral fraud was protested in the streets, civil society was divided and relatively weak. The opposition's failure to unite to protest against fraud played an important role in allowing the PRI to get away with stealing votes from Cárdenas.[15] The right-wing opposition party, the PAN, reasoned that its interests were better served by supporting the regime despite the PRI's misdeeds than rallying behind Cárdenas. Lastly, even in the realm of ideas, many public intellectuals were still willing to defend the idea of Mexico as an uncommon democracy, but a democracy nonetheless.[16]

Some of these factors changed after the 1988 presidential elections. With the end of the Cold War, the signing of NAFTA, and the Chiapas uprising in December of 1993, international pressure for Mexico's democratization increased. But the subsequent democratization cannot be attributed to external forces. Internal events during the year of the 1994 presidential elections critically shaped the democratic transition. In December 1993 the Zapatista uprising erupted in the South of Mexico. Just after the guerrilla uprising, the government announced its intention to reform the institutions so as to guarantee the transparency of the elections. The Chiapas uprising triggered the creation of an independent electoral institute, the IFE, which offered credible guarantees to the opposition that the 1994 presidential elections would not be manipulated. Six citizens endorsed by the three major political parties, the PRI, the PAN, and the PRD, were elected to the board of the IFE and were given sufficient institutional resources to organize and monitor the elections. The 1994 electoral reform was essentially created to prevent postelectoral protests and violence from erupting after the elections.

But the reform also had an international audience in mind. This time the international media had ample presence in covering the Zapatista uprising, which also meant that Mexico's coming presidential elections would be more prominently observed in the world. Carlos Salinas, his economic advisers, and the PRI cared deeply about how a protested election would harm their international reputation and contribute to capital flight. After the Zapatista uprising, and especially after the killing of the PRI's presidential candidate, Luis Donaldo Colosio, national and international investors had given clear signals that they would leave if more violence erupted. Moreover, the Zapatista uprising had received ample international media coverage, and this put the coming presidential elections at the center of attention in the United States and Europe, increasing the costs for the PRI of a protested election. The creation of an independent electoral board can be understood primarily as a consequence of domestic processes, but buttressed by international reputation costs. Furthermore, the granting of the independence of the IFE came about because the PRI was confident that it would win the coming elections, and this party wanted to give credibility to its victory before its national and international audiences.[17]

CONCLUSION

A transition to democracy in Mexico failed to materialize in 1994 because the PRI successfully defeated the other contenders in those elections. The elections were clean but not fair. In particular, although the vote count was transparent, access to campaign finance and media was seriously lopsided. All major opposition forces agreed after 1994 that the issue of transparency of the vote count had been successfully addressed and that what still needed reform was campaign financing and access to the media. A second major electoral reform in 1996 corrected the unfair competitive conditions between competitors. This reform was carried out while the country struggled with one of its worst economic recessions in the twentieth century that erupted after the abrupt devaluation of the peso in December of 1994. As a consequence, voters bitterly turned against the PRI in one local election after another, and by the 1997 congressional elections the PRI lost the majority in the Lower Chamber of Deputies. The loss of the majority in the Lower Chamber obliged the PRI for the first time in its history to gain the opposition's support in the legislature to pass laws. By the time the PRI lost the presidential race in 2000, the transition to democracy was complete.

NOTES

In writing this chapter we profited from interviews with key experts regarding the Mexican transition. These individuals include Andres Albo, President of the Council of the Federal Electoral Institute; Benito Nacif, Councilor of the Federal Electoral Institute; Helena Hofbauer, Director of FUNDAR, an NGO devoted to transparency; Michael Layton, Federico Estevez, and Vidal Romero, as well as journalists, public officials, and some key advisors to the IFE board. None of them are responsible for our interpretations or any errors contained here.

1. Josefina Zoraida Vazquez and Meyer, Lorenzo, *The United States and Mexico* (Chicago: University of Chicago Press, 1985); Robert A. Pastor and Jorge Castañeda, *Limits to Friendship: The United States and Mexico* (New York: Knopf Doubleday, 1989).

2. Peter Smith and Rosario Green, *Foreign Policy in U.S.-Mexican Relations* (San Diego: Center for US-Mexican Studies, UCSD, 1989).

3. *El País* (México/Madrid), January 9, 1990, our translation.

4. It might be noted that intellectually Vargas Llosa's indictment was not altogether new: the acerbic critique of communist rule offered by Vaclav Havel in *The Power of the Powerless* (Armonck, N.Y.: M. E. Sharpe) made a similar point. The originality lay in offering the critique to the Mexican regime, which had always prided itself on offering a middle way, far short of communism.

5. To be sure, one of the reasons why so many Mexicans felt insulted by the critique was the arrogance with which Vargas Llosa assumed that citizens did not even realize they were not living under a free regime—hence, the "perfection" of the Mexican autocracy.

6. Beatriz Magaloni, *Voting for Autocracy* (Cambridge: Cambridge University Press, 2006).

7. Ibid.; and Beatriz Magaloni, "The Game of Electoral Fraud and the Ousting of Authoritarian Rule," *American Journal of Political Science* 54, no. 3 (2010): 751–65.

8. Magaloni, *Voting for Autocracy*.

9. Beatriz Magaloni, "Catching-All-Souls: The PAN and the Politics of Catholicism in Mexico," in Timothy Scully and Scott Mainwaring, eds., *Christian Democracy in Latin America* (Stanford, Calif.: Stanford University Press, published with Alejandro Moreno, 2003), 247–74; and Magaloni, *Voting for Autocracy*.

10. Magaloni, *Voting for Autocracy*.

11. Kenneth Greene, *Why Dominant Parties Lose: Mexico's Democratization in Comparative Perspective* (Cambridge: Cambridge University Press, 2007).

12. Terry L. Karl, "Dilemmas of Democratization in Latin America," *Comparative Politics* 23, no. 1 (1990): 1–23.

13. Larry Rohter, *New York Times*, June 4, 1990.

14. With regard to democratic consolidation (which is not a central aspect of this inquiry), by 2006 international forces had only a marginal influence or presence, at a time when the young Mexican democracy might have required greater international attention, as

it was challenged by a highly polarized electoral race that resulted in a very slim margin of victory and accusations of electoral fraud. In that election, however, there were few international observers or other international actors, given that it was assumed that Mexico already had the institutional scaffolding of a consolidated democracy.

15. Magaloni, *Voting for Autocracy*; and Magaloni, "The Game of Electoral Fraud and the Ousting of Authoritarian Rule."

16. Pempel's book on "uncommon democracies," which was swiftly translated into Spanish by the Fondo de Cultura Económica in 1991, allowed many scholars to place Mexico in the company of dominant party regimes, such as Sweden, Japan, Israel, or Italy. See T. J. Pempel, *Uncommon Democracies* (Ithaca, N.Y.: Cornell University Press, 1990).

17. Magaloni, *Voting for Autocracy*; and Magaloni, "The Game of Electoral Fraud and the Ousting of Authoritarian Rule."

CHAPTER ELEVEN

South Korea

The Puzzle of Two Transitions

A. David Adesnik and Sunhyuk Kim

In October 1979 the conditions were ripe for a transition to democracy in South Korea, also known as the Republic of Korea (ROK). After two decades of stunning economic growth, the plunge toward recession had begun. Labor unions launched a wave of strikes and demonstrations. Korean students also filled the streets in protest. Churches also lent their support to the movement. Finally, the workers, students, and clergymen were joined by the parliamentary opposition, which had prestige but not power. Although the United States customarily favored stability in South Korea, the Carter administration resented the Park dictatorship, because of both its human rights violations and its apparent efforts to bribe American legislators. Under pressure, the Park dictatorship found itself beset by internal divisions, with hard-liners calling for the use of force and soft-liners advocating a measure of compromise with the protesters. This division culminated in the assassination of Park by his own intelligence chief. The reins of power then passed to a provisional government that committed itself to democratic elections and the protection of civil liberties. Yet just six months later, General Chun Doo Hwan, a protégé of Park, violently consolidated his control of the government, ushering in another seven years of dictatorship.

In June 1987 Chun Doo Hwan found himself in a situation that would have been familiar to Park. Students, workers, church leaders, and opposition leaders united once again to oppose the regime. Yet this time, the economy kept growing and the regime remained united. Chun also had an excellent relationship with President Reagan, who hosted Chun at the White House as recently as 1985. Nonetheless, Chun surrendered to the protesters' demand for free and fair elections and for the restoration of civil liberties. South Korea today is a full-fledged democracy. The puzzle that remains is why South Korea became a democracy specifically in 1987, even though the prospects for a transition were so much more favorable in 1979. Chun clearly had the power to deploy the armed forces in defense of the regime, yet he chose not to do so.

Why not? Three factors account best for the failed transition of 1979–80 and the success of 1987. First, the personal situation and interests of both Chun Doo Hwan and Roh Tae Woo, his second-in-command, had changed significantly over the years. In 1979–80, both men were ambitious young generals whose mentor and patron, Park Chung Hee, had just been assassinated. They had no qualms then about shooting their way into power. By 1987, Chun and Roh were political veterans who had presided over a return to the spectacular growth rates of the Park era. They were also determined to cement their legacy both by presiding over the first peaceful transfer of power in the history of the ROK and by hosting the 1988 Summer Olympics. Roh also recognized that he could prevail in a free and fair election, because of a divided opposition. Although reluctant at first, Chun and Roh accepted that compromise best served their interests.

A second factor that accounts for the different outcomes in 1979–80 and 1987 is the increased unity of the protest movement. The four main constituents of the movement—students, labor unions, churches, and the parliamentary opposition—were the same during both transitions. In both instances, these constituents sought to establish umbrella organizations, or *chaeya*, that would effectively coordinate the strategy and resources of the movement.[1] In 1987, however, the *chaeya* achieved a much greater degree of efficiency and solidarity because they learned from the mistakes of the failed transition in 1979–80.

The third factor that explains the difference between South Korea's two transitions is the contrast in how the Carter administration and the Reagan administration approached both US-ROK diplomacy and the challenge of democracy promotion. Although strongly committed to human rights, the Carter administration hesitated to challenge the legitimacy of authoritarian governments, preferring to focus on preventing specific actions, such as torture and unjust imprisonment. Thus, while the Carter administration welcomed the democratic opening of 1979, it remained passive when Chun wrested power back from the civilians. Initially, the Reagan administration rejected democracy promotion, preferring to focus on the solidarity of anticommunist governments, both authoritarian and democratic. Yet over time, the administration reversed its course. Thus, at a critical moment in 1987, President Reagan sent a personal letter to Chun Doo Hwan, insisting that

Chun find a peaceful solution to the prevailing crisis. Ironically, Reagan's word carried considerable weight precisely because Reagan had embraced Chun without hesitation during the early and uncertain days of his regime.

THE TWO TRANSITIONS

Park Chung Hee ruled South Korea for 18 years. As a young general, he led a coup d'etat that overthrew a recently elected government in 1961. His coup represented a bid for personal power, not an ideological statement. After more than two years in power, Park suddenly called for elections. In spite of the considerable benefits of incumbency, Park prevailed over his opponent by the razor-thin margin of 1.4 percent. Economic growth rapidly accelerated in the mid-1960s, enabling Park to win reelection by a much safer margin in 1967, although the gap narrowed again when Park sought a third term in 1971. In 1972, Park declared martial law. He dissolved the National Assembly, banned political parties, and closed the universities. Park then promulgated a new "revitalizing reform" (*Yusin*) constitution, which lent its name to the final, or *Yusin*, period of his tenure.

After more than a decade and a half of continuous and rapid growth (table 11.1), a brief interval of economic turbulence brought on the demise of the Park dictatorship. When the price of oil spiraled out of control in 1979, it drove prices higher throughout the South Korean economy, damaging the welfare of millions of wage earners who were ill-equipped to deal with inflation. In the second half of 1979, the economy entered a deep recession. Workers rapidly mobilized against the regime.

Efforts to suppress the protests only provoked further mobilization, which led to a fatal split among Park's closest advisers. They disagreed about whether to respond to the pro-democracy movement with intensified force or with an offer of compromise. The main advocate of compromise was Kim Chae Kyu, head of the Korean CIA. On the evening of October 26, 1979, Kim had dinner with President Park. The discussion at dinner led Kim to believe that Park had come down decisively in favor of a hard-line approach. In desperation, Kim paid a brief visit to his nearby office, returning with a .38 Smith & Wesson hidden in his pocket. Back in the dining room, Kim shot both Park and his chief bodyguard at point-blank range. When his gun jammed, Kim borrowed another .38 from one of his men to finish off the victims.[2]

Prime Minister Choi Kyu Ha quickly assumed the role of acting president and formed a transitional government. On November 10, Choi announced that the constitution would be amended "to promote democracy" and that new elections would be held. In addition, Choi revoked many of the "emergency decrees" issued

TABLE II.I.
GDP Growth and Inflation Rates, 1966–1980
(in percentages)

Year	Real GDP Growth	Inflation
1966	n/a	11.3
1967	n/a	10.9
1968	n/a	10.8
1969	n/a	12.4
1970	n/a	16.0
1971	8.2	13.5
1972	4.5	11.7
1973	12.0	3.2
1974	7.2	24.3
1975	5.9	25.3
1976	10.6	15.3
1977	10.0	10.1
1978	9.3	14.5
1979	6.8	18.3
1980	−1.5	28.7

Source: Bank of Korea Economic Statistics System, http://ecos
.bok.or.kr, and Korean Statistical Information Service, www.kosis
.kr/index.jsp.

by Park and restored the civil rights of Park's rivals, such as former president Yun Po Sun and opposition leader Kim Dae Jung.

The transition suffered its first setback on December 12, when Major General Chun Doo Hwan and Major General Roh Tae Woo, in concert with other members of their secret military society, the Hanahoe, launched a rapid and violent operation to arrest the Army's pro-democracy chief of staff, thus consolidating their control of the military. Chun and Roh gradually reduced Prime Minister Choi and the other civilians to a set of figureheads. On April 14, 1980, Chun illegally appointed himself head of the Korean CIA, provoking a violent wave of student demonstrations. The protests culminated on May 15, when 70,000 to 100,000 students demonstrated in the heart of Seoul. Chun responded by declaring martial law, suspending all political activity, arresting opposition leaders, and closing the universities.[3] This brought an end to the protests, except in Kwangju, where an uprising took control of the city from government forces. On May 27, a brutal assault by 20,000 military personnel retook the city.[4] Chun's control was now complete. In the months after the Kwangju uprising, Chun imposed a new constitution on the ROK and elevated himself to president.

According to the new constitution, the president would serve a single, nonrenewable term of seven years in office. In light of Chun's continual assertions that he would step down from office on schedule, South Koreans began to think of the end of Chun's term as a potential moment of transition. Chun also implemented a measured agenda of liberalization once the economy recovered. As part of the agenda, Chun pardoned or rehabilitated hundreds of political prisoners, lifted the ban on political activity by more than 200 opposition figures, and allowed more than 1,000 students expelled for political reasons to return to their universities. Chun ultimately sought to construct a convincing democratic façade that would enhance his legitimacy without reducing his power. In February 1985 the regime held legislative elections designed to produce a docile majority in the National Assembly. The balloting process was fair, although the regime's unusual process for distributing seats enabled its loyalists to win a majority in spite of receiving only 35 percent of the vote, as opposed to 29 percent for the main opposition party, led by Kim Dae Jung and Kim Young Sam. In the court of public opinion, the election represented a massive victory for the opposition, because the playing field tilted so heavily toward the government. Turnout at the polls was 84.6 percent, the highest in 30 years. Thus, the electorate interpreted the results as an authentic expression of the will of the people.

Chun clearly understood that his electoral gambit was a failure. Knowing the opposition would demand free and fair elections for president in 1987, Chun sought to evade deliberations about the succession process. If the 1980 constitution remained in force, Chun would be able to install Roh as his successor. In February 1986, the opposition marked the anniversary of the legislative elections by launching a campaign to revise the constitution.[5] After extensive protests and rioting, Chun compromised by allowing the formation of a special committee in the National Assembly to propose a set of constitutional revisions. The committee's negotiations dragged on until April 1987, when Chun suspended the process. The streets remained calm.

Chun attempted to cement his victory on June 10 by announcing the nomination of Roh Tae Woo to become the next president. This time, the opposition exploded. Violent protests erupted across South Korea on the day of Chun's announcement. Led by students, the crowds attacked the police with fists, blunt objects, and gasoline bombs. The police responded with nightsticks and tear gas, clouds of which rolled through the streets of South Korea. The two Kims called for nonviolent protests against the regime, of which there were many, yet it was student violence that pushed the regime to the brink. In spite of their fury, the protests and riots resulted in few fatalities on either side. Yet the police were rapidly becoming exhausted, whereas the students' numbers and energy seemed inexhaustible. Chun still had the option of mobilizing the armed forces, yet this approach carried with it the risk of extreme violence, perhaps bloodier than the Kwangju Uprising of 1980. Nine days into the riots, Chun issued an order for military mobilization but rescinded it later that day. As the riots surged into their third week, Chun accepted that he would have to surrender to the protesters' principal demands: direct presidential elections and the restoration of civil liberties.

On June 29, 1987, Roh Tae Woo announced the reforms the protesters had demanded.[6] This marked the moment of transition, when the regime accepted that a new system of government would be put in place in South Korea. Yet from Chun and Roh's perspective, their government had lost the battle in order to win the war. It was public knowledge that both Kim Young Sam and Kim Dae Jung considered themselves to be the democratic opposition's natural candidate for president. As Chun and Roh correctly calculated, the Kims would split the opposition vote, allowing Roh to prevail with a small plurality. In the months leading up to the presidential vote in December, the opposition sought to reconcile its two candidates and produce a unified ticket, but to no avail. In the meantime, the constitution was revised to replace the electoral college with a single round of voting for president. Had the opposition insisted on a two-round election, in which the top two finishers in the first round had to compete in a run-off, one of the Kims would presumably have prevailed. But the opposition showed no interest, allowing Roh to prevail with 35.6 percent of the vote, just several points more than each of the two Kims.[7] Initially, both Kims responded to their defeat by alleging a corruption of the vote, yet the charges were soon withdrawn.

In 1992, Kim Young Sam won the next presidential election by forging an alliance with Roh. In spite of his alliance with Roh, Kim moved aggressively to implement democratic reforms. In 1996, a South Korean court convicted both Chun and Roh of treason and mutiny, sentencing Chun to death and Roh to many years in prison. In 1997 Kim Dae Jung prevailed in the ROK's third free presidential election. His inauguration resolved the last concerns that the transition might be reversed. As president-elect, Kim pardoned both Chun and Roh.

DOMESTIC CAUSES OF SUCCESS: THE *CHAEYA*

In both 1979 and 1987, South Korea's authoritarian regimes had to face down broad and deep coalitions committed to a democratic opening. The 1987 coalition was much more tightly organized, however. In 1979 the diverse array of groups opposed to the regime struggled to establish umbrella organizations, or *chaeya*, that could coordinate the coalition's efforts. In 1987 the effort to establish *chaeya* organizations was far more effective. A second critical difference between the two coalitions was the challenge they faced. Initially, both coalitions sought to overthrow dictatorship led by former generals. After the fall of the *ancien régime*, the respective challenges faced by the two coalitions diverged. In 1987, the struggle basically ended with Chun and Roh's capitulation to the opposition's demands. In

1979 the opposition still had to contend with a bloody-minded army determined to restore its control by any means necessary. This challenge was more than the *chaeya* could bear, at least in the short term.

The first *chaeya* began to emerge in the early 1970s, after Park Chung Hee imposed the *Yusin* constitution.[8] In November 1974 the National Congress for the Restoration of Democracy was founded. It was followed in 1978 and 1979 by the National Coalition for Democracy and the National Coalition for Democracy and Reunification. The organizations participating in these *chaeya* associations included "religious groups (for example, the Catholic Priests' Association for Justice), intellectual groups such as the Council of Dismissed Professors, human rights organizations like the Korean Council for the Human Rights Movement, and writers' groups (the Council of Writers for Practicing Freedom, for instance)." The leadership of the *chaeya* in the 1970s included "former politicians, religious leaders, scholars, and other professionals and were widely respected for their morality, integrity, experience and caliber."[9]

The *chaeya* enjoyed a cooperative relationship with the parliamentary opposition led by Kim Young Sam and Kim Dae Jung. However, "the cooperation and alignment between civil society and political society was not through institutionalized channels such as joint organizations. It was aligned instead through individual connections and commitments. Furthermore the main cooperation occurred between religious leaders and opposition party politicians."[10] In contrast, student groups and labor unions had few close links with the parliamentarians. This notable absence represented a significant organizational flaw, because the students and the unions were so critical to the mass mobilization that threatened the dictatorship.

In spite of its initial defeat by Chun, civil society began to reawaken when the regime began to relax various restrictions on political activity in 1983. In March 1985 two smaller *chaeya* combined to form the People's Movement Coalition for Democracy and Reunification (PMCDR). The unity of the opposition also benefited strongly from the decision of student groups, such as the Youth Coalition for Democracy Movement (YCDM), to explicitly support the parliamentary opposition in advance of the 1985 legislative elections. This was the first time since the early 1960s that students identified themselves with a political party.[11]

In late 1985 the PMCDR and the democratic opposition in the National Assembly launched a campaign to collect 10 million signatures in support of revising the constitution. Together, they formed the National Coalition for Democracy Movement (NCDM). This tight alliance allowed the pro-democracy coalition to prevail when the government sought to disrupt the campaign with a barrage of raids and arrests. Such tactics were met with massive rallies that forced the government back onto the defensive. However, the PMCDR broke with the NCDM when the two Kims agreed to negotiate with the regime on the subject of the constitution. After Chun suspended those negotiations, a new umbrella organization emerged, known as the National Movement Headquarters for a Democratic Constitution (NMHDC). In the critical period between June 10 and June 29, 1987, the NMHDC organized several massive demonstrations, including the June 26 Peace Parade that mobilized 1 million protesters across South Korea.[12] Three days later, Roh Tae Woo announced that the government would surrender to the opposition's demands.

INTERNATIONAL INFLUENCES ON DEMOCRATIC TRANSITIONS

Democracy assistance programs—from training journalists and union organizers to funding exchange programs for teachers and students—are the standard prescription for promoting democratic change. Although, in rare instances, democratic change has followed a foreign invasion, few responsible voices condone violence in the name of democratization. Often, both scholars and practitioners assume that slow-moving assistance programs and unwanted invasions are the only methods for promoting democratic transitions from abroad. Yet the case of South Korea clearly demonstrates that there is a third path—diplomacy—that observers have persistently overlooked in spite of its potential to catalyze democratic transitions.

The words of American envoys, in both public and private, made a significant contribution to the democratic transition in South Korea. In the 1980s, there were no democracy assistance programs to speak of. The United States garrisoned ample forces in South Korea, yet the threat of force against the ROK, let alone its actual use, were unthinkable in light of the common threat that the United States and the ROK faced from North Korea. Diplomacy was the only path open to American officials interested in democratic change, but it was an effective one.

One of the drawbacks of promoting democracy via diplomacy is that it is an intensely political and uncertain process. Foreign service officers and civil servants can implement democracy assistance programs once they have been approved by host and donor governments. In contrast, effective diplomacy requires senior officials—up to and including the head of state—to make affirmative decisions in favor of exerting pressure on behalf of democratization. Sometimes, senior officials are simply unwilling to exert such pressure, because they consider other objectives to be more important than democratization. At other times, they may be willing to pay lip service to democratic ideals, but little more. Even when a government begins moving toward a strategy of promoting democratization via diplomacy, factionalism within the cabinet or executive branch may hinder its implementation. In the case of South Korea, it was a fortunate coincidence that

American strategic interests and domestic politics aligned to favor support for democratization in the mid- to late 1980s, when just a few years earlier, exerting such pressure was simply out of the question.

Under what conditions can diplomacy affect the course of a democratic transition? Friendly and trustful relations between the intervening power and the state in transition are extremely important. Chun Doo Hwan and his advisers took the words of American officials seriously because they believed that the Reagan administration was deeply committed to the security of South Korea. Ironically, Reagan's initial disinterest in any sort of political reform in South Korea played an essential role in fostering this belief. There was also a considerable imbalance of power between the United States and South Korea, with the latter depending on the former for its security. Yet, if the United States had sought to pressure Chun in the early and uncertain days of his regime, he may have responded as intransigently as Park Chung Hee did to American criticism of his record on human rights. Sometimes, no amount of diplomatic pressure will make a difference if internal conditions militate against a transition.

As illustrated by South Korea, the potential for diplomacy to promote democratic change is greatest when the authority and legitimacy of a regime begin to falter. When democratic activists begin to challenge an authoritarian regime, its dependence on allied governments, especially the most powerful ones, is heightened. The allied government can begin to exert pressure in a way that might have provoked a backlash at another time. The tactics available to the allied government are many. Visiting officials may publicly call for change, either directly or through the news media, as Gaston Sigur and George Shultz did in Seoul. Ambassadors may counsel against specific actions, such as James Lilley's warning not to use force against the protesters inside of Myungdong Cathedral. Legislatures may issue condemnations or call for free and fair elections, as Congress did in the midst of the June riots. Yet sometimes, a quiet letter, such as Reagan's missive to Chun, may carry the most weight. The tactics available are manifold. Their effectiveness depends intimately and ultimately on the situation.[13]

THE INTERPLAY BETWEEN DOMESTIC AND INTERNATIONAL FACTORS IN TRANSITION: THE UNITED STATES AND DEMOCRACY IN SOUTH KOREA

Regime change in South Korea has always reflected the influence of American diplomacy alongside the imperatives of South Korean domestic politics. Since the founding of the ROK, South Korean actors have initiated every transition from one regime to another. South Korean actors have also exerted the greatest influence on the course and outcome of those transitions. Yet American decisions, expressed in terms of both actions and acts of omission, have made certain outcomes far more or far less probable than they would have been otherwise.

The United States' influence on South Korean politics was greatest in the immediate aftermath of the Second World War. The arrival of Allied forces in 1945 brought an end to 35 years of Japanese colonialism on the Korean peninsula. Whereas American forces occupied the peninsula south of the 38th parallel, Soviet forces held the territory north of that line. As in Germany, the onset of the Cold War resulted in the emergence of two separate republics, each one diplomatically aligned with its respective occupying power. On May 10, 1948, Koreans on the southern half of the peninsula cast their votes in a US-supervised election. Before the election, on April 5, the US commander in Korea, Lieutenant General John R. Hodge, issued a "Proclamation on the Rights of the Korean People" that is similar both to the American Bill of Rights and to the chapter on rights and duties of the US-drafted Japanese Constitution. Hodge's proclamation declared, among other things, that all Koreans "are equal before the law and entitled to equal protection under the law, and no privileges of sex, birth, occupation or creed are recognized." Hodge's proclamation influenced the constitution adopted by the newly elected National Assembly on July 12. However, the Koreans responsible for drafting the constitution were already inclined in a democratic direction as a result of the Allied victory in World War II and the imperative of distinguishing South Korea from its communist counterpart to the north. On August 15, 1948, the ROK was officially founded by President Syngman Rhee, winner of an election within the Assembly. Rhee was a veteran nationalist who had spent many years in the United States but had rarely gotten along well with American policy makers.[14]

From the founding of the ROK through the mid-1970s, the US government displayed an uneven interest in South Korean democracy. Always concerned with stability, the United States tended to favor democratization when it advanced the cause of stability. After the outbreak of the Korean War in 1950, Rhee's government became progressively less democratic. Preoccupied with the threat from the North, the US government made little effort to restrain Rhee authoritarian tendencies in the 1950s. Yet when the ROK government rigged the 1960 elections and protesters poured into the streets, the United States helped ease Rhee out of office, paving the way for a democratic transition. When Park Chung Hee launched his coup d'etat in 1961, the United States did not contest the outcome, but did pressure Park to hold elections, which he did in 1963. Park's declaration of martial law in 1972 coincided with a period of US retrenchment in Asia, during which it withdrew from Vietnam and reached out to China. As a practitioner of *Realpolitik*, President Nixon was not inclined to confront Park about internal matters.

The contrasting outcomes of the South Korean transitions in 1979–80 and 1987 are attributable in part to the very different approaches to those events taken by the Carter administration and the Reagan administration, respectively. Although the Carter administration welcomed the democratic opening of 1979 and lent its support to the interim government, the administration shied away from an active effort to ensure the transition's success. The turbulence of the US-ROK relationship in 1977 and 1978 was one reason. In addition, the crisis in US-Iranian relations made the administration extremely averse to any course of action that risked further instability.

The Reagan administration approached the US-ROK relationship from a different perspective. Initially, the Reagan administration rejected democracy promotion in principle, preferring to focus on the solidarity of anticommunist governments, both authoritarian and democratic. As a result, Reagan developed a relationship of trust and confidence with Chun Doo Hwan. Yet, over time, the administration came to favor democratic transitions even at the expense of strongly anticommunist dictatorships. Thus, at a critical moment in 1987, President Reagan sent a personal letter to Chun Doo Hwan, insisting that Chun find a peaceful solution to the prevailing crisis. Ironically, Reagan's word carried considerable weight precisely because Reagan had embraced Chun without hesitation during the early and uncertain days of his regime.

The mutual antagonism of Jimmy Carter and Park Chung Hee resulted in a low point in US-ROK relations. As a candidate for president, Carter spoke in favor of a phased withdrawal of US forces from Korea, planned in consultation with both the ROK and Japan. Yet during his first months in the White House, Carter surprised the ROK by announcing a schedule for the withdrawal of all US combat forces within 4–5 years. The humiliation for Park was considerable, even though Carter ultimately abandoned his plans in response to congressional opposition. Carter also antagonized the Park regime by describing its human rights violations as "repugnant." In addition, the US-ROK relationship suffered as a result of congressional investigations into the influence-buying operations of South Korean businessman Park Tong Son. After the Department of Justice indicted Park on 36 counts of bribery and similar offenses, Carter requested his extradition. Park Chung Hee refused. President Park also denied that he had any knowledge of Park Tong Son's activities, although that denial lacked credibility. The legal ramifications of the scandal were minimal, yet once again both presidents felt insulted by the other.[15]

After Park's assassination, the United States sought to present itself as unobtrusive but supportive of reform. Two days after the killing, William Gleysteen, the US ambassador in Seoul, sent a cable to Washington elaborating his preferred approach:

I urge that we resist the temptation to suggest architectural designs to the Koreans in favor of: (A) providing reassurance against the threat from the North, (B) urging the observance of "constitutional processes" and (C) gently working through all channels toward political liberalization. We should avoid critical public comment or punishing actions unless and until the new regime has blotted its copybook.[16]

The challenge facing the United States was how to favor liberalization both gently and effectively when the partisans of authoritarianism imposed no such restraints on themselves. Chun and Roh's violent takeover of the ROK military on December 12, 1979, represented the first test of the United States' good intentions. General John Wickham, the US commander in Korea, was furious because Chun and Roh had brazenly ignored their obligation to inform the national headquarters before effecting the movement of troops. Yet the only price Chun had to pay for his actions was to sit through a lecture from Ambassador Gleysteen and General Wickham two days after the takeover. According to the cable Gleysteen sent back to Washington, the ambassador told Chun "bluntly and directly" that his actions had threatened the ROK's progress toward freedom and stability. Gleysteen then informed the State Department that "Chon [sic] understood our message clearly."[17]

General Wickham was less confident. He reported back to the Pentagon that "Chun impressed me as a ruthlessly ambitious, scheming and forceful man who believes he is destined to wear the purple [presidential sash]. . . . He is on the make, has a taste for power, and knows how to use it." Nonetheless, Wickham argued for a "hands-off-response" because he believed neither that it was Washington's place to interfere in Korean domestic politics nor that Washington could do so effectively.[18] In January and February 1980, Wickham and Gleysteen gave some consideration to supporting a countercoup within the military by anti-Chun generals but ultimately decided against it. By March, Gleysteen had even begun to defend Chun, reporting back that the United States "should resist oversimplifying Korean politics by making Chun Doo Hwan the sinister source of all evil."[19]

Even after Chun imposed martial law in May, the United States hesitated to question his authority. Meeting on May 22, 1980, in the midst of the violence in Kwangju, the National Security Council decided that the American approach to the ROK government should entail "in the short term support, in the longer term pressure for political evolution."[20] A memo for the national security adviser prepared the day before the meeting laid out the justification for this approach in greater detail. It listed the United States' objectives in South Korea as:

1. Maintain security on the Korean peninsula and strategic stability in Northeast Asia. (Do not contribute to "another Iran"—a big Congressional concern.)

2. Express a carefully calibrated degree of disapproval, public and private, towards

recent events in Korea. (But not in a way which could contribute to instability by suggesting we are encouraging opposition to the Government.)[21]

Despite its initial confidence that the defense of human rights could enhance American security, the Carter administration had now succumbed to the fear that the defense of human rights would damage American security.[22] Ironically, the Carter administration found itself in a position where defending human rights might "contribute to instability" precisely because it had done so little to strengthen democracy and deter a military coup in the months after Park's assassination.

In its final months in office, the Carter administration cooperated with incoming Reagan administration officials to save the life of Kim Dae Jung, who had been sentenced to death for his dissidence against Chun's new regime. This surprising instance of cooperation effectively illustrates how little difference remained between the Carter and Reagan approaches, even though Carter embraced human rights in principle whereas Reagan prioritized anticommunism. In August 1980, Carter wrote a private and impassioned letter to Chun asking him to spare Kim's life.[23] This effort to save an individual without challenging the system responsible for his repression had become characteristic of Carter's human rights initiatives. Also characteristically, the Reagan administration sought to save Kim's life because of outside pressure, not because of an actual concern for Kim. Richard Allen, the incoming national security adviser, recognized that Kim's death would provoke outrage at home and abroad. In the midst of such outrage, it would become impossible for the United States to help Chun consolidate his four-month-old regime, strengthen the US-ROK security relationship, and prevent North Korea from taking advantage of tensions in the West. Thus, Allen negotiated a reprieve for Kim in exchange for an invitation for Chun to visit the White House. According to Richard Armitage, who served as a member of Reagan's transition team in the months before his inauguration, "It was an easy deal."[24] Both sides were willing to compromise in order to promote their shared interest in a stronger US-ROK relationship. On January 21, 1981, the day after Reagan's inauguration, the administration announced that Chun would soon be arriving for a visit. Less than two weeks later, Chun became the first head of state to visit Reagan at the White House.[25]

In June 1982 Reagan reversed his public stand against democracy promotion. In a speech before the British Parliament, Reagan described the spread of democracy across the globe as essential to the free world's ultimate victory over communism. Reagan also observed that democracy rested on a broad foundation of rights and liberties, not just on fair elections. The practical implication of Reagan's new stance was the founding, in 1983, of the National Endowment for Democracy (NED). Even so, few journalists or scholars—let alone Democrats—attributed much credibility to Reagan's claim that the United States would oppose not just dictatorships of the left but also of the right. Archival evidence suggests, however, that Reagan, as usual, meant exactly what he said in public but did not have a clear sense of how to implement the sweeping commitment he had made.[26]

In the months before Reagan's visit to South Korea in November 1983, there was little discussion of how his new commitment to democracy promotion would affect his close relationship with Chun Doo Hwan. In the weeks just before Reagan's departure, the White House focused its energy on arms control issues that threatened to divide the United States from Western Europe. This brief interval was a memorable one for Robert McFarlane, who had just been promoted to national security adviser.[27] Richard Armitage, then serving as the Pentagon executive responsible for military relations with the Asia-Pacific region, recalls that political reform in South Korea was not a major concern at the time.[28] Speaking before the National Assembly in Seoul, Reagan withheld direct criticism of the regime but firmly insisted that democracy was the goal toward which South Korea must strive in spite of the ever-present threat from the North. The American president declared:

> The development of democratic political institutions is the surest means to build the national consensus that is the foundation of true security. . . . We welcome President Chun's farsighted plans for a constitutional transfer of power in 1988. . . . Now, this will not be a simple process because of the ever-present threat from the North. But I wish to assure you once again of America's unwavering support and the high regard of democratic peoples everywhere as you take the bold and necessary steps toward political development.[29]

The State Department's internal summaries of Reagan's discussions with Chun show that Reagan expressed his clear support for liberalization. In a preparatory memo for the meeting, Robert McFarlane informed Reagan that "your second meeting with President Chun should focus on political liberalization and economic issues. Although Chun will not welcome a discussion of the Korean domestic political situation, he will expect you to refer to it and to express support for further liberalization."[30] McFarlane recalls that Reagan's polite and friendly manner softened the pro-democracy message given to Chun. According to McFarlane, "President Reagan's tendency was . . . to never lecture an ally." Reagan's emphasis remained on the brutality and unpredictability of North Korea and its Soviet patrons. Moreover, Reagan "wanted this to be a visit without rancor in any way, or seeming to hector the government."[31]

Surprisingly, Chun did not resist a discussion of political reform. Instead, the South Korean president told Reagan that the ROK's turbulent postwar history had led "the people [to] believe that a change of presidents is only possible through violence. This is a very dangerous way of thinking. . . . My term is scheduled to end in 1988 and it will."[32] Of course, Chun did not specify how his successor would be chosen, nor is there any indication that Reagan pressed for a clarification.

The tension between Reagan's friendship with Chun and his commitment to democracy promotion did not flare up again until just before South Korea's legislative elections in February 1985. Days before the election, Kim Dae Jung returned to South Korea from his exile in the United States. Kim arrived with an entourage of prestigious American observers, including scholars, retired diplomats, and Democratic members of Congress. The observers' purpose was to prevent Kim from sharing the fate of Filipino opposition leader Benigno "Ninoy" Aquino, who was murdered on the tarmac of the Manila airport after his return from exile in the United States. Although Kim arrived safely, ROK security officers beat and threw to the ground a number of the American observers.[33] Reagan told journalists that the melee had resulted from "bad judgment on both sides" and that the incident "tended to hide the fact that Korea, South Korea, has made great strides toward democracy. . . . Their democracy is working."[34] Yet as the *Washington Post* pointed out, the assault on Kim's entourage took place just one day after Reagan had declared in his State of the Union address, "Freedom is not the sole prerogative of a chosen few; it is the universal right of all God's children . . . our mission is to nourish and defend freedom and democracy, and to communicate these ideals everywhere we can." If so, then the assault on Kim's entourage was an assault on the principles that Reagan had so passionately sworn to defend. And so, the *Post* asked, "What is [Reagan] going to do about it?"[35] Just four days later, after the opposition's stunning performance in the legislative elections, the *Post* offered Reagan an apology. Its editors asked:

> Did some of us perhaps give too much importance to the well-publicized drama of Kim Dae Jung's return? The image of him as a banned and abused politician seems not to square with the reality of the leeway offered his party in the campaign and with its success at the polls. . . . It remains, however, that President Chun, partly in response to American "quiet diplomacy," has been opening up the system somewhat: releasing prisoners, readmitting banned people to academic and political life.[36]

It is unknown whether Reagan understood that legislative elections were about to take place when he said of the South Koreans, "Their democracy is working." Nonetheless, the elections validated Reagan's confidence that change was underway. In April, Chun visited the White House for a second time, where Reagan praised "the steps his government has taken to further promote freedom and democracy."[37] This time, there were no negative editorials and Chun's visit did not even make the front page of either the *Washington Post* or the *New York Times*.

Reagan demonstrated no apparent interest in the protracted negotiations over the presidential succession process that consumed South Korea politics in late 1986 and early 1987. Midranking officials in the administration monitored the negotiations carefully, however. Gaston Sigur, the assistant secretary of state for East Asian and Pacific affairs, actively sought to extract concessions from Chun's regime. On February 6, 1987, during a public address in New York devoted entirely to the situation in South Korea, Sigur declared that the time had come for the military's permanent withdrawal from the nation's politics. According to Sigur, the security of the ROK in the midst of constant threats from the North demanded a popular government no less than it did a strong army.[38] Somewhat recklessly, Sigur delivered his address without prior approval from any of his superiors. At first, Secretary of State George Shultz was outraged by Sigur's insubordination. Yet just a few weeks later, when Shultz visited Seoul to meet with Chun, Shultz said of Sigur's speech that "every sentence, every word, every comma is the policy of our government."[39] In public, Shultz was less animated but no less firm. At a press conference following his discussions with Chun, Shultz announced, "The United States, as a friend and ally, supports the aspirations of all Koreans for continuing political development, respect for basic human rights and free and fair elections."[40]

In the spring of 1987, Washington paid little attention to the situation in South Korea, in part because the capital was consumed with the scandal known as Iran-Contra. In Seoul, however, US ambassador James Lilley sought to lay the foundation for gradual reform without compromising the ROK's stability. In November 1986 Lilley had replaced Ambassador Richard "Dixie" Walker, Reagan's first ambassador to Seoul. Walker was a staunch advocate of close relations between the US and ROK governments. Walker also had a habit of making flippant remarks that antagonized his critics. According to Don Oberdorfer, the *Washington Post*'s correspondent for Northeast Asia at the time, "Dixie, he was not the easiest person for a correspondent to deal with. . . . He had his own agenda, so to speak. . . . He was a decent guy, he was a kind of avuncular figure. . . . I never had the sense he was telling me what he was really thinking."[41] Ambassador Lilley recalls that Walker was unpopular with the professional diplomats at the US Embassy in Seoul and that even State Department officials in Washington "took hard hits" at Walker. In addition, Walker bore the resentment of prominent scholars of East Asian affairs in the United States, who were fierce critics of the Chun dictatorship. Upon his arrival in Seoul, Lilley was scarcely more popular than his predecessor. Most of Walker's critics objected to Lilley's appointment as ambassador, in the expectation that his diplomacy would resemble Walker's.[42]

During the process of his confirmation as ambassador, Lilley concluded, "Voices from the legislative corridors of Washington as well as from the halls of the State

Department were pushing, loudly and crudely, for the primacy of democracy in the South Korean equation." Lilley resented those who insisted that the pursuit of security and reform were mutually exclusive. Among those he singled out was Senator John Kerry (D-MA), who asked Lilley at his confirmation hearings, "What do you place first: security or democracy?"[43] Lilley's approach to the US-ROK relationship stood in contrast to the approach of both his subordinates at the embassy and his superior in Washington, Gaston Sigur. Whereas Sigur made a point of visiting Kim Dae Jung on all of his trips to Korea, Lilley resisted the pressure to meet with Kim during his first months as US ambassador in Seoul. Lilley recalls that many of his colleagues wanted him to follow the example set by Ambassador Harry Barnes, a forceful advocate of democracy and human rights during his tenure in a number of South American capitals in the 1980s.[44]

In the final weeks before the explosion of protests and riots that brought down the dictatorship, Sigur and Lilley continued to serve as the two faces of American diplomacy in South Korea. Although not apparently by design, Sigur and Lilley performed a sort of "good cop, bad cop" routine, in which the assistant secretary demanded concessions from the regime, while the ambassador assured Chun and Roh of America's friendship. During his several visits to Seoul in this period, Sigur continued to make a point of meeting with Kim Dae Jung, who remained under house arrest at the time. On one occasion, the government sought to intimidate Sigur by having the security detail guarding Kim's house rock Sigur's car so hard that it almost flipped over. Lilley describes this as "a scare tactic of the crudest form." Yet rather than granting Sigur's requests to join the assistant secretary for his meetings with Kim Dae Jung, Lilley held back. He later wrote:

> I kept more quiet about my work, reassuring leaders that they had US support and then making sure they understood our hope that democratic change would come in the form of open elections, greater freedom of the press, and genuine opposition parties. I couldn't be effective as the US ambassador if alienated from my Korean counterparts.[45]

Among Lilley's most controversial decisions in this period was to attend the electoral convention of Chun and Roh's Democratic Justice Party (DJP) in early June 1987. The US Embassy's own political counselor told Lilley that his attendance amounted to complicity in a democratic charade. Sixty other ambassadors boycotted the convention. Yet Roh Tae Woo personally expressed his gratitude to Lilley for his attendance, observing that there had been considerable pressure for Lilley to join the boycott.[46]

In keeping with Chun's wishes, the convention nominated Roh to succeed Chun as president. When announced in public on June 10, 1987, Roh's nomination sparked the wave of protests and riots that ultimately brought about a democratic transition. On the evening of June 10, student protesters occupied the Myungdong Cathedral in downtown Seoul. The government considered evicting the students by force.[47] Lilley, however, counseled against such a reckless move. Meeting with the ROK foreign minister on June 13, Lilley said flat out, "Don't go into the cathedral with troops. It will reverberate all over the world." The government stood down and resolved the situation peacefully by relying on priests to serve as intermediaries with the students.[48]

The explosion in South Korea caught Washington off guard. Neither the president nor the secretary of state nor any other high-ranking official made a public statement about the events in South Korea. Although some within the administration suggested sending a presidential emissary to Seoul, others felt that confronting Chun in a public manner might provoke a backlash. Eventually, a consensus emerged around a proposal to send a private letter from Reagan to Chun counseling restraint.[49] The precise origins of this approach are difficult to identify. During Reagan's second term, the White House, State Department, and Pentagon coordinated their policies toward East Asia by means of a weekly meeting on Monday afternoons known as the "EA [East Asia] informal." The principal participants in these meetings were Gaston Sigur from the State Department, Richard Armitage from the Pentagon, and James Kelly from the National Security Council staff at the White House. A critical influence on this group's thinking with regard to Korea was its successful and bloodless effort to facilitate a democratic transition in the Philippines in 1986.[50]

The group had several reasons to believe that a letter from Reagan to Chun, rather than a more confrontational approach, might be sufficient to prevent bloodshed and promote reform in Seoul. First of all, "The South Korean military . . . had a big hangover from Kwangju." Although Chun was hardly repentant, many officers were ashamed of the military for killing hundreds of the civilians they were supposed to protect. Chun himself was constrained by the upcoming Olympics and the potential for the games to be canceled in the event of major violence. The members of the EA informal also believed that Roh Tae Woo was "far more flexible" than Chun Doo Hwan. In several discussions with Roh, members of the group had suggested that Roh would be able to prevail in free and fair elections as a consequence of the opposition's inability to unite behind a single candidate, either Kim Dae Jung or Kim Young Sam.[51] The EA informal's perception of Roh as more flexible than Chun was shared by others. Lilley recalls that "Roh was a different kind of man."[52] In addition, Roh cultivated a close relationship with Don Oberdorfer, the correspondent for the *Washington Post*, in spite of the paper's constant condemnations of the dictatorship. Oberdorfer recalls that Roh's "eagerness" to talk was "extraordinary." Oberdorfer adds that "I always had hopes for [Roh]. . . . He was an open-minded guy who wanted to talk."[53]

Reagan's letter to Chun was moderate in tone but delivered in a forceful manner. Composed by the president's advisers, "the missive was couched in sympathetic, gentle, and inoffensive language, which Reagan preferred when dealing with allies." Moreover, the contents of the letter were vague and referred to the crisis at hand indirectly at best. For example, the letter observed, "Dialogue, compromise, and negotiation are effective ways to solve problems and maintain national unity."[54] Delivering the letter in a time of crisis presented a challenge. The South Korean ambassador to Washington, Kim Kyung Won, advised Ambassador Lilley to present the letter to Chun in person, rather than dispatching it through the corridors of the Foreign Ministry. The letter from Washington arrived in Seoul on the night of Wednesday, June 17. On Thursday, the Foreign Ministry informed the US Embassy via phone that Chun would not receive Lilley. The US political counselor, the third-ranking official at the embassy, then demanded a meeting with a ministry representative, only to be given the same reply as before. Only after the political counselor lost his temper and began to yell at one of his South Korean counterparts did the foreign minister himself place a phone call to Lilley. Chun would agree to meet with the American ambassador on Friday, June 19.[55]

Lilley was invited to meet Chun at the Presidential Palace at 2 pm on Friday. At 10 am, Chun had met with his defense minister, intelligence chief, and uniformed chiefs of staff. Chun ordered the deployment of battle-ready troops across the country by 4 am the next morning. Plans were made to arrest opposition leaders. Before visiting Chun at the Palace, Lilley conferred with the commander of US forces in Korea, General William J. Livesey. The ambassador informed the general of his intention to advise Chun against the use of force. Livesey said nothing. In an unusual departure from his conservative style, Lilley chose to interpret the general's silence as consent for a forceful demarche to President Chun. Lilley was determined to reinforce "Reagan's amicable letter with firm and unambiguous statements about the US position regarding the declaration of martial law."[56] Lilley ventured to Chun that the imposition of martial law would risk undermining the US-ROK alliance and result in another massacre as disastrous as the one at Kwangju. Lilley told Chun, "This is the American position. The [US military] command is with me. I speak for all of the United States."[57]

In addition to the administration, Congress sought to send its own message to Chun and his supporters. Resolutions calling for free and fair elections in South Korea passed both houses without a single dissenting vote. Remarkably, both Republicans and Democrats embraced the Wilsonian proposition that promoting democracy enhanced US national security rather than sowing chaos. Sen. Claiborne

Pell (D-RI), observed that "If the South Korean people are able to freely choose their own government, they will not hesitate to defend it."[58] Some Democrats went further and sought to deploy economic sanctions against the Chun regime. On June 18, the day before Lilley presented Reagan's letter to Chun, Senator Ted Kennedy (D-MA) introduced the "Democracy in South Korea Act," which would have imposed sanctions on the ROK because "there is no justification for American trade assistance that subsidizes dictatorship in South Korea." Senator Kerry, a cosponsor of the act, added, "Quiet diplomacy and the familiar refrain of nonintervention in Korea's internal affairs' are simply not adequate responses to the present crisis . . . I am cosponsoring and avidly support the proposed sanctions against South Korea."[59] The call for sanctions never gathered much support, however. Of course, when Roh announced on June 29 that there would be direct presidential elections, the question of sanctions became irrelevant.

Just two or three hours after Lilley met with Chun, Foreign Minister Choi Kwang Soo informed the ambassador by phone that Chun had decided not to declare martial law.[60] To what degree might one say that American diplomacy promoted the democratic cause in South Korea? More specifically, to what degree might American diplomacy have influenced Chun's decision not to use the military to crush the pro-democracy movement in 1987 as he had in 1980? Was it a coincidence that Chun made his decision just hours after Lilley delivered Reagan's letter, or can a direct, causal relationship be established? Lilley himself cautions against believing that American diplomacy was dispositive. He writes that "it was likely the South Koreans themselves," both generals and diplomats, who "may have influenced President Chun the most." As Armitage observed, the military itself would not countenance another Kwangju.[61] Oberdorfer suggests that the younger colonels and generals in the ROK military made known to Chun and Roh their adamant opposition to the use of lethal force against the protesters. Among authors who have scrutinized the South Korean transition, the most widely cited explanation for Chun's restraint is that if the violence escalated, the International Olympic Committee might have called off the 1988 Summer Games or awarded them to another host.[62] For Chun, the games symbolized the success of his effort to transform South Korea into a truly modern republic. Although Chun had taken power in the midst of deep recession, he presided over a return to double-digit economic growth. Chun also took power at an unprecedented low point in US-ROK relations and proceeded to restore an alliance that many South Koreans considered essential to their security. Resorting to the brutal methods of 1980 would have jeopardized that achievement. Finally, given that Roh had strong prospects of winning a free and fair election, Chun could be confident that neither the economic nor the diplomatic pillar of his agenda would crumble as a result of a democratic transition.

Ultimately, there is no way to separate and quantify the significance of these critical influences on Chun's thinking. One can only speculate whether Chun might
still have kept the army in its barracks if there were no Summer Games scheduled
for 1988, if the United States signaled that violence was acceptable, or if Roh were
not a viable candidate in a free and fair election.

CONCLUSION

In the context of the Cold War, the willingness of the United States to pressure its
authoritarian allies was closely related to the risk that destabilizing the incumbent
dictatorship would facilitate its replacement with a Marxist or pro-Soviet regime.
Today, the willingness of the United States to exert pressure relates closely to the
risk that destabilizing the incumbent dictatorship will facilitate its replacement
with a hostile Islamic regime. The fundamental dilemma is the same. How can
democratic governments promote democratic transitions abroad without compromising their own security? Even though scholars have not paid much attention to
the role of diplomacy in encouraging transitions, American diplomats have begun
to rediscover the subject. In a 2006 address at Georgetown University, Secretary
of State Condoleezza Rice coined the phrase "transformational diplomacy" to describe her efforts to implement the Bush administration's ambitious but controversial democracy promotion agenda.[63] The implications of Rice's efforts remain
unclear, especially now that there is a Democratic president in the White House.
Yet diplomacy has constituted an essential component of democracy promotion
efforts in the past and can be expected to do so in the future. It is advisable for
scholars to explore the history of such efforts in order to assess what impact they
may have in the years ahead.

NOTES

1. The literal meaning of *chaeya* is "out in the field" or "in the opposition."

2. The most detailed account of these events in English can be found in Don Oberdorfer,
The Two Koreas: A Contemporary History (New York: Basic Books, 1991), 109–11.

3. Research Group on Korean Politics, *Hanguk chongchisa* [Korean Political History]
(Seoul: Paeksan sodang, 1994), 373.

4. There has been persistent disagreement about the number of civilian fatalities in
Kwangju. Whereas government figures put the number at under 200, human rights organizations long insisted that the real death toll was as high as 2,000. Recent research suggests
that the actual toll may have been approximately 300. See Bruce Cumings, *Korea's Place in
the Sun: A Modern History* (New York: W. W. Norton, 1997), 377–78; Linda Lewis, *Laying
Claim to the Memory of May: A Look Back at the 1980 Kwangju Uprising* (Honolulu: University
of Hawaii Press, 2002), 69–71.

5. Koon Woo Nam, *Korean Politics: The Search for Political Consensus and Stability* (Lan-
ham, Md.: University Press of America, 1989), 302.

6. For a full text of Roh's announcement, see Manwoo Lee, *The Odyssey of Korean Democracy: Korean Politics, 1987–1990* (New York: Praeger, 1990), 145–48.

7. Sang Chol Yun, *1980 nyondae hangugui minjuhwa ihaeng kwajong* [Process of Democratic Transition in Korea in the 1980s] (Seoul: Seoul National University Press, 1997), 176–97.

8. Jang-Jip Choi, *Hanguk hyondae chongchiui kujowa pyonhwa* [Contemporary Korean Politics: Structure and Change] (Seoul: Kkachi, 1989), 191–92.

9. Sunhyuk Kim, *The Politics of Democratization in Korea: The Role of Civil Society* (Pittsburgh: University of Pittsburgh Press, 2000), 59.

10. Ibid., 73.

11. Ibid., 85.

12. Ibid., 91–92.

13. For a more detailed set of policy prescriptions relating to diplomacy and democratization, see David Adesnik and Michael McFaul, "Engaging Autocratic Allies to Promote Democracy," *Washington Quarterly* 29, no. 2 (2006): 7–26.

14. John K. Oh, *Korean Politics: The Quest for Democratization and Economic Development* (Ithaca, N.Y.: Cornell University Press, 1999), esp. chap. 2.

15. Lee Chae-Jin, *A Troubled Peace: US Policy and the Two Koreas* (Baltimore: Johns Hopkins University Press, 2006), 81–102. Lee provides the most detailed and thoroughly researched account of US-ROK relations under Carter.

16. Cable, Seoul to Washington, October 28, 1979. Available via the Declassified Documents Reference System (hereafter DDRS). The DDRS is an online database, available via subscription from Gale/Cengage Learning, designed to facilitate access to documents declassified by the federal government.

17. Cable, Seoul to Washington, December 15, 1979, Doc. CK3100116064, DDRS.

18. John A. Wickham, *Korea on the Brink: A Memoir of Political Intrigue and Military Crisis* (Washington, D.C.: Brassey's, 2000), 64–65, 114–18.

19. Cable, Seoul to Washington, March 17, 1980, Doc. CK3100128699, DDRS.

20. NSC Memorandum, "Summary of Conclusions," n.d., cited in Oberdorfer, *The Two Koreas*, 129.

21. Memo, Gregg to Brzezinski, May 21, 1980, Doc. CK3100466142, DDRS.

22. South Korean movement activists almost unanimously point out that the US government's support for Chun after Kwangju—in addition to the widespread speculation in South Korea that the United States might have endorsed or condoned the massacre—was the main reason for the consequential alignment of democracy movement and anti-Americanism. After Kwangju, democracy movement in South Korea took an unambiguously anti-American tone. Interviews with Ki Pyo Chang, Hee Yeon Cho, Se Ung Hahm, Dong Choon Kim, and Choong Il Oh, Seoul, April 21–23, 2008.

23. Letter, Carter to Chun, August 1980, Doc. CK3100117778, DDRS. See also Zbigniew Brzezinski's memo to Carter from September 1980, Doc. CK3100499249, DDRS.

24. Richard Armitage, interview Arlington, Va., April 29, 2008.

25. In public, the Reagan administration denied that it had offered the ROK any incentive to spare Kim's life. This was not wholly untrue, since Reagan and his advisers had always intended to welcome to Washington the most prominent of the right-wing dictators from whom Carter had kept his distance. Thus, in a sense, Allen negotiated a concession from the South Koreans in exchange for an invitation that would have been extended in any event.

26. A. David Adesnik, "Reagan's 'Democratic Crusade': Presidential Rhetoric and the

Remaking of American Foreign Policy" (Ph.D. diss., Oxford University, 2005). Although little noticed either at the time or thereafter, Reagan's conversion to the democratic cause came in response to the unexpected success of free elections in El Salvador, a small country that had an outsized influence on Reagan's thinking about global politics (ibid., 164–214).

27. Robert McFarlane, interview, Arlington, Va., April 28, 2008. McFarlane's predecessor was William "Judge" Clark. McFarlane had served as Clark's deputy.

28. Armitage interview. Armitage's title was Deputy Assistant Secretary of Defense for International Security Affairs.

29. "Address before the Korean National Assembly in Seoul," November 12, 1984, in *Public Papers of the Presidents of the United States* (Washington, D.C.: US Government Printing Office, 1984).

30. Memo, McFarlane to Reagan, November 5, 1983, Doc. CK3100497051, DDRS.

31. McFarlane interview.

32. Memo, Wolfowitz to Shultz, November 19, 1983, National Security Archive—South Korea Collection, Washington, D.C. In contrast to the archive's extensive online and microform holdings, the South Korea Collection is available only to on-site visitors.

33. Cumings, *Korea's Place in the Sun*, 381. Cumings, a historian at the University of Chicago, was one of the members of Kim's entourage. Initial reports claimed that the officers had beaten Kim as well, but Kim later said that this was not so.

34. "Interview with Bernard Weinraub and Gerald Boyd of the New York Times," February 11, 1985, in *Public Papers*.

35. "A Challenge to Mr. Reagan," unsigned editorial, *Washington Post*, February 11, 1985, A22.

36. "The Elections in Korea," unsigned editorial, *Washington Post*, February 15, 1985, A24.

37. "Remarks Following Discussions with President Chun Doo Hwan of the Republic of Korea," April 26, 1985, in *Public Papers*.

38. *American Foreign Policy—Current Documents* (Washington, D.C.: Department of State, 1987), February 6, 1987, Doc. 366. Sigur ensured greater exposure for his address by delivering it on the day before a memorial service for Park Chong Chol, a student who had died in police custody.

39. Oberdorfer, *The Two Koreas*, 166.

40. David K. Shipler, "Seoul Gives Shultz a Democracy Vow," *New York Times*, March 7, 1987, A3.

41. Don Oberdorfer, interview, Washington, D.C., April 28, 2008.

42. James Lilley, interview, Washington, D.C., April 28, 2008. Ambassador Walker passed away in 2003. He himself was a scholar of East Asian affairs who received his doctorate from Yale in 1950 and continued to teach at the university until 1957. Lilley recalled that those on the East Asia faculty at Yale were the most vocal critics of Walker in the 1980s.

43. James Lilley (with Jeffrey Lilley), *China Hands: Nine Decades of Adventure, Espionage, and Diplomacy in Asia* (New York: Public Affairs, 2004), 265–66.

44. Lilley interview.

45. Lilley, *China Hands*, 270–71.

46. Ibid.

47. Se Ung Hahm, a prominent Catholic priest who led the pro-democracy movement in the 1980s who currently serves as president of the Korea Democracy Foundation, recollects that he was told that Catholic countries in Europe and Latin America would consider

boycotting the Olympic Games if the Korean government used force to evict the student protestors from the Myungdong Cathedral. Hahm, interview, Seoul, April 22, 2008.

48. Lilley, *China Hands*, 274.

49. Oberdorfer, *The Two Koreas*, 168.

50. Armitage, interview, April 29, 2008. The successful transition in the Philippines also served as a great inspiration to democracy activists and opposition leaders in South Korea. Interviews with Se Ung Hahm, Seoul, April 22, 2008, and Dong Choon Kim, Seoul, April 23, 2008.

51. Armitage interview.

52. Lilley interview.

53. Oberdorfer interview.

54. Quoted in Oberdorfer, *The Two Koreas*, 168.

55. Lilley, *China Hands*, 276.

56. Ibid., 277–78.

57. Oberdorfer, *The Two Koreas*, 170.

58. *Congressional Record*, June 27, 1987, 17916.

59. *Congressional Record*, June 18, 1987, 16652, 16662.

60. Lilley interview.

61. Lilley, *China Hands*, 278; Armitage interview.

62. Oberdorfer, *The Two Koreas*, 164; Cumings, *Korea's Place in the Sun*, 332–33.

63. Condoleezza Rice, "Remarks at the Georgetown University School of Foreign Service," January 18, 2006, www.unc.edu/depts/diplomat/item/2006/0103/rice/rice_georgetown.htm.

CHAPTER TWELVE

Turkey

The Counterintuitive Transition of 1983

Senem Aydin-Düzgit and Yaprak Gürsoy

On September 12, 1980, the Turkish Armed Forces overthrew their democratic government, claiming that anarchy, terror, separatism, and economic crises had crippled Turkish society. In a publicized speech, Chief of the General Staff Kenan Evren accused the political parties of inciting domestic terror between leftist and rights groups and not taking on the responsibility to prevent chaos. In the same speech, General Evren implied that the military would return to its barracks and lead a transition to democracy after the restoration of law and order and the preparation of a new constitution.[1] The military kept its promise to a limited degree and stayed in power for only three years. In 1982 a new constitution was written, and in November 6, 1983, new elections were held.

THE TRANSITION TO DEMOCRACY

The liberalization process, however, had serious shortcomings. Only three parties that were preapproved by the generals were allowed to run in the November elections. Additionally, most of the politicians before the 1980 coup and their parties were banned from politics. The military increased its political autonomy and received reserve and tutelary powers in the 1982 constitution. The constitution itself was highly criticized for its restriction of basic political, social, and minority rights.[2]

Despite these shortcomings, the November 1983 elections were the event that marked the transition to democracy in Turkey. This was because a center-right political party that was not favored by the military won 45 percent of the votes and received the mandate to form the first civilian government after the 1980 intervention. The military hierarchy preferred former General Turgut Sunalp; yet it still relinquished its control in favor of Turgut Özal, the founder and leader of the victorious Motherland Party. Four years later, the Özal government lifted the ban on political parties. Subsequently, free and fair elections were held in November 1987, with the participation of political leaders and parties of the pre-1980 coup. Even though it was the 1987 elections that truly qualified Turkey as a minimal electoral democracy, formal military rule ended in 1983. The victory of a civilian in these elections also set the background for the lifting of political restrictions four years later. Therefore, Turgut Özal's electoral success in 1983 denotes a democratic breakthrough.

In this chapter, we argue that the Turkish military intervention of 1980 did not face significant opposition from international actors and there was no major international intervention for democracy in Turkey. Despite lack of sanctions and only a minimal degree of pressure on the Turkish military, international actors still played important but perhaps counterintuitive roles in the democratic transition. International actors (especially the United States) did not provide assistance to domestic opposition forces and continued to provide aid to the military. As a result, the relative balance of power among domestic groups was kept in favor of the military. The Turkish military was successful in restoring order and repressing opposition forces. This, in turn, gave the military generals confidence that they had achieved their initial goals when they first planned the intervention and therefore could lead a transition to democracy.

Second, economic accomplishments during military rule with considerable American, World Bank, and International Monetary Fund (IMF) assistance contributed to the democratic transition. Relatively good economic performance increased the confidence of the generals and contributed to their decision to lead a transition to democracy. Additionally, implementation of a successful adjustment program in coordination with the World Bank and IMF increased the popularity of Turgut Özal, who served in the military government until 1982 as the minister responsible for the economy. This facilitated his triumph in the 1983 elections. Özal's contacts with Western political actors made it difficult for the generals to keep Özal out of the race and ignore the electoral results once the ballot was cast.

Finally, the Europeans pressured the military to keep its word and return the country to democracy. The military was pushed to declare a timetable for return to democracy approximately one year after the coup. These gestures that were taken to satisfy the international community increasingly bound the military rulers by their own words to eventually hold elections and consent to its results.

DOMESTIC FACTORS IN THE 1983 TRANSITION TO DEMOCRACY

The 1980 coup and the 1983 transition to democracy were not the first of their kind in Turkey. In fact, Turkey made its first transition to democracy in 1950, when the single-party rule of the Republican People's Party (RPP) came to an end with national elections. The RPP founded the Turkish Republic in 1923 and carried out several political, social, and economic reforms that molded a secular republic in a predominantly Muslim country. The Kemalist ideology of the party envisioned a modern Turkish society that would be part of the politically and sociologically more advanced Western countries. Even though the military was not directly involved in government during this period, it took on the responsibility to support the policies and reforms of the RPP and serve as the guardian of the Kemalist, secular, nationalist, and pro-Western revolution. Indeed, the RPP included significant numbers of retired military officers, and the founder of the Republic, Mustafa Kemal Atatürk, was a commander of the armed forces.

After the first transition to democracy, Turkey witnessed two military interventions in 1960 and 1971. Ironically, these interventions resulted in the perception that the Turkish Armed Forces were not greedy. The military did not hold on to power for long periods of time despite having had the opportunity to do so. It justified each of its interventions by its self-declared role as the guarantor of the Kemalist reforms, secularism, democracy, and Turkey's Western orientation. Even though both actions in the 1960s and the 1970s resulted in coups, most outside observers and significant segments of the Turkish public had come to believe that it was not in the Turkish Armed Forces traditional character to establish a long-term military dictatorship and that they were in fact the true guardians of the Kemalist republic.

Similar sentiments led to the public endorsement of the coup in 1980. The military enjoyed support from the majority of society because of the instability of the 1970s and the relative success of the military in power.[3] The 1970s was identified with increasing terrorism and street violence. The ideological conflict between the Left and the Right in parliament and on the streets was combined with increasing religious fundamentalism throughout Turkey and Kurdish separatist movements in the eastern regions. Violence had reached such proportions that there were on average 20 deaths per day during the weeks that preceded the military intervention.

Another source of concern before the intervention was the economic crisis. The exhaustion of import substitution industrialization strategy coincided with the 1973 oil crisis, increases in prices, and a drop in the volume of imports. The result was widespread scarcity of basic commodities, accumulation of foreign debt, and increasing inflation and unemployment. People from all walks of life were affected by the crisis. While strike activities and radicalism intensified among the lower income groups, the leading business enterprises and associations were also dissatisfied and blamed the politicians for giving in to radical groups and failing to readjust the economy. As a final attempt to save the economy, in January 1980, the last government formed by the Justice Party initiated a major economic program, which would start a new export-led growth period, in accordance with the suggestions of the IMF. Even though this program was welcomed by the business community, labor and some inefficient sectors resisted liberalization. Because of its unpopularity, the government failed to fully implement the program.

Thus, when the military took over on September 12, 1980, Turkey faced several challenges, the most important ones being terrorism, lack of personal safety, and economic crisis. In all of these issues, the military was relatively successful.[4] Until the transition to democracy in 1983, the military repressed what it perceived as threatening groups and put an end to violence and terrorism. The generals perceived the mainstream political parties as one of the primary reasons for the instability of the 1970s. According to the military hierarchy, even though the terrorist organizations had relatively few supporters, they still had an important destabilizing effect because of the lenient attitudes of the center-left and center-right parties. Indeed, the coup was against mainstream politics as much as it was against radical groups. As a result, for the first time the military closed down all parties, including the founding party of the Republic, the RPP.

In the economic sphere, the military gave the responsibility of readjustment to Turgut Özal, who was a former employee of the World Bank, a well-known figure in business circles, and the chief architect of the economic program announced in January. This unpopular program could now be implemented under martial law, which restricted worker activities. As a result, in a short period of time, the economy picked up and grew on average close to 4 percent per annum (thanks mainly to the growth in industry). Exports boomed, Turkey's balance of payments was enhanced, tax revenue doubled, and inflation declined to around 30 percent.[5]

These political and economic policies of the coup were welcomed by some elite groups. Özal's economic solutions were perceived positively "by the private sector, in general, and big business, in particular," and became one of the reasons why the business community supported the 1980 intervention.[6] Even though the activities of the politicians were severely restricted, most political leaders also chose not to actively oppose the military.[7] The military's intervention was seen as a bitter pill that needed to be swallowed for stability.

The main domestic reasons in explaining the transition to democracy in Turkey are the relatively weak opposition the military faced during its rule and its success in achieving its goals in accordance with the Kemalist ideology. The military was successful in restoring law and order by suppressing opposition groups and stabilizing the economy. The commanders of the armed forces became confident that democracy would not produce the same results as it did in the 1970s, since the former political forces, including mainstream ones, were now repressed. A return to democracy did not signal to the generals the continuation of major societal upheavals.

An additional factor that contributed to the decision of the incumbent officers to initiate the transition after a short term of rule was the belief that their power and influence would not be damaged. The military hierarchy was directly involved with the writing of the new constitution, which guaranteed increased autonomy and reserve and tutelary powers to the armed forces. The military high command also received personal immunity from prosecution in the 1982 constitution, and Chief of the Staff Kenan Evren assumed the presidency of the Republic for seven years, while the commanders of the armed forces became members of the Presidential Council until 1989.[8]

In conclusion, the military rulers believed that their withdrawal would not threaten the military's interests and their personal well-being and security. Moreover, because the repression of the old political forces was successfully achieved, there was belief that the reforms the armed forces instituted would not be upset and reversed.

EXTERNAL ACTORS: REACTIONS TO MILITARY RULE AND PRESSURES FOR REDEMOCRATIZATION

The most crucial foreign actors for Turkey at the beginning of the 1980s were the United States and several Western European countries, the North Atlantic Treaty Organization (NATO), World Bank, the IMF, Organization for Economic Cooperation and Development (OECD), Council of Europe (COE), and the European Community. Several human rights organizations, such as the Helsinki Human Rights Watch based in the United States and Amnesty International, also played vital roles in reporting issues of torture, cases against freedom of speech, and unjust imprisonment during military rule.[9]

The Turkish military between 1980 and 1983 did not face any major external influences and pressures for democratic transition emanating from these groups. There were no overt, tangible, and coercive forms of international intervention in Turkey. Even the minimal amount of economic, political, and diplomatic sanctions that the Turkish military faced was not substantial and significant taken as a whole.

The Support of the United States, US-Based Institutions, and NATO

Turkey's alliance with the United States, which dates back to the end of the Second World War, continued during the military rule of 1980–83. Before the coup d'etat American officials believed that the situation in Turkey was chaotic and potentially dangerous for US interests, especially if the leftist or Islamic terrorist organizations were to gain the upper hand.[10] Reflecting this view, in its first official declaration about the military coup in Turkey, the Carter administration stressed that "for the last several years, Turkey has been beset by increasing politically motivated terrorism and severe economic difficulties." In the statement, the United States pledged to continue its assistance to Turkey and declared its hope that Turkey will have economic and political stability.[11]

This initial "low-key" response to Turkey contrasted with the US reaction to other military interventions in the world at around the same time.[12] In his daily report to President Jimmy Carter on September 12, Secretary of State Edmund Muskie commented that "the press will rightly note the clear difference in tone between this statement and those we have made about situations in Korea and Bolivia. . . . [T]here is no junta mentality in Turkey."[13] Indeed, American newspapers *did* pick up on this difference and argued that "US officials seemed almost relieved that the interruption of democracy came not from such extremist forces as Turkey's communists or fundamentalist Moslems, but from the armed forces." It was noted that the administration perceived the Turkish military as "moderate, pro-Western and committed to Turkey's role as NATO's strategically important southern anchor in the Mediterranean."[14] In addition, there was strong belief in the administration that the military would return to its barracks after restoring order, as it did before.

The positive assessments of the State Department officials were shared by the US National Security Council. In a memorandum sent to National Security Advisor Zbigniew Brzezinski, a Turkey specialist argued that

> proposals [are being made by] people with little judgment on Turkey . . . for gestures of disapproval for the military takeover. Most of this simply adds up to the petty sanctimoniousness which would needlessly irritate the military leadership in Turkey which has shown every sign of responsibility and good judgment and hardly needs nattering from us in schoolmarmish fashion. We should not boycott meetings or other scheduled international undertakings in which Turkey is playing a role nor should we encourage NATO allies to do this sort of thing. Other gestures that serve no concrete purpose should be avoided. . . . The basic posture [that the US government] has taken

so far is exactly right. Let's not muddy our record by unnecessary self-righteousness! The Turkish generals are not Greek colonels or African master-sergeants. Let's make it clear to them that we understand that![15]

Cordial exchanges took place between the military rulers, the US Embassy, high-ranking diplomats, and even President Jimmy Carter in the early days. In early October, President Carter sent a message to General Evren through the US ambassador in Ankara and appeared "understanding" of the military coup. Evren replied to this message and reminded Carter that "the Turkish Armed Forces have always been committed to democratic rule" and that they "are determined . . . to remove all obstacles which have, in the past, hindered the healthy functioning of the democratic order."[16]

Similar to the US administration, NATO officials took a controlled stance in their initial reaction to the Turkish coup. A NATO spokesman argued that the intervention was "'strictly an internal matter,' but said a strong, stable and violence-free Turkey [was] vital to the Western alliance." The official stated that NATO hoped Turkey would return to democracy, similar to the 1960 and 1971 military interventions.[17] Despite NATO's democratic credentials and the agitation of some European members about the legitimacy of Turkish military rule, there were no discussions of expelling Turkey from NATO or any substantial pressure for democratization as a result of the military takeover.

After the first warm response of the American government and NATO to the military coup, good relations between the allies continued. The Turkish-US Defense and Cooperation Agreement (DECA), which was renewed in March 1980 before the coup, was ratified after the military took over in Turkey.[18] With the DECA, the United States pledged to provide general economic assistance and military aid to renovate Turkey's armed forces. As promised, Turkey received substantial amounts of economic and military aid during the junta years. There was gradual increase in economic and military assistance during military rule when compared with the three years leading up to the coup (table 12.1). Between 1980 and 1983, Turkey received a total of $2.253 billion in economic and military assistance. This amount was the third largest American aid to a foreign country after Israel and Egypt.[19]

Turkey also received economic aid from the World Bank and IMF, which had already committed to Turkey's economic readjustment before the military coup. International donors aided Turkey before 1980 by rescheduling its external debt. After the declaration of the January 1980 readjustment plan by the democratically elected Demirel government, the World Bank provided a $200 million structural adjustment loan. In June 1980, Turkey and the IMF signed a three-year standby agreement which provided approximately $1.6 billion worth of assistance.[20]

TABLE 12.1.
Assistance to Turkey (in millions of current US dollars)

	1977	1978	1979	1980	1981	1982	1983	1984	1985
Economic assistance	0.2	1.1	69.6	198.1	201.0	301.1	286.0	139.5	175.9
Military assistance	125.0	175.4	180.3	208.2	252.8	403.0	402.8	718.3	703.6
Total	125.2	176.6	250.0	406.3	453.8	704.1	688.8	857.8	879.5

Source: US Agency for International Development (USAID) Overseas Loans and Grants, Obligations and Loan Authorizations (Greenbook), http://qesdb.usaid.gov/gbk.

Support continued after the military took over. Özal's presence in the military's cabinet persuaded the IMF and World Bank that the Turkish Armed Forces were dedicated to the implementation of the liberalization program. The suppression of worker activities during the military regime was also a positive sign that the reform program could be carried out.[21] In October 1980, the World Bank approved a supplement of $75 million to the first structural adjustment loan (SAL). In April 1981 the second SAL for $300 million was sanctioned. The third structural adjustment loan, worth $304.5 million, was also endorsed during the military regime.[22] The World Bank also gave other types of assistance, such as "project loans, economic and sector work leading to policy recommendations, and technical assistance."[23] The bank collaborated closely with the IMF, which in 1983 signed another one-year standby agreement with Turkey, supplying around $75 million. Both institutions guided and monitored the economic liberalization reforms and aided the military government in continuing to restructure the economy by providing monetary assistance.

American support to Turkey between 1980 and 1983 was not always in monetary terms. In their speeches and visits to Turkey, US officials also approved the actions of the military leaders. In December 1981, Defense Secretary Caspar W. Weinberger visited Turkey and met with Chief of the General Staff Kenan Evren. Two leaders agreed that a "high-level joint defense group" would be established to " 'enlarge and improve defense cooperation' between two nations."[24] Perhaps more importantly than this agreement, Weinberger openly praised General Evren, stating, "We admire greatly the way in which order and law have been restored in Turkey under your very able direction."[25] In May 1982, Secretary of State Alexander Haig made a similar visit to Turkey and met with high level officials. Haig brought with him a letter from President Ronald Reagan and congratulated the junta for restoring law and order. Haig also "encouraged the military leaders to move ahead with their timetable for a return to democracy."[26] However, such calls for democratization by US officials did not go further than "encouragement" since, even behind closed doors in these meetings, Turkish military leaders were not pressured to make a transition.[27]

Such political support from American officials was critical in balancing international opposition to the military.[28] For instance, Secretary of State Alexander Haig angrily responded to a British reporter in Brussels, who asked if "the United States was using a 'double standard' in condemning martial law in Poland . . . while increasing aid to Turkey." Haig argued that "the question itself 'reflects a double standard' by Europeans equating Poland and Turkey." The secretary of state reminded the reporter that Turkey was in chaos before the military intervention.[29] In his visit to Ankara, Haig also discussed the attitudes of the Europeans with

General Evren, who extensively complained about Europe's negativity toward Turkish domestic politics.[30]

When the issue of expelling Turkey from the Council of Europe came up, American officials were worried that Turkey would be isolated from Europe.[31] On this issue, the Reagan administration "pressed the Europeans to relax their stand on Turkey and resume economic aid."[32] When in July 1982 several European countries applied to the European Commission of Human Rights in Strasburg against the Turkish junta, the United States officially defended Turkey once again. A State Department announcement said, "While there are human rights problems in Turkey, it would be shortsighted to forget that the current government has nearly eliminated the human rights violations due to terrorism that were rapidly eroding the viability of democracy in Turkey."[33]

The official policy of the US administration in dealing with the rift between Europe over Turkey's military rule is reflected in Secretary of State Haig's message to West German foreign minister Hans-Dietrich Genscher in December 5, 1981. Haig responded to a letter written by Genscher after the minister's visit to Turkey and shortly before Haig's own visit to Ankara as follows:

> Geography, history, and shared values make Turkey a major partner for Europe and the United States. We fully support efforts to overcome the current estrangement between Turkey and certain sectors of Western Europe, in the interest of a stronger alliance, a stronger Europe, and a stronger Turkey. . . .
>
> The supreme goal which all friends of Turkey share is that the current regime return the country to stable democracy in a reasonable timeframe. General Evren and his colleagues are determined to achieve that goal. . . . The United States of America, the Federal Republic of Germany, and other allied and friendly states must assure that Turkey continues to receive sufficient support to achieve its objective. It is noteworthy in this regard that the former politicians whom you met agreed that the Evren regime must not be isolated. That is our view as well.
>
> . . . Continued frank exchanges between friends offer the best means to achieve the results we all seek. Your visit to Ankara served that purpose, as will mine.[34]

The US administration did not defend Turkey only against the Europeans but also against some American critics. On April 14, 1983, a congressional hearing on human rights in Turkey was held before the US Congress. Several human rights activists criticized the restrictive manner in which democracy was being reestablished and argued that torture was widespread in Turkey. Assistant Secretary of State Elliott Abrams and former ambassador to Turkey James Spain were witnesses who defended the Turkish military government and American policy. In their testimony, these State Department officials argued that Islamist and leftist terrorist organizations in Turkey before the military intervention challenged strategic interests. They noted that generals would eventually return to full democracy because of their Western, Kemalist orientation and because they had never intended to stay in power for a long period of time.[35] The results of the staff report written by the US Commission on Security and Cooperation in Europe (CSCE) was also presented in the hearing. The report highlighted that non-Muslim minorities in Turkey felt more secure after the military intervention, implying that repression was not widespread as claimed by the other witnesses.[36] In addition, electoral monitoring by the CSCE was pointed out to demonstrate that the 1982 constitutional referendum was "a fair one, fairly counted, and the results reflect[ed] the views of the people of Turkey."[37]

Even though in the hearing human rights activists pleaded for the aid to Turkey to be cut, Assistant Secretary of State Abrams and Ambassador Spain advocated a different strategy:

> In the case of Turkey, circumstance and unwise policy among those outside . . . could put the essential allegiance to the West in doubt. Many decades ago, Turks chose the West, but they have sometimes felt the West rejected their very choice of the West. . . . If, in properly emphasizing human rights concerns, we isolated Turkey from the Western human rights tradition, the result would be tragedy.
>
> Instead, the United States has sought to protect human rights in Turkey by frequent dialogue with the Government of Turkey, by seeking to protect Turkey's place as a valued Western ally and by keeping Turkey closer to the West rather than pushing it further away.[38]

Thus, the US administration believed that support for Turkey should continue even if the transition to democracy was restrictive. It was argued that sensitivities on human rights should be raised gently only in private meetings. The overall US policy on Turkey during the military intervention suggests that these views of the State Department officials were implemented.

From the initial days of the military intervention in September 1980 to the November 1983 elections, the United States, NATO, and American-based financial institutions supported Turkey militarily, economically, and politically. Criticisms in the United States increased toward the end of the military junta. However, the Reagan administration did not oppose the manner of the transition. Turgut Özal's victory was welcomed by the Americans because of his previous commitment to liberal reforms and experience in the United States as a World Bank employee. However, even if the results were different, support for Turkey would have continued as long as (and to guarantee that) Turkey stayed committed to the Western alliance against the Soviets, was stable and without the risk of an Islamic or leftist takeover, and maintained a healthy liberal economy. In addition, the Turkish Armed Forces were popular and successful at home, and they had a reputation of returning to their barracks. From the perspective of American officials, there was no need to pressure Turkey to democratize. Such pressure might even push away a valuable ally. The counterintuitive US policy was that supporting the Turkish generals and defending them against European and other critiques would hasten the return to a stable democracy.

Reactions of the European Community, the Council of Europe, and the West European Governments

Turkey became a founding member of the Council of Europe in 1949 and signed an Association Agreement with the European Economic Community in 1963. The Turkish military has traditionally viewed Europe as the ultimate destination for the country's Kemalist trajectory of modernization and accorded high primacy to Turkey's membership to these European organizations as an affirmation of the country's European credentials. In contrast to the United States, European governments and institutions were highly critical of the military coup and the policies of the military regime. The pressure for a rapid transition to democracy intensified in time with the exacerbation of human rights conditions in the country, although the extent of the vocal criticism and the ensuing policies aimed to promote transition to democracy in Turkey were not uniform among different Western European states and in the different configurations of the West European institutional settings.

The initial reactions from Europe to the military intervention can in general be regarded as cautious, yet critical. The foreign ministers of the European Community, Commission, and Parliament issued statements expressing concern over the developments in the country.[39] The COE also responded to the military intervention with a recommendation that expressed that the Parliamentary Assembly was "gravely concerned at the military intervention in Turkey." What set the COE recommendation apart from its counterparts in the European Community was its explicit threat of political sanctions on Turkey. In the document, the Parliamentary Assembly recommended to the Committee of Ministers to "remind the Turkish government that the Committee of Ministers has to take action in conformity with Article 8 of the Statute of the Council of Europe if the Turkish government does not take prompt steps as mentioned in paragraph 10." This implied that Turkey could be expelled from the COE if it did not respect the provisions of the European Convention on Human Rights, release all elected politicians who had not gravely violated any law before the coup, and take rapid steps for transition to democracy.[40]

Regarding economic aid, the European Commission officially adopted the position that contractual commitments to Turkey under the Association Agreement, namely the Third Financial Protocol ($400 million) and the Special Aid Package ($100 million), would be honored.[41] The policy of continued economic aid to Turkey was, however, becoming more and more difficult to sustain, especially after the first year of military rule. The European Council and the European Commission were under constant attack from the European Parliament for not freezing EC aid to Turkey in the face of massive human rights violations and rising concerns over a speedy return to democracy in the country.[42] In addition to Turkey's worsening human rights record, the accession of Greece in 1981 to the EC and the efforts of Greek members to freeze relations with Turkey were also influential in the rising criticisms by the Parliament.[43] It was argued that the European Community had to freeze the Association Agreement with Turkey, just like it did with Greece in May 1967.[44] Thus, throughout 1981, the European Parliament—particularly upon the initiatives of the socialist, communist, and liberal parliamentary groups—delivered tough warnings to the military regime through its resolutions. The most significant of those was the one delivered on April 10, 1981 where the European Parliament called on the Commission, Council, and the member states to suspend economic aid to Turkey.[45]

The Council of Ministers and the European Commission, however, paid little attention to Parliament's requests. In fact, in the four debates held at the European Parliament between January and August 1981, both the Council of Ministers and the European Commission preserved their mild attitude to the deeds of the military government and reiterated the importance of continuing cooperation with Turkey, with the hope of aiding the transition to democracy.[46] In line with this, the Council of Ministers approved the terms of the European Commission negotiating mandate in May 1981 for the Fourth Financial Protocol of $625 million, and the Commission completed the formal negotiations with the Turkish representatives within the framework of the Association Committee in June 1981.[47]

This attitude of the Council of Ministers and the European Commission began to change in the second half of 1981, particularly as a reaction to the military government's November 1981 decision to abolish all political parties that existed before the coup and the imprisonment of former prime minister Ecevit for publicly criticizing the military regime.[48] The Fourth Financial Protocol was scheduled to come into force on November 1, 1981. However, the European Commission refused to pass the file concerning the protocol to the Council for final conclusion, and the Council never formally insisted on receiving the file from the Commission, which in effect led to the freezing of EC economic aid to Turkey. The freezing of aid was reinforced further by an initiative of the Socialist members of the European

Parliament Budgets Committee, which ensured that the Council could no longer approve any expenditure under the heading of the Protocol without the consent of the Parliament, which shares budgetary authority.

Turkey's economic relations with individual West European countries were also hampered in 1981. Germany, as the second biggest supplier of military and economic assistance to Turkey after the United States, was the West European country with which Turkey had enjoyed closest economic links. In March 1981, German parliamentarians declared at a news conference that continued economic and military aid to Turkey "would speed up the period of a return to democracy."[49] Nevertheless, mainly owing to pressure from public opinion fueled by the worsening of human rights conditions, the ban on former political parties, and the persecution of the former Social Democratic leader in Turkey, Germany delayed bilateral aid to the country in both 1981 and 1982.[50] What is significant here is that, despite these setbacks, bilateral aid was eventually renewed in both years. In fact, Germany was even reported to undertake the residual financing of some selected national projects that were to be funded under the EC's Fourth Financial Protocol.[51] Germany also continued to be the primary foreign investor in Turkey with 25 companies, ranking above the United States, Switzerland, and France.[52]

The Netherlands, Austria, Luxembourg, and the Nordic countries (Denmark, Finland, Norway, and Sweden) were more adamant in applying economic sanctions on Turkey. They all ended program and project aid under the OECD consortium for Special Assistance to Turkey in 1982. In 1980 and 1981, the total contribution of these countries to the consortium was $65.5 million and $56 million respectively.[53] Since these states were among the smallest contributors to the consortium, while the highest contributor was Germany (with a total of $620.55 million in both years), the economic sanctions imposed were not of high significance for the country. Germany's economic assistance to Turkey in 1982 ($79.63 million) exceeded the total aid dispersed by all seven European states in both 1980 and 1981. Given also the continued US economic assistance to Turkey, reaching high proportions as discussed earlier, it can be argued that the amount of economic sanctions applied by European governments and the European Commission was considered negligible by Turkish officials, who could rely on their main beneficiaries of economic aid, namely the United States and Germany.[54] This was expressed succinctly by a European Commission official when he highlighted that these economic sanctions were merely "pocket money" for the Turkish government.[55]

More so than economic aid, political relations were being used to mount pressure on the military government to make the transition to democracy. In December 1980, European Commission president Thorn expressed his concerns over a rapid transition to democracy in Turkey in a meeting with Foreign Minister Türkmen. Two years later, in January 1982, Foreign Minister Türkmen met Thorn to present the timetable for a transition to democracy and ask for the Fourth Financial Protocol to be resumed, where he was refused on grounds of human rights violations.[56] Leo Tindemans, the president of the European Council, visited Turkey in April 1982. On this visit, General Evren presented Tindemans the timetable for transition to democracy, and Tindemans expressed the Council's concern for the human rights situation in the country.[57] No EC member state suspended bilateral political relations with Turkey. In fact EC states, especially Germany, made use of its political links to promote democratic change in Turkey. As early as March 1981, German Parliament's Foreign Affairs Committee visited Turkey to encourage the Turkish military to achieve a rapid transition to democracy.[58] German foreign minister Genscher first visited Ankara in November 1981 to discuss the delay of German financial assistance to Turkey, where he was assured by General Evren of his intention to hold elections in a reasonable time.[59] Genscher also met Evren in November 1982 to discuss the delay of economic aid and express his concerns at the slow steps toward transition.

As opposed to the Council, the European Commission, and the individual member states, the European Parliament froze political relations with Turkey. The European Parliament adopted a resolution on January 22, 1982, which formally suspended its participation in the Joint Parliamentary Committee and in effect froze political relations between the European Parliament and the Turkish Grand National Assembly.

The COE demonstrated even more opposition to the military regime than did particular European governments or the EC to the extent of considering severe political sanctions. At the May 1981 session of the Council of Europe Parliamentary Assembly, it was decided that the credentials of the Turkish delegates to the Assembly were not to be renewed for the 1981–82 session and that there could be no Turkish delegation in the Assembly until it was "elected and properly constituted."[60] A joint subcommittee of the Political and Legal Committees was also established to monitor developments in Turkey and to deliver regular reports on the political situation in the country.

What was most notable, however, was the debate over the suspension of Turkey's membership to the COE, which had been on the agenda of the COE since the immediate aftermath of the intervention. The possibility of expulsion had been consistently brought up in almost every COE order, resolution, and recommendation on the situation in Turkey between 1980 and 1983. Thus delegations were sent to Turkey to undertake "fact finding missions" and then report their findings to the Assembly in relation to Turkey's membership. The delegations were also forcing the military regime to explain and justify itself under mounting pressure. The best-known delegation visit, which was also widely covered by the international press, took place in January 1982, following rising criticisms in Europe over the imprisonment of Ecevit, the trial of former leftist trade union leaders, and restricted freedom of press. The delegation, which was first rejected by the Turkish authorities, was, upon pressure by West European States, later received at the highest level by General Evren and Foreign Minister Türkmen, who highlighted that "Turkey places importance on its relations with the Council of Europe and wants these relations to continue."[61] A member of the delegation—Ludwig Steiner, conservative member of Parliament from Austria—stated afterward that the delegation had left the talks with a "positive impression," but this would not come to mean that the COE would vote in favor of sustaining Turkish membership.[62]

Despite all the criticism, however, the COE did not vote for Turkey's expulsion, neither after the January 1982 delegation visit nor on any other occasion. This did not come to mean that relations were improving. In fact, just the opposite was the case. In the course of 1982 and 1983, political groups from the left (socialists, communists) and the Greeks were pushing strongly for Turkey's expulsion.[63] On top of that, in the immediate aftermath of the January 1982 visit of the COE delegation, the COE adopted a resolution on Turkey calling member states to invoke Article 24 of the European Convention of Human Rights. The article permits any contracting state to report to the Commission of Human Rights any infringement of the provisions of the Convention.[64] This resolution caused a major uproar in Turkey and even led to considerations among the generals to withdraw Turkey from the Council.[65]

In line with this resolution, in July 1982 five Member States of the COE—namely, Norway, Sweden, Denmark, France, and the Netherlands—filed a case against Turkey at the European Commission of Human Rights on grounds of continuing political repression, violation of human rights and trade union rights, and the torture of prisoners.[66] Although a friendly settlement was eventually reached in December 1985 between these states and Turkey, the case contributed to increasing resentment of Europe by the Turkish authorities.[67] The threat of expulsion from the COE reached its peak in January 1983, when the Parliamentary Assembly published a resolution "to give serious consideration to making a recommendation to the Committee of Ministers aiming at application of Article 8 of the Statute of the Council of Europe," which regulates the expulsion of member states.[68] The resolution was particularly critical of the undemocratic provisions of the recently adopted constitution in November 1982, continuing human rights abuses, restrictions on participation in political activity, and mass trial of union members. Nevertheless, in the Assembly vote, the proposal to expel Turkey was turned down with 35 votes in favor and 75 votes against. However, in the same voting session, it was also decided that Turkey would lose its voting rights in the Committee of Ministers.[69]

In order to understand why the COE did not expel Turkey from membership, despite all its criticisms and threats, the two main approaches in the Assembly need to be considered. One, taken up mostly by socialists, communists, and the Greeks, pressed for expulsion, often in reference to the suspension of Greek membership after the Colonels' coup in 1967.[70] The second approach emphasized the need to keep Turkey in the COE in order to be able to exert leverage and thus aid the process of transition in the country.[71]

In the end, the second approach prevailed. Despite the accompanying threat of expulsion, the concern held by the second approach was also officially expressed in the January 1982 and January 1983 resolutions on Turkey. The January 1982 resolution declared that "Turkey's continued membership of the Council of Europe gives the latter the opportunity as well as the obligation to watch over the restoration of democratic institutions and the respect of human rights in that country."[72] Similarly, the January 1983 resolution stated that the Assembly is "conscious that the Council of Europe's influence will be more effective so long as Turkey's links with the Council of Europe are maintained."[73]

Another factor that contributed to the decision of not expelling Turkey from the COE was the role played by the opponents of the coup in Turkey. As expressed above, there was no strong and unified resistance to the military rule in Turkey. Nevertheless, individual democrats, most notably former social democrat delegates to the Parliamentary Assembly, kept in close contact with the COE and expressed the necessity of sustained membership for the transition to democracy in Turkey.[74] The same arguments were also put forward by former political leaders like Demirel and Ecevit.[75] Thus, in a similar logic with the European Community, "neither the total severing of relations, nor the unquestioning and uncritical continuance of relations as before" was perceived as a helpful option in guiding the COE's relations with Turkey.[76]

INTERACTIONS BETWEEN EXTERNAL ACTORS AND DOMESTIC CONTEXT IN EXPLAINING THE DEMOCRATIC TRANSITION IN 1983

The Turkish military declared from the start and reiterated on various occasions that its main goal was to achieve transition to democracy in the shortest time possible. The Turkish military perceived itself as the guardian, not the ruler, of the Kemalist regime. At the time, both domestic and international actors believed that the Turkish military would return to its barracks. Indeed, the transition to democracy in 1983 can partly be explained by the initial aims of the military intervention. The "costs of adapting" to democracy were low for the military, given that Turkey was democratic since 1950 and the military already had its own road map to transition, which also empowered the armed forces in the new democratic regime. Given the expectation that there would not be a return to chaos after the mainstream parties were closed down and radical groups were oppressed, the benefits of sustaining an authoritarian regime for a long period of time did not outweigh the costs of continued repression and European pressure.

The domestic reasons and the motivation of the military from the very beginning to lead a transition to democracy (albeit a restricted one) make it rather difficult to asses the true impact of external factors on democratic transition in the Turkish case. A closer look at events suggests that external actors mattered. However, in all likelihood the Turkish military would have returned to democracy as long as it achieved its initial goals of restoring order and establishing new rules for democracy.

In fact, this was the assessment of the external actors and especially the US administration at the time as well. Imposing sanctions against Turkey or empowering domestic actors against the Turkish Armed Forces seemed counterproductive. As a result, the United States and American-based financial institutions, such as the World Bank and IMF, continued to provide assistance and aid to the Turkish government and, hence, the military. Strengthening the military helped the generals attain internal security and relative economic stability, the two major ills of the precoup period in Turkey. Successful domestic governance, in turn, promoted public support for the military government, facilitating an easier transition. Hence, perceiving their goals as having mostly been achieved, the military proceeded with the transition.

If, instead, in the name of promoting democratic forces, the external actors had attempted to revitalize the previous ideological groupings on the left and/or the right, this would have most likely provided a strong justification for the military to remain in power in order to prevent further domestic chaos and bloodshed in the country. Withholding economic support at a time of massive economic instability would have produced similar results. Domestic resistance and upheaval with foreign support would have also made it difficult to reach an agreement on the new constitution, especially on articles that ensured military autonomy. Such failure of the military could have delayed transition for a few more years or more possibly, lead to its postponement for an indeterminate period. This could also go hand in hand with a potential reversal of Turkey's Western orientations, as often hinted by the military leaders through more frequent visits to Eastern Europe or improved economic relations with Middle Eastern countries.[77] Thus, American support affected the military's success during the coup years and, thereby, facilitated the transition to democracy.

Another result of American support was Turgut Özal's rise to power as the civilian prime minister. Özal's victory in the November 1983 elections prevented the sustenance of military rule via blocking the election of the military's preferred candidate, Turgut Sunalp. This victory was partly a result of Özal's successful liberal economic policies—backed by the United States, World Bank, and IMF—which significantly increased his popularity among the electorate and especially among the business community. Only days before the elections, in a publicized speech, the leader of the junta, Kenan Evren, urged the Turkish electorate not to vote for Özal. Yet, despite this aversion, the military accepted his candidacy in the elections (while it put a ban on almost all of the former politicians) and agreed to transfer control over to him after the ballots were cast. Özal had strong ideological and political ties with the United States both because of his previous experience as a World Bank employee and because of his preference for liberal policies.[78] Rejecting his victory could have seriously undermined American, World Bank, and IMF financial support to Turkey, which the country needed after the economic crises of the 1970s.[79] Given that the military frequently announced in the international and domestic arena that it would eventually return to democracy, declaring the electoral results null and void would also bring about a significant loss of credibility and opposition at home and abroad, even in the United States. Losing US support at a time when relations with Europe were already strained could have left the country in total isolation. Thus, the military was bound by its own pledges and by Özal's close ties with the West to follow through the transfer of power from the armed forces to the civilians.

Whereas American military and financial support for the Turkish Armed Forces played important roles in democratic transition, the impact of the economic and political sanctions employed by Europe should be regarded with caution in the Turkish case. European economic sanctions were not substantial enough to exert serious pressure, thanks to sustained economic support by the two main creditors, namely the United States and Germany. Political sanctions on the part of the European Community were mostly limited to the European Parliament, which did not enjoy high decision-making power in the EC at the time. Besides, Turkish membership in the European Community was a too distant possibility to be utilized for democratic conditionality.

Under these conditions, there was little incentive for the military government to comply with pressure from the European Community or its individual member states. It still needed to be reminded, however, that the limited sanctions from the

EC and some of the member states were pushing the government to justify itself in the international arena. Foreign Minister Ilter Türkmen's visit to Europe only three days after the referendum on the new constitution, to explain the new state of affairs in Turkey and to ask for the suspension of the Fourth Protocol provides a clear example in this respect.[80]

The situation with the Council of Europe was more different. The military's historic commitment to Westernization and to its ties with Europe as part and parcel of the Kemalist legacy that it upholds led it to bestow a highly symbolic importance on COE membership.[81] Thus, the threat of expulsion could be expected to have an impact on the transition to democracy. The evidence available suggests that the willingness to end military rule existed earlier, but it was slightly accelerated as a result of COE pressure. In his memoirs, General Evren highlights that he envisaged a three- to four-year military rule before achieving transition.[82] He also underlines the firm belief he held that COE would not expel Turkey but would instead use conditionality through membership to exert pressure.[83] Thus, the dominant tendency in the COE was well understood by the military rulers.

However, the series of events in the country in 1981 changed the picture. In February 1981, the Council of Europe's Parliamentary Assembly convened to decide whether to impose any sanctions against Turkey or to expel it from the COE. On the eve of its assembly meeting, the government announced that an inquiry into four cases of alleged torture had led to the arrest of the members of the security forces found responsible.[84] Similarly, pressure from the COE was found to be influential in the reduction of the detention period from 90 to 35 days.[85] Although these can be considered as cosmetic gestures, they also demonstrate that the military rulers still cared about the country's European prospects and were willing to take some steps in that respect.

A more notable impact can be observed regarding the declaration of a timetable on transition to democracy. COE (along with the EC) had been demanding a timetable of transition from the early days of the military rule, with no concrete result.[86] Dissolution of political parties and the imprisonment of Ecevit at the end of 1981 had led to severe responses from Europe. This was the period when the prospect of expulsion began to be discussed as a strong possibility. Just a week before the COE delegation responsible for drafting the report that would determine the state of Turkey's membership arrived in Turkey, Evren announced an approximate date for general elections. This announcement was made almost two years in advance of the scheduled general elections and a month after having dissolved all political parties.[87] Regarding the postponement of the decision on the expulsion of Turkey from the Council of Europe, Evren wrote in his memoirs that "now we have gained three more months."[88]

CONCLUSION

Various external actors were at work in attempting to aid the transition process in Turkey. The way in which these actors interacted with domestic conditions and developments suggest that the case of Turkey introduces new dimensions to the debate on external influence on transition to democracy.

It demonstrates that external actors do not necessarily aid transition through the imposition of sanctions. It shows that economic and political support through constant, but cautious, expression of criticism and concern can also help a country to achieve a smooth transition to democracy. Military and economic support from the United States and financial organizations, coupled with a "wait and see" attitude in Europe, can be emulated in cases where the military (or authoritarian rulers) pledge to return to democracy relatively quickly and take concrete steps— like declaring a timetable and drafting a constitution—to make a transition. Although foreign support and relative economic and political success could lead to authoritarian stability and not to democratization, it is still possible for the rulers to initiate the transition voluntarily in cases like Turkey where they are powerful enough to mold a new political landscape, dictate the terms of the regime after the transition, guarantee their personal interest, and assure autonomy for their institutions. Surely the newly founded democratic regime would be restrictive under those circumstances; but if the domestic opposition to be fostered by the international actors is weak and not necessarily democratic, imposing sanctions on the authoritarian rulers, while empowering other domestic actors, might lead to ultimately worse and counterproductive results.

NOTES

We acknowledge the valuable inputs of Ali Çarkoğlu, Sabri Sayarı, Alain Servantie, İlter Turan, and all interviewees.

1. Milli Güvenlik Konseyi Genel Sekreterliği, *12 Eylül Öncesi ve Sonrası* (Ankara: Türk Tarih Kurumu Basımevi, 1981), 196–203.

2. See, for instance, *Human Rights in Turkey's "Transition to Democracy": A Helsinki Watch Report* (New York: US Helsinki Watch Committee, 1983), 66–75.

3. Foreign newspapers reported the public support for the military intervention. Because the Turkish newspapers could not have been entirely impartial during this period, these foreign reports provide the best neutral account of public opinion during this period. For examples of such articles, see Don A. Schanche, "Most Turks Believe Military Rulers Will Keep Pledge to Cede Power," *Los Angeles Times*, May 13, 1982, E1; Eric Morgenthaler, "Conventional Coup: In Turkey, a Takeover by Military Is Almost Normal Part of Politics," *Wall Street Journal*, September 15, 1980, 1; Edward Walsh, "Turkey Tests 'Controlled Democracy,'" *Washington Post*, November 6, 1983, A17.

4. Kevin Michel Cape, "Turkey: Leftover Challenges for New Leaders," *Christian Science*

Monitor, November 9, 1983, 20; Metin Demirsar, "Turkey Gets Capital Infusion by Coaxing Foreign Creditors to Invest Funds Owed," *Wall Street Journal*, December 4, 1981, 38; Paul Henze, "Turkey Pulling Itself Together," *Christian Science Monitor*, August 13, 1981, 12; Barry Newman, "At the Crossroads: Turkey Seems to Be on the Road to Democracy, but Its Route There Appears Very Undemocratic," *Wall Street Journal*, June 15, 1982, 56; "Turkey Chooses Democracy," *Wall Street Journal*, November 8, 1983, 34.

5. C. H. Dodd, *The Crisis of Turkish Democracy* (Beverley: Eothen Press, 1990), 58–61.

6. Yeşim Arat, "Politics and Big Business: Janus-Faced Link to the State," in Metin Heper, ed., *Strong State and Economic Interest Groups: The Post-1980 Turkish Experience* (Berlin: Walter de Gruyter, 1991), 141–42.

7. Major exceptions to this indifference were Bülent Ecevit and Süleyman Demirel, the leaders of the major parties, the RPP and JP, respectively. For the appeals of the Turkish politicians to the Europeans and their belief that the military would make a transition to democracy, see Marvine Howe, "Turkey's Junta Lobbies to Stay in European 'Club,'" *New York Times*, March 9, 1981, A9.

8. For more on the reasons why the military disengaged voluntarily, see Yaprak Gürsoy, "Civilian Support and Military Unity in the Outcome of Turkish and Greek Military Interventions," *Journal of Political and Military Sociology* 37 (Summer 2009): 47–75.

9. Amnesty International contributed to the Political Affairs and Legal Affairs Committee in the Parliamentary Assembly of the Council of Europe. Its reports were frequently referred to in the debates and reports of these European institutions. However, its criticisms (along with those of others such as Human Rights Watch) toward the military regime were found to have no significant direct repercussions in Turkey.

10. There is strong belief among some circles in Turkey that the United States was involved in the coup. A controversial interview conducted in 1997 by Paul Henze, a US National Security Council country specialist, have perpetuated the belief that the Americans in Ankara staged the coup. However, no concrete evidence has yet come to light that supports overt US involvement in the coup. In fact, even though an intervention was expected in the United States, it still came as a surprise. State Department reports and congressional hearings show that the probability of a military takeover was seen as low only a few months before September 1980. See *Turkey, Greece, and NATO: The Strained Alliance; Staff Report to the Committee on Foreign Relations United States Senate* (Washington, D.C.: US Government Printing Office, 1980), 30; *United States-Turkey Defense and Economic Cooperation Agreement, 1980: Hearing before the Subcommittee on Europe and the Middle East of the Committee on Foreign Affairs House of Representatives* (Washington, D.C.: US Government Printing Office, 1980), 27–28.

11. The full text of the declaration is available in Fahir Armaoğlu, *Belgelerle Türk-Amerikan Münasebetleri (Açıklamalı)* (Ankara: Atatürk Kültür, Dil ve Tarih Yüksek Kurumu Türk Tarih Vakfi Kurumu Yayınları, 1991), 364.

12. John M. Goshko, "From the Allies: Patience," *Washington Post*, September 13, 1980, A1.

13. "Memorandum for the President from Edmund S. Muskie," *The Secretary of State*, September 12, 1980, Library of Congress electronic archives.

14. Goshko, "From the Allies: Patience."

15. "Memorandum for Zbigniew Brzezinski from Paul Henze, Subject: Turkey—Things to Keep in Mind at Next MBB," National Security Council, September 17, 1980, Library of Congress electronic archives.

16. "Letter to President Jimmy Carter from General Kenan Evren," *White House*, October 10, 1980, Library of Congress electronic archives.

17. "NATO Designated Turkey Coup as Internal Matter," *Los Angeles Times*, September 12, 1980, A2.

18. *United States-Turkey Defense and Economic Cooperation Agreement*, 24.

19. Metin Demirsar, "U.S. Upgrades Military Links to Turkey with Eye to Soviet Union and Mideast," *Wall Street Journal*, January 12, 1983, 32.

20. Jayanta Roy, "The Turkish Economy: Assessment of a Recovery under a Structural Adjustment Program," *EDI Working Papers* (Washington, D.C.: Economic Development Institute of the World Bank, 1989), 13–14, 48.

21. Sina Pamukçu, former vice-secretary-general of the Confederation of Progressive Trade Unions of Turkey (DİSK), has even argued that the coup was supported by the IMF and the World Bank due to its potential to suppress worker movements. Sina Pamukçu, interview, Brussels, April 2008.

22. *Program Performance Audit Report: Turkey—Second and Third Adjustment Loans (Loans 1987-TU and 2158-TU)*, no. 5763 (Washington, D.C.: World Bank, 1985), i–iii.

23. Roy, "The Turkish Economy," 47.

24. Marvine Howe, "U.S. and the Turks Agree to Create Joint Defense Unit," *New York Times*, December 6, 1981, 1.

25. David Wood, "Weinberger Tightly Guarded in Turkey," *Los Angeles Times*, December 6, 1981, 23.

26. Bernard Gwertzman, "Haig Ends 'Warm' Talks in Turkey," *New York Times*, May 13, 1982, 3.

27. İlter Türkmen, former minister of foreign affairs, interview, Istanbul, September 2007.

28. As military rule continued in Turkey, anti-junta reports against human rights violations, often critical of the US policy toward Turkey, started to appear in American newspapers. See, for example, Jeri Laber (executive director of Helsinki Watch), "Turkey's Electoral Farce," *New York Times*, October 19, 1983, A1; Stuart Schaar (human rights activist), "Turkey: Democracy Deferred," *Christian Science Monitor*, December 24, 1981, Pierre Schori (international secretary of the Swedish Social Democratic Party), "U.S. Policy toward Turkey," *New York Times*, December 13, 1981, E29.

29. Leonard Downie Jr., "Council of Europe Votes for Probe of Rights in Turkey," *Washington Post*, January 30, 1982, A24.

30. Kenan Evren, *Kenan Evren'in Anıları*, vol. 3 (Istanbul: Milliyet Yayınları, 1991), 166–67. On February 16, 1983, similar discussions took place between General Evren and US ambassador Vernon Walters, who brought a letter from President Reagan. Kenan Evren, *Kenan Evren'in Anıları*, vol. 4 (Istanbul: Milliyet Yayınları, 1991), 94–96. General Evren had similar meetings in Ankara with former secretary of state Henry Kissinger in June 1983 and with former president Richard Nixon in 1985. Both leaders discussed the negative attitudes of the Europeans toward military rule in Turkey with contempt. Kenan Evren, *Kenan Evren'in Anıları*, vol. 5 (Istanbul: Milliyet Yayınları, 1991), 238–40, 285–86.

31. Metin Demirsar, "Europe's Tiff with Turkey Worsens," *Wall Street Journal*, December 29, 1981, 25.

32. Downie, "Council of Europe Votes for Probe of Rights in Turkey."

33. "U.S. Defends Turkey on Human Rights," *New York Times*, July 10, 1982, 5.

34. "Text of Secretary of State Alexander Haig, Jr.'s Message to West German Foreign

Minister Hans-Dietrich Genscher, Subject: Reply to Genscher on Turkey," *White House Situation Room*, December 7, 1981, Library of Congress electronic archives.

35. "Statement of Hon. Elliot Abrahams, Assistant Secretary of State, Bureau of Human Rights and Humanitarian Affairs, Accompanied by Charles Faribanks, Deputy Assistant Secretary" and "Statement of Hon. James Spain, Former Ambassador to Turkey," in *Human Rights in Cyprus, Greece, and Turkey: Hearing before the Subcommittee on Human Rights and International Organizations of the Committee on Foreign Affairs House of Representatives* (Washington, D.C.: US Government Printing Office, 1983), 2–18.

36. "Statement of Elliot Abrahams," in ibid., 7.

37. Ibid., 15.

38. Ibid., 6.

39. See "Speech by Lord Carrington (President-in-Office of the Council) Delivered at the European Parliament on 8 July 1981" and "European Parliament Resolution on the Events in Turkey on 18 September 1980," *Official Journal of the European Communities*, no. C 265/55, October 13, 1980.

40. "Recommendation on the Situation in Turkey," *Council of Europe*, no. 904, October 1, 1980.

41. "Speech by Lorenzo Natali (Vice-President of the European Commission) Delivered at the European Parliament, 17 September 1980," European Parliament archives, Luxembourg.

42. See, in particular, the debates of the European Parliament on April 10, 1981; July 6, 1981; July 8, 1981; and November 18, 1981, European Parliament archives, Luxembourg.

43. Manfred Michel, former secretary-general of the Socialist Group, European Parliament, and Richard Balfe, former member of the European Parliament, interviews, Brussels, September 2007.

44. See in particular, the speeches delivered in the debate of the European Parliament on April 10, 1981.

45. "European Parliament Resolution on the Military Junta in Turkey on 10 April 1981," *Official Journal of the European Communities*, no. C 101/110, May 4, 1981.

46. See the debates of the European Parliament on January 14, 1981; April 10, 1981; July 6, 1981; and July 8, 1981.

47. "Statement Submitted by the European Parliament Socialist Group Regarding the Human Rights Situation in Turkey and Turkey's Relations with Western Europe," in *Human Rights in Cyprus, Greece, and Turkey*, 116.

48. Richard Cox, retired commission official, interview, Brussels, March 2008. See also Wood, "Weinberger Tightly Guarded in Turkey."

49. Howe, "Turkey's Junta Lobbies to Stay in European 'Club.'"

50. See the "Statement Submitted by the European Parliament Socialist Group."

51. "Speech by Mr. von Hassel (Member of the European Parliament from the German Christian Democrat Party (CDU) Delivered at the European Parliament on 13 October 1983," European Parliament archives, Luxembourg.

52. Metin Demirsar, "Turkey Gets Capital Infusion by Coaxing Foreign Creditors to Invest Funds Owed," *Wall Street Journal*, December 4, 1981, 38.

53. See "Chart on Organization on Economic Cooperation, and Development, and Special Aid to Turkey, 1979–82, Submitted by Hon. Ludwig Fellermaier (Socialist Member of the European Parliament)," in *Human Rights in Cyprus, Greece, and Turkey*, 80.

54. Türkmen interview.

55. Alain Servantie, European Commission official, interview, Brussels, September 2007.

56. Ibid.

57. "Conclusions of the European Council, Brussels, 29–30 March 1982," *Bulletin of the European Communities*, no. 3 (1982): 21.

58. Howe, "Turkey's Junta Lobbies to Stay in European 'Club.'"

59. "Conclusions of the European Council, London, 26–27 November 1981," *Bulletin of the European Communities*, no. 11 (1981): 55.

60. "Order on the Term of Office of the Turkish Parliamentary Delegation," *Council of Europe*, no. 398 (1981): May 14, 1981.

61. Martin Howe, "Group Said to Seek Changes in Turkey," *New York Times*, January 14, 1982.

62. Ibid.

63. Klaus Schumann, retired Council of Europe official, interview, Strasbourg, March 31, 2008.

64. "Resolution on the Situation in Turkey," *Council of Europe*, no. 765 (1982): January 28, 1982.

65. Sam Cohen, "Though Angry, Turkey Sticks with Council of Europe," *Christian Science Monitor*, February 4, 1982, 7.

66. "Statement Submitted by the European Parliament Socialist Group," 114.

67. Kenan Evren, *Zorlu Yıllarım*, vol. 2 (Istanbul: Milliyet Yayınları, 1994), 15.

68. "Resolution on the Situation in Turkey," *Council of Europe*, no. 794 (1983), January 27, 1983.

69. Evren, *Zorlu Yıllarım*, 15.

70. İhsan Dağı, "Democratic Transition in Turkey, 1980–83: The Impact of European Diplomacy," *Middle Eastern Studies* 32 (April 1996): 134.

71. Schumann interview.

72. "Resolution on the Situation in Turkey," no. 765 (1982).

73. "Resolution on the Situation in Turkey," no. 794 (1983).

74. Anonymous Council of Europe official, Interview, Strasbourg, April 2008.

75. Howe, "Turkey's Junta Lobbies to Stay in European 'Club.'"

76. "Statement Submitted by the European Parliament Socialist Group," 114.

77. Demirsar, "Europe's Tiff with Turkey Worsens," 25; Sam Cohen, "Turkey—a Key NATO Member Looks to the Middle East for New Economic Ties," *Christian Science Monitor*, March 24, 1982, 3.

78. Several American officials have agreed that Turgut Özal was well-known and highly respected in the United States. George Harris, former Director of Analysis for Near East and South Asia, US Department of State, anonymous National Security Council Official, and anonymous State Department Official, interviews, Washington, D.C., September 2007.

79. In our interview, Jayanta Roy (lead economist for Turkey in the World Bank between 1979 and 1986) stressed that the only implicit political conditionality for World Bank support to Turkey was to maintain Turgut Özal in charge of economic affairs. If Özal had been removed from power, the World Bank officials would have been at least concerned. Interview, Washington, D.C., September 2007.

80. Dağı, "Democratic Transition in Turkey," 135.

81. Türkmen interview.

82. Kenan Evren, *Unutulan Gerçekler* (Ankara: Tisamat, 1995), 8.

83. Ibid., 16.

84. Sam Cohen, "Turkey Upset over Western Critics," *Christian Science Monitor*, February 3, 1981, 10.

85. Schaar, "Turkey: Democracy Deferred," 27.

86. See, for example, "Resolution on the Situation in Turkey," *Council of Europe*, no. 395 (1981), January 29, 1981.

87. Dağı, "Democratic Transition in Turkey," 138.

88. Evren, *Kenan Evren'in Anilari*, vol. 2, 408.

PART THREE

Failed Transition Cases

CHAPTER THIRTEEN

Algeria

An Aborted Transition

KRISTINA KAUSCH AND RICHARD YOUNGS

Beginning in the late 1980s liberalizing reforms were implemented in Algeria that led the country to a moment of potential democratic breakthrough in 1991. At this moment election results were revoked, and authoritarian control reestablished, with many measures of deliberalization introduced by a military-led junta. A severe economic crisis triggered by long-standing structural deficits, combined with a fall in world oil prices and price rises for basic goods imposed under an International Monetary Fund (IMF) stabilization plan, provoked public riots in October 1988. Algeria's single-party socialist National Liberation Front (FLN) government saw its position increasingly weakened as its reliance on high oil prices started to backfire. As a result of the riots, it shifted course in an effort to stabilize the country and secure its own rule. In 1989 the government introduced a new democratic constitution that abolished references to socialism and one-party rule, and made a commitment to multiparty elections. Between 1989 and 1991, a range of measures of political liberalization was implemented. During this time, the newly founded Islamist party Front Islamique du Salut (FIS) was able to establish itself as the most effective and successful opposition party. The FIS's victory in the June 1990 local elections was the first time an Islamist party gained a majority in a free vote in any Arab country.

Algeria's putative transition to democracy came to a sudden halt soon after the FIS emerged as the strongest force in the first round of national legislative elections held in January 1991. The army intervened on February 11, 1992, in a violent coup in the name of safeguarding democracy from religious extremism. President Chadli Benjedid was forced to resign. On March 5, the FIS was officially banned, and eventually its leadership and thousands of followers were jailed in desert detention camps. Political rights and freedoms were curtailed, reversing the process of political liberalization. Violent confrontations between the army and Islamists ensued, and within months a civil war had broken out. The perpetuation of violence throughout the rest of the decade, which claimed more than 150,000 victims, impeded any resumption of political liberalization.

This chapter argues that the manner in which the process of political liberalization occurred in Algeria predetermined an outcome that worked against a successful democratic transition. Domestic hindrances were so significant in this case that firmer external support for democratization may not have made a definitive difference. While the "Islam factor" has received most attention in assessments of the Algeria case, the "oil factor" was if anything more influential in shaping the underlying interest calculations of external actors. Breaking down the components of Algeria's internal dynamics helps understand the precise ways in which a range of international factors lengthened the odds against democratization. The interplay between domestic and international variables was deeply symbiotic. Internal obstacles magnified external concerns over the consequences of Algeria's transition. These concerns in turn reinforced antidemocratic domestic forces. In the context of this comparative volume, Algeria stands as a case where domestic and international factors combined to ensure that democracy stood little chance of embedding itself.

CHRONICLE OF A TRANSITION FRUSTRATED: DOMESTIC FACTORS

While the Algerian regime committed itself to democratic reform, underlying factors acted as long-term impediments to liberalization. The negative effects of high natural resource revenues on democratic development have been widely studied, and in particular in the Arab world government-controlled oil and gas reserves have been seen as a major obstacle to democratization. Algeria's 1991 experience strongly corroborates such explanations.[1] The overwhelming dependency of the Algerian economy on hydrocarbon revenues (amounting to an estimated 98.5 percent of all state revenues) made Algeria "a wretched poster child"[2] for the rentier theory of the petrostate and a "bunker state *par excellence*."[3] The hydrocarbons sector had long lacked substantial linkages with the broader economy, choking off the prospect of broader economic modernization.[4]

When world oil markets plunged in the mid-1980s, Algeria's oil and gas dependency momentarily became a pro- rather than antireform variable. With the fall in revenues, the regime and army could "no longer deliver on their promises of a just and equal society [and] Algeria faced the dilemma of 'performance le-

gitimacy' common to authoritarian regimes."[5] Massive structural deficits appeared
when state services toward an expanding and increasingly demanding population
diminished with the decline in oil revenues. This was a key factor in pushing the
government to contemplate reform, but the energy factor was ultimately and over
the longer term an obstacle to democratic dynamics taking firmer root.

The structure of the Algerian economy ensured the salience of economic interests hostile to democratization. Key economic actors (both domestic and international) with privileged political linkages had high stakes in maintaining the
regime.[6] These actors had supported the gradual development of a market economy, but most did not want this to facilitate the development of major productive
capacities outside the hydrocarbon sector that would limit the scope for their im-
porting activities. Economic actors also saw political reform as risking instability.[7]
The linkage was tight between Algeria's hydrocarbon dependence and the army's
continued political role: oil rents helped entrench the military's position, making
the shift from political liberalization to democratization more difficult.[8] The lack
of economic diversification before the 1991 elections also meant that few independent and diversified economic actors had emerged to act in favor of democracy.
Although radical Islam is often cited as having been the decisive factor in Algeria,
this structural imbalance of the country's economy was if anything even more
relevant in shaping underlying political dynamics.

An additional factor militating against a full-fledged democratic transition was
the traditionally dominant role of the army (i.e., the organization's politically engaged senior leadership rather than the entirety of its rank and file). The army's
role in Algeria's independence struggle had imbued it with a store of legitimacy.[9]
The military was said to identify itself with the people, the revolution, the unity of
the state, and a strong state structure, values that were also important for Algerian
citizens.[10] According to one expert, the army was seen by many Algerians as "the
mirror of the people, a reliable model and an example to be followed."[11]

Crucially, this helped ensure that the process of political liberalization that took
Algeria to the point of transition did not in practice significantly weaken the power
of the army. With its harsh repression of the 1988 Black October riots, the Algerian
military lost some of its popularity and stepped back from direct political rule.
However, the army was not brought under formal and firm constitutional rule but
had agreed to withdraw from the forefront of politics only temporarily, maintaining a watching brief over events.[12] Chadli's choice as president was a compromise,
giving the military leadership control over the incipient process of liberalization.[13]

Civil and military structures had become tightly intertwined, predicated on a
threefold, largely blurred structure consisting of the military, the bureaucracy, and
the FLN. These three strongly interwoven institutions were dependent on each

other for the continuation of the regime and shared a common "socializing background."[14] The army's sanctioning of a process of political liberalization has to be understood as having been granted within such ideational parameters. While the FLN in its political platform emphasized the primacy of the political over the military, this view was "rapidly . . . contradicted by discourse and practice."[15] Behind the political reforms implemented from 1989 onward, army generals retained a strategy of manipulating the new sphere of political parties.[16] By 1991, many in the West believed democratizing Algeria was a question of dislodging the FLN, while in reality the FLN rule in itself was a façade power structure constructed by the army, which had never relinquished guardianship.[17]

More generally, the government's reform process lacked robust popularity. The Chadli government intended democratic liberalization not out of a genuine commitment to democracy but to protect its own position. But by the time the process of democratization was launched, the government's legitimacy was profoundly weakened. As pointed out, by the mid-1980s the FLN's socialist development model had engendered rampant unemployment and housing shortages. After having opened political space in the hope of self-survival, the Chadli government failed to respond to citizens' grievances and demands. Some observers concluded that the Algerian transition failed because it was initiated in an undemocratic manner and in the absence of a previously negotiated agreement on the basic political rules.[18]

Rather than gaining credit for committing to democratization, the Chadli government hemorrhaged support to the FIS. The FIS succeeded in challenging the state's legitimacy in moral terms through the prism of Islam. The FIS took on the same discourse and basis of socioeconomic legitimacy as the FLN. FIS leader Abassi Madani was indeed a founding member of the FLN at the very beginning of the revolution. The FIS succeeded in spreading the notion that the government's whole reform project was a perversion of the values of the revolution. By the late 1980s, generational change had made the link to the struggle for independence as the main source of governmental legitimacy increasingly weak.[19] The government lacked a pool of strong support for its reform project; there was no mass mobilization when that democratizing project was interrupted. Indeed, many commentators argued that much of the popularity of the FIS was not rooted in the people's enthusiasm for the Islamists but constituted mainly a protest vote against decades of FLN misrule. A profound polarization of Algerian society contributed significantly to the reversal of the country's democratic opening. The radicalization of public opinion led to the rise of and support for the FIS, a group that opposing sectors of society were acutely fearful of. Algeria lacked a consensus on the basic political rules of the game as it stood on the cusp of potential democratic transition.

Algerian democrats feared that a potentially undemocratic party was about to come to power by democratic means and were accordingly torn over what response to the FIS was appropriate. Some argued that the party's victory in a democratic election process must be respected. Others claimed that the FIS was not to be trusted; that its program was not compatible with a democratic, pluralist society; and that, as much as their victory represented in itself a success for democracy, it would soon lead to an eradication of the very pluralism and openness that brought the party to power (this fear being symbolized by the subsequently much-repeated line "One person, one vote, one time").[20] It is impossible to know to what extent a FIS government would have reversed the democratic opening. Although some sections of the FIS (notably Ali Belhaj and his broad base of followers) had been notably antidemocratic in their statements, the party's official stance was pro-democracy.[21]

A manifestation of this polarization was the failure of those opposing the coup—the FIS, other Islamist and secular opposition parties, as well as parts of the FLN government and party leadership—effectively to respond to the army's 1992 takeover. This incapacity was due not only to the opposition's failure to unite but to the opposition forces' lack of institutional and organizational capacity. In addition, the lack of a significant secular opposition front with broad public support allowed the regime to portray the FIS as the fundamentalist threat to a secular-oriented democratic government.[22]

Secular opposition parties also failed to unite for the cause of democratization. The FIS refused to acknowledge that a successful social rebellion required a wider alliance that included both the religious and the nonreligious opposition. It was not until 1995 that the FIS sought such a rapprochement, under the aegis of the Sant'Egidio mediators in Rome.[23]

Tactics were adopted that widened rather than tempered differences between the regime elite and the FIS. During the 1988–92 period, the relationship between the Algerian regime and the FIS became increasingly antagonistic, with the regime shifting from an initially accommodating to a confrontational approach. The military leadership behind the Chadli administration was opposed to a "pacted" arrangement in which Islamists along with other oppositional tendencies would work out new rules of the game with the government, army, and state bodies.[24]

From the mid- to late 1980s, the regime adopted an increasingly repressive policy toward Islamists, which included mass arrests of militants. This radicalized many Islamists.[25] After political liberalization had been set in motion, the government then belatedly attempted various means of containing the FIS.[26] This included manipulation of the electoral process, whereby elections were delayed to allow the regime to modify electoral laws to the apparent disadvantage of the FIS, and the withdrawal of funds from local councils to undermine the FIS's credibility. Such measures widened the breach between government, army, and the FIS in the crucial period before the 1991 elections.

The FIS feared that if it fought the election under the new rules it would suffer defeat. On May 25, 1991, it announced that it would boycott the elections due on June 27. The FIS then called its supporters out onto the streets to demonstrate and participate in a general strike. The strike call was neither well received nor generally obeyed, but the call for antigovernment demonstrations turned Algiers into a city under siege during the first week of June. The whole affair precipitated the resignation of the Hamrouche government and its replacement by an administration under the leadership of Sidi Ghozali, who agreed to rescind the new electoral laws. The FIS consequently agreed to participate in the parliamentary elections arranged for December 1991–January 1992, despite the internment of its leaders.[27]

However, when the first round of national elections of December 26, 1991, gave the FIS 47.3 percent of the votes—with the FLN winning only 23.4 percent—a moderate response failed to win out. It became known later that Chadli and some FLN leaders did approach the FIS to propose a power-sharing scheme according to which Chadli would keep the presidency, the Islamists would control nonstrategic ministries such as education, justice, and religious affairs, and the FLN would run the technical ministries. But the military leadership rejected such an arrangement.[28] Notwithstanding his own reservations regarding the FIS, Chadli claimed that he was prepared, as the head of state, to work with it as a partner in government if need be; but the upper echelons of the FLN and the armed services saw any concession to the FIS victory as "beyond the pale."[29]

After the military coup in January 1992, the FIS, FLN, and the Socialist Forces Front (FFS) announced their joint opposition to the High State Committee (Haut Comité d'Etat or HCE) and called for a return of the electoral process. After Chadli's decommission, the first talks on an official basis between the FLN and the FIS were held, involving also the FFS, but talks failed to lead to an agreement. The FIS even announced the formation of a second, parallel parliament composed of the 231 candidates elected in the first round of the elections (188 of whom were FIS members). Later attempts at dialogue between the FIS and the government failed, as the military-political nomenklatura remained split over whether the FIS should be engaged, and if so, under which conditions this could take place.[30] With escalating rhetoric and confrontation, police and troops countered with massive arrests. The FIS was banned and dissolved, its (remaining) leadership put in jail and thousands of activists interned in detention camps in the Sahara. Violent confrontations between the army and Islamist militants ensued, with each side blaming the other for having started the violence. Between 1992 and 1998, an estimated 150,000 people lost their lives and 1.5 million citizens were displaced.

POSITIONS OF INTERNATIONAL ACTORS

The international community responded uncritically when the army revoked the electoral process in January 1992. Equally important was that in the run-up to the 1991–92 elections external actors' policies failed to make successful transition more likely as they supported a political reform process aimed at stability rather than democracy, without seeking to challenge the army's continuing power.

The key international actor was France. The interruption of Algeria's electoral process engendered deep divisions within the French political elite. Many critical French voices were raised, especially initially. But the French government eventually retained a normality of relations with the new Algerian government in the wake of the coup.

Before the elections, France even sent advisers to engage in gerrymandering, to help the FLN win the majority of seats.[31] According to the resident correspondent of *Le Monde* (who was expelled from Algeria a few months after the coup), shortly after the results of the first round of elections were known an envoy of the Algerian regime was sent discreetly to find out what the French reaction would be in case of an interruption of the Algerian electoral process. The French government was reported to have given only very guarded responses, limiting itself to a series of noncommittal remarks on the virtues of democracy. It remained in the role of a passive observer. This passivity was also influenced by concerns that the National Front might exploit the discourse of an Islamist regime one hour's flight from France in the upcoming French elections. Algeria's political situation might entail the need for massive additional aid, which neither France (with its high unemployment rates close to elections) nor its European neighbors (which were either engaged on other fronts or not particularly interested in the Maghreb) were willing to bear.[32]

There was also concern that the coup allowed the return to power of more nationalist figures than those of the Chadli era—a political development that was seen as adversely affecting French vested interests in Algeria. The French government did not call for a formal integration of the FIS in the government but suggested that a political personality capable of engineering a synthesis between the Islamist and secular nationalist traditions be propelled to the forefront of Algerian politics.[33] But ultimately the legacy of the complex colonial past made French intervention difficult and potentially counterproductive.

When French president François Mitterrand suggested that the coup was "abnormal" he was immediately "slapped on the wrist by the Algerian government which told him to mind his own business—which he then did."[34] France had supported reform of a type that would not risk the "sacro-sainte unité des forces armées."[35] In the first official statement after the first round of elections in December 1991, a spokesman of the French Ministry of Foreign Affairs had proclaimed that, "whatever the choice of the Algerian people," relations between Algeria and France "should be maintained" and even "deepened."[36]

President Mitterrand's public reaction to the 1992 coup was a master class in obfuscation. As said, he recognized that the coup was "at the least abnormal"; on the other hand, "with the demission of the president there has been what one could call a constitutional vacuum, and the Algerian authorities had to improvise a response," and it was not up to him as a Frenchman to "judge what is happening in Algeria" and what exit was best for the country.[37] After this initial response, which provoked furious reactions in the Algerian leadership, Mitterrand limited himself to issuing messages of "friendship" to Algeria and the government.[38] After the January 1992 coup, official reactions from France not only largely abstained from criticism but even cautiously endorsed Chadli's demission and the interruption of the electoral process. The official reaction to the coup from the French Ministry of Foreign Affairs expressed "preoccupation" over the events in Algeria, reaffirming its "solidarity" with the Algerian people, and qualifying Chadli Benjedid's resignation as an event that was "important and heavy in consequences." Foreign Minister Dumas would say only that he hoped Algeria could "rediscover a climate of compromise."[39]

In contrast, Bernard Kouchner, then state secretary for humanitarian affairs, rather bluntly said that "coups d'etat are not good . . . they always turn against us." A few months later, Kouchner again provoked diplomatic tensions with the Algerian Ministry of Foreign Affairs when, in an interview with *Jeune Afrique*, he announced his intention to visit Algerian detention camps in the Sahara in which Islamist militants had been held for several months. Criticism of the coup from the opposition was also more pronounced. Alain Juppé, secretary-general of the Rally for the Republic (RPR), expressed the hope that "this regime of emergency will be accompanied by economic and political reforms which allow, when the moment has come, the Algerian people to express itself with [the necessary] knowledge," adding that France "could not do otherwise" than end its development cooperation with Algeria "if human rights were violated." Gérard Longuet, president of the Republican Party, stated that the FLN had "completely failed in its mission" but that the FIS was "not an inevitable element in Algeria." Valérie Giscard d'Estaing, president of the Union for French Democracy (UDF), said in a television interview that the interruption of the electoral process was "antidemocratic" and "dangerous." "It is a mistake to interrupt an ongoing electoral consultation because the results are not convenient for you," he added, and called on the French government to adopt an attitude of "vigilance" vis-à-vis the further evolution of the situation in Algeria and to judge the new regime according to its "respect for democratic rules and human rights." Most outspoken against the interruption of the electoral process was Jean-Marie Le Pen, head of the Front National, who called the new Algerian regime a "camarilla of dictatorial military," which had "just, in a very cynical way, ridiculed the Algerian people's will to give itself a democratic authority." He emphasized the possible repercussions in Europe's large immigrant community and suggested a pact with the FIS to repatriate Algerian migrants.[40]

The call for a reconsideration of national and European aid policies toward Algeria was voiced by several politicians across the board as a possible reaction to the coup but was not put into practice. The French government agreed to a new set of financial accords, albeit not offering such generous increases as previously. Despite a certain frostiness in relations with the new regime, the French government declined to put in question existing aid cooperation or energy contracts.[41]

Several French politicians even suggested that punitive conditionality should be applied if Algeria *respected* the democratic process: before the second round of elections, RPR president Jacques Chirac and Charles Pasqua, head of the RPR parliamentary group, argued that aid should be suspended to Algeria if the Islamists came to power. Pasqua argued that this would imply a refusal of human rights. Chirac said that if the FIS came to power, "France and Europe must, of course, respect the Algerian decision" but that they "must not be hesitant . . . to review completely our cooperation policy with Algeria." Jacques Delors, president of the European Commission, neither supported nor opposed such a possibility.[42]

Several other European governments (including Italy and Germany) also increased bilateral aid levels to Algeria after 1990.[43] A document issued by the 12 members of the European Communities (EC) regarding the situation in Algeria emphasized the EC's willingness to cooperate with the Algerian authorities in their economic recovery, at the same time asking the Algerian regime to practice "respect for human rights, tolerance and pluralism."[44]

Reactions to the coup from Spain were also ambivalent, clearly showing more signs of relief over being spared an Islamist-run neighbor than concerns over democratic procedures. The Spanish government expressed regret over the demission of President Chadli, to whom it ascribed an important "reformist role," but abstained from insisting on respect for the electoral process, instead expressing its faith in the "good sense of Algerians to continue the reform process."[45] Francisco Fernández Ordoñez, minister of foreign affairs, did qualify the cancellation of the electoral process in Algeria as a "coup d'etat" but at the same time advocated

reinforced dialogue and cooperation with the new Algerian regime. In an appearance before the Spanish congress, he affirmed that the European posture was to
wait and see how things developed: "The version I get from Ghozali is that this is
an instrumental coup d'etat to allow a viable democracy, not a chaos." However,
he confirmed that Spain and France had (successfully) opposed other European
countries' attempts to suspend EC aid to Algiers. This was despite the minister
having held meetings with the FIS "at the highest level," which he insisted had
given him "reassurances" regarding the future of economic relations in the case
of a FIS ascent to power.[46] On an earlier occasion, the minister said that the coup
had diverted "a certain bad outcome."[47] The Spanish foreign minister also pushed
for European Union (EU) member states, largely submerged in efforts to assist
transition in Europe's East, to pay more attention to its "southern flank," including an assessment in financial terms, to overcome the current crisis in Algeria.[48]

The United States was not strongly engaged in Algeria at this juncture. Washington expressed its concern and hope for a quick return to democracy. On February 13, a State Department spokeswoman issued a statement asking for a dialogue
among all the parties and for a return to democratic elections, while implying that
the establishment of a High Security Council in Algeria conformed to the constitution. With regard to the latter, protests by the Algerian opposition and diplomatic
circles in Washington led the State Department a day later to "modify" its previous statement by saying it had "decided not to get involved in the constitutional
debate." After the coup, State Department officials also declared their intention to
remain aloof from the new Algerian regime, while noting the silence from Southern European states such as France, Spain, and Italy in reaction to the coup.[49]
In a 2000 interview, Ronald Neumann, US ambassador to Algeria from 1994 to
1997, admitted, "We had scarcely awoken to Algeria in the period 1988–1992. . . .
And this period of transition out of the single-party dictatorship . . . which was a
tremendously vital period for Algeria, was one that we, no doubt unfortunately, did
not notice."[50] The United States still considered Algeria, in fact the entire Maghreb,
as a French preserve.[51]

Among Arab governments, only Sudan (run by a military junta largely made
up of Islamic fundamentalists) and Libya sided with the FIS. Other Arab governments in North Africa, such as Egypt, Jordan, Morocco, and Tunisia, feeling threatened by the rise of Islamist forces on their own soil, had reason for relief when
the Algerian military circumvented a FIS government. In Egypt, Hosni Mubarak
explicitly appealed to the international community to respect Algeria's sovereignty
and not to interfere in the country's internal affairs. The Egyptian minister of the
interior Abdel Jalim Musa expressed his concern regarding the situation in Algeria

and noted that the military would not tolerate any action that may alter the stability of the country. Hassan II of Morocco said: "The Algerian people are a responsible and grown-up people, and I am convinced that, independently of the election results, the Algerian government will respect the agreements Algeria has subscribed to with its allies and partners."[52]

THE INTERPLAY OF DOMESTIC AND INTERNATIONAL FACTORS

This overview of external actors' positions serves as background for examining how a range of international variables interacted specifically with the domestic dynamics identified. Viewing the chronicle of Algeria's internal politics from a wider perspective enables us to identify the interplay between domestic and international factors—how these two levels were mutually conditioning. Various factors can be identified that manifest such interplay.

The Absence of International Pressure

Quite apart from the question of their political will, critics accused Western governments of having misunderstood the problem of authoritarianism and arbitrary rule in the Algerian context. It was assumed that these problems were rooted in the FLN's formal political monopoly, when the issue at stake was the far more pervasive hegemony of the military.[53] One Frenchman involved at the time argued that Paris had failed to understand the nature of the reform process: "The French elite do not understand the Algerian reality . . . the true nature of the system" in part because it retained "an admiration for the successes of these Third World Gaullists."

This meant that international actors misdiagnosed the challenge, while also finding their room for maneuver limited by the complex nature of Algeria's internal politics. Indeed, these domestic complexities were so great that external actors may not have been able to change the outcome even if they had been fully committed to pushing for democratic transition. A week after the coup, the Algerian government withdrew its ambassador to France in reaction both to the extremely mild criticisms coming from Paris and to the visit of a French diplomat whose message the Algerian regime viewed as a French-Iranian conspiracy. This reaction fed back into French internal politics. Domestically, the French government was under sharp attack for its failure to criticize the army's repression of the October 1988 riots. Reluctance to criticize the sovereign government of a former colony was often mentioned as the main reason for this and was reinforced by the fact that many of the political figures in the French socialist government had been supporters of the FLN in its struggle for Algerian independence. Several petitions signed by French and Algerian intellectuals called on the French government to voice stronger criticism toward the Algerian government.[54]

One expert maintains that French security forces were directly behind the Algerian army's intervention to halt a democratic transition that would lead to FIS rule; with the officers responsible having been "France's protégés, . . . [a] clique of former officers of the French army who rallied to the ALN at a late stage in the war."[55] Arms and tank sales from Southern Europe had directly enhanced the military's position and capacity. Army positions were directly empowered by external factors.

Two weeks after the coup, Ali Harun, an envoy from the newly established ruling High State Council, was sent to Europe to speak to leaders in various European capitals to give explanations and to lobby for understanding for the interruption of the electoral process. In Spain, he met with Fernández Ordoñez and Prime Minister Felipe González. On his visit the envoy sought to win European acceptance of the coup by portraying the military coup as a courageous act of resistance and comparing the Algerian situation in January 1992 to the situation in Germany in 1933 when Hitler's NSDAP was on the verge of coming to power. His Spanish interlocutors advocated a resumption of the democratic process and asked for human rights and pluralism to be respected, but without referring to the second round of elections or specifying that the coup should be reversed.[56] Previous links with and support for the army had emboldened the latter, which in turn raised the stakes of a belated change in European positions.

Economic Positioning

On the economic front, the Algerian government and international investors sought to double-guess each others' intentions. Key international actors had an interest in continued stability to secure energy supplies. In June 1992 the Spanish gas company Enagas and Algeria's Sonatrach signed a 25-year contract for the annual delivery of 6 million cubic meters of gas to Spain, via a new pipeline transiting Morocco. In 1991 Gaz de France extended three major supply contracts with Algeria from 10 to 15 years. By this time, Algeria provided one-third of French gas supplies. The role played by political Islam cannot be understood without reference to these energy interests, which constituted international actors' most concrete and immediate concerns.

Some degree of economic opening was deemed important for Western energy interests. The fact that the nationalization of foreign assets was no longer perceived to be a risk helped trigger several new joint ventures with Western companies. But at the same time privileged protection and treatment from the political system continued to be important. Algerian security officers were provided to guard foreign plants, often outnumbering foreign workers. State-of-the-art technology was used to provide secure compounds, in dramatic contrast to the rudimentary domestic conditions of production. In short, collaboration with the security apparatus provided positive benefits.[57] International oil deals directly replenished the army's coffers, reducing its incentives to compromise with the opposition and withdraw definitively from politics.[58]

European governments and the United States pressed for the 1988 IMF structural adjustment plan and thus contributed to the Algerian government's initial decision to commit to democratic transition. Here, an apparently pro-democratic interplay of domestic and international variables could be seen. Indeed, Mouloud Hamrouche's project of rapid liberalization of the Algerian economy was said to be "the brainchild of Parisian advisers."[59] But experts observed that the international community did not press for structural adjustment in either the hope or expectation that it would assist democratic transition.[60] Western governments did not seek an economic reform process that would endanger the political management of the hydrocarbons sector that formed the basis for the privileged relationship between the regime and powerful external interests.

In part because of economic fears, Southern European governments were also increasingly concerned with migration flows and the risk of a mass exodus to France, Spain, and Italy in the case of an Islamist takeover in Algeria. At the same time, the possible impact of instability in Algeria on the large Algerian immigrant community worried European governments, particularly France, which at the time was home to a million Algerian residents. "Any excessive commentary [i.e., critical comment of events in Algeria] could incite them, even to fight among themselves on our own territory," argued French prime minister Michel Rocard, at the same time noting the wrath that the many French citizens still living in Algeria may face if the French government were perceived to be interfering in the country's domestic affairs.[61] After the results of the first round of elections were released, the French Embassy in Algiers reportedly prepared for a massive influx of refugees, taking stock of tents and blankets available. The external impact of Algeria's cautious opening precluded further international support for democratization.

The Gulf War

The Gulf crisis erupted during the Algerian elections and temporarily had a strong emotional impact on the Algerian population, as political competition momentarily focused on foreign policy issues. Both Islamists and secular parties advocated strong pro-Iraqi positions, and two parties (FIS and the Movement for Democracy in Algeria) called on the government to dispatch volunteers to defend Iraq when the United States started sending troops to Saudi Arabia in August 1990. The demands of the opposition contrasted with the more cautious position of the Chadli government, which criticized the American intervention in the crisis and scale of hostilities against Iraq but refrained from inflammatory rhetoric and sought a mediated solution by rallying international support in the Middle East and in France. When Chadli's diplomatic efforts failed and hostilities commenced in Iraq, the FIS was able to lead protests and channel inflamed passions in its favor.[62]

The UN war against Iraq in 1991 forced the FIS, in order to stay popular with its constituency, to end its tacit alliance with Chadli and Hamrouche, who were pressed by the French government not to object to the Iraq invasion. This in turn fed into France's decision to back the army's intervention against the strike in June 1991, "which overthrew Hamrouche and decapitated the FIS, well before the later coup against Chadli and the canceling of the legislative elections."[63] At the time of the army's cancellation of the 1991 elections, the war in Iraq further increased polarization in Algeria, as the Algerian government's neutrality was at odds with Algerian public opinion which strongly opposed the war.

The Iran Factor

Iran was a factor that influenced events in Algeria at several levels. The experience of the Iranian Revolution, Iran's international diplomatic isolation, and frequent Western clashes with the Iranian regime during the 1980s, including the much publicized 1989 Salman Rushdie *fatwa*, increased European fears of Islamic rule and a possible Iranian model taking root in the immediate European neighborhood. This fear, though judged unfounded by many observers, was reinforced by some FIS members' assertions that Iran was indeed their political model.[64]

In early 1992 Algeria withdrew its ambassador from Iran and expelled the Iranian envoy to Algiers, in reaction to Tehran's support of the FIS. Criticisms of the Algerian regime in the Iranian official press during the week after the coup, which warned the Algerian regime not to "abuse the people's power" by disrespecting an Islamist victory in the elections, had led the new Algerian leadership to demand a "clear and public" repudiation of these criticisms by the Iranian government. A visa ban was issued for Iranian citizens, including diplomats. Indications seemed to confirm that the FIS had multiplied its contacts with the Iranian government, although FIS officials vehemently denied a report in the *Independent*, which reported that Iran had given the party $3 million in financing.[65]

Finally, a French attempt to bring Iran into the negotiations for a pacted solution provided the final prompt for the Algerian regime to take drastic steps against

Iran and expel the Iranian ambassador from Algeria. The French government brought Iran into the picture arguing that the mullahs could cool the FIS's ardor. Reportedly France hoped that the Iranians would be able to win from the FIS guarantees that French interests would be protected in the event of the Islamists winning power.[66] Rumors spread of contacts between the Iranian and French secret services. In some Algerian papers, the FIS was referred to as standing for the axis "France, Iran, Sudan."[67] In short, French efforts to involve Iran in Algerian politics to exert influence on the FIS in the aftermath of the 1991–92 legislative elections contributed to the Algerian military's rejection of a pacted solution.

Lack of Support for Civil Society and Opposition Forces

If Western governments were reluctant to criticize the Algerian military, it comes as no surprise that they were even more reluctant proactively to fund democracy projects. There was no formal evidence of the secular opposition receiving funds from Western governments. There was little external support at this stage to build civil society organizations—donors would lament that there were few such autonomous organizations to back anyway, as a potential means of bridging the Islamist-secular divide. The international community did little proactively to assist in the formation of the type of inclusive and robust civil and political society normally seen as a prerequisite to smooth transition. None of the type of logistical support provided in Eastern European revolutions, for example, was offered in Algeria. Some analysts indeed lamented the absence of any attempt by Western powers to forge alliances with the potential advocates of democratic change within civil society.[68] The dearth of such support compounded the fractious uncertainty of civil society groups; such splits in turn made it harder for external actors to identify obvious and effective reformist interlocutors.

In contrast, the FIS reportedly received substantial funds from Islamist networks in other countries to counter leftist groups. Although the precise amounts and actors cannot be formally identified, "it is clear that *zakat* (charity) funds and logistical support made their way to Algerian Islamists from Iran, Pakistan and Saudi Arabia."[69] The Algerian government accused European countries and the United States of allowing Algerian supporters of the FIS to transfer funds and arms through their territories.

Weak International Mediation Efforts

Some analysts accuse the international community of having failed to understand the overriding need for political reconciliation as a prior step toward democratic transition. The EC did little to seek to engage with army moderates to win these over to a pacted solution. French emissaries, however, did engage and negotiate with the FIS leadership, but ultimately the French attempt to convince the Algerian military leadership to consider a pacted solution failed.

Far from seeking to mitigate polarization, some external policies stoked the growing divisions within the Algerian polity. One critic argues that the West sought to undermine "modernist nationalism" and simply saw an initial stirring up of political competition as useful for that.[70] France initially backed the emergence of the FIS. The FIS did not emerge as a spontaneous reaction to FLN misrule but reportedly as a deliberate ploy by the Chadli regime, backed by Mitterrand's France, to use the Islamists to channel popular disaffection in a way that would undermine Chadli's nationalist critics in the FLN. France was made responsible for "spring[ing] a pluralist constitution upon a society entirely unprepared for this transition as a pretext for . . . instrumentalizing [the Islamists] against the nationalists in the FLN. It was only when the FIS escaped Chadli's control in 1991 that the army intervened to slap it down and Paris adopted secularist rhetoric to justify its support for the resort to repression."[71]

Support to Consolidate the New Regime

Much debate in the aftermath of the coup was dominated by debates over a prospective IMF package. With foreign debt estimated at $26 billion, it seemed that the regime desperately needed a new debt rescheduling agreement to stabilize the economy and leave sufficient resources to fund social programs. In the event, the international community enthusiastically offered an IMF support package, only for the Algerian government to refuse the offer. This deprived the regime of new credits amounting to an estimated $1.6 billion.[72] Instead of formally rescheduling its debt, the Ghozali government eventually decided to sell several oil fields to foreign companies to fill the holes in its budget.[73] Expansionary monetary and fiscal policies were adopted, and prices and trade were returned to administrative control. But by 1994 Algeria was again on the edge of financial disaster, facing another balance-of-payments crisis. This time, in April 1994, Algeria did agree to a comprehensive structural adjustment program as a precondition to rescheduling approximately two-thirds of its foreign debt.[74]

The lack of political pressure on the Algerian regime to revive the democratic process continued after 1992, reducing the prospect of the coup being only a temporary interruption in the process of democratization. After 1991, France continued to be especially reluctant to press coercively and was concerned to retain stability, rather than leaning on the army to reopen the process of democratic transition. Algerian migration to Europe was by then growing fast and almost exclusively to France, with the latter hosting nearly 4 million immigrants of Algerian descent in the mid-1990s. Terrorist attacks in the mid-1990s by Algerian Islamists had been aimed primarily at France and French citizens. France was uniquely susceptible to charges of neocolonialism in Algeria and remained the state whose intervention was most likely to provoke counterproductive reaction. French policy makers continued to judge that France would be the state most at risk from any instability engendered by a renewed and conflictive process of political liberalization. During the turbulent years of the early 1990s, other EU states heeded Paris's strictures against any form of coercive pressure against the Algerian government. The Common Foreign and Security Policy (CFSP) statements were diluted at Paris's insistence that there be no more than a vague expression of "hope" that democratization be able to proceed, while unequivocal support be given to official efforts firmly to suppress terrorism.[75]

French authorities kept the EU—and its potentially more pro-democracy northern states—at arm's length from any political intervention; François Mitterrand stated at the end of the Extraordinary Meeting of the Council of Europe of October 27, 1993: "I do not think that the current drama in Algeria is in the domain of the European Union. As far as that is concerned, France is acting as she must in respect of this neighboring country."[76]

Algeria was soon offered a fourfold increase in EU aid.[77] Indeed, Algeria was one of the biggest gainers, in both proportionate and absolute terms, in the distribution of European aid during the early 1990s. In the immediate aftermath of the interruption of the democratic process, the European Parliament sanctioned increases in EC aid to Algeria within the very same vote that suspended the allocation of aid to Morocco and Syria. During the FIS-led strikes in mid-1991, the governments of the EC adopted a plan to extend $125 million in emergency aid to Algeria to buy food and other essentials. Additionally, World Bank loans to Algeria between 1990 and 1995 were more than double the US$1.4 billion extended in the period 1985–89.[78]

European conditionality tightened at this stage was economic, not political, relating to structural economic reforms. In the period after the elections, European governments' strong and unequivocal pressure, in particular through the IMF and including the use of conditionality, for the process of economic liberalization to be reinitiated contrasted with the absence of a similar stance in relation to political liberalization. One expert sustains that at this pivotal political moment, the EU's primary goal was the narrowly self-interested one of getting the Algerian government to accept the rescheduling of Algeria's debt—and hence the obligation to undertake a structural adjustment program dictated by the IMF.[79]

As violence flared after 1992 and the regime adopted increasingly repressive measures against Islamists, the EU's silence was perceived by many in Algeria as complicit. European Union statements did not urge the regime to include Islamists in dialogue but merely welcomed the faintest of moves in this direction once these had already occurred.

The United States did not adopt a more balanced approach until the mid-1990s when it started holding meetings with FIS representatives in Europe and the United States and calling for reconciliation between the FIS and the Algerian government, as a tentative first step in moving back toward some degree of political reform. Even then it was not unreservedly backed by France in this shift in approach.[80] European governments both refrained from critical diplomacy and themselves desisted from formalized contact with the FIS.[81] The EU made no effort to secure a removal of the ban on the FIS engaging in political activity. No firm pressure was exerted even on issues of good governance and increasingly rampant FLN corruption.[82]

CONCLUSION

The failure of Algeria's transition in 1991–92 derived from powerful domestic variables, a series of international factors, and the way in which domestic and external factors interacted with one another in symbiotic fashion.

The range of domestic factors presented here suffices to demonstrate that, while Algeria appeared to stand on the brink of democratic breakthrough in 1991, it did so with many factors still undermining such a possibility. If IMF structural reforms had unleashed a period of change, these were not harnessed specifically for genuine democratization. On balance, long-term structural variables militated against far-reaching political change, in particular the preponderance of the hydrocarbon sector in the national economy and the continued legitimacy of the Algerian military among a significant proportion of the population. These were compounded by a range of short-term factors that acted more specifically close to the moment of potential transition: no broad constituency of strong support for democracy had emerged; democracy's broad ideational appeal was circumscribed; a "secular versus Islamist" polarization undermined agreement on the "rules of the game," cutting across support for democratization; divisions grew between secular opposition parties; and a lack of engagement with the FIS in turn was reflected in and related to the weak legitimacy of reform. It is difficult to ascertain with precision whether Islam or oil was the most potent obstacle; but the energy factor should certainly not be underplayed, despite Algeria being routinely cited as the most emblematic case of concerns derived from radical Islam.

In terms of external variables, even if the international community did argue in favor of democratic transition, it is not clear how influential this was in taking Algeria to the foothills of transition. While some believe that enhanced international pressure could have had a serious impact, others argue that such pressure simply led the "proud" Algerian political elite to become more determined to demonstrate autonomy by resisting democracy. It remains unclear whether the international community's nominal backing for democracy increased or undermined the legitimacy of Chadli's reforms. Some critics assert that Western pro-democracy rhetoric lowered the esteem of the Algerian government in the eyes of the people and that "authoritarianism [was] more permissible than . . . identification with Western powers."[83] Both the Gulf War and Iranian "meddling" further tipped the scales against democracy. The Algerian government's relatively neutral, reconciliatory stance toward the 1990–91 Iraq War, which initially gave Chadli the air of a "major Arab statesman," ended up conflated in the eyes of many Algerians with a broader pro-Western agenda, damaging the latter's credibility. In this context, democratic transition probably stood little chance; the approach adopted in this volume of "zooming out" from an understanding of domestic factors helps explain why international factors simply fed into this doomed national scenario.

France sought to keep transition on track, but in a controlled fashion that would produce the "right result." It was widely judged in Algeria that democratic transition was a stage-managed means of helping the regime survive, with manufactured Western-backed legitimacy. It is generally acknowledged that this drove more people into the clutches of the FIS, despite the latter's ambiguity toward democratic values. Because some FIS representatives were critical of democratic norms, Western governments were able to claim that their indulgence of the coup in fact safeguarded the prospect of democratization.[84] For some critics, ambivalent policies and lack of political will to support genuine democratization was compounded by external actors simply misunderstanding the nature of the "reform" process in the years leading up to the 1991 elections.

Crucially, this account demonstrates how there was strong interaction and mutual conditioning of domestic and international positions. International concern intensified as the FIS's support base expanded; this in turn further reinforced that same support for the FIS as democracy became equated with Western anti-Islam. France reacted to the regime's tactics; the regime reacted in turn to the change in the international community's concerns about the FIS. Increasing polarization within Algeria made the international community more nervous about intervening or cutting aid; this reluctance in turn informed the military's drift toward hardline confrontation, which increasingly closed off any possible mediation space for external actors to work in.

Situating this case study within the context of this volume, it might be said that Algeria represents one of the most overdetermined cases of failed transition. Despite the existence of some variables pulling the country toward reform, most explanatory factors pushed in the opposite direction. In this case, the notion of considering a wider focus than just domestic variables is useful. The preceding account demonstrates how there was in fact a complex mutual conditioning in play between domestic and international variables. But were international factors really crucial in accounting for the failure of transition? Our account shows that the military-led regime was certainly conscious of international reactions. But it is difficult to ascertain in this case whether transition would have failed *even if* external variables were pushing more unequivocally in democracy's favor. As we have shown, there was certainly a wide range of domestic variables impeding reform that might well have sufficed on their own as spoilers; among these, the uncertainty over the FIS's own commitment to democracy and the country's rapid spiral into civil war still stand as the most evocative lessons from the Algerian case. Perhaps we might at most be able to conclude that the regime might have felt more obliged to return to some degree of reformist path in the midterm period *after* the 1991 coup had international pressure during this period been greater.

NOTES

1. Clement M. Henry, "Algeria's Agonies: Oil Rent Effects in a Bunker State," *Journal of North African Studies* 9, no. 2 (Summer 2004): 68–81; Michael L. Ross, "The Political Economy of the Resource Curse," *World Politics* 51, no. 2 (January 1999): 297–322; Hazem Biblawi, "The Rentier State in the Arab World," in G. Luciani, ed., *The Arab State* (Berkeley: University of California Press, 1990), 85–98; Kiren Aziz Chaudhry, *The Price of Wealth: Economies and Institutions in the Middle East* (Ithaca, N.Y.: Cornell, 1997); Terry Karl, *The Paradox of Plenty* (Berkeley: University of California Press, 1997).

2. Michael Bonner, Megan Reif, and Mark Tessler, *Islam, Democracy and the State in Algeria: Lessons for the Western Mediterranean and Beyond* (London: Frank Cass, 2004), 69.

3. Henry, "Algeria's Agonies: Oil Rent Effects in a Bunker State," 74.

4. Ibid.

5. Mohammed Akacem, "The Role of External Actors in Algeria's Transition," *Journal of North African Studies* 9, no. 2 (Summer 2004): 153–68.

6. Ibid.

7. Hugh Roberts, "The Bouteflika Presidency and the Problems of Political Reform in Algeria," transcript of a presentation at Fundación para las Relaciones Internacionales y el Diálogo Exterior (FRIDE), Madrid, February 3, 2005, www.fride.org.

8. M. Akacem, "The Role of External Actors in Algeria's Transition," 154.

9. Ibid.

10. John P. Entelis, "Algeria: Technocratic Rule, Military Power," in I. William Zartman, Mark A. Tessler, John P. Entelis, Russell A. Stone, Raymond A. Hinnebush, and Shahrough Akhavi, eds., *Political Elites in Arab North Africa: Morocco, Algeria, Tunisia, Libya, and Egypt* (New York: Longman, 1982), 110.

11. Robert Malley, *The Call From Algeria: Third Worldism, Revolution, and the Turn to Islam* (Berkeley: University of California Press, 1996), 12.

12. Aylin Güney and Aslihan Çelenk, "The European Union's Democracy Promotion Policies in Algeria: Success or Failure?" *Journal of North African Studies* 12, no. 1 (March 2007): 112.

13. Robert Mortimer, "State and Army in Algeria: The 'Bouteflika Effect,'" *Journal of North African Studies* 11, no. 2 (June 2006): 155–71.

14. Entelis, "Algeria: Technocratic Rule, Military Power," 93.

15. Güney and Çelenk, "The European Union's Democracy Promotion Policies in Algeria," 110; Malley, *The Call From Algeria*, 127.

16. Roberts, "Bouteflika's Presidency."

17. Ibid.

18. Yahia H. Zoubir, "Stalled Democratization of an Authoritarian Regime: The Case of Algeria," *Democratization* 2, no. 2 (Summer 1995): 109–39.

19. Claire Heristchi, "The Islamist Discourse of the FIS and the Democratic Experiment in Algeria," *Democratization* 1, no. 4 (August 2004): 115–17.

20. Bonner, Reif, and Tessler, *Islam, Democracy and the State in Algeria*, 2–3.

21. Heristchi, "The Islamist Discourse," 111–32.

22. John P. Entelis, "Lisa Arone: Algeria in Turmoil; Islam, Democracy and the State," *Middle East Policy* 1 (1992): 23–35.

23. Azzedine Layachi, "Political Liberalisation and the Islamist Movement in Algeria," *Journal of North African Studies* 9, no. 2 (Summer 2004): 46–67.

24. John Entelis, "Islamist Politics and the Democratic Imperative: Comparative Lessons from the Algerian Experience," *Journal of North African Studies* 9, no. 2 (Summer 2004): 202–15.

25. Heristchi, "The Islamist Discourse," 116.

26. Ibid., 117.

27. Jonathan G. Farley, "Algeria: Democracy 'On Hold,'" *Contemporary Review* 262, no. 1526 (March 1993): 130–35.

28. Layachi, "Political Liberalisation," n. 11.

29. Farley, "Algeria: Democracy 'On Hold,'" 3.

30. Jacques de Barrin, "Algerie: après la proposition du porte-parole du FIS peut-il avoir dialogue avec des 'islamistes de bonne foi'?" *Le Monde*, September 19, 1992; Ferran Sales, "Los integristas argelinos amenazan con crear un Parlamento paralelo," *El País*, January 16, 1992.

31. M. Akacem, "The Role of External Actors in Algeria's Transition," 158.

32. Marion Georges, "Le mutisme craintif de Paris," *Le Monde*, January 9, 1992.

33. Camille Bonora-Waisman, *France and the Algerian Conflict: Issues in Democracy and Political Stability, 1988–1995* (London: Ashgate, 2000).

34. Ulla Holm, "Algeria: France's Untenable Engagement," *Mediterranean Politics* 3, no. 2 (Autumn 1998): 104–14.

35. Alain Chenal, "La France rattrapée par le drame algérien," *Politique Etrangère* 60, no. 2 (March 1995): 415–25.

36. "Paris souhaite mantenir et 'approfondir' ses relations avec Alger," *Le Monde*, January 1, 1992.

37. François Mitterrand responding to the press at the European Council in Luxemburg on January 14, 1992, quoted in Chenal, "La France rattrapée par le drame algérien," 415.

38. Ibid., 415–25.

39. Interview with M. Roland Dumas, minister of foreign affairs, French Ministry of Foreign Affairs, in *Figaro*, February 17, 1992.

40. "L'interruption du processus électoral en Algérie est observée avec bienveillance en France," *Le Monde*, January 14, 1992; "En France, le gouvernement reste prudent, l'opposition est partagée," *Le Monde*, January 15, 1992; Jacques de Barrin, "Algérie: démocatisation et relance économique; M. Merbah, ancien premier ministre, reproche au pouvoir de faire cavalier seul," *Le Monde*, May 9, 1992.

41. Melanie Morisse-Schilbach, *L'Europe et la question algérienne* (Paris: Presses Universitaires de France, 1999), 62.

42. "Reactions en France FACE au succes du FIS en Algérie: Mr. Pascua souhaite une révision de la politique de coopération," *Le Monde*, January 7, 1992; "L'interruption du processus électoral en Algérie est observée avec bienveillance en France"; "En France, le gouvernement reste prudent, l'opposition est partagée"; de Barrin, "Algérie: démocatisation et relance économique"; "Appel de M. Chirac à la 'vigilance,'" *Le Monde*, January 10, 1992.

43. Morisse-Schilbach, *L'Europe et la question algérienne*, 52.

44. "El golpe en el país maghrebí evitó un 'mal seguro,' según Fernández Ordoñez," *El País*, February 18, 1992.

45. "España destaca el papel reformador de Chadli Benyedid," *El País*, January 13, 1992.

46. "Fernández Ordoñez califica de 'golpe de Estado' la toma de poder por una junta en Argelia," *El País*, January 29, 1992.

47. "El golpe en el país maghrebí evitó un 'mal seguro,' según Fernández Ordoñez."

48. "Fernández Ordóñez insta a la CE a que preste ayuda urgente a Argelia," *El País*, January 23, 1992.

49. "La crise algérienne: nuances américaines et menace iranienne," *Le Monde*, January 16, 1992.

50. "Our aim has been first and foremost stability of the Maghreb." Ronald Neumann, interview by Roger Kaplan, Washington-Algiers, *African Geopolitics*, September 6, 2000.

51. Azzedine Layachi, "Algerian Crisis, Western Choices," *Middle East Quarterly* 1, no. 3 (September 1994): 62.

52. "España destaca el papel reformador de Chadli Benyedid," *El País*, January 13, 1992.

53. Hugh Roberts, "Demilitarizing Algeria," Carnegie Paper no. 86, Carnegie Endowment for International Peace, May 2007.

54. Steven Greenhouse, "French Government Is Criticized for Failing to Condemn Algeria," *New York Times*, October 18, 1988.

55. Hugh Roberts, *The Battlefield: Algeria, 1988–2002; Studies in a Broken Polity* (London: Verso, 2003), 308.

56. "Un emisario de Argel pedirá hoy comprensión a González, El País, 28.02.1992; El régimen argelino compara el FIS con los nazis," *El País*, February 29, 1992.

57. Richard Youngs, *The European Union and the Promotion of Democracy* (New York: Oxford University Press, 2001), 94–114.

58. M. Akacem, "The Role of External Actors in Algeria's Transition," 154.

59. Roberts, *The Battlefield: Algeria, 1988–2002*, 313.

60. Hugh Roberts, "Dancing in the Dark: The European Union and the Algerian Drama," in R. Youngs and R. Gillespie, eds., *The European Union and Democracy Promotion: The Case of North Africa* (London: Frank Cass, 2002), 106–34.

61. Greenhouse, "French Government Is Criticized for Failing to Condemn Algeria."

62. Robert Mortimer, "Islam and Multiparty Politics in Algeria," *Middle East Journal* 45, no. 4 (Autumn 1991): 586–87.

63. Roberts, *The Battlefield: Algeria, 1988–2002*, 314.

64. Youssef M. Ibrahim, "Algeria Arrests a Senior Islamic Leader," *New York Times*, January 23, 1992.

65. Ibid.

66. "D'Europe ne sont ignorées des plus hautes autorités de l'Etat," *Humanité*, July 3, 1992.

67. Bonora-Waisman, *France and the Algerian Conflict*, 50.

68. Andrew Pierre and William Quandt, "Algeria's War on Itself," *Foreign Policy* 99 (Fall 1995): 131–48.

69. M. Akacem, "The Role of External Actors in Algeria's Transition," 163–64.

70. Roberts, *The Battlefield: Algeria, 1988–2002*, 305–15.

71. Ibid.

72. Marion Georges, "Algérie: les négotiations avec 240 banques à Paris—L'avenir du régime est lié à la signatura d'un accord sur la dette," *Le Monde*, February 22, 1992.

73. De Barrin, "Algérie: démocatisation et relance économique."

74. Kada Akacem, "Economic Reforms in Algeria: An Overview and Assessment," *Journal of North African Studies* 9, no. 2 (Summer 2004): 115–25.

75. Youngs, *The European Union and the Promotion of Democracy*, 100.

76. Jean-Francois Daguzan, "French-Algerian Relations or the Search for Friendly Incomprehension," *AFRI* 2 (2001): 5.

77. Youngs, *The European Union and the Promotion of Democracy*, 95.

78. www.country-data.com.

79. Roberts, "Dancing in the Dark," 106–34.

80. M. Akacem, "The Role of External Actors in Algeria's Transition," 116.

81. C. Spencer, "The Roots and Future of Islam in Algeria," in C. A Sidahmend and A. Etheshami, eds., *Islamic Fundamentalism* (Boulder, Colo.: Westview Press, 1996).

82. Youngs, *The European Union and the Promotion of Democracy*, 96.

83. Entelis, "Islamist Politics and the Democratic Imperative," 213.

84. Roger Diwan, "Fareed Mohamedi: Paris, Washington, Algiers," *Middle East Report* 25, no. 1 (January–February 1995): 25–27.

CHAPTER FOURTEEN

Iran

The Genealogy of a Failed Transition

ABBAS MILANI

The Iranian revolution of 1979 was a failed transition to democracy. The purpose of this chapter is to answer an enduring set of enigmatic and interrelated questions: How did Iran's democratic movement came about, what was its morphology, what role did domestic and international factors play in its evolution, and why did it end in a politically despotic, ideologically sclerotic, and economically incompetent regime?

The first section of the chapter will search for the roots of the democratic movement in the shah's rapid, skewed authoritarian modernization project. His increasingly despotic demeanor, his gross mismanagement of the oil windfall, his misunderstanding of his regime's foes and friends, and inconsistent American pressure for democratization combined to beget the democratic movement of 1978.

The shah consistently tried to ignore domestic and American pressures to democratize. In the fifties and early sixties, when he was politically weak and dependent on the United States, he at least paid lip service to these pressures. In the seventies, when buoyed by increased petrodollars, he felt strong and independent of America, he railed against democracy as a disease befitting only the "blue-eyed world." His new dismissive disposition coincided with the years of the Nixon administration, when American pressure for democratization in Iran had ended and when socioeconomic developments had redoubled the need for democracy. During the Carter administration, American pressure for democratization commenced again, but by then the shah was sick with cancer, the Iranian economy was mired in "stagflation," and there was no organized moderate democratic force left in the country capable of managing and leading a successful transition to democracy.

The shah's rapid but undemocratic modernization effort not only created the key elements of the democratic coalition that ultimately overthrew him but ironically helped determine Khomeini's victory as the unlikely head of that democratic coalition. The shah stubbornly believed that communists and liberal democrats were his main enemies; toward them he pursued a scorched-earth policy. When in the early seventies he had a chance to create a moderate democratic alternative, he scuttled it in favor of a pseudofascist one-party system in 1975.

Islam and the clergy, the shah believed, were his natural allies. He at best unwittingly allowed the growth of a remarkably nimble, multifaceted network of religious institutions that ranged from mosques and lecture halls to secret clerical groups and Islamic terrorist organizations. He saw them as the expedient antidotes to the Marxist threat.

The second part of the chapter describes how the democratic coalition that overthrew the shah had as its leader a man with a clear undemocratic past. The unwieldy coalition he lead was composed of an alliance of traditional members of the bazaar, modern industrialists, urban middle and technocratic classes, women's movement, students, workers, and millions of the conservative poor villagers who had converged on the cities in the decade before the revolution. Neither the economic interests nor the political or cultural visions of these disparate groups could cohere into a unified vision or consistent political structure. They nevertheless all coalesced around an inchoate desire for the overthrow of the shah, a more open polity, and the spiritual leadership of Ayatollah Khomeini. The convulsions in Iranian politics for the past 30 years have been the direct result of the eventual reckoning of these inchoate demands and the peoples' continued insistence on their democratic rights.

Khomeini's ability to beguilingly put on the mantle of a democratic leader, his discipline in keeping silent about his concept of *Velayat-e Fagih* (Guardianship of the Fagih) in the months before the revolution, and finally his charisma allowed him to improbably lead what was an inherently incongruent democratic coalition.

A combination of domestic and international factors facilitated Khomeini's success. Carter's human rights policies, international media and their criticism of the shah for his human rights abuses, the role of international human rights organizations (such as Amnesty International, the Red Cross, and the International Committee of Jurists) after being allowed for the first time to visit Iranian jails in 1977, a romantic attachment to Khomeini as the sage of the Orient, and finally machinations by the Soviet Union all encouraged the democratic opposition, and weakened the shah's regime. Moreover, the majority of the Iranian democrats as well as the American government at the time concluded that only Khomeini and his nimble network of allies and institutions could hold the country together, stave off any Soviet encroachment, and deliver something close to a democratic polity. A handful of Iranian democrats, including Shapour Bakhtiyar and Gholam-Hossein Sadighi, tried to forestall Khomeini's rise to power. In December 1978 Bakhtiyar tried to create a democratic government of national reconciliation. Behind the scenes, he was helped by moderate clerics like Shariat-Madari. He was to the Iranian Revolution what Kerensky was to the Russian Revolution of 1917. That is why Iran's failed transition to democracy is for America one of the great intelligence failures of twentieth century and for Iranian democratic forces, a miscalculation of historic consequences.

The last part of the chapter describes how the incongruent democratic coalition broke asunder and led to the creation of a new despotic Islamic regime. The Iranian Left, particularly those who followed the Soviet Union, played a crucial role in this process. How was it that a surprising coalition of radical and democratic forces came together to overthrow absolutism, and how did a militant, organized, and ruthless minority use and abuse the illusions of its erstwhile democratic allies to establish a new despotism?

AUTHORITARIAN MODERNIZATION AND THE ROOTS OF THE 1979 DEMOCRATIC MOVEMENT

In a meeting with Mohammad Reza Shah Pahlavi in October of 1978, the British ambassador Anthony Parsons offered the shah a brilliant analysis of the social movement that had befuddled him. The shah, Parsons said, "had kept the country under severe discipline for 15 years while he had pursued his policy of rapid modernization. It was inevitable that when this discipline was relaxed, there would be a violent release of popular emotion. Thanks to the fact that the modernization program had ridden roughshod over the traditional forces in Iran, and thanks to the inequalities of wealth and appalling social conditions for the urban poor which had resulted from the boom, it was not surprising that this wave of emotion had become a wave of opposition."[1] In an earlier meeting, Parsons referred to the "massive influx into the cities from the rural areas," creating a "rootless urban proletariat of dimensions hitherto unknown in Iran." The people had nothing to look forward to and "in this state of mind, it was natural for them to turn back to their traditional guides and leaders, the religious hierarchy."[2]

The shah had ignored the task of socializing this new urban class, particularly the millions who converged onto the cities and shantytowns from the countryside, into the ethos of modernity. Nor was he willing to share power with them or the burgeoning middle classes. According to a CIA profile of the shah, he believed democracy "would impede economic development" in Iran.[3] He promised that the time for democracy would come in the future. He wagered that he, and only he, could and should determine the timetable for such a democratic transition; it was, he believed, a "gift" only he could give to the nation. He lost the bet, and the result was the failed 1979 transition to democracy. According to the CIA, the shah had a concept of "himself as a leader with a divinely blessed mission to lead his country from years of stagnation . . . to a major power, supported by a large military establishment."[4]

His success in consolidating in his hand the absolutist power of a potentate was particularly remarkable in the context of the monarchy's history at the moment he ascended the throne in 1941. By then, for more than a century, the institution of Iranian monarchy had been clearly in a historic crisis. In Europe, the crisis of monarchy had been even older. In Iran since mid-nineteenth century, every king, save one, had been either assassinated or forced to live his last years eating "the bitter bread of banishment." The sole exception to this pattern, the only king who died peacefully and in Iran, was Mozzafer-al Din Shah, who in response to the 1905–7 Constitutional movement agreed to sign a decree that allowed Iran to become a democratic constitutional monarchy. In Europe, too, since the rise of modernity and its incumbent idea of democracy, the only monarchies that survived were those willing to accept Rousseau's concept of popular sovereignty and resigned themselves to a simply ceremonial role for the king.[5]

The last Iranian reminder of monarchy's institutional crisis was the fate of the shah's own father, who was forced to abdicate and died in exile, forlorn and heartbroken. It was a clear indication of the shah's obsolete and absolutist concept of power that, in spite of the institutional crisis of monarchy, and in spite of the fact that he had commissioned hundreds of books chronicling the accomplishments of his regime, he never commissioned even one substantive treatise that offered a convincing argument about the merits of monarchy in the modern age—one that would answer the question why monarchy is the best regime for Iran in the twentieth century. This failure was rooted in his "divine right" conception of royal power. His first memoir was called *Mission for My Country*, and in it he unabashedly made the claim that his rule was divine in origin, and his decisions divine in inspiration.[6] It was, he believed, simply "natural" for Iranians to accept his absolutist power.

In contrast, during the age when the British monarchy was experiencing a similar crisis, rooted in the political challenge of modernity, British kings and queens either wrote themselves or commissioned others to write virtually hundreds of monographs, essays, and books in defense of monarchy.[7] James I himself wrote dozens of treatises arguing why monarchy is the best possible system for England. Shakespeare, who better than anyone captures the anxieties and intellectual challenges of his time, seems obsessed with the question of kings and their claim to power in the modern age. The shah, in stark contrast, never articulated a theory about how and why monarchy can survive in the age of modernity and democracy. He only repeated that monarchy is a "natural system" and deeply rooted in the Persian *Geist*.

By late 1978 when the shah realized he had been wrong in his assessment of this *Geist* and understood the gravity of the situation, the armed forces and even the dread secret police (SAVAK) were in disarray, the generals were in despair, and the opposition was emboldened by what it perceived was the West's new critical disposition toward the shah. As is often the case with revolutionary movements, every concession the beleaguered shah made only fed the emboldened opposition's appetite for more concessions and undermined the regime's cohesion and ability to survive. By December 1978, British and American embassies were both detecting "signs of dissention and disarray at the top of the armed forces." Commanders complained that the shah was infirm of purpose, suggesting that his father was made of sterner mettle and that such a crisis "would have never happened under Reza Shah."[8]

The dynamic Parsons was referring to and the generals were complaining about had in reality begun more than two decades earlier. As early as 1958, the CIA and the State Department were convinced that unless something drastic was done in the realms of politics and economy, Iran was heading toward a revolution. In September of 1958, the National Security Council met to discuss a new "Special National Intelligent Estimate," which claimed that the shah's regime "is not likely to last long." It was decided that the United States must work hard to "convince the Shah that the most immediate threat to his regime lays in internal instability rather than external aggression."[9] He must, in other words, reduce his "preoccupation with military matters" and focus more on social development. The shah was to be pressed for prompt, "meaningful, political, social and economic reforms." The main opposition to the shah was decided to be "the growing educated middle class" as a result of its discontent with "Iran's antiquated feudal structure and the privileges of the ruling classes."[10] They were further angered by the corruption of the military, political, and civil service authorities, including members of the royal family and the shah himself. It was further decided that should the shah resist these proposed changes, the United States should take immediate steps toward "developing appropriate contacts with emerging non-communist groups."[11] Unless there was a controlled revolution toward democracy and a market economy from the top, the United States was convinced, a radical revolution from the bottom, one that might benefit the Soviet Union, would be inevitable. As early as 1966, the State Department's Bureau of Intelligence and Research "pointed to basic difficulties for the Shah. . . . The realities of the future will not include the indefinite polarization of one-man rule; in some fashion that cannot yet be discerned, it appears likely that the Shah will confront a choice between allowing greater participation in government or seriously risking a fall from power."[12] Much the same language could be used, indeed was used, in 1978 by Parsons and American Embassy dispatches to describe the shah's options on the eve of the failed transition to democracy.

The changes the United States proposed between 1958 and 1962 altered the economic and political face of Iran and the foundations of the shah's basis of support. A market economy would replace the semifeudalism of the postwar years, and the authoritarianism of the period would also give way to a more democratic polity, with the shah assuming more and more the role of a symbolic figurehead, as stipulated in the constitution. Though the shah too had long believed that, unless he led such a "controlled revolution," chaos and radicalism would be unavoidable, the CIA had concluded that "Mohammad Reza Pahlavi is incapable of taking necessary actions to implement" the needed reforms.[13]

It was a measure of America's anxieties about the future of Iran and of its desire to convince the shah about the urgent need for more democracy that the US Embassy in Tehran chose to keep silent when it was contacted by General Valiollah Qarani about his intended coup.[14] Qarani, at the time the head of military intelligence, was along with a group of more than 30 officers and officials planning to seize power, implement the letter of the 1906 constitution, and force the shah to play a merely symbolic role. They also wanted to appoint as prime minister an old nemesis of the shah, Ali Amini. The coup attempt failed—most probably because British intelligence informed the shah[15]—and Qarani was given a surprisingly light sentence. The American Embassy, as well as some of the top Shiite clergy at the time, was working behind the scenes to lessen his sentence. The connection between Qarani's failed constitutional coup in 1958 and the democratic coalition that overthrew the shah two decades later was both personal and political. Qarani had become close allies of the Freedom Movement (the group entrusted by Khomeini to form the first postrevolution provisional government) and was appointed by Khomeini as the first chairman of the joint chiefs of the Iranian army after the revolution.

Moreover, in spite of his arrest, Qarani's effort was not altogether futile: within two years of his failed coup, as a direct result of US pressures, the same Ali Amini that Qarani wanted to name as prime minister was indeed appointed by a reluctant shah to head a new government. Amini's mandate was to bring about political and economic reforms and a rapprochement with the shah's opponents.

Amini, supported by the Kennedy White House, insisted on having more power and independence than previous prime ministers. The most controversial member of his cabinet was easily Hassan Arsanjani. Like Amini, Arsanjani was an old hand in Iranian politics, but unlike Amini he had been unabashed in his criticism of the shah. He was a charismatic orator, a muckraking journalist and a self-styled socialist by avocation, and a lawyer by vocation. In the Amini cabinet he was in charge of land reform and the Ministry of Agriculture. If Qarani had not failed in his coup attempt, Arsanjani was slated to lead the same ministry. There is somewhat of a consensus among scholars and politicians that Arsanjani's radicalism and charisma, his ambitions and his political acumen, made the Amini plan for land reform more radical than initially intended.[16]

Although the shah reluctantly supported Amini's reforms—a process that he eventually took over and called the White Revolution or the Shah and People Revolution—there was considerable opposition to it from members of the landed gentry who were losing their properties, from clerics who objected to any policy that questioned the sanctity of private property or allowed women the right to vote, and finally from military officers who believed Amini would cut the military budget and pave the way for Soviet influence.[17]

Most of Iran's moderate democrats also dismissed the land reform and other changes eventually made by Amini and the shah as mere cosmetics. Therein was created the embryo of the incongruent coalition that overthrew the shah less than two decades later: secular and Islamist democrats and moderate socialists who opposed to the reforms because they found them superficial united with the clerics, lead by Khomeini, who opposed them because they were supposedly against fundamental tenets of Islam. Modernizing democrats began uniting with antimodern clergy to oppose the shah's reforms and despotism in 1962. This coalition challenged the shah in June 1963 and was brutally suppressed. It is an often overlooked sign of the power of the democratic movement and ideas that two decades later, the same Ayatollah Khomeini who had opposed women's right to vote was now taking on the mantle of a democratic movement and openly advocated women's suffrage. Like the 1905 Russian Revolution that was said to be the dress rehearsal for the 1917 revolution, in Iran too, events in 1963 became the dress rehearsal for the emergence of an even more powerful but similarly incongruent democratic coalition in 1979.

One man, however, questioned the wisdom of the land reform from the perspective of long-term economic and political development. He was known as a planning and economic prodigy, and thus his democratic vision has been eclipsed by the substance and often-stern style of his management. His name was Abolhassan Ebtehaj, and ever since his appointment as the director of the plan organization in 1955, he had survived in power simply because of the shah's continued support. By 1961 Ebtehaj's luck ran out, and he ended up in prison.

But even in prison, Ebtehaj never shied away from expressing his often unique, sometimes contrarian's views. When he learned about plans for a land reform and the shah's upcoming trip to the United States, he decided to write a pithy "Personal and Confidential" letter from prison to his "friends in America" hoping to convince them to stop the Iranian government's plans for a land reform. Ebtehaj was easily the most relentless advocates of an Iranian market economy, a viable middle class and a capitalist class sure of its investments, and democracy as a smithy wherein these forces could best interact and grow.

In his letter, Ebtehaj offered ten reasons why the land reform was detrimental to Iran's long-term capitalist and democratic developments. Under a "capitalist system of free enterprise," he wrote in his letter from prison, "it is not right and just that a person may own any number of factories . . . but be denied the right to own more than a certain amount of farm land." He agreed that absentee landlordism was a curse and a problem for the Iranian agriculture and economy, but he suggested searching for ways to overcome "the drawbacks . . . without resorting to sequestration." Instead of confiscating property, he offered a land reform brought about through a system of taxation, where farms would be taxed on the basis of not "actual but optimum yields." He proposed a simple but sophisticated system of taxation that would ultimately bring about the desired changes in the country's agricultural system without undermining the idea of private property.[18]

Ebtehaj's critique is particularly important in its contrast with the shah's willingness, indeed eagerness, to use the discourse of revolution and the practice of forced sequestration to promote his own political ends and his vision of economic development. Not long after the Ebtehaj letter, the shah began to incessantly talk of the White Revolution, and all manner of "sequestration" became part and parcel of his "White Revolution." The shah had a pseudosocialist, "statist" vision of the economy where the state could and should become an economic Leviathan. As Ebtehaj had predicted, not long after the land reform, the shah proved willing to forcefully expropriate the country's only private television, the first private university, and the country's richest private mine. By the mid-1970s, industrialists were ordered, by royal fiat, to give at least 50 percent of their company's share of stocks to their workers. In the months before the rise of the democratic movement, he used an army of university students, deputized to punish, even imprison, those who allegedly contributed to inflation. He threatened to use the military to bring down prices.

Not only Iranian students and much of the technocratic classes wanted change and democracy, but members of the bazaar—the traditional heart of trade in Iran and a source of support for democratic change in modern Iran—and even members of the modern industrialist class were disgruntled with the shah's economic policies. A speech to the senate by Gassem Lajevardi, a scion of one of the most important industrialist families in Iran and at the time himself a senator embodied this disgruntlement. What Lajevardi discreetly demanded was more democracy and rule of law as a way to guarantee long-term investment.[19] No one, in his words, paid any attention to his speech.

The speech was important from a different perspective. There was an unwritten contract between the shah and Iran's entrepreneurial class, particularly those in modern sectors. They would not engage in politics and would accept the shah's absolute leadership; in return, they could count on the government's pro-business policies. For two decades, buoyed by rising oil prices, the covenant worked. As a result, even independent organizations that could represent the political interests of the entrepreneurial class were not tolerated by the shah. All unions and merchant or industrialist associations were either banned or dominated by the regime. Iran witnessed impressive socioeconomic growth and was in fact among the fastest-growing developing economies in the world. But the covenant came back to haunt the regime and the entrepreneurial class when the system went into a crisis. The entrepreneurs themselves were in 1978 either critical of the shah (from Amid-Hozour and the Moghadam brothers to the Farmanfarmaian and Lajevardi families),[20] or politically inactive, impotent, and unable to successfully defend the regime or their own investments. To what extent did the shah's constant conjuring of revolutionary rhetoric make the idea and concept of revolution an accepted part of the Iranian political discourse? Did these appropriations undermine the ability or resolve of Iran's private sector to come to the shah's defense when his regime went into a crisis in 1978? How much did these grandiose promises of rising standards of living, of surpassing Germany and Japan, fuel the population's rising expectations and contribute to the classical J-curve of expectations rising faster than the government's ability to satisfy them?[21] In other societies, the word *revolution* brings to mind cataclysmic changes. By 1978, the word had been a constant part of Iran's political vocabulary for almost two decades. By then, the idea of expropriating successful businesses had also become "normal." When in the months after the revolution, the regime confiscated the properties of 52 of Iran's largest industrialist families, the decision was only a surprise because of the size of the confiscation and not for the confiscation itself.

At the same time, it was a measure of the shah's resilience as a politician that in spite of the great chasm that separated his vision from the new policy proscribed by the United States since 1959 that he not only stayed a close ally of the United States for the next 17 years but also gradually forced even the Kennedy administration to rethink some key elements of its policy. At the end of his state visit to the United States in 1962 in a joint press conference with the shah, Kennedy insisted that "a modern political leader" must work "not just with the upper elements of society" but "with the ordinary mass of people." The shah in return accepted the premise but added that in "Iran firm action is necessary and he was sure that the United States would not insist on absolute constitutional legality within Iran." Kennedy responded by accepting that "special situations" sometimes exist in different countries and that in Iran, "the Shah was the key stone of . . . security and progress."[22] The shah and his supporters and even some among the Iranian democrats understood these words as a green light for the shah's authoritarianism and the recognition of the Kennedy White House that their ideas of democracy are obsolete in a country like Iran.

The irony is that ultimately the shah's success in defying US pressure for democratization proved to be his undoing. Had the shah remained a constitutional monarch, as the American policy proposed during the Eisenhower and Kennedy administrations, instead of becoming a modernizing albeit authoritarian monarch, as he was in the seventies, he might have been able to save his throne, and the monarchy. As early as 1975, Richard Helms, onetime head of the CIA and then US ambassador to Iran, wrote in his end-of-tour report that "the conflict between rapid economic growth and modernization vis-à-vis a still autocratic rule . . . is the greatest uncertainty of Iranian politics." Helms went on to say that "alas history provides discouraging precedents" for a peaceful resolution of this conflict. "I can recall no example of a ruler," he said, "willingly loosening the reins of power."[23] By the time the shah was willing—or was pressured by Carter—to make some of those concessions, he was already deemed too vulnerable and weak by his opponents. They now wanted his throne, not an offer of a democratic opening.

During his days of power, the shah had followed a political scorched-earth policy, eliminating or curtailing all moderate opposition. All genuine political parties were declared illegal and in their place, he willed into existence first a two-party system and then something called the "Progressive Circle"—the group eventually became a political party (Iran Novin or New Iran) and its founding members, Mansur and Hoveyda, were Iran's prime ministers from 1964 to 1976. CIA state chief in Tehran, Gratian Yatsevitch, played a crucial role in creating and strengthening the Progressive Circle, initially intended to "take the wind out of the sail" of the National Front and other moderate opposition forces who refused to make peace with the shah.[24]

Once in power, however, members of the Progressive Circle, particularly Hoveyda—the prime minister for 13 years—not only made no effort to promote democracy but also became a great facilitator of the shah's increasing authoritarianism. As the price of oil jumped and the social fabric of Iranian society changed with stunning rapidity, and as the need for a more democratic polity increased, the shah became more and more authoritarian. The rapidity of these changes fueled his grandiosity and his belief that he was "anointed" to defy the age-old dictum that modern middle classes want a share of power. The faux moderates of the Progressive Circle became his sycophantic servants, and the real moderates, whether inside the National Front or among the ranks of Iran's burgeoning middle class, swelled the ranks of the opposition. These were conveniently the days of the Nixon administration, and his Nixon Doctrine. The shah was, according to this doctrine, the designated guarantor of security in the Persian Gulf, and the US government was required to sell the shah as much arms as he desired and to stop pressuring him for more liberalization. Prudent moderates, advocating reform and democracy, as well as radical advocates of change, from every political persuasion, were shunned or barred from politics. The brunt of these despotic measures was taken against the Iranian Left and moderate democrats, as the shah believed them to be the main foes to his regime.

On the other hand, the shah believed the clergy—with the exception of the few Khomeini supporters—were his reliable allies in the fight against communists or secular nationalists. His scorched-earth policy left the clergy and its vast nimble network of organizations an opportunity to grow and to monopolize the public domain. When in October 1969, "moderate religious leaders" sent a message to the shah and to the US Embassy that they were worried "about the situation" in the country and "angry at Khomeini" for putting them in a difficult position of either choosing his radicalism or being branded as a "reactionary mullah of the court," the shah chose to ignore their warnings. More than once, similar warnings from the moderate clergy (about everything from the shah's sudden decision to change the calendar and make it begin in a "royal" rather than Islamic event to new progressive laws about women and family protection laws) were ignored. Open letters and declarations from secular moderate politicians—from leaders of the National Front to independent moderate opposition figures like Khalil Maleki and Mozzafer Baghai—were either ignored or, more often, punished. Assadollah Alam, the powerful court minister for more than a decade, constantly reminded the shah that radical clerics like Khomeini had been deracinated in 1963, when Alam was the prime minister.[25] The more the shah ignored the moderate clergy, the easier it became for Khomeini and his radical allies to gain and consolidate hegemony over religious forces in Iran.[26]

In the meantime, the clergy began building a vast, nimble network of organizations that ranged from the most successful terrorist organization in modern Iran (Fedayan-e Islam) to schools that trained students in a strictly Islamic curriculum. Clerics published magazines with tens of thousands of subscribers and books that promulgated religious points of view. With encouragement from the shah's regime, there was a boom in the building of mosques and seminaries in the sixties and seventies. It is estimated that by 1977, there were more than 75,000 mosques in the country.[27] The number did not include the hundreds of *takiyeh*—the temporary structures or tents set up around religiously important days to house religious rituals—that sprung to action when needed. Each mosque became a potential party-cell for training dedicated members, accumulating funds, and promoting religious ideas. As early as 1962, followers of Khomeini organized a nationwide network of telephone connections they could use to send an action message, or to read over the phone the text of a Khomeini statement that needed to be distributed around the country. By 1978, they used the network to distribute overnight hundreds of thousands of tapes, containing Khomeini's most recent sermon invariably railing against the shah and sometimes a new promise of a more democratic tomorrow.

The ever-watchful SAVAK either looked the other way or encouraged these religious institutions and networks. They hoped it would temper the influence of the communists—in their mind, their biggest foes. Only in the most radical cases, when open allegiance to Khomeini was shown, did SAVAK ever come into action against these mushrooming institutions. As a result, when the regime went into a crisis in 1977, the clerical network, by then dominated by Khomeini and his allies, turned out to be the only force capable of offering itself as a viable alternative to the status quo.

Religious forces had by then also developed the idea of a Hosseiniye—a lecture hall that used modern trappings, to cultivate religious ideas, shorn of superstitions. The halls usually allowed people to sit on chairs, by then a habit of the middle classes, and forego the more cumbersome mosque practice of sitting on the floor. The most famous of these halls, called Hosseiniye Ershad, was built in one of Tehran's upper-class neighborhoods. The financial support came from members of the bazaar close to the Freedom Movement, and the ideological management of the center was in the hands of Khomeini supporters. Every move they made, we now know, they made after consultation with Khomeini, who was in those days exiled in Najaf.[28] At this Hosseiniye, more moderate clergy, like Ayatollah Mottaheri, or fiery Islamists orators, like Ali Shariati, offered a version of Shiism more amenable to modernity and democracy. Among those influenced by Shariati's rhetoric was Mir-Hossein Mousavi, who now leads the Green Movement and his influential wife, Zahra Rahnavard.[29] Though Shariati was known partially by his fierce critique of the Shiite clergy as a symbol of a despotic and stale Islam, he usually praised Khomeini as an exception, a "progressive" cleric fighting relentlessly against despotism and colonialism. More than any other ideology, the writings of the likes of Shariati prepared the context for Khomeini's leadership of the democratic movement. Today, the roots of the reform movement can at least partially be sought in followers of Shariati who joined the revolution on the basis of his ideas, were disappointed by the clerical despotism that emerged, and are still trying to create a more democratic Shiism. By promoting economic changes that created a new more wealthy and educated middle class, the shah, inadvertently created the forces necessary for a democratic transition. His scorched-earth political policy, however, denied these forces either a share of power or an opportunity to organize, even within the limits clearly set out by the constitution. Through a modern iteration of Shiism, the clergy succeeded in uniting with many in this critical social class.

Ironically, by the early 1970s even the shah realized that his regime faced serious political challenges. In 1973, he learned of his serious illness, and as he grew disgruntled with or became afraid of the newfound arrogance in the New Iran Party[30]—with party congresses looking more like communist party rituals, with requisite delegations from fraternal parties and party songs performed by comrades, arms locked in unity—he began to search for a remedy. He asked to meet with Mehdi Samii, one of Iran's most respected technocrats, with extensive connections among middle-class moderate intellectuals and the leaders of the National Front. The shah told Samii of his worries about the future and about the "problem of transition"—particularly after his death—and asked Samii to launch a new political party that would indeed succeed in soliciting the support of the Iranian educated middle classes for a peaceful transition.

For almost five months, Samii met regularly with the shah, discussing and setting out the parameters of what the new party would be allowed to do. Fortunately, Samii took copious notes every time he met with the shah. As these notes indicate, what the shah had in mind was a loyal opposition party, a centrist party with hints of social democratic ideas in its proposed platform. It could participate in elections and even attempt to directly negotiate with the opposition, including the clergy. Ten of the country's most respected technocrats, with impeccable reputations for financial probity and centrist political inclinations, had already signed on as the new party's founding members.

But then the price of oil suddenly quadrupled, and in Samii's words, "suddenly His Majesty changed his mind and pulled the plug on the party."[31] Instead of facilitating the creation of such a genuine centrist democratic party, one that might have been an alternative to the status quo when the regime went into a crisis in 1977, one that could have conceivably obviated the crisis had it been put in charge of the government in 1975, when the shah was at the height of his power, the shah instead opted for the disastrous idea of a one-party system. All other parties were dismantled in favor of the new Rastakhiz (Resurgence) Party. Everyone in the country was expected to join—otherwise, the shah offered them a free passport to leave the country! When 15 years earlier, a grass-roots loyal opposition movement called Rastakhiz was launched by a dependable ally of the shah, it had been dismantled on the shah's orders simply because in its meetings it sported no pictures of the shah.[32]

The new Resurgence Party of 1975 was a stillborn monster and an immediate source of discontent and even ridicule. The fact that key party ideologues were often from the ranks of lapsed Stalinists made the organization more and more behave like a pseudo-Stalinist monstrosity of bad ideas and bad politics.[33] Some believe the idea for the party first came to the shah from Sadat in Egypt; others point the finger to a group of five, mostly American-trained technocrats who suggested the one-party system on the basis of Huntington's prescription for political development in developing countries.[34] Whatever the source, the idea was a political disaster. Instead of creating "political participation," as the shah kept promising, it became a political albatross that created nothing but discontent.

Not long after the creation of the party, the Carter administration came to power, and began to pressure the shah to democratize and show more respect for human rights. Moreover, in the last years of the Nixon administration and for much of the Ford administration, Iran and United States had been fighting an open, often bitter war of diplomacy on the price of oil. When the shah refused to use his influence in the Organization of Petroleum Exporting Countries (OPEC) to reduce the price of oil, the United States made a covert pact with Saudi Arabia to bring the price down. Although the shah claims that this refusal—and not the democratic aspirations of the people—was the real source of his downfall, some scholars have suggested that the sudden drop in the price of oil indeed helped the fall of the shah.[35] Just as Iran's revenues were drastically reduced with stagnant oil prices, Carter administration resumed pressure on the shah to democratize and liberalize. The timing could not be worst: the shah was sick, and the economy was in a downturn. The normal instabilities that accompany any authoritarian regime's attempt to democratize only aggravated the effects of the economic crisis. By 1978, Iran's GNP growth in real terms dropped to 2.8 percent. This recessionary slowdown was exacerbated by unusually high inflationary rates. Like much of the West, Iran too faced the strange hybrid phenomenon of "stagflation." Some in the US Congress began to worry about Iran's budgetary priorities (and the fact that, in line with the shah's views, precedence was given to military matters over social needs). These anxieties lead to ideas to "link Iran's human rights performance with arms transfer."[36] It is hard not to ask what might have happened if, in 1975, instead of clamping down the system with a pseudofascist party, the shah had continued his own effort to create the Samii party? What might have happened if in 1976, when he still wielded much power, he had made substantive concessions to the opposition, instead of waiting for 1978, when he was politically vulnerable and weak?

Even this unusual constellation of stars was not enough to end the shah's regime and shatter the dream of a democratic transition. In the last two years of his rule before the 1979 failed transition to democracy, in each moment of crisis the shah made arguably the worst possible choice. He showed weakness when he was supposed to be strong, and he feigned power when he in fact had none. The reason for this remarkable series of errors was not tactical but strategic, rooted in his view that the whole revolution was a conspiracy of outside forces against him. He changed his mind about who masterminded the conspiracy but never wavered in his belief that the conspiracy was the causal root of the revolution. Even in his last book, *Answer to History*, written in exile, and long after he had been "un-kinged," he argues with surprising certainty that it was a conspiracy of Western and Communist forces that overthrew him. To "understand the upheaval in Iran . . . one must understand the politics of oil." He goes on to claim that as soon as he began to insist on a fair share of oil wealth for Iran, "a systematic campaign of denigration was begun concerning my government and my person . . . it was at this time that I became a despot, an oppressor, a tyrant. . . . This campaign began in 1958, reached its peak in 1961. Our White Revolution halted it temporarily. But it was begun with greater vigor in 1975 and increased until my departure."[37] What he failed to understand was that it was the democratic aspirations of the Iranian people that begot the movement against him and that his own social and economic policies of the sixties and seventies helped create the very social forces—particularly the middle class and the new technocratic class—that united to overthrow him. He dismisses nearly every opposition to his rule as a tool of Western governments to bring pressure on him.[38] In 1977, as the movement was picking up momentum, he ordered some of his top oil negotiators to meet with Western oil companies and "give them what they want."[39] In the months leading up to the revolution, he was desperate in trying to understand what the United States and Britain "wanted of him."

During the same weeks as the shah grew more desperate for a sign of support from the West, particularly the United States, the messages he got from America were contradictory. For example, the British Embassy was "told in strictest confidence that when Bill Sullivan," the American ambassador, returned to Tehran from a leave, "he was asked if he would seek a personal message of support for the Shah from President Carter. Sullivan fobbed [the shah] off by saying that such a message would be unusual and inappropriate the present time."[40] The response depressed the shah, but a few weeks later, when he was told that he would be in fact "receiving a telephone call" from the president, "the Shah was clearly delighted, and according to Sullivan, 'his chin moved up from his knees to at least his chest."[41] In reality, there were profound differences between directions the embassy was receiving from the White House, the National Security Council, and the State Department. The vacuum created a space wherein Sullivan seemed to have followed his own "foreign policy." Whereas Zbigniew Brzezinski suggested an iron fist policy to establish law and order to be then followed by concessions to the opposition, the State Department insisted on the continuation of the liberalization policy. The shah, caught between these differing words of advice, went from one extreme to another, invariably to disastrous results. On the other hand, Khomeini, dangling a tactical but tantalizing democratic platform, used each of the shah's moves to his own profit. No wonder then that in the weeks before the collapse of the regime, American officials, including General Huyser (sent by Carter on a special mission to Iran) and "General Gast (the MAAG chief in Tehran), were in close touch with the military . . . [and] were working to facilitate contact between them and Khomeini's forces." By then it was US policy that there should be no coup in Iran. The decision was made after "questions" were put to "Khomeini forces in Iran and Paris"; satisfied by the response they received, US officials were facilitating Khomeini's rise to power.[42]

Even when the shah sought domestic sources of the revolution, he had a myopic vision. He concluded he should have exercised more authoritarianism and not less. "Today, I have come to realize that the events of 1978–9 are attributable in part to the fact that I moved too rapidly in opening the doors of the universities, without imposing more severe preliminary selection. The entrance exams were too easy."[43] He calls the students "spoiled children" who helped wreck havoc on Iran.

The students were of course "not spoiled" children. Nor was it "written" that they as well as much of Iran's democratic forces would join an alliance with Khomeini. It is not, in short, impossible to imagine a scenario for a transition to democracy, but in reality that effort begot a despotism even more brutal than the one it replaced. Why? And how?

A DEMOCRATIC COALITION WITH A DESPOTIC LEADER?

It is hard to pinpoint the moment the unwieldy democratic coalition that eventually overthrew the shah began to coalesce. One thing is certain: Carter's human rights policies had an impact in reinvigorating the dormant democratic movement. As early as May 1977, 53 of the country's top lawyers and law professors wrote a letter to the shah, accusing his government of interfering in the work of an independent judiciary. Less than a month later, three top leaders of the National Front (Karim Sanjabi, Darius Forouhar, and Shapour Bakhtiyar) wrote an open letter of their own. They criticized the regime's economic policies and, in a language reminiscent of Ebtehaj's 1962 critique of the land-reform, suggested that the mishandled land reform and subsequent bad policies have wrecked the country's agricultural sector. They demanded an end to despotism, respect for the constitution and for the Universal Declaration of Human Rights, an end to the one-party system, freedom of the press, and release of all political prisoners. In quick order, other groups of lawyers, professors, and political activists entered the epistolary fight for democracy.

One of the most important of these was a letter signed by 98 prominent writers, poets, and translators that marked essentially the reemergence of the Iranian Writers Association—a group that played an important role in the subsequent democratic struggle in Iran. With every passing day, as it became evident that the regime was no longer punishing those who signed these daring declarations, their numbers suddenly increased. The Iranian Committee for the Defense of Freedom and Human Rights was founded and had in its ranks not only most leaders of the National Front but also Mehdi Bazorgan—the future prime minister of the Islamic regime.

Some in SAVAK claim that the announcement of the Carter candidacy was for them the first warning shot. In fact, they prepared a new intelligence estimate. It warned of a potentially serious crisis and demanded a free hand to use the full force of their power to confront and contain the crisis. It indicated that some of the same coalition of opponents that challenged the regime in 1963—Marxist groups, students, members of the bazaar, the urban poor, and radical clergy—are readying themselves for yet another, more serious challenge. In 1963, the report claimed, the opposition was buoyed by the Kennedy administration's talk of democracy and reform, and in 1977 Carter's human rights policies were giving them a new lease on life. The report went on to claim that this time the challenge is far more serious than in 1963: there are more Marxists in more groups and many more workers in cities, more cadres for revolutionary groups (many trained by Palestinian groups in armed struggle), many more college students, and more moderate democrats willing to join the opposition, if they sense any weakness in the regime. The conclusion of the report was that any hint of weakness in the regime, of succumbing to the human rights policies of the new Carter administration, could trigger a rapid slide into a systemic crisis.[44]

The shah was incensed. He accused those in SAVAK who had prepared the report of treasonously overlooking the fruits of his labor and of the "revolution" he had made. Do they mean to say, he reportedly asked, that we have accomplished nothing in the past two decades? The underlying premise of the SAVAK report and the shah's angry retort captured the core of his illusion and SAVAK's delusion: economic progress, he believed, will mollify people's demand for democracy, while his secret police, even when anticipating a crisis, sought the solution only in an iron fist.

In spite of the role his own policies had in the creation of the crisis, the shah felt betrayed not just by the West but also by the people of Iran. Sometimes he claimed that his opponents were nothing but "Marxists, terrorists, lunatics and criminals." He believed that only with the help of Western intelligence institutions could the Iranians organize into the large democratic movement of 1978 and considered the West's "betrayal" of him something that far exceeded the "giveaway at Yalta."[45]

The shah's paranoid view about the endogenous roots of discontent were augmented by the Persian malady of conspiracy theories, attributing every major event in the modern history of the country to some pernicious and pervasive foreign force—the British, the Free-Masons, the communists, and in the past thirty years the "Zionist-American" conspiracy, and more recently the "velvet revolution" conspiracy.[46] The shah in 1978 and Iran's supreme leader Ali Khamenei today refuse to see the domestic roots of discontent or accept the people's ability to organize themselves into a powerful and disciplined movement.

Belief in conspiracy theories, or "heated exaggerations, suspiciousness, and conspiratorial fantasy" is, as Richard Hofstadter has argued, founded on a "paranoid style of politics."[47] Such beliefs and theories are themselves an enemy of democracy. They posit and produce a passive citizenry, willing to accept that forces outside society shape and determine the political fate of the community.[48] A responsible citizenry, cognizant of its rights and responsibilities, is a foundational prerequisite for democracy, but conspiracy theories absolve citizens of responsibility for their own action and fate, and place all the blame on the "Other."[49] The anticolonial rhetoric of the Left, with its tendency to place all the blame on the "Orientalist" West, helped nurture this "nativist" tendency to forego self-criticism, opting instead to blame the Other.[50] In 1978 the shah and most Iranian government officials had an exaggerated view of the power of America and England to "to direct events" in Iran. A few critical reports by the BBC and critical comments in the American media were more than enough to convince both the people and the regime that the shah was now vulnerable and that the West was out to get him. Even Khomeini was reported to listen to nightly broadcasts of the Voice of America, the BBC, and Radio Israel. So pervasive was this perception that American and British media, particularly the BBC and the Voice of America, represent the views of their governments that both countries' ambassadors worked hard to dispel the notion. More than once Iran "semiofficially" objected to the British government about the content of BBC broadcasts. It threatened to end some contracts with British companies if the BBC continued its critical comments. At one time, some of the shah's generals from the air force came up with the idea of using the cover of night "to take out the relay towers of the BBC."[51] The shah rejected the idea, but in recent accounts offered by the BBC itself, it admits to having a "critical" disposition toward the shah. According to the broadcaster, "the image of the BBC changed in the collective perception of the population. It was no longer the voice of 'British colonialism' but a trusted friend."[52]

Tensions over these broadcasts reached such a level that by September 1978, the British ambassador, in meetings with the shah and the prime minister (at the time Sharif-Emami) informed them of his decision to dispatch an "entirely trustworthy" emissary to meet with Ayatollah Shariat-Madari, "as leader of the most important moderate opposition," and reassure them that the BBC does not reflect official British policy and that Great Britain's "true position" was in fact full support for the shah.[53]

The US government too took many steps to reassure the shah and his regime that, in spite of what American media writes and reports, American officials continue to support the regime. But as Karl Popper has argued,[54] an indispensable characteristic of all historicist antidemocratic theories are that they are not falsifiable;[55] any attempt to offer empirical or rational proof critical of the theory is already "explained" and dismissed by the theory—and conspiracy theories become forms of historicism when they reduce the complicated flux of history to the machinations of one actor or conspirator.

Like a traditional Oriental potentate, the shah felt the society owed him a debt of gratitude for the progress and the freedoms he had "given them." In reality, in the past 15 years of his rule, there was unprecedented cultural and religious tolerance and freedom in Iran. Private lives were free from virtually any governmental interference. The only exceptions were the lives of those who in any way actively opposed the regime (in which case their phones were tapped, their mail was opened, and their movements monitored).[56] Jews and members of the Baha'i faith enjoyed virtual equality with Muslims. But for most in Iran's opposition, these cultural and economic freedoms were either a form of "decadent libertinism" or merely cosmetic to cover the more fundamental lack of political democracy. On the eve of the revolution, it was this political freedom that was, more than any other liberty, the focus of the democratic movement.

Moreover, most Iranians touched by modernity—and its notions about the natural rights of citizens—considered the freedoms the shah thought he had "given" them their inalienable rights.[57] He was, in the words of a confidante, "like a man who had lavished everything on a beautiful woman for years, only to find that she had been unfaithful all along."[58] The authoritarian system the shah had established placed him as the sole "decider" for nearly every major economic, political, and military decision in the country. As a report by the State Department's Bureau of Intelligence and Research made clear,

the Shah is not only king, he is de facto prime minister and is in operational command of the armed forces. He determines or approves all important governmental actions. No appointment to an important position in the bureaucracy is made without his approval. He personally directs the work of the internal security apparatus and controls the conduct of foreign affairs, including diplomatic assignment. No promotion in the armed forces from the rank of lieutenant up can be made without his explicit approval. Economic development proposals—whether to accept foreign credit or where to locate a particular factory—are referred to the Shah for decision. He determines how the universities are administered, who is to be prosecuted for corruption, the selection of parliamentary deputies, the degree to which the opposition will be permitted, and what bills will pass the parliament.[59]

When his deteriorating health and mood and his failing grip on power rendered him incapable of making any decisions, as it did in late 1978, the entire machinery of the state came to a grinding halt.

The regime's policy and practical lapses were no match for Khomeini's clear and early appreciation of the structural nature of the crisis and the democratic nature of the movement. The shah's paralysis—induced as much by his endogenous paranoia as by the medications he was taking while undergoing chemotherapy to fight his cancer—could not compete with Khomeini's resolute and ruthless Machiavellian guile. Around the time George Ball, dispatched to Iran by President Carter in December of 1978, concluded that the shah was not likely to survive, the British government too had, on October 30, 1978, decided that the shah did not have any chance to survive and that they "should start thinking about reinsuring."[60] When both countries began to "reinsure" and tried to establish ties with leaders of the opposition, the only force they found that could, in their judgment, keep the country from chaos or falling into the Soviet orbit and creating a government "responsive" to the demands of the people was Khomeini and his coterie of clerics, and the surprisingly large and swelling ranks of his democratic and even leftist followers.

The movement that overthrew the shah was democratic in nature and aspirations. Some 11 percent of the country's population of 38 million at the time participated in the movement, compared to 7 and 9 percent in the French and Russian Revolutions.[61] Slogans of the day were unmistakably democratic as well. Anywhere between 38 to 50 percent of the slogans were directed against the shah, while about 16 to 30 percent favored Khomeini personally. At best, 38 percent asked for an

Islamic Republic (and none for a clerical regime).[62] The most common slogan was "Independence, Freedom and an Islamic Republic."

In the months leading to the collapse of the shah, Khomeini grabbed the mantle of a populist and democratic leader, and instead of espousing his ultimate goal and true ideology, he took on the guise of a leader befitting a democratic movement. From his first book in Persian, written in the aftermath of the fall of Reza Shah to the collection of his sermons on an Islamic government, compiled by his students in Najaf in late sixties, Khomeini had made it clear that in his mind the only genuine form of government is the absolute rule of the jurist who rules not in the name of people and for the goal of democracy but for implementing Islamic *sharia*.[63] He called the theory *Velayat-e Fagih*, or the rule of jurist. Even in the annals of Shiite history, Khomeini's view was a minority, espoused only by a handful of ayatollahs.[64] In the months leading to the revolution, however, Khomeini never referred to his own concept of *Velayat-e Fagih*. The fact that the shah and his SAVAK had banned Khomeini's books for decades made them unavailable to Iranian readers or critics. Moreover, Khomeini was nothing if not a disciplined politician. Even his book on the subject of *Velayat-e Fagih* was compiled by his students from their lecture notes, affording him always "plausible deniability."

Velayat-e Fagih claims humans are incapable of sound decisions on their own, and like minors who need the "guardianship" (*Velayat*) of parents, people too need the guardianship of the jurist. It is a theological incarnation of the Platonic idea that the people are incapable of sound political judgment and need the guardianship of a philosopher. If in Plato human reason is the key to this philosophical wisdom, for Khomeini it is revelations in the Qur'an, and in the Hadith[65]—words and deeds attributed to the prophet and his 12 male progeny, called the imams— that are the keys to justice in this passing world and salvation in the other infinite realm.

Velayat-e Fagih is equally undemocratic in its "language of legitimation,"[66] or the way it purports to achieve and maintain its legitimacy. Khomeini posits that legitimacy for this guardianship is divine in origin and not dependent on the consent of the guarded.[67] In Iran, he eventually changed his theory even more, and by introducing the concept of *Maslahat* (expediency) he posited that his words and *fatwa*—and after him those of his successor—trump even the fundamentals (*Usul*) of *sharia* and Islam.[68] In the years after the clerical heist of power, some of the more conservative members of the clergy—like Mesbah-Yazdi—have openly pointed to the incompatibility of democracy and *Velayat-e Fagih*, even conjuring such ideas as the "discovery" of the *Fagih*, rather than his election or appointment, and of an "acquired" sacred sagacity once he is "discovered."

But in the months before the revolution, Khomeini made no reference to *Ve-layat-e Fagih*, but he repeated more than once that the next government after the shah will be democratic and that the clergy will have no role in any of its political institutions. There will be freedom for all, and coercion on none, he promised more than once. In an interview on November 7, 1978, he even claimed that "personal desire, age and my health do not allow me to personally have a role in running the country." On the same day, he told the German *Die Spiegel* that "our future society will be a free society, and all the elements of oppression, cruelty and force will be destroyed." A few days earlier, on October 25, he had said that "the ranking Shiite religious clergyman do not want to govern in Iran themselves," promising at the same time that women will "be free . . . in the selection of their activities, and their future and their clothing."[69]

To add further poignancy to this democratic pose, Khomeini allowed a few ambitious Western-trained aides (like Abol-Hassan Bani-Sadr, Sadeq Gotb-Zadeh, and Ebrahim Yazdi)[70] to become in Paris the public face of his movement. The three were his de facto spokespersons and helped consolidate the democratic façade. At the same time, unbeknownst to much of the world, in Tehran Khomeini had already appointed a few trusted clerics—nearly all his students in earlier years—into a covert "Revolutionary Committee" that managed the day-to-day affairs of Khomeini's followers. Some members of this committee, particularly those from the Freedom Movement, were in close contact with American Embassy officials in Tehran, and they eventually convinced the ambassador that, contrary to what they had been told by the shah, the clergy is both capable and willing to establish a democratic polity in Iran.

It was a measure of the democratic nature of the movement and of Khomeini's democratic façade that in 1979 the first draft of the new proposed constitution made no mention of *Velayat-e Fagih*. It was modeled on France's Fifth Republic constitution. Moreover, even a year after his return home, when the first elected president was impeached and a new election was scheduled, Khomeini still resisted efforts by the clergy, specifically by Ali Khamenei, to run for the job of president.[71]

Eventually, Khomeini's democratic promises transubstantiated into the clerical despotism of *Velayat-e Fagih*. There was in the style and substance of his Paris pronouncements an air of "Chauncey Gardner"—simple-minded innocence masquerading as profound saintly wisdom. But beneath this appealing, albeit disingenuous façade, there lurked the steely determination of a despot keen on riding a democratic wave to the deeply undemocratic shores of *Velayat-e Fagih*. The Chauncey Gardner turned into a modern day Savonarola, railing against the corruptions of modernity and democracy. How?

THE FAILURE OF THE DEMOCRATIC TRANSITION IN IRAN
AND THE ROLE OF FOREIGN FORCES

By the time of the 1979 failed transition to democracy, no country was deemed as powerful in Iran as the United States—blamed by the royalists for the revolution and for betraying the shah, and considered a foe by the new regime, accused of conspiring to bring back the monarchy, or fomenting a civil war in Iran. As a US Embassy Memorandum, written on the eve of the revolution made clear, "the 'secret hand' theory which is deep in the Iranian grain . . . blames the US (among others) for Iran's many problems."[72] The controversial George Ball report, prepared in December 1978, captures these dynamics. "All parties are looking to the United States for signals,"[73] he writes. "We made the Shah what he has become. We nurtured his love for grandiose geopolitical schemes and supplied him the hardware to indulge his fantasies." Ball goes on to say, "Now that his regime is coming apart under the pressures of imported modernization," the United States should pressure the shah to give up much of his power and "bring about a responsible government that not only meets the needs of the Iranian people but the requirement of our own policy."[74] In reality, American efforts to create a more "responsible" government go back to the Kennedy and Eisenhower administrations and the roles they played in the evolution of democratic forces.

Ever since 1958, when the State Department talked of middle-class and moderate opposition to the shah, they meant more than any group the National Front, created by Mossadeq in 1949 and brutally suppressed after the August 1953 coup. Though the United States was involved in the overthrow of the Mossadeq government—for many the "original sin" of US policy in Iran—from the late fifties US policy changed, and it began to see Mossadeq's followers as the harbingers of democracy and political reform in Iran. From 1959 the shah was under pressure from the United States to reconcile with this group. In 1978, on the eve of the failed transition to democracy, these pressures reached fever pitch. The National Front leaders tragically failed to capitalize on these pressures; Khomeini, on the other hand, cleverly if not deceptively used them to his own benefit. The fact that his appointed prime minister for the provisional revolutionary government in 1979 and nearly every one of the ministers in that cabinet were from the ranks of the religious elements of the National Front, the fact that in contact with American officials—much of which he himself initiated—he and his aides presented a democratic façade, and finally the fact that the US Embassy in Tehran had since 1965 been barred from contacting opposition figures and was in 1978 dangerously misinformed about the Shiite clergy all combined to help Khomeini in his subtle game plan and also underscored his ability for tactical compromise.

Though in the early 1960s, Bazorgan and other members of the new government had split from the National Front and created their own party—the Freedom Movement—they nevertheless remained de facto members of the National Front. Moreover, throughout their tumultuous brief tenure in power, they remained dedicated to the pursuit of democratic values. But no sooner were they in power than they encountered Khomeini's constant meddling into the details of running the new state.

The secular National Front leadership decided in 1978 against either making a coalition with the shah or forming a government of its own. It deferred to Khomeini. Though they were ostensibly representatives of Iran's moderate middle class, the leaders of the National Front preferred the puritan politics of uncompromising opposition to the shah over the pragmatic realism of unity with a weakened shah as a possible first step toward establishing democracy in Iran. In the famous words of Khalil Maleki, himself a supporter of Dr. Mossadeq and a onetime leader of the National Front, "these [National Front] leaders are not even demagogues; they are merely followers of the demos."[75] The National Front leadership not only refused to form a national unity government itself but tried to block and succeeded in helping defeat efforts by two of its leaders—Gholam-Hossein Sadighi and Shapour Bakhtiyar—who tried to form just such a coalition government. In 1978 Karim Sanjabi, the presumptive leader of the National Front, decided to defer leadership of the movement to Khomeini. When he traveled to Paris, on his way to a convention of Social Democratic parties of the world, he met with Khomeini and abdicated all pretense of leading an independent secular movement. In a communiqué he issued after his meeting with Khomeini (a statement Khomeini refused to sign lest the presumptive leader of secular forces developed delusions that he was on par with the ayatollah), Sanjabi accepted not only Khomeini's leadership but also the increasing role of Islam in shaping the ideology of the movement. No wonder then that, upon his return to Tehran, Sanjabi told the shah "that no solution would work without a green light from Khomeini," and he would accept nothing short of the shah's abdication.[76] The "moral midgetry" of his argument became even more evident when in the same meeting he told the shah that he should keep a military government in power a few more months and in the process reduce Khomeini's influence. And then Sanjabi suggested he will be able to act on his own and form a government of national reconciliation.

The failure of a secular democratic coalition was not entirely the fault of the National Front and its zeal for puritan politics. The shah, too, was adamantly against reconciliation with a force he had long deemed his intractable foes. Ever since American pressures for such an alliance with the National Front began, the shah, more than once, told the American officials that a National Front government "would be a precursor of communist takeover." The leaders of the National Front, the shah went on to say, have "no purpose except to come to power." Moreover, their organization has been "badly infiltrated by communists."[77] When American officials raised the issue of the National Front's membership in a new coalition government, the shah stated, "Flatly . . . he could not live with a National Front Government whose first act would be to abolish SAVAK."[78] Even in 1978, faced with the end of his dynasty, he was less than enthusiastic about forming such a coalition. In June 1978, in a private meeting with British officials, in describing his decision to liberalize, he went on a "vitriolic denunciation of the old National Front" and made it clear that it was beyond "the lines of political acceptability."[79] Later on when he had no choice but to seek—indeed beseech from a much weakened position—a coalition with the same leaders, he refused to abide by Sadiqi's request that he stay in Iran but out of politics. He also declined the request by a key member of the Bakhtiyar cabinet to turn over the operational command of the armed forces. He in fact "stubbornly insisted not only on retaining his role . . . of commander-in-chief . . . but also on controlling the military budget."[80] The shah thus rebuffed General Jam, the charismatic officer who could have potentially held the military together and under the command of a Bakhtiyar government. He left Iran in disgust. It took the military 36 days before it turned against Bakhtiyar and tried to make its peace with the mullahs who seemed poised to take over the reins of power.

Other than Britain and the United States, the Soviet Union, too, was imagined by both the shah and the secular opposition to play a key role in determining developments in Iran. In the months leading to the 1979 failed transition to democracy, the shah's Cold War fears of Soviet machinations were augmented by a series of events that convinced him that the Soviet Union, too, was out to overthrow him. In 1977 the Iranian secret police (SAVAK) arrested the KGB's top spy in Iran. He was a two-star general of the Iranian military and had been, for almost three decades, a paid agent of the KGB.[81] For much of his political life, the shah had an exaggerated view of the KGB's power in Iran.[82] As it happened, the general was in fact one of only two paid agents of the KGB.[83] In 1975, even rumors of his philandering were, according to the shah, a "KGB operation." For its part, the KGB worked hard to fan the flames of these fears. They circulated the rumor that it had even "influenced the Shah's choice of his third wife."[84] Exaggerated as these claims were, in 1978 Soviet moves left little room about its intentions.

On November 19, 1978, Brezhnev threatened an invasion of Iran, if "anti-Soviet" elements were to gain the upper hand in the country. The statement was, in short order, followed by a confidential letter to President Carter "suggesting that because the Soviets have a long border with Iran, they should enjoy a special position of influence."[85] Ever since 1917, Soviet leaders had tried to turn Iran into another Finland, where "anti-Soviet activities" could trigger a Russian invasion. They used Article 5 or 6 of the Soviet's 1921 agreement with Iran—or, more accurately, their self-serving interpretation of these articles—as a legal basis for their attempted "Finlandization." Iran had initially agreed to the article only in the context of the tumultuous situation in the years after the 1917 revolution. The article in fact allowed Soviet intervention only if White Russian forces used Iran as a base of attack against the newly established Bolshevik government. But in subsequent years the Soviets had their own, "expanded" interpretation of the article and used it many times to threaten an attack on Iran. The 1978 Brezhnev letter was only the latest iteration of this attempt.

Moreover, leaders of the Soviet-backed Tudeh Party, who had been living in Eastern Europe or the Soviet Union for three decades, and from 1965 had been angling to return to Iran as a "constitutional" opposition party, were rapidly returning to Iran in 1978, but this time with a platform that called for the overthrow of the monarchy. They began to quickly revive the old party apparatus. From their first moment of arrival, the party leaders supported Khomeini and the most anti-democratic, anti-American wings within the clergy. Tudeh Party members infiltrated the new Islamic bureaucracy, including the newly formed Revolutionary Committees that took over the security of neighborhoods and workplaces.[86] The party further tried to endear itself to the clergy by passing on "intelligence" on opposition activities. At one time, the commander of the Iranian navy was a party "sympathizer." As Rafsanjani makes clear in his daily journals, top party leaders (including Noural-Din Kianouri, first secretary of the party central committee) met with him intermittently and passed on information that was sometimes new and important—such as the time the party informed the clergy of a pending coup originating in one of Iran's air force bases—and sometimes only an excuse to keep their contacts with high-ranking officials of the regime.[87] The party used its extensive propaganda apparatus to promote anti-American and antidemocratic slogans.

The party leaders' ardor for Khomeini was more than mere tactical unity in face of a common enemy. There were profound structural undemocratic affinities between their ideology and Khomeini's brand of Shiism; both had a messianic sense of history, both claimed a monopoly of truths, both desired to remake society in the image of some utopian perfection, and both used anti-Americanism as a pillar of their ideology. In their theoretical scheme, Khomeini was Iran's Kerensky and they wanted to do in Iran what the Bolsheviks did in the Russian Revolution of 1917. But Khomeini out-Lenined the Leninists; he used them to destroy the democratic opposition and then brutally suppressed them.

Aside from these returning old Tudeh Party cadres, Jimmy Carter's promotion of human rights convinced the shah to release nearly all of the almost 4,000 political prisoners in Iran. Nearly every one of these newly released prisoners had long experience in underground organizational techniques. Dozens had been trained by radical Palestinian groups and knew the methods of terrorism—romanticized in those days of Franz Fanon and his apotheosis of violence, as the art of urban guerrilla warfare. Their release strengthened the opposition, weakened the resolve of the regime and SAVAK, but also weakened the prospects of democracy in Iran. Most of these recently released prisoners were schooled in Stalinist models of Marxism and dismissed liberal democracy as a "frivolous" and "fraudulent" bourgeois gimmick. Even forces loyal to the Mojahedeen-e Khalg-e Iran (MEK), though ostensibly following an Islamic ideology, were in fact supporting an eclectic mix of Leninism and their own version of Islamic "liberation theology."[88] Before long, in the Iranian political discourse even the word "liberal" became synonymous with decadence and servile disposition to "colonialism." The dominant discourse was one of radical revolution and the purgative power of violence and not democracy and the rule law. When the regime's "revolutionary Courts" began to execute members of the ancien regime after summary trials, when grotesque pictures of their bullet-ridden bodies were published all over the front papers of the country's daily papers, it was these radical groups, many enjoying the political capital of having been in the forefront of the fight against the old regime, who not only applauded this violence but demanded even more. Their "revolutionary" blood lust ended only when the same courts began to execute hundreds from their ranks. Nothing united these disparate forces as their opposition to "imperialism," particularly that of the United States.

Another factor facilitating Khomeini's façade and his assumption of the movement's leadership was the Confederation of Iranian Students. From the late fifties, thousands of Iranian students had begun to converge on European and American universities. Till then, educational sojourns to the West had been a privilege limited to the children of the elite. Indispensable to the shah's modernization plans was a large, trained technocratic class. But Iran lacked the educational infrastructure to train such a class. Sociologists have called the late fifties the age of the technocrats. American policy in Iran also advocated that new young technocrats must gradually take the place of traditional politicians. From the late fifties, cheap bus and train service from Iran to Europe became available then, and before long students from all social classes began to arrive in the West. The more radical elements used their newfound freedom in Western democracies to create the Confederation of Iranian Students[89]—an international organization that became a formidable foe of the shah throughout the rest of his tenure.

Throughout the seventies, the confederation became a powerful source of propaganda against the shah, and in favor of Khomeini as an embodiment of the overdetermined "anti-imperialist" struggle. Dominated by the Left and structured along the lines of a "United Front" suggested by Stalin in the thirties—communists leading the largest number of democratic forces in a common battle—the Confederation of Iranian Students was instrumental in turning the students' democratic aspirations into a force for radicalism and critical of "bourgeois democracy." As the shah's regime showed signs of collapse, leaders of the confederation returned to Iran, joining forces advocating not a democratic transition but a radical revolution. No sooner did they began to oppose the rising clerical despotism—some foolishly taking arms against the regime in quixotic uprisings—than more than 200 of them were executed by the regime's firing squads.[90] The student movements' leftist tendencies and Khomeini's abilities to pitch his ideas in a language that made it part of the "anti-imperialist discourse" made it easier for this strange alliance of modernizing students and a demodernizing cleric. An unfortunate romance developed—and even continues to exist till today—between leftist Western intellectuals and the clerical regime that came to power in Iran. Some of the most renowned Western intellectuals also fell prey to this strange romance. The regime's egregious breaches of democratic rights of the Iranian people were often overlooked by these Western leftists because of what they alleged was the regime's "struggle against imperialism." Michel Foucault's brief infatuation with Khomeini as the embodiment of a radically new "critique of modernity" is arguably the most risible and tragic example of this romantic folly.[91]

About six months after Khomeini's return home, the American Embassy in Tehran reported that he and a handful of clerics in Qom were "now making decisions on about all matters of importance including public security, the press, commerce and the military."[92] In Iran, realizing the fractured feuding, and the relative weakness of the democratic forces, and using not only a militant anti-Americanism as a motto to neutralize or co-opt many among the radical forces of the Iranian Left—foremost among them the Soviet-backed Tudeh Party and the Maoist Ranjbaran Party—but also the chaos and crisis caused by Saddam Hussein's decision to attack Iran and by the occupation of the American Embassy by his ardent student supporters, Khomeini pressed a pliant Constituent Assembly to pass not the promised democratic constitution but a new one founded on his ideas about *Velayat-e Faqih*, a constitution where he was granted more despotic powers than arguably any despot in any constitutional government, and certainly more than the shah he had just replaced. As many recent memoirs, reports, and interviews by Iranian politicians of the time have revealed, it was Khomeini more than anyone else who prolonged the occupation of the American Embassy. According to Mousavi, for example, who in those days was an ardent supporter of Khomeini and today is a leader of the Green Movement, it was Khomeini "who changed what was initially supposed by the students occupying the embassy to be a three- or four-day event into what he himself called a new 'second revolution.'"[93] The occupation of the embassy, along with the eight-year-long war with Iraq—which again Khomeini was instrumental in prolonging—allowed him to force through the constituent assembly a new constitution that placed disproportionate despotic powers in his hands. It was, in the words of one scholar, "the constitution of the hierocratically oriented Islamist camp, the product of a social stratum which, in the decades of modernization had been forced to relinquish more and more of its positions of power and were, after the revolution able to expand a scarcely hoped for historical chance not only to retrieve lost ground but to realize [new powers] not ever dared to speak of openly in bygone centuries."[94]

Iran's democratic dream was once again delayed. Revolutionary terror tried to deracinate the democratic flowering that had come about with the revolution. In the months after the shah's fall, there was no censorship in the country. Hundreds of papers and magazines, each presenting a different perspective, were published. *Ayandegan*, created in the mid-sixties with help from Iranian government (SAVAK, in fact) and American companies and intended to offer a new language of politics, was taken over by its editorial board and soon became the most read and relentless voice of democracy in the country. Books banned for the past 30 years suddenly flooded in what came to be known as "The White Cover" series—for their use of simple white covers, free of any fancy designs. The series was heavy on translations of second-rate Soviet tracts and pamphlets written by radical underground groups, and light on democratic tracts. In cities and villages, no less than in governmental or private offices, committees elected by people took over the daily management of the machinery of power and management. Political parties were free to operate. A "hundred flowers" were abloom, and it was precisely their power and promise that frightened Khomeini.

Gradually and sometimes violently Khomeini dismantled the democratic machinery, replacing it instead with a complicated despotic clerical structure. When in March 1979 women tried to organize a demonstration to protest what turned out to be the regime's first step in forcing Islamic attire on women—requiring them to wear the Islamic *hijab* if they wanted to enter government offices— Khomeini ordered the demonstration suppressed, calling those opposed to the new regulars "harlots." A few weeks later, in August 1979 when the newly formed New Democratic Front, composed of left of center Iranian democrats, tried to organize a demonstration to oppose the closure of *Ayandegan*, the peaceful gathering was viciously attacked by a new force of chain-wielding thugs that had taken on the name of Hizbollah—the party of god. In Iranian nomenclature, it was a new name, and in 1979 carried something of a negative aura—gangs-cum-militia composed of urban poor, plus elements of the lumpen-proletariat, keen on proving their piety, and invariably led by clerics. This was the birth of what became a nemesis of democracy in Iran and is called the Basij. The spontaneous neighborhood committees, as well as the elected management committees in institutions that had emerged on the eve of the revolution, were either dismantled or replaced by committees dominated by clerics appointed by Khomeini, invariably housed in mosques. Before long, these new committees were placed in charge of surveillance and suppression.

In the country, as in each institution, a dual power structure emerged. There was a provincial government and its appointed ministers and managers who invariably defended democratic values, but real power was in the hands of anointed "Imam's Representatives" (*Namayandeye Imam*). The government of Bazorgan had a fate not unlike Kerensky in Russia and the Weimar Republic of Germany. It was attacked from the right by Khomeini and other clerics who wanted to seize power and from the left by virtually every organization who disparagingly accused it of "liberalism." Revolutionary Courts, with their leaders appointed directly by Khomeini, began to rapidly execute members of the *ancien régime*. Sadeq Khalkhali, a student of Khomeini who later declared more than once that he never killed anyone without Khomeini's approval, came to be known as "the hanging judge." His trials of high-ranking officials of the regime often lasted no more than a few moments. The same Khomeini who a few months earlier had promised the rule of law in a democratic Iran now, when faced with criticism of the kangaroo courts and summary trials and speedy executions, declared in brazen disregard for both, "All one needs do with criminals is to establish their identity, and once this has been established, they should be killed right away."[95] The trial and execution of Amir-Abbas Hoveyda, the shah's prime minister for 13 years, became a test of wills between the government and its hope of establishing the rule of law and Khomeini's revolutionary committees that had started a blood bath. Ultimately, as the government prepared the ground for a public trial, Khomeini ordered Khalkhali to convene a speedy trial and moments after the death verdict was rendered, Hoveyda was executed—not by a firing squad but by a cleric whose father had died in prison in the sixties.[96]

The power and authority of these courts and committees was increasingly ensured by the growing military might of the newly created Islamic Revolutionary Guard Corp (IRGC). Instead of dismantling the predominantly royalist army—and creating 500,000 armed and trained potential foes of the regime—Khomeini kept the military intact but simply retired, exiled, or executed nearly the entire class of generals. Younger more zealous officers were placed in command positions. At the same time, more and more money and power were placed in the IRGC. Before long, poets and political activists were writing eulogies to the failed experiment in democracy in Iran.

Events in Iran since June 12, 2009, and the stolen presidential election manifest the perseverance of Iran's democratic movement. The same coalition of forces that overthrew the shah in 1979 is now trying to establish democracy in Iran. Mir-Hossein Mousavi, onetime prime minister of the Islamic regime, is today the nominal leader of the Green Movement that has emerged since June. In his recent pronouncements, he has rightly declared that developments in Iran since June are the continuation of the effort that began during the Constitutional Revolution of 1905. Everything from the language and logic of democracy to institutions of civil society are today far more developed than they were in 1905, or 1979. Khamenei today is not only repeating some of the shah's errors of three decades ago but refusing to draw the right conclusions from the outcome of the revolution. Like the shah, he too believes that the roots of the democratic movement are not in Iran but in some "American-Zionist" conspiracy. The abducted revolution of 1979 has only delayed but not destroyed the quest for democracy. Khamenei has wrongly concluded that what ended the shah's reign was his willingness to make compromises with the opposition. More than once, he has declared that he will not repeat the errors of the shah and will not cave to the opposition's demands. The real lesson of the 1979 revolution in fact is that had the shah accepted some of the opposition's demands in 1975, when he was still very strong, and if he had allowed the development of moderate democratic forces during the sixties and seventies, the revolution could well have been avoided. Iranian democrats insist they want no revolution, but Khamenei's intransigence can only beget more radicalism. International forces, acting with prudence and patience can be a crucial ally of Iranian democrats in what has so far seemed like a Sisyphean struggle.

NOTES

1. Public Record Office (hereafter PRO), "Iranian Internal Situation, 12 October 1978," PREM 16/1719.

2. PRO, "Iranian Internal Situation, 16 September 1978," PREM 16/1719.

3. CIA, Mohammad Reza Pahlavi, Shah of Iran, October 23, 1978. I obtained a copy through a Freedom of Information Act request.

4. Ibid.

5. For a brilliant analysis of the inherent incongruence between monarchy and modernity, see Ernst H. Kantrowicz, *The King's Two Bodies: A Study in Mediaeval Political Theology* (Princeton, N.J.: Princeton University Press, 1957).

6. Mohammed Reza Pahlavi, *Mission For My Country* (London: Hutchison Publishers, 1962). More than once, he claims divine protection and revelation. In later years, he repeated these claims, suggesting that many of his decisions are made after divine inspiration.

7. For a discussion of some of the theories developed in Europe in legitimizing monarchy, see Kantrowicz, *The King's Two Bodies.*

8. PRO, "Iranian Internal Situation, 12 December 1978," PREM/16/1719.

9. US Department of State, "Statement of US Policy toward Iran," *Foreign Relations of the United States, 1958–1960* (Washington, D.C.: US Government Printing Office, 1993), 613.

10. Ibid., 606.

11. Ibid., 613.

12. National Security Agency, (hereafter NSA), no. 369, "Political Internal Issues."

13. CIA, "Stability of the Present Regime in Iran: Secret Special National Intelligence Estimate," August 25, 1958, NSA, no. 362. Much the same sentiment is reflected in another National Intelligence Estimate; see "The Outlook for Iran: Secret National Intelligence Estimate NIE 36–40," NSA, no. 385.

14. For the story of the Qarnai Affair from the perspective of his life, see Abbas Milani, *Eminent Persians: Men and Women Who Made Modern Iran, 1941–1979* (Syracuse, N.Y.: Syracuse University Press, 2008), 1:445–51.

15. See the chapter on Qarani in ibid. I have also interviewed General Alavi-Kia, the deputy director of SAVAK at the time, and been involved in the investigation of the case. Interview, San Diego, September 3, 2006.

16. There are several scholarly reports about the land reform and they are more or less in consensus that Arsanjani had a radicalizing effect. See, for example, Afsaneh Najmabadi, *Land Reform and Social Change in Iran* (Salt Lake City: University of Utah Press, 1987), 83.

17. For a detailed account of the landed gentry's attempt to fight the land reform, and its de facto alliance with the clergy, see Mohammad Gholi Majd, *Resistance to the Shah: Landowner and Ulama in Iran* (Gainesville: University of Florida, 2000). For the role of the clergy, see *Baresi va Tahli Nehzat-e Imam Khomeini* [Analysis of the Khomeini Movement] (Tehran: n.p., n.d.). The book has as its author S.H.R., reported to be a chief of staff to Khomeini during his years of exile. Whereas the latter book borders on the hagiography, the former is sometimes overly personalized in its attack on the Pahlavi regime.

18. Abolhassan Ebtehaj, *The Memoirs of Abolhassan Ebtehaj* (London: Paka Print, 1991), 853–57.

19. A copy of his speech was given to me, courtesy of Senator Lajevardi.

20. For a discussion of these families and their politics, see A. Milani, *Eminent Persians.*

21. James Davies, "The J-Curve of Rising and Declining Expectations as a Case of Some Great Revolutions and a Contained Rebellion," in Hugh Davis Graham and Ted Robert Gurr, eds., *Violence in America* (New York: Praeger, 1969), 690–730. For a brief discussion of the Curve in relations to Iran's revolution, see, for example, Mohsen Milani, *Iran's Islamic Revolution: From Monarchy to Islamic Republic* (Boulder, Colo.: Westview, 1988), 16.

22. This was the most important result of the shah's visit to the White House in 1962. For details of their last joint press conference, see JFK, NSC, box 116, "Robert Komer to Bundy, April 23, 1962."

23. NSA, no. 9799, US Embassy, Tehran, "End of Tour Report, August 4, 1975."

24. For a detailed account of the US Embassy's and CIA's role in these developments, see Abbas Milani, *Persian Sphinx: Amir Abbas Hoveyda and the Riddle of the Iranian Revolution* (Washington, D.C.: Mage, 1999), particularly the chapters on "Progressive Circle," and the "White Revolution," 135–71.

25. Alam recounts other episodes in the fifth volume of his memoir. I have discussed the letters and the response, and how the government's decision to ignore them strengthened

Khomeini. See Abbas Milani, "Alam and the Roots of the Iranian Revolution," in *King of Shadows* (Los Angeles: Ketab Corp, 2005), 46–79.

26. NSA, no. 2048, "Religious Leaders Fear Departure of the Shah," January 1, 1969.

27. The figure is provided by the Ogaf (religious endowment) office. See "Amaken Moghadass" [Sacred Institutions]. A copy of the report was provided to me courtesy of an employee of the organization.

28. For an account of this center's management, see Ali Rahnama, *Islamic Utopian: A Political Biography of Ali Shariati* (London: I. B. Tauris, 2000).

29. For an account of their lives, See *New Republic*, March 11, 2010, 12–15.

30. Manuchehr Shahgoli, a close ally of Hoveyda went to the American Embassy at the time and told diplomats that the shah dismantled the party and opted for the one-party system because he "realized how strong the party itself was getting. . . . the Shah decided it was time to crush yet another organization." NSA, no. 2177, "US Embassy, Tehran, Iran, Hoveyda Loyalist Lets off Steam, 25 January 1977."

31. Mehdi Samii has kindly provided me with his notes, taken at the time of his meetings with the shah. They are a remarkable document in the honesty of their discussion.

32. See the chapter on Mesbah-Zadeh in A. Milani, *Eminent Persians*, 1:399–406.

33. For a tragic-comical narrative of these lapsed Stalinists fighting on behalf of their patrons—Hoveyda and Alam—in developing party structure and ideology, see Hamid Shokat's interview with Kourosh Lashai, in his series on the oral history of the Iranian New Left. See also Hamid Shokat, *Goftegou Ba Kourosh Lashai* (Tehran: Akhtaran, 2002).

34. I have written at some length about the origins of the one-party idea in *Persian Sphinx*, 275–87.

35. For a detailed account of these behind-the-scene activities, see Andrew Scott Cooper, "Showdown in Doha: The Secret Deal That Helped Sink the Shah of Iran," *Middle East Journal* 62, no. 4 (Autumn 2008): 567–90.

36. NSA, "A Brief Overview of the US-Iran Relations," 27. The report was prepared in the early eighties; it has no author, or other indications about who commissioned it.

37. Mohammad Reza Pahlavi, *Answer to History* (New York: Stein and Day, 1980), 93–97.

38. Ibid., 146.

39. Mohammad Ali Movvahed, interview, London, September 17, 2009. He was one of the top negotiators for Iran. He has written a two-volume authoritative history of the oil movement, from the time of Mossadeq till the fall of the shah.

40. PRO, "Embassy in Tehran to Foreign Office, 8 September 1978," FCO 8/3184.

41. PRO, "Embassy in Tehran to Foreign Office, November 9, 1978," FCO 8/3184.

42. PRO, "Embassy in Tehran to Foreign Office, January 20, 1979," PREM 16/2131.

43. Pahlavi, *Answer to History*, 116.

44. Parviz Sabeti, interview, September 3, 2005.

45. William Shawcross, *The Shah's Last Ride* (London: Pan Books, 1989), 99.

46. The first attempt to study conspiracy theories from a scholarly perspective was undertaken by Hamid Ashraf, "The Appeal of Conspiracy Theories to Persians," *Princeton Papers* 5 (Winter 1997): 57–88.

47. Richard Hofstadter, "The Paranoid Style in American Politics," *Harper's*, November 1964, 77–86. The seminal essay was later republished as a part of a book, in *The Paranoid Style in American Politics and Other Essays* (Cambridge, Mass.: Harvard University Press, 1996), 1.

48. For conspiracy theories as a form of political participation, see Jon W. Anderson, "Conspiracy Theories, Premature Entextualization, and Popular Political Analysis," *Arab*

Studies Journal 4, no. 1 (Spring 1996): 96–102. For a brilliant depiction of what engagement in conspiracy theorizing, particularly about the British, does to the fabric of life and political thought in an average middle-class family in Iran, read the now classic novel *My Uncle Napoleon*, written by Iraj Pezeshkzad, and translated into English by Dick Davis (Washington, D.C.: Mage, 1996). The book was also made into one of Iran's most acclaimed television series. There is now a small library of books and articles written about whom and why the novel was written—many seeing a British hand in its publication!

49. For a thorough discussion of conspiracy theories in Iran, read Houchang E. Chehabi, "The Paranoid Style in Iranian Historiography," in Touraj Atabki, ed., *Iran in the 20th Century: Historiography and Political Culture* (London: I. B. Tauris, 2009), 155–205; for a psychological approach to this proclivity, see Marvin Zonis and Joseph Craig, "Conspiracy Thinking in the Middle East," *Political Psychology* 15, no. 3 (1994): 443–59.

50. For a description of the nativist tendency in Iran as well as the Othering process, see Mehrzad Boroujerdi, *Iranian Intellectuals and the West* (Syracuse, N.Y.: Syracuse University Press, 1996), 1–76.

51. I interviewed some of the generals who told me about their plans. The shah demurred. General Azar-Barzin, interview, Los Angeles, September 2006.

52. www.bbc.co.uk/Worldservice/History/Story/2007/02/070123_1930s.shtml.

53. PRO, "British Embassy to Foreign Office, September 29, 1978," PREM 16/1716.

54. Karl Popper, *The Poverty of Historicism* (London: Routledge, 2002).

55. Before Popper, theories were deemed scientific simply if they were verifiable. Popper added the added qualification that they must also be falsifiable, or allow for new data to disprove the theory. See Karl Popper, *Conjectures and Refutations* (London: Routledge, 2002).

56. Documents of SAVAK, published after the revolution, reveal the extent of this monitoring over the lives of artists, activists, and even moderate politicians like Amini. Their every move was monitored by SAVAK.

57. Mehdi Samii, a prominent technocrat, describes an angry shah telling him and a few others gathered in a meeting, "After all we have given them, why are they still opposing us." Samii dared to declare that the problem is that they consider what the shah thinks he has given them their inherent rights. Mehdi Samii, interview, September 3, 2008.

58. PRO, "British Embassy to Foreign Office, 25 September 1978," PREM 16/1719.

59. NSA, Bureau of Intelligence and Research, Department of State, "Studies in Political Dynamics in Iran," Secret Intelligence Report, no. 13, 603.

60. PRO, "30 October 1978, Prime Minister's office to Foreign Ministry," PREM 16/1719.

61. Charles Kurzman, *The Unthinkable Revolution in Iran* (Cambridge, Mass.: Harvard University Press, 2004).

62. Two different studies, one by Mohammad Mokhtari, and the second by Mehdi Bazorgan, the first a poet and the second the first prime minister of the IRGC, come up with slightly different percentages about the content of the slogans. For a discussion of the two studies, see Mohsen Milani, *The Making of the Islamic Revolution*, 2nd ed. (Boulder, Colo.: Westview, 1999), 136.

63. For a collection of Khomeini's books, see *Islam and Revolution: Writings and Declarations of Imam Khomeini*, trans. Hamid Algar (Berkeley: Mizan Press, 1981). For a brief biographical sketch of his life and intellectual development, see the chapter on Khomeini in A. Milani, *Eminent Persians*.

64. For a brilliant exposition of this history, see Ayatollah Mehdi Haeri Yazdi, *Hekmat va Hokumat* (London: Shadi, 1995).

65. For a discussion of Shiite Hadith literature, see Abbas Milani, "Kafi Is Kafi," in *Lost Wisdom: Rethinking Persian Modernity* (Washington, D.C.: Mage, 1997), 13–27.

66. For a discussion of every regime's need of a language of legitimation, see Jean François Lyotard, "Notes on Legitimation," *Oxford Literary Review* 9, nos. 1–2 (1987): 106–18.

67. For a discussion of similarities between Plato and *Velayat-e Fagih*, see Vanessa Martin, *Creating an Islamic State: Khomeini and the Making of a New Iran* (London: I. B. Tauris, 2000).

68. Arash Naraghi presented a paper on this subject at the Hoover Institution's Iran in the Transition lecture series organized by Mike McFaul, Larry Diamond, and myself. Earlier, inside Iran, Hajjarian had written an article on the implications of the concept of *Maslahat* for governance in Iran.

69. All quotes from Jalal Matini, "The Most Truthful Individual in Recent History," *Iranshenasi* 14, no. 4 (Winter 2003): 1–8.

70. Today, Bani-Sadr lives in exile after being impeached as the first president; Gotb-Zadeh was executed on the charge of conspiring to launch a coup; and Yazdi, the leader of the Freedom Movement is in jail, following the postelection demonstrations.

71. Rafsanjani's daily journal (*Khaterat*) for the year 1982, as plans for impeaching Bani-Sadr are being made behind the scenes; there is also an attempt to convince Khomeini to change his mind and allow Khamenei to run. Rafsanjani, *Khaterat*, no. 1360 (1981–82): 240–82. The book is available online in Rafsanjani's website.

72. US Embassy in Tehran, "Alternative Views from the Province," in *Asnad-e Laneye Jasusi* [Documents from the Den of Spies], vol. 16 (Tehran: n.p., n.d.).

73. George Ball, "Issues and Implication of the Iranian Crisis, December 1978," 16, George Ball Papers, Princeton University Library, Seeley G. Mudd Manuscript Library, box 30, doc. no. MC031.

74. Ibid., 2.

75. Khalil Malwki, *Do Nameh* [Two Letters] (Tehran: Roshan, 1357/1958). Both letters are addressed to Dr. Mossadeq and in them Maleki describes the situation and offers biting criticism of the National Front leadership.

76. PRO, "Tehran to Foreign Office, 19 December 1978," PREM 16/1720.

77. John F. Kennedy Presidential Library, "Tehran to State Department, May 13, 1961."

78. Ibid.

79. PRO, "Tehran to Foreign Office, 6 July 1978," FCO 8/3184.

80. Ball, "Issues and Implications," 3.

81. For an account of his arrest and life, see A. Milani, *Eminent Persians*, 1:462–68.

82. For an account of the KGB in Iran, see Christopher Andrew and Vasili Mitrokin, *The World Was Going Our Way: The KGB and the Battle for the Third World* (New York: Basic Books, 2005), 165–76.

83. For an account of the KGB in Iran, see Vladimir Kuzichkin, *Inside the KGB: My Life in Soviet Espionage*, trans. Thomas B. Beattie (New York: Pantheon, 1990), 115–41.

84. Andrew and Mitrokin, *The World Was Going Our Way*, 175.

85. Ball, "Issues and Implications."

86. For an account of how the Tudeh vision gradually dominated much of the Left, see Maziar Behrooz, *Rebels with a Cause: The Failure of the Left in Iran* (London: I. B. Tauris, 2000). Many memoirs of members of the Tudeh Party and of the Fedaeeyane Khalg, a leftist guerrilla group that gradually gave up its radical ways and adopted the ideology of the

Tudeh, have since been published. For example, see Mehdi Aslani, *The Crow and the Red Rose: Memoirs of Prison* (Koln: Arash Publishers, 2009), 3–60.

87. Rafsanjani's daily journals include numerous reports about such meetings. For example, *Khaterat*, no. 130 (1981–82): 276.

88. For a more or less impartial description of the group, see Ervand Abrhamian, *The Iranian Mojahedin* (New Haven: Yale University Press, 2009). The famous Murphy Report prepared for the State Department describing the group as a terrorist organization is a critical account of its work. The group has taken the State Department to federal court four times to have its name removed from the list, all to no avail.

89. There are now two histories of the confederation, one in Persian and in two volumes, and the second a shorter, one-volume account in English. See Hamid Shokat, *Confederation Daneshjuyan Iran* [Iranian Confederation of Students] (Los Angeles: Ketab, 2000).

90. A couple of books have chronicled these efforts. The quixotic fervor of the movement, its use of "revolutionary violence" and its tragic results can be seen particularly in *Parandeye No-Parvaz* [The New Flying Bird] (Koln: Sarbedaran, 1383/2004).

91. For a detailed account of this romance, see Janet Afary and Kevin Anderson, *Foucault and the Iranian Revolution: Gender and the Seductions of Islamism* (Chicago: University of Chicago Press, 2005).

92. US Embassy, Tehran, "Moves toward Government Unification, 8/3/79," in *Asnad-e Laneye Jasusi* [Documents from the Den of Spies].

93. See Mousavi's fourteenth statement, available in most Web sites. See www.rahesabz .net/story.3332.

94. Asghar Schirazi, *The Constitution of Iran: Politics and State in the Islamic Republic of Iran*, trans. Jon O'Kane (London: I. B. Tauris, 1997), 293.

95. NSA, no. 244, "Current Foreign Relations," April 11, 1979.

96. In A. Milani, *Persian Sphinx*, I have described this process in detail.

CHAPTER FIFTEEN

China

The Doomed Transitional Moment of 1989

MINXIN PEI

The bloody suppression of the pro-democracy movement in Beijing on June 4, 1989, marked a turning point in contemporary Chinese political history.[1] This historic—and tragic—event brought China closest to the only possible democratic breakthrough since the founding of the People's Republic. Before the violent crackdown, during which at least several hundred students and ordinary citizens were killed and even more protestors were wounded, peaceful pro-democracy demonstrations, organized mostly by college students, swept Beijing and nearly all the major Chinese cities. At the height of the protest movement, several million individuals participated in pro-democracy demonstrations in 132 major cities, including 27 provincial capitals (only 3 provincial capitals did not report demonstrations).[2] The spontaneous pro-democracy movement began on April 15, 1989, when college students in Beijing went to Tiananmen Square to honor the death of Hu Yaobang, a liberal former general secretary of the Chinese Communist Party (CCP) who was dismissed in January 1987 for refusing to suppress student-led pro-democracy demonstrations at that time. With the top leadership paralyzed by the division between hard-liners (led by Deng Xiaoping and Li Peng, the premier) and soft-liners (headed by Zhao Ziyang, the general secretary of the CCP), the Chinese government failed to take forceful measures to put an end to the student-led movement in April.[3] Enraged by an official statement (in the form of an editorial in the *People's Daily*) published on April 26 that labeled the student-led movement as "perpetrators of chaos," thousands of college students began to go on a hunger strike in Tiananmen Square, as a means to pressure the Li Peng–led government to enter into negotiations regarding several key demands raised by the students.[4]

However, the Li government refused to respond, even as thousands of students were fainting from hunger and exhaustion in the square. The stalemate—and the escalation of political tension—rallied the public in Beijing to the cause of the students. As a result, other social groups, workers, journalists, teachers, government officials, and ordinary citizens spontaneously organized relief missions to care for the students and also called for the government to concede to the students' demands.

By pure coincidence, Mikhail Gorbachev, then the Soviet leader, arrived in Beijing on May 15 for a three-day state visit, accompanied by thousands of foreign journalists. The presence of Gorbachev further tied the hands of the Chinese government, making it impossible for the authorities to use force to clear the square during the Deng-Gorbachev summit. It was only after the departure of Gorbachev that Premier Li Peng declared martial law in Beijing and ordered the People's Liberation Army (PLA) to enforce it.[5] By then, Zhao had been purged, and the hard-liners had assumed total control of the main levers of the CCP and the government.[6] However, in a scene reminiscent of the "people power" in Manila in 1986, ordinary citizens of Beijing blocked PLA convoys, preventing the troops from entering the central parts of the city for nearly two weeks. Faced with such unprecedented mass defiance and determined to defend its power with all available means, the CCP leadership gave order to the PLA troops to use deadly force on June 4, ending a 50-day political upheaval that could have led to a dramatic democratic breakthrough in China.[7]

In retrospect, the dramatic events in the spring of 1989 did not take place in a political vacuum. China's transition from Maoist totalitarian rule officially began in 1979, when a reformist coalition led by Deng Xiaoping gained political supremacy within the CCP.[8] In the 1980s, economic reform gradually loosened the state's control over society. More important, driven by pent-up demands from below and encouraged by some of the liberal leaders in the CCP, China had experienced a decade of unprecedented intellectual freedom.[9] Occasional backlash by the conservatives, such as the infamous antispiritual pollution campaign in 1983, failed to stop the trends of political and social liberalization. Within the Communist Party, even top leaders, including Deng Xiaoping, seriously considered various options of political reforms to facilitate China's economic development.[10] On the eve of the failed transition in 1989, several liberals, such as general secretary of the party Zhao Ziyang and Hu Qili, a member of the Politburo Standing Committee slated to succeed Zhao, occupied key positions in the government and the Communist Party. In 1986–87, Zhao himself chaired a task force that produced a blueprint for limited political reform.[11] Had the pro-democracy movement forced the hard-liners out of power in May 1989 and enabled the liberals within the CCP to gain control, history would have been different. Even though the CCP might continue to stay in power, a CCP led by reformers like Zhao Ziyang could have started a gradual process of democratic reform that would have substantially, if not fundamentally, transformed the Chinese political system.

Of course, the crackdown on June 4 changed history. The liberals at the top echelon of the party were quickly removed from power. Leading intellectuals advocating democratic reforms were exiled, imprisoned, or silenced. The conservatives and technocrats quickly rallied behind a neo-authoritarian strategy championed by Deng, who viewed rapid economic growth, not democratic reform, as the only option to keep the Communist Party in power. Since Tiananmen, China has experienced two decades of double-digit economic growth and made itself a global economic power. Politically, the post-Tiananmen regime has not only successfully resisted the global onslaught of democratization that was unleashed by the fall of the Soviet empire but also adapted its tactics of rule and acquired new and more effective instruments of power.[12]

THE ROAD TO TIANANMEN

The Tiananmen crisis did not arise out of a political vacuum. In fact, it was the culmination of the political tensions accumulated through many years of draconian radical rule and conflict between pro-democracy elements in Chinese society and the defenders of one-party rule inside the CCP. Before the failed transition in June 1989, China was ruled by what might be called a "liberalizing post-totalitarian autocracy." In many respects, the regime displayed several unique characteristics that appeared to have contributed to the build-up of demands for democratic reforms before the events in the spring of 1989. First, the CCP leadership in the 1980s consisted of a finely balanced grand coalition of liberals, moderate technocrats, and conservatives (who were victims of Mao's despotic rule but opposed radical market-oriented reforms and political liberalization). It was the combined political strength of this grand coalition that eased Mao's loyalists from power in 1977–78. Because the liberals, headed by Hu Yaobang, spearheaded the campaign to repudiate Maoist policies and provided the intellectual firepower for legitimizing market-oriented reform, they were given significant portfolios in the CCP's Central Committee (Hu headed the important Organization Department before becoming the general secretary, and his protégé, Zhu Houze, was the chief of the Propaganda Department in the mid-1980s).[13] With the liberals assuming the most political risks, the moderate technocrats were able to pursue market-oriented policies that were far more progressive than otherwise possible.[14] The conservatives had a different agenda. They yearned to return to the pre-Cultural Revolution era and opposed both economic and political reforms. Their primary objective was the restoration of a political order characterized by communist-bureaucratic rule and economic planning.[15] Deng Xiaoping himself, however, played a careful balancing role. A pragmatic but risk-taking leader who wanted to save the CCP by adopting market-oriented economic reforms, he was forced constantly to use the liberals to delegitimize the conservatives (who opposed Deng's economic reforms) and rely on the conservatives to constrain the liberals (who threatened Deng's goal of maintaining the rule of the CCP). Such fluid political dynamics at the top in the 1980s provided a series of opportunities both for the liberals to push for greater political reform and for the conservatives to stage counterattacks.[16]

Second, the "liberalizing post-totalitarian autocracy" faced an acute crisis of legitimacy and confidence. The devastation of Mao's leftist radicalism was responsible for China's economic backwardness, which became all the more visible once China opened its doors to the outside world after 1979. The CCP itself was demoralized as well, having suffered itself as a victim of Mao's Cultural Revolution. Millions of the cadres of the CCP were persecuted in one form or another during the decade-long chaos (1966–76). Within Chinese society, the abysmal failure of radical communism was felt even more directly. Mass political terror, economic deprivations, and restrictions on personal freedoms had fatally undermined the trust of the ordinary people in their rulers. In the early 1980s, the so-called Scar Literature, which detailed the heart-rending sufferings of ordinary Chinese during the Cultural Revolution, had a powerful effect on delegitimizing the CCP rule.[17] Obviously, the crisis of legitimacy of the *ancien régime* allowed new ideas, especially those associated with Western liberalism, to gain appeal on college campuses and in intellectual communities in the 1980s.

Third, the economic reforms launched in the late 1970s had begun to produce some political effects.[18] The gradual dismantling of the planned economy directly contributed to the loosening of restrictions on many individual freedoms (such as travel, residence, and employment). The access to information also grew. Such liberalizing trends produced the paradoxical effects of whetting the appetites of those who believed that the progress was too slow and more liberalization was needed. At the same time, faster progress on the front of economic reform contrasted sharply with the government's failure to open up the political system. However, as market-oriented reforms began to demand deregulation, decentralization, and greater policy predictability, China's liberal intelligentsia began to turn its sights on the unreformed one-party regime and demanded commensurate political reforms. While the calls for "political modernization" (shorthand for democratization) were made in 1979 by dissidents who insisted that China's economic modernization could not succeed without a fundamental change in its political system, the linkage between economic reform and political reform was not explicitly made until the mid-1980s, when Deng himself grew increasingly frustrated with the slow pace of economic reform and blamed the entrenched bureaucracy.[19] In 1986 Deng personally called for political reform, although he was primarily interested in streamlining bureaucracy and increasing administrative efficiency and was adamant about not endangering the CCP's rule. However, the political discourse initiated by Deng took off in a different direction. Immediately, Chinese elites began the most extended and serious debate on political reform—a debate that soon sparked the first large-scale student-led pro-democracy movement in the 1980s: in December 1986, students in several key cities, including Beijing, Hefei, and Shanghai, organized street demonstrations calling for immediate democratic reforms and setting off a confrontation with the CCP.[20]

Although Deng sided with the hard-liners in crushing the 1986 student-led pro-democracy demonstrations and fired Hu Yaobang as the CCP general secretary, he appointed Zhao Ziyang as the new CCP general secretary and prevented the conservatives from rolling back the economic reform. Zhao also acted quickly to end the conservative backlash in the aftermath of Hu's dismissal. The trends of political liberalization continued and even picked up speed in 1988, on the eve of the Tiananmen tragedy.

The Brewing Crisis

The impressive achievements of China's economic reform and restoration of political order boosted the legitimacy of the party, but within the fragile grand coalition new tensions and fissures had begun to emerge and escalate. Toward the late 1980s, the delicate balancing act by Deng alone could no longer contain these tensions and risks because much more powerful forces were at play. In retrospect, the crisis of 1989 took place amid a deteriorating economy wrecked by high inflation, rising disunity within the elite, deep frustrations felt by the pro-democracy liberals, and tactical blunders committed by the conservatives in handling the incipient crisis.

During the 1980s, the half-reformed Chinese economy could not escape the boom-to-bust cycle: each round of economic liberalization led to loosening credit control, which in turn caused run-away investment and soaring inflation (table 15.1). Moreover, economic reform in the urban sector, centered on making state-owned enterprises more responsive to market forces, encountered far stronger resistance than anticipated, which prompted Deng to toy with the idea of using democratic reform to overcome bureaucratic resistance. In 1988, to reenergize the sagging economic reform, Deng decided to take a risky gamble on price reform.

TABLE 15.1.
Macroeconomic Performance, 1985–1989 (in percentages)

	1985	1986	1987	1988	1989
GDP growth	17.1	10.1	14.1	15.8	5.2
Growth in fixed investment	39	19	21	22	–7
Annual inflation	8.8	6.0	7.3	18.5	17.8

Source: *Statistical Yearbook of China, 1990* (China Statistics Press, 1990), 51, 153, 249.

Unfortunately, the timing could not have been worse. In terms of public support, the regime did nothing to prepare the Chinese public. It launched its price reform in the style of "shock therapy," a huge tactical mistake that only compounded an originally flawed policy decision. Cyclically, the investment boom that began in 1985 caused persistently high inflation on the eve of the ill-fated price reform. The central authorities failed to rein in investment growth despite a dramatic reduction in fixed investment in 1986. As a result, hyperinflation hit China in 1988, with the consumer price index (CPI) reaching 18.5 percent (more than double the rate for 1987); inflation remained high into 1989. The price liberalization reform implemented in 1988 added fuel to the inflationary spiral of consumer goods. There were reports of widespread panic buying in urban areas.[21] The government was eventually forced to abandon its price reforms.

The runaway inflation in 1988 and the abandonment of price reform had profound political consequences. To the Chinese public, hyperinflation reduced its standard of living, eroded its confidence in the future, and undercut the CCP's political legitimacy. At the elite level, Deng's political authority declined because his decision to push ahead with price reform was considered reckless. The political weakening of Deng allowed the conservatives to seize this opportunity to attack economic reform and try to pin the blame on the liberal general secretary of the CCP, Zhao Ziyang. Along with Deng, Zhao's political fortune suffered as a result of the poor macroeconomic performance. (Indeed, one of the charges against him after he was removed after the Tiananmen crackdown was that he was responsible for the macroeconomic mismanagement of the late 1980s.)[22]

Although the hyperinflation might have provided a political opening for the conservatives within the CCP to attack the liberals, the fissures within the CCP long preceded this development. As observed earlier, the reformist grand coalition Deng formed after returning to power in the late 1970s consisted of, by necessity, conservatives, moderates, and liberals, all of whom helped Deng defeat the surviving Maoists in the brief interval between the Cultural Revolution and the launch of the reform (1977–78). But differences over ideology, policy, and personnel soon began to plague this grand coalition. Despite Deng's skillful balancing act, he could not prevent such differences from escalating into an eventual showdown during the Tiananmen crisis. Specifically, after the fall of Hu Yaobang in January 1987, Zhao Ziyang became, by default, the standard-bearer of the reformist forces. Although by temperament and ideological inclinations, Zhao was considered a moderate technocrat (whereas Hu was an arch liberal), he gradually was forced to take up the cause of the liberals in fending off the constant efforts by the conservatives to roll back the reform. On the eve of the Tiananmen Crisis, the top leadership could be described as split in three ways: liberals (headed by Zhao Ziyang and Hu Qili, who was a member of the Politburo Standing Committee), the conservatives (led by Chen Yun, Li Peng, and Yao Yilin, who was the executive vice-premier), and the balancers (such as Deng and President Yang Shangkun). The liberals were by far the weakest force and had to depend on Deng's support to counter the conservatives. During the initial four weeks of the Tiananmen crisis, the regime's reaction was paralyzed by its internal split.[23] However, once Deng switched sides and threw his support behind the conservatives, the liberals were doomed. The split among the various institutions of the regime and the state was less important than the split among individual leaders at the top. Because of Zhao's previous position in the State Council, he had personal ties with liberal economic reformers based in a key research institute, which played a minor role in trying to rally public support for Zhao during the crisis. Significantly, there was no overt split between the CCP and the military. Because of Deng's personal authority as the commander in chief, he was able to maintain the loyalty of the military. Within the CCP, only one provincial party chief, Yuan Geng, who was the CCP secretary in Hainan, openly supported Zhao. In addition, perhaps a few thousand of midlevel officials publicly broke with the hard-liners.[24]

Mass Protest and Regime Response

Clearly, the Tiananmen Crisis became such a pivotal event mainly because of the massive protest that swept across the nation in mid-May. Such popular outpouring of support for the pro-democracy students marked the high point of the failed transition in 1989. Specifically, the mass protest, involving tens of millions of people from all walks of life across China, was triggered by a rapid succession of coincidental events and botched response by the CCP. (However, pro-democracy activists and some analysts argue that the conservatives deliberately provoked a confrontation with the students in order to force Deng to show his hands and remove Zhao.) In mid-April, college students in Beijing spontaneously went to Tiananmen Square to lay wreaths at the Monument to People's Heroes as their tribute to Hu Yaobang, the liberal former CCP chief who unexpectedly died of a heart attack on April 15. This spontaneous act quickly turned into a loosely organized student movement calling for more democracy in China. As fate would have it, when the crisis was brewing, Zhao Ziyang had to leave Beijing on a scheduled visit to North Korea, thus giving the archconservatives the effective authority to manage the crisis. The conservatives branded the student movement as subversive, and their stance got the support of Deng, who himself harbored deep antipathy toward student movements. The conservative-engineered reaction to the student movement escalated tensions. Students began to demand that the government retract its condemnation of the student movement (expressed in an editorial in the *People's Daily*, the official CCP paper, on April 26). Because Zhao was out of the country, he had little influence over how the crisis was handled. Predictably, the government rejected the students' demands, thus setting up a confrontation.

Again by pure coincidence, the Soviet leader Mikhail Gorbachev was about to begin his historic visit to Beijing in mid-May. Sensing a strategic opportunity to use Gorbachev's visit as a pressure point on the government, the students in Beijing began a mass hunger strike on Tiananmen Square. But the government's initial response was total indifference and continued rejection of the demands of the students. Angered by the government's inaction, the ordinary citizens of Beijing began to rally behind the students and more than a million poured into the streets of the capital to demand that the government respond to the students' demand. By that time, students in other major cities began to stage sympathy demonstrations in support of the students in Beijing. Many colleges in the provinces also sent their representatives to Beijing to join the hunger strikers and demonstrators in Tiananmen Square. The nature of the protest movement had changed as well. Instead of focusing on the students' original (modest) demand for retracting the editorial and for permission to form their own unions, the expanded protest movement denounced corruption in government and openly called for more democracy.[25] The arrival of Gorbachev provided another, albeit short-lived, boost to the movement.

At the height of the movement, the regime effectively lost its control over much of the print media although it retained the control over television and radio. The journalists in Beijing were among the most active supporters of the protest movement. Even the *People's Daily* gave sympathetic coverage to the students because its top editors were liberals.[26] The apparent loss of control by the regime over the print media obviously emboldened the demonstrators and signaled, to the public at large, that the regime itself was either paralyzed or deeply divided. More important, before Zhao was removed from power, he gave several media interviews that showed he favored negotiation and compromise, thus also suggesting publicly a split within the regime.

Although China had no large nongovernmental organizations (NGOs) that could rally public support for the demonstrators in Tiananmen Square, *official* organizations, ranging from the Labor Federation to various government agencies, suddenly became the conduit through which support was mobilized. Scenes of the demonstrations in Beijing in mid-May showed red flags identifying the institutional affiliations of a diverse group of supporters, all of them spontaneously organized. Some intellectual leaders also tried to get the Standing Committee of the People's Congress, nominally the supreme constitutional body, to intervene in the crisis. Unfortunately, the head of the committee, Wan Li, who was a moderate liberal, was away on a state visit to North America. (Wan cut short his visit but was prevented from returning to Beijing after his plane landed in Shanghai.) The most fascinating aspect of the prominent role played by official organizations during the crisis was that the leaders of these organizations either became supporters of the protest movement or lost their authority and failed to prevent their employees from taking to the street. This suggested that, while preexisting NGOs are desirable in mobilizing support for mass protest, they are always indispensable. Protesters can always seize existing institutions and organizations and turn them into vehicles of mobilization.

Because the Tiananmen pro-democracy movement took the CCP leadership by complete surprise, the regime undertook no preventive or preemptive measures before the event, and its initial response to the crisis was hampered by an internal split and miscalculation. What saved the CCP during the crisis was the personal will and authority of the paramount leader, Deng Xiaoping. Even though by that time Deng himself had become the target of the protesters and lost his popularity, he retained the control of the Chinese military in his capacity as the commander in chief of the PLA. This enabled him to bring in several field armies from faraway provinces to quash the pro-democracy movement. Politically, he threw his weight behind the conservatives and changed the balance of power at the top, thus ensuring the defeat of the liberals. Wang Juntao, a leader of the pro-democracy movement, argued that Deng played the most crucial role in saving the CCP during the crisis.[27]

UNORGANIZED DOMESTIC OPPOSITION AND MASS MOBILIZATION

What made the pro-democracy movement in 1989 unique—and doomed its fate— was that it was driven by an *unorganized* opposition formed on an ad hoc basis.[28] Given the tight restrictions that the CCP imposed on independent social and political organizations, no organized political opposition could exist. Nevertheless, the liberal fervor that swept Chinese college campuses and intellectual communities in major cities in the 1980s, it can be argued, created an elite-based virtual opposition group that pushed for political liberalization. In fact, before 1989, the liberal intelligentsia had been engaged in a constant contest with the CCP over the issue of political reform. As a virtual opposition, the Chinese liberal intelligentsia in the 1980s had no elected leaders, but it did have more than a dozen prominent spokesmen, such as Fang Lizhi (an astrophysicist and vice-president of the Chinese University of Science and Technology), Liu Bingyan (a well-known investigative reporter), Wang Ruoshui (deputy editor of the *People's Daily*), and Bai Hua (a writer). The elite intellectual community was connected by liberal publications (such as the Shanghai-based *World Economic Herald*, *Dushu*, a leading journal of book reviews, and *Shouhuo*, a literary magazine) that were under the control of liberal editors.[29]

However, the pro-democracy forces in the 1980s had no broad social base within Chinese societies. As a virtual opposition group, it was restricted to the elite college students, university professors, journalists, writers, and academics in government-run research institutions. Without its fixed organizational network, this group could not reach out to or develop substantive ties with other social groups, such as industrial workers. In any case, the development of organizational linkages among different social groups would have been an impossible task because none of these groups had genuinely independent organizations.[30]

In retrospect, mass mobilization was made possible during the crisis by existing organizational channels and structures embedded in Chinese society, the economy, and the political system. Ironically, nominally officially affiliated organizations and institutions (such as state-run colleges, government agencies, state-owned enterprises, and official labor unions) quickly turned themselves into efficient conduits of mass mobilization. Technologically, mass mobilization in 1989 did not require sophisticated equipment or systems. Protestors relied on old-fashion fixed-line telephones, hand-held megaphones, and crudely printed leaflets as means of communication. Importantly, part of the official media (major newspapers) had their editorial control effectively taken over by journalists and editors sympathetic to the protestors and became critical channels of information dissemination, thus facilitating mass mobilization. Mass mobilization during the crisis was also facilitated by the opposition movement's adroit exploitation of issues to put the regime on the defensive and rally support from a sympathetic public. Initially, college students seized on the issue of the CCP's unjust treatment of Hu Yaobang, who had played a pivotal role in the reform movement in the late 1970s and early 1980s. Then they focused on the retraction of the *People's Daily* editorial on April 26 that branded the students as "creators of chaos"; because they had organized orderly demonstrations, college students in Beijing felt they were unjustly maligned by the government. During their hunger strike, the pro-democracy forces used the issue of government indifference to the plight of the students to rally the public. Finally, after martial law was declared, the rallying issue was "no troops in the city."[31]

As an ad hoc opposition movement, the pro-democracy forces were by no means ideologically coherent. The college students occupying Tiananmen Square were divided among moderates and radicals. The moderates wanted to seek realistic, albeit small, gains, such as greater autonomy for student unions and some form of government acknowledgment of the just cause represented by the student movement. Although the moderates started the protest movement, they soon lost the control to the more radical elements (such as Wuer Kaxi and Cai Ling), who gained spotlight with their more confrontational tactics and rhetoric. In addition, a small group of midlevel government officials who had worked for Zhao had another agenda—trying to salvage Zhao's political future. As for the general public, it was galvanized not so much by democratic ideological values as by a sense of justice—ranging from the government's mishandling of the students' hunger strike and official corruption. On the basis of its rhetoric, it was unclear what the pro-democracy movement's grand objective was. No one was openly calling for the overthrow of the CCP. In all likelihood, the pro-democracy movement was demanding liberalizing political reform undertaken and led by the CCP. To that extent, the objective was not regime change but leadership and policy change under the same regime.

With the exception of a small number of seasoned democracy activists (such as Chen Zimin and Wang Juntao, who had participated in or led protest and electoral campaigns before), the leaders of the pro-democracy student movement were inexperienced. While numerous senior and midlevel officials in the CCP were sympathetic to the cause of the protestors, only a few openly broke with the regime during the crisis. The leadership deficit of the pro-democracy movement was not compensated by the strength of civil society in China at the time. The CCP's tight control made it impossible for either organized opposition or strong civil society groups to emerge. Nevertheless, the 1980s did experience a mini-revival of civil society in China. Tens of thousands of civic associations, mostly professional and leisure groups, were formed in the decade. But the most potent civil society groups, such as independent labor unions, religious groups, public advocacy groups, private foundations, and business associations, could not be formed because of government restrictions.[32] In any case, China's emerging but still tiny civil society had practically no political impact both before and during the Tiananmen crisis.

The role of the Chinese media, by contrast, was far more powerful than that of civil society. The media sector experienced tremendous growth in the 1980s. More important, the print media grew increasingly liberalized owing to the pressures from market forces and liberal journalists.[33] Consequently, the print media—newspapers, magazines, and books—emerged as the most important conduit through which liberal values were disseminated and discourse on democratic reform was carried out. Notably, the Chinese media went through an unusually open and lively debate about Chinese culture and political orientations in 1988, the year preceding the Tiananmen crisis.[34] Liberal academics heatedly debated the political and economic influence of Chinese culture and launched a frontal assault on the conservative values embedded in traditional Chinese culture. The "culture fever" even spread to television, which the CCP had guarded with extraordinary vigilance. A multipart series, called *River Elegy*, which boldly asserted that China's economic backwardness was caused by its self-centered and parochial Confucian culture, was broadcast in late 1988 and became an instant national sensation. Influenced by the "culture fever" in the media, college students were also drawn into the debate on culture and China's future. Intellectually, it appeared that the relative freedom in the media and the openness on college campuses in 1988 must have played an important role in fomenting the pro-democracy demands among the urban elites.[35]

THE ROLE OF EXTERNAL FACTORS

For China's pro-democracy forces, the overall external environment in the 1980s offered more encouragement than discouragement. Even though the major Western powers, especially the United States, did not adopt a policy of actively promoting democracy in China, a host of positive factors contributed to the emergence of the pro-democracy movement in the 1980s.

Economically, China's growing ties with the West directly expanded cultural and intellectual exchanges. Worries about negative reaction from the Western business community acted as a powerful brake on the Chinese government when its conservatives tried to roll back reform and reimpose tight political control (as in the case of the infamous but short-lived "Anti-spiritual Pollution" campaign in 1983). In the area of education, China hired thousands of foreign scholars to teach on its campuses and imported (or copied without permission) a very large number of textbooks used in Western universities. Western movies and translated works of Western literature and philosophy became very popular in China, especially among the younger generation. Intellectually, the economic success of the democratic West, in contrast with the economic failure of the communist countries, gave a powerful boost to democracy-advocates in Chinese society.[36]

Regionally, China was located in a "democratizing neighborhood."[37] Politics in Taiwan, the mainland's archrival across the Taiwan Strait, underwent a gradual and successful process of transition in the 1980s, culminating in the lifting of the martial law and the ban on political parties in 1986. South Korea experienced a democratic breakthrough in 1987. In the Philippines, the People Power overthrew the Marcos regime in 1986. These regional trends had a profound impact on the Chinese intellectual community. In 1988, in addition to the "culture fever," the most discussed topic in Chinese intellectual circles was the "East Asian model."[38] Although the dominant thinking on the "East Asian model" was that effective authoritarian rule was required to promote rapid economic growth during the initial phase of economic take-off, the idea that a transition to democracy would take place in due course under this model was viewed as a plausible or even desirable outcome. Additionally, the global nondemocratic hegemon, the Soviet Union, was itself undergoing *glasnost* and *perestroika*, a process of political liberalization that also significantly influenced China's political and social elites. The benign external security environment was a necessary condition for a relatively permissive political environment inside China in the late 1980s.

International Socialization

In the 1980s, China's integration into the international community was just beginning. With its leadership's focus on economic development, Beijing understandably gave priority to learning about and adjusting to international commercial norms. In this respect, its international socialization quickly led to the reform of domestic policies and institutions to attract foreign investment. The learning of prevailing international democratic norms was a far more uneven and difficult process. The most eager proponents within China for democracy were liberal intelligentsia. Although they were small in number, they occupied strategic positions in the media and academia and became influential voices among China's younger generation. Throughout the 1980s, they constantly urged the CCP to adopt political reform alongside economic reform. But their efforts were seldom successful. Within the CCP, the liberal reformers were mostly in the tradition of Western European democratic socialism: while they advocated greater tolerance and political openness, they consistently envisioned a political system that would be dominated by a reformed Communist Party (which would enjoy greater popular legitimacy and behave more democratically in the party's internal affairs and in its governing practices). Thus, one could argue that society-based liberals were fully identified with Western democratic values, whereas liberals within the regime were partially identified with such norms. Politically, this coalition was pitted against a far more powerful conservative and neo-authoritarian coalition that was determined to defend the CCP's political monopoly. To be sure, the conservatives were not even identified with the prevailing commercial norms of the international community. Their goal was to restore the pre–Cultural Revolution order. The neo-authoritarians represented by Deng were identified with the market-oriented economic norms of the West but rejected Western democratic norms. Thus, even though the conservatives (led by Chen Yun) and the neo-authoritarians constantly clashed over economic reform, they never failed to form a winning coalition against the liberals when the latter attempted to push for democratic reforms.

Moreover, the Chinese government viewed the West with political ambivalence throughout the 1980s. Though it aggressively sought to integrate China into the Western-dominated economic order, seen as the only route to modernization, Beijing rejected "full Westernization" in general and Western democracy in particular. The conservatives and Deng regarded Western democracies as intent upon subverting the rule of the CCP by a subtle process of "peaceful evolution." This official attitude contrasted sharply with that of China's liberals, who viewed the West, both politically and economically, as a desirable order in which they wanted China to participate. As analyzed earlier, the democratic transitions in East Asia (the Philippines, South Korea, and Taiwan) sparked heated intellectual debate on China's own future on college campuses and in public media in China prior to Tiananmen. Although it is impossible to establish causality, the interaction between a quick succession of successful democratic transitions in East Asia and the forward-looking public discourse on Chinese culture and its political future in 1988 clearly existed. If anything, the successful transitions, particularly in South Korea and Taiwan, should have set up powerful normative examples for China's pro-democracy elites.

The transmission of liberal norms to China, again as noted earlier, occurred unimpeded throughout the 1980s as Western governments, companies, universities, and nongovernmental organizations developed and expanded various channels of engagement with their Chinese counterparts. For the most part, however, these exchanges did not have an explicit political agenda (even though they produced, to varying degrees, similar political effects). The degree of the intensity of these efforts varied as well. In the 1980s, the efforts by Western democracies to encourage China to move toward a more liberal political system were low-key because the West focused its resources mostly on the former Soviet Union and gave China less priority. (Another explanation might be that the West thought China was moving in the right direction and needed less direct assistance or push.) The penetration of the Chinese economy by Western firms was by far the most intense, but it was the least political. The most effective and efficient form of engagement was by Western universities and nongovernmental organizations (especially foundations and cultural establishments) that supplied China with much-needed intellectual and financial resources. The cultural and educational programs sponsored by these foreign nongovernmental actors were eagerly embraced by China's artistic and intellectual communities (despite onerous government restrictions). Even though none of the leaders of the Tiananmen movement was associated with such programs, these activities substantively contributed to the vibrant intellectual debate that raged in China before the crisis.

Marginal Role of External Actors during the Crisis

The pro-democracy movement in 1989 caught all concerned by surprise. Neither the CCP leadership nor Western intelligence saw it coming.[39] As a result, to the extent that external variables influenced the pro-democracy movement, they did so prior to the onset of the crisis, and their impact was mostly on shaping a conducive economic, political, and intellectual environment in which pro-democracy forces could grow and assert themselves. However, once the pro-democracy forces were engaged in a high-risk confrontation with the regime, external variables played only a marginal role.[40]

To be exact, during the height of the Tiananmen crisis, positive external incentives were offered at best in implicit terms (such as greater international respect and better ties with the West), whereas negative incentives (sanctions) were suggested more explicitly by Western political leaders (especially those in the US Congress). In any case, for a regime facing the real possibility of its demise, external incentives, vaguely expressed as they were, were not compelling enough for the CCP to adapt. To be sure, for the CCP hard-liners and Deng, the costs of adaptation—accepting the students' demands and starting a gradual course of political opening—were high, but not necessarily prohibitive. The risk that the CCP could eventually lose power was real, but this process was likely a long one because the pro-democracy movement was not calling for an immediate overthrow of the regime. Some senior officials could face charges of corruption, but most senior CCP leaders would have been safe from criminal prosecution in a gradual regime transition. However, while the positive incentives would benefit many (and certainly avert a bloody confrontation), the costs of adaptation (gradual democratic reforms) would fall mostly on the hard-liners and Deng—they would be the first to lose power to the liberals if the pro-democracy forces won the battle in Tiananmen. Zhao would have strengthened his position. Deng's influence would certainly have waned a great deal because he would have borne the responsibility for backing the hard-liners in late April. Not surprisingly, as the paramount leader, Deng had a veto on whether to adapt or fight—and he chose to fight.

In terms of "change agents," those domestic actors with close ties with foreign players, China had few before the Tiananmen crisis. Although the country had by that time developed extensive and growing ties with the West, organizational linkage between domestic actors (either as individuals or as members of civic groups or the government) and foreign actors was extremely weak, even nonexistent. Only a few Western NGOs had just begun to operate in China; most Western governments were cautious in reaching out to prominent dissidents or liberal intellectuals for fear of offending the Chinese government. China's pro-democracy activists were similarly wary of being identified as agents of the West, a label that would discredit them with the Chinese public. (Thus, during the Tiananmen crisis, the pro-democracy activists emphasized their "patriotism" and steered away from any direct association with external actors, except for supporters from Hong Kong, which was considered part of China.)

Despite its role in providing extensive global coverage of the Tiananmen crisis, the Western media played a useful but perhaps not an essential role in mobilizing Chinese students and ordinary citizens during the crisis. Some scholars claim that Western media outlets such as the Voice of America and the BBC became the principal sources of news for Chinese citizens, while others discount their effects on student mobilization.[41] In retrospect, the foreign media performed several important functions. First, the presence of a large number of foreign journalists clearly constrained the Chinese government's ability to take more drastic and decisive steps in dealing with the demonstrators in Tiananmen Square, thus prolonging and intensifying the crisis. Second, blanket coverage of the crisis in progress helped attract international attention to and sympathy for the students, thus forcing the international community to exert pressures on Beijing (even though such pressures were not enough to prevent the eventual bloody crackdown). Third, the presence of the Western media in Beijing during the crisis evidently boosted the morale of the students, who waved signs in English and even erected a replica of the Statue of Liberty (called "Goddess of Democracy" in Chinese) on Tiananmen Square. Last, but not the least, the Chinese-language coverage of the drama of the crisis by the Western media became a reliable source of information for residents outside Beijing.

As briefly mentioned before, Western governments were largely powerless in influencing the behavior or decision-making process during the crisis. Besides issuing calls for moderation and hinting at serious consequences should Beijing use force, the West did little else. Intriguingly, the lack of the West's capacity to intervene at the most critical moments during the Tiananmen crisis was reflected in how China's ruling elites viewed external actors. According to the recollections of Zhao Ziyang, it was clear that China's top leadership, in fact, rarely thought about the international consequences of its decisions. During the crisis, the most

decisive factors influencing the calculations of the key leaders involved were domestic, such as the power struggle within the top leadership, Deng's own public
image, and the culpability of missteps made by the conservatives that led to the
escalation of the crisis.[42]

External Sanctions after Tiananmen

In the wake of the regime's violent suppression of the pro-democracy movement,
an act captured by live television coverage by the Western media, the West imposed
economic and political sanctions on China. Aware of their limited leverage, the
United States and its allies avoided the most severe punitive measures, such as
severance of diplomatic ties or an economic embargo. Instead, Western powers
opted for relatively restrained and symbolic sanctions against Beijing. Such sanctions were coordinated at the G-7 Summit in July 1989. Diplomatically, they ended
top-level contact with Chinese leaders. Western countries gave asylum to dozens
of the leaders of the pro-democracy activists who had escaped China. Tens of thousands of Chinese students studying in the West received permanent residence.
Economically, the West reduced (though only temporarily) the World Bank's lending to China and cut off credit made available through the US Ex-Im Bank. The
most severe sanctions were imposed on the Chinese military, an institution viewed
as directly culpable in the suppression of the pro-democracy movement. The limited assistance to the PLA provided by the United States was ended immediately.
The West also imposed an arms embargo that banned the exports of military and
law-enforcement equipment and technology to China. But the West refrained from
completely isolating China or destroying the strong economic relationship with
China. As a result, China's access to Western markets (under the terms of the Most
Favored Nation status) was preserved. To further ensure that the Chinese leadership exercise restraint in the postcrisis crackdown and to limit the damages done
by the sanctions on US-China relations, the administration of George H. W. Bush,
sent secret envoys immediately after the Tiananmen crackdown (in July 1989) and
also at the end of 1989.

The economic sanctions, mild as they were, remained for only a very short
period of time. They were gradually lifted in the 1990s after China's economy
began its spectacular growth run following Deng's tour of southern China in
1992. The pressure of the Western business community and signs that China
was at least back on track in its pro-market reforms made it increasingly difficult
to maintain the (symbolic) economic sanctions. The West's diplomatic sanctions
similarly became unsustainable in the early 1990s. After Iraq invaded Kuwait

in August 1990, the West's need for China's cooperation at the United Nations Security Council (in which China has a veto) gave Beijing an opening to break the Western diplomatic isolation. By abstaining at the crucial Security Council vote on approving the use of force against Iraq in October 1990, China was able to extract crucial diplomatic concessions from the West later.[43] Within a few years, top-level contact with the West resumed. The United States' threat to end China's Most Favored Nation status unless Beijing improved its post-Tiananmen human rights record, made by Bill Clinton during the presidential campaign in 1992, was ignominiously abandoned in 1994 when President Clinton was forced to delink China's trade status from its human rights record. In November 1994, Clinton met Chinese president Jiang Zemin at a summit for the leaders of the Asia-Pacific Economic Cooperation, marking the end of the Tiananmen diplomatic sanctions against China.

Only the arms embargo against China stayed in place long after the failed transition in 1989. But its effects were limited. After the collapse of the Soviet Union, the new Russian government under Yeltsin began to export advanced weapon systems and defense technologies to China (such as fighter jets, missiles, and warships), mainly to earn hard currency. Western firms also transferred to China many crucial dual-use technologies not covered by the arms embargo. Supported by expanded access to new technologies and weapon systems and funded by a double-digit increase in military spending, the PLA made significant gains in its capabilities in the two decades after it crushed the pro-democracy movement.

The post-Tiananmen sanctions did not achieve much in terms of punishing the Chinese government for its suppression of the Tiananmen movement or forcing Beijing to improve its human rights record and adopt political reforms (even though the interventions by Western governments did succeed in freeing individual dissidents and leaders of the pro-democracy movement).[44] The West was hobbled by many factors in designing an effective strategy in dealing with China after the Tiananmen crackdown. Most important, the United States and its allies all had competing strategic priorities that acted to moderate the pressure to enact more drastic punitive sanctions against China. Strategically, a hostile China could destabilize Asia and threaten vital Western interests (especially in the area of nonproliferation). China's cooperation with the West at the United Nations Security Council was another desirable objective. Economically, Western businesses were afraid to lose their billions of dollars in investment in China and access to a fast-growing market with huge potential. Realistically, Western governments all understood that external pressure in the wake of the Tiananmen crackdown could accomplish very little.

CONCLUSION

The democratic transition in China in 1989 failed for many reasons. But negative external influence was not one of them. This study shows that, if anything, a full range of external factors was highly positive for the prospect of a democratic transition in China in the late 1980s. In fact, it is argued in this study that these positive factors helped create a conducive environment in the 1980s for the pro-democracy forces in China. To the extent that external factors failed to influence the outcome of the 1989 transition, that was largely due to the fact that external forces could not be brought to bear on the closed decision-making process at the very top of a besieged Chinese regime. Although external factors were instrumental in fostering a liberalizing political, economic, and cultural environment in a sovereign state, the same factors were practically irrelevant in a crisis situation. Therefore, the causes of the failed transition in 1989 were exclusively domestic.

When we examine the balance of power of the hard-liners and soft-liners during the Tiananmen crisis, it is obvious that the hard-liners had almost insuperable advantage. First, the conservatives and neo-authoritarians were closely allied against the liberals. With the paramount leader, Deng, firmly in the camp of the hard-liners, the soft-liners' cause was doomed. Second, the hard-liners had the support of the military, which ultimately was called upon to crush the protest movement. Third, even during the crisis, the CCP continued to control the most important segments of the media (television and most newspapers), denying the pro-democracy an efficient means to rally the public. Fourth, the pro-democracy forces lacked the organizational bases within Chinese society to sustain the protest movement or mobilize enough population to change the outcome of the power struggle at the top.

That external factors could not influence the outcome of a crisis-driven transition in China in 1989 should not come as a surprise. After all, these factors have rarely determined the outcome of pivotal political events in large countries. With its population, military strength, huge territory, and long history, China presented a particularly difficult "target country" even under the best circumstances. In 1989 its hard-liners showed the West that, when faced with the prospect of regime demise, they would not be constrained by international public opinion or threats of sanctions. Unfortunately, the continual survival, if not the resilience, of the CCP regime since Tiananmen appears to have vindicated the hard-liners.

NOTES

1. Many scholarly books and documents have been published on this historic event. See Dingxin Zhao, *The Power of Tiananmen: State-Society Relations and the 1989 Beijing Student Movement* (Chicago: University of Chicago Press, 2004); Tony Saich, *The Chinese People's*

Movement: Perspectives on Spring 1989 (Armonk, N.Y.: M. E. Sharpe, 1990); Craig Calhoun, *Neither Gods nor Emperors: Students and the Struggle for Democracy in China* (Berkeley: University of California Press, 1994); James Miles, *The Legacy of Tiananmen: China in Disarray* (Ann Arbor: University of Michigan Press, 1996); Michel Oksenbert et al., eds., *Beijing Spring, 1989: Confrontation and Conflict: the Basic Documents* (Armonk, N.Y.: M. E. Sharpe, 1990); George Hicks, *The Broken Mirror: China after Tiananmen* (Chicago: St. James Press, 1990).

2. James Tong, "The 1989 Democracy Movement in China: A Spatial Analysis of City Participation," *Asian Survey* 3 (March 1989): 310–27; Jonathan Unger, *The Democracy Movement in China: The View from the Provinces* (Armonk, N.Y.: M. E. Sharpe, 1990).

3. Zhao Ziyang gave his account of the power struggle during the Tiananmen crisis in his memoirs, *Prisoner of the State: The Secret Journal of Premier Zhao Ziyang* (New York: Simon and Schuster, 2009).

4. The key demands included retracting the infamous April 26 editorial in the *People's Daily*, an official declaration that the students were patriots, and the recognition of independent student unions.

5. Martial law was declared on May 19. Gorbachev departed Beijing on May 18.

6. The most important meeting of the Politburo Standing Committee was convened on May 17 in Deng's home. The decision to declare martial law was made at that time over Zhao's objections. Zhao threatened to resign but did not tender his resignation in a formal letter. He was effectively dismissed on May 19 and barred from attending any top-level meetings afterward. See Zong Fengming, *Captive Conversations* (Hong Kong: Open Publishing House, 2007), 13–14.

7. No reliable record indicates who actually gave the order to use deadly force. The decision to bring in PLA troops was reached at a meeting convened in Deng Xiaoping's home on May 17.

8. For an overview of the early stage of the post-Mao reforms, see Harry Harding, *China's Second Revolution: Reform after Mao* (Washington, D.C.: Brookings Institution, 1987).

9. See Merle Goldman, *Sowing the Seeds of Democracy in China: Political Reform in the Deng Xiaoping Era* (Cambridge, Mass.: Harvard University Press, 1995).

10. Wu Guoguang, *Political Reform under Zhao Ziyang* (Taipei: Yuanjing Publishing, 1997).

11. According to Wu Guoguang, a member of the task force, Zhao's blueprint was endorsed by Deng even though Deng thought it went a bit too far in trying to institute separation of powers. See ibid.

12. See David Shambaugh, *The Chinese Communist Party: Atrophy and Adaptation* (Berkeley: University of California Press, 2008); Andrew Nathan, "Authoritarian Resilience," *Journal of Democracy* 1 (January 2003): 6–17; Minxin Pei, "How China Is Ruled," *American Interest* 3, no. 4 (March–April 2008): 44–52.

13. Zhao Ziyang began as a moderate technocrat but became the leader of the liberals within the CCP after he assumed the position of the general secretary following Hu Yaobang's ouster in January 1987.

14. Yasheng Huang argues that the reform in the 1980s produced far more impressive results than the 1990s. See Huang, *Capitalism with Chinese Characteristics: Entrepreneurship and State during the Reform Era* (New York: Cambridge University Press, 2008).

15. Chen Yun, a veteran revolutionary who was effectively Deng's political equal, was the leader of the conservatives. For a discussion of the conservative economic strategy, see

398 FAILED TRANSITION CASES

Nicholas Lardy and Kenneth Lieberthal, *Chen Yuan's Strategy for China's Development: A Non-Maoist Alternative* (Armonk, N.Y.: M. E. Sharpe, 1983). Zhao Ziyang also detailed how Chen was firmly opposed to market reforms in his secret journal, *Prisoner of the State*.

16. Many books detail the political struggle among various groups in the 1980s. See Yang Jishen, *Zhongguo gaige niandai de zhengzhi douzheng* [Political Struggle in the Era of Reform in China] (Hong Kong: Excellence Culture Press, 2004).

17. See X. L. Ding, *The Decline of Communism in China: Legitimacy Crisis, 1979–1989* (New York: Cambridge University Press, 1995).

18. See Deborah Davis, ed., *Chinese Society on the Eve of Tiananmen* (Cambridge, Mass.: Harvard University Press, 1990).

19. For an overview of the tensions between economics and politics in the 1980s, see Joseph Fewsmith, *Dilemmas of Reform in China: Political Conflict and Economic Debate* (Armonk, N.Y.: M. E. Sharpe, 1994).

20. For a brief overview of Deng and political reform, see Minxin Pei, *China's Trapped Transition: The Limits of Developmental Autocracy* (Cambridge, Mass.: Harvard University Press, 2006), 46–56.

21. Barry Naughton, "Why Has Economic Reform Led to Inflation?" *AEA Papers and Proceedings* 81 (May 1991): 207–17.

22. Zong Fengming, *Zhao Ziyang: Captive Conversations* (Hong Kong: Kaifang Publishing, 2007), 17.

23. According to Yuan Yue, a protest leader at the Ministry of Justice, for three weeks (from the end of April to mid-May), there was no clear signal from the central government. The minister of justice himself did not know what to do when his subordinates requested permission to go to Tiananmen to demonstrate. Yuan, interview, Shanghai, August 12, 2007.

24. In Shanghai, for example, 500 CCP members signed on May 20 a petition against the declaration of martial law in Beijing. They were organized by two bureau-level cadres. Zhu Xueqin, interview, August 15, 2007. Zhu was a participant in the demonstrations in Shanghai in 1989.

25. See Yan Sun, "Chinese Protest of 1989: The Issue of Corruption," *Asian Survey* 31 (August 1991): 762–82.

26. Lu Chaoqi, a deputy editor of the People's Daily, gave an account of how the liberal editors of the paper gave sympathetic coverage to the protest. Lu Chaoqi, *June 4: An Internal Diary* (Hong Kong: Zuoyue Publishing House, 2006).

27. Remarks made at a conference on mass protest at Oxford University in March 2007.

28. Xueguang Zhou analyzed how unorganized groups can mobilize for collective action in China in Xueguang Zhou, "Unorganized Interest and Collective Action in Communist China," *American Sociological Review* 58 (February 1993): 54–73.

29. See Merle Goldman, Timothy Cheek, and Carol Lee Hamrin, eds., *China's Intellectuals and the State: In Search of a New Relationship* (Cambridge, Mass.: Harvard University Press, 1987).

30. For a discussion on the role of civil society in the Tiananmen protest, see Barret McCormick, Su Shaozhi, and Xiaoming Xiao, "The 1989 Democracy Movement: A Review of the Prospects for Civil Society in China," *Pacific Affairs* 65 (Summer 1992): 182–202.

31. Lucian Pye provides a cultural analysis of the protestors' tactics during Tiananmen. See Lucian Pye, "Tiananmen and the Chinese Political Culture: The Escalation of Confrontation from Moralizing to Revenge," *Asian Survey* 30 (April 1990): 331–47.

32. Minxin Pei, "Civic Associations in China: An Empirical Analysis," *Modern China* 2

(July 1998): 285–318; Thomas Gold, "The Resurgence of Civil Society in China," *Journal of Democracy* 1 (January 1901): 18–31.

33. For a study of the changes in the Chinese media in the reform era, see Daniel Lynch, *After the Propaganda State: Media, Politics, and "Thought Work" in Reformed China* (Stanford, Calif.: Stanford University Press, 1999); for a study of the changes in the television industry, see James Lull, *China Turned On: Television, Reform, and Resistance* (London: Routledge, 1991).

34. See Seth Faison, "The Changing Role of the Chinese Media," in Saich, *The Chinese People's Movement*, 145–63.

35. For an account of the intellectual atmosphere in Beijing on the eve of Tiananmen, see Perry Link, *Evening Chats in Beijing: Probing China's Predicament* (New York: W. W. Norton, 1992).

36. Yuan Yue, the official in the Ministry of Justice, argued that the most influential support from the West came before the eruption of the crisis in the form of disseminating the ideas of liberty, justice, human rights, and democracy. Yuan interview.

37. For a study of the democratic transitions in East Asia, see Larry Diamond and Marc Plattner, eds., *Democracy in East Asia* (Baltimore: Johns Hopkins University Press, 1998).

38. See Barry Sautman, "Sirens of the Strongman: Neo-authoritarianism in Recent Chinese Political Theory," *China Quarterly* 129 (1992): 72–102.

39. Zhu Xueqin, a protest organizer in Shanghai, said that to the extent there was any warning at all, it was very vague and referred only to possible "irregular removal" of liberal leaders (most probably Zhao). Zhu interview.

40. According to Chen Zimin, one of the protest leaders in Beijing, there was no communication between the protestors and the West during the crisis. Chen, interview, Beijing, August 11, 2007. Zhu Xueqin in Shanghai and Yuan Yue in Beijing also said that there was no Western material support for or involvement in the protest movement. Yuan interview; Zhu interview.

41. Zhao, *The Power of Tiananmen*, 302–6.

42. Zhao, *Prisoner of the State*.

43. According to Chen Zimin, a leader of the Tiananmen movement, he was detained immediately after June 4, 1989, but was not formally arrested until the day the United Nations Security Council began to debate the first Gulf War resolution. Chen interview.

44. Chen Zimin recalled that the US diplomatic pressures on China led to a significant improvement in his treatment in prison. Chen interview.

CHAPTER SIXTEEN

Azerbaijan

Losing the Transitional Moment

VALERIE J. BUNCE AND SHARON L. WOLCHIK

The 2005 elections in Azerbaijan qualify as a failed transition. Opposition political leaders mounted election campaigns but were outmaneuvered by President Ilham Aliyev's New Azerbaijan Party (YAP) and its allies, which allegedly won an overwhelming victory in parliamentary elections that were seriously flawed. Although several opposition parties formed a preelection bloc, and some nongovernmental groups attempted to mount citizens' campaigns, regime harassment and intimidation, coupled with the ability of the Aliyev government to use patronage to shore up support, prevented the development of any widespread challenge to the ruling party. International and domestic election monitors documented blatant fraud and falsification of election results.[1] As a result, the YAP, affiliated parties, and so-called independents accounted for all but 8 of the 115 seats in the legislature. Of the eight opposition candidates elected, several boycotted parliament to protest the fraudulent nature of the elections.

The ability of the Aliyev regime to maintain its hold on power reflected both internal and external factors. We begin our analysis of the interplay of these factors in leading to this failed effort to use elections to create a democratic opening in Azerbaijan with a discussion of the political and economic context of the regime on the eve of the elections in order to assess the degree of vulnerability of the regime and the tools available to it to preserve its power, as well as its actions during the election campaign and after. We then turn to internal factors that influenced the opposition and civil society, and the efforts of both groups to unite, organize, and contest the elections. After setting the context for these elections, we examine the most important international influences and then turn to the interaction of domestic and international actors. The chapter concludes with a discussion of what this case tells us about electoral continuity and change in semi-authoritarian states.

TRANSITIONAL CONTEXTS

Azerbaijan presents an interesting case from the perspective of transitions, as it experienced a brief period after the end of the Soviet Union in 1991 that raised hopes that democratic politics would take root. As Azeris proudly point out, Azerbaijan was a parliamentary republic during its brief period of independence from 1918 to 1920. Although this fledgling government was quickly conquered by the Red Army, its multiparty system, civil and political liberties, and national versus religious orientation are a legacy that democrats in Azerbaijan cherish.[2] However, it soon became clear that this brief democratic legacy would have little impact on postcommunist politics. From June 1991 to March 1992, Ayaz Mutalibov served as president. In March 1992 Mutalibov was forced to resign as the result of the situation in Nagorno-Karabagh. In June 1992 the nationalist leader Abulfaz Elchibey won 60 percent of the vote in presidential elections that were generally judged to have been democratic,[3] after several months of political turmoil.[4]

Elchibey's government, however, also soon fell victim to the war in Karabagh. With the "victory" of Armenia, supported by Russia, Azerbaijan lost 16 percent of its territory and gained 700,000 refugees from the newly occupied areas.[5] Defeat provided the pretext for a referendum on Elchibey's presidency, in which more than 90 percent of those voting expressed a lack of confidence in the president. Forced to flee to Nakhchivan by a paramilitary uprising in 1993, Elchibey was replaced by Heydar Aliyev, who was elected president in 1993 and remained in that office until shortly before his death in 2003. The former head of the Communist Party of Azerbaijan and member of the Politburo of the Communist Party of the Soviet Union, Aliyev presided over a regime that became increasingly autocratic. Able to rely on oil revenues, his government oversaw a complicated system of patronage networks, often described as clans, that came to control most of Azerbaijan's wealth, including privatized state enterprises and new businesses, as well as the country's sizable oil and gas resources. The transfer of power to Heydar's son, Ilham, who was elected president in October 2003, raised hopes that the regime would become more moderate. However, Ilham disappointed these hopes, despite his talk of the need to cooperate with NATO and the European Union, and enact economic reform, and instead continued many of his father's practices, including his strategy of rule. International assessments of the degree of democratization, such as Freedom House rankings, in fact found that Azerbaijan had regressed on all measures except corruption, which remained the same between 2003 and 2005. The country's overall ranking fell from "partly free" to "not free."[6]

As has been the case in many of the countries that experienced the democratic breakthroughs commonly termed electoral revolutions, Azerbaijan has a semi-authoritarian political system.[7] The ruling elite concentrated around the president controls all of the levers of power and most of the country's economic resources. The media are also largely in the hands of the regime, which maintains its rule by a combination of material, coercive, and normative incentives.[8] Despite its authoritarian character, the Aliyev regime, like most other political systems, feels compelled to organize elections, even though these are rigged and their results falsified, in order to maintain the myth of popular support, reaffirm its power, and give lip service to the internationally accepted norm of democratic rule.[9] As a result, there are regular opportunities for the opposition to focus on the failings of the regime and attempt to come to power. To date, however, the authorities have been successful in manipulating and falsifying the election results, and preventing the opposition from mounting an effective challenge. They have also succeeded to a large extent in deflecting international criticism of election irregularities.

The structure of Azerbaijan's economy clearly strengthened the hand of the regime. Nearly a classic case of a resource-dependent country, 50 percent of GDP and 90 percent of foreign exports in Azerbaijan came from energy exports.[10] GDP grew an astonishing 26 percent in 2005 (and a more astonishing 36 percent in 2006). Growth was highest in the oil and gas sectors, which account for around one-third of GDP. However, non-oil output has also increased at an annual average rate of 15 percent since 1999.[11] According to the World Bank and United Nations Development Program (UNDP), Azerbaijan ranks in the lower middle-income level on per capita income, which was $1,240 in 2005 and as a middle-income country in terms of human development.[12] However, the phenomenal growth in GDP due to foreign investment in the energy sector in recent years has not trickled down to any great extent to the populace as a whole. The Gini index for inequality in the early 2000s was slightly higher than the average of that in other non-Baltic former Soviet republics. Despite the country's high growth rates, the World Bank estimates that more than 29 percent of the population lived in poverty in 2006, and 8 percent of this group in extreme poverty.[13] The International Labor Organization estimates that approximately 30 percent of the labor force is employed by the government in one capacity or another. The government thus has and frequently uses cutbacks in working hours or loss of jobs as threats against those who support the opposition.[14]

The structure and performance of the economy allowed Aliyev to reward his supporters at all levels and punish his enemies. Real GDP growth and continued foreign investment in the energy sector provided ample resources to retain the regime's support among the elite, and there were no Azeri equivalents of the Ukrainian businessmen who supported the Orange Revolution. At the same time, however, the high degree of inequality and the large proportion of citizens who live in poverty provided a potential pool of voters for the opposition to mobilize.

The regime's hand was also strengthened by the nature of Azeri society and the intertwining of political and economic power. The country's social structure reflects the development that occurred under communism as well as the changes since 1991. There is near universal (98.8 percent) literacy among those 15 and older, and education levels have increased. As in other postcommunist states, the past decade has seen a change in the social structure as previously forbidden groups such as capitalists and entrepreneurs have reappeared. In contrast to the situation in many formerly communist countries in which the structure of the economy has shifted from its former emphasis on heavy industry to focus on the service sector, industry (particularly nonmanufacturing sectors) in Azerbaijan has grown considerably faster than agriculture or the service sector.[15] However, nearly half of all households still depend on agriculture, which contributes only 8 percent of GDP, for their livelihoods.[16]

Unlike many of the former Soviet republics which have sizable ethnic, and particularly Russian, minorities, Azerbaijan's population is primarily ethnically Azeri (95.8 percent). There are relatively few Russians (2.8 percent of the population). There is a small (1.5 percent) Armenian minority, as well as very small representation of other minorities, including Ukrainians, Avars, and Turks.

Azerbaijan's society is widely held to be characterized by clan relationships. Based in part on kinship and in part on geography, these patronage networks play an important role in the country's economic as well as political life. The ability to start a business or run an economic enterprise depends on membership in one of these networks. The clans that dominate the regime, including the clan centered around the Aliyev family, make use of the sizable revenues from oil and gas to keep their networks intact. The very close links between politics and economics mean that political office holding is also tied very directly to the officeholder's economic status. Strong ties, and preferably, kinship, are required to engage in large-scale economic activity. Entrepreneurs are dependent on higher-level state officials to maintain control of their enterprises and provide protection against efforts to extort money from them.[17]

Opponents argue that the power of the Aliyev regime rests on a set of intertwined hierarchies. These include a regional hierarchy reflected in the fact that Azeris from Armenia and Nakhchivan hold the key positions in the government and also monopolize key industrial and business sectors. The regime also rests on

404   FAILED TRANSITION CASES

a clan hierarchy centered on the Aliyev family. Numerous state officials are direct members of this family.[18] The families or clans of other top state officials staff lower level bureaucratic positions. Finally, there is a hierarchy based on corruption, which is endemic. State positions are filled as the result of bribery, which links officials or their proxies at various levels.[19]

These relationships are embedded in and center on competition for resources and wealth. Opposition activists argue, in fact, that it is this feature of the cleavages in the regime that holds the system together. Because those involved in these networks, which reach down to the lower layers of the apparatus and permeate all sectors of the economy, realize that all will lose if the regime changes, they unite to resist pressure to change or threats to the regime.[20] Since Heydar Aliyev's consolidation of his power in 1993, the regime has had near exclusive control of the economic and financial resources of the country. Since then, access to a political office has been a prerequisite for engaging in business activity, as well as the source of illicit financial resources. In fact, because of the systemic control of the regime's bureaucracy over almost all of the financial resources generated in the country, financial power in Azerbaijan has been described as "bureaucratic capital."[21] Before the 2005 elections, Aliyev further tightened his control over the country's financial resources by imprisoning and persecuting several wealthy and influential members of his regime.[22]

In addition to the importance of political linkages in the economy and the power of clan networks, the excesses of the regime also make top leaders reluctant to peacefully relinquish power and contribute to the unity of the regime. In the communist era, as after the death of Stalin, many top party leaders were reluctant to allow even relatively minor changes because of their own complicity in the crimes of that era. Similarly, members of the current ruling group in Azerbaijan now have good reason to fear that they would be prosecuted should they lose power. As a dissident intellectual who wished to remain anonymous stated, "During the 12 years since Heydar Aliyev's post-communist advent to power, the regime has built its wealth on violent means, tortures, assassinations, and a widespread destitution. The regime members know that they would not be left untouched if they are overthrown. Their property would be confiscated; some of them deserve hanging in the main square in Baku. If a successor government would fail to punish the culprits who oppressed us, then ordinary citizens, the relatives, sons or daughters, of the regime victims would do this. The upper echelons of Azerbaijan's government do not really have an alternative to holding on to power. Theirs is a 'win-or-die' situation and they know this. This is the source of their unity in crisis."[23]

Not only did Aliyev have such supports for his regime, but he also did not hesitate to use coercion against the opposition and independent activists. Although they had some freedom of action, leaders of the opposition were occasionally arrested. The use of violence was not widespread, but the regime used force against demonstrators on numerous occasions. Several opposition activists, including the editor and technical director of the opposition Azadliq bloc were beaten and then photographed in compromising positions with prostitutes,[24] and one, Elmar Huseynov, editor of the journal *Monitor*, was murdered.

Aliyev's ability to carry out such acts reflected his firm grip on the police and security forces as well as on the country's military. The state, dominated by the Aliyev clan, retained considerable capacity in 2005. Aliyev and the clan leaders loyal to him were able to use patronage and coercion to maintain the loyalty of the bureaucracy as well as of the security and military forces. The police, for example, received salary increases, at times seven-fold, and new cruisers before the start of the 2005 election campaigns. But, while the coercive organs of the state functioned very effectively to carry out Aliyev's orders, infrastructure has been neglected, and in some locales religious organizations are providing social services customarily provided by government.

Some analysts have suggested that there were tensions in the ruling group between those who served Heydar Aliyev, Ilham's father, who are more conservative, and younger, Western-oriented "reformists."[25] Shortly before the November 2005 elections, the ministers of Health and Economic Development, as well as several officials and businessmen who had kinship and friendship ties to them, were arrested on charges of attempting a coup against the president. It was later revealed that the charges were related not to a real attempt to unseat the president but to a long-standing feud between these ministers and another member of the cabinet. Observers note that there were long-standing tensions between former minister of health Ali Insanov and his group, the Yeraz, or "Yerevan Azerbaycanlisi" (Azerbaijanians from Yerevan who were deported in the 1980s) and the Nakhchivan group that has surrounded Ilham Aliyev since he came to power in 2003.[26] Although such episodes indicate that there are divisions among the supporters of the regime that erupt from time to time, the complicity of all factions and the potential loss of benefits to all that would result from regime change have, to date at least, limited significant defections. These factors also made it difficult for the opposition to challenge the regime effectively.

Reliance on material incentives and the occasional use of coercion against the opposition and intellectuals were supplemented in Azerbaijan by the use of normative incentives, in this case, the unresolved situation of Nagorno-Karabagh. The unsettled state of Nagorno-Karabagh and the widespread perception that Armenia unjustly "occupies" this region that should rightfully be part of Azerbaijan are powerful tools for the ruling elite to use in maintaining its power. As even a casual visitor to Azerbaijan can attest, the war and Azerbaijan's loss of territory to Armenia dominate conversation about politics and are used very adeptly to justify the need for a strong government. As the result of the war in Nagorno-Karabagh, there are approximately 700,000 refugees from the territory, which is currently occupied by Armenia with the support of Russia. The presence of these displaced persons is yet another factor that keeps the war a central issue in politics.

The country's geopolitical position including its proximity to Iran and Iraq, as well as its oil and gas, also had an important impact on political developments in the country. As we will discuss at greater length later, security and energy considerations led the United States and other Western democracies to soft-pedal their criticisms of the regimes of both Heydar and Ilham Aliyev and moderate their statements concerning electoral irregularities.

INTERNAL FACTORS
The Opposition and Civil Society

Despite the concentration of power in the hands of the Aliyev family and significant limits on the activities of the opposition, opposition political parties were able to exist, as was a small but important nongovernmental sector. Operating from rundown offices on the outskirts of the capital or in borrowed quarters, opposition political leaders were sometimes physically threatened, beaten or arrested. They nonetheless generally had the freedom of action to orchestrate meetings of their followers and contest elections, as well as meet with foreigners. However, they had neither the resources nor the opportunity to organize a large-scale civic movement.

The Azeri opposition in 2005 consisted of several political parties whose leaders occasionally attempted to cooperate in elections. Many opposition leaders had been involved in politics since the country's independence in 1991. Isa Gambar, the head of the Musavat party, for example, had served as speaker of parliament and had run for president against Ilham Aliyev in 2003, garnering an alleged 13.97 percent of the vote compared to the 76.84 percent Aliyev received in what were widely held to be fraudulent elections. Put under house arrest, Gambar and some 600 other opposition activists who were jailed in 2003 were the nucleus of the opposition in 2005. Inspired by the events in Georgia and Ukraine, where elections were used to mobilize citizens to oust semi-authoritarian leaders in 2003 and 2004, Gambar and other opposition leaders joined forces in 2005 in the Azadliq, or Freedom, alliance. Other members of the alliance included the Popular Front Party of Azerbaijan led by Ali Karimli and the Democratic Party of Azerbaijan. The Yeni Siyaset or New Policy bloc also participated. The Liberal Party of Azerbaijan, led by Lala Shovket, former state secretary with ties to the intellectual circles in

Moscow surrounding Gorbachev in the mid- to late 1980s, also fielded candidates. Voter choice in the 2005 elections was complicated by the pseudo-opposition: the many "independent" candidates who actually supported the Aliyev regime and the copy-cat parties the regime organized to parallel many of the opposition parties. In October the regime prevented the return to Azerbaijan of Rasul Guliyev, the former speaker of parliament, widely seen as someone who could appeal both to dissatisfied elements in the clans supporting the president and to certain elements of the opposition. Detained in Ukraine at Baku's request, Guliyev eventually left Ukraine for London and gave up his ambitions to run for office in Azerbaijan.

In contrast to the opposition in Ukraine in 2004, the Azeri opposition was unable to count on financial support from a strong dissatisfied element of the business sector at home or unequivocal moral support from abroad. Many opposition leaders had been involved in politics for at least a decade, and their ability to recruit younger leaders or to appeal to the population was hampered in some cases by their perceived complicity with the regime. Some were also hindered in their efforts to gain popular support by their association with Azerbaijan's losses in Nagorno-Karabagh. As with many other oppositions in the postcommunist world, ideological divisions were less important than personality differences and personal ambitions. The external limitations imposed by the regime on the ability of opposition leaders to build effective, mass-based political parties were paralleled by a reluctance to engage in many of the techniques outside experts on party development counsel, such as door-to-door campaigning, canvassing, and personal contact with voters and potential supporters.[27]

We should not minimize the efforts of the opposition, however. In the course of the 2005 campaign, both the Azadliq and the YeS coalitions held meetings with thousands of voters in the countryside. Azadliq, for example, held meetings with voters in 34 of the 65 rural districts. Some of these attracted more than 10,000 voters, according to party leaders.[28] However, the main base of support for the opposition was in the capital, where the regime finds it more difficult to apply surveillance techniques than it does in smaller towns and villages. Also, with fewer opposition dailies available outside the capital, it is more difficult to overcome the negative image of the opposition that the regime fosters in the official broadcast media.[29]

Numerous nongovernmental organizations (NGOs), many with outside funding, participated in election-related activities, including voter education and get-out-the-vote campaigns. During the elections, two coalitions of Azerbaijani NGOs, as well as some other NGOs, observed the elections. The first coalition, the Election Monitoring Center, united 14 NGOs and sent 2,315 observers to 124 of the 125 electoral districts. The second coalition, the Coordinative Advisory Council for Free and Fair Elections (CACFFE), which brought together 48 NGOs, sent out 2,237 observers to 80 districts. Members of CACFFE managed to obtain full election documentation in 32 districts. Both the Monitoring Center and CACFFE recorded enough falsification to conclude that a revote was needed.[30]

Several youth organizations also were active in the elections. These included Yeni Fikir (New Thinking), which opposition leader Ali Karimli of the Popular Front helped found in April 2004. Drawing their inspiration from youth organizations in countries that had experienced democratizing elections, Yeni Fikir activists participated in training sessions on nonviolent conflict and attempted to emulate the get-out-the-vote campaigns that had proved successful elsewhere. The young activists of Yeni Fikir, though closely associated with Karimli, were largely political neophytes. Generally students, many had been active in the Azerbaijan Popular Front Party before the founding of Yeni Fikir, which was often referred to as the "youth wing" of APFP.[31] Other youth organizations, including Magam (Moment, also translated as It's Time), Dalga (Wave), and Yokh (No) were also active, despite harassment by the regime.[32] The influence of youth movements in Serbia, Georgia, and Ukraine, as well as other outside experts in nonviolent conflict was evident in the fact that one of these organizations, Magam, launched its activities in April 2005 with a translation of Gene Sharp's 1993 book *From Dictatorship to Democracy*.[33] The book is considered a bible for Azerbaijan's youth organizations, and all four actively disseminated it. Hampered by the regime's repression and the arrest of Yeni Fikir's chairman, Ruslan Bashirli, in August 2005 on charges of attempting to overthrow the government and accepting funds from foreign NGOs and Armenian intelligence agencies, Yeni Fikir and other youth organizations were not successful in raising turnout, which dropped to 46 percent according to official results.[34]

The media were largely controlled by the regime. Observers estimate that the state-owned and "public" TV outlets devoted approximately 79 percent of their coverage to regime candidates. The few independent journals and newspapers of the opposition had limited circulation, and their editors and journalists often suffered beatings or harassment. Although the government remained in firm control of the broadcast media and also published numerous daily newspapers, there was greater diversity in the print media, and the opposition had access to several print outlets. The opposition paper *Yeni Musavat*, in fact, had the largest daily circulation (14,350) in 2003, a figure nearly twice that of the two state newspapers (*Khalg*, which had a daily circulation of 6,615, and *Azerbaijan*, with 7,534). *Azadliq*, another opposition outlet, had a daily circulation of 5,610.[35] Radio Free Europe analysts note, however, that because most of the population cannot afford the papers and most lack advertising, newspapers without state subsidies are usually published in only a few thousand copies. A public opinion poll cited by *Baku Today* found that less than 3 percent of the population read newspapers regularly; 70.8 percent read them rarely or not at all. Most Azeris get information about public events from the broadcast media, which were and are firmly under the control of the regime.[36]

The opposition in Azerbaijan had access to the electronic media, although Internet usage by the population remained limited, particularly outside the capital. In 2006, only 9.8 per 100 people used the Internet in Azerbaijan, and broadband subscribers numbered 0.03 per 100 people.[37] Ownership of personal computers was also low, only 2.3 per 100 persons in 2006.[38] The regime limited its opponents' use of the Internet to mobilize supporters by controlling the content of materials posted and the opposition's access.[39] There was a 50 percent increase in the number of people with mobile phones between 2004 and 2005 (from 18 to 27 per 100).[40] Mobile phone use in Azerbaijan was higher in 2004, 2005, and 2006 than in Armenia, similar to that in Georgia, and lower than that in Belarus and Ukraine.

Earlier Attempts

In contrast to the situation in several of the countries in which oppositions successfully used elections to oust autocrats, there was no single incident or series of incidents that demonstrated, as happened elsewhere, that the regime had so overstepped its boundaries as to be intolerable. Thus, unlike the situation in Serbia before 2000, where Milosevic was imprisoning members of the youth group Otpor as young as 12, or in Ukraine, where the murder of journalist Hrihoryi Gongadze and poisoning of Viktor Yushchenko illustrated the desperation of the regime and led many citizens to agree with the slogans It's Enough! and Time for a Change, in Azerbaijan the regime's level of repression remained relatively constant. Although it reacted violently against demonstrators at a June rally it permitted, the fact that it had allowed the demonstration to take place was viewed by certain outside observers at least as a sign of movement in the right direction. This lack of a precipitating event in turn made the opposition's task of mobilizing citizens to vote and to vote against the regime more difficult.

Nonetheless, as occurred in many of the cases in which the mobilization of citizens around elections succeeded in ousting semi-authoritarian leaders, the 2005 elections were preceded by earlier efforts to bring about democratic change in Azerbaijan. In the 2003 presidential elections, the opposition considered running a single candidate. However, the surprise addition of Ilham Aliyev as a second candidate in addition to his father for the YAP and Heydar's illness threw a new factor into the race. Some in the opposition felt that it would be easy to defeat Ilham. Isa Gambar, head of the Musavat party, termed the situation "original," and, along with Ali Karimli, head of the People's Front movement, and Etibar Mammadov, head of the Azerbaijan Istimal Party, claimed at least publicly to believe that confusion over the future of the regime and the presence of two candidates would split the ruling party and lead to an opposition victory. Others, however, argued that the structure of Heydar's regime would still be in place and would secure a victory for Ilham. Spokespersons for YAP disclaimed any problem with the dual candidates and adopted the slogan Two Candidates, One Campaign.[41]

Eight other candidates, including seven from opposition parties, eventually ran for president in 2003. Leaders of several of these parties met in London but decided not to run a single candidate. Rather, they agreed to support the candidate who garnered the most votes in what they anticipated would be the second round of the election. In the end, however, there was no second round, and Ilham was elected in elections that were widely condemned as not meeting the standards of the international community.

As it would in 2005, the Aliyev regime used intimidation and force against opposition leaders. Rallies and meetings with voters on the outskirts of Baku were broken up, and on several occasions police and other regime supporters (described frequently as "athletically built people" in civilian clothes) clashed with opposition supporters, with resulting serious injuries to supporters and some leaders. Widespread interference with the efforts of opposition leaders to post their materials or meet with voters continued throughout the campaign.[42]

Immediately after the election, a planned march and peaceful protest organized by opposition leaders led to violent clashes between police and opposition supporters in which many citizens were injured. The violence in turn was used by the Aliyev regime as an excuse for a massive crackdown on the opposition and the arrest of opposition leaders, including many at local levels. In addition, numerous election observers who refused to sanction the fraud they witnessed by signing documents that the elections had been free and fair and some civil society leaders were also arrested. Human rights groups called on Western leaders and the EU to protest the violation of political and civil liberties. Although the detainees and political prisoners were eventually released, the restrictions on public activity by the opposition remained in effect until the approach of the 2005 election. The impact of the crackdown and Ilham's consolidation of his own power after the death of his father in December 2003 set back the development of both the political opposition and civil society considerably.

After the 2005 elections, the opposition remained fragmented and conflicted about its role and how best to proceed. Marginalized by regime harassment and propaganda and forced to work in very difficult conditions, opposition leaders also were bitter about what they perceived to be the ambiguous stance of the United

States and other Western governments concerning the irregularities evident in the election and the regime in general.

EXTERNAL FACTORS

Numerous international actors influenced or attempted to influence the outcome of the 2005 elections in Azerbaijan. These included the US and other Western governments, the European Union, the Organization for Security and Cooperation in Europe and other international election monitoring bodies, and Western NGOs. Activists and "graduates" of the successful use of elections and protest to oust autocrats attempted to share their experiences and tactics, and the example of successful popular mobilizations elsewhere in the postcommunist region was an important inspiration for the opposition. Multinational corporations, by their investments in Azerbaijan's resource sector, also played a role, albeit indirectly.

As in previous elections, Western governments, including that of the United States, urged the Azeri government to take steps to ensure free and fair elections. President George W. Bush's statement during a May 2005 visit to Georgia—"Now, across the Caucasus, in Central Asia and the broader middle East, we see the same desire for liberty burning in the hearts of young people. They are demanding their freedom—and *they will have it*"[43]—was believed by many in Azerbaijan to be a signal to the Azerbaijani government that it must hold free and fair elections.[44] Some of the approximately 10,000 protestors who demonstrated in Baku in early June to call for free elections, for example, carried slogans addressing Bush.[45] US ambassador to Azerbaijan Reno Harnish stated that Washington would "issue a comprehensive warning" to the Central Election Committee and the Azerbaijani authorities if any attempt were made to falsify the vote.[46] On a visit to Azerbaijan in the summer of 2005, Madeleine Albright carried a similar message: that the Central Electoral Commission needed to be truly independent and ensure that elections were free and fair.[47] Ambassador Harnish noted in July 2005 that Washington was conducting talks with the authorities and the opposition to promote what he called a "new, evolutionary model of political change" in Azerbaijan that would allow the opposition to hold up to a third of the seats in parliament and would involve cooperation between opposition deputies and the more liberal members of the YAP.[48]

The US Agency for International Development implemented a variety of programs aimed at strengthening political parties, voter education, and support for independent media, as well as anticorruption and rule of law programs. Overall, however, USAID funding for democracy and governance programs in Azerbaijan has been lower than levels of funding in many other post-Soviet states. Azerbaijan was the recipient of official development aid, which totaled $224,500,000 in

2005.[49] Official aid was used primarily for economic and social development. Some funds were also used for government capacity building. Official aid gave priority to economic reform and the strengthening of government institutions. At the same time, USAID implemented a variety of programs aimed at political parties, voter education, and independent media. USAID also provided broadcast transmitters to seven regional TV stations.[50] In 2005 the agency focused on activities to ensure free and fair elections. Activities funded included training of political parties and domestic observers, a pilot exit poll during the municipal elections, and a national exit poll during the legislative elections. In 2004 USAID spent $38,782,000 on democracy, conflict, and humanitarian assistance. Its budget for civil society programs in Azerbaijan in 2004 and 2005 was $5,900,000 and $6,470,000 respectively, compared to $93,406,000 in Armenia, $94,339,000 in Ukraine, and $73,657,000 in Georgia. Its spending on democracy and governance programs actually decreased in Azerbaijan in 2005 to $3,735,500. Although USAID aid for these purposes also decreased in Armenia and Ukraine in 2005, the amounts ($74,938,000 and $81,250,000) remained substantially higher than those spent in Azerbaijan and increased significantly in Georgia to $10,850,000.[51]

The EU has been the main provider of aid to Azerbaijan: it granted 15 million euros to Azerbaijan for 2004–5 under the Tacis National Action Programme for support for institutional, legal, and administrative reform; private-sector and economic development; and the Institutional Building Partnership–Civil Society (IBPP) and Policy Advice (PAP), which were to be instruments for the preparation of further administrative reforms.[52] The EU decided to include Azerbaijan as well as Armenia and Georgia in the European Neighborhood Policy in 2004 and began the process of negotiating an action plan with each in 2005. Human rights groups hoped that Azerbaijan's inclusion in the ENP would provide the EU with leverage to improve respect for human and political rights in Azerbaijan.[53]

The Office for Security and Co-operation in Europe / Office for Democratic Institutions and Human Rights (OSCE/ODIHR) provided approximately 670 long- and short-term observers to monitor the 2005 elections. Observers noted some improvement in the preelection period regarding candidate registration, meeting of deadlines by the Central Election Commission (CEC) in regard to technical preparations, voter education campaigns by the CEC, and the decision to use invisible ink to mark voters' fingers, among others. The OSCE/ODIHR report also noted that candidates were able to make use of free airtime and hold rallies with their supporters, although "many" opposition rallies were prevented or restricted by the regime. Overall, the report noted that significant irregularities were observed in 13 percent of polling stations observed and concluded that the elections overall did not meet OSCE and other international standards for democratic elections.[54] The

OSCE/ODIHR mission observed similar irregularities in the repeat elections held in May 2006 in the 10 districts in which the Central Election Commission and the Constitutional Court invalidated the November 2005 results.[55]

Numerous private and semigovernmental foundations provided aid to Azerbaijan. These included the Soros Foundation, the International Foundation for Electoral Systems (IFES), the National Democratic Institute (NDI), and the International Republican Institute (IRI), which funded activities related to democracy promotion as well as others that implemented projects related to socioeconomic development, community building, education, health, and refugee issues. The latter included the Eurasia Foundation, CHF International, Counterpart International, the Foundation for International Community Assistance (FINCA), the International Red Cross and Red Crescent, the International Health Group, the International Medical Corps, the International Finance Corporation, International Relief and Development (IRD), Pathfinder International, Relief International, World Hope International, UNDP, Transparency International, World Vision International, Oxfam, and Save the Children.[56]

Election monitor and observer training and voter education topped the list of activities funded by the Open Society Institute (OSI), IFES, NDI, and IRI in Azerbaijan before the 2005 elections. IRI claims to have trained 900 local election observers, and OSI about half of that number through its grants to several local NGOs.[57] IFES's activities included efforts to promote change in the election code through work with the presidential apparatus and the Central Election Committee, together with the Council of Europe's Venice Commission and the OSCE/ODIHR. IFES also focused on capacity building at the Central Election Committee and work on the national voter registry,[58] and provided comprehensive election and voter education training to 48 young people from seven regions with the expectation that they would transfer their knowledge to their communities through small projects.[59] These preelection activities were very meager compared to IFES's activities before the 2003 presidential elections when it had trained approximately 10,000 election officials sitting on electoral commissions at the precinct, district, and central levels.[60]

International NGOs also focused on get-out-the-vote activities and fighting voters' alienation from the political system in the preelection period. One of the goals of the civil society program of OSI for 2005, for example, was to "streamline the atmosphere of frustration and depression in public sentiments in order to keep people still believing in their ability to influence the democratization process."[61] IFES in turn carried out a special voter education program designed to motivate those groups supposedly least likely to vote: youth, women, people with disabilities, and internally displaced people.[62] None of these four organizations carried out parallel vote tabulation during the elections, but OSI supported such activity for the additional elections held May 16 for the 10 constituencies where the vote was annulled.[63] All of these organizations organized some preelection activities in rural areas, but none had a program covering all of the rural regions of Azerbaijan, with the exception of IRI's campaign-training programs. IRI reports indicate that it provided message development, get-out-the-vote tactics, leadership, door-to-door canvassing, and media training for "over 1400 participants from the election headquarters of representatives of both ruling and opposition political parties, as well as independent candidates."[64]

Many of the programs of private, semiofficial organizations focused on civil society and the NGO sector. The Soros Foundation funded three main sets of programs: civil society, education, and information technologies. The civil society programs included projects focused on increasing transparency concerning oil revenues, media building, gender, health, civil society, electoral monitoring, rule of law, judiciary/courts, legal aid, decentralization and aid to local government, fundamental freedoms advocacy, and art.[65]

We do not have complete data on the total amount these groups spent in Azerbaijan before the 2005 elections, but it appears that aid for civil society development was smaller than the $224.5 million official development aid spent on economic development and strengthening of the government apparatus.[66] The Soros Foundation, for example, which was the largest of the nonofficial donors focused on civil society building, spent $140,411 on projects related to law, $118,449 on media projects, and $47,525 on projects to strengthen civil society in 2001. In addition, the foundation spent $136,281 on women's empowerment projects and $92,085 on cooperation among NGOs in former communist countries. Total aid to civil society, including the latter activities, amounted to $543,751.[67] Between 2001 and 2005, the organization's total grants budget in Azerbaijan increased from $1,678,107 to $2,196,530.[68]

The National Endowment for Democracy (NED) focused its programs on support for groups such as the Azerbaijan Lawyers Association and think tanks such as the FAR Center for Economic and Political Research, which monitored religious freedom. It undertook campaigns to increase awareness of electoral rights and civil education and conducted public opinion polls. The NED instituted an Election Monitoring Center to inform the public about the electoral process and to produce radio and television announcements encouraging voters to participate in the elections; the Azerbaijan Foundation for the Development of Democracy, which sponsored debates among candidates and seminars for monitors and members of the electoral commissions and conducted a public opinion poll; and several other groups that encouraged voter turnout and sponsored civic education programs.

NED also supported development of the NGO sector and youth groups and provided funds for *Azadliq*, the country's oldest independent newspaper, to publish a report on human rights violations and the abuse of power before the 2004 municipal elections. NED funding for programs in Azerbaijan was $220,594 in 2000; $159,750 in 2001; $284,292 in 2002; $411,988 in 2003; $434,766 in 2004; and $525,506 in 2005.[69]

IRI's programs focused on political party development and campaign assistance, election surveys, women's empowerment, and youth involvement in politics. IRI officials put particular emphasis before the 2005 elections on encouraging party leaders to take their message to the voters in face-to-face meetings and door-to-door canvassing. Many party leaders resisted these methods, which were unusual in Azeri politics.[70] NDI's projects focused on many of the same issues, including civil society development, training for political party leaders, and election reform and monitoring. NDI also sponsored projects to increase women's empowerment and election monitoring.

As noted, the work of international NGOs in Azerbaijan before the 2005 elections was not easy. NDI came into conflict with the authorities during 2005 for funding youth groups.[71] IRI's relations with the government were also poor, and its Azerbaijan director was killed in 2000 under suspicious circumstances.[72]

INTERACTION OF EXTERNAL AND DOMESTIC FACTORS

The Orange and Rose Revolutions influenced the strategies of several opposition groups in 2005, particularly the youth organizations.[73] Several opposition leaders, including Isa Gambar, traveled to Ukraine to observe the 2004 events firsthand and were clearly aware of the lessons of these events. He and other opposition leaders explicitly referred to the Ukrainian developments as part of their strategy before the 2005 elections.[74]

Pora activists attempted to come to Azerbaijan to train Yeni Fikir supporters, only to be turned away by the authorities at the border. Knowledge of the activities and strategies of youth groups in other, successful, democratizing elections, however, was evident among the young activists in Azerbaijan, including those of Yeni Fikir.[75]

In their attempts to reach voters, opposition and NGO activists employed many of the same techniques used in other attempts to unseat autocrats by elections. Some of these, such as the orange t-shirts and orange flags, were taken directly from the experience of other successful electoral challenges, in this case, in Ukraine. Parties also sold or distributed other resistance symbols, such as badges and bandanas with YeS and Azadliq symbols to ordinary citizens.[76] These do not appear to have been as ubiquitous in Azerbaijan as in Serbia, Ukraine, Georgia, or Slovakia, however, where opposition logos, posters, t-shirts, and slogans were evident in massive numbers and played an important role in spreading awareness of the opposition campaign and gaining new supporters. Some of the posters prepared for protests were in English and addressed the US president: "Help us, Mr. Bush!"; and "Mr. Bush, do not lose a friendly Muslim country!"[77]

Just as the opposition drew lessons from Ukrainian and Georgian developments, Aliyev also took steps to consolidate his power and prevent any challenges similar to those that occurred in Ukraine in 2004 or Georgia in 2003 before the 2005 elections. As noted earlier, in October he dismissed several members of the government and had others arrested on charges that they had misused state funds, organized riots, and plotted a coup, lest they become potential rivals. Aliyev also took action against mass mobilization by the opposition, even going so far as to have police officers confiscate orange material in shopping centers in Baku in order to prevent the opposition, which had chosen it as the color of its campaign in reference to the Orange Revolution in Ukraine, from using it.[78] Youth activists were detained and accused of working with the Armenian intelligence services or accepting funding from foreigners to overthrow the government.[79] The government broke up meetings opposition candidates attempted to hold with their supporters and beat and arrested opposition supporters who tried to hold a rally in Baku in October before the election. Members of the opposition party were detained, and 27 were seriously injured at a rally organized by the Azadliq.

The regime also clearly had the Georgian case in particular in mind. Shortly before the elections, the minister of the interior stated in a widely publicized television appearance: "I am warning all those forces out there who hope to see a change in Azerbaijan. Azerbaijan is not Georgia. Our government is very well prepared to handle unrest."[80] As in Armenia, the regime painted a very negative picture of Georgia after the ouster of Shevardnadze, frequently referring to the "chaos" and alleging that living standards had declined.[81]

International organizations and outside governments did have some influence on the regime's behavior before the 2005 elections. As the result of a last-minute decision on the part of Aliyev in response to outside pressure, NGO activists and some youth leaders were able to act as election observers during the elections. Along with international observers, domestic election monitors documented numerous violations of proper procedure, complaints that eventually led to the invalidation of the results and new elections in a few constituencies.[82]

Again, because of international pressure, including that by the EU's Venice Commission, the regime agreed to some changes in the Election Code before the 2005 elections. Most of these were largely cosmetic and involved minor changes in wording. As the OSCE Final Opinion on the Amendments to the Election Code of Azerbaijan noted, "Unfortunately, the most important suggestions have not been implemented by the authorities of Azerbaijan in spite of the repeated recommendations from the Parliamentary Assembly and the Committee of Ministers of the Council of Europe. The adopted amendments . . . reflect the recommendations of 2004 only to a limited degree, dealing mostly with technical and minor issues."[83] The Election Commission agreed to maintain a Web site and publish lists of voters, without their addresses. But the commission remained under the control of those loyal to Aliyev and did not play an independent role.

In May 2005 the Aliyev government acknowledged certain mistakes in the conduct of elections and proposed steps to overcome problems resulting from a "post-Soviet mentality." In June 2005 the government yielded to international pressure and allowed the opposition to organize a rally in the Baku suburbs, the first officially permitted opposition rally since the 2003 presidential elections. However, these rallies could be held only for short periods of time and generally only outside the capital. In general, the opposition followed the procedure the government required for holding demonstrations. Thus, they organized peaceful protests outside of Baku, shortly after the November 2005 elections, which drew approximately 20,000 people. Another 30,000 protested at a similar rally held on November 19.[84] However, opposition leaders and participants in authorized demonstrations also suffered intimidation and, on occasion, beatings and detention. On November 26, 2005, Lala Shovket and Ali Karimli called on citizens at a protest that had been approved in Baku to remain where they were after the end of the approved time period. This demonstration was brutally repressed by the police, and numerous demonstrators were injured.[85] In October the government enacted certain measures, including lifting the ban on NGOs with substantial foreign support and lifting limitations on domestic election observers to comply with external demands, at least on the surface. However, these measures appear to have had little impact on the elections.

Support from external actors was critical for NGO activities related to the election. Before the election, numerous NGOs funded by outside actors engaged in activities to increase voter awareness, improve the quality of political party platforms and election monitoring, and monitor the media. The National Endowment for Democracy, for example, supported six regional resource centers that provided office support and informational resources for NGOs and activists, as well as the Election Monitoring Center and the Support Center for Democratic Elections to produce informative television and print materials about the rules and regulations governing the electoral process. NED also assisted the Azerbaijan Lawyers Association and the Azerbaijan Foundation for Development of Democracy in providing legal assistance to voters and candidates.[86] The Open Society Institute supported nine local NGOs to train voters and observers on their rights, and another nine local NGOs to monitor election legislation amendments and the securing of election rights. OSI also funded educational projects on elections run by local NGOs in four rural regions, three of which targeted youth.[87] Another local NGO, the Najafov Foundation, was also involved in preelection media monitoring.[88]

Despite its backing of Armenia in the conflict in Nagorno-Karabagh, Russia was an important player in Azerbaijan. Although the country's first two post-Soviet leaders had refused to become part of the Commonwealth of Independent States (CIS) that succeeded the Soviet Union, Heydar Aliyev brought Azerbaijan into that group. One of his first decisions, in fact, was to create a 10 percent share for Russian Lukoil in oil exploration at the expense of Azerbaijan's State Oil consortium.[89] All of the opposition leaders interviewed for this project and independent experts agreed that Russia had a strong interest in the maintenance of Azerbaijan's current regime, which defends and balances Russia's interest against Western influence in the country.[90] Opposition leaders in Azerbaijan are convinced that Russia provided diplomatic and unofficial support to the Aliyev government in falsifying the elections and suppressing mass protests.[91] These claims are supported by the report of the CIS election monitoring team and the subsequent strengthening of relations between the two countries.[92] Vladimir Putin visited Azerbaijan in February 2006, two months after the repression of postelection protests in Baku. During his visit, Putin congratulated Ilham Aliyev on the outcome of the 2005 elections and discussed improving the strategic and trade partnership between the two countries.[93]

Azerbaijan also had significant economic linkages to Russia at the time of the 2005 elections. Lack of publicly available data before 2006 makes assessing the degree of this linkage difficult; analysts estimate that Russia ranked third after Turkey and the United States in trade with Azerbaijan in 2005.[94] In 2006, after the elections, Russia was the largest single trading partner of Azerbaijan, after the EU, but before Turkey and the United States. In that year, trade with Russia accounted for 13 percent of Azerbaijan's total external trade, while trade with Turkey and the United States accounted for 6.6 and 2 percent, respectively.[95] Thus, either analysts underestimated Russia's share of Azerbaijan's trade in 2005, or there was a substantial increase in Russian-Azerbaijan bilateral trade after 2005.

As noted earlier, Western governments, including that of the United States, called for free and fair elections and used diplomacy and normative pressure and urged the Azeri government to take steps to ensure free and fair elections. However, despite the strong statements of President Bush and other leaders before the elections, the actual pressure exerted on the government in connection with the 2005 elections by the United States and other outside actors appears to have been minimal. Security and energy considerations have led the United States and other Western democracies to soft-pedal their criticisms of the regimes of both Heydar and Ilham Aliyev and moderate their statements concerning electoral irregularities. As former US ambassador Richard Miles noted in a 2009 interview, the United States kept in contact with Heydar Aliyev throughout the Elchibey period and found him easier to deal with than the fragmented fledgling democratic government.[96] Miles also noted the role the United States played in encouraging the establishment of the energy consortium that opened up Azeri oil and natural gas and thus provided the economic foundation for Heydar Aliyev's rule.[97]

A USAID report on the agency's activities in the country in the period leading up to the 2005 elections captures the US perspective shortly after Ilham Aliyev's election: "Since independence," it notes, "Azerbaijan has experienced a number of upheavals that have impeded its democratic progress. Political turbulence in the early 1990s made it difficult for democracy to take root. The new Ilham Aliyev government, which came to power in 2003, appears to be more open to democratic reform."[98] The report also reflects another critical aspect of the US approach to democratic development in Azerbaijan: "USAID has made great efforts to forge constructive relationships with the government and our implementing partners in order to bring the benefits of economic growth and political pluralism to an ever-increasing proportion of the Azerbaijani population."[99] The unwillingness of the United States and its allies to rock the boat in Azerbaijan, given other security, strategic, and energy considerations, was also evident in the comment of as a US foreign service officer interviewed in Baku in March 2007: "Why should we support regime change in Azerbaijan? The regime here has been a good friend of the United States."[100]

US evaluations of the 2005 elections noted irregularities but also progress from previous elections in certain areas but did not call for new elections.[101] When the Constitutional Court of Azerbaijan confirmed the results announced by the Central Election Committee (considered falsified by the observers and the polls) and annulled the election results in 10 constituencies (including the mandate of two key opposition candidates from these districts), the US Embassy issued a statement the next day congratulating the Constitutional Court for canceling the election results and expressing "optimism about working with newly elected members of parliament."[102]

Azeri opposition leaders protested the lack of the promised "harsh response" to the falsification of the election results, which they attributed to the US need for oil and the support of Azerbaijan's government because of the country's proximity to Iran.[103] In a meeting at the headquarters of the Azerbaijan Popular Front party after the elections between the US ambassador, the leaders of Azadliq, Lala Shovket, and Ali Karimli, Karimli noted that the US Embassy had welcomed changes in his constituency twice: once when the Central Election Commission named him the winner and once when the Constitutional Court overturned that decision.[104] Lala Shovket publicly asked, "Why is freedom and democracy not a top priority in Azerbaijan? . . . Is it because we are not Christian? . . . Or is it because we have oil?"[105]

There was no US pressure after the violent suppression of mass protests after the elections. Before the Constitutional Court of Azerbaijan approved the election results, the US Embassy expressed hope regarding the government's commitment to democratization. The official US statement applauded the decision of the Constitutional Court to annul the results in several constituencies in which fraud had occurred and urged the government to take additional action to address the concerns of the international community. However, it did not condemn the government's use of violence against peaceful protesters or deplore the violation of their human rights.[106]

Thus, US and other Western diplomats hinted at closer relations with Baku if the 2005 elections were free and fair, but they did not threaten the regime with concrete sanctions if they were not. Nor did they impose such penalties when the regime falsified the election. Competing foreign policy priorities, including security issues, the war in Iraq, and energy needs influenced these actions in the case of the United States and may have also influenced those of European countries.

European countries, through the Council of Europe, attempted to use normative sanctions to influence the regime, but to little effect. Thus, although several of the recommendations of the Venice Commission intended to improve the quality of voter participation in the elections and prevent fraud, such as the inking of fingers of voters, were adopted by the Aliyev regime, they proved to be ineffective in influencing the outcome, that is, in preventing widespread falsification of results or the intimidation of the opposition and its supporters.[107]

Both the United States and Europe tried to use democratic conditionality to influence the behavior of the regime. However, the "carrots" or benefits to be gained were diffuse, and the consequences of not complying with outside calls for free and fair elections were limited. The EU, for example, could not use a tool it used very effectively to encourage regime change in Slovakia and Croatia, the promise of eventual EU membership.[108] Similarly, given the country's scores (political rights, 37%; civil liberties, 41%; control of corruption, 18%; government effectiveness, 24%; rule of law, 48%; voice and accountability, 32%), the United States could not promise the possibility of participation in the Millennium Challenge.[109]

But the most important limit on the effectiveness of efforts to use democratic conditionality in Azerbaijan were two other factors we have discussed previously.

These were first, the limited interest of the US and other Western governments in seeing regime change in Azerbaijan, given the perceived value of stability in that country and the "good ally" reputation of the Aliyev regime, at least among US officials. Thus, the verbal support of President Bush and others for free and fair elections and the implicit threat of loss of the possibility of better relations with the United States were not credible to the regime, given other US interests and priorities. Second, the very high cost to Aliyev and those surrounding him of regime change also limited the ability of outside actors to use conditionality to support a democratic transition. In the face of the economic benefits they would have lost and likely threats to their personal security should they have allowed free and fair elections in which the opposition had a chance at defeating them, it is not clear what benefits outside actors would have had to offer the Aliyev leadership to have had a real influence on regime actions.

CONCLUSION

Despite the hopes of some in the opposition that Azerbaijan would experience a democratic breakthrough similar to those that happened in several other post-communist states, the 2005 elections did not lead to a regime transition. There are several explanations for this failure. As numerous scholars have pointed out, one of the preconditions for a democratic transition by way of elections is a vulnerable autocrat. Many analysts argue that Ilham Aliyev would have been likely to have won the 2003 presidential elections, and his party the 2005 parliamentary elections, even if they had been free and fair, though by a smaller margin than the "official" results. The regime's ability to buy the support of the country's business elite because of petrodollars, the clan ties that link politicians and others, and the role the government plays in providing employment all served to co-opt potential opposition to the regime. The government's control of most media outlets, as well as of the police and army, and Ilham's preemptive moves against potential rivals within the leadership further insulated the regime from challenge. And, as the numerous attacks on the opposition before and in the course of the election campaign illustrated, the regime did not hesitate to defend its interests with force against its opponents.

The threat to Aliyev and chances of a democratic victory were further reduced by the nature of the opposition. The opposition did learn from successful uses of elections to oust semi-authoritarian leaders in other postcommunist countries to some degree by 2005. Thus, there was a united opposition that cooperated in the election campaign. But, many of the leaders of the opposition were tainted in the public eye by association with the government that "lost" Karabagh. Former government officials themselves in some cases, they were also suspect because of the opportunities they were perceived to have had to pilfer public resources and suspicions that their chief aim in running for office was to have such opportunities again. In addition, the opposition parties were small, with poor organizational development and weak links to the population, particularly outside the capital. The opposition also lacked a figure capable of capturing the popular imagination or articulating a radically different vision of politics. There was no one who could accomplish what Slovak democracy activist Pavol Demes terms the central task of those who seek to use elections to democratize: inspire hope that real change is possible and move ordinary citizens from pessimism and passivity to optimism and action. Imitation parties and pseudo-"independents" who actually supported the regime cluttered the field and further alienated voters from the process.

In addition, there was no broad-based campaign to get out the vote by civil society groups, which were generally very weak. Youth organizations based on the Ukrainian and Georgian models were small and were not able to mobilize large numbers of people. The media remained largely in state hands, and use of cell phones and the Internet, which played important mobilizing roles in Ukraine in particular, was not as widespread.

Azerbaijan also lacked several of the external influences that weakened autocrats and strengthened democrats in successful democratic breakthroughs in postcommunist countries. Chief among these were interest and support for regime change on the part of the United States and European governments. Stability and strategic considerations clearly trumped democratic change as a US goal. There is thus little evidence of the kind of pressure the United States exerted in Ukraine or Georgia on leaders to allow the opposition to assemble and refrain from using force, to say nothing of the proactive course of the United States in ousting Vladimir Meciar in Slovakia in 1998 or Slobodan Milosevic in Serbia 2000. US funding for democracy-related programs and civil society development was relatively modest in Azerbaijan and did not increase markedly in the run up to the 2005 elections. The EU played a similarly cautious role. Despite clear evidence of fraud and failure to heed the prescriptions of international election monitoring bodies before or after the 2005 elections, progress continued on extending the European Neighborhood Policy to Azerbaijan. In both cases, officials noted violation of the procedures for free and fair elections, but criticism was muted and reports also noted improvements in several areas, despite evidence of widespread intimidation and coercion of the opposition and electoral fraud. "Graduates" of previous successful democratizing elections attempted to play a role in Azerbaijan but generally gave less emphasis to activities involving this country than to those in Belarus, for example. Those who did attempt to be active were frequently thwarted by the authorities.

As this brief summary indicates, it is not only factors that weaken autocrats and strengthen the opposition that are important in considering the outcome of elections in countries such as Azerbaijan. As we have argued in other venues, the primary way in which a transition from semi-authoritarian regimes has occurred in the postcommunist world has been through the use of elections and, in some cases, protests centered around flawed elections. In fact, in the postcommunist world, this path, which has involved the full implementation of a specific model of regime change, the electoral model, has been the only one to date that has led to democratic breakthroughs.[110] For postcommunist cases at least, then, the critical issues are those that facilitated or hindered the full application of the electoral model. In Azerbaijan, conditions have not been favorable for the full implementation of this model. On the other hand, there is also little evidence that the hopes of outside actors that gradual, evolutionary change, without the use of this model, will lead to a democratic breakthrough will be fulfilled. A question that can only be posed, rather than answered, is whether the failed attempt to produce a transition in the 2005 elections in Azerbaijan will be just one more in a series of failures or whether it, like failed attempts before the successful use of elections to create democratic breakthroughs in other postcommunist countries, will serve as a dress rehearsal for later efforts that will succeed. The efforts of opposition and youth activists in Azerbaijan to emulate the protests of the Arab Spring in 2011, though harshly repressed by the regime, raise another possibility—that protests not related to elections may eventually produce regime change.

NOTES

1. See Anar M. Valiyev, "Parliamentary Elections in Azerbaijan: A Failed Revolution," *Problems of Postcommunism* 53, no. 3 (May–June 2006): 17–35, for more details.

2. See Leila Alieva, "Azerbaijan's Frustrating Elections," *Journal of Democracy* 17, no. 2 (April 2006): 147–60.

3. See Valiyev, "Parliamentary Elections in Azerbaijan."

4. See Audrey L. Alstadt, "Azerbaijan's Struggle toward Democracy," in Karen Dawisha and Bruce Parrott, eds., *Conflict, Cleavage, and Change in Central Asia and the Caucasus* (New York: Cambridge University Press, 1997), 110–55, for discussion of politics in the early years after independence.

5. See Valiyev, "Parliamentary Elections in Azerbaijan," 18.

6. See ibid., table 2, for these scores from 1996 to 2005.

7. See Valerie Bunce and Sharon Wolchik, "Defeating Dictators: Electoral Change and Stability in Competitive Authoritarian Regimes," *World Politics* 63, no. 1 (January 2010): 43–86, for discussion of the range of regime types that experienced democratizing elections in the postcommunist world between 1998 and 2006.

8. See Zvi Gitelman, "Power and Authority in Eastern Europe," in Chalmers Johnson, ed., *Change in Communist Systems* (Stanford, Calif.: Stanford University Press, 1970), 235–63, for a discussion of the use of these incentives during the communist period.

9. See Valerie Bunce and Sharon Wolchik, "Electoral Revolutions and International Diffusion," *Communist and Post Communist Studies* 39, no. 3 (September 2006): 283–304, for a discussion of the importance of elections in the modern world and the opportunities they provide for popular mobilization and democratization.

10. See Daniel Heradstveit, "Democratic Development in Azerbaijan and the Role of the Western Oil Industry," *Central Asian Survey* 20, no. 3 (2001): 261–88, and Pauline Jones Luong and Erika Weinthal, "Prelude to the Resource Curse: Explaining Oil and Gas Development Strategies in the Soviet Successor States and Beyond," *Comparative Political Studies* 34, no. 4 (May 2001): 367–99.

11. World Bank, "Country Brief 2006: Azerbaijan" (September 2006).

12. Ibid.

13. Ibid., 1.

14. See Human Rights Watch, "Azerbaijan Parliamentary Elections, 2005: Lessons Not Learned," *Human Rights Watch Briefing Paper*, October 31, 2005.

15. World Bank, "Azerbaijan at a Glance," September 2, 2007, 1.

16. World Bank, "Country Brief 2006: Azerbaijan."

17. See Togrul Juvarli and Ali Abasov, "Economic Implications of the Parliamentary Elections: Symbiosis of Politics and Economics," in Stina Torjesen and Indra Øverland, eds., *International Election Observers in Post-Soviet Azerbaijan* (Stuttgart: ibidem-Verlag, 2007), 169–220; Joseph A. Kechichian and Theodore W. Karasik, "The Crisis in Azerbaijan: How Clans Influence the Politics of an Emerging Republic," *Middle East Policy* 4 (1995): 57–71; Nazim Imanov, "Ilk on ilin yekunlari: iqtisadiyyat" [Summary of the First Ten Years: The Economy], in Ali Abasov, ed., *Musteqilliyimizin On Illiyi: ugurlarimiz, itkilerimiz*, trans. Sara Rzayeva (Baku: Yeni Nesil, 2003), 136–50.

18. Baheddin Heziyev, a prominent contributor to the *Azadliq*, opposition, and newspaper, interview, Baku, January 2006.

19. Ibid.

20. Ibid.

21. Juvarli and Abasov, "Economic Implications of the Parliamentary Elections," 169–220.

22. See Alieva, "Azerbaijan's Frustrating Elections."

23. Baku State University professor, interview Baku, January 2006.

24. See Valiyev, "Parliamentary Elections in Azerbaijan," 23.

25. See Swante Cornell, "Democratization Falters in Azerbaijan," *Journal of Democracy* 12, no. 2 (2001): 118–31; and Liz Fuller, "Azerbaijan: Leadership Ignoring Election Pressure," *Radio Free Europe Radio Liberty*, June 29, 2005, www.rferl.org/featuresarticle/2005/06/0794b2b2-2a83-4b9e-b9fl-44445599e8el.html.

26. See Rovshan Ismayilov, "Azerbaijan: Two More Officials Sacked," *EurasiaNet*, October 20, 2005, http://eurasianet.org/departments/civilsociety/articles/eav 102005.shtml; and Liz Fuller, "Azerbaijan: Political Shock Waves Continue," *EurasiaNet*, October 29, 2005, www.eurasianet.org/departmens/insight/articles/ppl02905.shtml.

27. NDI representative, interview, Baku, March 2007.

28. Interviews with Ali Karimli and Ali Aliyev, Baku, January 2006.

29. Karimli and Masimov interviews. Also see Rufat Abbasov and Mina Muradova,

"Azerbaijan: Television Is a Campaign Battleground," *EurasiaNet*, October 28, 2005, www
.eurasianet.org/departments/civilsociety/articles/eav102805a.shtml.

30. Alieva, "Azerbaijan's Frustrating Elections,"153–54.

31. Asim Oku, "Revolution in Azerbaijan May Begin on 21st of August," *Axis Information and Analysis Turkish and Caucasian Section*, August 15, 2005, www.axisglobe.com/article.asp
?article=317.

32. Khadija Ismayilova and Shahin Abbasov, "Young Activists Poised to Assume Higher Political Profile in Azerbaijan," *EurasiaNet*, June 14, 2005, www.eurasianet.org/departments/
insight/articles/eav061405.shtml.

33. Gene Sharp, *From Dictatorship to Democracy: A Conceptual Framework for Liberation*, 4th ed. (East Boston, Mass.: Albert Einstein Institute, 2010).

34. Alieva, "Azerbaijan's Frustrating Elections."

35. Ilgar Khudiyev, "Coverage of the 2003 Post-Election Protests in Azerbaijan: Impact of Media Ownership on Objectivity" (Master's thesis, Manship School of Mass Communication, Louisiana State University), http://etd.lsu.edu/docs/available/etd-11152005–113447/
unrestricted/Khudiyev_thesis.pdf.

36. Liz Fuller, "Azerbaijan: Authorities Intensify Pressures on Independent Media," *Radio Free Europe Radio Liberty*, November 29, 2006, www.rferl.org/content/article/1073092
.html.

37. World Bank, "ICT at a Glance: Azerbaijan," http://devdata.worldbank.org/ict/aze_
ict.pdf.

38. Ibid.

39. See Fuller, "Azerbaijan: Authorities Intensify Pressures on Independent Media"; Open Net Initiative Azerbaijan Report (2007), http://opennet.net/research/profiles/azerbaijan.

40. World Bank, World Development Indicators—WDI online database, www.worldbank
.org/data.

41. See EurasiaNet, "Election Watch: Guide to the Azeri Presidential Elections," October 15, 2003, www.eurasianet.org; and Human Rights Watch, "Azerbaijan: Presidential Elections 2003: Obstruction of Opposition Rallies," *Human Rights Watch Briefing Paper*, October 13, 2003, for more information.

42. See EurasiaNet, "Election Watch"; and Human Rights Watch, "Azerbaijan: Government Launches Crackdown after Election, Hundreds of Opposition Members Arrested," October 22, 2003, www.eurasianet.org.

43. Cited in Haroutiun Khachatrian and Alman Mir-Ismail, "Sizing Up the 'Bush Effect' in Azerbaijan and Armenia," *EurasiaNet*, June 9, 2005, www.eurasianet.org/departments/
insight/articles/eav060905.shtml.

44. Ibid.

45. Natalia Antelava, "Azeri Faith in Opposition Falters," *BBC News*, Baku, November 12, 2005, http://news.bbc.co.uk/1/hi/world/europe/4432254.stm.

46. Fuller, "Azerbaijan: Leadership Ignoring Election Pressure."

47. Antoine Blua, "Azerbaijan: West Maintaining Strong Pressure for Democratic Ballot," *Radio Free Europe Radio Liberty*, July 13, 2005, www.rferl.org/featuresarticle/2005/
07/2ddd2753-76f1-449c-96a1-c05483654efd.html.

48. Liz Fuller, "Azerbaijan: Will the Real Closet Liberals Please Stand Up?" *Eurasia Insight*, July 24, 2005, www.eurasianet.org/departments/insight/articles/pp072405.shtml.

49. World Bank, World Development Indicators—WDI online database, www.world
bank.org/data.

50. USAID, *Country Profile: Azerbaijan,* January 2007.

51. USAID 2006 Assistance Budget for Europe and Eurasia, www.usaid.gov/policy/budget/cbj2006/ee/.

52. European Union: "Azerbaijan Action Program, 2004–2005," http://ec.europa.eu/europeaid/where/neighbourhood/regional-cooperation/enpi-east/documents/annual_programmes/azerbaijan_2004_en.pdf.

53. See Human Rights Watch, "Azerbaijan and the European Neighbourhood Policy," *Human Rights Watch Briefing Paper,* June 15, 2005; and Commission of the European Communities, "European Neighbourhood Policy: Country Report Azerbaijan," *Commission Staff Working Paper,* March 2, 2005.

54. OSCE, Office for Democratic Institutions and Human Rights, "Republic of Azerbaijan. Parliamentary Elections 6 November 2005," *OSCE/ODIHR Election Observation Mission Final Report,* February 1, 2006, 2–3.

55. See OSCE/ODIHR, "Republic of Azerbaijan. Partial Repeat Parliamentary Elections, 13 May 2006," *Annex to the Final Report on the 6 November 2005 Parliamentary Elections,* June 23, 2006.

56. Azerweb, Online Database and Resource Center for the Non-profit Community in Azerbaijan, www.azerweb.com.

57. IRI Azerbaijan Web site, www.iri.org.az/; Information from the Civil Society program of OSI, January 2006.

58. IFES, "Past Projects" Report on Azerbaijan, www.ifes.org/azerbaijan.html?page=past.

59. "Report on Voter Education Activities for the 2005 Parliamentary Elections," IFES Azerbaijan (2005), www.ifesaze.org/pdf/voter/voter_edu_report.pdf.

60. NDI report on Azerbaijan, published on World Movement for Democracy (WMD) Web site, September 15, 2003, www.wmd.org/documents/DemNews-Oct2003/NDIReport1-1010.doc.

61. Fuad Suleymanov, director of the Civil Society Program at OSI-Azerbaijan, interview, January 2006.

62. "Report on Voter Education Activities for the 2005 Parliamentary Elections."

63. Suleymanov interview.

64. IRI activity report, January 2006, www.iri.org.az/pps.php#ot.

65. Open Society Institute Azerbaijan Foundation Web site, www.osi-az.org.

66. World Bank, World Development Indicators—WDI online database, www.worldbank.org/data.

67. Open Society Institute's Latest Online Report (2002), www.osi-az.org/figure.shtml.

68. On the basis of OSI-AF annual public reports for 2001, 2002, 2003, 2004 and 2005, www.osi-az.org.

69. From NED annual reports for the years 2000–5, www.ned.org/publications/publications.html.

70. Dallas Frohrib, IRI, interview, Baku, March 2006.

71. "NDI under fire in Azerbaijan," *Democracy Guy,* August 5, 2005, http://democracyguy.typepad.com/democracy_guy_grassroots_/2005/08/ndi_under_fire_.html.

72. "NDI under fire in Azerbaijan."

73. Yeni Fikir activists, interview, Baku, March 2007.

74. Isa Gambar, interview, Baku, March 2007. See also Human Rights Watch, "Azerbaijan Parliamentary Elections, 2005."

75. Interview with Yeni Fikir activists, Baku, March 2007.

76. Lower level Azadliq bloc member, interview, Baku, January 2006.

77. C. J. Chivers, "Crowd Protests Fraud in Azerbaijan Vote," *New York Times*, November 10, 2005, www.nytimes.com/2005/11/10/international/asia/10azerbaijan.html.

78. Larissa Momryk, "Azerbaijan through Western Eyes," *Ukrainian Weekly*, January 8, 2006, 8.

79. Valiyev, "Parliamentary Elections in Azerbaijan," 24.

80. Ramil Usubov, Minister of the Interior, Azerbaijan state TV (AzTV) news, October 2005.

81. Insaf Intizar, "Xalqa 'pachka,' efire puf, cibe para" (a folk saying, "blowing ashes into one's eyes," that used to indicate distorting or denying what is obvious), *Azadliq*, January 10, 2008, 9.Translated by Sara Rzayeva.

82. See Alieva, "Azerbaijan's Frustrating Elections"; and Valyieva, "Parliamentary Elections in Azerbaijan."

83. OSCE, "Final Opinion on the Amendments to the Election Code of the Republic of Azerbaijan," 2, www.osce.org/documents/odihr/2005/11/16895_en.pdf.

84. Momryk, "Azerbaijan through Western Eyes."

85. See Alieva, "Azerbaijan's Frustrating Elections."

86. National Endowment for Democracy, "Eurasia Program Highlights," www.ned.org/grants/05programs/highlights-eurasia05.html.

87. OSI-AF Azerbaijan Report on the Progress of Election Program, www.osi-az.org/election.shtml.

88. "Azerbaijan's 2005 Elections: Lost Opportunity," Crisis Group Europe Briefing no. 40, November 21, 2005, 5, www.caei.com.ar/es/programas/cei/P09.pdf.

89. Angeliki Spatharou, "Political Role of Oil in Azerbaijan, 1989–1994," *Journal of Southern Europe and the Balkans* 4, no. 1 (May 2002): 29–35.

90. Interviews with Ali Karimli, Lala Shovket, Ali Aliyev, Khaleddin Ibrahimli, Baku, January 2006.

91. Interviews with Ali Karimli, Lala Shovket, Ali Aliyev, Khaleddin Ibrahimli, and Baku State University professor.

92. See Robert Parsons, "Analysis: Putin Seeks to Draw Azerbaijan Back into Russian Orbit," *Radio Free Europe Radio Liberty*, February 21, 2006, www.rferl.org/features article/2006/02/0335ec2e-489b-4be6-b5f0-f52d0c96226b.html.

93. Rovshan Ismayilov "Trade, Investment Take Center Stage at Russia-Azerbaijan Summit," *EurasiaInsight*, February 28, 2006, www.eurasianet.org/departments/business/articles/eav022806.shtml; Parsons, "Analysis: Putin Seeks to Draw Azerbaijan Back into Russian Orbit."

94. See Ismayilov, "Trade, Investment Take Center Stage at Russia-Azerbaijan Summit."

95. Ministry of Economic Development of Azerbaijan, Foreign Trade Report, 2006 (in Azeri),www.economy.gov.az/.

96. Richard Miles, interview, Washington, D.C., September 2009.

97. Ibid.

98. US Agency for International Development, Democracy and Governance: Azerbaijan, http://azerbaijan.usaid.gov/sehife.php?lang=eng&page=0201.

99. Ibid.

100. US foreign service officer, interview, US Embassy, Baku, March 2007.

101. Adam Ereli, deputy spokesman for the US Government, "Azerbaijan Parliamentary Elections," US Official Press Statement no. 2005/1047 (Washington, D.C., November 7, 2005), www.state.gov/r/pa/prs/ps/2005/56574.htm.

102. Rovshan Ismayilov, "Azerbaijan Opposition Charges US with 'Double Standards,'" *EurasiaNet*, December 7, 2005, www.eurasianet.org/departments/insight/articleseav120705 .shtml.

103. Interviews with Ali Karimli, Lala Shovket, Ali Aliyev, Khaleddin Ibrahimli.

104. Ismayilov, "Azerbaijan Opposition Charges US with 'Double Standards.'"

105. C. J. Chivers, "Police Break Up Peaceful Demonstration in Azerbaijan," *New York Times*, November 27, 2005, www.nytimes.com/2005/11/27/international/asia/27azer.html?.

106. Sean McCormack, spokesman for the US Government, "Azerbaijan Elections," US Official Press Statement no. 2005/1128 (Washington, D.C., December 2, 2005).

107. "Azerbaijan's 2005 Elections: Lost Opportunity."

108. Milada Anna Vachudova, *Europe Undivided: Democracy, Leverage, and Integration after Communism* (Oxford: Oxford University Press, 2005). Also see Valerie J. Bunce and Sharon L. Wolchik, "Defining and Domesticating the Electoral Model: A Comparison of Slovakia and Serbia," in Valerie J. Bunce, Kathryn Stoner-Weiss, and Michael McFaul, eds., *Waves and Troughs in Communist and Post-Communist Europe and Eurasia* (Cambridge: Cambridge University Press, 2009).

109. Millennium Challenge Corporation, Azerbaijan Report, www.mcc.gov/selection/ scorecards/2004/score_fy04_azerbaijan.pdf.

110. See Valerie Bunce and Sharon Wolchik, "Favorable Conditions and Electoral Revolutions," *Journal of Democracy* 17, no. 4 (October 2006): 5–18.

Contributors

EDITORS

Kathryn Stoner, Stanford University

Michael McFaul, Stanford University; and Senior Director for Russia and Eurasia, National Security Council, US Government, 2009–11; United States Ambassador to Russia, 2011

CONTRIBUTING AUTHORS

A. David Adesnik, American Enterprise Institute, Washington, D.C.

David Altman, Political Science Institute, Pontificia Universidad Católica, Chile

Edward Aspinall, Australian National University

Senem Aydın-Düzgit, Istanbul Bilgi University, Turkey

Valerie J. Bunce, Cornell University

Larry Diamond, Stanford University

Alberto Diaz-Cayeros, University of California, San Diego

Gregory F. Domber, University of North Florida

Desha Girod, Georgetown University

Yaprak Gürsoy, Istanbul Bilgi University, Turkey

Antoinette Handley, University of Toronto, Canada

Ray Salvatore Jennings, Visiting Researcher, Center on Democracy, Development and the Rule of Law, Stanford University

Kristina Kausch, FRIDE, Spain

Sunhyuk Kim, University of Southern California

Beatriz Magaloni, Stanford University

Marcus Mietzner, Australian National University

Abbas Milani, Stanford University

Minxin Pei, Claremont-McKenna College

Rafael Piñeiro, Political Science Institute, Pontificia Universidad Católica, Chile

Timothy D. Sisk, Josef Korbel School of International Studies, University of Denver

Sergio Toro, Political Science Institute, Pontificia Universidad Católica, Chile

Sharon L. Wolchik, George Washington University

Richard Youngs, FRIDE, Spain

Index

Atatürk, Mustafa Kemal, 292
Atwood, Brian, 55
Aurora Foundation, 76
Austria, 303
Aydın-Düzgit, Senem, 12, 290–315
Aylwin, Patricio, 194, 212
Azadliq, 408, 415
Azerbaijan, 13, 400–428; authoritarianism
   in, 401, 402; civil society organizations in,
   407–8, 417–18, 422; clan hierarchies in,
   403–4, 405, 421; communist era in, 404; corruption in, 21, 403–4, 422; democracy indices
   in, 401–2; economy of, 402–3; elections in, 15,
   400, 406, 407–8, 409–11, 412–13, 419, 421;
   electoral fraud in, 21, 400, 402, 406, 410,
   420, 422; Europeans and, 411, 412, 416–17,
   420, 422; failed democratic transition in,
   400, 421–23; international election monitors
   in, 412–13, 416; international NGOs and,
   411, 413–14, 415; media in, 16, 402, 408–9;
   military and security forces in, 405; and
   Nagorno-Karabagh conflict, 401, 405–6, 407,
   418, 421; and oil, 18, 401, 421; political opposition in, 406–7, 410–11, 417, 419–20, 421, 422;
   repression and coercion in, 404–5, 409, 410,
   420; and Russia, 418; US and, 411, 418–20,
   421, 422

Babbitt, Bruce, 201
Baghai, Mozzafer, 352
Bai Hua, 387
Bakhtiyar, Shapour, 344, 357–58, 365
Ball, George, 361, 364
Bangermann, Martin, 89n56
Bani-Sadr, Abol-Hassan, 363, 376n70
Barnes, Harry, 282
Bashirli, Ruslan, 408
Bazorgan, Mehdi, 358, 365, 371, 375n62
BBC (British Broadcasting Corporation), 100,
   124, 359–60, 393
Belhaj, Ali, 323
Berger, Samuel, 60n96
Bessmertnykh, Aleksandr, 40
Biko, Steven, 176
bin Laden, Osama, 8
Black Sash, 183
Blustein, Paul, 154–55, 161
Boafo-Arthur, Kwame, 224, 232, 233
Boakeye, Daniel, 234–35

Boeninger, Edgardo, 203, 207, 213, 217n34
Booth, Anne, 165n16
Botha, Pieter W., 177, 180
Boutros Ghali, Boutros, 183
Bratton, Michael, 228
Brezhnev, Leonid, 30, 43, 47, 366–67
Britain. *See* United Kingdom
Brown, Archie, 58n31
Brynn, Edward, 243n82
Brzezinski, Zbigniew, 142n44, 295–96, 357
Bunce, Valerie J., 13, 109, 400–428
Burns, Nicholas, 60n96
Busch, Andrew, 41
Bush, George H. W. (and administration): and
   China, 394; and Poland, 73–74; and Soviet
   Union, 27, 50–52, 60n92
Bush, George W. (and administration): and
   Azerbaijan, 418, 420; democracy promotion,
   286, 411; and Ukraine, 127, 129, 136
Buthelezi, Mangosutho, 177, 185, 191n57

Cai Ling, 388
Camdessus, Michel, 154
Canada, 125, 206
Canadian International Development Agency
   (CIDA), 103, 231
Cárdenas, Cuauhtémoc, 246, 251, 262
Carothers, Thomas, 22n1, 97
Carrington, Lord, 184
Carter, Jimmy (and administration): and Chile,
   197; and foreign radio broadcasting, 45; and
   human rights, 278, 343, 357, 358, 367–68;
   and Iran, 342, 355, 356, 357, 361, 367–68; and
   Poland, 70; and South Korea, 266, 267, 276,
   277–78; and Soviet Union, 48; and Turkey,
   295, 296
Castillo Velasco, Jaime, 210
Center for Conflict Resolution, 183
Center for Economic Research and Education
   (CIDE, Chile), 209, 218n49
Center for Free Elections and Democracy
   (CeSID), 103, 110, 114
Center for Policy Studies, 183
Center for Social and Economic Studies
   (FECTOR, Chile), 209
Center for Social and Educational Studies (SUR,
   Chile), 209
Center for Socio-Economic Research (ISEC,
   Chile), 209

Özal, Turgut, 291, 293, 298; US support for, 300, 308, 314n78

Pahlavi, Mohammad Reza Shah: authoritarianism of, 345–46, 351–52, 354–55, 360–61, 372n6; conspiracy theories of, 356, 358–59, 360; crushing of opposition by, 351–52, 354, 365–66, 372, 374n30; illness of, 354, 361; on Islam and clergy, 343; modernization program of, 342, 343, 344–45; opposition to democracy by, 342, 344–45; and US, 347, 350–51, 357, 368; and White Revolution, 348, 349, 356

Pamukçu, Sina, 312n21

Pan Africanist Congress (PAC, South Africa), 170, 172, 175

Paris Club, 232, 235

Park Chung Hee, 266, 267, 268, 275, 276

Park Tong Son, 276

Parsons, Anthony, 344, 347

Parta, Eugene, 45

Partido Acción Nacional (PAN, Mexico), 257, 262

Partido Revolucionario Institucional (PRI, Mexico), 245, 246, 261, 264

Pasqua, Charles, 327

Pastrana, Misael, 201

Pathfinder International, 413

Pei, Minxin, 13, 378–99

Pell, Claiborne, 284–85

Pelton, Robert S., 209–10

People's Daily, 378, 385, 387, 397n4

People's Movement Coalition for Democracy and Reunification (PMCDR, South Korea), 272–73

Perez de Cuellar, Javier, 89n56

Pertini, Allessandro, 89n56

Philippines, 16, 147, 280; democratic transition in, 283, 289n50, 390

Pinchuk, Viktor, 127

Piñeiro, Rafael, 192

Pinochet, Augusto, 193, 195, 196, 198

Pinto-Duschinsky, Michael, 206

Pipes, Richard, 43

Poland, 9–10, 62–90; Catholic Church in, 64, 68; civil society organizations in, 18, 64; economy of, 65, 66, 83; elections of 1989 in, 69, 81–82; foreign debt of, 71–72, 79; independent media in, 16, 64, 66, 75–76, 81; international sanctions against, 62–63, 70–71,

77; martial law in, 49, 62, 64–65; release of political prisoners in, 62, 65, 66, 78, 79, 83, 88n53; Round Table negotiations in, 63, 67–69, 79–80; Solidarność-led government in, 69; and Soviet Union, 64, 65, 84; strikes and labor disturbances in, 64, 66–67, 82–83, 84; successful democratic transition in, 19, 63, 77–83; and Ukraine, 126–27, 129, 132, 136; and US, 18, 62–63, 70–78, 80–81, 84, 88n45; and Western Europe, 62–63, 78–79, 83, 89n56

POLCUL, 76

Polish America Congress Charitable Foundation (PACCF), 76

Polish-American Enterprise Fund, 73–74

Polish Helsinki Watch Committee, 76

Polish Legal Defense Fund, 76

Polish United Workers' Party (PZPR), 64, 65, 68; negotiations with opposition by, 64, 67, 68–69, 82; political control and repression by, 62, 67, 84; and political liberalization, 62, 73, 77, 79

Polish Workers Aid Fund (PWAF), 74, 87nn38–39

Pontis Foundation, 110

Popovic, Srdja, 97, 110

Popper, Karl, 360, 375n55

Popular Front Party of Azerbaijan, 406

Pora (Ukraine), 122, 132, 134, 135, 415

Poroshenko, Petro, 124

Prabowo Subianto, 157

Price, Robert M., 181–82

Pridham, Geoffrey, 23n10

Program for Work Economy (PET, Chile), 209

Progressive Circle (Iran), 351–52

Provisional National Defense Council (PNDC, Ghana), 221, 223, 225, 227, 229, 240n23

Prueher, Joseph W., 159

Przeworski, Adam, 116

Puryear, Jeffrey, 209, 212

Putin, Vladimir, 27, 28, 418; and Ukraine, 128–29, 130, 137

Qarani, Valliollah, 347

Radio Free Europe, 17, 18, 20, 44, 408

Radio Liberty, 17, 44, 45, 46, 124

Rafsanjani, Akbar Hashemi, 367, 376n71

Rahnavard, Zahra, 353

Ramphosa, Cyril, 184

Ranjbaran Party (Iran), 369

Rawlings, Jerry, 223–24, 228, 241n40; and
Ghana democratization, 17, 221–22, 223, 225,
235, 236, 238, 243n87; popularity of, 221, 225;
rise and fall of, 223, 227; US and, 232, 243n87

Reagan, Ronald (and administration): military
buildup by, 39–40; and Poland, 62, 70–71;
and South Africa, 181; and South Korea,
266–68, 274, 276, 278–81, 283, 284,
287nn25–26; and Soviet Union, 48–49;
and Turkey, 298, 299–300

Red Crescent, 413

Relief International, 413

Republican People's Party (RPP, Turkey), 292

Resurgence Party (Iran), 354–55, 374n33

Rhee, Syngman, 275

Rice, Condoleezza, 286

Roberts, Kenneth M., 211

Rocard, Michel, 331

Rockefeller Foundation, 206

Roh Tae Woo, 267, 269, 270, 282–83, 285; US
and, 282, 283–84

Romania, 116

Rowland, Paul, 99

Roy, Jayanta, 314n79

Rubin, Robert, 155

Rushdie, Salman, 332

Russia, 8, 9, 27–61, 91–92, 395, 418; autocratic
rollbacks in, 27, 28; conflict between Yeltsin
and parliament in, 37–38; constitution in,
28, 29–30, 35–36, 38, 57n1, 58n22; economic
reforms in, 37, 54; elections in, 17, 38, 58n22;
IMF and, 54, 61n100; sovereignty from Soviet
Union, 35; successful democratic transition
in, 17, 19, 27, 28–30, 55–56; and Ukraine, 126,
128–29, 130, 137; and US, 17, 27, 51, 52–55, 56.
See also Soviet Union

Rutskoi, Aleksandr, 37

Rwanda, 238

Saddam Hussein, 369

Sadighi, Gholam-Hossein, 344, 365

Sakwa, Richard, 36

Salinas de Gortari, Carlos, 262, 263

Samii, Mehdi, 354, 375n57

Sandbrook, Richard, 225

Sanguinetti, Julio María, 202

Sanjabi, Karim, 357–58, 365

Saudi Arabia, 43

Save the Children, 413

Schaff, Adam, 78

Schmitter, Philippe, 6, 23n9

Schoen, Douglas, 99

Schröder, Gerhard, 129

Schweitzer, Peter, 40, 49

Scowcroft, Brent, 51–52

Sejersted, Francis, 184

Serbia, 10, 91–119; alternative media in, 20,
100–102, 107, 113, 115; Bulldozer Revolution
in, 91–92, 117, 131; civil society organizations
in, 16, 102–4; consensus for regime change
in, 91–92, 109, 112; and diffusion, 109–11,
114; direct democracy assistance to, 92,
111–14; elections in, 91, 93–94, 95–96,
99, 107, 117; ethnic chauvinism in, 91, 93,
95–96, 115; international aid for opposition
in, 98–100, 113–14; international sanctions
against, 105–9, 114–15; and Kosovo, 94, 104;
mass mobilizations in, 15, 91–92, 96, 116;
Milošević regime character in, 94–95; NATO
bombing campaign against, 94, 101, 104–5,
114; OTPOR in, 92, 95, 97–98; repression in,
94, 95, 409; security forces' defection in, 92,
114; successful democratic transition in, 19, 91,
97, 100, 116–17, 422; US and, 100–101, 107–8,
422; Western diplomacy and, 108–9, 115

Serbian Renewal Movement (SPO), 93

Se Ung Hahm, 288–89n47

Shahgoli, Manuchehr, 374n30

shah of Iran. See Pahlavi, Mohammad Reza
Shah

Shakespeare, William, 345–46

Shariati, Ali, 353, 354

Shariat-Madari, Ayatollah, 344, 360

Sharp, Gene, 98, 408

Shevardnaze, Eduard, 35, 40

Shouhuo, 387

Shovket, Lala, 406, 417, 419–20

Shultz, George, 274, 281

Sigmund, Paul, 203, 212

Sigur, Gaston, 274, 281, 282, 288n38

Silva Henríquez, Raúl, 209

Singapore, 147

Sisk, Timothy D., 10–11, 168–91

Slovakia, 109, 416, 422

Slovenia, 93

Smolar, Eugeniusz, 75